Tort Law

Ninth Edition

Tort Law

Catherine Elliott and
Frances Quinn

PEARSON

Harlow, England • London • New York • Boston • San Francisco • Toronto • Sydney
Auckland • Singapore • Hong Kong • Tokyo • Seoul • Taipei • New Delhi
Cape Town • São Paulo • Mexico City • Madrid • Amsterdam • Munich • Paris • Milan

Pearson Education Limited
Edinburgh Gate
Harlow CM20 2JE
United Kingdom
Tel: +44 (0)1279 623623
Fax: +44 (0)1279 431059
Web: www.pearson.com/uk

First published 1996 (print)
Second edition published 1999 (print)
Third edition published 2001 (print)
Fourth edition published 2003 (print)
Fifth edition published 2005 (print)
Sixth edition published 2007 (print)
Seventh edition published 2009 (print)
Eighth edition published 2011 (print)
Ninth edition published 2013 (print and electronic)

ISBN: 978-0-273-78578-1 (print)
978-0-273-78583-5 (PDF)
978-0-273-78579-8 (etext)

British Library Cataloguing-in-Publication Data
A catalogue record for the print edition is available from the British Library

Library of Congress Cataloging-in-Publication Data
A catalog record for the print edition is available from the Library of Congress

10 9 8 7 6 5 4 3 2 1
16 15 14 13 12

Cover image: Getty Images

Print edition typeset in 9/12.5pt Frutiger LT Pro by 35
Printed by Ashford Colour Press Ltd., Gosport

NOTE THAT ANY PAGE CROSS REFERENCES REFER TO THE PRINT EDITION

Brief contents

Contents

Lecturers *Teach your course, your way.*

MyLawChamber is a powerful teaching tool which you can use to assess your students, and improve their understanding.

Make the interactive Pearson eText a 'live' teaching resource by annotating with your own commentary, linking to external sources, critique, or updates to the law and sharing with your students.

Set quizzes and mini-assessments using the bank of over 450 multiple-choice questions to gauge your students' understanding.

Use Case Navigator, a case reading resource we offer in conjunction with LexisNexis, to assign student seminar work.

For information about teaching support materials, please contact your local Pearson sales consultant or visit **www.mylawchamber.co.uk**.

The regularly maintained mylawchamber site provides the following features:

- Search tool to help locate specific items of content.
- Online help and support to assist with website usage and troubleshooting.

Case Navigator access is included with your mylawchamber registration. The LexisNexis element of Case Navigator is only available to those who currently subscribe to LexisNexis Butterworths online.

Guided tour

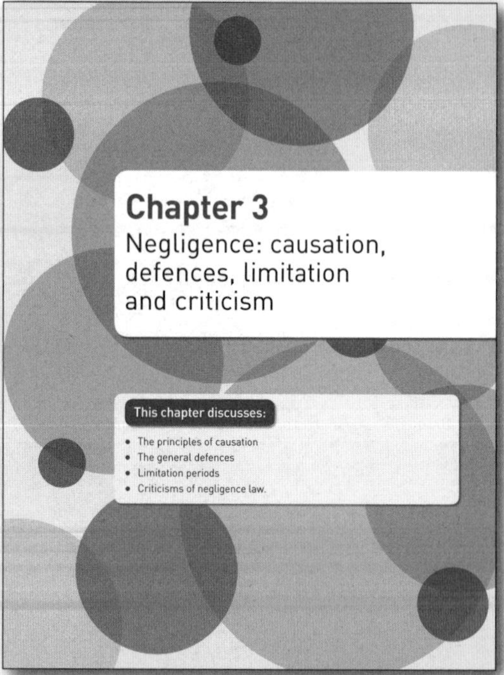

Chapter 3

Negligence: causation, defences, limitation and criticism

This chapter discusses:

- The principles of causation
- The general defences
- Limitation periods
- Criticisms of negligence law.

Chapter contents briefly outline the key themes/concepts to be covered in the following chapter. Ideal for focusing your learning, and for navigating around the book.

Chapter 9 Defamation

Section 9 of the Act provides that cases brought by claimants from outside the countries stated may not be heard here, unless the court is satisfied that, of all the places where the defamatory statement has been published, England and Wales is 'clearly the most appropriate place in which to bring an action'. This is quite a wide and flexible test, so how far it restricts libel tourism will depend very much on how the courts interpret the test: there might be difficult judgements to make where, for example, a defamatory statement was published more widely abroad than in the UK, but the claimant lives here for much of the time, or has important business interests here. Check this book's website for when this comes into force.

Topical issues

Libel tourism

Compared to most other countries, our defamation laws give far more protection to reputation than to freedom of speech, which makes it easier for a claimant to win here than in most other countries. In addition, the cost of a libel action is much higher here than elsewhere, so there is pressure on defendants to settle a claim, even if there is a chance they could have won it, rather than risk the huge cost of going to court. As a result, in recent years, increasing numbers of claimants from abroad have brought libel cases here, even if the defamatory statements were made in newspapers or magazines that are primarily published in a different country. Known as 'libel tourism', this practice has earned London the nickname of 'the libel capital of the world'.

Claimants have been able to do this because the UK courts have traditionally imposed very few restrictions in cases from abroad. Until the Defamation Act 2013 was passed, claimants from abroad only had to show two things in order to be able to sue under English law:

- They have a reputation in this country. This effectively means little more than that a number of people in this country know who they are.
- The defamatory statement was circulated here. The arrival of the Internet means that the second requirement is also very easy to satisfy, since material published all over the world can be downloaded here.

By contrast, defamation claims in the USA can only be heard if the publication was 'expressly aimed' at readers/listeners in that country.

As a result of these lax rules, cases were accepted by the English courts even where, in common-sense terms, there was no real link to the UK. In **Mahfouz** *v* **Ehrenfeld** (2004), for example, a Saudi Arabian billionaire sued an American academic in London, over a book which was not published in the UK, but was only available if bought from America via the Internet. Only 23 copies were bought by UK buyers. Similarly, in **Mardas** *v* **New York Times** (2008), the claimant was a Greek citizen, suing two American newspapers. One of the papers has a UK edition but did not publish the article there, the other only sold 177 copies in the UK, and only 31 people in the UK read the article on the Internet. Mr Mardas did not pursue a claim in the US courts, where he would have been unlikely to win.

The UK courts were increasingly criticised for allowing libel tourism, because it effectively means that claimants can bypass the laws in their own countries, and avoid any protection for free speech that those laws may give. In response, some US states passed new laws, providing that libel judgments won in the UK are unenforceable.

236

Topical issues boxes demonstrate how the law works within newsworthy, topical or contentious situations.

Key case boxes summarise the leading cases in the area, and identify the related principle of law.

Key Case **McGhee *v* National Coal Board** (1972)

As an example, take the facts of **McGhee** *v* **National Coal Board** (1972). The claimant's job brought him into contact with brick dust, which caused him to develop the skin condition dermatitis. It was known that contact with brick dust could cause dermatitis, but it was not suggested that merely exposing workers to the dust was negligent, as that was an unavoidable risk of the job they did. However, it was known that the risk of developing dermatitis could be reduced if workers could shower before leaving work, as this would lessen the amount of time the dust was in contact with their skin. The defendants had not installed any showers, and the claimant argued that they had been negligent in not doing so. To succeed in his claim, he had to prove that this negligence had caused his dermatitis – but because showers would only have lessened the risk, not removed it, the 'but for' test did not work. It was impossible to say that the damage would not have happened 'but for' the defendant's negligence, but equally impossible to say that it would definitely still have happened without the negligence.

As a result, in cases where there is more than one possible cause of damage, the courts have modified the 'but for' test, in an attempt to find a fair way to decide whether liability

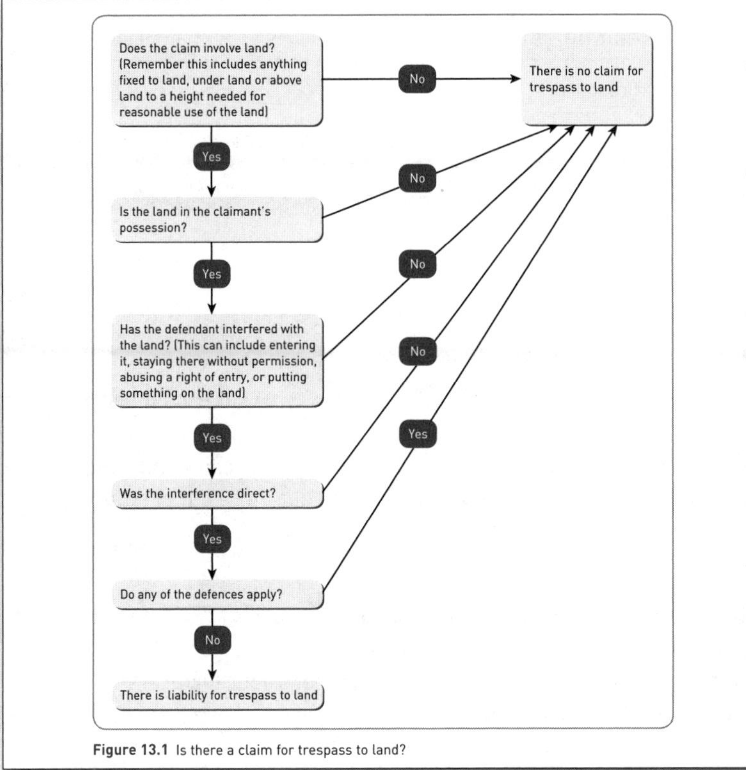
Does the claim involve land? (Remember this includes anything fixed to land, under land or above land to a height needed for reasonable use of the land)
No
There is no claim for trespass to land
Yes
No
Is the land in the claimant's possession?
Yes
No
Has the defendant interfered with the land? (This can include entering it, staying there without permission, abusing a right of entry, or putting something on the land)
No
Yes
Yes
Was the interference direct?
Yes
Do any of the defences apply?
No
There is liability for trespass to land

Figure 13.1 Is there a claim for trespass to land?

Diagrams and **flow charts** are used throughout to highlight complex legal processes.

Exam style question and answer guidance help you to test your understanding and successfully prepare for assessments.

Answering questions

Siobhan and Brian are mechanics who work in a garage owned by Krafty Kars. The business has grown over the past year, and Siobhan and Brian's workload has increased. Brian also has to do a large amount of the firm's paperwork. Six months ago, he felt that the workload was becoming too much for him: he had not been sleeping well and was feeling very stressed at the long hours he was having to work. At the same time, his marriage was breaking up. He spoke to the garage owner about his workload, and asked if they could recruit a third mechanic, or take on someone to do the paperwork. The owner refused, saying that they could not afford extra help.

Last week Brian phoned in sick and his doctor has diagnosed a nervous breakdown. Siobhan was left to cope on her own and, during the day, she needed to lift a very heavy piece of

Summary of Chapter 6

There are three main ways to claim compensation for defective products:

- Breach of contract
- Negligence
- The Consumer Protection Act 1987.

Product liability in contract

The buyer of a defective product can sue the seller for breach of contract; this protection is strengthened by the terms implied into contracts by the Sale of Goods Acts.

- Only the buyer and third parties given the benefit of the contract can sue.
- Only the seller can be sued.
- All types of product are covered.

Chapter summaries enable you to identify, recap and focus on the key points from the chapter you've read.

Further reading sections contain reference to relevant articles government papers and Internet resources that you may wish to use for further study.

Reading list

Text resources

Atiyah, P S (1997) *The Damages Lottery*. Hart Publishing
Better Regulation Task Force (2004) *Better Routes to Redress*. Cabinet Office Publications
Cane, P (2006) *Atiyah's Accidents, Compensation and the Law*, 7th edn. Cambridge University Press
Conaghan, J and Mansell, W (1993) *The Wrongs of Tort*, Chapters 4 and 5. Pluto Press

Visit **www.mylawchamber.co.uk** to access a wealth of tools to help you develop and test your knowledge of tort law, strengthening your understanding so you can excel.

The Pearson eText is a fully searchable, interactive version of *Tort Law*. You can make notes in it, highlight it, bookmark it, even link to online sources – helping you get more out of studying and revision.

Learning tools in MyLawChamber:

- Interactive multiple choice questions to test your understanding of each topic
- Practice exam questions with guidance to hone your exam technique
- Weblinks to help you read more widely around the subject and really impress your lecturers
- Glossary flashcards to test yourself on legal terms and definitions
- Legal newsfeed to help you read more widely, stay right up to date with the law and impress examiners
- Legal updates to help you stay up to date with the law and impress examiners

Case Navigator provides in-depth analysis of the leading cases in tort law, improving your case-reading skills and understanding of how the law is applied.

Use the access card at the back of the book to activate MyLawChamber. Online purchase is also available at **www.mylawchamber.co.uk**.

Preface

If there is one thing you can count on when studying tort law, it is that things do not stand still for long. During the two years since the last edition, a number of key cases have been decided, and are featured here, including **Wright** *v* **Cambridge Medical Group** (2011) on loss of a chance in medical negligence; **Sienkiewicz** *v* **Greif (UK) Ltd** (2011) on causation; **Delaney** *v* **Pickett** (2011), on illegality; **AB and others** *v* **Ministry of Defence** (2012), on limitation periods; **Thornton** *v* **Daily Telegraph Media Group** (2011) and **Flood** *v* **Times Newspapers** (2012) in defamation; **ETK** *v* **News Group Newspapers** (2011), **Rio Ferdinand** *v* **MGN** (2011) and **Von Hannover** *v* **Germany** (2012) in privacy; **Barr and others** *v* **Biffa Waste Services** (2012) and **Coventry** *v* **Lawrence** (2012) in nuisance; and **Weddall** *v* **Barchester Healthcare** (2012) and **Wallbank** *v* **Wallbank Fox Designs** (2012) on vicarious liability. We also cover the changes made to the law on defamation in the Defamation Act 2013, and have expanded the section on issues in defamation. In response to feedback from students and lecturers, this edition also contains more diagrams and flowcharts, and more 'Topical issues' boxes, which aim to set the law in context and bring it alive for the reader.

As with the previous editions, our aim is to provide a clear explanation of the law of tort. As well as setting out the law itself, we look at the principles behind it, and discuss some of the issues and debates arising from tort law. We hope that the material here will allow you to enter into that debate and develop your own views as to how the law should develop.

One of our priorities in writing this book has been to explain the material clearly, so that it is easy to understand, without lowering the quality of the content. Too often, law is avoided as a difficult subject, when the real difficulty is the vocabulary and style of legal textbooks. For that reason, we have aimed to use 'plain English' as far as possible, and explain the more complex legal terminology where it arises. There is also a glossary of legal terms at the back of the book. In addition, chapters are structured so that material is in a systematic order for the purposes of both learning and revision, and clear subheadings make specific points easy to locate.

Although we hope that many readers will use this book to satisfy a general interest in the law, we recognise that the majority will be those who have to sit an examination in the subject. Therefore, each chapter features typical examination questions, with detailed guidance on answering them, using the material in the book. This is obviously useful at revision time, but we recommend that when first reading the book, you take the opportunity offered by the Answering questions sections to think through the material that you have just read and look at it from different angles. This will help you both understand and remember it. You will also find a section at the end of the book which gives useful general advice on answering exam questions on tort law.

This book is part of a series that has been written by the same authors. The other books in the series are *The English Legal System*, *Criminal Law* and *Contract Law*.

We have endeavoured to state the law as at 1 January 2013.

Catherine Elliott and Frances Quinn
London 2013

Table of cases

Case Navigator provides in-depth analysis of the leading cases in tort law, improving your case-reading skills and understanding of how the law is applied.

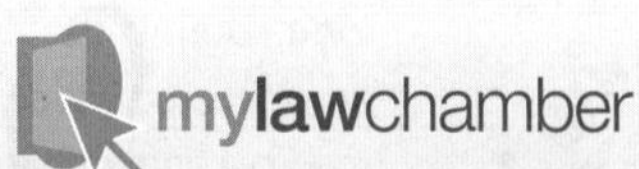

Visit **www.mylawchamber.co.uk** to access unique online support:

- **Direct deep links** to the core cases in **tort** law
- **Short introductions** provide guidance on what you should look out for while reading the case
- **Questions** help you to test your understanding of the case, and provide feedback on what you should have grasped
- **Summaries** contextualise the case and point you to further reading so that you are fully prepared for seminars and discussions

Case Navigator cases are highlighted in **bold**.

Case Navigator access is included with your mylawchamber registration. The LexisNexis element of Case Navigator is only available to those who currently subscribe to LexisNexis Butterworths online.

Tables of statutes, statutory instruments and European legislation

Table of statutes

Table of statutory instruments

Table of European legislation Conventions

Directives

Chapter 1
Tort law: an introduction

This chapter discusses:

- What a tort is
- How torts compare to other legal wrongs
- The roles of policy and fault in tort law
- Alternative compensation methods for personal injury
- Proposed reforms of the tort system.

The law of tort covers a wide range of situations, including such diverse claims as those of a passenger injured in a road accident, a patient injured by a negligent doctor, a pop star libelled by a newspaper, a citizen wrongfully arrested by the police, and a landowner whose land has been trespassed on. As a result, it is difficult to pin down a definition of a tort; but, in broad terms, a tort occurs where there is breach of a general duty fixed by civil law.

When a tort is committed, the law allows the victim to claim money, known as damages, to compensate for the commission of the tort. This is paid by the person who committed the tort (known as the tortfeasor). Other remedies may be available as well or instead. In some cases, the victims will only be able to claim damages if they can prove that the tort caused some harm, but in others, which are described as actionable *per se*, they only need to prove that the relevant tort has been committed. For example, landowners can claim damages in tort from someone trespassing on their land, even though no harm has been done by the trespasser.

Comparing tort with other legal wrongs

Torts and crimes

A crime is a wrong which is punished by the state; in most cases, the parties in the case are the wrongdoer and the state (called the Crown for these purposes), and the primary aim is to punish the wrongdoer. By contrast, a tort action is between the wrongdoer and the victim, and the aim is to compensate the victim for the harm done. It is therefore incorrect to say that someone has been prosecuted for negligence, or found guilty of libel, as these terms relate to the criminal law. Journalists frequently make this kind of mistake, but law students should not!

There are, however, some areas in which the distinctions are blurred. In some tort cases, damages may be set at a high rate in order to punish the wrongdoer, while in criminal cases, the range of punishments now includes provision for the wrongdoer to compensate the victim financially (though this is still not the primary aim of criminal proceedings, and the awards are usually a great deal lower than would be ordered in a tort action).

There are cases in which the same incident may give rise to both criminal and tortious proceedings. An example would be a car accident, in which the driver might be prosecuted by the state for dangerous driving, and sued by the victim for the injuries caused.

Torts and breaches of contract

A tort involves breach of a duty which is fixed by the law, while breach of contract is a breach of a duty which the party has voluntarily agreed to assume. For example, we are all under a duty not to trespass on other people's land, whether we like it or not, and breach of that duty is a tort. But if A refuses to dig B's garden, A can only be in breach of a legal duty if she had already agreed to do so by means of a contract.

In contract, duties are usually only owed to the other contracting party, whereas in tort, they are usually owed to people in general. While the main aim of tort proceedings is to compensate for harm suffered, contract aims primarily to enforce promises.

Again, there are areas where these distinctions blur. In some cases liability in tort is clarified by the presence of agreement. For example, the duty owed by an occupier of land to someone who visits the land is greater if the occupier has agreed to the visitor's presence, than if the 'visitor' is actually a trespasser. Equally, many contractual duties are fixed by law, and not by agreement; the parties must have agreed to make a contract, but once that has been done, certain terms will be imposed on them by law.

A defendant can be liable in both contract and tort. For example, if a householder is injured by building work done on their home, it may be possible to sue in tort for negligence and for breach of a contractual term to take reasonable care.

The role of policy

Like any other area of law, tort has its own set of principles on which cases should be decided, but clearly it is an area where policy can be seen to be behind many decisions. For example, in many tort cases one or both of the parties will, in practice, be insurance companies – cases involving car accidents are an obvious example but this is also true of most cases of employers' liability, medical negligence and occupiers' liability. The results of such cases may have implications for the cost and availability of insurance to others; if certain activities are seen as a bad risk, the price of insurance for those activities will go up, and in some cases insurance may even be refused. There is, therefore, an argument for saying that this fact should be taken into account when tort cases are decided. In some cases, judges do specifically refer to the issue of insurance, but more often, it is not overtly mentioned yet still appears to be given consideration.

In terms of simple justice, it may seem desirable that everybody who has suffered harm, however small, should find it easy to make a claim. In practical terms, however, the tort process is expensive and it is difficult to justify its use for very minor sums. The courts therefore have to strike a balance between allowing parties who have suffered harm to get redress, and establishing precedents that make it too easy to get redress with the result that people make claims for very minor harms. The English courts have often been resistant to upholding claims that would 'open the floodgates' for a large number of new cases, which again brings policy into the decision.

There are other practical concerns too: it has been suggested, for example, that in the USA, where ordinary individuals are much more likely to sue than here, medical professionals are inclined to avoid new techniques, or to cover themselves by ordering costly and often unnecessary tests, because of the danger of legal action. While it is clearly a good thing that dangerous techniques should not be used, medical science has always had to take certain risks in order to make new discoveries, and it may be that fear of litigation can stunt this process.

These are difficult issues to weigh up, and traditionally English judges avoided the problem by behaving as though such considerations played no part in their decisions, referring only to established principles. However, in recent years they have been more willing to make clear the policy implications behind their decisions: certainly the 'floodgates' argument mentioned above has been overtly referred to in the case law on both nervous shock and the recovery of economic loss in negligence.

The Compensation Act 2006 now gives judges specific permission to address one particular aspect of policy when deciding cases involving negligence or breach of statutory duty. Section 1 of the Act states that when considering whether a defendant should have taken particular steps to meet a standard of care, a court

> may . . . have regard to whether a requirement to take such steps might –
> (a) prevent a desirable activity from being undertaken at all, to a particular extent, or in a particular way, or
> (b) discourage persons from undertaking functions in connection with a desirable activity.

The clause was a response to claims that Britain has developed a 'compensation culture' in which people are too ready to sue over trival events.

Topical issue

A compensation culture

Over the past decade, both the media and politicians have frequently argued that Britain has a 'compensation culture', in which people have become too ready to sue over trivial events, and in which it has become common to try to blame someone for events which would once have been seen as nothing more than accidents. The media in particular give the impression that the number of cases is constantly rising, and the courts are flooded with trivial claims; it is, for example, widely believed that the British courts allowed a claim against McDonald's by a woman who was scalded because her coffee was too hot. In fact, when the government set up a taskforce to investigate the issue, its report, *Better Routes to Redress* (see Reading on the Internet at the end of this chapter), found that the number of people suing for personal injury has gone down in recent years, and there was no statistical evidence that the compensation culture actually exists. As you will discover when you read the next chapter, it is not legally possible in England to claim in negligence for trivial accidents that are nobody's fault, and while it is true that McDonald's were sued for selling too-hot coffee in the USA, an attempt to bring a similar claim in the English courts failed.

Tort and the requirement of fault

Most torts require that the defendant was at fault in some way. This means that, in order to be liable, the defendant must have either deliberately acted wrongfully, or there must have been something they could reasonably have been expected to do to prevent the harm they caused, which they failed to do. However, there are a few torts which can be committed without the defendant being at fault in any way. These are known as **strict liability** torts. An example can be found in the Animals Act 1971, which states that someone who keeps an animal that is classified as a dangerous species under the Act is liable for any damage that animal does, even if there was nothing they could have done to prevent it. In some cases, a strict liability tort will include defences which provide that, despite the strict liability, there are still some circumstances in which a defendant will not be liable. Under the Animals Act 1971, for example, the keeper of a dangerous animal will not be liable if the harm done was completely the fault of the claimant. Whether or not a tort requires fault has an impact on how easy it is to claim under that tort, since it is clearly much easier simply to prove that a defendant has done a particular act, or caused a particular sort of damage, than it is also to have to prove that they acted deliberately, or could have taken steps to avoid the damage. There is therefore a certain amount of debate about whether more torts should be made no-fault (and therefore strict liability) in order to give better protection to potential claimants. In some countries, for example, there are no-fault systems for claims involving car accidents and for medical negligence. This issue sometimes comes up in exam questions, so it is useful to understand some of the arguments for and against a requirement of fault.

Reasons for a requirement of fault

Control of tort actions

The fact that a claimant must usually prove fault limits the number of tort actions brought, and helps prevent the courts from being overloaded and potential defendants being exposed to very wide liability.

Laissez faire policy

The modern tort system arose in the nineteenth century, when the doctrine of *laissez faire* was prominent. This argued that individuals should be responsible for their own actions, with as little intervention from the state as possible. People were not required actively to look after each other, only to avoid doing each other harm, and they would only be expected to make amends for such harm as they could reasonably have avoided doing – in other words, not for harm caused when they were not at fault. It was considered best for the state to provide a framework of rules so that people could plan their affairs, but to intervene in those affairs as little as possible.

Deterrence

The requirement of fault is said to promote careful behaviour, on the basis that people can take steps to avoid liability, whereas under strict liability it would be beyond their control, leaving little incentive to take care.

Wider liability would merely shift the burden

Compensation is designed to shift the burden of harm from the person who originally suffered the harm to the person who pays the compensation. It moves, rather than cancels out, the loss. As a result, it can be argued that it is better to let the loss lie where it falls unless some other purpose can be served by providing compensation. A fault requirement adds an additional purpose, that of punishing the wrongdoer.

Accountability

The requirement of fault is a way of making people pay for what they have done wrong, which appears to be a deep-seated social need – even though in many cases it is actually an insurance company which pays, and not the person responsible.

Strict liability merely reverses the burden of proving fault

Almost all strict liability torts allow the defendant to plead the contributory fault of the claimant as a defence, or a factor which should reduce damages. In practice, therefore, strict liability often amounts to nothing more than a reversal of the burden of proof.

Arguments against a requirement of fault

Unjust distinctions

The result of the fault principle is that two people who have suffered exactly the same injuries may receive very different levels of compensation. For example, John and Jim both lose the use of their legs in separate car accidents; in Jim's case the driver is proved to be at fault, in John's, the driver is not. They both suffer the same degree of pain, they both end up with the same disability and the same problems. Yet Jim may win thousands of pounds in damages to help him cope with those problems, while the most John can hope to receive are benefits provided by the social security system. As we shall see further on, some countries have partially replaced tort law with no-fault compensation schemes aimed at dealing with this problem. A no-fault scheme could compensate not only accidents, but also hereditary and other disabilities and illnesses, on the basis that the problems are the same, regardless of cause.

Illogical distinctions

Even if it is admitted that the potentially huge number of tort actions has to be limited in some way, proof of fault is not the only grounds by which this could be done, nor a particularly logical choice. It appears to be the result of a policy decision that it is sometimes just to reward defendants who have been careful, by protecting them from liability for the consequences of their actions. Quite apart from the fact that fault is difficult to prove, and failure to prove fault does not mean that fault did not occur, it is difficult to see the logic of this approach when the wrongdoer is insured, and would not personally lose anything by paying damages.

Lack of deterrence

The practical deterrent effect of fault liability is debatable. First, the generalised duty to take care is too vague to influence behaviour much. Secondly, in many cases the tortfeasor will be well aware that damages will be paid by their insurance company. Motorists are obliged by law to take out insurance against accidents, as are most employers, and many professional organisations run negligence insurance schemes for their members. It can be argued that defendants also know that a claim may result in higher premiums, but it is debatable whether this is actually much of a deterrent, especially in business situations where the cost can simply be passed on to consumers in higher prices.

Of course, cost may not be the only deterrent; bad publicity can be equally powerful, if not more so. However, large corporations with good lawyers can largely avoid such publicity by negotiating an out-of-court settlement which includes a condition that the claimant does not reveal details about the case or the settlement. In such a case, claimants' chances of recovery seem to depend not on fault, but on the amount of pre-trial publicity they can drum up.

Tort should compensate and not punish

It can be argued that it is not the job of tort to punish wrongdoers; that function properly belongs to the criminal law.

Damages can be disproportionate to fault

As we will see when we look at negligence, there are cases in which a very minor level of fault can result in very serious consequences. There can be a huge disproportion between defendants' negligence (which may only be a momentary lapse in concentration) and the high damages that they subsequently have to pay.

Expense

The need to prove fault increases the length, and so the cost, of tort cases. This increases the proportion of money that is spent on operating the tort system rather than compensating claimants.

Unpredictability

The fault principle adds to the unpredictability of tort cases, and increases anxiety and pressure on both sides. The practical result is that claimants may feel pressurised into accepting settlements worth much less than they could have won if they had gone to court.

Problems with the objective standard

Fault is judged by reference to an objective standard of behaviour, which ignores the knowledge or capacity of the individual; this can mean that someone is legally at fault, when we would not consider that they were at fault morally, or at least not to the degree suggested by the law. For example, the law requires an objective standard of care from drivers, and it expects this equally after 20 years of driving, or 20 minutes.

Alternative methods of compensation for personal injury

A hundred years ago, the law of tort, with all its flaws, was almost the only way of gaining compensation for accidental injury, but its role has declined with the development of insurance and social security. For these the issue of fault is usually irrelevant.

The social security system

The vast majority of accident victims who need financial support get it not from the tort system, but through social security benefits. This is because most accident victims do not sue anybody, either because the accident was not (or cannot be proved to be) someone else's fault, or because they do not realise they could sue, or because for some reason (often cost) they decide not to. They may be unable to work for a long period or even permanently and, unless they have insurance, state benefits will be their only means of financial support. Benefits vary depending on the person's needs, and how much they have paid into the system while working, but are unlikely to provide for more than the bare essentials of life – unlike tort compensation, which is designed as far as possible to give an accident victim back the standard of living he or she enjoyed before the accident.

The social security system tends to provide support for injury victims more quickly, and with less uncertainty than the tort system, but its drawbacks are the very low levels of support, and the continuing stigma attached to accepting state benefits – tabloid newspapers, for example, routinely refer to benefits as 'handouts', when the recipients may in fact have been paying into the social security system for years through tax and national insurance.

Insurance

A whole range of policies provide insurance cover in many potentially dangerous situations. Two of the most important sources of accidents are road traffic and industry, and statute makes it a criminal offence for either vehicle users or employers to be without adequate insurance (under the Road Traffic Act 1988 and the Employers' Liability (Compulsory Insurance) Act 1969 respectively). In addition, the Motor Insurers' Bureau, an organisation set up by the insurance industry, gives money to traffic victims where the driver is either uninsured or unidentified (as in the case of a 'hit and run' accident).

Many people take out household insurance, which usually covers occupier's liability. Three main types of policy provide compensation where accidental death or injury occurs: life assurance, personal accident insurance and permanent health insurance.

In many cases, employers provide a variety of benefits which may also be of use to accident victims. There may be lump sums payable under occupational pension schemes where death or injury lead to premature retirement. Some employers offer sick pay at higher rates and for longer periods than the statutory scheme, though this rarely exceeds six months on full pay.

Compensation for victims of crime

There are additional sources of financial help for those who are injured as a result of crime. The Criminal Injuries Compensation Scheme compensates victims of violent crime, and those injured while trying to prevent crime, for pain and suffering and loss of amenity (meaning loss of the ability to lead a full life through injury).

The sums awarded are based on a tariff, which allocates specific sums to different levels of injury. Traditionally, the tariff amounts were similar to those which a court would pay out for the same sort of injury if a tort claim was made, but in 2012, against a great deal of opposition, the Government made radical changes to the scheme, removing compensation for the lowest levels of injury, and cutting the amounts given to those in the middle range. The Criminal Injuries Compensation Scheme also offers compensation for loss of earnings, for those unable to work after an injury, but at a lower level than a tort claim would. In practice the scheme provides a remedy where a person's rights in tort are useless because the assailant has not been identified, or would be unable to pay substantial damages if sued.

A second source of compensation for crime victims is the compensation order, which courts can make against those convicted of crimes, in order to pay for any damage they have done in committing the crime. The orders can cover compensation for personal injury, or loss of or damage to property; in practice most are for theft, handling stolen goods and criminal damage.

The NHS complaints system

Since the mid-1990s, claims against the NHS for medical negligence have been increasing, and currently cost the NHS over £700 million a year in compensation and legal fees. As a result, in 2001, the National Audit Office looked into the issue of negligence claims against the NHS, and concluded that money could be saved, and complaints dealt with more efficiently, if a new system specifically for NHS complaints was created.

The Commission pointed out that research showed that, in many cases, financial compensation was not the patient's main aim. Often, they were more interested in getting a genuine explanation of what had gone wrong, an apology, and some kind of reassurance that action would be taken to prevent other people being injured by the same sort of mistake. It was when the NHS failed to meet these needs that attitudes tended to harden, leading people to sue for compensation. The Commission concluded that if measures were put in place to address these issues, fewer legal cases might be brought.

A further report was produced in 2003 by the Chief Medical Officer, Liam Donaldson. In *Making Amends*, he too recommended the creation of a new scheme for NHS complaints, which would make it easier to get not just compensation, but also acknowledgement of mistakes, and care and rehabilition to deal with the results of the medical negligence. The emphasis in the report was on creating a system in which, instead of the patient having to prove fault, and the NHS attempting to fight claims, NHS staff would be encouraged to admit mistakes, and the organisation would take responsibility for improving practice by learning from such mistakes.

The government's response to *Making Amends* was the NHS Redress Act 2006. It allows the creation of an NHS Redress Scheme which, the explanatory notes to the Act state, will 'provide investigations when things go wrong, remedial treatment, rehabilitation and care where needed, explanations and apologies, and financial compensation in certain circumstances' without the need to go to court. Patients who accept redress offered under the scheme will have to waive their right to take legal action.

The Act is what is known as an enabling Act, which sets out a broad framework for the scheme and then permits the detailed rules to be put in place by means of secondary legislation. It was passed in November 2006, and the government then began consulting with interested parties before deciding on the details of how the scheme will work. It was eventually decided that the scheme would be piloted in Wales, and a new NHS redress scheme began operating there in April 2011. The idea of the scheme is to encourage the NHS to be more receptive of complaints, rather than taking a defensive attitude, and to simplify the way straightforward, relatively low-value claims are dealt with.

The scheme only applies to claims worth up to £25,000, and allows patients to make a claim verbally, by post or by email. The scheme obliges the relevant NHS trust to investigate the complaint, respond to the patient, and assess whether the actions complained of have caused harm to the patient. Where there is negligence, as well as financial compensation, which can include the cost of any remedial treatment required, the trust should give an apology and a clear explanation of what went wrong, and have an action plan in place to make sure the same thing does not happen again to someone else. No studies have yet been done to assess how well the scheme is working, but there have been criticisms that allowing trusts to investigate themselves means that the investigations cannot be considered fully independent and unbiased. No plans have yet been made to extend the scheme to England.

Special funds

Highly publicised accidents involving large numbers of victims, such as the sinking of the *Herald of Free Enterprise* ferry off Zeebrugge and the King's Cross underground fire, sometimes result in the setting up of special funds to compensate the victims.

No-fault systems

The social security and insurance arrangements run alongside the tort system in England. However, in some countries, tort liability in particular fields has been completely replaced by a general no-fault scheme of compensation. The main benefits of this are that similar levels of harm receive similar levels of compensation, regardless of whether fault can be proved, and that the money spent on administering the tort system, and providing legal aid in tort cases, can instead be spent in compensating those who have suffered harm. It should be pointed out here that tort is a notoriously uneconomical way of delivering benefits to those who need them: the 2001 survey of medical negligence claims by the National Audit Office found that in nearly half the cases studied, the costs of the case would be higher than the damages awarded to the claimant. In cases where the claim was for more than £500,000, 65 per cent cost more than the eventual damages.

The most notable no-fault scheme is that which was created in New Zealand in 1972. The system, run by a body called the Accident Compensation Corporation (ACC), is funded by a combination of money from the state, and levies on earnings, petrol prices, businesses and car tax. It provides compensation for injury which is caused by any kind of accident, or which develops gradually as a result of the victim's job, or which is caused by medical treatment or sexual assault or abuse. It pays for the cost of medical treatment and rehabilitation, and provides those who cannot work as a result of their injuries with compensation amounting to 80 per cent of what they would have been earning before the injury. Where an accident victim dies, it pays compensation to their dependants, again amounting to 80 per cent of what the victim was earning. There may also be payments towards other costs resulting from the injury, such as home adaptations, help at home or, for child victims, help with schooling. The scheme requires claimants to prove their injuries, using medical evidence, but they are not required to prove that anyone else was at fault, and they can claim compensation even if the injury was partly their fault. The role of the ACC is to provide such practical help as is needed for victims to get back to work and everyday life as soon as possible, rather than to provide the kind of large payouts that tort systems tend to do. They also have an accident prevention role, advising the public, companies and organisations on how to stop accidents happening in the first place.

In the USA, approximately half of all the states have established no-fault schemes for victims of road accidents, though there is considerable variation between these schemes and their effect on any potential tort claim. In most of these states, motorists have to buy no-fault insurance cover up to the limit imposed by their state, and the driver and anyone else injured by the vehicle can make a claim. Non-pecuniary loss such as pain and suffering is still covered by the tort system and in some states, claims for non-pecuniary loss can only be brought if the case is particularly serious. The US schemes seem to have led to a lowering in the cost of motor insurance, and the award of compensation to many victims who would have received no compensation under the old system.

In the Australian state of New South Wales, tort liability for transport accidents has been replaced by a scheme which only pays compensation if the accident was caused by the fault of someone, and for these purposes the victim's fault is not sufficient. The practical effect of this has simply been that cases which would in the past have been dealt with as tort cases in the civil courts are now being heard by administrative tribunals; and because statute imposes limits on the payments that can be made under the scheme, there has been a decrease in the amount of compensation for the serious cases.

Although most no-fault schemes have been created in the context of transport accidents, in Sweden there is a no-fault scheme for victims of medical accidents.

Alternative methods of making wrongdoers accountable

There are also alternatives to the tort system in terms of holding wrongdoers to account for what they have done. The criminal law is an obvious example, though it does not cover all activities which would lead to redress in tort. Highly publicised accidents, such as the thalidomide tragedy, the sinking of the *Herald of Free Enterprise* and the King's Cross fire often result in public inquiries, which aim to investigate why they happened and provide recommendations to prevent similar accidents.

Reform of the tort system

In the 1970s, the then government put in place a Royal Commission to study the various systems for compensating personal injury. The Royal Commission on Civil Liability and Compensation for Personal Injury, known as the Pearson Commission, reported in 1978, and remains the last large-scale examination of personal injury compensation. It considered several alternative recommendations for reform, including a no-fault scheme, and the abolition of fault-based tort liability, to be replaced by a system which would place responsibility on the party best placed to insure against the risk. Where, for example, a pedestrian is knocked down by a car, it is obviously much more practical for the motorist to insure against such an accident than for the pedestrian to do so. Equally, it is easier for an employer to take out one insurance policy covering the whole workforce than for each employee to buy their own accident insurance. However, there would be cases where it might be reasonable to expect the victim to insure themselves against the risk, and in this case an uninsured victim would have to bear the loss.

The Commission concluded that, given the social security system in England, it was unnecessary to establish a full no-fault compensation system. It recommended that the tort system should still provide accident compensation, alongside the benefits provided by the social security system, but that there should be a shift in the balance between the two, towards increased social security benefits. In particular, the report advocated that there should be improved benefits for the victims of industrial injuries, and that a dedicated scheme should be set up for injuries caused by motor vehicles, as these were by far the largest category of accidental injury studied by the Commission and were also likely to be serious. The scheme would be financed by a levy on petrol.

The Commission considered the idea of no-fault schemes for other particular types of accident but, given the possible difficulties in defining the scope of such schemes, and in financing them, felt there were too many practical problems to make these a sound proposition.

The idea of a general compulsory insurance was also rejected, on the grounds that it would be difficult to enforce, that some might find it unaffordable, and that it was not desirable to expect people to insure themselves against harm caused by others. Such a system would retain the high operational costs of the tort system, yet lose the advantage of making wrongdoers pay for the harm they cause.

The Commission recommended that the tort system should be kept because of its deterrent effect and because '[t]here is an elementary justice in the principle of the tort action that he who has by his fault injured his neighbour should make reparation' (Pearson Report of the Royal Commission on Civil Liability and Compensation for Personal Injury, Cmnd 7054, 1978, paras 245–63). It envisaged, however, that many small tort cases would no longer be brought if its recommendations on social security benefits were put into action.

The Commission also suggested that two measures be taken to reduce tort damages. Non-pecuniary damages would be available only in the most serious cases, and the value of any social security benefits obtained as a result of injury should be offset against the damages awarded. This, it was suggested, was justified by the fact that both social security benefits and tort damages were ultimately derived from society at large, and should not be paid twice.

The Pearson Commission was not a success, and its proposals were heavily criticised. The suggestion for a road accident compensation scheme, for example, was criticised as creating yet another *ad hoc* category in an already complex and fragmented system, when in fact road accident victims appeared to be one of the categories best served by the tort system. Shortly after the Pearson Commission reported, a Conservative government was elected, and rather than increase social security benefits as the Commission had suggested, it set about cutting them, so there was no real opportunity for the social security system to play a larger role in accident compensation as the Commission had envisaged. By the late 1980s, it was generally assumed in the majority of Western industrialised countries that social security spending should be curtailed, and, despite changes of government in the UK, controlling expenditure on welfare benefits is still seen as a priority; against this background, the Commission's overall approach is obviously not going to be adopted. Only one significant move has been made in their direction, with the advent of legislation to allow the value of social security benefits received by accident victims to be claimed back by the state from tortfeasors (see p. 406).

Answering questions

Compensation for personal injury arising from negligence relies on the claimant being able to prove that their injury is someone else's fault. How satisfactory is a system based on proof of fault and are there better alternatives?

To answer this question, you will need to have studied negligence, as well as the issues raised in this chapter. A good way to start this essay would to be to look at what we mean when we say that compensation for personal injuries caused by negligence depends on fault. Explain the ways in which the law of negligence judges fault: relevant issues here would be the **Caparo** test, the standard of reasonableness; and the rules on causation and remoteness of damage, all of which are designed to ensure that a defendant will only be liable for damage which can be said to be their fault.

In order to decide whether dependence on fault creates a satisfactory system, you should work through the reasons why fault might be thought desirable, as explained in this chapter, and explain how those factors contribute to the system we have. You could then work through the disadvantages of the fault principle (as explained on p. 5) again relating them to their practical impact on the tort system. Other useful material, specifically relating to the strengths and weaknesses of the law on negligence can be found on page 137. Remember, though, that you are only being asked about personal injury claims, so the material on economic loss is not relevant here.

You should then look at the alternatives to a fault-based system, which are covered in this chapter, and give an assessment of their strengths and weaknesses. Finally, you should offer a conclusion which, based on the arguments you have put forward, states whether you think a fault-based system is the best option, or whether it should be replaced by an alternative, either completely or in certain types of case.

Summary of Chapter 1

Tort law covers breaches of a duty owed under civil law, and usually allows the victim to claim financial compensation.

Tort and other legal wrongs

- Tort and crime: crimes are punished by the state; torts are a dispute between the person committing the tort, and the victim.
- Tort and breach of contract: torts involve breach of a duty fixed by law; breach of contract involves breaching a duty agreed between the parties.

The role of policy

Policy can be seen to be behind many tort law decisions, because the rules made can have important effects on social issues such as the availability of insurance, or the willingness of doctors to try new techniques.

The requirement of fault

Most torts require proof of fault, but a small number of torts impose strict liability.

Reasons for a fault requirement:

- control of tort actions;
- laissez faire policy;
- deterrence;
- wider liability merely shifts costs;
- accountability;
- strict liability only reverses the burden of proof.

Arguments against a fault requirement:

- unjust distinctions;
- illogical distinctions;
- lack of deterrence;
- tort should compensate, not punish;
- damages disproportionate to fault;
- expense;
- unpredictability;
- problems with an objective standard.

Alternative methods of personal injury compensation

Other systems include:

- social security;
- compensation for crime victims;
- the NHS complaints system;
- insurance;

➜

- special funds;
- no-fault systems in other countries.

Reform of the tort system

The Pearson Commission recommended a shift towards better compensation through social security for accident victims, but was not followed.

Reading list

Text resources

Atiyah, P S (1997) *The Damages Lottery*. Hart Publishing

Better Regulation Task Force (2004) *Better Routes to Redress*. Cabinet Office Publications

Cane, P (2006) *Atiyah's Accidents, Compensation and the Law*, 7th edn. Cambridge University Press

Conaghan, J and Mansell, W (1993) *The Wrongs of Tort*, Chapters 4 and 5. Pluto Press

Genn, H (1987) *Hard Bargaining*, Clarendon

Gooderham, P (2007) 'Special treatment?' *New Law Journal* 694

Harlow, C (2005) *Understanding Tort Law*, 3rd edn, Chapters 2–4. Sweet & Maxwell

Harris, D et al. (1984) *Compensation and Support for Illness and Injury*. Oxford University Press

Harris, P (2006) *An Introduction to Law*, 7th edn, Chapter 9. Cambridge University Press

Henderson, J (1981) 'The New Zealand accident compensation reform' 48 *University of Chicago Law Review* 481

Jacobs, J (2006) 'Reforming personal injury compensation' *Solicitors Journal* 586

Lewis, R (2005) 'Insurance and the tort system' 25(1) *Legal Studies* 85

Morgan, J (2004) 'Tort insurance and incoherence' 67(3) *Modern Law Review* 384

Morris, A (2007) 'Spiralling or stabilising? The compensation culture and our propensity to claim damages for personal injury' 70 *Modern Law Review* 349

Parker, A (2006) 'Changing the claims culture' *New Law Journal* 702

Report of the Royal Commission on Civil Liability and Compensation for Personal Injury (The Pearson Report) (1978) Cmnd 7054

Slapper, G (2005) 'Compensation culture' 46 *Student Law Review* 28

Stapleton, J (1995) 'Tort insurance and ideology' 58 *Modern Law Review* 820

Towler, A (2005) 'Time to redress' *Solicitors Journal* 652

Williams, K (2005) 'State of fear: Britain's compensation culture reviewed' 25(3) *Legal Studies* 499

Reading on the Internet

The NHS Redress Act, and its explanatory notes, can be read at:
http://www.opsi.gov.uk/acts/en2006/2006en44.htm

The report, *Better Routes to Redress*, into the alleged compensation culture, can be read at:
http://www.brc.gov.uk/downloads/pdf/betterroutes.pdf

The government's response to *Better Routes to Redress* can be read at:
http://www.dca.gov.uk/majrep/bettertaskforce/better-task-force.pdf

The Chief Medical Officer's report *Making Amends* can be read at:
http://www.dh.gov.uk/Consultations/ClosedConsultations/ClosedConsultationsArticle/fs/en?CONTENT_ID=4072363&chk=qXY2KS

Visit **www.mylawchamber.co.uk** to access tools to help you develop and test your knowledge of tort law, including interactive multiple choice questions, practice exam questions with guidance, weblinks, glossary flashcards, legal newsfeed and legal updates.

Chapter 2
Negligence: elements of the tort

This chapter discusses:

- How negligence is committed
- The tests for a duty of care
- Breach of a duty
- Damages.

Negligence is the most important tort in modern law. It concerns breach of a legal duty to take care, with the result that damage is caused to the claimant. Just a few examples of the type of case which might be brought in negligence are people injured in a car accident who sue the driver, businesses which lose money because an accountant fails to advise them properly, or patients who sue doctors when medical treatment goes wrong.

Torts other than negligence are normally identified by the particular interest of the claimant that they protect. For example, nuisance protects against interference with the claimant's use and enjoyment of land, while defamation protects against damage to reputation. By contrast, negligence protects against three different types of harm:

- personal injury;
- damage to property;
- economic loss.

In practice, the rules of the tort may differ according to which type of harm has been suffered, but all of them are protected by negligence.

The tort of negligence has three main elements:

- the defendant must owe the claimant a duty of care;
- the defendant must breach that duty of care;
- that failure must cause damage to the claimant.

The duty of care

Negligence is essentially concerned with compensating people who have suffered damage as a result of the carelessness of others, but the law does not provide a remedy for everyone who suffers in this way. One of the main ways in which access to compensation is restricted is through the doctrine of the duty of care. Essentially, this is a legal concept which dictates the circumstances in which one party will be liable to another in negligence: if the law says you do not have a duty of care towards the person (or organisation) you have caused damage to, you will not be liable to that party in negligence, no matter how serious the damage.

It is interesting to note that in the vast majority of ordinary tort cases which pass through the court system, it will usually be clear that the defendant does owe the claimant a duty of care, and what the courts will be looking at is whether the claimant can prove that the defendant breached that duty – for example, in most of the road accident cases that courts hear every year, it is already established that road users owe a duty to other road users, and the issues for the court will generally revolve around what the defendant actually did and what damage was caused. Yet flick through the pages of this or any other law book, and you soon see that duty of care occupies an amount of space which seems disproportionate to its importance in real-life tort cases. This is because when it comes to the kinds of cases which reach the higher courts and therefore the pages of law books, duty of care arises frequently, and that in turn is because of its power to affect the whole shape of negligence law. Every time a potential new duty of care is accepted (or ruled out), that has implications for the numbers of tort cases being brought in the future, the types of situations it can play a part in, and therefore the role which the tort system plays in society.

As a result, the law in this field has caused the courts considerable problems as they have often found themselves torn between doing justice in an individual case, and preventing a vast increase in the number of future cases. We can analyse the development of the law on duties of care in three main stages: the original neighbour principle as established in **Donoghue** *v* **Stevenson** (1932); a two-stage test set down in **Anns** *v* **Merton London Borough** (1978), which greatly widened the potential for liability in negligence; and a retreat from this widening following the case of **Murphy** *v* **Brentwood District Council** (1990). Although much of the following section describes historical development, it is worth taking time to get to know the background, as this will help you make sense of the reasoning in many later cases.

Development of the duty of care

The neighbour principle

Key Case **Donoghue** *v* **Stevenson** (1932)

The branch of law that we now know as negligence has its origins in one case: **Donoghue** *v* **Stevenson** (1932). The facts of **Donoghue** *v* **Stevenson** began when Mrs Donoghue and a friend went into a café for a drink. Mrs Donoghue asked for a ginger beer, which her friend bought. It was supplied, as was customary at the time, in an opaque bottle. Mrs Donoghue poured out and drank some of the ginger beer, and then poured out the rest. At that point, the remains of a decomposing snail fell out of the bottle. Mrs Donoghue became ill, and sued the manufacturer.

Up until this time, the usual remedy for damage caused by a defective product would be an action in contract, but this was unavailable to Mrs Donoghue, because the contract for the sale of the drink was between her friend and the café. Mrs Donoghue sued the manufacturer, and the House of Lords agreed that manufacturers owed a duty of care to the end consumer of their products.

For the benefit of future cases, their Lordships attempted to lay down general criteria for when a duty of care would exist. Lord Atkin stated that the principle was that 'You must take reasonable care to avoid acts or omissions which you can reasonably foresee would be likely to injure your neighbour.' This is sometimes known as the neighbour principle. By 'neighbour', Lord Atkin did not mean the person who lives next door, but 'persons who are so closely and directly affected by my act that I ought to have them in contemplation as being so affected when I am directing my mind to the acts or omissions which are called in question'. The test of foreseeability is objective; the court asks not what the defendant actually foresaw, but what a reasonable person could have been expected to foresee.

The claimant does not have to be individually identifiable for the defendant to be expected to foresee the risk of harming them. In many cases, it will be sufficient if the claimant falls within a category of people to whom a risk of harm was foreseeable – for example, the end user of a product, as in **Donoghue** *v* **Stevenson**. The ginger beer manufacturers did not have to know that Mrs Donoghue would drink their product, only that someone would.

Legal Principle

There is a duty in tort to take reasonable care to avoid acts or omissions which you can reasonably foresee would be likely to injure your neighbour.

A two-stage test

The issue of reasonable foresight was never the only criterion for deciding whether a duty of care is owed. As time went on, and a variety of factual situations in which a duty of care arose were established, the courts began to seek precedents in which a similar factual situation had given rise to the existence of a duty of care. For example, it was soon well established that motorists owe a duty of care to other road users and employers owe a duty to their employees, but where a factual situation seemed completely new, a duty of care would only be deemed to arise if there were policy reasons for creating one. 'Policy reasons' simply mean that the judges take into account not just the legal framework, but also whether they believe society would benefit from the existence of a duty. This approach began to be criticised, and the apparent need to find such reasons was said to be holding back development of the law.

This view was addressed in **Anns** *v* **Merton London Borough** (1978), where Lord Wilberforce proposed a significant extension of the situations where a duty of care would exist, arguing that it was no longer necessary to find a precedent with similar facts. Instead, he suggested that whether a duty of care arose in a particular factual situation was a matter of general principle. In order to decide whether this principle was satisfied in a particular case, he said, the courts should use a two-stage test. First, did the parties satisfy the neighbour test – in other words, was the claimant someone to whom the defendant could reasonably be expected to foresee a risk of harm? If the answer was yes, a *prima facie* duty of care arose. The second stage would involve asking whether there were any policy considerations that meant it would not be desirable to allow a duty of care in this situation. If there were no policy considerations that argued against establishing a duty of care, then a duty could be imposed.

This two-stage test changed the way in which the neighbour test was applied. Previously, the courts had used the neighbour test to justify new areas of liability, where there were policy reasons for creating them. After **Anns** *v* **Merton London Borough**, the neighbour test would apply unless there were policy reasons for excluding it. This led to an expansion of the situations in which a duty of care could arise, and therefore in the scope of negligence. This expansion reached its peak in **Junior Books** *v* **Veitchi** (1983), where the House of Lords seemed to go one step further. The House appeared to suggest that what were previously good policy reasons for limiting liability should now not prevent an extension where the neighbour principle justified recovery. They therefore allowed recovery for purely economic loss (see p. 25) when previously this had not been permitted.

As the first stage was relatively easy to pass, it seemed likely that the bounds of liability would be extended beyond what was considered to be reasonable, particularly given the judiciary's notorious reluctance to discuss issues of policy – a discussion that was necessary if the second stage was to offer any serious hurdle. As a result, the growth in liability for negligence set all sorts of alarm bells ringing. Eventually, the problems of insuring against the new types of liability, and the way in which tort seemed to be encroaching on areas traditionally governed by contractual liability, led to a rapid judicial retreat and, in a series of cases, the judiciary began restricting new duties of care.

The judicial retreat

In 1990, the case of **Murphy** *v* **Brentwood District Council** came before a seven-member House of Lords. The House invoked the 1966 Practice Statement (which allows them to depart from their own previous decisions) to overrule **Anns**. They quoted the High Court of Australia in **Sutherland**

Shire Council *v* **Heyman** (1985), a case in which the High Court of Australia had itself decided not to follow **Anns**:

> It is preferable, in my view, that the law should develop novel categories of negligence incrementally and by analogy with established categories, rather than by a massive extension of a *prima facie* duty of care, restrained only by indefinable 'considerations which ought to negative, or to reduce or limit the scope of the duty or the class of person to whom it is owed'.

The broad general principle with its two-part test envisaged in **Anns** was thereby swept aside, leaving the courts to impose duties of care only when they could find precedent in comparable factual situations.

Rejection of the **Anns** test did not mean that the categories of negligence were closed, but the creation of new duties of care was intended to involve a much more gradual process, building step by step by analogy with previous cases involving similar factual situations.

The law today

Over the years, case law has established that there are a number of factual situations in which a duty of care is known to be owed. For example, drivers owe a duty to take care not to injure pedestrians, and employers owe a duty of care to take reasonable steps to protect their employees from injury. However, there are still situations in which it is not clear whether there is a duty of care, and, following the moves towards a tighter test after **Anns** was overruled, the House of Lords set down a new test in **Caparo Industries plc** *v* **Dickman** (1990).

Case Navigator

The case is explained in more detail below, but, essentially, it requires the courts, when faced with the question of whether a duty of care should be imposed, to ask:

- Was the damage caused reasonably foreseeable?
- Was there a relationship of proximity between claimant and defendant?
- Is it just and reasonable to impose a duty?

The **Caparo** test is now accepted as the basic test to be applied when a court is presented with a new factual situation in which it needs to decide whether a duty of care exists. However, the courts have developed more detailed, and more restrictive, rules which apply in certain types of case:

- where the damage caused is psychiatric, rather than physical, injury;
- where the damage caused is purely economic loss;
- where the damage was caused by a failure to act (known as liability for omissions);
- where the damage was caused by a third party, rather than the defendant;
- whether the defendant falls within a range of groups who have become subject to special rules on policy grounds.

We will look first at the basic **Caparo** test, and then afterwards at the special types of case.

Procedural issues

Before we move on to look at the rules surrounding where and when a duty of care will be found, there is one important procedural point which will help you make sense of some of the cases discussed in this chapter. Where a case raises an issue of law, as opposed to purely issues of fact, the defendant can make what is called a striking out application, which effectively argues that even if the facts of what the claimant says happened are true, this does not give them a legal claim against the defendant. Cases where it is not clear whether there is a duty of care are often the subject of striking out applications, where essentially the defendant is saying that even if they had caused the harm alleged to the claimant, there was no duty of care between them and so there can be no successful claim for negligence.

Where a striking out application is made, the court conducts a preliminary examination of the case, in which it assumes that the facts alleged by the claimant are true, and from there, decides whether they give rise to an arguable case in law – so in a case involving duty of care, they would be deciding whether, on the facts before them, the defendant may owe a duty of care to the claimant. If not, the case can be dismissed without a full trial. If the court finds that there is an arguable case, the striking out application will be dismissed, and the case can then proceed to a full trial (unless settled out of court). The claimant will still have to prove that the facts are true, and that the complete case is made out, so a case which is not struck out can still be lost at trial. For an example of this, see **Swinney** *v* **Chief Constable of the Northumbria Police** (p. 61). Recent cases brought before the European Court of Human Rights have raised important questions about the use of striking out applications (see p. 63).

Duties of care: the **Caparo** test

Key Case **Caparo** *v* **Dickman** (1990)

As explained above, the basic test for a duty of care is now the one set down in **Caparo** *v* **Dickman** (1990). This will usually be applied to duty of care questions in cases involving physical injury and/or damage to property, and those which do not fall into any of the special categories listed above. In some cases, it is also applied alongside the special rules in those categories, and some experts suggest that those special rules are in fact simply a more detailed application of the principles in the **Caparo** test.

The test requires the courts to ask three questions:

- Was the damage reasonably foreseeable?
- Was there a relationship of proximity between defendant and claimant?
- Is it just, fair and reasonable to impose a duty in this situation?

As we shall see from the cases in this section, in many situations one or more of these elements may overlap, and so the test is not always applied as a clear, three-step process.

Legal Principle

The basic test for a duty of care is whether the damage was reasonably foreseeable, whether there was a relationship of proximity between claimant and defendant, and whether it is just and reasonable to impose a duty.

Reasonable foreseeability

This element of the test has its foundations in the original 'neighbour principle' developed in **Donoghue** *v* **Stevenson** (see p. 18). Essentially, the courts have to ask whether a reasonable person in the defendant's position would have foreseen the risk of damage. A case which shows how this part of the test works is **Langley** *v* **Dray** (1998), where the claimant was a policeman who was injured in a car crash when he was chasing the defendant, who was driving a stolen car. The Court of Appeal held that the defendant knew, or ought to have known, that he was being pursued by the claimant, and therefore in increasing his speed he knew or should have known that the claimant would also drive faster and so risk injury. The defendant had a duty not to create such risks and he was in breach of that duty.

In order for a duty to exist, it must be reasonably foreseeable that damage or injury would be caused to the particular defendant in the case, or to a class of people to which he or she belongs, rather than just to people in general. In other words, the duty is owed to a person or category of persons, and not to the human race in general. A good example of this principle can be seen in **Palsgraf** *v* **Long Island Railroad** (1928). The case arose from an incident when a man was boarding a train, and a member of the railway staff negligently pushed him, which caused him to drop a package he was carrying. The box contained fireworks, which exploded, and the blast knocked over some scales, several feet away. They fell on the claimant and she was injured. She sued, but the court held that it could not reasonably be foreseen that pushing the passenger would injure someone standing several feet away. It was reasonably foreseeable that the passenger himself might be injured, but that did not in itself create a duty to other people.

That does not, however, mean that the defendant has to be able to identify a particular individual who might foreseeably be affected by their actions; it is enough that the claimant is part of a category of people who might foreseeably be affected. This was the case in **Haley** *v* **London Electricity Board** (1965). The defendants dug a trench in the street in order to do repairs. Their workmen laid a shovel across the hole to draw pedestrians' attention to it, but the claimant was blind, and fell into the hole, seriously injuring himself. It was agreed in court that the precautions taken would have been sufficient to protect a sighted person from injury, so the question was whether it was reasonably foreseeable that a blind person might walk by and be at risk of falling in. The Court of Appeal said that it was: the number of blind people who lived in London meant that the defendants owed a duty to this category of people.

The duty must also relate to a particular kind of harm which the defendant could reasonably foresee arising from their actions, rather than to the possibility of causing any kind of harm whatsoever. As Lord Oliver explained in **Caparo** *v* **Dickman**, 'It is not a duty to take care in the abstract, but a duty to avoid causing to the particular plaintiff [the old word for claimant] damage of the particular kind which he has in fact sustained.' The Court of Appeal was faced with an interesting question on this issue in **Bhamra** *v* **Dubb** (2010). The case arose from a very sad story in which the claimant's husband, who had a severe egg allergy, collapsed and died after unknowingly eating a dish containing eggs, which was served at a wedding. The wedding was a Sikh one, and the Sikh religion bans its followers from eating certain foods, including eggs. The defendant, who was the caterer, knew this, but it appeared that at some point the food at the wedding had run out, and he had sourced extra from another supplier. The dish supplied would not usually have contained eggs in any case, but, for some reason which was never quite established, they had been used on this occasion.

It was clear that the defendant owed Mr Bhamra and all the other guests a duty not to serve them food that would generally be considered harmful, such as mouldy or 'off' food. The Court said it was also clear that the caterer owed Mr Bhamra and the other guests a duty not to offend their religious sensibilities by serving eggs (you might well ask where this particular duty comes from, since offence to religious sensibility is not a form of damage recognised in a negligence claim, but the court glossed over this point). But did the defendant owe Mr Bhamra a duty not to cause him physical harm by serving him eggs? The Court of Appeal held that there were four factors that meant he did owe such a duty. First, he was under a duty not to serve food containing eggs, because of the nature of the event. Secondly, he would have known that some people are allergic to eggs, and would suffer serious injury if they ate food containing them. Thirdly, he knew that anyone attending the wedding would expect the food to be free of eggs and so would believe they could safely eat any dish served, even if they had an egg allergy. Finally, Mr Bhamra had every reason to rely on the caterers not serving food containing eggs, and would not have seen any reason to ask whether any dish contained egg. Taken together, 'this very unusual combination of circumstances' meant that there was a duty of care not to cause Mr Bhamra physical harm by serving him eggs.

Proximity

In normal language, proximity means closeness, in terms of physical position, but in law it has a wider meaning which essentially concerns the relationship, if any, between the defendant and the claimant. In **Muirhead** *v* **Industrial Tank Specialities** (1985), Goff LJ pointed out that this does not mean that the defendant and claimant have to know each other, but that the situations they were both in meant that the defendant could reasonably be expected to foresee that his or her actions could cause damage to the claimant.

In this sense, proximity can be seen as simply another way of expressing the foreseeability test, as the case of **Caparo** *v* **Dickman** itself shows. The claimants, Caparo, were a company who had made a takeover bid for another firm, Fidelity, in which they already owned a large number of shares. When they were deciding whether to make the bid, they had used figures prepared by Dickman a firm of auditors, for Fidelity's annual audit. The figures showed that Fidelity was making a healthy profit. However, when the takeover was complete, Caparo discovered that Fidelity was in fact almost worthless. They sued Dickman, and the House of Lords had to decide whether Dickman owed them a duty of care. They pointed out that the preparation of an annual audit was required under the Companies Act 1985, for the purpose of helping existing shareholders to exercise control over a company. An audit was not intended to be a source of information or guidance for prospective new investors, and therefore could not be intended to help existing shareholders, like Caparo, to decide whether to buy more shares. The audit was effectively a statement that was 'put into more or less general circulation and may foreseeably be relied on by strangers to the maker of the statement, for any one of a variety of purposes which the maker of the statement has no reason to contemplate'. As a result, the House of Lords held that there was no relationship of proximity between Caparo and Dickman, and no duty of care.

Case Navigator

Proximity may also be expressed in terms of a relationship between the defendant, and the activity which caused harm to the claimant, defined by Lord Brennan in **Sutradhar** *v* **Natural Environment Research Council** (2004) as 'proximity in the sense of a measure of control over and responsibility for the potentially dangerous situation'. An example of this kind of proximity can be seen in **Watson** *v* **British Boxing Board of Control** (2000), where the claimant was the famous professional boxer Michael Watson, who suffered severe brain damage after being injured during a match. He sued the Board, on the basis that they were in charge of safety arrangements at professional boxing matches, and evidence showed that if they had made immediate medical attention available at the ringside, his injuries would have been less severe. The Court of Appeal held that there was sufficient proximity between Mr Watson and the Board to give rise to a duty of care, because they were the only body in the UK which could license professional boxing matches, and therefore had complete control of and responsibility for a situation which could clearly result in harm to Mr Watson if the Board did not exercise reasonable care.

In **Sutradhar** *v* **Natural Environment Research Council** (2006), the claimant was a resident of Bangladesh, who had been made ill by drinking water contaminated with arsenic. The water came from wells near his home, and his reason for suing the defendants was that, some years earlier, they had carried out a survey of the local water system, and had neither tested for, nor revealed the presence of arsenic. The claimant argued that the defendants should have tested for arsenic, or made public the fact that they had not done so, so as not to lull local people into a false sense of security. The House of Lords, however, held that the defendants had no duty of care to users of the water system, because there was insufficient proximity. Mr Sutradhar himself had never seen the defendants' report, and so his claim had to be based on the idea that they owed a duty to the whole population of Bangladesh. The House of Lords said this could not be the case: the defendants had no connection with the project that had provided the wells, and no one had asked them to test whether the water was safe to drink. They had no duty to the people or the government of Bangladesh to test the water for anything, and were simply doing general research into the performance of the type of wells that happened to be used in that area. The fact that someone had expert knowledge of a subject did not impose on them a duty to use that knowledge to help anyone in the world who might require such help. Proximity required a degree of control of the source of Mr Sutradhar's injury, namely the drinking water supply of Bangladesh, and the defendants had no such control.

Justice and reasonableness

In practice, the requirement that it must be just and reasonable to impose a duty often overlaps with the previous two – in **Watson** and **Sutradhar**, for example, the arguments made under the heading of proximity could equally well be seen as arguments relating to justice and reasonableness. It was obviously more just and reasonable to expect the Boxing Board to supervise a match properly, since that was their job, than it was to expect the researchers in **Sutradhar** to take responsibility for a task that was not their job, and which they had never claimed to have done.

Where justice and reasonableness are specifically referred to, it is usually because a case meets the requirements of foreseeability and proximity, but the courts believe there is a sound public policy reason for denying the claim. An example is **McFarlane** *v* **Tayside Health Board** (1999). The claimant had become pregnant after her partner's vasectomy failed, and claimed for the costs of bringing up the child. The courts denied her claim, on the basis that it was not just and reasonable to award compensation for the birth of a healthy child – something most people, they said, would consider a blessing.

Case Navigator

In **Commissioners of Customs and Excise** *v* **Barclays Bank plc** (2006), the government's Customs and Excise department was owed large sums in unpaid VAT by two companies, who had accounts with the defendant bank. Customs and Excise had gone to court and obtained what are called 'freezing' injunctions, which restricted the two companies' access to the money they had in the bank. The bank was notified of the orders, and should have prevented the companies from withdrawing money, but, apparently because of negligence, they failed to do so, which meant that the two companies were able to take out over £2 million, and Customs and Excise were unable to recover all the money owed. They sued the bank, claiming that it owed them a duty of care. The House of Lords held that it was foreseeable that Customs and Excise could lose money if the bank was negligent in handling the freezing injunction, and that this suggested there was also a degree of proximity. However, the decisive issue was whether it was just and reasonable to impose a duty. The House stated that where a court order was breached, the court had power to deal with that breach; this would usually be enough to ensure that banks complied with such orders, and there was nothing to suggest that the order created any extra cause of action. In addition, it was unjust and unreasonable that the bank should become exposed to a liability which could amount to very much more than the £2 million that was at stake in this case, when it had no way of resisting the court order, and got no reward for complying with it.

In **Mitchell** *v* **Glasgow City Council** (2009), the claimants were the wife and daughter of a man who had been killed by their neighbour. The neighbour rented a house from the defendant council, and had a history of abusing the claimants' family, including making threats to kill them. In an attempt to solve the problem, the council called the defendant to a meeting, and told them that if his behaviour did not improve, they would consider evicting him. Within an hour, he had gone back home and attacked his neighbour, inflicting injuries which proved fatal. The claimants argued that the council were aware that he had made death threats, and had a duty of care to warn them about the meeting, because they had reason to suspect he might attack anyone he suspected of complaining about him to the council. The House of Lords said that it was not fair, just and reasonable to impose such a duty, because that would mean that a similar duty must apply to all other landlords, and to social workers, in similar situations. Imposing a duty to warn, and liability if warnings were not issued, would deter landlords from taking steps to deal with anti-social behaviour by tenants, which would not be desirable. In this case the council had done their best to deal with the problem, and it was better that they took those steps than did nothing at all. The situation might have been different if the council had, by their words or behaviour, undertaken responsibility for the claimants' safety, but, as they had not, no duty should be imposed.

In **West Bromwich Albion Football Club** *v* **Medhat El-Safty** (2006), the case concerned a knee injury to a West Brom player, Michael Appleton. The club arranged for him to see the defendant, an orthopaedic consultant, who advised surgery. The operation was unsuccessful, and Mr Appleton could no longer play; it was established that the advice was negligent, as other treatment should have been tried first. As well as being a personal disaster, losing a player meant that the club lost money, and they sought to sue the defendant for their losses. The defendant clearly had a duty towards the player, as his patient, to take reasonable care to give competent medical advice, but the club could only claim if he also had a duty to take reasonable care not to damage their financial interest in the player. The Court of Appeal said that it was not just and reasonable to impose such a duty because there was nothing to suggest that the defendant should have realised he would be taking on that responsibility, and to take on this additional duty could have conflicted with his duty towards the player who was his patient, if, for example, aggressive treatment could have enabled him to play on, but led to problems later in life. The defendant was therefore not liable to the club.

Duties of care: pure economic loss

Many losses resulting from tort could be described as economic; if the claimant's house is burnt down because of the defendant's negligence, the loss is economic in the sense that the claimant no longer has an asset they used to have. Similarly, a claimant who suffers serious injury which makes them unable to work suffers a financial loss. The law of tort has always been willing to compensate for these losses with damages.

However, economic loss also has a more precise meaning in tort. The term is usually used to cover losses which are 'purely' economic, meaning those where a claimant has suffered financial damage that does not directly result from personal injury or damage to property – for example, where a product bought turns out to be defective, but does not actually cause injury or damage to other property. In cases of pure economic loss, the law of tort has been reluctant to allow a claim.

A case which illustrates the difference between the types of loss is **Spartan Steel** *v* **Martin** (1972). Here the defendants had negligently cut an electric cable, causing a power cut that lasted for 14 hours. Without electricity to heat the claimants' furnace, the metal in the furnace solidified, and the claimants were forced to shut their factory temporarily. They claimed damages under three heads:

- damage to the metal that was in the furnace at the time of the power cut (physical damage to property);
- loss of the profit that would have been made on the sale of that metal (economic loss arising from damage to property); and
- loss of profit on metal which would have been processed during the time the factory was closed due to the power cut (pure economic loss).

A majority of the Court of Appeal held that the first two claims were recoverable but the third was not. The defendants owed the claimants a duty not to damage their property, and therefore to pay for any loss directly arising from such damage, as well as for the damage itself, but they did not owe them any duty with regard to loss of profit.

Economic loss and policy

There are two main reasons for the traditional reluctance to compensate pure economic loss. The first is that, traditionally, contract was the means by which economic loss was compensated, and the courts were reluctant to disturb this. Contract was seen as offering certainty; defendants could only be liable for losses caused by their own failure to fulfil a freely undertaken agreement, and this clearly had benefits in the commercial world.

The second reason, linked to the first, is the much-quoted 'floodgates' argument. This reasons that while, as a general rule, an act or omission can only cause personal injury or property damage to a limited number of people, the possible economic loss from the same act may be vast and in practice incalculable. In **Spartan Steel**, for example, had the defendants been liable to compensate for profit lost as a result of the power cut, the number and amount of claims might in theory have been astronomical. Although this does not provide much of a moral reason why such losses should not be compensated, an accepted part of law's role in a market economy like ours is to provide industry and commerce with a framework within which they can plan their activities, and preventing unlimited claims for economic loss obviously assists in this.

Development of the law

The issue of economic loss in negligence has been the subject of much legal activity over the past 40 years or so, and the law has swung backwards and forwards over the issue. The result is that claims for pure economic loss are now allowed in certain situations, but the law surrounding them is complex, fragmented and still has an unsettled air. However, it is more easily understood if we first look at the traditional position on economic loss, and the developments that have taken place in the past four decades.

Origins of the claim for economic loss

The initial position on pure economic loss in negligence was laid down in the case of **Candler** *v* **Crane, Christmas & Co** (1951). Here a firm of accountants had done some work for a client, knowing that the figures produced would also be considered by a third party. As a result of relying on the figures, the third party suffered financial loss, but the Court of Appeal held that the accountants owed no duty of care regarding economic loss to the third party; their responsibility was only to the client with whom they had a contractual relationship.

This remained the situation until 1963, when the extremely important case of **Hedley Byrne** *v* **Heller** provided that there were some situations in which negligence could provide a remedy for pure economic loss caused by things the defendant had said, or information they had provided; essentially, there needed to be a 'special relationship' between the parties, which would arise where the defendants supplied advice or information, knowing that the claimants would rely on it for a particular purpose. This is sometimes known as 'negligent misstatement'. (The case is discussed more fully below.)

Following this came the case of **Anns** *v* **Merton London Borough** (1978) which, as we discussed on p. 19, was part of the judicial expansion of negligence liability during the 1970s. The case concerned economic loss arising from the claimant's house being badly built; defective foundations had caused cracking in the walls. This might at first sight appear to be a case of damage to property, but the courts have traditionally been insistent that a defect is not the same thing as damage: where a product is defective in its manufacture, claims may be made for any personal injury caused as a result of the defect, or any damage to other property, but not for the defect itself, which is considered economic, since the loss arises from the reduced value of the object. In **Anns**, however, the House of Lords decided that the cracks in the walls could be viewed as damage to property rather than economic loss, and therefore compensated.

This was followed by the case which is generally viewed as forming the peak of the expansion in negligence liability, **Junior Books** *v* **Veitchi** (1983). The claimants in the case had had a factory built for them under a contract with a building firm. The factory needed a special type of floor in order to support the kind of machinery the claimants wanted to use, and the claimants requested that the builders use a particular flooring firm to provide this, which they did. After the floor was laid, it was found to be defective. If the factory owners had themselves contracted with the flooring company, they could have sued them in contract for the price of replacing the floor, but their only contract was with the builders; the builders had contracted with the flooring company. It was possible to make out a case that the builders had been negligent, but a potential stumbling block was that the factory owners' loss was purely economic: the defect in the floor posed no threat to safety, nor any risk of damage to the fabric of the building, and so the only loss was the cost of replacing it. However, a majority of the House of Lords held that there was nevertheless a duty of care between the builders and the factory owners with regard to the defect in the floor.

The situation after this was that claimants could recover for economic loss caused by statements under **Hedley Byrne**, and, following **Anns** and then **Junior Books**, it was also possible to recover for economic loss caused by negligent acts. However, as we saw on p. 19, the general expansion of negligence liability was much criticised and it was at this point that the courts began to draw back, with the eventual overruling of **Anns** in **Murphy** *v* **Brentwood District Council** (see p. 19). Like **Anns**, **Murphy** concerned a defective building, and, as well as laying down general principles for the way in which the law on negligence should develop, the House of Lords put a stop to the possibility that defects in products could be seen as damage to property; it reaffirmed that they were to be regarded as economic loss and that they could not be compensated in negligence.

Junior Books was not overruled in **Murphy**, but in a series of later cases on defective products the courts declined to follow it and eventually it was considered that **Junior Books** was to be regarded as unique to its facts, and in particular the idea that, by specifying that the flooring company should be used, the claimants created a relationship of proximity between themselves and the defendants, even though there was no contract.

From there on, both the courts and academic commentators began to develop an approach to economic loss which distinguished between such loss when caused by negligent acts, and when caused by negligent statements or advice. Aside from the apparent anomaly of **Junior Books**, it appeared that economic loss arising from acts was not recoverable in negligence, whereas such loss arising from statements and advice was, if it could be fitted into the requirements of **Hedley Byrne**.

The current position

Case Navigator

During the 1990s, a new mood of cautious expansion was visible in a number of cases. These extended **Hedley Byrne** beyond liability for negligent statements or advice, and established that it can, in some circumstances, also cover negligent provision of services. This was specifically stated in **Henderson** *v* **Merrett Syndicates Ltd** (1994), and confirmed in **Williams and Reid** *v* **Natural Life Health Foods Ltd and Mistlin** (1998) (both cases are discussed below). The result now appears to be that when the **Hedley Byrne** principles are fulfilled, pure economic loss is recoverable where it is caused by either negligent advice or information, or by negligent provision of services. There is also a category of cases where compensation has been given for economic loss caused by negligent provision of services, even though the requirements of **Hedley Byrne** were not entirely fulfilled (these are discussed on p. 34).

Economic loss is still not, however, recoverable where it is caused by defective products, where **Murphy** still applies. Nor is it recoverable when caused by negligent acts other than the provision of services.

We will now look in more detail at **Hedley Byrne** and its effects.

The Hedley Byrne principles

Key Case **Hedley Byrne** *v* **Heller (1964)**

The claimants in **Hedley Byrne** *v* **Heller** (1964) were an advertising agency, who had been asked by a firm called Easipower Ltd to buy substantial amounts of advertising space on their behalf. To make sure their clients were creditworthy, Hedley Byrne asked their own bank, the National Provincial, to check on them. National Provincial twice contacted Heller, who were Easipower's bankers and were backing them financially, to enquire about Easipower's creditworthiness. Heller gave favourable references on both occasions, but each time included a disclaimer stating that the information was being supplied 'without responsibility on the part of this Bank or its officials'.

The second enquiry asked whether Easipower was 'trustworthy, in the way of business, to the extent of £100,000 per annum', and Heller answered that Easipower was a respectably constituted company, considered good for its ordinary business engagements. This message was conveyed to Hedley Byrne, and, relying on that advice, they entered into a contract with Easipower Ltd. Easipower later went into liquidation, leaving Hedley Byrne to pay the £17,000 due to companies from whom they had bought advertising space. Hedley Byrne claimed this amount from Heller.

In view of the words disclaiming liability, the House of Lords held that no duty of care was accepted by Heller, and none arose, so the claim failed. However, the House also considered what their conclusion would have been if no words of disclaimer had been used, and this is where the importance of the case lies. Their Lordships stated *obiter* that, in appropriate circumstances, there could be a duty of care to give careful advice, and that breach of that duty could give rise to liability for negligence. The fact that the sole damage was economic loss did not, they said, prevent this.

The House of Lords laid down a number of requirements which claimants would need to satisfy in order to establish a duty of care under **Hedley Byrne**. There must be:

- a 'special relationship' between the parties;
- a voluntary assumption of responsibility by the party giving the advice;
- reliance on that advice by the party receiving it; and
- it must be reasonable for that party to have relied on the advice.

The requirements are to a large extent interlinked, but some specific principles can be drawn out from the cases.

Legal Principle

There is a duty of care not to cause economic loss where there is a special relationship between the parties, the defendant voluntarily assumed a responsibility to the defendant, the claimant relied on the defendant's advice, and it was reasonable to do so.

The 'special relationship'

This was described by Lord Reid in **Hedley** as arising where 'it is plain that the party seeking information or advice was trusting the other to exercise such a degree of care as the circumstances required, where it was reasonable for him to do that, and where the other gave the information or advice when he knew or ought to have known that the enquirer was relying on him'.

Lord Reid made it plain that the 'special relationship' requirement meant that **Hedley Byrne** only covers situations where advice is given in a business context:

> Quite careful people often express definite opinions on social or informal occasions, even when they see that others are likely to be influenced by them; and they often do that without taking the care which they would take if asked for their opinion professionally, or in a business connection . . . there can be no duty of care on such occasions.

Advice given off the cuff in a social setting will therefore not, as a rule, give rise to a duty of care. For example, both doctors and lawyers frequently complain that as soon as they disclose their profession at parties, fellow guests want to discuss backaches or boundary disputes; they can at least take comfort that, tedious though those conversations may be, they will not result in a negligence suit if the advice given is careless. Curiously, there is, however, one case in which a duty of care under **Hedley** was found in a purely friendly setting. In **Chaudry** *v* **Prabhakar** (1988), the defendant had advised the claimant, a friend, to buy a particular second-hand car, without noticing that it had been in an accident. It was in fact unroadworthy, and the claimant successfully sued for negligence. The case has, however, been heavily criticised, and is unlikely ever to be followed; it certainly appears wrong in the light of Lord Reid's statement.

An example of the special relationship can be seen in **Esso Petroleum Co Ltd** *v* **Mardon** (1976). Here the claimant had leased a petrol station on the strength of Esso's advice that he could expect to sell at least 200,000 gallons a year. In fact he only managed to sell 78,000 gallons in 15 months. The Court of Appeal held that, in making the prediction, the petrol company had undertaken a responsibility to Mr Mardon, and he had relied on their experience in the petrol market; his claim was allowed.

The person giving the advice need not be a professional adviser. In **Lennon** *v* **Commissioner of the Metropolis** (2004), the claimant was an officer in the Metropolitan Police, who was changing jobs to go and work in the police force in Northern Ireland. He had been entitled to a housing allowance, and wanted to make sure this continued, so he asked an executive in the personnel department whether it would affect his housing allowance if he took time off between finishing one job and starting the other. She advised him that it would not. In fact, the time off counted as a break in service, which resulted in his losing entitlement to the housing allowance for ever. He sued the Metropolitan Police, who were vicariously liable (see Chapter 16) for the personnel officer's acts. The Court of Appeal upheld his claim, stating that even though the personnel officer was not a professional adviser, she had a managerial job in the police service, and had, or had access to, special complex knowledge about the effects of transfers on police allowances of the kind in question. She had led the claimant to believe he could rely on her advice, rather than telling him the question was outside her sphere of experience and suggesting that he took advice from elsewhere.

Voluntary assumption of responsibility

As Lord Reid pointed out in **Hedley Byrne**, a person asked for advice in a business context has three choices: they can opt to give no advice; choose to give advice, but warn that it should not be relied on; or give the advice without giving any such warning. In general, someone who chooses the third option will be considered to have voluntarily assumed responsibility for that advice.

An example of where the courts will find such an assumption of responsibility can be seen in **Dean** *v* **Allin & Watts** (2001), where the Court of Appeal held that the defendant, a solicitor who had acted for some clients who were borrowing money, had also assumed responsibility for the other party to the transaction – Mr Dean, the person lending the money. Mr Dean was a mechanic, and not widely experienced in business finance. He was approached by two borrowers seeking funding for their property company, and agreed to lend them £20,000, with a particular property being put up as security for the loan. The borrowers suggested that their solicitors draw up the necessary documentation, and met all the legal costs. Mr Dean made it clear that he would not be involving his own solicitor, and it was never suggested by the borrowers' solicitor that he should take independent legal advice.

The solicitor advised that the security could be dealt with by way of a deposit of the deeds to the property; this was in fact incorrect, and deposit of the deeds did not give Mr Dean any rights over the property. Eventually, the borrowers defaulted on the loan, and the mistake was discovered. Mr Dean now had neither his money, nor the property. He sued the solicitor, and the

Court of Appeal held that, in knowing that Mr Dean was not taking independent advice, the solicitor knew that he was being relied on to ensure that there was effective security for the loan, and therefore in continuing to act, without recommending that Mr Dean take independent advice, he was assuming a responsibility to him. The court stressed the fact that the defendant knew Mr Dean was inexperienced in business matters, and also pointed out that there was no conflict of interest between his interests and those of the defendant's clients, who also wanted to put in place effective security for the loan. Had the solicitor advised Mr Dean to consult a solicitor of his own, the result would, the court said, have been different.

In **Calvert** *v* **William Hill Credit Ltd** (2008), the case concerned the question of how far a bookmaker could be liable for economic losses caused to a problem gambler. The claimant was a greyhound trainer who had initially made a lot of money from gambling, but whose gambling habits eventually became compulsive, leading to losses of over £2 million. Realising that he had a problem, he had asked the bookmaker, William Hill, to close his telephone betting account and not to allow him to open another one (an arrangement known as 'self-exclusion'). The bookmaker had in place procedures to do this, which were part of a social responsibility policy that was designed to protect problem gamblers, but in Mr Calvert's case the system failed and he was able to go on gambling with William Hill, as well as with other bookmakers.

He argued that there were two possible grounds on which it could be said that William Hill owed him a duty of care. The first was that, by putting in place a social responsibility policy that was designed to protect problem gamblers, they had voluntarily assumed a responsibility towards such gamblers. The court rejected this idea, on the grounds that it was not reasonable to expect the bookmaker to identify all problem gamblers; that gamblers who signed up to the self-exclusion arrangement also agreed to a disclaimer absolving William Hill of legal responsibility for their economic losses; and that it was unfair to allow a situation in which problem gamblers could take their winnings if they were successful, but expect the bookmakers to compensate them if they were not.

The second argument was that, by agreeing to include Mr Calvert in the self-exclusion arrangement, the bookmaker assumed responsibility for carrying out that arrangement properly. The court found that he had identified himself to William Hill as a problem gambler, had asked for their help in excluding him from betting for six months, and had been told that he would get that help. That being the case, the court found that William Hill did have a duty of care to carry out the self-exclusion arrangement, and they had breached this duty. However, Mr Calvert's claim failed because the House of Lords found that William Hill's negligence did not ultimately cause his losses: even before he knew that the self-exclusion policy was not in place, he was still betting heavily through other bookmakers, and, given the extent of his gambling problem, the losses he sustained would have happened anyway.

Claimants not known to the defendant

More complex problems arise when the claimant is not known to the defendant, but claims to be, as Lord Bridge put it, 'a member of an identifiable class'. In **Goodwill** *v* **British Pregnancy Advisory Service** (1996), an attempt was made to use **Hedley Byrne** in a new factual context. The claimant, Ms Goodwill, had become pregnant by her boyfriend. Three years before their relationship began, he had undergone a vasectomy performed by the defendants. They had advised him after the operation that it had been successful and he would not need to use contraception in the future. He told Ms Goodwill this when they began their relationship, and she stopped using any contraception. In fact the vasectomy had reversed itself, and she became pregnant. She sued the defendants for negligence, claiming the cost of bringing up her daughter.

The Court of Appeal held that in order to claim successfully for pure economic loss arising from reliance on advice provided by the defendants, a claimant had to show that the defendants knew (either because they were told or because it was an obvious thing to assume) that the advice they supplied was likely to be acted on by the claimant (either as a specific individual or one of an ascertainable group), without independent enquiry, for a particular purpose which the defendants knew about at the time they gave the advice, and that the claimant had acted on the advice to his or her disadvantage.

In the case before them, the Court of Appeal held that at the time when the advice was given, the claimant was not known to the defendants, and was simply one of a potentially large class of women who might at some stage have a sexual relationship with the patient before them. They could not be expected to foresee that, years later, their advice to their patient might be communicated to and relied on by her for the purpose of deciding whether to use contraception; therefore the relationship between the defendants and Ms Goodwill was not sufficiently proximate to give rise to a duty of care. The court pointed out, however, that the situation might be different where a man and his partner were advised at the same time, or possibly even where their relationship was known to those giving the advice.

In common-sense terms, the distinction is a difficult one. Clearly, as Ms Goodwill pointed out, in this day and age it was not unlikely that a man of her boyfriend's age would have a sexual relationship with future partners, and, while the class of possible future partners might be large, the number who would end up pregnant was not, given that once pregnancy had occurred, it would be known that the vasectomy had reversed itself. Furthermore, the purpose to which such partners would put the advice was exactly the same as the purpose for which the patient would use it: as a statement that if they had sexual relations, no pregnancy would result. What we see in cases like this one is the courts struggling to balance the need to compensate loss where justice demands it and no other means of redress is available, and yet avoid opening those much-mentioned floodgates and opening defendants to unreasonable liability. The theme is continued in the 'wills cases' (discussed on p. 34).

The effect of disclaimers

Where a defendant has issued some kind of disclaimer (as in **Hedley Byrne** itself), this would appear to suggest that they are not accepting responsibility for their advice. However, the courts have stated that merely issuing a disclaimer will not always prevent liability under **Hedley Byrne**. Cases in this area are very fact-dependent, but the general approach seems to be that a disclaimer is more likely to prevent liability in cases where the claimant could reasonably be expected to understand what it meant, such as where the claimant is a business, or someone experienced in the kind of transaction taking place. This was the case in both **Omega Trust Co Ltd** *v* **Wright Son & Pepper** (1997), where the case involved a valuation of commercial property, and **McCullagh** *v* **Lane Fox & Partners Ltd** (1996), which concerned information given by an estate agent to a purchaser at the upper end of the housing market; and, in both cases, the courts found that the disclaimer issued by the defendant could be taken to mean there was no assumption of responsibility under **Hedley Byrne**.

However, in **Smith** *v* **Eric S Bush** (1990), the case involved advice given by surveyors to the buyers of an ordinary family home and, in this case, the House of Lords found that the existence of a disclaimer did not mean there was no assumption of responsibility towards the buyers. The claimants' home had been negligently surveyed by the defendants, and was worth much less than they had paid for it. The survey had been commissioned by the building society from which the claimants had sought a mortgage, as part of its standard practice of ensuring that the property was worth at least the money that was being lent. However, such surveys were routinely relied upon by purchasers as well, and in fact purchasers actually paid the building society to have the survey done, although the surveyors' contract was always with the building society. The House of Lords held that in such situations surveyors assumed a duty of care to house purchasers; even though the surveys were not done for the purpose of advising home buyers, surveyors would be well aware that buyers were likely to rely on their valuation, and the surveyors only had the work in the first place because buyers were willing to pay their fees. An important factor was that this did not impose particularly wide liability: the extent of the surveyors' liability was limited to compensating the buyer of the house for up to the value of the house.

Reliance by the claimant

Reliance under **Hedley Byrne** requires that the claimant depended on the defendant using the particular skill or experience required for the task which the defendant had undertaken; it is not merely general reliance on the defendant exercising care.

The claimant must prove not only that they relied on the defendant, but that it was reasonable to do so, and the courts have held that this will not be the case where the claimant relies on information or advice for one purpose, when it was given for a different purpose. In **Caparo Industries plc** *v* **Dickman** (1990) (see p. 23 for the full facts) Caparo relied on an auditor's report prepared by Dickman when deciding whether to invest in Fidelity. The House of Lords held that as auditors' reports were not prepared for the purpose of giving such guidance, Dickman were not liable.

Lord Bridge held that there was no special relationship between Caparo, as potential investors, and the auditors. He drew a distinction between situations where 'the defendant giving advice or information was fully aware of the nature of the transaction which the claimant had in contemplation' and those in which 'a statement is put into more or less general circulation and may foreseeably be relied upon by strangers to the maker of the statement, for any one of a variety of purposes which the maker of the statement has no specific reason to contemplate'.

This approach was followed in **Reeman** *v* **Department of Transport** (1997). Mr Reeman was the owner of a fishing boat that required an annual certificate of seaworthiness from the Department of Transport (DoT), without which it could not be used at sea. The boat was covered by such a certificate when Mr Reeman bought it, but it was later discovered that the surveyor who inspected it for the DoT had been negligent; the certificate should not have been issued and would not be renewed, making the boat practically worthless.

Mr Reeman sued for his economic loss, but the Court of Appeal held that, following **Caparo**, the provision of information for a particular purpose could not be taken as an assumption of responsibility for its use for a different purpose. The purpose of issuing the certificate was to promote safety, not to establish a boat's commercial value, even though the boat effectively had no commercial value without it. In addition, the class of person likely to rely on the statement had to be capable of ascertainment at the time the statement was made, and not merely capable of description; when the certificate was issued, there was no reason to identify Mr Reeman as someone who was likely to rely on it.

However, the courts are willing to look very closely at the circumstances in which advice was given, and there are cases where they have held that the fact that advice was given for one purpose does not mean it is unreasonable for the recipient to rely on it for another purpose at the same time. In **Law Society** *v* **KPMG Peat Marwick** (2000) the defendants were accountants to a firm of solicitors, and were asked by them to prepare the annual accounts which were required by the Law Society. The accountants failed to uncover the fact that a senior partner in the firm was defrauding hundreds of clients. When the frauds eventually came to light, over 300 clients claimed compensation from a fund set up for this purpose by the Law Society, and the Law Society sued the accountants, claiming that the accounts had been prepared negligently. The accountants argued that their duty was only owed to the solicitors' firm; the Law Society held that the accountants owed a duty to them, by virtue of the Law Society's reliance on the information given in the accounts. The Court of Appeal analysed the situation using the three-step **Caparo** test. They held that if accountants' reports failed to highlight improprieties in the way a firm dealt with clients' money, it was clearly foreseeable that loss to the fund would result. There was sufficient proximity between the reporting accountant and the Law Society, and it was fair and reasonable to impose a duty. On this last point, the court made use of similar reasoning to that in **Smith** *v* **Eric S Bush** (see p. 32), pointing out that the imposition of a duty did not expose the accountants to unrestricted liability; the amount of compensation that could be claimed was restricted to the amount of clients' money that had been lost in the frauds, and the time within which it could be claimed was also limited, given that reports were delivered annually, so negligence in any one year could be uncovered by a non-negligent report the following year.

Recovery without reliance – the 'wills' cases

The 1980s and 1990s brought a crop of cases which have allowed compensation for economic loss caused by negligent advice or services, yet which do not sit quite comfortably within the principles of **Hedley Byrne**. In **Ross** *v* **Caunters** (1980), a solicitor had been negligent in preparing a client's will, with the result that it was in breach of probate law and the intended beneficiary was unable to receive her inheritance. She successfully sued the solicitor for the value of her loss. Although the loss was purely economic, and caused by an act rather than a statement, the case was not considered especially significant at the time, since it took place in the period after **Anns** *v* **Merton London Borough** (1978), when the wider approach to the issue of a duty of care was in place, and before **Murphy** *v* **Brentwood District Council** (1990) tightened up the requirements again. However, the significance comes from the fact that it was followed in the post-**Murphy** case of **White** *v* **Jones** (1995). Here, two daughters had had a quarrel with their father, and he cut them out of his will. The family was later reconciled, and the father instructed his solicitors to renew the £9,000 legacies to his daughters. A month later, he discovered that the solicitors had not yet done this, and reminded them of his instructions. Some time afterwards, the father died, and it was found that the will had still not been changed, so the daughters could not receive their expected inheritance. They sued the solicitors, and the House of Lords allowed the claim, even though the loss was purely economic and the result of negligent work rather than a negligent misstatement.

White *v* **Jones** proved somewhat difficult to explain on **Hedley Byrne** principles. Wills are prepared in order to put into practice the wishes of the person making the will (the testator), and, as Lord Goff stated in **White** *v* **Jones**, in many cases, beneficiaries will not even be aware that they stand to gain, so it is hard to see how they can be said to rely on the solicitor's skill as required under **Hedley Byrne**. Clearly the solicitors in both cases had assumed the responsibility for preparing the wills correctly for the testators, but could they also be said to have accepted a responsibility towards the beneficiaries? The House of Lords admitted that it was difficult to see how this could be argued, but, even so, they were prepared to allow a remedy.

What appears to have swayed them was the practical justice of the claimant's case: the solicitor had been negligent, yet the only party who would normally have a valid claim (the testator and his estate) had suffered no loss, and the party who had suffered loss had no claim. As Lord Goff pointed out, the result was 'a lacuna [loophole] in the law which needs to be filled'. The exact *ratio* of the case is difficult to discover, as the three judges were divided on how the assumption of responsibility problem was to be got over. Lords Browne-Wilkinson and Nolan argued that, in taking on the job of preparing the will, the solicitor had voluntarily accepted responsibility for doing it properly, and it was for the law to decide the scope of that responsibility and in particular whether it included a duty to the claimants. Both held that it did. Lord Goff held that the solicitor had in fact assumed responsibility only to the testator, but that the law could and should deem that responsibility to extend to the intended beneficiaries.

However, even if the decision in **White** *v* **Jones** did no more than use practical justice to fill a loophole in the law, the case of **Carr-Glynn** *v* **Frearsons** (1998) extended it beyond this approach. Here a woman had made a will leaving the claimant her share in a property. The defendants, the solicitors who had drawn up the will, had advised her that there was a problem with the ownership of the property which could result in her share automatically passing to the other part-owners on her death, so that any bequest of it would be ineffective. They told her what to do to avoid the problem, but she died before taking the advice. The claimant therefore received nothing under the will, and the estate also suffered a loss since the share in the property passed to the co-owners.

The case was different from **Ross** *v* **Caunters** and **White** *v* **Jones**, where the estate had suffered no loss and the party who had suffered loss had no claim; here, allowing a duty of care to the disappointed beneficiaries might give rise to two claims for the same loss, one from the intended beneficiaries and one from the estate. However, the Court of Appeal held that although the estate had a claim, any damages it recovered by bringing that claim would not go to the claimant, who was therefore still left without a remedy unless the principle of **White** *v* **Jones** was extended to cover her. The court stated such an extension was reasonable; there was a duty of care, and it required that the solicitor should have taken action herself to ensure that the will would take effect as expected.

How far do the 'wills' cases go?

In the years since **White** *v* **Jones**, there has been great debate about how far the principles laid down in that case will go. Could they apply to agreements other than wills? The case of **Gorham** *v* **British Telecommunications plc** (2000) would seem to suggest that they can. The case involved a pension plan taken out by a Mr Gorham, on the advice of an insurance company. They told him he would be better off opting out of his employer's pension scheme and taking out his own pension instead; this was untrue. One of the advantages of the employer's scheme was the insurance benefits that would be paid to Mr Gorham's family if he died while working for the company. These were lost when he switched pensions, so when he did die, still an employee of the firm, his widow sued. The Court of Appeal found that the position of intended beneficiaries of an insurance policy was comparable to that of the intended beneficiaries to a will, and that the adviser had therefore undertaken a responsibility to the family, as well as to Mr Gorham himself.

Negligence and references

A case which, it has been suggested, reveals an expansion of liability for economic loss is **Spring** *v* **Guardian Assurance** (1994). The claimant, Mr Spring, had been employed by the defendant, but was sacked. When seeking a new job, he needed a reference, but the one supplied by the defendant said that Mr Spring was incompetent and dishonest. Not surprisingly, he failed to get the new job. He sued the defendant for negligence, claiming the economic loss caused by not getting the job. The trial judge found that Mr Spring was not dishonest, and that, while the defendant had genuinely believed that what he had written was true, he had been negligent in the way he reached that conclusion. The House of Lords agreed that a duty of care existed, and the defendant had breached it.

Two key factors make **Spring** different from the usual **Hedley Byrne** case. First, the information which caused the loss was not given *to* the person who relied on it, as it was in **Hedley**, but was *about* him. Secondly, it is hard to see how there can be a truly voluntary assumption of responsibility where someone is asked to give an employment reference, because this is one situation where the three options outlined by Lord Reid in **Hedley** (see p. 30) do not apply. Someone who refuses to give a reference is, effectively, giving a bad one, because the prospective new employer will assume there must be something to hide; equally, saying that the reference should not be relied on is likely to set alarm bells ringing. An ex-employer asked for a reference is therefore forced to assume responsibility, whichever option he or she chooses. A third issue is that claims involving damage to reputation would usually be considered to fall within the tort of defamation, which has its own rules; it was argued in the case that allowing a claim in negligence would subvert these rules. What swayed the House of Lords to allow the claim, however, seems to be very much, as in the wills cases, the practical justice of the situation.

Negligent misstatement and contract

Because contract was traditionally seen as the method for resolving disputes involving pure economic loss, it was originally thought that where two parties had made a contract, a negligence action could not be used to fill in any gaps in that contract. However, in **Henderson** *v* **Merrett Syndicates Ltd** (1994), it was established that the existence of a contract between the parties did not prevent a **Hedley Byrne** special relationship arising. The case arose when the Lloyd's insurance organisation made considerable losses on many of its policies. The losses had to be borne by people who had invested in Lloyd's by underwriting the policies. Known as Lloyd's Names, these people were grouped into syndicates and invested on the understanding that they were assuming unlimited liability; if big losses were made, the Names could lose everything they had. They were willing to take on this liability because becoming a Name was seen as a sure way of making money for those who were wealthy enough to be able to invest, and in previous years it had proved to be exactly that.

However, in the early 1990s, a series of natural and man-made disasters led to unusually big claims, and the Names were called upon to pay; many were ruined financially as a result. They alleged that the agents who organised the syndicates had been negligent; many of the Names had entered into contracts with these managers, but, by the time the actions were brought, the three-year limitation period for a breach of contract action had expired. Could they then take advantage of the longer (six-year) limitation period for tort actions? The House of Lords held that they could; the syndicate managers had assumed responsibility for the Names' economic welfare, and the existence of a contract could only prevent liability in tort if such liability would contradict the terms of the contract. Lord Goff explained:

> liability can, and in my opinion should, be founded squarely on the principle established in **Hedley Byrne** itself, from which it follows that an assumption of responsibility coupled with the concomitant reliance may give rise to a tortious duty of care irrespective of whether there is a contractual relationship between the parties, and in consequence, unless his contract precludes him from doing so, the plaintiff, who has available to him concurrent remedies in contract and tort, may choose that remedy which appears to him most advantageous.

Negligent misstatements often take place in a pre-contractual situation, where one party is trying to persuade the other to enter a contract. **Hedley Byrne** can apply in such situations, but in practice it has been made less important in this area by the Misrepresentation Act 1967, which imposes its own liability for false statements made during contractual negotiations.

Problems with the law on economic loss

Too many restrictions – or too few?

The case of **Spartan Steel** *v* **Martin** (1972) illustrates that the distinction between pure economic loss and other kinds of loss can be a very fine one – and one that in common-sense terms is difficult to justify. The defendants' negligence caused all three of the types of loss that resulted from the power cut, and all three types of loss were easily foreseeable, so why should they have been liable to compensate two sorts of loss but not the third? To the non-legal eye, distinguishing between them seems completely illogical – as indeed it must to a claimant who is left with a loss caused by someone else, and has no redress unless they have a contract. In many cases this can be seen as allowing a defendant to get away with seriously careless behaviour, regardless of the loss caused to others.

On the other hand, it can be argued that rather than not allowing sufficient redress for pure economic loss, the tort system in fact allows too much. In most cases of pure economic loss, what we are really talking about is not loss, but failure to make a gain. This is obvious in the wills cases, for example, but also applies to cases such as **Smith** *v* **Eric S Bush** (1990), where it can be argued that in buying the house the claimants were simply entering into a market transaction, and these always run the risk of creating loss as well as the possibility of making a gain. They did not have money taken from them, they simply bought a house which was worth less than they thought.

Traditionally, the role of tort law is to compensate those who have actually suffered loss; it can be argued that those who wish to protect their expectation of gain should do so through contract, and those who have given nothing in return for a service should not be compensated when that service lets them down financially. One answer to the latter view is that in most of the cases where claimants have not given anything in return for provision of advice or services, the defendants nevertheless gain a commercial benefit from the situation. This is most clear in **Smith** *v* **Eric Bush**, where the surveyors only had the work in the first place because house buyers were willing to pay for it, albeit indirectly, but it can also be found in less obvious situations. In **Hedley Byrne**, Lord Goff pointed out that in establishing whether the necessary special relationship existed in a particular case:

> [i]t may often be a material factor to consider whether the adviser is acting purely out of good nature or whether he is getting his reward in some indirect form. The service that a bank performs in giving a reference is not done simply out of a desire to assist commerce. It would discourage the customers of the bank if their deals fell through because the bank had refused to testify to their credit when it was good.

Overlap with contract law

The issue of the relationship between contract and tort causes particular problems, and in particular, the assertion in **Henderson** that a claimant who has a contractual remedy as well as a possible action in negligence should be able to choose between them. As well as rendering the limitation period for contractual actions essentially meaningless in these situations, it allows the claimant to pick and choose in other ways. For example, in contract a loss will only be compensated if there was a very high degree of probability that it would result from the defendant's breach of contract; is it necessarily right that a claimant who cannot satisfy that requirement should get another bite of the cherry in tort, where liability can be allowed for even extremely unlikely losses if they were reasonably foreseeable?

Lack of clarity

Perhaps the most significant practical problem in this area is that in their anxiety to avoid opening the floodgates to massive liability, yet allow redress where justice seems to demand it, the courts have resorted to over-complex and not entirely logical arguments. The wills cases are an obvious example of this, and the result is uncertainty about their scope, and the possibility of further fragmentation in the way the law treats economic loss.

Duties of care: psychiatric injury or 'nervous shock'

It is well established that physical injury can give rise to a claim in tort, but what about psychiatric damage? The concept of a duty has been used to limit compensation claims for psychiatric damage (often called nervous shock), in the same way as it has been used to limit claims for economic loss. In the past, where there was no physical harm the courts were slow to accept claims for mental, rather than physical, injury caused by negligence. Such claims are now recognised but are subject to a number of restrictions.

What is 'nervous shock'?

Psychiatric injury has traditionally been known by the courts as 'nervous shock', a label which adds to the confusion surrounding this area of the law by being completely misleading. The term implies that claimants can seek damages because they are shocked at the result of a defendant's negligence, or perhaps upset, frightened, worried or grief-stricken. This is not the case. In order to claim for so-called 'nervous shock', a claimant must prove that they have suffered from a genuine illness or injury. In some cases, the injury or illness may actually be a physical one, brought on by a mental shock: cases include a woman who had a miscarriage as a result of witnessing the aftermath of a terrible road accident (**Bourhill** *v* **Young** (1943), though the woman's claim failed on other grounds), and a man who was involved in an accident but not physically injured in it, who later suffered a recurrence and worsening of the disease myalgic encephalomyelitis (ME), also known as chronic fatigue syndrome, as a result of the shock (**Page** *v* **Smith** (1995)).

If the shock has not caused a physical injury or illness, the claimant must prove that it has caused what Lord Bridge in **McLoughlin** *v* **O'Brian** (1983) (see below) described as 'a positive psychiatric illness'. Examples include clinical depression, personality changes and post-traumatic stress disorder, an illness in which a shocking event causes symptoms including difficulty sleeping, tension, horrifying flashbacks and severe depression. It is important to be clear that this category does not include people who are simply upset by a shock, regardless of how badly; they must have a recognised psychiatric illness, and medical evidence will be needed to prove this. Consequently, we will use the term psychiatric injury from now on, though 'nervous shock' is referred to in many judgments.

Claimants who can prove such injury can only claim in negligence if they can establish that they are owed a duty of care by the defendant, with regard to psychiatric injury (and of course that the defendant's negligence actually caused the injury). This will depend on their relationship to the event which caused the shock, and case law has developed different sets of rules, covering different categories of claimant. The number of categories has varied at different stages of the law's development, but since the most recent House of Lords case, **White and others** *v* **Chief Constable of South Yorkshire** (1999), there are now three:

- those who are physically injured in the event which the defendant has caused, as well as psychiatrically injured as a result of it. These are called primary victims;
- those who are put in danger of physical harm, but actually suffer only psychiatric injury. These are also called primary victims;
- those who are not put in danger of physical injury to themselves, but suffer psychiatric injury as a result of witnessing such injury to others; these are called secondary victims. A duty of care to secondary victims will arise only if they can satisfy very restrictive requirements.

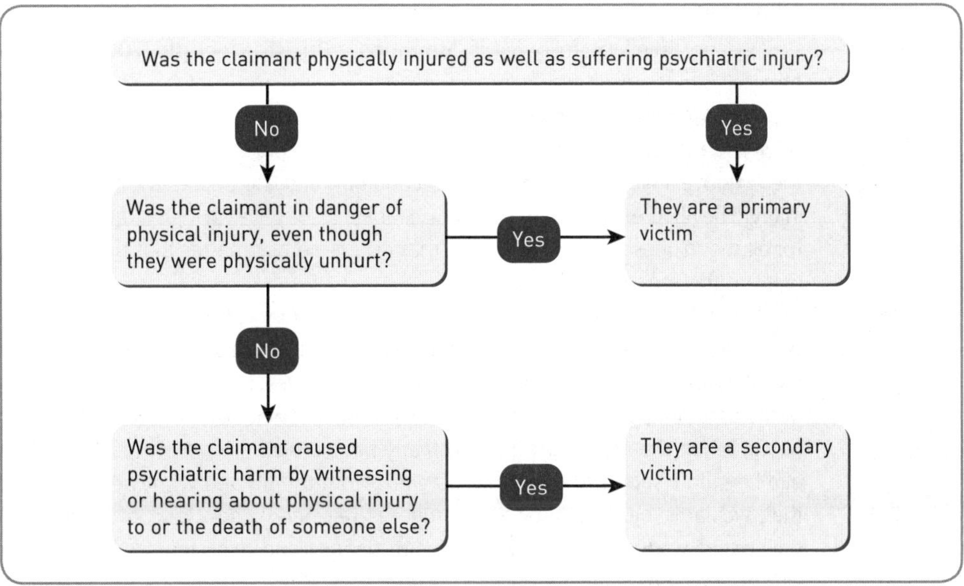

Figure 2.1 Primary and secondary victims in psychiatric injury claims

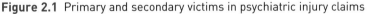

Primary victims

An accident victim who suffers physical injury due to the negligence of another can recover damages not just for the physical injuries but also for any psychiatric injury as well. The ordinary rules of negligence apply to such cases. The category of primary victims also includes those who are put at risk of physical injury to themselves, and who do not actually suffer physical injury but do suffer psychiatric injury as a result of the dangerous event. **White and others** (1999) confirms that if a person negligently exposes another to a risk of physical injury, they will be liable for any psychological injury that this may cause the other person, even if the threatened physical injury does not in fact happen.

This was originally established by the case of **Dulieu** *v* **White & Sons** (1901). The claimant was serving in a pub when one of the defendant's employees negligently drove his van and horses into the premises. The claimant feared for her safety, and although she was not actually struck she was badly frightened and suffered a miscarriage as a result. The defendant was found liable even though there was no physical impact, as he could have foreseen that the claimant would have suffered such shock.

The leading modern case on primary victims who are exposed to the risk of injury, but not actually physically hurt, is **Page** *v* **Smith** (1995). The claimant was involved in an accident which could have caused physical injury, but fortunately he escaped unhurt. Some years earlier, he had suffered from a serious illness called myalgic encephalomyelitis. He had had this illness for several years but, before the accident happened, it had gone into remission. After the accident, his old symptoms began to recur, and he claimed that this had been caused by the shock of being involved in the accident.

The House of Lords held that where it was reasonably foreseeable that a defendant's behaviour would expose the claimant to a risk of physical injury, there was a duty of care with regard to any injury that the claimant suffered, including psychiatric injury. It was not necessary that pyschiatric injury itself was foreseeable.

This approach was followed in **Simmons** *v* **British Steel plc** (2004). The claimant had been physically injured in a workplace accident, and as a result of his shock and anger at what had happened to him, he developed a severe skin condition. This led to him having to take a lot of time off work and, as a result of that, he developed a depressive illness. The House of Lords held that the employers were liable for the skin condition and the depressive illness, as well as the original injury. They had exposed him to a foreseeable risk of physical injury, and they were therefore liable for all the injuries that resulted from that risk. It did not matter that the actual type of the injuries was not foreseeable.

Although a claimant can claim for psychiatric injury caused by fears for their own safety even though no physical injury actually occurred, there must be some basis for the fears. In **McFarlane** *v* **Wilkinson** (1997), the Court of Appeal held that the fear must be reasonable, given the nature of the risk and the claimant's situation. The case arose out of the terrible events on the *Piper Alpha* oil rig, when the rig caught fire and many people died as a result of the explosion. The claimant had been in a support boat about 50 yards from the rig and witnessed the disaster. His claim for the psychiatric injury suffered as a result was rejected by the Court of Appeal, on the ground that the boat he was on was clearly never in any danger, and so his fear for his safety was unreasonable. (For reasons which will be obvious when we look at the witness cases below, merely seeing the disaster would not have been sufficient ground for this claimant's claim.)

What is unclear is whether a claimant can be considered as a primary victim if they were not actually in physical danger, but had reasonable grounds for thinking that they might be. The two leading judgments in **White** differ slightly in this area: Lord Steyn says the claimant must have 'objectively exposed himself to danger or *reasonably believed* that he was doing so' (our italics); on the other hand Lord Hoffmann refers only to primary victims being 'within the range of foreseeable physical injury'. Of course, in the majority of cases the reasonable belief that the claimant was in danger will arise from the fact that they actually were; but, in the throes of an emergency situation, it is not difficult to imagine making out a case for believing oneself to be in some danger when in fact there is no physical risk at all, and it is a pity that their Lordships did not make themselves clearer on this crucial point.

In **CJD Group B Claimants** *v* **The Medical Research Council** (1998), it was suggested that there might be a group which could not be considered primary victims in the usual sense, but who nevertheless should be treated in the same way. The claimants in the case had all had growth problems as children, and they had been treated with injections of growth hormone which, it was later discovered, may have been contaminated with the virus which causes Creutzfeldt–Jakob Disease (CJD), a fatal brain condition (this is the brain condition recognised as the human form of BSE or mad cow disease, but the events in this case have no link with the controversy over BSE-infected beef). It was established that those who had received the contaminated injections were at risk of developing CJD, but it was not possible to discover which batches had been contaminated, nor to test the recipients to discover whether a particular individual was harbouring the virus. As a result, the claimants were having to live with the fear of knowing that they might develop the disease, and some of them suffered psychiatric injury as a result of this.

It was established that the defendants had been negligent in allowing the injections to continue after the risk of contamination was suspected, and the claimants claimed that they were owed a duty as primary victims with regard to psychiatric injury, as the injections they were negligently given made them more than mere bystanders, and could be compared to the car accident in which the claimant in **Page** *v* **Smith** was involved. Morland J disagreed with this analysis, holding that they were not primary victims in the normal sense, because the psychiatric injury was not actually triggered by the physical act of the injections, but by the knowledge, which came later, that they might be at risk of developing CJD. Even so, he allowed their claim, on the basis that there was a relationship of proximity between the parties, that the psychiatric injuries were reasonably foreseeable, and there was no public policy reason to exclude them from compensation.

However, this approach was not followed in the case of **Rothwell** *v* **Chemical & Insulating Co Ltd** (2007). The claimants in the case were a group of workers who had been negligently exposed to asbestos while working for the defendants. If asbestos gets into the lungs, it can cause one of a range of fatal diseases. At the time the case was brought, none of the defendants had any of these diseases, but they did have what are known as pleural plaques. These are a form of scarring on the lungs, which show that asbestos has been inhaled. The plaques do not cause any symptoms, or make it more likely that the person will get one of the asbestos-related illnesses, but, because they are evidence that asbestos has entered the person's lungs, having them is a sign that that person may be at risk of asbestos-related illness. This naturally caused great anxiety among the claimants, but, as we have seen, this is not enough to make a claim for psychiatric injury. However, one of the claimants had gone on to develop clinical depression, which is a recognised psychiatric illness, as a result of the worry, and so the House of Lords had to consider whether the defendants owed him a duty of care with regard to psychiatric illness. They held that there was no duty of care in this case, stating that the question should be decided on the usual principles applicable to psychiatric illness caused at work (see p. 152). On this basis, the defendants could not reasonably have been expected to foresee that the claimant would suffer a psychiatric illness as a result of exposure to asbestos, so there was no duty of care and his claim failed.

Secondary victims

Key Case **White and others *v* Chief Constable of South Yorkshire (1999)**

White and others (1999) establishes that sufferers of psychiatric injury who are not either physically injured or in danger of being physically injured are to be considered secondary victims. Among the important cases which have fallen within this group are claims made by:

- people who have suffered psychiatric injury as a result of witnessing the death or injury of friends, relatives or work colleagues;
- those whose psychiatric injury has been caused by them unwittingly bringing about death or injury to others, where the ultimate cause was someone else's negligence (known as 'unwitting agents';
- those who have suffered psychiatric injury as a result of acting as rescuers, both those who have voluntarily given assistance to others in danger, and those who have done so as a result of their jobs, such as police officers.

Legal Principle

A claimant who suffers psychiatric injury but is not physically injured or at risk of physical injury is a secondary claimant who must pass the tests set down in Alcock. This category includes rescuers and employees of the defendant.

Until **White**, each of these groups had been subject to different treatment, but **White** establishes that they are all to be subject to the same rules, namely those developed in two key cases, **McLoughlin** *v* **O'Brian** (1982) and **Alcock** *v* **Chief Constable of Yorkshire** (1992). These cases established that secondary victims could only claim for psychiatric injury in very limited circumstances, and **White** confirms these limitations.

In **McLoughlin** *v* **O'Brian**, the claimant's husband and children were involved in a serious car accident, caused by the defendant's negligence. One of her daughters was killed and her husband and two other children badly injured. The claimant was not with her family when the accident happened, but was told about it immediately afterwards, and rushed to the hospital. There she saw the surviving members of her family covered in dirt and oil, and her badly injured son screaming in fear and pain. She suffered psychiatric injury as a result, including clinical depression and personality changes.

The House of Lords allowed her claim, even though up until then only witnesses who were actually present at the scene of a shocking incident had been allowed to recover for psychiatric injury. The decision itself was rather confused, in that Lord Bridge suggested that the sole criterion was still reasonable foresight, and the claimant could recover because her psychiatric injury was reasonably foreseeable, but Lords Wilberforce and Edmund-Davies favoured a different approach. They suggested that while psychiatric injury did have to be reasonably foreseeable, this in itself was not enough to create a duty of care towards secondary victims. Unlike other types of claimant, secondary victims would have to satisfy a series of other requirements, concerning their relationship to the primary victims of the shocking incident and their position with regard to that incident. This second approach is the one which has since found favour with the courts, and it was explained in detail in **Alcock** *v* **Chief Constable of South Yorkshire** (1992).

Alcock *v* **Chief Constable of Yorkshire** (1992)

Alcock *v* **Chief Constable of Yorkshire** (1992) arose from the Hillsborough football stadium disaster in 1989. The events which gave rise to the case (and to **White and others** *v* **Chief Constable of South Yorkshire** (1998)) took place during the 1989 FA Cup Semi-Final match between Liverpool and Nottingham Forest. All tickets for the match had been sold, and it was being shown on live television. However, play had to be stopped after six minutes because so many spectators had been allowed onto the terraces that some were being crushed against the high fences that divided the terraces from the pitch. A total of 95 people died in the tragedy that followed, and another 400 needed hospital treatment for their injuries.

The South Yorkshire police were responsible for policing the ground, and a public enquiry found that the incident was caused by a negligent decision on their part, which allowed too many people into the ground. Claims for physical injury and death were settled by the police, as were others for psychiatric injury which clearly fell within the accepted categories of those who could make a claim for this type of damage. This left two further groups who claimed psychiatric injury as a result of the tragedy: relatives and friends of those injured or killed, whose claims were examined in **Alcock**; and police officers on duty for the events of that day, who were represented in **White** (the fate of their claim is discussed later).

Alcock was a test case in that the specific claimants were chosen because between them they represented a range of relationships to the dead and injured, and positions in relation to the incident at the ground, which were held by around 150 other people who claimed to have suffered psychiatric injury as a result of the tragedy. They included parents, grandparents, brothers, brothers-in-law, fiancées and friends of the dead and injured, who had either been at the stadium when the disaster occurred and witnessed it at first hand, seen it live on television, gone to the stadium to look for someone they knew, been told the news by a third party, or had to identify someone in the temporary mortuary at the ground.

The claimants argued that the test for whether they were owed a duty of care was simply whether their psychiatric injuries were reasonably foreseeable, as Lord Bridge had suggested in **McLoughlin**. The House of Lords took a different view, pointing out that while it was clear that deaths and injuries in traumatic accidents commonly caused suffering that went well beyond the immediate victims, it was generally the policy of the common law not to compensate third parties. They held that although some exceptions could be made, they should be subject to much stricter requirements than those which applied to primary victims.

The starting point, they said, was that a secondary victim must prove that psychiatric injury to secondary victims was a reasonably foreseeable consequence of the defendant's negligence. **White** confirms earlier cases in stating that this will only be established where a bystander of reasonable fortitude would be likely to suffer psychiatric injury; if the claimant only suffers psychiatric injury because they are unusually susceptible to shock, reasonable foreseeability is not proved. However, it was pointed out that this rule should not be confused with the 'eggshell skull' situation seen, for example, in **Page** *v* **Smith**, where as a result of psychiatric injury the damage is more serious than might be expected. So long as a bystander of normal fortitude would be likely to suffer psychiatric injury, it does not matter that that psychiatric injury is made more serious by some characteristic personal to the claimant; but if the psychiatric injury would not have occurred at all to someone without the claimant's particular susceptibility, there is no claim.

→

Once reasonable foreseeability is established, there are three further tests which the courts must consider:

- the nature and cause of the psychiatric injury;
- the class of person into which the claimant falls, in terms of their relationship to the primary victim(s);
- the claimant's proximity to the shocking incident, in terms of both time and place.

The strength of restrictions which these tests place on claims can be seen in the fact that every single claimant in **Alcock** failed on at least one of them. Below we look at each in turn.

Legal Principle

Claimants who suffer psychiatric injury as a result of witnessing a shocking incident, but are not physically injured or at risk of physical injury, are owed a duty of care only if their psychiatric injury is caused by a sudden shock; they have a sufficiently close emotional tie to the primary victims; and they were sufficiently close in space and time to the shocking incident.

The nature and cause of the psychiatric injury

Like primary victims, secondary victims must prove that their psychiatric damage amounts to a recognised psychiatric illness. They are also subject to an additional requirement, that the psychiatric damage must have been caused by the claimant suffering a sudden and unexpected shock caused by a 'horrifying event'. This excludes, for example, cases in which people suffer psychiatric illness as a result of the grief of bereavement, or the stress and demands of having to look after a disabled relative injured by the negligence of another. In **Sion** *v* **Hampstead Health Authority** (1994), the claimant had developed a stress-related psychiatric illness as a result of watching his son slowly die in intensive care as a result of negligent medical treatment. It was held that as the father's psychiatric illness had not been caused by a sudden shock, he could not recover damages for it.

A contrasting case is **North Glamorgan NHS Trust** *v* **Walters** (2002). Here the claimant was the mother of a baby boy who died after receiving negligent treatment for which the defendants were responsible. The little boy, Elliott, was ill in hospital. Unknown to his mother at the time, the hospital had misdiagnosed his illness. She woke up to find him choking and coughing blood, and was told by the doctors that he was having a fit, but that he was very unlikely to have suffered any serious damage. Later that day, he was transferred to another hospital, where she was told – correctly – that he had in fact suffered severe brain damage and was in a coma; she was asked to consider switching off his life support machine. She and her busband agreed to this on the following day.

The events caused her to suffer a psychiatric illness, but the hospital argued that they were not liable for this as it was not caused by a sudden shock, but by a sequence of events that took place over 36 hours. The Court of Appeal disagreed: it said that the 'horrifying event' referred to in **Alcock** could be made up of a series of events, in this case, witnessing the fit, hearing the news that her son was brain-damaged after being told that he was not, and then watching him die. Each had their own immediate impact, and could be distinguished from cases where psychiatric injury was caused by a gradual realisation that a child was dying.

The courts have held that shock can be the result not just of injury or death to a loved one but also of damage to property. In **Attia** *v* **British Gas** (1988), British Gas were installing central heating into the claimant's house. She had spent many years decorating and improving her home and she was very attached to it. When she returned home in the afternoon she found her house on fire. It took the fire brigade four hours to get the blaze under control, by which time her house was seriously damaged. The fire was caused by the negligence of the defendants' employees. British Gas accepted their liability for the damage to the house but the claimant also sought damages for the nervous shock she had suffered as a result. The Court of Appeal accepted that she could make a claim for nervous shock resulting from the incident.

In many cases, causation will be difficult to prove, since, in addition to the required shock, claimants will have experienced the grief of bereavement, which could equally well have caused their psychiatric injury. In **Vernon** *v* **Bosley (No 1)** (1996), it was made clear that so long as a sudden shock is at least partly responsible for the claimant's psychiatric injury, the fact that grief has also played a part in causing it will not prevent a claim. In that case, the claimant had witnessed his children drowning in a car that was negligently driven by their nanny. The Court of Appeal accepted that his psychiatric illness might have been partly caused by his grief at losing his children, but, since the shock of witnessing the accident had also played a part, it was not necessary to make minute enquiries into how much of his illness was attributable to each cause, if indeed it was even possible to find out.

The class of person

If a secondary victim can prove that, as a result of the defendant's negligence, they have suffered a recognisable psychiatric injury because of a sudden shock, the next hurdle they face is to prove that they fall within a class of people which the law allows to claim compensation for such injuries. The key cases have focused on four possible classes of people:

- relatives and friends of those killed or injured as a result of the defendant's negligence;
- rescuers at the scene of accidents;
- employees of the party causing the accident;
- 'unwitting agents' – people who cause death or injury to others, not through their own fault but as a result of someone else's negligence.

Relatives and friends

Alcock makes it clear that relatives are the people most likely to succeed in an action for psychiatric damage as a secondary victim. But there is no set list of relationships; whether or not a claim succeeds will depend on the facts of each particular case. In **McLoughlin** *v* **O'Brian** Lord Wilberforce said:

> As regards the class of persons, the possible range is between the closest of family ties – of parent and child, or husband and wife – and the ordinary bystander. Existing law recognizes the claims of the first; it denies that of the second, either on the basis that such persons must be assumed to be possessed of fortitude sufficient to enable them to endure the calamities of modern life, or that defendants cannot be expected to compensate the world at large . . . other cases involving less close relationships must be very carefully scrutinized. I cannot say that they should never be admitted. The closer the tie (not merely in relationship, but in care) the greater the claim for consideration. The claim, in any case, has to be judged in the light of the other factors, such as proximity to the scene in time and place, and the nature of the accident.

On the same subject, Lord Keith said in **Alcock**:

> As regards the class of persons to whom a duty may be owed . . . I think it sufficient that reasonable foreseeability should be the guide. I would not seek to limit the class by reference to particular relationships such as husband and wife or parent and child.

He said that friends and engaged couples could potentially be included, for, '[i]t is common knowledge that such ties exist, and reasonably foreseeable that those bound by them may in certain circumstances be at real risk of psychiatric illness if the loved one is injured or put in peril.'

Despite these liberal-sounding statements, on the actual facts of the case, brothers, brothers-in-law, grandparents, uncles and friends were all found not to have a sufficiently close relationship with the deceased or injured person to succeed in their action. This is partly because the House of Lords emphasised that a claimant would not only have to prove that the *type* of relationship was one that would generally be assumed to be close, such as brother and sister, but also that the relationship was *as a matter of fact* close: there also needed to be a close relationship in terms of love and affection. This point had merely been made in passing by Lord Wilberforce in **McLoughlin** *v* **O'Brian** when he said that ties had to be close 'not merely in relationship, but in care'.

The result in **Alcock** was that a claimant who was present at the stadium at the time of the disaster at which his brother was killed failed in his action because he had not supplied evidence to prove that he was as a matter of fact close to his brother. Lord Keith said that the closeness of the tie could be presumed in 'appropriate cases', giving as examples the relationship between parent and child and that between an engaged couple. But if the relationship of a brother is not an appropriate case it is difficult to imagine many other examples.

Rescuers

Until **White**, it had been assumed that rescuers, meaning people who suffered psychiatric injury as a result of helping the primary victims of a shocking incident, were a special case, on the ground of public policy – the theory being that such selfless behaviour should be encouraged and supported, and therefore not subjected to rules stricter than those of ordinary personal injury. This was generally viewed as the position taken in the classic rescuer case of **Chadwick** *v* **British Railways Board** (1967), where the claimant spent 12 hours helping victims of a terrible train disaster which occurred near his home, and in which over 90 people were killed. He successfully claimed for psychiatric injury which occurred as a result of the experience.

White, as stated earlier, arose from the Hillsborough disaster, and here the claimants were police officers who had been on duty at the ground on the day of the tragedy. Like **Alcock**, **White** was originally a test case in that the four claimants had performed different roles which between them represented the experiences of a number of other officers. Three of them had actually been at the scene of the crushing incident: PC Bevis had spent time attempting to resuscitate fans, who were in fact already dead, close to the fences; Inspector White had passed dead and injured fans from the fenced-in areas; as had PC Bairstow, who had also helped in giving a victim heart massage. The fourth officer, PC Glave, had moved bodies into a temporary morgue set up at the opposite end of the ground from the incident, and obtained first aid for some of the injured.

The claimants claimed on two alternative grounds: first, that the police force owed them a duty of care as employees, and this covered the psychiatric injuries they had suffered (this claim is discussed at p. 47); or, secondly, that they were owed a duty of care as rescuers. They argued that either of these situations meant they were not secondary victims at all, and therefore not subject to the **Alcock** restrictions. The House of Lords rejected both arguments. It stated that only those who were in danger of physical injury (or, according to Lord Steyn, reasonably believed themselves to be so) could be viewed as primary victims; everyone else was a secondary victim. Rescuers were not to be considered as a special category of secondary victim either, but had to be subject to the normal rules on secondary victims, as stated in **Alcock**. This meant that none of the officers could have a claim on the basis of being rescuers, since they had no pre-existing close relationships with the primary victims.

In looking at the question of whether the officers could claim as rescuers, the House of Lords could easily have limited itself to considering whether professional rescuers should be treated in the same way as those who volunteer their help. It would have been easy to keep the special treatment of voluntary rescuers, yet deny the officers' claim on the grounds that the public policy reasons did not apply to them, since there should be no need to encourage them to act in ways that were already required by their jobs. However, the House chose to go further than this and consider the whole area of rescuers who suffer psychiatric shock. It stated that even voluntary rescuers were not, and should not be, a special category. Where acting as rescuer put a claimant in danger of physical injury, they could claim as a primary victim, but, where no risk of physical injury was caused to the rescuer, they would be a secondary victim, and therefore subject to all the restrictions in **Alcock**.

Two main reasons were given by Lord Hoffmann for the ruling. First, that allowing rescuers to be a special case would sooner or later lead to difficult distinctions: once rescuers includes those who help without putting themselves in any physical danger, the line between rescuers and bystanders may become difficult to draw. How much help would someone have to give to be considered a rescuer? Lord Hoffmann's second reason was that allowing the claims of professional rescuers would appear unjust, given that the police officers' conditions of service provided for them to be compensated in other ways for the psychiatric injury they had suffered, while, on the other hand, the bereaved relatives in **Alcock** had been given nothing. While it is difficult to argue with the justice of this point, Lord Hoffmann's reasoning does not explain why volunteer rescuers should be treated in the same way as professional ones. Interestingly, Lord Hoffmann claimed that this was not a change in the law, stating that existing rescuer cases were merely examples of the standard rules on recovery for psychiatric shock, because the claimants in those cases were all at risk of physical injury to themselves and therefore primary victims. In the leading case of **Chadwick**, at least, this is debatable: while a theoretical risk of a wrecked train carriage collapsing on the claimant was mentioned in that case, it is by no stretch of the imagination a keystone of the judgment.

This reasoning makes the impact of the judgment less clear than it seems at first sight. If Mr Chadwick can be considered a primary victim on the facts of his case, it may be that what the decision actually does is to allow the courts to take a wide view of whether voluntary rescuers were subject to physical danger, and use that reasoning to allow or deny a claim, rather than explicitly mentioning public policy.

Employees

The second argument made by the police officers in **White** was that they were owed a duty of care as employees of the party whose negligence caused the shocking event. It is well established that employers owe a duty of care towards employees, which obliges them to take reasonable care to ensure that employees are safe at work, and, although police officers are not actually employed by their Chief Constable, the court accepted that, for the purposes of their argument, the relationship was sufficiently similar to the employer–employee relationship. The claimants in **White** argued that this meant they could not be considered secondary victims, and were not subject to the **Alcock** restrictions. This argument was rejected by the House of Lords.

The House stated that the employers' duty to employees was not a separate tort with its own rules, but an aspect of the law of negligence, and therefore subject to the normal rules of negligence. This meant that where a type of injury was subject to special restrictions on when a duty of care would exist, these rules applied where the injury was caused by an employer to an employee, just as they would in any other situation. So, for example, just as there was no general duty not to cause economic loss to others, there was no duty for an employer not to cause economic loss to employees, by, for example, reducing opportunities to earn bonuses. In the same way, there was no special duty of care regarding psychiatric damage caused by employers to employees, just the normal rules, and these meant that there was no duty of care towards the claimants in **White**.

An attempt to widen employers' liability for psychiatric injury caused by a shocking event was firmly rejected by the House of Lords in **French and others** *v* **Chief Constable of Sussex Police** (2005). The claimants were all police officers who had been involved in events leading up to a raid on a suspect's premises. The raid went wrong, and the suspect was fatally shot by one of the defendants' colleagues. None of the defendants were present at the time, but, after the shooting, four of the five faced criminal charges concerning their part in the raid. They were acquitted, but then internal disciplinary procedures were brought against them. These too were either dropped or dismissed, but the whole process lasted around five years, and the men alleged that, as a result of the stress it put them under, they had all suffered psychiatric injury. Their case was that the police force had failed to provide adequate training, and this failure had led to the shooting, and the subsequent consequences for the defendants. They held that the psychiatric injuries they had all suffered were a foreseeable consequence of the failure to provide proper training.

The House of Lords rejected this argument. The claimants were clearly not primary victims, and, since they had not witnessed the shooting, they were not even secondary victims, and had no sustainable claim in law. In addition, if the foreseeability argument were to succeed, it would mean that the Chief Constable should have foreseen that if the police force failed to offer adequate training, an event such as the shooting would occur, and criminal and/or disciplinary proceedings would be brought against the officers involved, and the stress of that process would cause psychiatric injury. The House of Lords held that this chain of events was not a foreseeable result of the original failure to provide training.

Employees are therefore only able to claim for psychiatric injury caused by a shocking event where they can satisfy the rules on claims by secondary victims, or where they can be considered primary victims. An example of the latter type of case is **Cullin** *v* **London Fire and Civil Defence Authority** (1999), where the claimant was a firefighter who suffered psychiatric injury after an incident in which two colleagues became trapped inside a burning building. The claimant was among those who went into the building to attempt a rescue which proved impossible; he later witnessed their bodies being carried out. The fire authority applied to have his action struck out on the ground that the situation was similar to those of the police officers in **White**, in that the claimant was a professional rescuer and the risk of psychiatric injury he had been exposed to was a normal part of his job. The court disagreed, and said that this approach was too narrow. Relying on remarks made *obiter* by Lord Goff in **White**, they said that a professional rescuer who could establish that they were exposed to danger and the risk of physical injury, or reasonably believed that they were, even if only in the aftermath of the event, could qualify as a primary victim. In this case it was at least arguable that the firefighter had been a primary victim and so the action could not be struck out.

There is also a category of cases in which employees sue for psychiatric injury caused not by accidents but by stress at work. These are considered in Chapter 4.

Unwitting agents

There remains one category of claimant whose position is left unclear in **White**, namely those who witness a shocking accident caused by someone else's negligence and, while they are in no physical danger themselves, might be considered more than mere bystanders because some action of theirs physically brings about death or injury to another. The best-known example is **Dooley** *v* **Cammell Laird** (1951). Here the claimant was operating a crane at the docks where he worked, when, through no fault of his, it dropped a load into the hold of the ship being unloaded. He successfully claimed for psychiatric injury caused through fearing for the safety of a colleague working below. Until **White**, the case, along with a couple of similar decisions, was viewed as establishing the right of an employee to recover for psychiatric injury caused by witnessing or fearing injury to colleagues as a result of their employers' negligence. In **White**, Lord Hoffmann maintains that there is no such right, and that the cases, all of which were first instance judgments, were decided on their facts, and before the **Alcock** control mechanisms were in place. However, he concedes that there may be grounds for treating unwitting agent cases as exceptional, and exempting them from the **Alcock** restrictions, though the point is *obiter* since, as Lord Hoffmann points out, the facts of **White** do not raise the issue.

The issue was examined in **Hunter** *v* **British Coal** (1998). Here the claimant was a driver in a coal mine, who accidentally struck a water hydrant while manoeuvring his vehicle. He went to try to find a hose to channel the water away safely, leaving behind a colleague, C. When the claimant was about 30 metres away, he heard the hydrant explode and rushed to find the valve to turn it off, which took about 10 minutes. During that time he heard a message over the tannoy that a man had been injured, and on his way back to the accident scene another colleague told him that it looked as though C was dead. This proved to be the case, and the claimant's belief that he was responsible for his colleague's death caused him to suffer clinical depression.

When it became clear that in fact the accident had occurred because of his employer's failure to put certain safety features in place, he sued. The Court of Appeal held that, in order to be owed a duty of care of psychiatric injury, the claimant would have to have been at the scene of the accident when it happened, or seen its immediate aftermath; his depression had been caused by hearing about it and that was not sufficient. The case therefore seems to suggest that unwitting agents may have a claim if they satisfy the requirements of proximity in space and time.

Other bystanders

The cases make it clear that bystanders who have no relationship with the primary victims of an accident are very unlikely ever to be able to sue successfully for psychiatric injury experienced as a result. This approach approves the traditional position in cases such as **Bourhill** *v* **Young** (1943), where it was held that a woman who suffered psychiatric injury as a result of seeing the aftermath of a horrific motorcycle accident involving a stranger could not recover damages; the court held that an ordinary bystander could be expected to withstand the shock of such a sight, which meant that it was not reasonably foreseeable that the claimant would in fact suffer psychiatric damage as a result.

However, in **Alcock** the point was made that there might be very rare occasions when an incident was so horrific that psychiatric damage to even uninvolved bystanders was foreseeable, and there a duty of care would arise. The House of Lords gave the rather lurid and imaginative example of a petrol tanker crashing into a school playground full of children and bursting into flames.

Proximity

The third test which secondary victims must pass in order to have a claim concerns proximity, which in this case means how close they were to the shocking event, in terms of both time and place. In **Alcock** some claimants had seen the disaster from other stands inside the stadium; one of the claimants was watching the match on a television nearby and when he saw the disaster begin went to find his son (who had been killed); others saw the tragedy on the television at home or heard about it on the radio. **Alcock** established that to succeed in a claim for nervous shock, the witness must have been sufficiently proximate to the accident, which normally means that they must have been present at the scene of the accident or its immediate aftermath; hearing it on the radio or seeing it on the television will not usually be enough.

The House of Lords was not prepared to specify exactly what was the immediate aftermath, but the interpretation they give to the issue is narrower than that advocated in some of the *obiter dicta* in **McLoughlin** *v* **O'Brian**. Lord Keith appears to approve of the *dicta* in the Australian case of **Jaensch** *v* **Coffey** (1984), which stated that the aftermath continues for as long as the victim remains in the state caused by the accident, until they receive immediate post-accident treatment. **McLoughlin** was considered to be a borderline case by Lord Ackner and it was stated that identifying the body of a loved one at a temporary mortuary eight hours after the accident did not fall within seeing the immediate aftermath of the tragedy.

The House made it clear that merely being informed of the incident by a third party was not sufficiently proximate. This was confirmed in the very sad case of **Tan** *v* **East London and City Health Authority** (1999). The claimant was telephoned by a member of hospital staff and told that his baby had already died in its mother's womb, and would be stillborn. He went to the hospital for the birth, which took place around three hours later. He sued the hospital for psychiatric injury, but the court rejected his claim. It held that the shocking event that caused the psychiatric damage was the death of the baby before birth, rather than seeing it being born dead. The claimant had not witnessed the death itself, but been told about it over the phone, and therefore was not sufficiently proximate to the event.

In **Alcock**, the House also had to deal with the question of whether watching an incident on television could be sufficiently proximate to impose liability to secondary victims for nervous shock, as the Hillsborough disaster had been broadcast live on television to millions of people. The pictures did not pick out individuals, as broadcasting guidelines prevented the portrayal of death or suffering by recognisable individuals. On the facts, the House of Lords did not find that watching the television broadcasts was sufficiently proximate, though it did not rule out the possibility that sometimes television viewers could be sufficiently proximate. The House of Lords drew a distinction between recorded broadcasts and live ones. The former were never sufficiently proximate to give rise to a duty of care. With the latter they said that a claim was unlikely to arise because of the broadcasting guidelines which meant that normally even live broadcasts of disasters could not be equated with actually having been present at the scene of the tragedy. Lord Jauncey stated:

> I do not consider that a claimant who watches a normal television programme which displays events as they happen satisfies the test of proximity. In the first place a defendant could normally anticipate that in accordance with current television broadcasting guidelines shocking pictures of persons suffering and dying would not be transmitted. In the second place, a television programme such as that transmitted from Hillsborough involves cameras at different viewpoints showing scenes all of which no one individual would see, edited pictures and a commentary superimposed.

If pictures in breach of broadcasting guidelines were shown, their transmission would normally break the chain of causation as a *novus actus interveniens* (see p. 112). This would mean that the instigator of the incident would not be liable because they could not have foreseen that such pictures would be shown.

In rare situations, the chain of causation would not be broken and liability on the original instigator could be imposed. The example the judges gave was of a publicity-seeking organisation arranging an event where a party of children were taken in a hot-air balloon, the event being shown live on television so that their parents could watch. If the basket suddenly burst into flames, the suddenness of the tragedy might mean that it was impossible for the broadcasters to shield the viewers from scenes of distress and this would be reasonably foreseeable to those whose negligence caused the accident.

Psychiatric injury not caused by accidents

Though most of the cases on psychiatric injury involve accidents, there are of course other ways in which negligence can cause such injury. The most significant area for litigation is psychiatric injury caused by prolonged exposure to stress at work, and the courts have treated this in a different way to psychiatric injury caused by accidents and sudden events, notably by not requiring that the illness be triggered by a sudden shock. This area is discussed more fully in the chapter on employers' liability (see p. 152).

In **W** *v* **Essex County Council** (2000), the House of Lords was prepared to allow that there might be a claim for negligence causing psychiatric shock after the defendant council negligently placed a foster child who had a history of abusing other children into a family with four young children. He then abused those children, and both they and their parents suffered psychiatric injury as a result. Clearly there was no sudden shock, nor, certainly in the parents' case, any physical injury which would make them primary victims, nor did they directly witness the abuse. This would seem to set the case apart from other decisions on psychiatric injury, and the House of Lords did comment that the parents might well have difficulties making their claim, but they were not willing to strike out the case. However, it is important to note that the case took place shortly after **Osman** *v* **UK**, which put into question the use of striking out applications (see p. 73), and this may explain the courts' reluctance to dismiss the action. Whether it would have succeeded must now remain a mystery, as the case was settled out of court in January 2002, with the council paying £190,000 in compensation.

Statutory provision

In addition to the common law remedy for psychiatric injury, emotional distress can occasionally be compensated under statute. For example, there is a statutory award for bereavement contained in the Fatal Accidents Act 1976. There is no need to prove proximity to the incident that caused the death nor for evidence of a medically recognised mental illness. However, it has its own limitations as it is only awarded to a very small class of people, is for a fixed sum of money and is only available on death, not serious injury.

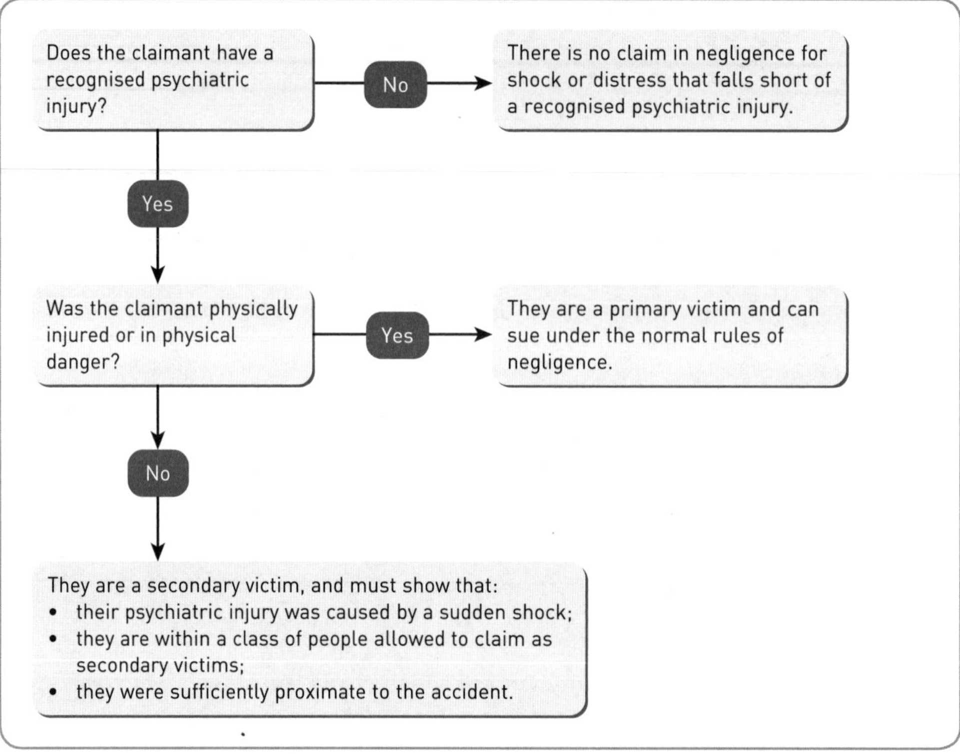

Figure 2.2 Liability for psychiatric injury

Problems with the law on psychiatric damage

The position of rescuers

As explained earlier, rescuers were traditionally thought to be a special case with regard to psychiatric shock, and a rescuer who suffered psychiatric shock as a result would not be subject to the same restrictions as a mere bystander. **White** of course changes this, and this aspect of the decision was comprehensively criticised in the dissenting judgments of Lords Goff and Griffiths in that case. Lord Hoffmann's claim that rescuers had never been a special case, and that the main authority, **Chadwick**, fitted in with his analysis because there was a danger of the train collapsing, is disputed by Lord Goff. He points out that the trial judge in **Chadwick** treated the potential danger as irrelevant, and was right to do so, because it was clearly not the threat of danger to himself that caused Mr Chadwick's psychiatric injury, but the horror of spending hours surrounded by the terrible sights and sounds that were the aftermath of the accident.

Lord Goff also pointed out that making rescuers' claims dependent on whether they were at risk of physical injury could create unjust distinctions. He gave the example of two men going to help in the aftermath of a train crash, where the situation happened to be that helping victims in the front half of the train involved some threat of physical danger, and working in the back half did not. Each of the two men might perform the same service, suffer the same trauma and end up living with the same degree of psychiatric injury, yet if they happened to be helping at opposite ends of the train one would be able to claim compensation for his psychiatric injury and the other would not, a distinction which his Lordship said was 'surely unacceptable'.

The 'closeness of relationship' rules

As you will remember, it was established in **Alcock** *v* **Chief Constable of South Yorkshire** (1992) that one of the requirements for recovery by a secondary victim was that they should have a relationship with a primary victim that was 'close in care', meaning that it is not sufficient to establish, for example, that the primary and secondary victims were brothers; it must also be proved that the relationship between them was close in terms of the way they felt about each other.

The requirement must make the trial more traumatic for the claimant, yet quite how it contributes to the law is difficult to see. Clearly it would be ridiculous for a claimant who was the brother of a primary victim to claim damages if in fact they disliked each other intensely and rarely had any kind of contact – but in such cases, is it likely that the claimant would be able to prove that he had suffered a psychiatric illness as a result of his brother's death or injury? This requirement alone provides a limiting mechanism that makes the test of factual closeness unnecessary.

In addition, it is hard to see why this should affect the defendant's duty, which is still initially based on foreseeability; how can a defendant be said to foresee whether or not the person they injure will have a close relationship with their relatives, and therefore to owe a duty only if they do?

The proximity requirements

As you will recall, the decision in **Alcock** regarding proximity was that in order to claim for psychiatric injury, a secondary victim would have to have been present at the incident which endangered, injured or killed their loved one, or to have witnessed its 'immediate aftermath'.

In **McLoughlin**, the deciding factor seemed to be that the injured were in much the same state as when the accident happened, covered in oil and dirt, and so the implication seems to be that this made the sight of them more devastating, and therefore more likely to mentally injure Mrs McLoughlin. While it is clear that these factors could make a sight more distressing and shocking, it is difficult to make out why exactly the courts believe this should be the dividing line between experiences which can and cannot cause psychiatric injury. Sight is not the only way in which human beings perceive suffering: hearing about the circumstances of an accident, particularly when the outcome is not known, can surely be equally devastating. Similarly, the House of Lords in **Alcock** were emphatic that those seeing the incident on television should not be able to claim, yet the claimants who saw the TV coverage would have known, right at the time when the incident was happening before their eyes, that their loved ones were there. Even if they could not identify them by sight, it is hard to see that this was less distressing than coming upon the aftermath of an accident, and if it was equally distressing, there seems no reason why it should be less likely to cause psychiatric injury.

Nor is the courts' emphasis on the time between the accident and the perception of it easy to justify. Among the **Alcock** claimants, for example, was one man who had gone to the ground and searched all night for the brother he knew had been at the match. It is difficult to see why those long hours of searching and worrying should be less likely to cause psychiatric injury than sight of a loved one immediately after an accident.

The 'sudden shock' requirement

As with the proximity requirements, it is difficult to find a rational basis for the line drawn between psychiatric injury caused by a sudden shock and the same injury caused by, for example, the stress of caring for a seriously injured relative, or the grief of being bereaved. So long as the psychiatric shock is a foreseeable result of the defendant's negligence, why should the precise aspect of the claimant's situation which triggered it off make any difference?

Take the case of **Sion** *v* **Hampstead Health Authority** (1994), for example (see p. 43). Had the son died suddenly of a fatal heart attack caused by his poor medical treatment, and his father been there to witness it, the father might very well have been able to secure compensation for any psychiatric illness he suffered as a result. Why should the fact that he watched his son die slowly, with all the stress and grief that must cause, change his situation? The defendant's treatment of his son is no less negligent; his own psychiatric injury is no less real, and nor is it less foreseeable. Furthermore, if sudden shock is a logical requirement, how are we to explain the decisions allowing claims for psychiatric injury after prolonged stress at work? Why is this stress coinsidered more harmful than the stress of caring for a relative injured by someone else's negligence? Clearly the law has to draw a line somewhere, but the justification for making a sudden shock the defining factor is hard to see.

Reform

The Law Commission has been looking at this area of the law for some time, and in 1995 began consulting with interested parties. The results of their consultations were published in 1998. The Commission argues that the current rules on compensation for secondary victims are too restrictive. They agree that the requirement for a close tie between primary and secondary victim is justified and should remain, but believe this alone would be sufficient; they recommend that the requirements of proximity (both in time and space, and in method of perception) should be abolished. They also suggest that the requirement for psychiatric injury to be caused by sudden shock should be abandoned. To date, however, there has been no sign of these changes being likely.

Duties of care: omissions

As a general rule, the duties imposed by the law of negligence are duties not to cause injury or damage to others; they are not duties actively to help others. And if there is no duty, there is no liability. If, for example, you see someone drowning, you generally have no legal duty to save them, no matter how easy it might be to do so (unless there are special reasons why the law would impose such a duty on you in particular, such as under an employment contract as a lifeguard). This means tort law generally holds people liable for acts (the things they do), not omissions (the things they fail to do).

However, there are some situations in which the courts have recognised a positive duty to act, arising from the circumstances in which the parties find themselves. Although the categories are loose and at times overlap, the following are the main factors which have been taken into consideration.

Control exercised by the defendants

Where the defendants have a high degree of control over the claimant, they may have a positive duty to look after them which goes beyond simply taking reasonable steps to ensure that the defendants themselves do not cause injury. A key case in this area is **Reeves** *v* **Commissioner of Police for the Metropolis** (1999). The case was brought by the widow of a man who had committed suicide while in police custody. Although previous case law had accepted that the police had a duty of care to prevent suicide attempts by prisoners who were mentally ill, Mr Reeves was found to have been completely sane, and the police therefore argued that while clearly they had a duty of care not to cause his death, they could not be held responsible for the fact that he chose to kill himself, and had no duty to prevent him from doing so. However, the Court of Appeal held that their duty of care to protect a prisoner's health did extend to taking reasonable care to prevent him or her from attempting suicide; they accepted that to impose a positive duty like this was unusual, but explained that it was justified by the very high degree of control which the police would have over a prisoner, and the well-known high risk of suicide among suspects held in this way.

The 2001 prize for the cheekiest legal action must surely go to the claimant in another case in this area, **Vellino** *v* **Chief Constable of Greater Manchester** (2001). Mr Vellino was a career criminal, with an extensive record, and was well known to the local police. On several occasions the police had gone to his flat to arrest him, and he had tried to escape by jumping from the second floor windows to the ground floor below. On the occasion that gave rise to the case, the police arrived and Mr Vellino jumped, as usual, but this time he seriously injured himself, ending up with brain damage and paralysis, which made him totally dependent on others for his needs. He sued the police, arguing that they were under a duty to prevent him from escaping, and their failure to do so had caused his injuries. It was, his counsel argued, foreseeable that he would try to escape, and foreseeable injury could result.

The Court of Appeal rejected the argument entirely, pointing out that it would mean that arresting officers had a duty to hold a suspect in the lightest possible grip, just in case he or she wrenched a shoulder in struggling to break free. Equally, it would mean prisons could be sued if prisoners hurt themselves jumping off high boundary walls, since it was foreseeable that prisoners might try to escape and that jumping off high walls tends to cause injury. In any case, the court said, Mr Vellino was not actually under the control of the police when he jumped. He was trying to escape police custody, which was a crime, and therefore the defence of illegality (see p. 128) applied.

Assumption of responsibility

Although in English law people generally have no duty to actively help each other, such a duty will be implied where the courts find that one of the parties has assumed responsibility for the other in some way. A common reason for finding such an assumption is where a contract implying such responsibility exists, or where such responsibility clearly arises from the defendant's job.

In **Costello** *v* **Chief Constable of Northumbria Police** (1999), the claimant was a police constable who was attacked by a prisoner in a police station cell. A police inspector was nearby, but despite her screams he failed to come to her aid. The claimant sued the Chief Constable, alleging that the inspector had a duty of care towards her in that situation (the Chief Constable was sued as being vicariously liable – see Chapter 17). The Court of Appeal agreed; as a police officer, the inspector had assumed a responsibility to help fellow officers in circumstances like these, and where a member of the police force's failure to act would result in a fellow officer being exposed to unnecessary risk of injury, there was a positive duty to act.

A defendant may also be deemed to have assumed responsibility for another person by virtue of his or her actions towards that person. In **Barrett** *v* **Ministry of Defence** (1995), the Ministry of Defence (MOD) was sued by the widow of a naval pilot, who had died by choking on his own vomit after becoming so drunk that he passed out. He had been found unconscious and an officer had organised for him to be taken up to his own room, but nobody had been told to watch over him and make sure he did not choke. The court heard that extreme drunkenness was common on the remote Norwegian base where the death happened, and the officer in charge admitted that he had not fulfilled his responsibility, imposed by Royal Navy regulations, of discouraging drunkenness at the base. At trial, the judge found the defendant was negligent in tolerating the excessive drinking, but reduced the damages by one-quarter because the dead man had been contributorily negligent in getting so drunk. The MOD appealed.

The Court of Appeal disagreed with the first instance court's finding that the officer could be liable for failing to prevent drunkenness, and held that it was fair, just and reasonable to expect an adult to take responsibility for their own consumption of alcohol and the consequences of it. However, the court stated that once the officer had ordered the unconscious man to be taken up to the room, he had from that point assumed responsibility for his welfare, and had been negligent in not summoning medical help or watching over him. Bearing in mind that the defendant would never have had to assume this responsibility had it not been for the dead man's own actions, they decided that there was contributory negligence, and damages were reduced accordingly.

Creation of a risk

Where a defendant actually creates a dangerous situation – even if this risk is created through no fault of the defendant – the courts may impose a positive duty to deal with the danger. This issue was explored in **Capital and Counties plc** *v* **Hampshire County Council** (1997). The case (which is discussed more fully on p. 65), concerned the question of whether fire brigades had a duty of care towards people whose property was on fire. The court concluded that in general they did not, but said that where a fire brigade had actually done something which either created a danger or made the existing danger worse, they then had a positive duty to take reasonable steps to deal with that danger. In the case itself, this meant that a fire brigade whose employee had ordered the claimant's sprinkler system to be turned off, and thereby enabled the fire to spread more rapidly than it would otherwise have done, was liable in negligence.

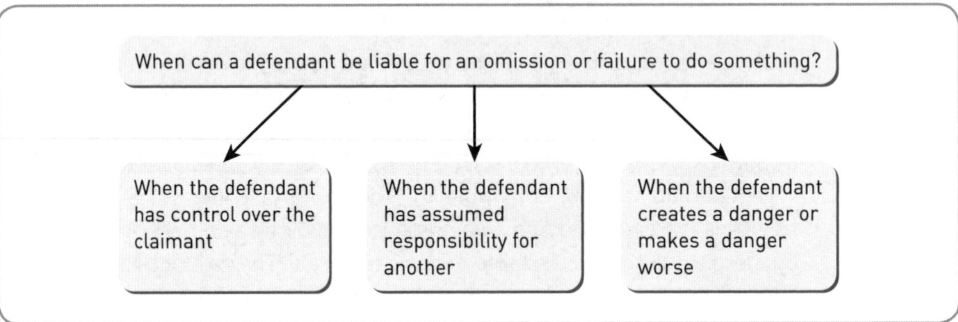

Figure 2.3 Liability for omissions

Duties of care: liability for the acts of third parties

In general, tort law is designed to impose liability on those who have caused damage, and so it does not usually impose liability on one person or body for damage done by another. This is the case even if the defendant could have foreseen that their own acts might make it possible or likely that someone else might cause damage as a result of them. In **P Perl (Exporters)** *v* **Camden London**

Borough Council (1984) the defendant council owned two adjoining buildings, numbers 142 and 144. The first was rented by the claimant, and the second was empty. There was no lock in the door of number 144, making it possible for thieves to enter, and, by knocking a hole in the wall, some thieves got through to number 142 and burgled it. The Court of Appeal held that the council was not liable for negligence: they might have foreseen the risk of harm in leaving the property without a lock, but that was not sufficient to make them responsible for the acts of the burglars.

There are, however, five circumstances where a duty of care regarding the acts of third parties may arise. The first and perhaps most common is where the law imposes vicarious liability, which is discussed in Chapter 17. The other four are:

- where there is a relationship of proximity between the claimant and the defendant;
- where there is a relationship of proximity between the defendant and a third party who causes damage to the claimant;
- where the defendant has negligently created a source of danger; and
- where the defendant knew or had reason to know that a third party was creating a risk to others on the defendant's property.

As you will see from the discussion of cases below, there are links between liability of the acts of third parties and liability for omissions, discussed in the previous section, since many cases will essentially concern an omission to prevent damage being done by a third party.

The defendant–claimant relationship of proximity

The term 'relationship of proximity' is essentially legal shorthand for the existence of circumstances relating to the particular defendant and the particular claimant, which may provide reasons why a duty of care should exist between them. This is a horribly slippery concept, but becomes clearer if we look at some examples.

The relationship can often arise from the existence of a contract between the parties. In **Stansbie** *v* **Troman** (1948), the defendant was a decorator, working on the claimant's premises. The claimant, leaving him alone in the house when she went out, specifically requested that he should be sure to lock the house before he left. He failed to do this, with the result that she was burgled. The existence of a contractual relationship between them was enough in this case to establish a relationship of proximity and so impose a duty of care to take reasonable steps to prevent a burglary.

The relationship may also arise from things the parties have said and done. This was the case in **Swinney** *v* **Chief Constable of Northumbria Police** (1996) (discussed on p. 61) where the police were held to have a duty of care to a particular claimant because she had supplied them with information regarding a criminal and stressed that it should be kept confidential, and it was clear that, if they did not do so, there was a serious risk that the criminal who the information concerned would try to take revenge on the claimant. This case can be contrasted with **Hill** *v* **Chief Constable of West Yorkshire** (1988). In that case, the mother of one of the women killed by Peter Sutcliffe, better known as the Yorkshire Ripper, sued the police, arguing that they had been negligent in failing to catch him earlier and so prevent her daughter's murder. It was held in this case that there was no relationship of proximity between the police and the claimant's daughter, since there was no reason for them to believe she was in special danger from Sutcliffe; she was simply in the same general danger as any member of the female public in the area where the murders were being committed. In both these cases, issues of public policy were also important (these are discussed on p. 60).

The defendant–third-party relationship of proximity

The main way in which a relationship of proximity can arise between the defendant and a third party who has injured the claimant is where the defendant had a right or responsibility to control the third party. However, this will rarely be enough in itself to create a duty of care: in addition, the claimant will need to be someone who was at a particular risk of damage if the defendants were negligent in controlling the third party, over and above the general risk such negligence might pose to the public at large.

This can be seen in the case of **Home Office** *v* **Dorset Yacht Co** (1970). Here prison officers (employed by the Home Office) were in charge of a youth custody centre, called a Borstal, situated on an island. Due to their negligence, some boys escaped from the Borstal and took boats belonging to the claimants to try to get away from the island, damaging the boats in the process. The House of Lords found that the Home Office was liable for the acts of the boys because the boys were under the officers' control (or at least they were supposed to be!). However, that did not mean that the Home Office owed a duty to anyone who might suffer damage caused by the boys, only those at particular risk; the yacht owners were held to come into this category because it was clearly foreseeable that if the boys escaped, they would try to get off the island by stealing boats.

Creating a risk of danger

A defendant who negligently creates or allows the creation of a risk of danger may be liable if a third party's actions cause that danger to injure the claimant. An example arose in **Haynes** *v* **Harwood** (1935), where a horse was left unattended in a busy street and bolted when some children threw stones at it. The defendant was held to owe a duty of care to a police officer who, seeing the danger, ran after the horse and caught it, injuring himself in the process.

In such cases it is not sufficient that the defendant creates a situation which might make it possible for a third party to injure someone else: there must be the creation of a special risk. This can be seen in **Topp** *v* **London Country Bus (South West)** (1993), where a bus was left unattended outside a pub by the defendant's employee, with the keys left in the ignition. When the pub closed, somebody got into the bus and drove it away. There was evidence that the bus was being driven erratically and without headlights, and ultimately it hit and killed the claimant. The Court of Appeal held that the defendant's leaving the bus as he did was not sufficient to amount to creating the kind of risk which would create a duty of care as in **Haynes**. It was no more a source of danger than any other vehicle parked on the road (unlike the horse, which might well have bolted even without the intervention of the children).

Risks created on the defendant's property

Where a defendant knows, or has the means of knowing, that a third party has created a risk to others on the defendant's property, the defendant has a duty to take reasonable steps to prevent danger to others. In most such cases, the danger will be to people on adjacent land. Such a situation was the subject of **Smith** *v* **Littlewoods Organisation** (1987). Here, Littlewoods were the owners of a disused cinema. While it stood empty, vandals set the building on fire, and the fire spread, causing damage to neighbouring buildings. The House of Lords held that an occupier of land could owe a duty to prevent risks caused on it by third parties, although on the facts of the case Littlewoods had not been negligent, since they had not known about the vandals and the precautions they had taken to keep trespassers out were reasonable.

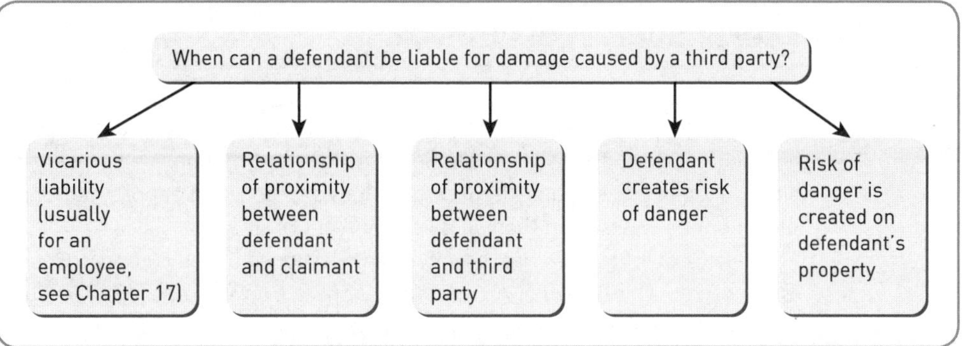

Figure 2.4 Liability for third parties

Topical issues

Compensation and community events

The so-called 'compensation culture' is never far from the headlines and, in 2009, a Court of Appeal case brought the issue into the news once again. In **Glaister and others** *v* **Appleby-in-Westmorland Town Council** (2009), the claimants were members of a family who had visited Appleby Fair, a week-long gathering of gypsies and travellers, mainly for the purpose of selling horses. The fair has been held for centuries, and become something of a tourist attraction. The council did not own the land where the fair was held, but did allow travellers attending the fair to stay on land it owned, and promoted the fair as an attraction to visitors.

The Glaisters were watching horses race along the public highway when a runaway horse came towards them. Mr Glaister tried to catch it, and was kicked, causing him serious head injuries. His wife and daughter suffered psychiatric injury from witnessing the incident. It was not possible to determine whose the horse was, or how it had broken free, so the Glaisters sought to sue the local council, claiming that they had a duty of care towards visitors to the fair, because they promoted it, and stood to gain from the extra visitors it attracted. They argued that the council had breached this duty by not putting in place insurance cover so that if anyone was injured, they would be compensated. The Court of Appeal rejected this argument, confirming that there is no general duty to prevent injury or damage caused by a third party just because the defendant could have prevented that damage, and no duty to ensure that third parties had insurance.

The claim was criticised as being an example of the compensation culture, which it is claimed is making it more and more difficult to organise public events like the fair, because the organisations running them are so afraid of being sued, and insurance premiums are becoming impossibly high. The Court of Appeal addressed this issue in its judgment, saying that imposing liability on the organisers of events like the fair for the acts of others would act as a deterrent to those who freely gave their time and energy to organise events that benefited the community.

Duties of care: special groups

A number of occupational and other groups have become subject to particular rules concerning negligence claims. This is generally because there are thought to be policy reasons why these groups should have immunity from certain types of action, and/or policy reasons why a duty of care should not be imposed on them in particular types of situation.

The issue of immunities has recently been questioned by the European Court of Human Rights, as being in possible breach of Art. 6 of the European Convention on Human Rights, concerning the right to a fair trial (this question is discussed on p. 63).

The police

Negligence cases involving the police generally fall into one of two categories: those involving operational matters, which basically means the way the police actually carry out their work; and those involving policy issues, such as the allocation of resources, or the priority given to different types of work.

Where a case involves purely operational matters, police officers are liable in just the same way as anyone else (in practice, the case will be brought against the relevant Chief Constable, under the principle of vicarious liability, explained in Chapter 17, and if the claim is successful, damages are paid out of a special fund). However, where a case involves policy issues, slightly more complicated rules apply. Before we look at these rules, the case of **Rigby** *v* **Chief Constable of Northamptonshire** (1985) is a useful guide to the distinction between operational matters and policy issues. Here a building owner sued the police for fire damage to his property, caused when the police used CS gas, which is inflammable, to oust a gunman who had taken refuge there. The court held that the police could not be held liable for equipping themselves with the gas, even though a non-flammable alternative was available, because that was a policy decision; however, they could be liable for negligence in failing to bring firefighting equipment to the scene, since this was an operational matter.

The basic position on police liability in cases involving policy decisions was laid down in **Hill** *v* **Chief Constable of Yorkshire** (1988). This was the case (referred to on p. 57), where the mother of one of a serial killer's victims sought to sue the police for failing to prevent her daughter's murder. As well as pointing to the lack of proximity between the police and the young lady who was killed, the House of Lords indicated that there were good policy reasons for not imposing a duty of care on the police in such cases: the fear of being sued might cause the police to compromise the way they work, in order to avoid liability; the decisions they made were likely to be partly policy-based; and the business of defending claims would take up money and manpower, distracting the police from the job of dealing with crime.

For these reasons, it was held in **Alexandrou** *v* **Oxford** (1993) that the police could not be held liable to a member of the public who was burgled after they had dismissed a message that his burglar alarm had been activated as a false alarm, and so failed to go to the scene and investigate. They owed him no duty of care even to turn up and check.

The position in **Hill** was confirmed by the House of Lords in **Brooks** *v* **Commissioner of Police for the Metropolis** (2005). The claimant in the case was Duwayne Brooks, a friend of Stephen Lawrence, who was murdered in a racist attack. Duwayne was with Stephen at the time, and was himself attacked by the gang who killed Stephen. The police investigation into the murder was grossly mishandled, and eventually became the subject of an official inquiry. Its report concluded that one of the problems was that when the police found Mr Brooks at the scene, agitated and, in their words, aggressive, they assumed that there had been some kind of fight, rather than that he and Stephen had been attacked and that he was understandably disturbed by what he had seen, and by the delay in an ambulance arriving. This mistake, the report said, was a result of racist stereotyping and, because of it, the police failed to treat him as a victim and did not, at first, take his evidence seriously.

Mr Brooks suffered post-traumatic stress disorder after the incident, and, although it was accepted that this was initially caused by witnessing the murder, he claimed that his treatment by the police had made it worse, and sued them for negligence. The basis of his case was that the police owed him a duty of care to:

- take reasonable steps to work out whether he was a victim and, if he was, to treat him appropriately;
- take reasonable steps to give him the appropriate support and protection for a witness to a serious violent crime;
- give reasonable weight to his account of what happened, and act accordingly.

The House of Lords was unanimous in finding that the police owed no such duty to someone in Mr Brooks's position. In doing so, they relied almost completely on the policy arguments put forward in **Hill**, pointing out that the primary duty of the police was to suppress and investigate crime, and that police time and resources would be diverted from that duty if they had to take the steps outlined above every time they dealt with someone who was a potential victim or witness. The House accepted that it was desirable for the police to treat victims and witnesses with respect, but held that imposing this as a duty that could give rise to liability for damages was going too far.

However, by the time **Brooks** was decided, the cases of **Osman** *v* **UK** (1998) and **Z** *v* **UK** (2002) had come before the European Court of Human Rights, both of which challenged the immunities given to public bodies (and are discussed at p. 63). Against this background, the House of Lords said that it was no longer appropriate to think in terms of a blanket immunity for the police and, even where cases involved policy issues, they should be assessed on the basis of whether there was a duty of care. Although they said it would still be rare to find a duty of care in cases involving the investigation of crime, the House agreed that there might be 'exceptional cases', or, as Lord Keith put it, 'cases of outrageous negligence by the police' which could fall outside the general principle in **Hill**.

In fact, there had already been a small number of cases in which the circumstances were such that the **Hill** principle was not applied. In **Swinney** *v* **Chief Constable of Northumbria Police (No 2)** (1999), the claimant was a pub landlady who had given the police information concerning the identity of a hit-and-run driver who had killed a police officer. The person she identified was known to the police as a violent and ruthless criminal. The claimant made it very clear to the police that, understandably, she was giving them the information confidentially and did not want to be identified as its source, and they agreed to this. Nevertheless, the police recorded her as the informant in a document containing the details she had supplied. This document was left in an unattended police car, from where it was stolen, and eventually reached the hands of the hit-and-run driver. The result was a campaign of terrifying threats of violence against the claimant. She was so badly affected by this that she suffered psychiatric illness and was forced to give up running her pub.

When the claimant tried to sue the police for negligence concerning the information she supplied, the police argued that there was no relationship of proximity between them and the people who had made the threats that would justify making the police liable for the actions of this third party; and that there were policy reasons, similar to those described in **Hill**, why they should not be held to have a duty of care towards the claimant. The Court of Appeal disagreed.

On the proximity question, the Court of Appeal held that the case could be distinguished from **Hill**, where the claimant's daughter had not been at any special risk from the murderer, but was simply one of many women in the area who were his potential victims. In **Swinney**, it was clear that if the information was allowed to fall into the wrong hands, the claimant was in particular danger, and, in recognising and agreeing to the need for confidentiality, the police had undertaken a responsibility towards this particular person. The court stated that informers were not to be considered merely as members of the public with regard to their relationship with the police; where someone gave information like this to the police, it created a special relationship, which gave rise to sufficient proximity to establish a duty of care.

As far as the policy issues were concerned, the Court of Appeal held such arguments were indeed relevant, but that in this case, the policy arguments favoured the claimant's case. They pointed out that the imposition of a duty of care to keep confidential information secure would encourage informants to come forward, and so help rather than hinder the fight against crime. On the facts, it was held that the actions of the police had not in fact breached their duty of care towards the claimant, so she lost her case.

Similarly, in **Waters** *v* **Commissioner of Police for the Metropolis** (2000), the House of Lords held that the immunity did not apply to a negligence action brought by a police officer who claimed that she had been raped by another officer, and, as a result of making a complaint about him, had been ostracised and bullied by other officers, which had resulted in her suffering psychiatric injury. She claimed that the police had failed to deal properly with her complaint, and had caused or allowed the other officers to victimise her. The House of Lords stated that the issue of whether the immunity should apply had to be considered in the light of all the relevant considerations in each case. It was true that, as in **Hill**, the negligence action would take officers and other resources away from the primary job of dealing with crime, but this had to be balanced against other issues of public interest, namely the fact that if the claimant's allegations were true, there was a serious problem with the police, which should be brought to public attention so that steps could be taken to deal with it.

However, both **Swinney** and **Waters** involved claimants who were in a special position regarding their relationship to the police, one as an informant and the other as an employee, and it was not clear quite what else would amount to the kind of 'exceptional case' referred to in **Brooks**. The case of **Smith** *v* **Chief Constable of Sussex** (2008) now suggests that, as far as ordinary members of the public are concerned, cases will have to be very exceptional indeed before the police can be held liable for failing to protect an individual. The claimant, Mr Smith, had told the police about a succession of death threats he had had from his former partner, Gareth Jeffrey, but the police took no action, and even refused to look at the threatening e-mails and texts. Eventually, Mr Jeffrey attacked Mr Smith with a hammer, so violently that he was arrested for attempted murder. Mr Smith survived, and sued the police for negligence. Despite the fact that the police had had clear information that Mr Smith was under threat from a particular individual (as opposed to the situation in **Hill**, where there was no way of knowing who the killer's next victim would be), the House of Lords held that the police were not liable. Although they admitted that it was a difficult balance to strike, they accepted the arguments in **Hill** and **Brooks** that creating a specific duty to an individual would be against the public interest, because it would skew the way in which police resources were used. They also pointed out that there would be many cases, especially in the area of relationship breakdown, where one person claimed to be under threat from another, and imposing a duty to protect the accuser could mean taking unjustified action against the person accused, who might well be innocent. As in **Brooks**, the House did not rule out the idea that there might be situations where the police would have a duty to protect a specific individual, but said this was not such a case.

In **An Informer** *v* **A Chief Constable** (2012), an attempt was made to establish that the police could owe a duty to informers to protect them from economic loss as well as physical harm. The claimant in the case, who, owing to the sensitive nature of what had happened, was only referred to as C, had told the police about an acquaintance who was involved in criminal activity. He then became an informer, regularly supplying information about the other man, referred to the court as X. To protect C from X, the police officers investigating X were not told who the informer was, and the officers who accepted information from C were not involved in the investigation against X. During the investigation of X, the officers carrying out that investigation began to suspect that C (whom they knew had dealings with X) was also involved in crime, specifically money laundering, and so, not knowing he was their informant, they obtained a restraint order against him, which restricted his access to his money and property. In the event, the suspicions against C could not be proved and he was never charged. He sued the police, claiming that the restraint order had damaged his business and caused him economic loss, and that, because he was an informer, the police had a duty of care to protect him from such losses.

The Court of Appeal rejected the claim, though each judge offered a different reason for doing so. Toulson LJ said that there was no duty of care to protect an informer against pure economic loss, because to impose such a duty would conflict with the need to allow the police to investigate whether the informer had committed any crime. Arden LJ said that the police had assumed a responsibility to C to take care to protect his welfare, which included his financial interests, but that that duty could be, and in this case was, outweighed by the need to protect the police from being hindered in their ability to investigate crime by potential negligence liability. Pill LJ also agreed that the duty to protect C's welfare included his financial interests, but said the police had to have discretion to balance his interests against the interests of carrying out the investigation and, in the circumstances, it was not a breach of duty for those officers who knew that C was an informer not to tell those officers who were investigating him, and thereby avoid the restraint order being made. What we can draw from these different approaches is that, while there may theoretically be a duty to look after an informer's financial interests, this duty is unlikely to be allowed to take priority over the need to investigate crime.

Police liability and the Human Rights Act

Attempts have been made to sidestep the **Hill** issue, by basing a claim on the Human Rights Act, rather than negligence. In **Osman** *v* **UK** (1998), the case was brought by the wife of a man who was murdered by someone who had an obsession with their son. The police had for a long time been aware of both the obsession and of the eventual killer's threatening behaviour; he had, for example, attacked a friend of the Osmans' son, and threatened to 'do a Hungerford', referring to a gunman who went on a shooting spree in the Berkshire town of Hungerford in 1987, killing 14 people. However, although the police interviewed him twice, they took no other steps and eventually the man stole a gun, attacked the Osmans' son and shot and killed Mr Osman. Mrs Osman sought to sue the police for negligence in failing to protect them, despite the clear evidence that they were at risk. When the case was struck out on the grounds of the **Hill** immunity, she went to the European Court of Human Rights and sued the UK government, claiming that the **Hill** immunity was in breach of the Art. 6.1 right to a fair trial, and that the failure to protect her husband and son was a breach of the right to life under Art. 2. The ECHR agreed with the Art. 6.1 claim (though in a later case it pulled back slightly from this position) (see p. 72), but said that the right to life under Art. 2 was not breached. However, it did say that there were circumstances in which national authorities could have an obligation to take preventative action to protect an individual whose life was at risk from the criminal activities of another. This obligation would arise, they said, where the authorities knew or ought to have known of a real and immediate risk to the life of an indentified individual, from the criminal activities of someone else, but they failed to take measures which were within the scope of their powers, and might reasonably have been expected to protect the person concerned.

In **Van Colle** *v* **Chief Constable of Hertfordshire** (2008), a case was brought in the British courts, claiming a breach of Art. 2. The claimants were the parents of a man who was shot dead just before he was due to give evidence in a criminal trial. Their son, Giles Van Colle, had been called as a witness in the trial of a man called Daniel Brougham, on charges of dishonesty. During the run-up to the trial, there was a series of threats and incidents of interference with witnesses, and evidence was provided that the police officer in charge of the case was aware, or should have been aware, of this. Nevertheless, no protection was provided for Giles, and days before the trial he was shot by Daniel Brougham, who was convicted of his murder. The claimants argued that the state authorities had put Giles at risk by requiring him to give evidence, and that there were reasonable precautions that the police could and should have taken, which would have made it more likely than not that his death could have been avoided. They said that this meant the police had breached his right to life under Art. 2 of the Human Rights Act.

Mr and Mrs Van Colle won their case at first instance and in the Court of Appeal, but the House of Lords reversed the Court of Appeal decision. They said that the key question, based on the **Osman** decision, was whether the officer in charge of the case, making a reasonable and informed judgement in the circumstances known to him at the time, should have realised that there was a real and immediate risk to Giles' life. If he should have realised this, there would have been a breach of Art. 2 because appropriate steps to protect Giles were not taken. However, on the facts, the House held that there had been no breach.

Topical issue

'Osman warnings'

In June 2008, *The Times* reported that the **Osman** case has led to a change in the way that the police carry out their work. As we have seen, where the police know of a serious threat to a particular individual and do nothing about it, they could be liable under Article 2 if that person is killed or seriously injured. *The Times* found that where police forces receive information that a particular individual may be the subject of a murder plot, but do not have enough evidence to make an arrest, it has become standard procedure to warn that person about the threat to their safety, a practice known as issuing an 'Osman warning', after the case of **Osman** *v* **UK**. In some cases the people concerned will be potential witnesses to crime (and may enter the witness protection programme as a result of the warning); in others they are themselves known criminals, particularly drug dealers and gang members, who are under threat from rivals or former associates. Around 1,000 Osman warnings are thought to be issued each year.

Other emergency services

A number of cases have looked at the liability for negligence of the other emergency services – fire brigades, ambulance services and coastguards – with varying results.

The position of the fire services was examined in three cases, heard together by the Court of Appeal: **Capital and Counties plc** *v* **Hampshire County Council; John Munroe (Acrylics) Ltd** *v* **London Fire and Civil Defence Authority**; **Church of Jesus Christ of Latter-Day Saints (Great Britain)** *v* **West Yorkshire Fire and Civil Defence Authority** (1997). The cases were heard together because they raised similar issues of law, but their facts were each slightly different. Each claimant had suffered a fire which severely damaged their property, and each alleged that the damage was the result of the relevant fire brigade's negligence. In **Capital and Counties**, the negligence was said to be that fire officers had turned off the building's sprinkler system when they arrived, allowing the fire to get out of control; in **John Munroe**, the claimant's building was set alight by smouldering debris from a fire in a nearby building; the negligence was alleged to be that, after examining the adjacent building and deciding the fire there was out, the fire officers had neglected to check the claimant's building, where they would have found the debris; in **Church of Jesus Christ**, the fire brigade had been unable to fight a fire because the water supply from nearby hydrants was inadequate, and the negligence was alleged to arise from the brigade's failure to inspect these hydrants regularly, which they had a statutory duty to do.

The first issue the Court of Appeal looked at was whether the fire services owed a duty of care to members of the public who had called them out to fires, to turn up to those fires, or at least to take reasonable care to do so. Purely on the authority of **Alexandrou** *v* **Oxford** (1993) (see p. 60), they held that there was no such duty; if the police were not liable for failing to turn up in response to an emergency call, there was no reason to make the fire services subject to a different rule. This may sound odd, but remember that the Court of Appeal was not considering whether the fire services have a moral or social duty to attend fires when called, nor even a duty under their employment contracts; what they were considering was whether they owed a duty of care to the victims of fires that would enable those victims to sue if the duty was breached. The court found it quite easy to conclude that no such duty existed.

Bearing this in mind, the court went on to consider whether, assuming they had turned up and begun to deal with the fire, the fire services owed a duty of care regarding the way in which a fire was fought; if they did so negligently, were they liable to those who suffered damage as a result? In the first case, **Capital and Counties**, it was argued that turning the sprinkler system off was a positive act which made the fire spread further than it otherwise would have done, and so actually caused harm to the claimant's property over and above that which the fire would otherwise have caused. The Court of Appeal agreed that there was a duty of care not to cause or increase harm in this way.

In the other two cases, it was argued that by turning up at the fires, the fire services had assumed responsibility for fighting the fires and the claimants had relied on this assumption, thus creating the necessary relationship of proximity between them and imposing a duty of care. The Court of Appeal disagreed, for three reasons. First, that the fire service's primary duty was to the public at large, and imposing a duty to individual property owners might conflict with this. Secondly, it was difficult to see precisely who such a duty would actually be owed to. If it were only the owner of the building on fire, this would leave the owners of adjacent buildings unprotected, and suggest that the burning building should be saved at the expense of those around it, but if the owners of adjacent buildings were also owed a duty, then a duty might as well be owed to everyone in the vicinity, since they would all be potentially at risk (remember again that the point under consideration is not whose property should actually be protected by the fire services, but who should be entitled to sue if they fail to protect it). Thirdly, it would be irrational to impose a duty of care regarding the way in which a fire was fought, when it had been established that there was no duty to turn up and fight it at all. It would mean that fire brigades would be better off in terms of legal protection from negligence suits if they simply refused ever to attend fires! For these reasons, the Court of Appeal held that apart from situations where the fire services' actions positively increased the damage done to the claimant, there was not a sufficient relationship of proximity between fire services and members of the public who suffered fires to give rise to a duty of care.

The Court of Appeal then considered public policy, and pointed out that in order for public policy reasons to prevent a duty of care arising, it was necessary to establish that such a duty would clash with 'some wider object of the law or interest of the particular parties'. In cases like that of **Capital and Counties**, where the fire services had increased the harm done, they concluded that there was no policy argument to prevent the imposition of a duty of care. In the other two cases, they had already established that no duty existed because there was no relationship of proximity, but they nevertheless considered what the public policy position would have been if a relationship of proximity had been found. The main public policy arguments against such liability were the usual floodgates issue, plus the fact that damages would ultimately have to be paid by the tax-payer, thus diverting taxes from more socially useful purposes. The court rejected these arguments on the grounds that they were equally applicable to other public services, such as the National Health Service, and these bodies were not immune from negligence actions.

This reasoning leaves aside a rather stronger public policy argument, namely the existence and widespread use of a simpler method of compensation for fire damage: insurance. Most owners of property are likely to have such insurance, and, in practice, claims brought against fire brigades are likely to stem not from the owners of property themselves, but from their insurers, who bring such cases because they hope to avoid paying out the benefits they have been paid to provide, and instead to shunt the financial responsibility onto the taxpayer.

When the courts looked at the position of the ambulance services, they took a different view. The issue was examined in **Kent** *v* **Griffiths and others** (2000), which concerned the London Ambulance Service's failure to respond promptly to a call from the claimant's doctor. The claimant was a pregnant woman who had asthma. Having been called in to see her during a bad attack, her GP rang for an ambulance, and was told one was on its way; however, it took 38 minutes to arrive, despite two further calls from the GP. As a result of the delay, she temporarily stopped breathing, which caused her to lose her baby, and to suffer long-term memory problems and personality changes.

The ambulance service argued that, on the authority of **Capital and Counties**, they owed the claimant no duty of care, but the Court of Appeal disagreed. It said that the nature of the service provided by the ambulance service was not comparable with that provided by fire brigades or police, but was more like that provided by National Health Service hospitals, which are accepted as having duties of care towards individual patients. Whereas the fire brigades and the police tended to provide services to the public at large, the ambulance service, once called to the assistance of an individual, was providing a service to that individual, and that individual would be the only person who could be caused damage by their failure to provide the service properly. Therefore, the Court of Appeal held, the ambulance service did owe a duty of care to the claimant.

The Court of Appeal did, however, stress that the distinction between operational and policy matters (see p. 60) would still apply, as it did in other cases involving emergency services. This meant that where there was a question of ambulances being delayed because of lack of resources, or because of demand elsewhere which the Ambulance Service had decided to give priority to, the duty of care question might be decided differently. In this case those issues did not arise; the resources had been available, and what was alleged was a careless failure to use them.

The armed forces

In **Mulcahy** *v* **Ministry of Defence** (1996), the Court of Appeal considered whether a member of the armed forces, injured by the negligent behaviour of a colleague during battle conditions, could sue for that injury. The reason why this – presumably fairly common – situation had never come before the courts before was that until 1987 the situation was covered by a statutory immunity, but this was removed in the Crown Proceedings (Armed Forces) Act 1987. The Act provides that the immunity can be restored by the Secretary of State for Defence in respect of any particular 'warlike operations' outside the UK, but no such order was made regarding the Gulf War, in which the claimant met his injury when a fellow soldier negligently discharged a gun beside him, damaging his hearing.

The Court of Appeal held that there was no duty of care between fellow soldiers engaged in battle conditions. Following the **Caparo** approach (see p. 21 above), the court found that there was foreseeability and proximity, but that it was not just and reasonable to impose a duty in the circumstances, because military operations would be adversely affected if every soldier had to be conscious even in the heat of battle that their actions could result in being sued by a comrade. However, the case of **Bici** *v* **Ministry of Defence** (2004) makes it clear that this 'combat immunity' will only apply where the situation is such that soldiers are actually under threat of attack. The claimants in this case were two Kosovan Albanians who were shot by British soldiers during peace-keeping operations in Kosovo. The High Court held that the soldiers were negligent in shooting the men when they were not being threatened by them, and they had no reasonable grounds to think that they were. The Ministry of Defence argued that the soldiers were covered by 'combat immunity', but the court said this was an incident of street disorder, not a combat situation.

The armed forces can be sued by their members for damage occurring completely outside battle conditions: **Barrett** *v* **Ministry of Defence** (see p. 55) is an example of this.

Local authorities and public bodies

Local authorities and other public bodies pose special problems regarding negligence actions, for two main reasons. The first is that even where foreseeability and proximity can be established, there will very often be reasons why imposing a duty of care may not be just and reasonable: in particular, the problem of damages ultimately being paid by taxpayers, and the danger of employees being distracted from their main task, and possibly changing their working practices, in order to avoid being sued. In these respects the dilemma is similar to that regarding public services such as the police and fire brigades. But there is a further problem with many cases involving public bodies, and, in particular, democratically elected ones. This is the question of 'justiciability', which simply means suitability for examination by a court.

The justiciability issue arises because, in many cases, the actions and decisions of public bodies can only be properly examined by reference to factors which the court process is not equipped to assess. Public bodies are frequently given powers to act, but allowed a discretion as to how, when and even whether they exercise those powers. The exercise of such discretion may depend on many different factors: the availability of resources and the other demands on those resources; the weight given to competing aims and objectives; the preference given to different methods of solving a problem or meeting a need.

Case Navigator

As an example, take the facts of **Stovin** *v* **Wise** (1996). Here the claimant had been injured when the motorbike he was riding was hit by a car driven by the defendant. The defendant claimed that the accident was partly due to the negligence of the local authority, which he therefore joined to the action. The basis for his claim was that he had been unable to see the claimant because an overhanging bank of earth was obstructing his view; the authority had a statutory power to order the removal of such obstructions and had failed to do so. We will discuss the decision in the case further on in this section, but for our purposes here it illustrates very well the problem of justiciability. The council did know about the obstruction (in fact the council had asked the landowner to remove the obstruction, but had not followed up when this was not done), and it knew that previous accidents had happened in the same spot. But there were even worse accident black spots in other areas of the county; there were calls other than accident black spots on the authority's road maintenance budget; and this budget was limited. On what basis should a court decide whether the authority should have spent its money and manpower on removing this particular obstruction?

Restrictions on liability

Up until recently, these problems were generally taken by the courts to mean that it was desirable to protect local authorities and other public bodies from actions for negligence, for the reasons explained. The benchmark case establishing this approach was **X** *v* **Bedfordshire County Council** (1995), in which the House of Lords grouped together five separate cases which all raised the issue of local authority liability in negligence; in each case the local authorities had applied to have the actions struck out, arguing that there was no cause of action. Two of the cases were brought by claimants who alleged that their local authorities had acted negligently regarding their powers to prevent child abuse; the other three cases concerned local authorities' powers with regard to providing education for children with special needs.

The House of Lords held that it was not just and reasonable to impose a duty with regard to protection from child abuse, on the grounds that this was an area where a degree of discretion had to be exercised and there might well be different views as to the wisdom of any decision taken. Imposing a duty of care would mean local authority employees making such decisions with one eye on whether they might be sued, and would also divert public money and manpower away from child protection. In addition, private citizens had other means of challenging decisions made in this area, including statutory appeals procedures and the right to petition the local authority ombudsman.

In the education cases, however, the House of Lords found that it was arguable that a duty of care might arise, because here there was not the same danger of defensive practices, and because advice was being given directly to and relied upon by parents.

A similarly restrictive approach was taken in **Stovin** *v* **Wise**, the road accident case referred to above. The claimant argued that the existence of a statutory power to remove the obstruction was sufficient to create a relationship of proximity between the council and users of the road, which would not otherwise exist. The House of Lords compared the position regarding a statutory power to that regarding a statutory duty (see Chapter 7), and said the situation was similar. Therefore, in order to discover whether a statutory power was intended to give rise to an individual right to sue in negligence, it was necessary to look at the statute itself, and decide whether in making it Parliament intended to create a private right to compensation. On this point, the very fact that Parliament had granted a power to act, rather than a duty to do so, suggested it did not intend to create such a right.

This did not mean that a statutory power could never give rise to a right to compensation if the power was not exercised, but in order to do so, two fairly strict requirements would have to be satisfied. First, the non-exercise of the power must have been irrational in the circumstances. This term (sometimes known as 'Wednesbury unreasonableness' after the case in which it was first described) is borrowed from public law, and essentially applies when a public body or official makes a decision that is so unreasonable that no reasonable public body or official could have made it.

Secondly, there must be 'exceptional grounds' for imposing an obligation to pay compensation. This will only be the case if, as Lord Hoffmann explained, there is 'general reliance' on the power being exercised, to the extent that 'the general pattern of social and economic behaviour' is affected by this reliance (an example of this might be the setting of insurance premiums). Lord Hoffmann stressed that the doctrine was concerned with the general expectations of the community at large, not those of the defendant; defendants would not have to prove that they had relied on the exercise of the power, but, equally, the fact that they did so rely would be irrelevant unless shared by the general public. Lord Hoffmann also pointed out that general reliance could only exist where the benefit provided, if and when the statutory power was exercised, was of 'uniform and routine' nature, so that it is clear exactly what the defendant was expected to do.

The current approach

These cases seemed to establish that the courts intended strictly to limit the liability of public bodies for negligence. But in **W** *v* **Essex County Council** (2000), a shift of approach began to appear. The claimants were foster parents for the council. They had children of their own and, before accepting their first foster-child, they had told the council that they could not foster any child who was a known or suspected child abuser; the council had agreed to this condition. The council then placed a 15-year-old boy with them, who the council knew had indecently assaulted his sister; they did not tell the foster parents this. During his stay, he sexually abused the claimants' children. They sued the council for negligence on their children's behalf.

The Court of Appeal was asked to decide whether the case could go ahead, or should be struck out. It pointed out that there were good policy reasons why a duty of care should not be imposed on the council: the task of dealing with children at risk was a difficult and delicate one, and a duty of care might lead councils to protect themselves from liability, at the expense of their duties towards children needing fostering. However, it stated that in this case it was arguable that the policy reasons should not apply, since the children who had been abused were not actually subject to the council's powers under statute, but were living at home with their parents, and, in addition, the council had given express assurances which it had broken. For these reasons the Court of Appeal refused to strike out the case, and the House of Lords upheld their decision. In the event, as we stated earlier, the case was finally settled out of court.

After the decision in **W**, there was a decisive move away from the restrictive approach of **X** *v* **Bedfordshire**. In **Barrett** *v* **Enfield London Borough Council** (1999), it was argued that the local authority owed a duty to a child who it had placed in care. The claimant was taken into care by the local authority when he was 10 months old. He remained there until he was 17, and had had a thoroughly unpleasant and difficult childhood. He alleged that the authority had a duty to place him for adoption, locate suitable foster homes and oversee his re-introduction to his birth mother; the fact that none of this had been done, he claimed, had led to him suffering psychiatric damage. The case was initially struck out on the grounds that, following **X** *v* **Bedfordshire**, there were sound policy reasons why it was not fair, just and reasonable to impose a duty of care. The striking out decision was eventually appealed to the House of Lords, who held that the action should not be struck out because without a proper examination of the facts it was not possible to determine whether the decisions taken with regard to the claimant's upbringing were policy ones, which would not be justiciable and so could not give rise to a duty of care, or operational ones, which could.

Case Navigator

In four cases which ultimately ended up being considered together by the House of Lords, the courts looked again at the issue of the duties owed by local educational authorities to children using their educational services, which you will remember was one of the issues raised in **X** itself. The first case was **Phelps** *v* **Hillingdon London Borough** (1998), in which the claimant – now grown up – had had problems with learning as a child and was referred to an educational psychologist employed by the local authority, who said her difficulties were the result of emotional and behavioural problems. In fact it was later discovered that the claimant was dyslexic. She claimed that the psychologist's failure to diagnose this had prevented her getting the educational help she needed, help which would have improved her employment prospects.

The second of the four cases, **Jarvis** *v* **Hampshire County Council** (1999) also concerned a claimant with dyslexia, though in this case it had been diagnosed correctly; the alleged negligence concerned the education authority's failure to give appropriate advice on the right kind of school for him.

In the third case, **G (a child)** *v* **Bromley London Borough Council** (1999), the claimant had a progressive muscle disease which meant he needed special equipment in order to be able to communicate; this was not provided and he alleged that his education had suffered as a result, causing psychological damage.

The fourth case concerned a claimant, Anderton, who was seeking access to her educational records in order to prove that she had been damaged by inadequate education. **Phelps** was the only case of the four which had been tried; in the other three, the House of Lords was only required to decide whether there was a potentially arguable case. It refused to dismiss any of the four claims, holding that a local education authority has a duty of care to provide an education appropriate to a child's needs, and where this does not happen, as a result of the negligent actions of a teacher or educational psychologist, the council may be liable.

The House of Lords stressed that, although there was a duty of care, liability for negligence would not be imposed merely because a child had done badly at school – a teacher or educational psychologist would have to fall below the standards expected of a reasonable body of similarly professional people for negligence to be found. They argued that this requirement would ensure that the decision did not result in a flood of claims.

Case Navigator

In **D** *v* **East Berkshire Community NHS Trust** (2003); **MAK** *v* **Dewsbury Healthcare Trust**; **RK** *v* **Oldham NHS Trust** (2003), the Court of Appeal heard three cases dealing with local authority liability for preventing child abuse. The first, **Berkshire**, was brought by a mother who had been wrongly suspected of harming her daughter. In the second, **Dewsbury**, a father and his daughter sued the local council for taking the daughter into care on the – incorrect – suspicion that she was being abused by her father. The claimants in the third case, **Oldham**, were a mother and father whose daughter was taken into care for a year after they were wrongly accused of abuse.

The councils sought to rely on **X** *v* **Bedfordshire**, which had stated that it was not fair, just or reasonable to impose a duty of care on councils with regard to the decision on whether to take a child into care, because fear of being sued would adversely affect the way councils did their job in this area. This particular point had not been disturbed by subsequent cases. The Court of Appeal said that the situation had, however, been changed since the passing of the Human Rights Act 1998, which created the right to freedom from inhuman and degrading treatment (Art. 3) and to respect for family life (Art. 8). This means that a council who wrongly takes a child into care (or wrongly fails to do so) can be sued under the Human Rights Act. As a result, it no longer made sense to say that councils should be immune from being sued in tort for negligence so as to avoid the adverse effects of fear of being sued, since they could be sued under human rights law instead.

As a result, it was now fair, just and reasonable to impose on councils a duty to use a reasonable degree of care and skill in making the decision on whether to remove a child from its parents. However, this duty was owed only to the child, not the parents. The Court of Appeal said that, in this kind of case, the interests of the parent and the child might well be different, and to allow a duty to both would create a conflict of interest. The claimants then appealed to the House of Lords, on the issue of whether a duty should be owed to parents (**D** *v* **East Berkshire** (2005)). They argued that there was no conflict of interest, because it was in the interests of both parents and children that the authorities acted with due care and skill when deciding whether children should be taken into care. The House of Lords rejected this argument. They said that at the point where there was suspicion of abuse, it was in the interests of the child that any suspicions, even if they were slight, were reported and investigated. Those steps would not necessarily be in the interests of the parent. Therefore there was a conflict which made it undesirable that child protection authorities should owe a duty of care to the parents in such cases, as well as to the children.

In **Lawrence** *v* **Pembrokeshire County Council** (2007), an attempt was made to use the Human Rights Act 1998 to defeat the decision in **D** *v* **East Berkshire**. The claimant argued that, in putting her children on the at-risk register, her local council had breached her right to respect for family life, under Art. 8 of the Act. The Court of Appeal rejected this approach. They explained that the reason for the decision in **D** *v* **East Berkshire** was to make sure that councils could protect children who appeared to be at risk from their parents. Providing, in Art. 8, a right to respect for family life did not weaken or undermine the need for such protection, and so the court held that **D** *v* **East Berkshire** was compatible with Art. 8.

In **Selwood** *v* **Durham County Council** (2012), it was pointed out that the policy factors which sometimes mean local authority liability should be restricted can also work in the other direction. The claimant in the case was a social worker, who was stabbed by a mentally disturbed person. She later discovered that he had made threats to kill her, but nobody at the council (who were not her employers) had told her this. She argued that they had a duty of care to do so, but the council argued that they had no duty to prevent the actions of a third party. The Court of Appeal found that it was arguable that a duty of care could exist, because it was in the public interest that social workers who were working with dangerous people should be protected as far as possible, and this was something that might be necessary to take into account when deciding whether it was fair, just and reasonable to impose a duty. In addition, the policy reasons which might argue against a council having a duty to the world at large might not apply when, as here, the duty would be owed to a smaller class of claimants who had a special relationship with the council because of the work they did.

Topical issue

Child protection cases

As we saw above, the case of **D** *v* **East Berkshire** established that local authorities owed a duty of care to children at risk of abuse. The case opened the way for children who had been abused at home to sue for a local authority's failure to take them into care and, in 2008, newspapers reported on one of the first cases of this kind to reach the higher courts, **Pierce** *v* **Doncaster Metropolitan Borough Council** (2008). The claimant had been beaten by his parents almost daily since he was a baby, left naked outside for hours at a time, and warned that if he told anyone, he would be killed. When he was six months old, he was briefly taken into care but then returned to his parents. His aunt later contacted social services when she saw burns on his body, but her warnings were ignored. He was not taken into care until he was 14, and had run away from home after his father threatened him with a knife. By that time he had a severe personality disorder. He argued that the local council had failed in their duty to him, by returning him to his parents after his initial stay in foster care. The council argued that they were not in breach of their duty of care, but the Court of Appeal disagreed, and Mr Pierce won his case. He was awarded £25,000 in damages. After the case, *The Times* reported that between 200 and 300 similar cases were being prepared by lawyers. Most of them were expected to be settled, with damages of between £15,000 and £100,000.

The issue hit the headlines again in 2009, with the story of Baby P, later identified as Peter. The 17-month old died after months of vicious abuse, with eight broken ribs and a broken back, despite the fact that social services had regularly visited his home. They were criticised for failing to take him into care, and baby P's father, who did not live with his mother, threatened to sue the local council on his son's behalf. At the time of publication it was not known whether that claim is to go ahead.

Reasons for the change

Why was there such a change in approach in the years since **X** *v* **Bedfordshire**? While there may have been a genuine change of view on the part of the courts as to the proper legal liabilities of public bodies, a more likely explanation is the effect of the decision of the European Court of Human Rights in **Osman** *v* **UK** (see p. 63), where it took a very dim view of the use of blanket immunities from suit. The ECHR pulled back from this position in the subsequent case of **Z** *v* **UK** (2001), but there remains doubt over how the law will be developed. This issue is discussed below.

Other types of case

It is worth noting that the issue of immunity from suit for public bodies and local authorities only arises in cases where a local authority or public body is claimed to be negligent with regard to something they have done or failed to do in their specific role as a public body – usually this will concern a statutory power or duty. If a local authority or public body is alleged to be negligent because they have done something which would amount to negligence if it was done by a private individual or organisation, the normal rules apply and the fact that the defendant is a public body is not an issue.

An example of this is **Beasley** *v* **Buckinghamshire County Council** (1997). Here the claimant was a paid foster-parent to a handicapped teenager. The child was heavy and so badly handicapped that she needed a lot of help and, as a result of the work, the claimant was injured. She claimed that the council had been negligent in failing to give her the necessary equipment and training to protect herself from injury. The council sought to have the case struck out, relying on **X** *v* **Bedfordshire** to argue that on public policy grounds no duty of care should exist; they argued that their decision to use the claimant's services had been one of policy, and within the discretion allowed them by statute. The court disagreed: the alleged negligence arose not from the decision to use the claimant's services, but from the way the council acted once it had taken that decision, namely the refusal to provide proper training and equipment. The case was not comparable with

X, but was more like a case involving an employer's duty of care to provide a safe working environment. The court therefore refused to strike the case out.

The future for special-group immunities

As we have mentioned previously, the question of special-group immunities has been called into question during the past few years by the European Court of Human Rights. The court has considered whether such immunities could be a violation of Art. 6 of the European Convention on Human Rights, concerning the right to a fair trial, and in **Osman** *v* **UK** (1998) they concluded that this could be the case, causing some uproar in the British legal world. Three years later, in **Z** *v* **UK** (2001), they appeared to draw back from this position, though some questions remain, which is why we need to look at these two cases in detail.

As we saw earlier (p. 63), **Osman** concerned a family who had suffered a tragedy at the hands of a criminal, and sought to sue the police for negligence in failing to prevent it. The police successfully made an application to strike out their claim, on the ground that **Hill** established that the police could not be sued for negligence concerning the investigation and suppression of crime. The Osmans then brought a case against the British government before the European Court of Human Rights (ECHR). They made a number of different allegations but, as far as our discussion here is concerned, the important one was that the striking out of their case was in breach of Art. 6.1 of the European Convention on Human Rights, which provides a right to a fair trial. The argument was that the decision in **Hill** gave the police a blanket immunity from negligence suits in cases which involved the investigation and suppression of crime, and that this meant that the English courts would not even look at the merits of such a case. As a result, people in the position of the Osmans would be denied a fair trial of their claim.

The British government argued that the rule established in **Hill** did not confer a blanket immunity; it did not mean that an action against the police on the issue of their work against crime was always doomed to fail. However, the ECHR found that the way in which the rule had been used did confer a blanket immunity. The courts had not looked at the merits of the Osmans' claim, nor the facts on which it was based; their case was simply rejected by the Court of Appeal because it was found to fall squarely within the scope of the exclusionary rule formulated by the House of Lords in the **Hill** case. The Court of Appeal had assumed that this provided the police with a watertight defence.

The ECHR pointed out that the aim of the **Hill** rule – to promote the effectiveness of the police service and so prevent crime – might well be legitimate within the terms of the Convention, but its scope and the way it had been used in this case were problematic. In particular, in dealing with the case on the basis of a striking out application, the Court of Appeal had denied itself the chance to consider whether there were competing public interest issues which would outweigh the public interest argument for the **Hill** rule. The ECHR suggested that clearly there were other public interest issues: the applicants' case had involved the alleged failure to protect the life of a child; they alleged that that failure was the result of a catalogue of acts and omissions which amounted to grave negligence as opposed to minor acts of incompetence; and the harm sustained was of the most serious nature. The ECHR held that these were considerations which should have been examined on their merits and not automatically excluded by the application of a rule which amounted to the grant of an immunity to the police.

The government argued that the Osmans had available to them alternative routes for securing compensation, such as a civil action against the killer or the psychiatrist who had examined him during the period before the killing and concluded that he was not mentally ill. However, the ECHR argued that these remedies would not have met the Osmans' aim in bringing the action against the police, which was to secure answers to the question of why the police failed to take action soon enough to protect the victims. While the Osmans might or might not have succeeded in proving that the police were negligent, they were at least entitled to have the police account for their actions and omissions in a court hearing which would examine the facts and merits of the case.

For these reasons, the court concluded unanimously that the application of the **Hill** rule in the Osmans' case was a restriction on the applicants' right of access to a court and therefore a violation of Art. 6.1 of the Convention.

The implications of Osman

Osman seemed to have extremely important implications, both for procedure and for the substantive law of tort. In terms of procedure, it seemed to suggest that the use of striking out applications to decide whether a duty of care exists in a particular case would only be permissible in the clearest cases, where all the issues could be weighed in the pre-trial examination. Some commentators believed it might even be suggesting that such use of striking out actions was not ever to be permissible. It was also clear from the arguments made that the decision did not only apply to cases against the police: the statement that public policy arguments in favour of immunity must be balanced against public policy arguments against it would equally well apply to actions against any of the special groups mentioned above. As a result, as we noted earlier, after **Osman** the English courts began to show considerable reluctance to allow striking out applications in cases concerning immunity for special groups. In **Barrett** and **Phelps** they made specific reference to **Osman** in explaining this, though not without criticism of it.

As far as substantive tort law was concerned, the implications were perhaps even more important. As we have seen, the approach of English tort law to the duty of care issue is to lay down general rules regarding policy questions (such as the distinction between operational and policy matters in cases concerning how the police do their job) and to use these rules to decide whether a particular individual's case gives rise to a duty of care. The result of this is that if the rules say there is no duty of care in a particular situation, then nothing about the individual's case can affect that. The **Osman** decision takes a different view, suggesting that it is important to balance the policy considerations behind general rules against the circumstances of each case – so that, for example, the seriousness of the harm done and the degree of carelessness shown by the defendant might outweigh the policy considerations behind the immunity, as the court found to be the case in **Osman**. Clearly this had the potential to wreak profound changes in the development of duties of care.

A retreat from Osman?

There was something of a sigh of relief in the English legal world when the ECHR appeared to backtrack from **Osman** in **Z** *v* **UK**, though it is by no means clear that the situation has stabilised, let alone reverted back to pre-**Osman** days. The case involved four children who had suffered horrendous neglect at the hands of their parents. Neighbours, the police and teachers had all expressed concern about them to social services, over a period of years, but the social services department refused to take them into care. They eventually did so five years after first being made aware of the problem, and only then at the mother's own request. Three of the four children suffered psychiatric illness as a result of what had happened to them, and the social services department was sued on their behalf by the Official Solicitor. The claim was struck out by the House of Lords on the basis that, following **X** *v* **Bedfordshire**, the social services had no duty of care towards the children.

The Official Solicitor took the case to the ECHR, alleging that the striking out was a violation of Art. 6 of the Convention. The ECHR (more or less) admitted that their view in **Osman** had been based on a misunderstanding of English tort law, something which English lawyers, judges and academics had been pointing out since the decision was published.

Article 6 is concerned with procedural blocks to exercising the right to a fair trial, such as, for example, where a government might arbitrarily remove the courts' jurisdiction to deal with certain types of claim. The so-called immunity in negligence of public authorities, however, was not a procedural block, but a part of the substantive law of negligence in this country. Our law of tort says that if it is not just and reasonable to impose a duty of care, then no such duty should be imposed. By saying that it was not just and reasonable to impose a duty of care on local authorities in child abuse cases, the court was not saying that local authorities had a blanket immunity from liability, but that there was no liability in law for them to be immune from.

The ECHR found that in **Z** *v* **UK**, the striking out hearing had been an adversarial examination of the issues in the case. Although this hearing did not test whether the facts alleged were true, it did examine whether, if they were true, the claimant would have had an arguable case in law. Since the answer was no, a hearing to examine whether the facts were true would simply be a waste of time and resources. In the striking out hearing, the House of Lords had carefully balanced competing policy questions, and, as a result, this was a sufficient trial for the purposes of Art. 6.

It would save both us and you a lot of time and trouble if we could assume that **Z** *v* **UK** simply shows that **Osman** was wrong and can now be ignored. Unfortunately, the situation is not quite so simple. While the ECHR in **Z** admitted to a misunderstanding, it did not say that **Osman** should be regarded as wrong. In fact, the decision of the court was not unanimous (it was made by a majority of 12 to 5), and it was clear that some of the dissenters still felt that the **Osman** approach was correct. As a result, the position of special-group immunities in negligence is still not clear.

One view is that **Z** *v* **UK** means that denying a duty of care on the basis that it is not fair, just and reasonable to impose one on the defendant is part of substantive English tort law, and not a procedural block, and therefore Art. 6 has no application in this area. This was the approach taken by the Court of Appeal in **D** *v* **East Berkshire Community NHS Trust** (2003), the case concerning local authority liability for investigating child abuse (discussed on p. 70). Relying on **Osman**, the claimants argued that striking out their claims on the grounds that no duty was owed to them was a violation of Art. 6. The Court of Appeal disagreed, stating that establishing the existence of a duty of care was a precondition of being allowed to sue someone in negligence. A claimant who is prevented from suing a defendant because they cannot establish that there is a duty of care is not prevented by an immunity, but by the fact that, in law, it is not possible for the defendant to be liable to them. Therefore, Art. 6 could not apply.

The House of Lords seemed to approve this view in **Matthews** *v* **Ministry of Defence** (2003). The case did not actually concern duties of care, but a similar issue of Crown immunity, which provides that, where it applies, the Crown cannot be sued for acts that other parties would be liable for. Matthews tried to argue that this immunity was in breach of Art. 6, but the House of Lords said that, as it was a part of substantive law, Art. 6 could not apply.

However, it is not at all clear from **Z** *v* **UK** that this is the position the ECHR will take in future cases. The ECHR made it clear in that case that even where there was a legal rule which meant that a defendant could not be liable in domestic law, they would look at that rule in order to decide whether it in fact operated as the kind of procedural block covered by Art. 6 and, if so, they would assess whether its existence was a disproportionate interference with the claimant's right to a fair trial. They in fact did this in **Z** *v* **UK**, giving two reasons why the immunity did not act as a blanket immunity: first, that it applied only to one specific area of a local authority's functions, rather than protecting them from any type of claim; and, secondly, that the House of Lords had carefully weighed up both sides of the policy issue, in deciding whether or not it was fair, just and reasonable to exclude a duty of care.

The fact that the ECHR looked at the **Z** case in this way suggests that the **Osman** approach may not be dead after all. First, if it was important that the immunity only applied to a specific part of the council's work, does that mean that an immunity which covered all the functions of a particular type of public authority would be viewed as a procedural block in breach of Art. 6? Secondly, if the fact that the House of Lords balanced up the competing public interest issues helped justify the immunity, does that mean that every court in every case has to perform the same weighing-up exercise? If it does, that means that in practice many of the rules on where a duty of care will exist are virtually useless as a means of sketching out the limits of tort liability, or of creating predictability and equal treatment.

Whatever happens in future cases, **Osman** has already had a profound impact on one aspect of negligence law. During the period between **Osman** and **Z** *v* **UK**, the courts were noticeably reluctant to use the striking out procedure in cases involving public authorities, and as a result the cases brought in that period have increased the liability of public authorities quite substantially. **Z** *v* **UK** does nothing to change that.

Breach of a duty of care

At the very beginning of this chapter, we explained that negligence has three elements: a duty of care; breach of that duty; and damage caused by the breach. Now that we have looked at the various tests for establishing whether a duty exists between the claimant and the defendant, we can move on to consider what, assuming a duty has been found in any particular circumstances, will constitute a breach of that duty.

Breach of a duty of care essentially means that the defendant has fallen below the standard of behaviour expected in someone undertaking the activity concerned, so, for example, driving carelessly is a breach of the duty owed to other road users, while bad medical treatment may be a breach of the duty owed by doctors to patients. In each case, the standard of care is an objective one: the defendant's conduct is tested against the standard of care which could be expected from a reasonable person. This means that it is irrelevant that the defendant's conduct seemed fine to them; it must meet a general standard of reasonableness.

As the test is objective, the particular defendant's own characteristics are usually ignored. A striking example of this is that the standard of care required of a driver is that of a reasonable driver, with no account taken of whether the driver has been driving for 20 years or 20 minutes, or even is a learner driver. In **Nettleship** *v* **Weston** (1971) the claimant was a driving instructor, and the defendant his pupil. On her third lesson, she drove into a lamp post and the claimant was injured. The court held that she was required to come up to the standard of the

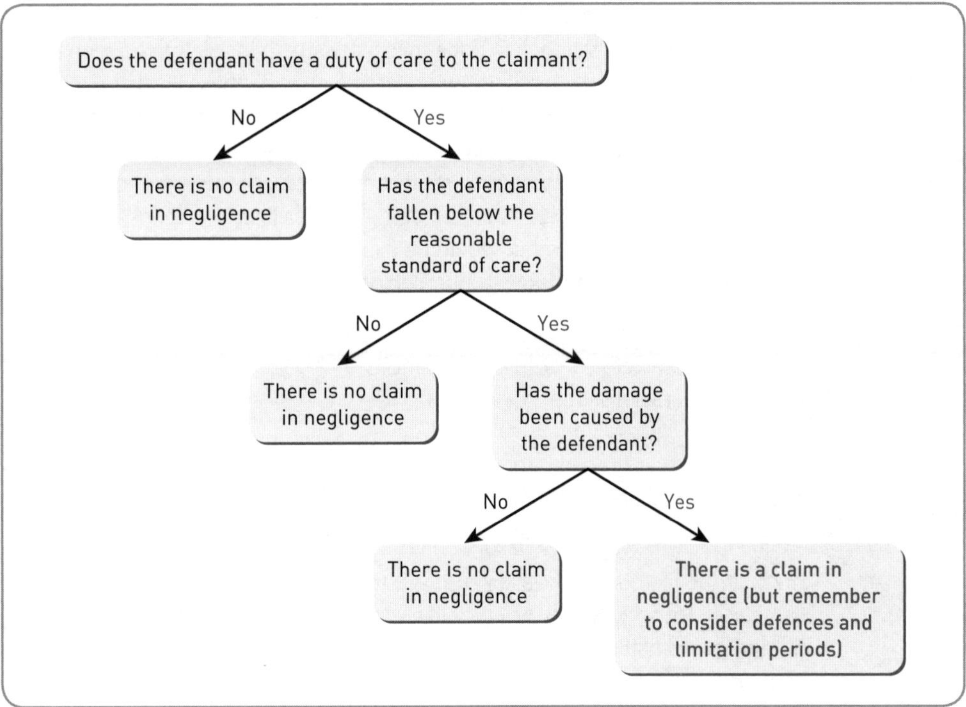

Figure 2.5 Is there a claim in negligence?

average competent driver, and anything less amounted to negligence. 'The learner driver may be doing his best, but his incompetent best is not good enough', the court said. 'He must drive in as good a manner as a driver of skill, experience and care.' However, there are a limited number of situations in which special characteristics of the defendant will be taken into account (see below).

The standard of reasonableness

It is important to realise that the standard of care in negligence never amounts to an absolute duty to prevent harm to others. Instead, it sets a standard of reasonableness: if a duty of care exists between two parties, the duty is to do whatever a reasonable person would do to prevent harm occurring, not to do absolutely anything and everything possible to prevent harm.

An example of this principle in operation is **Simonds** *v* **Isle of Wight Council** (2003). The claimant here was a five-year-old boy, who was injured while playing, unsupervised, on swings during a school sports day. The boy had had a picnic lunch with his mother near to where the sports day was taking place, and afterwards his mother sent him back to rejoin the supervised activities. Unknown to her, the little boy instead headed for some nearby swings. While playing there alone, he fell off and broke his arm. The court rejected the mother's claim that the school had a duty of care to prevent accidents happening on the swings. The sports day had been well supervised, and the school had in place measures to prevent children playing on the swings; it was not possible to make a playing field completely free of hazards, only to take reasonable precautions, and the school had done that. The same principle can be seen in **Holt** *v* **Edge** (2006). The defendant was a doctor, and the claimant a patient whose illness he misdiagnosed. The claimant had a bleed in her brain, but the defendant did not realise this because the symptoms she described were not typical of the condition. The condition then caused her to have a stroke. Her claim failed because the symptoms she talked about were unusual for that condition, and so the doctor did not fall below the expected standard in failing to diagnose it.

In deciding what behaviour would be expected of the reasonable person in the circumstances of a case, the courts consider a number of factors, balancing them against each other. These include:

- special characteristics of the defendant;
- special characteristics of the claimant;
- the size of the risk;
- how far it was practical to protect against the risk;
- common practice in the relevant field;
- any benefits to society that might be gained from taking the risk.

None of the factors is conclusive by itself; they interact with each other. For example, if a type of damage is not very serious nor very likely to occur, the precautions required may be quite slight, but the requirements would be stricter if the damage, though not serious, was very likely to occur. Equally, a risk of very serious damage will require relatively careful precautions even if it is not very likely to occur.

Special characteristics of the defendant

Children

Where the defendant is a child, the standard of care is that of an ordinarily careful and reasonable child of the same age. In **Mullin** *v* **Richards** (1998), the defendant and claimant were 15-year-old schoolgirls. They were fencing with plastic rulers during a lesson, when one of the rulers snapped and a piece of plastic flew into the claimant's eye, causing her to lose all useful sight in it. The Court of Appeal held that the correct test was whether an ordinarily careful and reasonable 15-year-old would have foreseen that the game carried a risk of injury. On the facts, the practice was common and was not banned in the school, and the girls had never been warned that it could be dangerous, so the injury was not foreseeable.

In **Orchard** *v* **Lee** (2009), the Court of Appeal stressed that where the claimant was a child, their behaviour would have to be 'careless to a very high degree' before they should be considered liable for negligence. The claimant in the case was a playground supervisor at a school, who was injured when a 13-year-old pupil ran into her, while playing tag with a friend. The Court of Appeal confirmed that the test in **Mullin** was the correct approach, but said it was not the whole story. Courts did need to ask what a reasonable and prudent child of the defendant's age would have foreseen, but only as part of the wider question of whether the child had fallen below the standard of behaviour that could reasonably be expected from a child of that age. Only if there was a high degree of carelessness should a child be liable. In this case, that did not apply where a child of 13 was playing a game within a play area, was not breaking any rules or acting to any significant degree outside the rules of the game.

Illness

A difficult issue is what standard should be applied when a defendant's conduct is affected by some kind of infirmity beyond their control. In **Roberts** *v* **Ramsbottom** (1980), the defendant had suffered a stroke while driving and, as a result, lost control of the car and hit the claimant. The court held that he should nevertheless be judged according to the standards of a reasonably competent driver. This may seem extremely unjust, but remember that motorists are required by law to be covered by insurance; the question in the case was not whether the driver himself would have to compensate the claimant, but whether his insurance company could avoid doing so by establishing that he had not been negligent. This is also one explanation for the apparently impossible standard imposed in **Nettleship** (p. 76).

Even so, in a more recent case, **Mansfield** *v* **Weetabix Ltd** (1997), the Court of Appeal took a different approach. Here the driver of a lorry was suffering from a disease which on the day in question caused a hypoglycaemic state (a condition in which the blood sugar falls so low that the brain's efficiency becomes temporarily impaired). This affected his driving, with the result that he crashed into the defendant's shop. The driver did not know that his ability to drive was impaired, and there was evidence that he would not have continued to drive if he had known. The Court of Appeal said that the standard by which he should be measured was that of a reasonably competent driver who was unaware that he suffered from a condition which impaired his ability to drive; on this basis he was found not to be negligent.

Professionals and special skills

Account will also be taken of the fact that a particular defendant has a professional skill, where the case involves the exercise of that skill. In such a case, the law will expect the defendant to show the degree of competence usually to be expected of an ordinary skilled member of that profession, when doing their duties properly. A defendant who falls short of that level of competence, with the result that damage is done, is likely to be held negligent. It would be ridiculous not to expect a surgeon carrying out an operation, for example, to have more skill than the untrained person in the street.

In **Vowles** *v* **Evans** (2003), a rugby player was injured as a result of a decision made by the referee. The Court of Appeal said that the degree of care a referee was legally expected to exercise would depend on his grade, and that of the match he was refereeing; less skill would be expected of an amateur stepping in to help out, than of a professional referee. This means that the same accident might amount to a breach of duty if the referee was a trained professional, but not if he was an amateur. The referee in the case was a professional and was found liable. Similarly, in **Horton** *v* **Evans** (2006), a pharmacist was held liable for the side-effects suffered by a customer whose GP had mistakenly prescribed drugs eight times stronger than her usual dose, on the grounds that a reasonably careful and competent pharmacist would have noticed the increased dosage and queried it with the claimant and/or the GP (the GP was also sued and settled out of court).

Differences of opinion

In assessing the standard of care to be expected in areas where the defendant is exercising special skill or knowledge, the courts have accepted that within a profession or trade there may be differences of opinion as to the best techniques and procedures in any situation.

Key Case Bolam *v* Friern Barnet Hospital Management Committee (1957)

This issue was addressed in **Bolam *v* Friern Barnet Hospital Management Committee** (1957), a case brought by a patient who had had electric shock treatment for psychiatric problems and had suffered broken bones as a result of the relaxant drugs given before the treatment. These drugs were not always given to patients undergoing electric shock treatment; some doctors felt they should not be given because of the risk of fractures; others, including the defendant, believed their use was desirable. How was the court then to decide whether, in using them, the defendant had fallen below the standard of a reasonable doctor?

Their answer was a formula which has been taken as allowing the medical profession (and to a certain extent other professions, as the test has been adopted in other types of case too) to fix their own standards. According to McNair J:

> A doctor is not guilty of negligence if he has acted in accordance with a practice accepted as proper by a responsible body of medical men skilled in that particular art.

Providing this was the case, the fact that other doctors might disagree could not make the conduct negligent. The practical effect of this decision (which was only given in a High Court case, but was adopted in several later House of Lords cases) was that so long as a doctor could find a medical expert prepared to state that the actions complained of were in keeping with a responsible body of medical opinion, it would be impossible to find him or her negligent.

Legal Principle

A doctor is not guilty of negligence if he or she has acted in a way which a responsible body of other doctors would consider to be correct.

Key Case Bolitho *v* City & Hackney Health Authority (1997)

The House of Lords has, however, now modified this much-criticised decision in **Bolitho *v* City & Hackney Health Authority** (1997). This case involved a two-year-old boy, who was admitted to hospital suffering breathing difficulties. He was not seen by a doctor. Shortly after his second attack of breathing problems, his breathing failed completely, he suffered a heart attack and died. His mother sued the health authority on his behalf, arguing that he should have been seen by a doctor, who should have intubated him (inserted a tube into his throat to help him breathe), and that it was the failure to do this which caused his death. The doctor on duty at the time maintained that even if she had seen the boy she would not have intubated him, which meant that the court had to decide whether she would have been negligent in not doing so. The doctor was able to produce an expert witness to say that intubation would not have been the correct treatment, and the claimant was able to produce one who said it would.

In this situation, the **Bolam** principle had always been taken as suggesting that the doctor was therefore not negligent – other medical opinion might disagree with what she did, but she could produce evidence that it was a practice accepted by a responsible body of medical opinion. Lord Browne-Wilkinson, delivering the leading judgment with which the others agreed, thought differently. While agreeing that the **Bolam** test was still the correct one to apply, he said that the court was not obliged to hold that a doctor was not liable for negligence simply because some medical experts had testified that the doctor's actions were in line with accepted practice. The court had to satisfy itself that the medical experts' opinion was reasonable, in that they had weighed up the risks and benefits, and had a logical basis for their conclusion. He then went on, however, to water down this statement by suggesting that in most cases the fact that medical experts held a particular view would in itself demonstrate its reasonableness, and that it would only be in very rare cases that a court would reject such a view as unreasonable. The case before the House of Lords, he concluded, was not one of those rare situations, and so the claimant's claim was rejected.

Legal Principle

Although the Bolam test still applies, a court is not obliged to find a doctor not liable for negligence purely because other medical experts have testified that his or her actions were correct.

However, there are some signs that **Bolitho** is being used more forcefully, to hold medical opinion to a proper standard of reasonableness. In **Marriott** *v* **West Midlands Regional Health Authority** (1999), the claimant had suffered a head injury after a fall at home; he spent the night in hospital but was discharged the next day after tests. After continuing to feel ill for a week, he called his GP, who could find nothing wrong but told Mrs Marriott to call him again if her husband's condition got any worse. Four days later, Mr Marriott became partially paralysed, and this was later discovered to be a result of the original injury. He claimed that the GP had been negligent in not referring him back to the hospital, given that the GP did not have the resources to test for the condition which he was eventually found to have. At trial, Mr Marriott's expert witness claimed that, given the symptoms Mr Marriott had shown, the GP should have sent him back to the hospital for more tests; however, the GP brought expert evidence to suggest that, although this would have been a reasonable course of action, keeping a patient at home for review was equally reasonable in the circumstances.

The old **Bolam** approach would have required the judge to find for the GP, given that he could prove that a reasonable body of medical opinion supported his actions, but, following **Bolitho**, the trial judge looked at the reasonableness of this opinion, given the risk to Mr Marriott, and concluded that, in the circumstances, deciding to review his case at home, without asking for further tests, was not a reasonable use of a GP's discretion. He therefore found the GP negligent. The Court of Appeal upheld his approach: a trial judge was entitled to carry out his own assessment of the risk in the circumstances, and was not bound to follow the opinion of a body of experts.

The use of the **Bolam** test has been extended to cover not just other professionals, but also defendants who do not have the skills of a particular profession, but have made a decision or taken an action which professionals in the relevant area might disagree about. In **Adams and another** *v* **Rhymney Valley District Council** (2000), the claimants were a family whose children died when fire broke out in the house they rented from the defendant council. The house had double-glazed windows which could only be opened with a key, and the claimants had been unable to smash the glass quickly enough to save the children. They argued that the council had been negligent in providing this type of window, and the issue arose of whether it was correct to decide this by applying the **Bolam** test, given that the council were not window designers. The court held that it was. They pointed out that, in deciding on the window design, the council had to balance the risk of fire against the risk of children falling out of a more easily opened window, and professional opinions varied on how this balance should be struck. If a reasonable body of experts in the field would consider that the council's window design struck this balance in an acceptable way, and the court accepted this view as reasonable, there was no negligence, even though other experts might disagree, and even though the council had neither consulted experts, nor gone through the same processes when choosing the design as an expert would have done.

Standards of skill

It was also established in **Bolam** (and **Bolitho** does not affect this point) that where a defendant is exercising a particular skill, he or she is expected to do so to the standard of a reasonable person at the same level within that field. No account is taken of the defendant's actual experience, so that a junior doctor is not expected to have the same level of skill as a consultant, but is expected to be as competent as an average junior doctor, whether he or she has been one for a year or a week. This principle was upheld in **Djemal** *v* **Bexley Heath Health Authority** (1995) where the standard required was held to be that of a reasonably senior houseman acting as a casualty officer (which was the defendant's position at the time), regardless of how long the defendant had actually been doing that job at that level.

The standard of care imposed is only that of a reasonably skilled member of the profession; the defendant is not required to be a genius, or possess skills way beyond those normally to be expected. In **Wells** *v* **Cooper** (1958) the defendant, a carpenter, fixed a door handle on to a door. Later the handle came away in the claimant's hand, causing him to fall backwards off an unfenced platform outside the door. It was held that the carpenter had done the work as well as any ordinary carpenter would, and therefore had exercised such care as was required of him; he was not liable for the claimant's injury.

In **Balamoan** *v* **Holden & Co** (1999) the defendant was a solicitor who ran a small town practice, in which he was the only qualified lawyer. The claimant consulted him over a claim for nuisance. During the following two years, he had two 30-minute interviews with non-qualified members of the solicitor's staff, but no contact with the defendant himself. At the end of that time, he was advised that his claim was worth no more than £3,000, and when he refused to accept that advice, his legal aid certificate was discharged and he stopped using the firm. He went on to conduct the nuisance case himself, and won a settlement of £25,000. He then sued the solicitor, arguing that, but for the solicitor's negligence in, for example, failing to gather all the available evidence at the time, he could have won £1 million in damages. The Court of Appeal held that the solicitor was only to be judged by the standard to be expected of a solicitor in a small country town (rather than, for example, a specialist firm which might have expert knowledge of big claims). However, if such a solicitor delegated the conduct of claims to unqualified staff who could not come up to that standard, the solicitor could be held negligent.

Case Navigator

A duty to explain?

In **Chester** *v* **Afshar** (2004), the House of Lords held that doctors had a duty not only to take reasonable steps to make sure their advice was right, but also to explain the thinking behind that advice. The claimant had been operated on by the defendent surgeon to treat a back problem.

When recommending the surgery, the surgeon had made no mention of any risk of things going wrong. After the operation, the claimant suffered severe nerve damage, which caused paralysis in one leg. She later discovered that this was a known, if unusual, risk of the surgery. She sued the doctor.

The House of Lords found that the doctor had not been negligent in the way he carried out the operation; the paralysis was something that could happen even when the surgery was carried out properly, as it had been here. But they stated that the surgeon had been negligent in not warning the claimant of the risk, however slight it might be. The patient had a right to choose what was or was not done to her, and she could only exercise this right if given full information. Providing such information was therefore part of the doctor's duty of care.

It was not clear from the judgment in **Chester** whether the duty to warn applied only in medical negligence cases, or in all cases involving professionals, but subsequent cases have suggested that it is, at the very least, much less likely that a duty to warn would be owed in non-medical situations. In **Moy** *v* **Pettman Smith** (2005), the defendant was a barrister, who was sued by a client. The claim arose out of another case in which the claimant, Mr Moy, was suing a health authority for medical negligence over an operation that went wrong, and the defendant was his barrister. Part of the evidence in the case was to be a report from an orthopaedic surgeon, but Mr Moy's solicitors failed to get it in time. The barrister's application to have the trial adjourned so that the report could be obtained had initially been refused, but she planned to apply again. At the door of the court, the health authority made a settlement offer of £150,000, but the defendant advised the claimant not to accept it, and said she was hopeful that there would be no problem getting time to present the medical report. In fact, she thought there was around a 50:50 chance of that application being accepted by the court, but reasoned that if the report could not be used, and the result was that Mr Moy won less than he should have, he could sue the solicitors. However, she did not explain any of this to Mr Moy.

On her advice, Mr Moy refused the offer, but, once the hearing got under way, it soon became obvious that the application to produce the extra evidence was not going to succeed, which would weaken the claimant's case. The barrister therefore advised Mr Moy to settle, but by this point the health authority had reduced their offer to £120,000. Mr Moy then sued the barrister, and the question arose as to whether she was negligent in failing to explain fully her thinking about the likelihood of the court accepting the application to submit the medical report. The House of Lords held that she was not. The advice she had given was within the range of advice that could be given by a reasonably competent barrister, and, as long as a barrister gave clear and understandable advice about their recommended course of action, it was not necessary to spell out all the reasoning behind that advice. Similarly, in **White** *v* **Paul Davidson and Taylor** (2004), the Court of Appeal considered whether the **Chester** duty to explain applied to a claim against a solicitor, and, in **Beary** *v* **Pall Mall Investments** (2005), to a claim against a financial adviser. In both cases, the answer was no.

Changes in knowledge

In areas such as medicine and technology, the state of knowledge about a particular subject may change rapidly, so that procedures and techniques which are approved as safe and effective may very quickly become outdated, and even be discovered to be dangerous.

Key Case Roe *v* Minister of Health (1954)

The case of **Roe *v* Minister of Health** (1954) established that where this happens, a defendant is entitled to be judged according to the standards that were accepted at the time when they acted.

The claimant in the case was left paralysed after surgery, because a disinfectant, in which ampoules of anaesthetic were kept, leaked into the ampoules through microscopic cracks in the glass, invisible to the naked eye. Medical witnesses in the case said that until the man's accident occurred, keeping the ampoules in disinfectant was a standard procedure, and there was no way of knowing that it was dangerous; it was only the injuries to the claimant that had revealed the risk. Therefore the defendant was held not to be liable and the claim failed.

Legal Principle

Where knowledge and practice within a particular area have changed over time, a defendant is entitled to be judged according to the standards accepted at the time the alleged negligence happened.

In **Maguire *v* Harland and Wolff plc** (2005), the claimant was a woman who had contracted the fatal disease mesothelioma, as a result of being exposed to asbestos fibres brought home on her husband's clothes. The husband worked for the defendant shipbuilding firm, and it was accepted that the firm had been in breach of their duty of care to him, in exposing him to asbestos. Could they also be expected to foresee injury to members of his family from exposure to his work clothes? Today, it is well known that such exposure can result in injury, but the court found that at the time when Mr Maguire was working at the shipyard there had been no information from specialists in workplace safety, or from the medical profession, to suggest that it was necessary or even sensible to protect family members from exposure. Therefore the defendants were not liable to Mrs Maguire and her claim failed.

However, once a risk is suspected, the position may change. In **N *v* UK Medical Research Council** (1996), the Queen's Bench Division looked at this issue. In 1959, the Medical Research Council (MRC) started a medical trial of human growth hormone, which involved giving the hormone to children with growth problems. The children were each given the hormone by one of four different methods. In 1976, the MRC were warned that the hormone could cause Creutzfeldt–Jakob Disease, a fatal brain disease. A year later, the MRC were told that two of the four methods of giving the hormone carried a particular risk of transmitting CJD. Ultimately, several of the children who received the hormone died from CJD, and their parents alleged that the MRC had been negligent in not investigating the risk when it was first suggested in 1976, and in not suspending the programme until it was proved safe.

The court held that the failure to look into the risk was negligent, and, if the MRC had looked into it then, failure to suspend the trial programme would also have been negligent.

Special characteristics of the claimant

If a claimant has some characteristic or incapacity which increases the risk of harm, the defendant may be expected to take that into account.

Key Case **Paris v Stepney Borough Council (1951)**

In **Paris v Stepney Borough Council** (1951), the claimant was employed by the defendants in a garage. As a result of a previous injury at work, he could see with only one eye. His job included welding, and, while doing this one day, a piece of metal flew into his good eye and damaged it. No goggles had been provided by the defendant. The House of Lords accepted that failing to provide goggles would not have made the defendants liable to a worker with no previous sight problems, but said that in this case the defendants were liable. The risk of injury was small, but the potential consequences to this particular employee if such injury did occur were extremely serious, as he could easily end up completely blind; moreover, the provision of goggles was not difficult or expensive.

Legal Principle

Where a claimant has some characteristic which increases the risk of harm, the defendant may have a duty to take extra precautions to protect them.

In a number of recent cases the courts have looked at the issue of claimants who are drunk, and whether this amounts to a characteristic which in some way increases a defendant's duty towards them. In **Barrett v Ministry of Defence**, the case of the drunken naval pilot (discussed on p. 55), the Court of Appeal took the view that there is no duty to stop someone else from getting drunk, but, once the claimant was drunk, it accepted that the defendant had assumed some responsibility for protecting him from the consequences of his intoxication, by virtue of the relationship between them and the fact that the defendant had ordered the claimant to be taken to lie down.

However, without such a relationship, it seems there is no general duty to give extra protection to a drunken claimant. In **Griffiths v Brown** (1998), the claimant had got drunk and asked a taxi driver to take him to a particular cashpoint machine. The driver dropped him off on the opposite side of the road from the machine, and he was injured while crossing. He argued that the driver, knowing he was drunk, had a duty not to expose him to the danger of crossing a road. The court rejected this argument: the duty of a taxi driver was to carry a passenger safely during the journey, and then stop at a place where they can get out of the car safely; that duty should not be increased by the fact that the claimant was drunk. However, the court accepted that the duty might be extended if, for example, a passenger who intended to spend the evening drinking arranged for a taxi driver to collect them and see them home safely; this clearly accords with the **Barrett** approach that there may be a duty to protect a drunken claimant where the defendant has actually done something which amounts to assuming responsibility for such protection.

Size of the risk

This includes both the chances of damage occurring, and the potential seriousness of that damage. In **Bolton v Stone** (1951), the claimant was standing outside her house when she was hit by a cricket ball from a nearby ground. It was clear that the cricketers could have foreseen that a ball would be hit out of the ground, and this had happened before, but only six times in the previous 30 years.

Taking into consideration the presence of a 17-foot fence, the distance from the pitch to the edge of the ground, and the fact that the ground sloped upwards in the direction in which the ball was struck, the House of Lords considered that the chances of injury to someone standing where the claimant was were so slight that the cricket club was not negligent in allowing cricket to be played without having taken any other precautions against such an event. The only way to ensure that such an injury could not occur would be to erect an extremely high fence, or possibly even a dome over the whole ground, and the trouble and expense of such precautions were completely out of proportion to the degree of risk.

A case in which the potential seriousness of an injury was decisive is **Paris** *v* **Stepney Borough Council** p. 85.

Practicality of protection

The magnitude of the risk must be balanced against the cost and trouble to the defendant of taking the measures necessary to eliminate it. The more serious the risk (in terms of both the chances of it happening and the degree of potential harm), the more the defendant is expected to do to protect against it. Conversely, as **Bolton** *v* **Stone** shows, defendants are not expected to take extreme precautions against very slight risks. This was also the case in **Latimer** *v* **AEC Ltd** (1952). Flooding had occurred in a factory owned by the defendants following an unusually heavy spell of rain. This had left patches of the floor very slippery. The defendants had covered some of the wet areas with sawdust, but had not had enough to cover all of them. The claimant, a factory employee, was injured after slipping on an uncovered area, and sued, alleging that the defendants had not taken sufficient precautions; in view of the danger, they should have closed the factory. The House of Lords agreed that the only way to eradicate the danger was to close the factory, but held that given the level of risk, particularly bearing in mind that the slippery patches were clearly visible, such an onerous precaution would be out of proportion. The defendants were held not liable.

Where the defendant is reacting to an emergency, they are then judged according to what a reasonable person could be expected to do in such a position and with the time available to decide on an action, and this will clearly allow for a lesser standard of conduct than that expected where the situation allows time for careful thought.

Common practice

In deciding whether the precautions taken by the defendant (if any) are reasonable, the courts may look at the general practice in the relevant field. In **Wilson** *v* **Governors of Sacred Heart Roman Catholic Primary School, Carlton** (1997), the claimant, a nine-year-old boy, was hit in the eye with a coat by a fellow pupil as he crossed the playground to go home at the end of the day. The trial judge had looked at the fact that attendants were provided to supervise the children during the lunch break, and inferred from this that such supervision should also have been provided at the end of the school day. The Court of Appeal, however, noted that most primary schools did not supervise children at this time; they also pointed out that the incident could just as easily have happened outside the school gates anyway. Consequently the school had not fallen below the standard of care required.

In **Thompson** *v* **Smith Shiprepairers (North Shields) Ltd** (1984), it was made clear that companies whose industrial practices showed serious disregard for workers' health and safety would not evade liability simply by showing that their approach was common practice in the relevant industry. The case involved a claimant who suffered deafness as a result of working in the defendants' shipyard, and the defendants argued that the conditions in which he worked were common across the industry and therefore did not fall below the required standard of care. Mustill J disagreed, stating that they could not evade liability simply by proving that all the other employers were just as bad. He pointed out that their whole industry seemed to be characterised by indifference to the problem of noise causing deafness, and held that there were some circumstances in which an employer had a duty to take the initiative to look at the risks and seek out precautions which could be taken to protect workers. He pointed out, however, that this approach must still be balanced against the practicalities; employers were not expected to have standards way above the rest of their industry, although they were expected to keep their knowledge and practices in the field of safety up to date.

Another area where common practice is taken into account is in accidents which take place during sports. In **Caldwell** *v* **Maguire and Fitzgerald** (2001), the claimant, Caldwell, was a professional jockey, as were the two defendants. All three were in a race with a fourth jockey, Byrne. At the point where the incident which gave rise to the case happened, Maguire, Fitzgerald and Byrne were neck and neck, with Caldwell close behind. As they approached a bend, Maguire and Fitzgerald pulled ahead in such a way as to leave no room for Byrne. Seeing its path ahead closed off, Byrne's horse veered across Caldwell's path, causing him to fall. The defendants were found to have committed the offence of careless riding under the rules of the Jockey Club, which regulates racing practice; this was the least serious of five possible offences concerning interfering with other riders.

Caldwell sued Maguire and Fitzgerald for causing his injuries, but the Court of Appeal found their conduct did not amount to negligence. They confirmed that a player of sports owes a duty to all the other players, and approved the test of negligence in sports used in the earlier case of **Condon** *v* **Basi** (1985), which stated that the duty on a player of sports is to exercise such care as is appropriate in the circumstances. The court went on to explain that this would depend on the game or sport being played, the degree of risk associated with it, its conventions and customs, and the standard of skill and judgement reasonably to be expected of players. As a result, the standard of care would be such that a momentary lapse of judgement or skill would be unlikely to result in liability and, in practice, it might be difficult to prove a breach unless the player's conduct amounted to a reckless disregard for others' safety. Therefore, in this case, the defendants were not negligent, as, within the circumstances of the horseracing world, careless riding was accepted as part of the sport, even if not approved of.

Players of sport also have a duty to spectators, but the court stated that as, in the normal course of events, spectators would be at little or no risk from players, a player would have to have behaved with a considerable degree of negligence before he or she could be said to have failed to exercise such care as was reasonable in the circumstances.

Potential benefits of the risk

Some risks have potential benefits for society, and it has long been the practice of the courts to weigh such benefits against the possible damage if the risk is taken. This principle was applied in **Watt** *v* **Hertfordshire County Council** (1954). The claimant was a firefighter. He was among others called to the scene of an accident where a woman was trapped under a car; a heavy jack was needed to rescue her. The vehicle in which the fire officers travelled to the scene was not designed to carry the jack, and the claimant was injured when it slipped. He sued his employers, but the court held that the risk taken in transporting the jack was outweighed by the need to get there quickly in order to save the woman's life. However, the court stated that if the same accident had occurred in a commercial situation, where the risk was taken in order to get a job done for profit, the claimant would have been able to recover.

The Compensation Act 2006 now confirms this position. Section 1 of the Act states that when considering whether a defendant should have taken particular steps to meet a standard of care, a court:

> may . . . have regard to whether a requirement to take such steps might –
> (a) prevent a desirable activity from being undertaken at all, to a particular extent, or in a particular way, or
> (b) discourage persons from undertaking functions in connection with a desirable activity.

As the case of **Watt** shows, s. 1 of the Act does not actually change the law, since the courts already considered the issue of public benefit where they felt it was necessary to do so, and s. 1 does not oblige them to take it into account, but merely confirms that they may.

The Act was passed in July 2006, so it is too early to see its impact, but critics have warned that it could lead to increased litigation. It has been suggested that it may end up being used to create two different standards of care, according to whether or not an activity is deemed 'desirable' or not. In his article 'What compensation?' (see Reading list), John Leighton Williams QC cites the example of a firefighter trying to claim compensation for being injured at work. Would the fact that fighting fires is likely to be considered a desirable activity mean that he or she would have to prove a higher degree of negligence than workers in other fields would have to? Firefighting might well be something society wants to encourage, but is preventing those injured as a result of such work from claiming compensation really the best way to do so?

Leighton Williams also makes the point that differentiating between desirable activities and others may lead individuals to believe they can take unacceptable risks, on the assumption that if anything goes wrong, they will not be held to account because they are leading Scouts on a climbing holiday, or taking a group of pupils skiing, and those activities would be considered desirable.

In **Cole** *v* **Davis-Gilbert** (2007), the Court of Appeal specifically mentioned the danger of setting standards of care so high that they discourage socially useful activities. The case arose after Ms Cole was walking across a village green, and stepped into a hole, breaking her leg. The hole had been used to hold a maypole for a village fête, and was dug by the local British Legion, who organised the fête. After the pole had been removed, they had filled in the hole, but, by the time of Ms Cole's accident, it had been left open again. It was not known how this happened, but the court assumed it was probably done by children playing on the green. The court held that the British Legion was not in breach of its duty to people walking on the green, because its members had taken reasonable steps to fill in the hole; equally, the landowners, who were also sued, were reasonable in assuming the hole had been filled in and were not liable either. The court commented that it was important not to set a higher standard of care than what was reasonable, because an unreasonable standard would eventually mean that events like village fêtes could not take place at all.

Table 2.1 The standard of reasonableness

Factors in favour of the defendant	*Factors in favour of the claimant*
The damage was not very likely to happen	The damage was very likely to happen
The damage was not very likely to be serious	The damage was very likely to be serious
It would have been difficult and/or expensive to take precautions against the risk	Taking precautions against the risk would have been simple and inexpensive
The precautions taken were in line with common practice, or it was not common practice to take precautions against this risk	It was common practice to take precautions against this risk, or better precautions than the defendant took
The risky activity had social benefits	There were no social benefits associated with the risky activity

Topical issue

Behind the headlines

Negligence cases often reach the news and, once you know a little about tort law, you will discover that they are often misrepresented. This certainly happened with much of the coverage of **Harris** *v* **Perry** (2008), a case in which a young boy was injured while playing in a bouncy castle that had been hired for a friend's birthday party. When, at first instance, the claimants won their case, it was widely reported in the press that the parents who had hired the castle would have to pay damages of over £1 million, and that the case was an example of the 'compensation culture', in which people seek to blame someone and get compensation for even the most minor injury. The facts of the case did not, however, fit this picture. First, the Perrys, like most householders, had home insurance, and it was their insurers who would have to pay the damages (in practice, it is extremely unlikely that an ordinary person without such insurance would be sued for negligence). In taking premiums from the Perrys, the insurance company was accepting the risk that they might, one day, have to pay out on the policy, which they would have assessed as a risk worth taking, in the knowledge that they might equally well have been able to take the premiums for years and years and never have to pay a penny on the policy. Secondly, the boy injured in the castle suffered severe brain damage, and will need 24-hour care for the rest of his life. His parents were not seeking to get rich at the expense of someone else, but to be able to pay for that care. Interestingly, when the case was appealed, and the defendants won, very few newspapers bothered to report the decision prominently.

Damage

The negligence must cause damage; if no damage is caused, there is no claim in negligence, no matter how careless the defendant's conduct. In the vast majority of cases this is not an issue: there will be obvious personal injury, damage to property or economic loss. However, there are cases where the claimant perceives that the defendant's negligence has caused damage, yet the law does not recognise the results of that negligence as damage. The cases discussed in this section give an insight into how the law decides what is damage and what is not.

Case Navigator

The issue of damage to property was the subject of **Hunter** *v* **Canary Wharf Ltd and London Docklands Development Corporation** (1997). The case arose from the construction of a tower block at Canary Wharf in East London. An action concerning the effects of the construction work was brought by local residents, and one of the issues that arose from the case was whether excessive dust could be sufficient to constitute damage to property for the purposes of negligence. The Court of Appeal concluded that the mere deposit of dust was not in itself sufficient because dust was an inevitable incident of urban life. In order to bring an action for negligence, there had to be damage in the sense of a physical change in property, which rendered the property less useful or less valuable. Examples given by the court included excessive dust being trodden into the fabric of a carpet by householders in such a way as to lessen the value of the fabric, or excessive dust causing damage to electrical equipment.

A very different issue was examined in **R** *v* **Croydon Health Authority** (1997) and **McFarlane** *v* **Tayside Health Board** (1999); could the birth of a child be considered damage? In **R** *v* **Croydon Health Authority**, an employee of the defendant had routinely examined the claimant, a woman of childbearing age, and found that she was suffering from a life-threatening heart condition, which could be made worse by pregnancy. The claimant was not told this, and went on to become pregnant and have a child. Although she did want a child, the claimant claimed she would not have become pregnant if she had known of the danger to herself in doing so. In addition to claiming for the fact that her heart condition was made worse by the pregnancy, she claimed for the expenses of pregnancy and the cost of bringing up the child, and was successful at first instance. The defendant appealed against the award of damages for the costs of pregnancy and bringing up the child. The Court of Appeal supported its view: where a mother wanted a healthy child and a healthy child was what she got, there was no loss. The court emphasised that a key factor in this case was that the claimant had wanted a child; the decision might be different, it was suggested, when a child was not wanted.

However, when this issue was addressed in **McFarlane** *v* **Tayside Health Board**, the House of Lords found it impossible to view as damage the birth of a healthy child, even to parents who had expressly decided that they did not want more children (the case is a Scottish one, but has been treated as representing English law too). The claimants were a couple who had four children, and decided that they did not want any more, so Mr McFarlane had a vasectomy. After he was wrongly advised that the operation had been successful, Mrs McFarlane became pregnant again, and gave birth to a healthy daughter. The couple sought to sue the health authority, with Mrs McFarlane claiming damages for the pain and discomfort of pregnancy and birth, and both claimants claiming for the costs of bringing up the child.

The House of Lords allowed the claim for pain and discomfort, pointing out that tort law regularly compensated for pain arising from personal injury, and there was no reason to treat pregnancy as involving a less serious form of pain. But they refused to allow the claim for the costs of bringing up the child, although there was some difference of opinion as to why. Lords Slynn and Hope simply argued that this was pure economic loss and it was not fair, just and reasonable to impose a duty on the health board to prevent such loss. Lords Steyn and Millett based their decision more on policy grounds, stating that the birth of a normal, healthy baby was universally regarded as a blessing, not a detriment, and therefore could not be viewed as damage. Lord Millett pointed out that although there were disadvantages involved in parenthood (cost being one), they were inextricably linked with the advantages, and so parents could not justifiably seek to transfer the disadvantages to others while themselves having the benefit of the advantages.

Both cases focused on the fact that the baby was healthy, and in **McFarlane** the House of Lords specifically declined to consider what the position is when a baby is born handicapped, who would not have been born at all if it were not for a defendant's negligence. The implication seemed to be that they might be prepared to allow that the birth of a child with disabilities could be considered damage in a way that having a healthy child did not, which said little for their approach to disabled people. (Note that what we are talking about here are cases where a disabled baby would not have been born at all, but for the defendant's negligence; this is not the same as cases where a baby would have been born healthy, but the defendant's negligence has caused its disability. There is no question that the latter type of case is accepted as damage, in the form of personal injury to the child.)

Not long afterwards, the question of whether the situation would be different if an unwanted child born as a result of negligence did turn out to be disabled arose before the Court of Appeal in **Parkinson** *v* **St James and Seacroft University Hospital** (2001). The claimant, Mrs Parkinson, and her husband had four children, and had decided they neither wanted nor could afford any more, so Mrs Parkinson was sterilised. Because of the hospital's admitted negligence, the operation did not work, and Mrs Parkinson became pregnant again. The child was born with severe disabilities, and Mrs Parkinson claimed for the costs of bringing him up. At first instance the court refused to allow her to claim the basic costs of his maintenance (the amount it would have cost to bring him up if he had not been disabled), following **McFarlane**. However, the judge said she could claim the extra costs which arose from her son's disability. The hospital appealed.

The Court of Appeal allowed Mrs Parkinson's claim for these extra costs (though not the basic costs), and, in her judgment, Hale LJ addressed the issue of whether the birth of a disabled child could be considered damage, if that of a healthy one could not. In doing so, she looked again at the reasoning in **McFarlane**. She argued that one of the most important rights protected by the law of tort was that of bodily integrity – the right to choose what happens to one's own body, and not to be subjected to bodily injury by others. The processes of pregnancy and childbirth, if unwanted, were a serious violation of this right, denying a woman the chance to decide what happened to her own body, and causing discomfort and pain. In addition, she pointed out that childbearing impacts on a woman's personal autonomy, saying that 'One's life is no longer just one's own, but also someone else's'. Mothers-to-be are expected to alter what they eat, drink and do to safeguard the baby, while after the birth there is a legal responsibility to look after the child, which includes a financial burden. As a result, she said, it was clear that where an unwanted pregnancy happened as a result of negligence, its consequences were capable of giving rise to damages. However, she went on, it was also necessary to take into account the fact that children bring benefits to their parents, and, since it was impossible to calculate these, the fairest assumption was that they were sufficient to cancel out the costs. This was what the House of Lords had assumed in **McFarlane**.

Applying this reasoning to the birth of a disabled child, she said that allowing a claim for the extra costs associated with disability made sense. It was acknowledging that a disabled child brought as much benefit to his or her family as any other child, but that, as he or she would cost more to bring up, the costs were not cancelled out. Therefore, the extra expense should be recoverable.

The same issue took a slightly different shape in **Rees** *v* **Darlington Memorial Hospital NHS Trust** (2002). Here the claimant was a disabled woman, who was almost blind as a result of a hereditary condition. Because of her disability, she did not want to have children, and so chose to be sterilised. The operation was performed negligently, and the claimant had a son, who was not disabled. She was a single parent, and claimed, not for the basic costs of bringing up her son, but for the extra costs of doing so that were caused by her disability.

The Court of Appeal had said that Ms Rees was entitled to compensation for these extra costs, but the House of Lords rejected the claim. As in **McFarlane**, they allowed the claimant compensation for the pain and stress of pregnancy and birth, but they refused to give compensation for any of the costs of bringing up a child. By a majority, they confirmed the reasoning in **McFarlane**, that a child should not be seen in terms of an economic liability, and that the benefits of having a child could not be quantified. They said that the idea of giving someone compensation for the birth of a healthy child would offend most people, especially as that money would come from the hard-pressed resources of the NHS.

However, they said that it was clear that where a defendant's negligence had brought about a pregnancy and birth which the mother did not want and had asked them to prevent, a legal wrong had been done that went beyond the pain and suffering of birth and pregnancy. As examples of the harm this could cause, Lord Bingham cited the situation of a single mother who might already be struggling to make ends meet and would now not only have another child to feed, but also face a longer period before she could work longer hours and earn more money; or the situation of a woman who had been longing to start or resume a much-wanted career, and was now prevented from doing so. The House of Lords held that there should be a financial recognition of this loss, and awarded Ms Rees £15,000 in addition to the compensation for pain and suffering.

The House also took the opportunity to consider whether **Parkinson** had been correctly decided, and said that it was; where a child born as the result of a defendant's negligence was disabled, the parents could claim for the extra costs associated with his or her disability.

The House of Lords recently shed some more light on how they assess the presence of damage in **Rothwell** *v* **Chemical & Insulating Co** (2007). This is the case (discussed on p. 41), where the claimants had been exposed to asbestos, which caused pleural plaques, a form of scarring on the lungs. Pleural plaques themselves cause no symptoms, nor do they make it more likely that a person will suffer an asbestos-related illness, but, because they show that asbestos has entered the lungs, they do indicate that a person is at risk of asbestos-related illness. As a result, they caused severe anxiety in the claimants. The House of Lords considered whether the plaques could be considered to be damage, and concluded that they could not. It was clear that the plaques were a physical change in the claimants' bodies; the court was shown photos of the scarring on the men's lungs. But, the House of Lords said, physical change in itself did not mean damage. For there to be damage, the change had to be something which made the claimants worse off in some way, whether physically or economically or both. The plaques themselves had no effect on the claimants' health, and so they could not be considered to be damage.

Topical issue

Is sperm property?

Advances in medical knowledge can result in novel questions coming before the courts, and this was the case in **Yearworth and others** *v* **North Bristol NHS Trust** (2009). The claimants in the case were all men who had undergone chemotherapy treatment for cancer. This kind of treatment can leave men sterile, and so it has become common for hospitals to offer patients the chance to have a sperm sample frozen under medical conditions, so that they still have at least a chance of having children if they later want to. The storage and use of such samples is regulated by the Human Fertilisation and Embryology Act 1990, which lays down rules about who can store the samples and how they can be used.

The claimants' sperm samples had been stored by one of the defendant's hospitals but, owing to negligence, they had been allowed to thaw, making them useless. The claimants sued the NHS Trust for negligence.

The Trust admitted that it had a duty of care to take reasonable care of the samples, and that it had breached this duty. However, it denied liability because, it argued, the loss of the samples was not damage of a kind that was recognised in the law of negligence. There were two possible ways in which the destruction of sperm could be classified as damage: either its destruction was a personal injury to the men who provided it, or, alternatively, the sperm could be considered to be the men's property. In making the argument that the damage was personal injury, the claimants' lawyer said that the sperm had been inside the men's bodies, and, if it had been damaged there, that would clearly have counted as a personal injury. Why, he argued, should the situation be any different because the sperm had been ejaculated? He went on to argue that the sperm was different from body parts which were intended to be discarded, such as nail clippings or amputated limbs, because it was always intended to be kept, the purpose of keeping it was exactly the same as the purpose it had while still in the men's bodies, namely to fertilise an egg and create a baby, and it was still biologically active and therefore had a 'living nexus' or connection with the men.

The Court of Appeal dismissed these arguments, stating that 'it would be a fiction to hold that damage to a substance generated by a person's body, inflicted after its removal for storage purposes, constituted a bodily or "personal injury" to him'. They provided little reasoned explanation for this conclusion, beyond saying that to accept destruction of the sperm as personal injury would 'generate paradoxes, and yield ramifications, productive of substantial uncertainty, expensive debate and nice distinctions in an area of law which should be simple, and the principles clear'.

The Court of Appeal therefore considered the alternative argument, that the sperm was the men's property. The Trust's lawyers had argued that the sperm could not be considered property, because the Human Fertilisation and Embryology Act 1990 had so restricted the rights that would normally go with ownership that it was no longer possible to say the men owned the samples. For example, the Act includes provisions that only organisations licensed under the Act can store the samples and use them to bring about a pregnancy, so it would not have been possible for the men to ask for the samples back and have them stored somewhere else, or to store them themselves. The Court of Appeal disagreed. They said that the men's bodies had produced the sperm, and the reason for giving the sperm samples was that it could later be used for their benefit. They agreed that the Act restricted the men's use of the samples, but pointed out that many statutes imposed restrictions on the use of property, without suggesting that this means the owner does not own it – for example, planning laws restrict a landowner's choice of how to use their land, but that does not mean that the land is not property or not owned. They further pointed out that, as well as placing restrictions on what they could do with the sperm, the Act also gave the men rights over it, such as that the men could at any time withdraw their consent to having the sperm stored, and no one else would have any right that could override that. They also pointed out that the men's recognised rights over the sperm, namely to decide its future use, exactly coincided with the result of the Trust's breach of duty, which was to prevent its future use. They therefore agreed that the sperm samples could be regarded as property, and so there could be liability in negligence for their destruction.

Answering questions

How far does the law of negligence impose a duty not to cause economic loss?

This essay question offers plenty of opportunity to use the information in the sections on economic loss. You should begin by talking about the nature of economic loss, and distinguishing between economic loss caused by physical injury or damage to property, and pure economic loss, perhaps using the case of **Spartan Steel** *v* **Martin** to illustrate the difference.

You can then go on to explain that as far as economic loss caused by personal injury or property damage is concerned, the existence of a duty of care is not problematic; if negligence causing these types of damage is proved, then the defendant will also be liable to compensate the claimant for resulting economic loss, within the rules of causation and remoteness. Then you can get into the real point of the essay: the issue of pure economic loss.

It would be useful to begin your discussion with a brief summary of the historical development of the law in this area, as discussed in this chapter, but do not get too bogged down: a simple recital of what happened first and what happened next and what happened after that will not earn you too many marks. Outline the development, but, in doing so, make it clear that you know not just what happened, but why, by discussing the reasons why the courts pulled back after **Junior Books** *v* **Veitchi**.

The biggest part of your essay should be a discussion of what the law on pure economic loss is now. Talk about those situations in which a duty of care will exist, looking in detail at the **Hedley Byrne** principles, as extended by **Henderson** *v* **Merrett Syndicates** and the 'wills cases'. You should also discuss the situations where a duty of care with regard to pure economic loss will not exist, namely defective products and negligent acts other than provision of services.

The question asks how far there *is* a duty not to cause economic loss, but to win yourself some more marks, finish your essay with a discussion of how far there *should* be such a duty. The material on problems with the law on economic loss will be useful here.

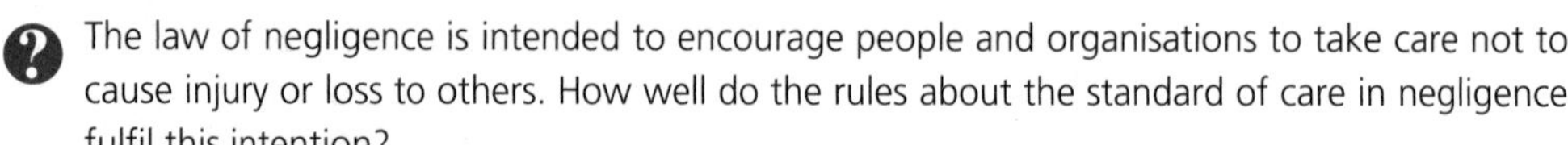

The law of negligence is intended to encourage people and organisations to take care not to cause injury or loss to others. How well do the rules about the standard of care in negligence fulfil this intention?

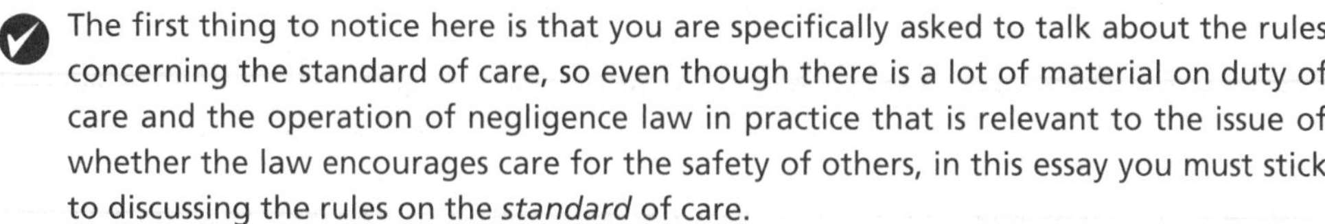

The first thing to notice here is that you are specifically asked to talk about the rules concerning the standard of care, so even though there is a lot of material on duty of care and the operation of negligence law in practice that is relevant to the issue of whether the law encourages care for the safety of others, in this essay you must stick to discussing the rules on the *standard* of care.

A good way to start would be to outline the basis of these rules: the standard of reasonableness; the objective approach; and the factors which the courts will weigh against each other to assess reasonableness. You can then go on to discuss each of these areas in more detail, stating how they operate to discourage dangerous behaviour, and highlighting any ways in which they fail to do this. As regards the objective standard, you could point to the fact that it can be vague, and in some cases unachievable. The case of **Nettleship** *v* **Weston** is relevant here, and in discussing it you should talk about the implications of insurance in negligence cases: the standard of driving imposed in **Nettleship** may not discourage unsafe driving, since a learner driver is unlikely to be able to reach that standard however hard they try, but what it does do is ensure that the financial risk is borne by the party who is insured and therefore able to pay. Similar comments apply to the rules on defendants whose conduct is affected by an infirmity over which they have no control, as in **Roberts** *v* **Ramsbottom**. You could contrast this with **Mansfield** *v* **Weetabix**, where the standard imposed seems more in keeping with the aim of promoting care, and yet its practical effect was to leave the injured claimant uncompensated, even though the defendant was insured.

In discussing the rules on special characteristics of the defendant, you should talk about the special rules for professionals, and in particular doctors. Discuss the criticisms made of **Bolam** *v* **Friern Barnet Hospital Management Committee**, and the idea that doctors are in effect allowed to set their own standard of care; how far can such rules effectively discourage medical negligence? Consider whether **Bolitho** *v* **City & Hackney Hospital Authority** has made a difference.

You should also point out that the rules on practicality of protection mean that defendants are not required to eliminate risk, only to take reasonable precautions. The cases of **Latimer** *v* **AEC** and **Bolton** *v* **Stone** are relevant here.

To extend the coverage of your essay, you could discuss the fact that in some cases the law's emphasis on promoting care in individuals ignores the wider picture and can result in injustice to claimants. On the issue of risks unknown at the time when the defendant acted, you can point out that there is no liability for damage caused as a result of such risks, and this can be justified by the argument that defendants cannot be expected to take care to avoid risks which are not known by anyone to exist. You can then go on to explain that this approach can be unfair to the claimant, whose injury will often result in some advance in knowledge that benefits others (as in **Roe** *v* **Minister of Health**) yet remains uncompensated because of the law's focus on individual fault.

Summary of Chapter 2

Negligence has three main elements:

- a duty of care;
- breach of the duty;
- damage caused by the breach.

Duty of care

Duty of care is a legal concept which dictates whether one party can be liable to another in negligence. The test for a duty of care has varied over the years, but the current main test comes from **Caparo** *v* **Dickman** (1990):

- Is the damage reasonably foreseeable?
- Was there a relationship of proximity between claimant and defendant?
- Is it just and reasonable to impose a duty of care?

The test has been modified for cases which involve:

- economic loss;
- psychiatric injury;
- omissions;
- acts of third parties;
- special groups.

Duties of care: economic loss

Cases involving pure economic loss use a duty of care test developed in **Hedley Byrne** *v* **Heller** (1963), which requires:

- a 'special relationship' between the parties;
- a voluntary assumption of responsibility by the defendant;
- reliance on that advice;
- that it was reasonable to rely on the advice.

Recent cases have allowed liability without reliance, in limited situations.

Problems with the law on economic loss:

- too few/too many restrictions;
- overlap with contract law;
- lack of clarity.

Duties of care: psychiatric injury

The initial duty of care test for psychiatric injury cases contains two elements:

- Is there a recognised psychiatric injury?
- Was the claimant:
  - physically injured as well as psychiatrically (a primary victim)?
  - in danger of physical injury (also a primary victim)?
  - a witness to the incident in some way while not themselves in physical danger (called a secondary victim)?

The first two types of claimant can claim under the normal rules of negligence. For secondary victims, three further tests apply:

- Do they have a recognised psychiatric illness, caused by a sudden shock?
- Are they within a class of people that the law allows to claim compensation for psychiatric injury as a secondary victim?
- What was their proximity to the shocking event?

Problems with the law on psychiatric injury:

- the position of rescuers;
- the 'closeness of relationship' rules;

- the proximity requirements;
- the 'sudden shock' requirement.

Duties of care: omissions

Negligence generally imposes liability for things people do, not things they fail to do, but there are some situations where a defendant may be liable for an omission to act:

- where the defendant has a high degree of control over the claimant;
- where the defendant has assumed responsibility for the claimant in some way;
- where the defendant creates a dangerous situation, and fails to deal with it.

Duties of care: acts of third parties

Negligence usually imposes liability only on the person who causes damage, but there are five situations where someone may be liable for damage done by another:

- vicarious liability;
- where there is a relationship of proximity between claimant and defendant;
- where there is a relationship of proximity between the defendant and the party causing damage;
- where the defendant negligently creates a source of danger;
- where the defendant knew/had reason to know a third party was creating a risk on their property.

Duties of care: special groups

A number of special groups have become subject to special rules on when they will owe a duty of care in negligence, although the **Caparo** test is still the basis of liability. They are:

- the police;
- other emergency services;
- the armed forces;
- local authorities and public bodies.

The European Court of Human Rights cases of **Osman** *v* **UK** (1998) and **Z** *v* **UK** (2001) have suggested that there may have to be some restrictions on the way the courts treat special groups.

Breach of a duty of care

A defendant will be in breach of their duty of care if their behaviour falls below the standard of behaviour reasonably to be expected in someone doing what they are doing.

The test is objective, and is known as the standard of reasonableness; it requires the defendant to take reasonable precautions, not to eliminate every possible risk.

In deciding on the standard to be expected, the courts weigh up a number of factors:

- special characteristics of the defendant;
- special characteristics of the claimant;
- the size of the risk;
- how far it was practical to prevent the risk;
- common practice in the relevant field;
- any potential benefits to society from the activity that caused the risk.

Damage

The defendant will only be liable if the negligence causes damage. The usual types of damage are:

- personal injury;
- damage to property;
- economic loss.

In a series of cases, the courts have decided that the birth of a baby, even if unwanted, is not damage.

Reading list

Text resources

Bailey, S (2006) 'Public authority liability in negligence: the continued search for coherence' 26 *Legal Studies* 155

Barker, C (2006) 'Wielding Occam's Razor: pruning strategies for economic loss' 26(2) *Oxford Journal of Legal Studies* 289

Barker, K (1993) 'Unreliable assumptions in the modern law of negligence' 109 *Law Quarterly Review* 461

Brazier, M and Miola, J (2000) 'Bye-bye Bolam: a medical litigation revolution?' 8 *Medical Law Reports* 85

Case, P (2001) 'Something "old", something "new", something "borrowed" . . . the continued evolution of Bolam' 17 *Professional Negligence* 75

Coke, Sir R (1991) 'An impossible distinction' 107 *Law Quarterly Review* 46

Conaghan, J and Mansell, W (1993) *The Wrongs of Tort*, Chapter 2. Pluto Press

Cooke, P J (2004) 'Primary victims: the end of the road?' 25(1) *Liverpool Law Journal* 29

Dias, R W M (1953) 'The duty problem in negligence' *Cambridge Law Journal* 198

Gearty, C (2002) 'Osman unravels' 67 *Modern Law Review* 87

Harlow, C (2005) *Understanding Tort Law*, 3rd edn, Chapter 2. Sweet & Maxwell

Hepple, B (1997) 'Negligence: the search for coherence' *Current Legal Problems* 69

Howarth, D (1991) 'Negligence after Murphy: time to rethink' *Cambridge Law Journal* 58

Howarth, D (2006) 'Many duties of care – or a duty of care? Notes from the Underground' 26(3) *Oxford Journal of Legal Studies* 449

Law Commission (1999) *Liability for Psychiatric Illness*, Law Commission Report No 249

Leighton Williams, J (2006) 'What compensation?' *Solicitors Journal* 934

Markesinis, B A (1987) 'An expanding tort law – the price of a rigid contract law' 103 *Law Quarterly Review* 354

Markesinis, B A (1989) 'Negligence, nuisance and affirmative duties of action' 105 *Law Quarterly Review* 104

Markesinis, B A and Deakin, S (1992) 'The random element of their Lordships' infallible judgment: an economic and comparative analysis of the tort of negligence from Anns to Murphy' 55 *Modern Law Review* 619

Mitchell, P and Mitchell, C (2005) 'Negligence liability for pure economic loss' 121 *Law Quarterly Review* 194

Morgan, J (2005) 'Slowing the expansion of public authority liability' 121 *Law Quarterly Review* 43

Mullany, N J (1992) 'Proximity, policy and procrastination' 9 *Australian Business Law Review* 80

Mullany, N J (1998) 'Liability for careless communication of traumatic information' 114 *Law Quarterly Review* 380

Posner, R A (1972) 'A theory of negligence' 1 *Journal of Legal Studies* 29

Smith, J C and Burns, P (1983) 'Donoghue and Stevenson: the not so golden anniversary' 46 *Modern Law Review* 147

Sprince, A (1995) 'Page v Smith, being "primary" colours' 11 *Professional Negligence* 124

Sprince, A (1998) 'Negligently inflicted psychiatric damage: a medical diagnosis and prognosis' 18 *Legal Studies* 59

Stapleton, J (1988) 'The gist of negligence' 104 *Law Quarterly Review* 213

Stapleton, J (1991) 'Duty of care and economic loss: a wider agenda' 107 *Law Quarterly Review* 249

Stapleton, J (1995) 'Duty of care: peripheral parties and alternative opportunities for deterrence' 111 *Law Quarterly Review* 301

Teff, H (1992) 'Liability for psychiatric illness after Hillsborough' 12 *Oxford Journal of Legal Studies* 440

Teff, H (1998) 'The standard of care in medical negligence – moving on from Bolam?' *Oxford Journal of Legal Studies* 473

Teff, H (1998) 'Liability for negligently inflicted psychiatric harm: justifications and boundaries' 57(1) *Cambridge Law Journal* 91

Teff, H (1998) 'Liability for psychiatric illness: advancing cautiously' 61 *Modern Law Review* 849

Todd, S (1999) 'Psychiatric injury and rescuers' 115 *Law Quarterly Review* 345

Trindade, F A (1996) 'Nervous shock and negligent conduct' 112 *Law Quarterly Review* 22

Weir, T (1998) 'The staggering march of negligence' in Cane, P and Stapleton, J (eds), *The Law of Obligations: Essays in Honour of John Fleming*. Oxford University Press

Witting, C (2000) 'Physical damage in negligence' *Cambridge Law Journal* 189

Witting, C (2005) 'Duty of care – an analytical approach' 25 *Oxford Journal of Legal Studies* 417

Woolf, Lord (2001) 'Are the courts unnecessarily deferential to the medical profession?' 9(1) *Medical Law Reports* 1–16

Reading on the Internet

The Compensation Act can be read at:
http://www.opsi.gov.uk/acts/acts2006/ukpga_20060029_en.pdf

The Law Commission's 1998 report on liability for psychiatric injury can be read at:
http://www.lawcom.gov.uk/lc_reports.htm

The House of Lords judgment in **Chester** *v* **Afshar** (2004) can be read at:
http://www.publications.parliament.uk/pa/ld200304/ldjudgmt/jd041014/cheste-1.htm

The European Court of Human Rights judgment in **Z** *v* **UK** (2001) can be read at:
http://www.echr.coe.int/ECHR/

The House of Lords judgment in **Sutradhar** *v* **Natural Environmental Research Council** (2006) can be read at:
http://www.publications.parliament.uk/pa/id200506/idjudgmt/id060705/sutrad-1.htm

The House of Lords judgment in **White** *v* **Chief Constable of South Yorkshire** (1998) can be read at:
http://www.parliament.the-stationery-office.co.uk/pa/ld199899/ldjudgmt/jd981203/white01.htm

The House of Lords judgment in **Alcock** *v* **Chief Constable of South Yorkshire** (1992) can be read at:
http://www.bailii.org/uk/cases/UKHL/1991/5.html

The House of Lords decision in **Van Colle** *v* **Chief Constable of Hertfordshire** and **Smith** *v* **Chief Constable of Sussex** (2008) can be read at:
http://www.parliament.the-stationery-office.co.uk/pa/ld200708/ldjudgmt/jd080730/vanco-1.htm

The Court of Appeal judgment in **D** *v* **East Berkshire NHS Trust** (2003) can be read at:
http://www.parliament.the-stationery-office.co.uk/pa/ld200405/ldjudgmt/jd050421/east-2.htm

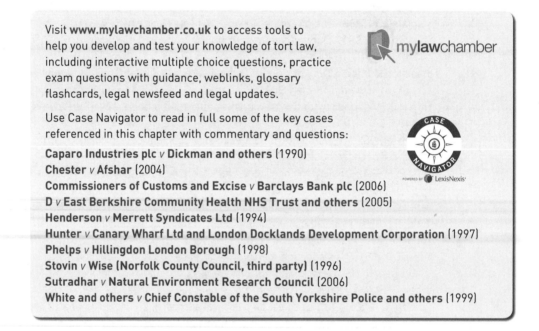

Visit **www.mylawchamber.co.uk** to access tools to help you develop and test your knowledge of tort law, including interactive multiple choice questions, practice exam questions with guidance, weblinks, glossary flashcards, legal newsfeed and legal updates.

Use Case Navigator to read in full some of the key cases referenced in this chapter with commentary and questions:

Caparo Industries plc *v* **Dickman and others** (1990)
Chester *v* **Afshar** (2004)
Commissioners of Customs and Excise *v* **Barclays Bank plc** (2006)
D *v* **East Berkshire Community Health NHS Trust and others** (2005)
Henderson *v* **Merrett Syndicates Ltd** (1994)
Hunter *v* **Canary Wharf Ltd and London Docklands Development Corporation** (1997)
Phelps *v* **Hillingdon London Borough** (1998)
Stovin *v* **Wise (Norfolk County Council, third party)** (1996)
Sutradhar *v* **Natural Environment Research Council** (2006)
White and others *v* **Chief Constable of the South Yorkshire Police and others** (1999)

Chapter 3
Negligence: causation, defences, limitation and criticism

This chapter discusses:

- The principles of causation
- The general defences
- Limitation periods
- Criticisms of negligence law.

In the previous chapter, we looked at the three basic elements of a negligence claim: a duty of care, breach of that duty, and damage. In this chapter, we look at three further factors which may come into a negligence claim, and most other kinds of tort claim:

- causation (did the breach cause the damage?), which divides into factual causation and legal causation, also known as remoteness of damage;
- defences (is there a legal reason why the defendant should not be held liable, or should have their liability reduced?);
- limitation (the set of legal rules that lay down time limits within which claims must be made).

So that you can get a complete overview of the first tort you study, this chapter talks mainly about negligence, but bear in mind that these rules do apply in other torts as well. Where the rules apply differently in another tort, this is explained in the relevant chapter.

At the end of this chapter, we also consider some of the problems with the law of negligence, and the criticisms made of it.

Causation

In order to establish negligence, it must be proved that the defendant's breach of duty actually caused the damage suffered by the claimant, and that the damage caused was not too 'remote' from the breach (a legal test which is covered on p. 114). The rules on causation covered in this section also apply to every other tort where proof of damage is required. In practice, the rules are also applied in torts which are actionable *per se* (which means actionable merely because they have been committed, whether or not damage is caused) because where no damage is caused, compensation is usually a token amount, known as nominal damages, so most cases are likely to involve damage of some kind and to require proof of it.

The 'but for' test

Causation is established by proving that the defendant's breach of duty was, as a matter of fact, a cause of the damage. To decide this issue the first question to be asked is whether the damage would have occurred but for the breach of duty. This is known as the 'but for' test.

The operation of the test can be seen in **Barnett** *v* **Chelsea and Kensington Hospital Management Committee** (1968). A night-watchman arrived early in the morning at the defendants' hospital, suffering from nausea after having a cup of tea at work. The nurse on duty telephoned the casualty doctor, who refused to examine the man, and simply advised that he should go home, and consult his GP if he still felt unwell in the morning. The man died five hours later, of arsenic poisoning: he had been murdered. The hospital was sued for negligence, but the action failed. The court accepted that the defendants owed the deceased a duty of care, and that they had breached that duty by failing to examine him. However, the breach did not cause his death. Evidence showed that, even if he had been examined, it was too late for any treatment to save him, and therefore it could not be said that but for the hospital's negligence he would not have died.

A similar result was reached in **Brooks** *v* **Home Office** (1999). The claimant was a woman in prison, who was pregnant with twins. Her pregnancy had been classified as high risk, so she needed regular ultrasound scans. One of these scans showed that one of the twins was not developing properly, but the prison doctor, who had little experience in this area of medicine, waited five days before seeking specialist advice. It was then discovered that the affected twin had died two days after the scan. Ms Brooks sued the Home Office (which is responsible for the prison service), arguing that she was entitled to receive the same standard of healthcare as a woman outside prison, and that the prison doctor's five-day delay in seeking expert advice fell below this standard. The court agreed with these two points, but it was found that a wait of two days before getting expert advice would have been reasonable for a woman outside prison and, as the baby had actually died within this time, the doctor's negligence could not be said to have caused its death.

Of course it is not always clear what would have happened but for the defendant's negligence. This was the situation in **Chester** *v* **Afshar** (2004), the case (described on p. 82) concerning the surgeon who failed to warn a patient of the possible risks of an operation. The defendants argued that causation could only be proved if the claimant could show that, had she been warned of the risk, she would have decided against having the operation at all. In that case, it could be said that, but for the surgeon's failure to warn, her injuries could not have happened. But the claimant did not say that she would definitely not have had the operation: she said that she would have sought further advice on what to do. As it was not possible to say what that advice would have been or how she would have responded to it, the defendants argued that causation was not proved. They said that surgeon's failure to warn that the operation could go wrong did not in any way increase the risk associated with the operation; that risk was there anyway, and it was a risk the claimant would have taken had she chosen to have the operation later, which she may well have done.

The House of Lords disagreed. They pointed out that the scope of the surgeon's duty of care to his patient included a duty to warn of any risks. Therefore, there had to be a remedy where a doctor failed to fulfil that part of the duty, and a patient was injured as a result of the risk, otherwise that aspect of the duty was meaningless. The House of Lords accepted that it was very difficult in this case to prove causation on conventional principles, and said that this was a case where legal policy required a judge to decide whether justice required the normal approach to causation to be modified. In this case it did. To find otherwise would mean that only those claimants who could categorically say that they would not have had the surgery would benefit from the existence of the duty of care, whereas those who needed time to think or more advice would not. This would leave the duty of care useless where it was needed most. On policy grounds therefore, the test of causation was satisfied and the claimant won her case.

The decision in **Chester** caused shockwaves through the legal profession, with several experts claiming that it meant the House of Lords had effectively abolished any meaningful requirement for factual causation. However, the subsequent case of **White** *v* **Paul Davidson** (2004) makes it clear that **Chester** should be viewed as an exceptional case, in which the House of Lords was prepared to play with the rules on causation for policy reasons because there was no other way to get justice for the claimant. The claimant in **White** was suing his solicitors, who he said had been negligent in giving him incomplete advice about a tenancy dispute. He admitted that he could not prove that he would have acted differently if given different advice and, on traditional principles, this meant he could not satisfy the 'but for' test. However, he argued that the effect of **Chester** was that he could still have a claim, on the basis that the solicitor had denied him the chance to make up his mind after being given the full facts. The Court of Appeal rejected this argument. Arden LJ stated that **Chester** did not establish a new general rule on causation, pointing out that the House of Lords in that case had not said they were overruling any traditional rules on causation.

There were policy reasons for the **Chester** decision, not least the fact that within medicine it is an established principle that patients asked to consent to surgery should have the risks explained to them. There were no such policy reasons in this case, and the general rule remained that a defendant can only be liable if their wrongful conduct actually caused harm.

An odd attempt to use the 'but for' test to a defendant's advantage was made in **Bolitho** *v* **City & Hackney Health Authority** (1997), the case (discussed on p. 81), concerning the little boy brought to hospital with breathing difficulties. The doctor in the case had argued that, even if she had turned up to examine the little boy, she would not have intubated him, so her failure to attend could not be a cause of his death. Had this argument been allowed to succeed, it would have meant that a patient who could prove that a doctor was negligent in not attending could lose the action on the basis that, even if the doctor had attended, she would have behaved negligently. The House of Lords rightly refused to accept this, and stated that causation could be established if the claimant proved either that the doctor would have intubated if she had attended, or that she *should* have intubated if she had attended, because it would have been negligent not to do so.

Topical issue

The Corby litigation

In 2009, an unusual negligence case, **Corby Group Litigation** *v* **Corby Borough Council** (2009), hit the headlines. The case was brought by a group of young people who all had birth defects, and claimed these had been caused by the council's negligence in allowing toxic substances to be released into the atmosphere during 15 years of decontamination and building work on a former industrial site. The case was referred to in the press as 'the UK's Erin Brocovich', after an American case in which a law clerk successfully took on a large company in a case about injuries caused by environmental contamination (the story was made into a film starring Julia Roberts).

The industrial site which the council was cleaning up was known to be contaminated with toxic materials, but, in removing these materials, it was alleged that the council took little care to prevent contamination of the wider area; contaminated soil was carried across public roads in uncovered lorries, spilling sludge and soil and dispersing dust into the air. During the works, the air locally was described as 'an atmospheric soup of toxic materials', and a red dust could be seen everywhere, including over the fruit and vegetables at the local market. The work took place from 1984 to 1999, and, by the late 1980s, there began to be a rise in the number of birth defects in children born in the area. It was eventually found to be three times higher than in the surrounding area, and ten times higher than would normally be expected in a town of Corby's size.

The council denied that the birth defects were caused by the work, and it took ten years for the claimants to be able to bring their claim to court. Much of this delay, their lawyers said, was caused by the council's unwillingness to disclose relevant information; on more than one occasion court action was needed to force disclosure. It was also alleged that the council was trying to portray the claimants' lawyer as an 'ambulance chaser'. When the case did reach the High Court, in 2009, Mr Justice Akenhead found, in assessing the expert evidence, that the increased number of birth defects was statistically significant, that the contaminants present on the site could have caused such defects, and that the council was negligent in the way it managed the site.

The ruling did not mean that the claimants had won, because it did not look at the facts of whether each claimant's birth defect had been caused by the council's negligence, but it meant that it was then open to each of them to sue. They would then have had to prove that the negligence had caused their particular birth defect, by showing that their mother had in fact been exposed to the contaminants and presenting medical evidence that their particular birth defect was more likely than not to have been caused by that exposure. However, although the council at first said it planned to appeal, it later decided to drop the appeal and settle with the claimants, and this happened in April 2010. One of the conditions of the settlement was that the amounts involved should not be revealed, so the full cost is not known.

Multiple causes

In some cases, damage may have more than one possible cause.

Key Case **McGhee** *v* **National Coal Board** (1972)

As an example, take the facts of **McGhee** *v* **National Coal Board** (1972). The claimant's job brought him into contact with brick dust, which caused him to develop the skin condition dermatitis. It was known that contact with brick dust could cause dermatitis, but it was not suggested that merely exposing workers to the dust was negligent, as that was an unavoidable risk of the job they did. However, it was known that the risk of developing dermatitis could be reduced if workers could shower before leaving work, as this would lessen the amount of time the dust was in contact with their skin. The defendants had not installed any showers, and the claimant argued that they had been negligent in not doing so. To succeed in his claim, he had to prove that this negligence had caused his dermatitis – but because showers would only have lessened the risk, not removed it, the 'but for' test did not work. It was impossible to say that the damage would not have happened 'but for' the defendant's negligence, but equally impossible to say that it would definitely still have happened without the negligence.

As a result, in cases where there is more than one possible cause of damage, the courts have modified the 'but for' test, in an attempt to find a fair way to decide whether liability should be imposed. Unfortunately, they have come up with not one test, but several. In many cases, the result will differ according to which test is applied, yet it remains difficult to predict which approach a court will take in a particular case. This is bad for litigants, but not quite as bad as it sounds for law students tackling problem questions; as long as you can say what the possible tests are, and what result each one is likely to lead to, you are not expected to be able to predict which a court would actually opt for.

The simplest approach is that which was actually taken by the House of Lords in **McGhee**. They said that in cases where there was more than one possible cause, causation could be proved if the claimant could show that the defendant's negligence had materially increased the risk of the injury occurring; it was not necessary to show that it was the sole cause. In

that case, the lack of showers was held to substantially increase the risk to Mr McGhee, and he won his case.

Legal Principle

Where there is more than one possible cause of injury, causation can be proved if the claimant can show that the defendant's negligence materially increased the risk of injury occurring.

A similar test was used in **Page** *v* **Smith (No 2)** (1996), which arose from the action discussed earlier, in the section on psychiatric injury (p. 40), involving an accident victim who claimed that the shock reactivated a previous physical illness, ME. The defendant claimed that the claimant had not proved that the accident had caused the recurrence of his illness. The Court of Appeal held that the question to be answered was, as in **McGhee**: 'did the accident, on the balance of probabilities, cause or materially contribute to or materially increase the risk of' the claimant developing the symptoms he complained of?

The 'material increase' approach was used by the Court of Appeal in the recent case of **Bailey** *v* **Ministry of Defence** (2008). The claimant, Miss Bailey, suffered brain damage while she was in a hospital run by the defendants. The defendants admitted that they had been negligent at an earlier stage of her care, but the brain damage was caused after this, when Miss Bailey suffered a heart attack due to inhaling her vomit. This was something which could have happened without any negligence, and the defendants argued that their breach of duty did not cause it to happen. But Miss Bailey's lawyers claimed that it had happened because she was in a weakened state, and that weakened state had been caused by the defendants' earlier negligence. The Court of Appeal found in favour of Miss Bailey, on the basis that but for their negligence, she would not have been in a weakened state, and so their negligence made a material contribution to what happened.

Although, as **Bailey** shows, the **McGhee** approach continues to be good law, the courts also use a different test, often in cases which would appear to be very similar to **McGhee**, and this test can lead to a quite different result.

Key Case **Wilsher** *v* **Essex Health Authority (1988)**

This alternative test was used in **Wilsher** *v* **Essex Health Authority** (1988), a tragic case concerning a claimant who was born three months early, with a number of health problems associated with premature birth. He was put on an oxygen supply and, as a result of a doctor's admitted negligence, was twice given too much oxygen. He eventually suffered permanent blindness, and the hospital was sued. However, medical evidence suggested that although the overdoses of oxygen could have caused the claimant's blindness, it could also have been caused by any one of five separate medical conditions which he suffered from. The House of Lords held that the claimant had to prove, on a balance of probabilities, that the defendant's breach of duty was a material cause of the injury; it was not enough to prove that the defendant had increased the risk that the damage might occur, or had added another possible cause of it. On the facts of the case, the defendant's negligence was only one of the possible causes of the damage, and this was not sufficient to prove causation.

Legal Principle

A claimant must prove, on a balance of probabilities, that the defendant's negligence was a material cause of their injury; it is not enough merely to increase the risk of damage.

'Loss of a chance' cases

A third approach is taken to causation in cases which involve what is called 'loss of a chance'. Often these are medical negligence cases, and a typical example might involve a claimant being diagnosed with cancer, who has a certain percentage chance of being cured, but has that chance reduced by their doctor's delay in diagnosing or treating the illness. In such cases the court then has to decide whether the delay can be said to have caused the patient not to have been cured, or whether that would have been the situation even if the doctor had not acted negligently. Loss of a chance can also involve financial losses, where a claimant misses out on the chance of a lucrative deal, or a well-paid job, because of the defendant's negligence.

Key Case **Hotson *v* East Berkshire Health Authority (1987)**

The key case on loss of chance with respect to injury or illness is **Hotson *v* East Berkshire Health Authority** (1987). Here the claimant, a young boy, had gone to hospital after falling from a rope and injuring his knee. An X-ray showed no apparent injury, so he was sent home. Five days later, the boy was still in pain, and when he was taken back to the hospital, a hip injury was diagnosed and treated. He went on to develop a condition known as avascular necrosis, which is caused when the blood supply to the site of an injury is restricted, and eventually results in pain and deformity. This condition could have arisen as a result of the injury anyway, but medical evidence showed that there was a 25 per cent chance that if he had been diagnosed and treated properly on his first visit to the hospital, the injury would have healed and the avascular necrosis would not have developed. The Court of Appeal treated this evidence as relevant to the issue of damages, holding that it meant his action could succeed but he should receive only 25 per cent of the damages he would have got if the condition was wholly due to the defendant's negligence.

The House of Lords, however, ruled that this was the wrong approach; what was really in issue was whether the claimant had proved that the defendant's negligence caused his condition. They concluded that he had not: the law required that he should prove causation on a balance of probabilities, which means proving that it was more likely that the hospital had caused his condition than that they had not. What the medical evidence showed was that there was a 75 per cent chance of him developing the condition even if the negligence had not occurred; proving causation on a balance of probabilities required at least a 51 per cent chance that the negligence caused the damage.

Legal Principle

In 'loss of a chance' cases, claimants must prove causation on a balance of probabilities, which means proving it was more likely than not that the negligence caused the injury.

This approach was challenged in **Gregg** *v* **Scott** (2005). The claimant had visited his GP, complaining of a lump under his left arm, but the doctor said it was nothing to worry about. Nine months later, the lump was still there, so the claimant consulted another GP, who referred him to a surgeon. The lump was diagnosed as cancer, and it was shown to have grown during the time between visiting the first and second GP. The claimant was treated, and the cancer went into remission, but it was not known whether he was actually cured.

The claimant sued the first GP on the basis that the delay had made it less likely that he would be cured, but it was not possible to prove this was the case. Statistics showed that out of every 100 people who developed the same kind of tumour, 17 would be cured if they had prompt treatment, but not if their treatment was delayed by a year; 25 would be cured even if their treatment was delayed by a year; and 58 would be incurable regardless of how much treatment they had and when. The claimant therefore argued that he had originally had a 42 per cent chance of being cured (adding together the figures for those who would be cured even if treatment was delayed, and those who would only be cured if they received prompt treatment). By delaying his treatment, the doctor had reduced his chances to 25 per cent.

The House of Lords rejected this argument, and said that the claimant could succeed only if he could prove that the defendant's negligence made it more likely than not that he would not be cured. Since the statistics showed that regardless of treatment, it was more likely than not that his cancer would not have been curable (a 58 per cent chance against a 42 per cent one), this had not been proved. The claimant also argued that even if it could not be proved that the doctor's negligence caused the spread of his cancer, he should be able to claim for 'loss of a chance', meaning a reduction in his chances of survival. The House of Lords said this could not form the basis of a claim in medical negligence.

Damages for loss of a chance have, however, been allowed in cases where the loss is purely financial. In **Stovold** *v* **Barlows** (1995), the claimant claimed that the defendant's negligence had caused him to lose the sale of his house. The Court of Appeal decided that there was a 50 per cent chance that the sale would have gone ahead had the defendant not been negligent, and on this basis they upheld the claimant's claim, but awarded him 50 per cent of the damages that he would normally have won (thus following the approach it had taken in **Hotson**, and not that taken by the House of Lords in that case).

In **Allied Maples Group** *v* **Simmons & Simmons** (1995), the claimants hoped to make a particular business deal, but were prevented from doing so by the defendant's negligence; it was possible that the deal might not have gone ahead for other reasons even if the negligence had not happened. The Court of Appeal held that where the damage alleged depends on the possible action of a third party (in this case the other party to the deal), the claimant must prove that the chance was a substantial one, as opposed to pure speculation on what might have happened. If so, the action can succeed on causation, and the evaluation of the chance will be taken into account when calculating damages.

Multiple tortfeasors

In the cases discussed above, the question has been whether damage was caused by the defendant, or by one or more non-negligent acts or situations, such as accident or illness. What happens when the damage was definitely caused by negligence, but there is more than one party which could have been responsible? This often arises in cases concerning work-related illnesses which take many years to develop, so that it is not always clear at which point during the claimant's working life the damage was done. In **Holtby** *v* **Brigham & Cowan** (2000), the claimant suffered asbestosis as a result of breathing asbestos dust at work over a long period. He had been employed by the defendants for approximately half that time, and by other firms doing similar work for the rest; for reasons which are not important here, he was only suing the defendants. The Court of Appeal stated that the defendants were liable if it was proved that their negligence had made a material contribution to the claimant's disability; their negligence did not have to be the sole cause of it. However, if the injury had also been partially caused by the negligence of others, the defendants would only be liable for the proportion they had caused. In deciding how big this proportion was, the judge followed the practice of insurance companies and related it to the amount of time the claimant had been exposed to the defendants' negligence and, erring on the side of the claimant, set the proportion of liability at 75 per cent.

Case Navigator

This approach can, however, work harshly against claimants, and this was revealed – and eventually to some extent corrected – in **Fairchild** *v* **Glenhaven Funeral Services** (2002). This case also concerned employees who had worked with asbestos, but here the disease caused was mesothelioma, an invariably fatal cancer that is almost always caused by asbestos. It is not entirely clear how mesothelioma is caused, but it is believed to be triggered by a single fibre of asbestos penetrating a cell in the lining of the lung, which then becomes malignant and eventually grows into a tumour. This makes it different from asbestosis, which generally gets worse the more asbestos the person is exposed to; with mesothelioma, the single event of the fibre entering the lung causes the disease. It may take up to 30 years to do so, but essentially the person's fate is sealed when the fibre enters the lung, and the amount of previous or subsequent exposure is irrelevant. This was what caused problems for the claimants in **Fairchild**.

The claimants (some of the men had already died, so their cases were brought by their widows) had been exposed to asbestos over long periods during their working lives, as a result of negligence by a series of different employers. By the time they sued, many of the companies were no longer in existence, so the claimants sued only those who were. Previously, in mesothelioma cases, the courts had taken the approach that all significant exposure to asbestos up to around 10 years before the symptoms developed could be said to have contributed to the causation of the disease. But in **Fairchild**, the High Court held that it was necessary for the claimant to prove which fibre had caused the disease, and only the employer that the claimant was working for at that time would be liable. Since it was impossible to know, let alone prove, which fibre had caused the disease, this ruling had the potential to mean that mesothelioma sufferers would never be able to sue those who had caused their disease unless they had only been exposed to asbestos by one employer.

As there are over 1,300 cases of the disease each year, and the figure is expected to more than double over the next 20 years, the decision caused considerable anxiety. But to many people's surprise, the Court of Appeal upheld the High Court's approach, and confirmed that where a claimant with mesothelioma has been exposed to asbestos by different employers at different times, and it cannot be proved, on a balance of probabilities, which period of exposure caused the illness, he or she cannot recover damages from any of the employers.

On a strict definition of causation, this at first sight looks plausible, if callous, but a closer look shows a number of problems. First, although the disease is caused by one inhalation of fibres and not cumulative exposure, you do not have to be a mathematical genius to work out that the more times you are exposed to asbestos, the higher the chance that on one of those occasions you will breathe some in. On this basis, it would not seem difficult to argue that each of the employers had increased the claimants' risk of getting the disease, just as the employer in **McGhee** did.

Secondly, the focus on the one 'guilty fibre' somehow suggests that only the employer who the claimant was working for at the time the fibre was inhaled did anything wrong – whereas in fact all of them had negligently exposed their employees to a substance which had the potential to kill them, prematurely and painfully. Ignoring this fact does not sit well with tort's claim to act as a deterrent to careless and dangerous behaviour. Thirdly, the parties who would actually be paying any damages would be insurance companies, who had been taking premiums for decades during which the risks of asbestos were well known, and now wanted to escape liability.

In the event, the House of Lords did hear the case, and came to a different view. They said that where an employee had been negligently exposed by different defendants, during different periods of employment, to inhalation of asbestos, a modified approach to proof of causation was justified. In such a case, proof that each defendant's wrongdoing had materially increased the risk of contracting the disease was sufficient to satisfy the causal requirements for liability. Applying that approach, the claimants could prove causation on a balance of probabilities, and the defendants were liable.

However, the benefits for claimants of the **Fairchild** decision were then restricted by the House of Lords decision in **Barker** *v* **Corus** (2006). In this case, a group of defendant employers sought to argue that, where an employee was negligently exposed to asbestos by more than one different employer, each employer's liability should be calculated according to the length of time the employee spent with them and, where relevant, to the type of asbestos involved (some kinds being more hazardous than others). In addition, one of the employees in the case had been self-employed for part of his career, and the companies which had employed him for the rest of the time argued that exposure to asbestos during his period of self-employment was his own responsibility, so they should not be liable for it.

The House of Lords rejected the argument about self-employment, basing their finding on the principle explained in **McGhee** (see p. 105). They pointed out that in **McGhee**, there had been both negligent and non-negligent exposure to brick dust. The firm was not negligent in exposing the claimant to the dust during his working hours, because it was an unavoidable part of the job, but they were negligent in allowing the exposure to last longer than necessary, by not providing showers. As **Fairchild** had built on **McGhee**, the same principle should apply here, so that the fact that the defendant had had some non-negligent exposure to asbestos did not mean that the **Fairchild** principle could not apply.

More controversially, the House accepted the argument that damages should be apportioned according to the extent to which each company had contributed to the claimants' exposure to asbestos. The practical effect of this on claimants was potentially devastating, as it meant that unless they were able to sue every employer who had exposed them to asbestos they could not hope to claim the full amount of damages appropriate to their illness. For example, where a claimant had worked for a roughly equal amount of time for three different employers and two had gone out of business by the time the claimant developed mesothelioma, the claimant would only be able to get a third of the damages that would normally be awarded for such a serious illness. The need, where possible, to trace all employers would add to the cost of cases, and the time they took, which was a particularly important issue given that by the time mesothelioma was diagnosed, claimants usually did not have many years left to live.

The decision was, not surprisingly, welcomed by the insurance industry, which stood to save millions of pounds as a result, but was widely criticised by personal injury lawyers as being unfair to claimants. The government agreed, and inserted an amendment into the Compensation Bill, which was going through Parliament at the time, effectively reversing the **Corus** decision. Section 3 of the resulting Compensation Act 2006 now provides that where a defendant is responsible for negligently exposing another to asbestos, and that person goes on to contract mesothelioma as a result of exposure to asbestos, the person responsible for the negligent exposure can be fully liable, even if it cannot be proved that it was that episode of exposure and not another that caused the disease. Where there are several parties who have negligently exposed the victim, the one who is sued can claim a contribution from the other(s), but there is no need for the victim to sue more than one of them.

A slightly unusual case involving two different tortfeasors in a non-workplace situation is **Wright** *v* **Cambridge Medical Group** (2011). The claimant was a child, Clarice Wright, who had contracted a serious bacterial infection. Her mother took her to her GP. Medical evidence showed that the GP should have referred Clarice to hospital immediately, but in fact she was not referred until 48 hours later. When she did get to hospital, she then suffered negligent treatment there, and ended up with permanent damage to her hip. For some reason which was not explained, her mother chose to sue the GP practice but not the hospital. The practice admitted their treatment (or lack of it) had been negligent, but said they could not be liable, because they had not caused the permanent injury; that was caused by the negligent treatment in hospital. Their argument was that if she had been referred to the hospital earlier, she would still have received negligent treatment then, and would still have been permanently injured.

The claimant's lawyers argued that she should have a claim for loss of a chance, in that by referring her late, the GP had lost her a chance to avoid the negligent treatment that she got because she was referred on that particular day. The Court of Appeal rejected this argument, saying that it was clear from **Gregg** *v* **Scott** that loss of a chance was not sufficient for this type of claim. However, they did allow the claim for other reasons. First, they said, once the claimant had shown that the GP practice was negligent, she was entitled to assume that she would have received proper hospital treatment if she had been referred at the right time, and it was up to the GP practice to disprove this, which they had not done. They could not simply put the blame on the hospital, who were not represented in the case. Secondly, that by cutting short the time the hospital had to treat Clarice correctly, the delay in referral was a cause of her injury; if she had been referred earlier, then, even if the hospital had still treated her negligently, they might, for example, have realised their mistake in time to put it right.

In **Sienkiewicz** *v* **Greif (UK) Ltd** (2011), the claimant had been exposed to asbestos by only one employer. There was evidence that he might have got mesothelioma from this exposure, but it was also possible that he got it from low-level exposure to asbestos in normal daily life. The evidence suggested that the exposure to asbestos at work only increased his risk of getting mesothelioma by 18 per cent. Nevertheless, the Supreme Court said that the rule set in **Fairchild** applied here too, because the employer had materially increased the risk. The court said that the only situation in which this would not be the case was where the negligent exposure was too insignificant to take into account.

Topical issue

The asbestos cases

We read a lot in the media about how negligence law is said to have created a 'compensation culture', in which people will sue over the most trivial incidents, and seek to blame someone for accidents that once would have been viewed as part of ordinary life. We hear much less about the way in which negligence law can provide a means of compensation for ordinary people who have been seriously injured by the (sometimes knowing) carelessness of big corporations – compensation which is not there to buy a

fancy car or a big house, but to replace the ordinary standard of living that their injuries have taken away. The asbestos litigation is one example of this.

The claimants and spouses of claimants in **Fairchild** *v* **Glenhaven** and **Barker** *v* **Corus** are just a few of the thousands of people who have suffered the effects of working with or near asbestos, a mineral that for many years was widely used in building materials, because it is very resistant to heat and fire. As well as mesothelioma, the disease referred to in these two cases, it also causes asbestosis, a serious and disabling lung illness, and lung cancer. The Health and Safety Executive estimates that there are currently over 3,500 deaths a year from asbestos-related disease and, because the illness takes so long to show symptoms, these rates are predicted to double over the next 20 years.

It was known that asbestos was a risk to health as far back as 1898, yet British companies continued to expose their workers to it until 1980. At the same time, insurers like those who stood to pay the claims in **Fairchild** and **Corus** were taking premiums from those companies, knowing that the risk existed. Yet when the results of exposure to asbestos began to be revealed, both the employers and the insurance companies did their level best to avoid liability. The way in which the insurance industry can manipulate the tort system can be seen in their behaviour regarding the **Fairchild** litigation. In the Court of Appeal, the defendants, who were funded by the insurers, had won their case. When the claimants decided to appeal to the House of Lords, the insurers offered them a full settlement. If the claimants had accepted it, that would have meant that the appeal would not be heard, preventing any chance of the Court of Appeal decision being reversed. As a result, the claimants in the case would have been compensated, but thousands of other victims would have been unable to succeed in a claim, unless someone else came along and took a case all the way to the House of Lords (which was not very likely to happen, since it is a difficult, time-consuming and expensive process, and any potential future claimants would, like the **Fairchild** ones, be very ill, with only a short time to live).

The then President of the Association of Personal Injury Lawyers, Frances McCarthy, called the offer to settle 'a cynical and underhanded attempt to prevent the cases being heard'. In the event, the claimants very bravely decided to continue with their fight (which, remember, they could have lost, leaving them with nothing), and, as a result, thousands of very ill people can now get the compensation they deserve.

Intervening events

What is the situation when, after the breach of duty has occurred, something else happens which makes the damage worse? Where such an event is said to break the chain of causation, the defendant will only be liable for such damage as occurred up to the intervening event. In such cases the intervening event is sometimes called a *novus actus interveniens*. Where there is an intervening event but the original tort is still a cause of the damage, however, the defendant remains liable. In **Baker** *v* **Willoughby** (1969) the claimant injured his left leg in a road accident as a result of the defendant's negligence. After the accident he was shot in the left leg by an armed robber, and ended up having his leg amputated. The robber was not caught and so could not be sued for the incident.

The defendant argued that his liability only extended to the point at which the armed robbery occurred, when the effects of his negligence were overtaken by the robber's shooting. However, in this context the 'but for' test is not strictly applied: it would be inaccurate to suggest that the damage would not have occurred but for the breach of duty, for the claimant's leg would have been damaged later anyway, as a result of the robbery. However, the House of Lords took the approach that tort law compensates as much for the inability to lead a full life as for the specific injury itself. This inability continues even where the original injury had been superseded by a later one.

However, **Baker** *v* **Willoughby** was not followed in the decision of **Jobling** *v* **Associated Dairies** (1982). As a result of the defendants' breach of duty, the claimant hurt his back at work in 1973, which rendered him disabled and reduced his earning capacity by 50 per cent. In 1976, the claimant was diagnosed as suffering from a back condition, known as myelopathy, which had no connection with the accident. By the end of that year he was unable to work. The defendants argued that they should only be liable for the effects of the back injury up to the point at which the myelopathy occurred, to which the claimant responded that the case of **Baker** *v* **Willoughby** should apply. The House of Lords found unanimously in favour of the defendants' argument, applying the 'but for' test strictly. The risk of unrelated medical conditions occurring was habitually taken into account when calculating damages for future loss of earnings. It could therefore not be ignored when it had already developed.

Intervening acts by the claimant

Where the intervening act is something the claimant does, the courts will look at whether it is fair to hold them responsible for the damage caused by that act. One aspect of this is whether the claimant's act was a reasonable one. In **McKew** *v* **Holland** (1969), the claimant had hurt his leg in an accident at work, caused by the defendant's negligence, and his leg was still very weak. When he walked down a very steep staircase with no handrail, his leg gave way, and he fell down the stairs, causing new injuries. The court held that he had chosen to put himself in a dangerous situation, knowing that his leg was weak, and that this was unreasonable behaviour which broke the chain of causation.

However, in **Spencer** *v* **Wincanton Holdings** (2009), the Court of Appeal made it clear that unwise behaviour by the claimant was not enough in itself to break the chain of causation; it would only do so if that was a fair result. The claimant was injured at work and because of the continuing pain of the injury, eventually decided to have part of his leg amputated. His car needed to be adapted to allow him to use it wearing his false leg, but until this could be done, he was able to drive around without the leg on because the car was an automatic so had only one foot pedal. Because putting the leg on was a cumbersome and time-consuming procedure, if he was only briefly getting out of the car, he would usually use sticks to help him walk instead. One day he stopped at a petrol station and, although he would usually have sounded the horn to get help from an attendant, he got out, without his sticks or his false leg, and, by steadying himself against a pump, was able to fill the car himself. His intention was to get back into the car and call an attendant to take his payment, but, as he was doing so, he caught his foot and fell, causing severe damage to his good leg. His employers accepted that their negligence had caused his original injury, and the amputation which clearly happened as a result of it, but were they liable for the fall at the petrol station as well? (It was established that the petrol station had not been negligent in any way.) The Court of Appeal said that the basis of the doctrine of *novus actus* was fairness: it was unfair to hold a defendant liable for something which was actually not a result of their negligence. Therefore, the fact that Mr Spencer had chosen to get out of the car without his leg or his crutches could only break this foreseeable chain of events if it would be unfair to hold the defendants responsible for the damage done by it. The court held that what happened to Mr Spencer was a foreseeable result of the defendants' negligence. They may not have been able to foresee the exact circumstances of the accident in the petrol station, but it was possible to foresee that if their negligence caused a man to lose his leg, that man would be more likely to hurt himself in an ordinary fall than someone who had two legs and would more easily be able to regain their balance. Therefore it was not unfair for the defendants to be held responsible for the injury caused by the fall. However, the Court of Appeal upheld the trial judge's decision to cut the damages by one-third for contributory negligence, in recognition of the fact that Mr Spencer had chosen not to use his leg or stick and increased the risk of falling.

Where the claimant's act is not an entirely voluntary one, the chain of causation will not be broken. In **Corr** *v* **IBC Vehicles** (2008), the claimant's husband had a horrific accident at work, which caused severe head injuries. As a result of the accident, he developed post-traumatic stress disorder and severe depression, and, six years after it, he committed suicide. His widow sued the employers, but they claimed that the suicide was an intervening act, which was not a reasonably foreseeable consequence of the accident. The House of Lords disagreed. They said that Mr Corr had suffered an accident for which IBC were liable, and it was agreed that his depressive illness had been caused by that accident, and that the depressive illness had led him to commit suicide. In taking his own life, Mr Corr had acted in a way that he would not have done if the original accident had not happened, and so that conduct was within the scope of IBC's duty of care to him. Although a voluntary act would break the chain of causation, Mr Corr's suicide was the result of the effects of depression, and so could not be considered an entirely voluntary act.

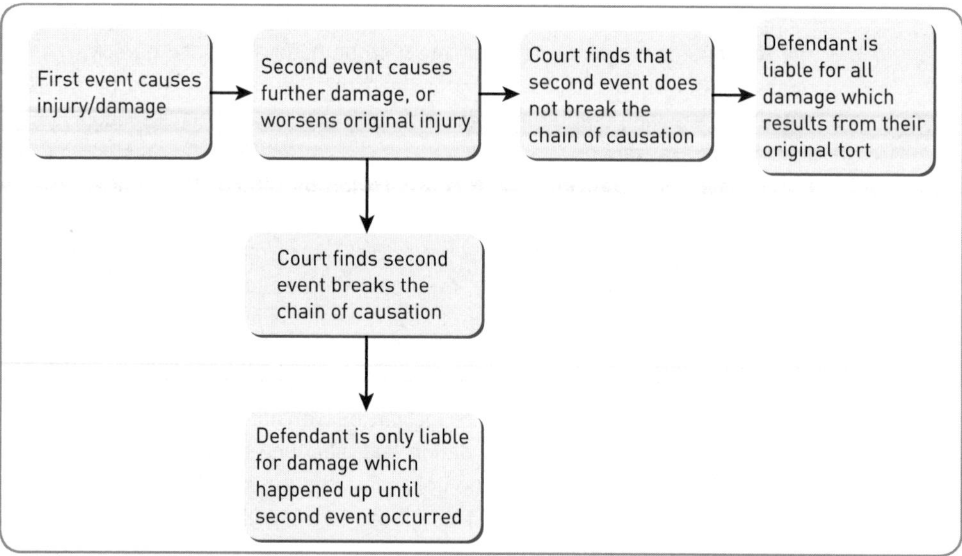

Figure 3.1 Intervening events

Remoteness of damage

As well as proving that the defendant's breach of duty factually caused the damage suffered by the claimant, the claimant must prove that the damage was not too remote from the defendant's breach. Like the issue of duty of care, the remoteness test is a legal test (rather than a factual one) which forms one of the ways in which the law draws the line between damage which can be compensated in law, and that which cannot. This means that there are some circumstances where the defendant will undoubtedly have caused damage in fact, but in law it is considered that they should not have to compensate the claimant for it (remoteness of damage also arises in other torts, but as the rules sometimes differ from those in negligence, the issue is also considered in the relevant chapters).

The tests for remoteness

There are two tests for remoteness in tort:

- the direct consequence test;
- the reasonable foreseeability test.

The test in negligence is now reasonable foreseeability, but the direct consequence test applies to some other torts, so for convenience it is explained here. The chapters on other torts detail which test applies to each one.

The direct consequence test

Key Case **Re Polemis (1921)**

The traditional test of whether damage was too remote was laid down in **Re Polemis** (1921), and essentially imposed liability for all direct physical consequences of a defendant's negligence; it became known as the direct consequence test. The case concerned the renting of a ship, an arrangement known as a charter. The people renting the ship, called the charterers, had loaded it with tins of petrol, and during the voyage these leaked, releasing large amounts of petrol vapour into the hold. The ship docked at Casablanca, and was unloaded. The workers unloading it had positioned some heavy planks as a platform over the hold and, as a result of their negligence, one of the planks fell into the hold. It caused a spark, which ignited the petrol vapour, and ultimately the ship was completely burnt, causing the owners a loss of almost £200,000. They sued the charterers.

The trial judge had found as a fact that the charterers could not reasonably have foreseen that the fire was likely to occur as a result of the plank falling into the hold, although they might reasonably have foreseen that some damage to the ship might result from that incident. However, the Court of Appeal held that this was irrelevant; the charterers were liable for any consequence that was a direct result of their breach of duty, even if such consequences might be different and much more serious from those which they might reasonably have foreseen. A consequence would only be too remote if it was 'due to the operation of independent causes having no connection with the negligent act, except that they could not avoid its results'.

Legal Principle

In torts which use the direct consequence test, defendants will be liable for any damage which is a direct result of their negligence, even if more serious than they could have foreseen.

The reasonable foreseeability test

Key Case

Overseas Tankship (UK) *v* Morts Dock & Engineering Co (The Wagon Mound) (1961)

As time went on and the tort of negligence grew, the direct consequence test came to be seen as rather hard on defendants. As a result, a new test was laid down in **Overseas Tankship (UK) *v* Morts Dock & Engineering Co (The Wagon Mound)** (1961), which is usually referred to as **Wagon Mound No 1** (a second case, **Wagon Mound No 2**, arose from the same incident, but raised different issues; it is discussed later). The incident which gave rise to the litigation was an accident which occurred in Sydney Harbour, Australia. In **Wagon Mound No 1**, the defendants were the owners of a ship which was loading oil there and, owing to the negligence of their employees, some of it leaked into the water and spread, forming a thin film on the surface. Within hours, the oil had spread to a neighbouring wharf, owned by the claimants, where another ship was being repaired by welders. It caused some damage to the slipway, but then, a few days later, further and much more serious damage was caused when the oil was ignited by sparks from the welding operations.

The trial judge found that the damage to the slipway was reasonably foreseeable but, given that the evidence showed that the oil needed to be raised to a very high temperature before it would catch fire, the fire damage was not reasonably foreseeable. Nevertheless, as the Australian courts were also following **Re Polemis**, he found the defendants liable for both types of damage.

The Privy Council, however, took a different view, stating that **Re Polemis** was no longer good law. The new test of remoteness was the foresight of the reasonable person: was the kind of damage suffered by the claimant reasonably foreseeable at the time of the breach of duty? Under this test, the defendants in **Wagon Mound No 1** were only liable for the damage to the slipway, and not for the fire damage. The reasonable foreseeability test as set down in **Wagon Mound No 1** is now the standard test for remoteness of damage in negligence.

Legal Principle

The test for remoteness in negligence is reasonable foreseeability, which means that a defendant will be liable for damage which was reasonably foreseeable at the time when the defendant breached their duty.

Type of damage

Under the reasonable foreseeability test as laid down in **Wagon Mound No 1**, a defendant will only be liable if it was reasonable to foresee the type of damage that in fact happened – in **Wagon Mound No 1**, it was clear that this covered the damage to the slipway, but not the fire damage. However, this has led to some difficult distinctions in other cases, as the contrasting decisions in **Doughty *v* Turner Manufacturing Co** (1964) and **Hughes *v* Lord Advocate** (1963) show.

In **Doughty**, the claimant was an employee who was injured when an asbestos cover was knocked into a vat of hot liquid. A chemical reaction between the asbestos and the liquid caused the liquid to bubble up and erupt over the edge of the vat, burning the claimant. The chemical reaction was not foreseeable, but the claimant argued that it was foreseeable that the lid falling in would cause some liquid to splash out, and the result of this was likely to be burning, the same injury as resulted from the liquid erupting. The court disagreed, holding that an eruption was different in kind to a splash, and so the damage was too remote.

In **Hughes**, Post Office employees had opened a manhole in the street, and left it open when they finished work for the day, covering it with a canvas shelter and surrounding it with paraffin lamps. The claimant, an eight-year-old boy, picked up one of the lamps and took it into the shelter. While playing there, he knocked the lamp into the manhole, and paraffin vapour from the lamp ignited, causing an explosion in which the claimant fell into the hole and was badly burnt. The defendants claimed that although they could have foreseen a risk that someone might be burnt, they could not have foreseen injuries caused by an explosion, and so the damage was too remote. The House of Lords rejected this view: if it was reasonably foreseeable that the damage would be burning, it did not matter that the burns were produced in an unforeseeable way.

More recent cases seem to suggest that the less narrow **Hughes** approach is gaining favour. In **Page** *v* **Smith (No 2)** (1996) (see p. 40), it was argued that where some form of personal injury was foreseeable, the fact that the damage suffered was psychiatric rather than physical did not make it too remote; they were both types of personal injury and that was foreseeable. Similarly, in **Margereson** *v* **J W Roberts Ltd** (1996), the Court of Appeal considered the case of claimants who had contracted the lung disease mesothelioma as a result of playing near the defendant's asbestos factory as children. The court held that it was not necessary for mesothelioma to be a reasonably foreseeable result of exposure to the asbestos dust, it was sufficient that some form of lung damage was reasonably foreseeable.

It is worth noting that although apparently conflicting cases like **Hughes** and **Doughty** can seem confusing, as a student you are not expected to know which path a court would take when faced with this issue; what you have to do is show that you are aware that the cases illustrate different approaches. So when you tackle a problem question, you can do this by stating that there are conflicting cases, and describing how the decision on the facts that are before you might go if the courts took, for example, the **Hughes** approach, and how this might differ if the view expressed in **Doughty** was preferred.

Extent of damage

So long as the type of damage sustained is reasonably foreseeable, it does not matter that it is in fact more serious than could reasonably have been foreseen. The extreme application of this principle is the gruesome-sounding 'eggshell-skull' rule, which essentially establishes that defendants will be liable even if the reason why the damage is more serious than could be expected is due to some weakness or infirmity in the claimant. In **Smith** *v* **Leech Brain & Co Ltd** (1962), the claimant was burnt on the lip as a result of the defendant's negligence. He had a pre-cancerous condition, which became cancerous as a result of the burn, and the defendant was held liable for the full result of the negligence.

Traditionally, it was considered that the 'eggshell-skull' rule did not apply in economic loss cases, where the claimant's lack of funds results in the financial loss being greater than it might otherwise have been. The view was that a defendant was not liable to pay any extra losses caused by the claimant's lack of money, as explained in **Liesbosch Dredger** *v* **S S Edison** (1933). The defendants negligently sank the claimants' ship and, because the claimants had already made contracts which required the use of the ship, they had to hire another vessel to do the work. It would have been cheaper overall to buy another ship, but the claimants could not at that point afford to do this. They therefore claimed for the cost of a new ship, plus the expenses of hiring the one they had used to fulfil their contractual obligations. The House of Lords refused to compensate them for the cost of the hired ship, on the ground that this loss was caused by their own financial circumstances, and was not foreseeable by the defendants.

However, a number of cases had seemed to suggest that a more generous view was appropriate, and, in **Lagden** *v* **O'Connor** (2003), the House of Lords confirmed that the 'thin skull' principle now applies to economic weakness as well as to physical. The claimant, Mr Lagden, was involved in a car accident which was the fault of the defendant, and needed a replacement car while his own was being repaired. In normal circumstances there would be no argument about the fact that the defendant would be liable to compensate the claimant for the cost of doing this, but the problem was that in this case Mr Lagden was unemployed and had very little money, and could not afford to pay to hire a car, or to take out a personal loan to buy a new one. His only option was to replace his car through what is called credit hire, where the payment is deferred for a long period. However, this option was more expensive than the other two, and the defendant, relying on **Liesbosch**, argued that they should not be liable for the extra costs, only for what it would have cost to hire a car in the normal way.

The House of Lords disagreed. While not saying that **Liesbosch** was wrong, they pointed out that it had been decided at a time when the test for remoteness of damage was direct causation (the **Polemis** test). The law had moved on since then and, as the test was now reasonable foreseeability, that meant that defendants had to take claimants as they found them, including their financial situation. If a claimant was hard up, and as a result of that they incurred extra costs, the defendant was liable to pay those costs, so long as they were reasonable. Costs would be considered reasonable if the claimant could not have avoided incurring them without making unreasonable sacrifices.

Risk of damage

Key Case **Overseas Tankship (UK)** *v* **Miller Steamship Co (The Wagon Mound No 2) (1967)**

The case of **Overseas Tankship (UK)** *v* **Miller Steamship Co (The Wagon Mound No 2)** (1967) establishes that so long as a type of damage is foreseeable, it will not be too remote, even if the chances of it happening were slim. The case arose from the accident in Sydney Harbour (discussed on p. 116) when we looked at **Wagon Mound No 1**; the defendants were the same, but in this case the claimants were the owners of some ships which were also damaged in the fire. When this case was heard, different evidence was brought which led the trial judge to conclude that it was foreseeable that the oil on the water would ignite, and when the case was appealed to the Privy Council, it held that on the evidence before that judge he was entitled to reach this conclusion. The risk was small but it clearly existed, and therefore the damage was not too remote.

Legal Principle

As long as the type of damage which occurred is foreseeable, it will not be too remote, even if the chances of it happening were small.

Intervening events

An intervening event will only make damage too remote if the event itself was unforeseeable. The old case of **Scott** *v* **Shepherd** (1773) is still one of the best illustrations of this. The defendant threw a lighted firework into a market hall while a fair was being held there. It landed on a stall, and the stall owner picked it up and tossed it away from his stall; it landed on another, whose owner did the same, and, after the firework had done a lively tour of the market, it eventually exploded in the claimant's face, blinding him in one eye. The court held that the defendant was liable; the actions of the stallholders were a foreseeable result of throwing the firework and therefore could not be considered intervening events.

In **Humber Oil Terminal Trustee Ltd** *v* **Owners of the Ship *Sivand*** (1998), the defendants' ship had damaged the claimants' wharf as a result of negligent navigation. The claimants engaged contractors to repair the wharf, and their agreement with the contractors included a clause that obliged the claimants to pay any extra repair costs which might be necessary if the repairers encountered physical conditions which could not have been foreseen. This in fact happened, as the seabed proved unable to take the weight of the jack-up barge the repairers used, and so the barge sank. The claimants were claiming against the defendants for damage caused to the wharf by their negligence, and they sought to add this increased cost to their claim. The defendants argued that the loss of the barge was not foreseeable, and was an intervening act which broke the chain of causation. The Court of Appeal disagreed: although the precise circumstances were not reasonably foreseeable, it was the kind of circumstance envisaged by the contract, and the loss of the barge was not caused by an intervening event, but an existing state of affairs, namely the condition of the seabed, so it did not break the chain of causation.

Proving negligence

The claimant normally has the burden of proof in relation to proving negligence, which can be a considerable obstacle. However, there are two exceptions to this rule: where the defendant has a criminal conviction related to the incident in question, and where the principle of *res ipsa loquitur* (see below) applies.

Criminal convictions

Under s. 11 of the Civil Evidence Act 1968, a defendant's criminal conviction is admissible evidence in a subsequent civil case based on the same facts. This means that if a defendant whose conduct is alleged to have been negligent has already been convicted of a crime for that conduct, that is evidence of negligence, and it is for the defendant to disprove it if they can. A common example is where a defendant in a motor accident case has already been convicted of dangerous driving as a result of the accident.

Res ipsa loquitur

There are circumstances in which the facts of the case are such that the injury complained of could not have happened unless there had been negligence, and, in such cases, the maxim *res ipsa loquitur*, which means 'the facts speak for themselves', may apply. One example is the case of

Scott *v* **London and St Katherine's Docks** (1865), where the claimant was injured by some bags of sugar which fell from the open door of the defendant's warehouse above. There was no actual evidence of negligence, but the Court of Appeal held that negligence could be inferred from what had happened, since the bags of sugar could not have fallen out of the door all by themselves. Similarly, in **Mahon** *v* **Osborne** (1939), it was held that a swab left inside the claimant after a stomach operation could not have got there unless someone had been negligent.

In **George** *v* **Eagle Air Services** (2009), the claimant's partner and the father of her children was killed when a plane operated by the defendants crashed as it was about to land. She claimed that the pilot must have been negligent in his handling of the plane. The defendants responded that the plane had been checked and found safe, and they had not authorised the pilot to carry out any activities that would be outside the safe operation of the plane. They offered no other evidence to show that they were not negligent. The Privy Council found that modern air travel had a reasonable safety record, and plane crashes would not normally occur without some kind of failure on the part of someone involved in flying, maintaining or designing the aircraft. Therefore, in the absence of any evidence to rebut the presumption, *res ipsa loquitur* could apply.

In cases like these, the courts may treat the facts themselves as evidence of negligence (but only evidence, which may be rebutted), provided that two other conditions are satisfied: the events are under the control of the defendant or the defendant's employees, and there is no direct evidence of negligence.

Under the control of the defendant

This point is illustrated by two contrasting cases. In **Gee** *v* **Metropolitan Railway** (1873), the claimant fell out of a train just after it left a station, when the door he was leaning against flew open. The railway staff clearly had a duty to ensure that the door was properly shut and, since the train had so recently left the station, it could be inferred from the fact of what happened that they had not shut it properly. However, in a similar case, **Easson** *v* **LNE Railway** (1944), the train was seven miles past the last station when the door flew open. In this case it was held that the fact that the door had opened in this way did not necessarily mean that railway staff had been negligent, because the situation was not under their exclusive control; any passenger could have interfered with the door during the time since the train had left the station. The staff might have been negligent, but the facts alone were not enough to act as reasonable evidence to that effect.

No direct evidence of negligence

If there is direct evidence of what caused the damage, the courts will examine that, rather than inferring it from the facts alone. In **Barkway** *v* **South Wales Transport Co Ltd** (1950), the claimant was injured when the bus he was travelling in burst a tyre and crashed. The tyre burst because of a defect that could not have been discovered beforehand, but there was evidence that the bus company should have told drivers to report any blows to their tyres, which could weaken the tyres, and they had not done so. The court held that it should examine this evidence rather than rely on *res ipsa loquitur*.

Rebutting the inference of negligence

What does a defendant have to do to rebut an inference of negligence under the doctrine of *res ipsa loquitur*? In **Ngu Chun Piu** *v* **Lee Chuen Tat** (1988), a coach driver swerved while travelling along a dual carriageway, and crossed the central reservation, hitting a bus that was moving in the opposite direction. A passenger on the bus was killed, and his personal representatives sued the driver and owner of the coach. The Privy Council ruled that on the facts negligence could be inferred, but the coach driver was able to rebut this inference by explaining that he had had to swerve to avoid a car which had cut in front of him. Therefore the claimant had to provide actual evidence to prove negligence.

In **Ward** *v* **Tesco Stores Ltd** (1976), the claimant slipped on some yogurt which had been spilt on the floor of the defendant's supermarket. She put forward evidence that three weeks later, another spill, this time of orange juice, was left on the supermarket's floor for 15 minutes, although she had no evidence of the circumstances leading up to her own accident. The defendant gave evidence that the floor was swept five or six times a day, and that staff were instructed that if they saw a spillage they should stay by it and call someone to clean it up. Nevertheless, the Court of Appeal relied on the doctrine of *res ipsa loquitur* to find that negligence could be inferred, and this inference was not rebutted by the defendant's evidence.

The Highway Code

Following the Road Traffic Act 1988, s. 38(7), where a road user fails to comply with any provision of the Highway Code, that fact may be submitted as evidence of negligence.

Defences

The defences described in this section are often called the general defences, because they apply to a range of different torts, as opposed to specific defences which are only applicable to particular torts. In this chapter we discuss their application to negligence. Not all of them can in fact be used in negligence cases; we have included some inapplicable defences which students commonly imagine might apply in negligence, and explained why they do not.

Where the defences described in this chapter are used in other torts, the rules detailed here will usually apply in the same way. Where there are differences, this information can be found in the relevant chapters, along with discussion of defences which are specific to torts other than negligence.

Contributory negligence

Common law traditionally provided that anyone who was partly responsible for the harm done to them could not recover in tort. Not surprisingly, this caused considerable injustice in some cases, and the Law Reform (Contributory Negligence) Act 1945 now provides that in such cases the claim need not fail but the defence of contributory negligence may apply. Where this defence applies, damages can be reduced to take account of the fact that the fault was not entirely the defendant's.

An example of the application of this defence can be seen in **Baker** *v* **Willoughby** (1969), the case discussed earlier, in which the claimant was run over by the defendant and then, in a separate incident, shot by a robber. In the first incident he was crossing the road; the defendant was driving carelessly, but the claimant had had a clear view of the road for the last 200 yards travelled by the car, and had taken no evasive action. The Court of Appeal found that he was 50 per cent contributorily negligent – in other words, that both parties were equally to blame. The result was that the claimant received 50 per cent of the damages he would have got if there had been no contributory negligence.

In much of the following discussion, we talk about the claimant taking care for their own safety, because many of the cases on contributory negligence in negligence actions concern accidents. However, contributory negligence can equally well be raised in an economic loss case, where the claimant has failed to take reasonable care of their own economic interests.

In many cases, the claimant's negligent behaviour will contribute to causing the accident which results in damage. An obvious example would be a pedestrian who walks out into the path of a car without looking. However, contributory negligence can also apply where the claimant's behaviour does not cause the accident itself, but contributes to the amount of damage done. For this reason, damages to drivers or passengers in road accidents are always reduced if seatbelts have not been worn, since this negligence would usually increase the injuries suffered.

This principle can be seen clearly in economic loss cases, such as **Cavendish Funding Ltd** *v* **Henry Spencer & Sons Ltd** (1998). Here the claimants had lent money for the purchase of a property which had been negligently valued by the defendants. The defendants had valued the building at over £1½ million, and the claimants had also had a valuation from another company, at around £1 million. The property was actually worth around £250,000. The claimants based their loan on the defendants' valuation and lost money as a result; they sued the defendants for the loss. The Court of Appeal held that the claimants had been contributorily negligent. The discrepancy between the two valuations should have made it clear that something might be wrong, and they should have checked; had they done so the valuation would have been reduced and they would not have lost so much. The court deducted 25 per cent from their damages for contributory negligence.

The damage to which the claimant's negligence has contributed must fall within the general scope of the risk they were taking, but the courts have been willing to give this a fairly wide interpretation. In **Jones** *v* **Livox Quarries** (1952), the claimant was riding on the back of a vehicle called a traxcavator at the quarry where he worked. The vehicle was not designed to carry passengers in this way. The claimant was injured when another vehicle drove into the back of the traxcavator. He argued that his contributory negligence amounted only to taking the risk that he might fall off the back of the traxcavator, but the court held that being hit from behind by another vehicle was also within the range of possible risks arising from riding on the traxcavator, and the claimant's negligence in doing so had contributed to his injury.

The standard of care

The standard of care which the claimant must show for their own safety (or economic circumstances) in order to avoid being found contributorily negligent is essentially the same as the standard of care required of a defendant in negligence: that of the reasonable person involved in the relevant activity. Like the standard of care in negligence, it is usually objective, but allowance is made for children, and probably for people with some type of disability which makes it impossible for them to reach the required standard.

In **Badger** *v* **Ministry of Defence** (2005), the claimant's husband had died of lung cancer. He had worked for the defendants for over 30 years, during which time he was negligently exposed to asbestos, which it was found was a cause of his lung cancer. He had also smoked all his life, and it was found that this was also a cause of the cancer. Did the smoking make him contributorily negligent? The Queen's Bench Division found that he was not contributorily negligent for starting to smoke, because he had started in 1955, when it was not widely known that smoking could cause cancer, or any other health problems. However, by the mid-1970s this connection was known, and the first government health warnings about smoking began to appear. In addition, Mr Badger had been specifically warned by his doctors that he ought to give up smoking from 1968 onwards. The court therefore concluded that a reasonably prudent person in Mr Badger's position would have given up smoking by the mid-1970s, and so he was contributorily negligent from that point onwards.

A claimant will not be contributorily negligent where they have only fallen below the standard of care as a result of an error of judgement: the courts have pointed out that reasonable people do make errors of judgement from time to time, and especially in emergency situations. In **Jones** *v* **Boyce** (1816), the claimant was riding on top of the defendant's coach when one of the horses' reins broke, and it looked as though the coach might topple over. The claimant jumped from the coach, breaking his leg. As it turned out, the coach was kept on the road, so if the claimant had kept his seat he would not have been injured. Clearly he had contributed to his own injury, but the court held that this did not amount to contributory negligence; he had acted reasonably in the face of what appeared to be a dangerous situation.

In **Revill** *v* **Newbery** (1996), the claimant had entered the defendant's land intending to steal from his shed, but was shot by the defendant, who had taken to sleeping in his shed because he was concerned, correctly as it turned out, about the risk of theft and vandalism. He was sued for negligence by the would-be burglar, and successfully raised the defence of contributory negligence.

The case of **Reeves** *v* **Metropolitan Police Commissioner** (1999) makes it clear that intentionally harming yourself can be contributory negligence. This, you may remember, is the case where police were found negligent in allowing a prisoner to commit suicide. The court found that the claimant's death was caused equally by two factors: the police negligence in allowing him to take his own life; and his action in doing so. Therefore he was 50 per cent contributorily negligent.

Children

Where the claimant is a child, the standard of care is that which could reasonably be expected, taking into account the child's age and development. In **Gough** *v* **Thorne** (1966) a 13-year-old girl was injured crossing the road. A lorry driver had stopped to let her cross, and signalled to her that she should cross, so the girl did so, without checking to see whether there was any other vehicle coming up from behind to overtake the lorry. In fact there was a lorry approaching, and it hit and killed her. The court held that, taking into account her age, she had not fallen below the expected standard of care and so was not contributorily negligent. Lord Denning explained:

> A very young child cannot be guilty of contributory negligence. An older child may be; but it depends on the circumstances. A judge should only find a child guilty of contributory negligence if he or she is of such an age as reasonably to be expected to take precautions for his or her own safety; and then he or she is only to be found guilty [of contributory negligence] if blame should be attached to him or her.

In **Yachuk** *v* **Oliver Blais Co Ltd** (1949), a nine-year-old boy bought some gasoline, a highly inflammable fuel, from the defendants, saying his mother needed it for her car. He took it away and played with it, and ended up being seriously burnt. The company was found to be negligent in supplying the gasoline to a child of that age, but the boy was not found contributorily negligent on the grounds that at his age he could not be expected to know the dangers of gasoline. By contrast, in **Evans** *v* **Souls Garage** (2000), the claimant was one of two 13-year-old boys who bought petrol from the defendant, intending to inhale the fumes. Spilled petrol caught light, burning the claimant badly. He successfully sued the defendant for negligence in selling the petrol to children, but damages were reduced by a third for his contributory negligence in playing with petrol, which he knew to be dangerous.

Very young children are unlikely ever to be found contributorily negligent, since they cannot be expected to have enough awareness and experience to guard their own safety at all.

Contributory negligence and causation

Contributory negligence will only provide a defence it if helped to cause the accident, or the damage, or made the damage worse. If a claimant does not take a reasonable standard of care for their own safety, but the accident would have happened anyway, and the damage would have been just the same, there is no defence. In **Smith** *v* **Finch** (2009), the claimant was a cyclist, injured when he was hit by the defendant's motorbike. The claimant was not wearing a helmet, and the defence alleged that this made him contributorily negligent. However, evidence showed that helmets do not protect the head if an accident happens at the speed at which the defendant was travelling, and that helmets did not protect against blows to the back of the head, which was what had happened here. The court found that it was not proved that wearing a cycle helmet would have reduced the claimant's injuries, and so there was no reduction in the damages.

Reduction of damages

Where contributory negligence is proved, the claimant's damages will be reduced 'to such extent as the court thinks just and equitable having regard to the claimant's share in the responsibility for the damage' (Law Reform (Contributory Negligence) Act 1945, s. 1(1)).

The exact calculations are at the discretion of the court and will vary according to the facts. An example of the kind of calculations that must be made can be seen in **Badger** *v* **Ministry of Defence** (2005), the case (referred to on p. 122), about the man whose lung cancer was caused partly by the defendants' negligence, and partly by his own failure to give up smoking. The defendants accepted that they were more to blame than the claimant, because they had breached safety laws by exposing him to asbestos at a time when the risks were already known. The court therefore found that even if the smoking and the asbestos had been equal causes, the claimant's liability should be no more than 50 per cent. However, there was a further factor to take into consideration, in that for the first 20 years that he smoked, Mr Badger could not be considered contributorily negligent, because he could not reasonably be expected to foresee that doing so could injure his health. Therefore, the court concluded, the appropriate reduction on damages for contributory negligence was 20 per cent.

In one of the most common examples of contributory negligence, failure to wear a seatbelt in road accident cases, the courts have laid down a standard set of reductions. In **Froom** *v* **Butcher** (1976), it was stated that in cases where using a seatbelt would have prevented the claimant's injuries from happening at all, damages should be reduced by 25 per cent. Where the injuries would have happened anyway, but wearing a seatbelt would have made them less serious, damages should be reduced by 15 per cent.

Volenti non fit injuria (consent)

This Latin phrase means 'no injury can be done to a willing person', and describes a defence which applies where the claimant has in some way consented to what was done by the defendant, on the basis that in giving consent the claimant was voluntarily taking the risk of harm. An obvious example is that of a boxer, who by entering a boxing match consents to being hit by an opponent. Unlike contributory negligence, it is a complete defence, rather than a means of reducing damages: if the claimant consented, the defendant is not liable at all.

The test of consent is objective: clearly it is impossible for the courts to see inside the minds of claimants, and so they judge whether there was consent on the basis of the claimant's behaviour. What they are therefore asking is not so much whether the claimant actually consented, but whether their behaviour was such that it was reasonable for the defendant to think that there was consent. As our boxer example shows, consent is easily signified by conduct: the boxer may not say 'I agree that you can hit me', but, by stepping into the ring at the start of the match, he makes it reasonable for his opponent to assume he has consented to being hit.

What will amount to consent?

As we have said, the courts are unable to look into the minds of claimants to see whether they consented, so they look to the claimant's outward behaviour as evidence of whether consent was given. Where a claimant clearly knew of a risk, this may be evidence that they consented to it, but it is not in itself conclusive proof. In addition, consent will only amount to a defence if it is freely given; consent given under pressure is not satisfactory.

Both these principles can be seen in the decision in **Smith** *v* **Baker** (1891). The claimant worked in the defendant's quarry. The defendant was negligently using a crane, so that stones swung above the claimant's head while he was drilling in the quarry. The claimant was aware of this happening, and of the risk that a stone could fall, and had complained about it to his employer, but with no success. Sure enough (you will have recognised by now that the stories leading up to tort cases tend not to have happy endings), one did fall, and seriously injured him. When he sued, his employers argued *volenti*, claiming that, in continuing to work when he knew of the risk, he was accepting it. The House of Lords said no: taking on work that was intrinsically dangerous might be acceptance of a risk, but continuing to do work that was not in itself dangerous, but was made so by the employer's negligence, did not qualify as consent merely because the claimant had known of the risk. They also recognised that the claimant in fact had little practical choice in the matter.

A contrasting case is that of **Imperial Chemical Industries** *v* **Shatwell** (1965). Here the claimant and his brother, James, were employed in the defendants' quarry. They needed to test some detonators, and had been told by the defendants to take certain precautions when doing so. However, they decided to do the test without taking these precautions and, as a result, there was an explosion which injured the claimant. He sued the defendants on the basis of their vicarious liability for James's negligence and for breach of their statutory duty regarding health and safety. The claim failed because James would have been able to rely on the defence of *volenti*: the claimant was fully aware of the risk he was taking, and had clearly consented to it.

The claimant must be mentally capable of giving consent. In **Kirkham** *v* **Chief Constable of Greater Manchester** (1990), the police were sued on behalf of a man who had committed suicide while in police custody; the police had known he was a suicide risk and failed to prevent him taking his own life. They tried to raise the defence of *volenti*, but the court said this could not apply where the claimant had not been of sound mind.

The case of **Reeves** *v* **Commissioner of Police for the Metropolis** (1999) in fact seems to suggest that *volenti* can never be a defence to a negligent failure to prevent suicide; in that case the facts were similar to **Kirkham**, but the dead man was found to have been of sound mind. Nevertheless, the Court of Appeal said *volenti* was not an applicable defence, given that the act the police were basing the defence on – the suicide – was the exact act they had a duty to prevent.

Disclaimers and exclusions

Where harm has come from an activity which arises from a contract between claimant and defendant, the defendant may try to use the existence of exclusion clauses in the contract to raise the defence of *volenti*. A common example might be that car parks frequently display notices disclaiming liability for negligence regarding any damage to cars parked there, and they may argue that any motorist who uses the car park is voluntarily assuming the risk that if their car is damaged, they will have no claim on the car park owners. Under common law, so long as the claimant was given sufficient notice of the relevant term of the contract (in our car park scenario, for example, this would require that the notices were clearly displayed and visible before the motorist was committed to parking there), the term would apply as a complete defence.

However, the use of exclusion clauses to avoid liability is restricted by the Unfair Contract Terms Act 1977. This provides that 'where a contract term or a notice purports to exclude or restrict liability for negligence, a person's agreement to or awareness of it is not of itself to be taken as indicating his voluntary acceptance of any risk'. In addition, the 1977 Act states that a defendant who is acting in the course of a business, or who occupies premises for business purposes, cannot use a contract term to avoid or restrict their liability for death or personal injury resulting from negligence. In the same circumstances, liability for other types of damage can only be avoided or restricted if it is reasonable to do so. The test of reasonableness is whether the term is 'a fair and reasonable one to be included having regard to the circumstances which were, or ought reasonably to have been, known to or in the contemplation of the parties when the contract was made'.

Special cases

Passengers in road accidents

The Road Traffic Act 1988, as interpreted by the courts, effectively excludes the use of *volenti* to allow drivers to avoid liability to passengers. Before the Act was passed, drivers who had not taken out insurance sometimes tried to exclude liability to passengers in the event of a crash by placing notices in their cars stating that they would not accept liability for injury to passengers. The Road Traffic Act 1988 makes insurance compulsory for motorists, and s. 149 further provides that any attempt to avoid liability to passengers will be ineffective.

Section 149 has been given a fairly broad interpretation by the courts, and held to prevent motorists relying on any form of *volenti* defence with regard to passengers. In **Pitts** *v* **Hunt** (1991), the claimant was a passenger on a motorbike being driven by the defendant. He knew that the defendant was uninsured and had been drinking, but encouraged him to drive in a dangerous way. The bike crashed, seriously injuring the claimant, who therefore sued the defendant. The Court of Appeal held that the defendant could not rely on the defence of *volenti* because of the Road Traffic Act (in fact the defence of illegality, discussed below, was successfully pleaded, so the defendant was not liable).

Sports

Where an injury is received by a player during a lawful game or sport, played according to the rules, the defence of *volenti* can apply, because players are deemed to have taken the risk of such injury voluntarily. In **Simms** *v* **Leigh Rugby Football Club** (1969), the claimant broke his leg when he was tackled and thrown against a wall. The court held that because the injury occurred during the course of the tackle, which was within the rules of the game, the defence of *volenti* applied and the defendants were not liable. Similarly, in **Wooldridge** *v* **Sumner** (1963), it was held that spectators at sporting events have voluntarily assumed the risk of any harm caused by the players, providing it does not result from intentional or reckless behaviour.

Where the game has not been played according to the rules, the defence is much less likely to apply. In **Smoldon** *v* **Whitworth** (1996), the claimant was a player in a rugby match. The match involved young players (under-19s) and the rules for this age group included a provision that there should be no collapsed scrums, as these could cause injury. However, the referee failed to prevent a collapsed scrum and the claimant was seriously injured as a result. He sued the referee, who claimed the defence of *volenti*, on the basis that the claimant had voluntarily participated in the scrum. The Court of Appeal refused to accept this: the player might have consented to the ordinary rules of the game, but that did not mean he had agreed to the defendant's breach of duty in failing to apply anti-injury rules.

Volenti can apply in a similar way to people who have consented to what the courts call 'rough horseplay', or what might more usually be called mucking around. In **Blake** *v* **Galloway** (2004), the claimant and defendant were two teenagers who were playing around on an area of ground covered in bark chippings. They were throwing the chippings at each other, when a piece of bark thrown by the defendant hit the claimant in the eye and seriously injured him. His action for negligence failed. The court held that someone who voluntarily takes part in vigorous sports, or (as here) rough horseplay, can only succeed in negligence if the other person's behaviour falls far below an acceptable level. When people lark about in the way the two teenagers were doing, said the court, there are 'tacit rules', meaning that, although they do not spell out the rules of the 'game', there are certain things they would not expect the other to do. In this case, the two teenagers were each accepting that the other would throw chippings at them in a playful way, but not, for example, that one might pick up a stone and throw that instead. If the defendant had departed from those tacit rules and done something which the claimant could not be said to have consented to, *volenti* would not offer a defence, but in this case he had not departed from the 'rules' of their game, but merely made an error of judgement.

Rescuers

Where a defendant's negligence causes an emergency, and as a result the claimant consciously and deliberately takes a risk in order to rescue someone in imminent danger, the defence of *volenti* will not apply. This is because a rescuer is deemed to be acting instinctively due to their moral or social conscience, and therefore not exercising genuine freedom of choice. In addition, in a rescue case, the defendant's negligence will have happened before the rescuer took a risk, and so the rescuer cannot really be said to have consented to what the defendant did; in fact they may not even know about it.

In **Haynes** *v* **Harwood** (1935), the defendant's employee left his van and horses unattended in a busy street and the horses bolted when a child threw a stone at them. The claimant was a police officer, on duty inside the nearby police station. Hearing the commotion, he ran out and managed to stop both runaway horses, but in the process one of them fell on him, causing him serious injury.

The defendant pleaded *volenti*, but the Court of Appeal said the defence could not apply, because the police officer was acting under a duty to protect the public.

Volenti was also put forward as a defence in the case of **Chadwick** *v* **British Railways Board** (1967), where the claimant suffered psychiatric injury as a result of the many hours he spent helping the injured victims of a terrible train crash near his home. The defendants argued that since he was not related to any of the victims, or involved in the crash himself, he could be said to be exercising a voluntary choice, but once again the court rejected the defence. On policy grounds alone, both decisions are clearly sensible: any other approach would effectively mean penalising those who risk their own safety to help others.

However, the defence may apply where the risk taken was actually unnecessary in the circumstances. In **Cutler** *v* **United Dairies (London) Ltd** (1933), a cab driver's horses bolted and ran into a field, and the claimant was injured when he went in to try to recapture them. The horses were in fact creating no risk to people or even property where they were, and so the claimant could not be said to be acting in an emergency. The court held that in this case *volenti* could apply.

Illegality

Where the claimant's case is connected with the fact that they have committed a criminal act, the defence of illegality (sometimes known as *ex turpi causa*) may apply. The basic reason for this defence is public policy: many people would find it offensive that a person committing a crime could sue for damages if they were injured as a result of doing so. An example of the defence in use is **Ashton** *v* **Turner** (1981), where both claimant and defendant had taken part in a burglary. The defendant had the job of driving the getaway car, but did it so badly that the claimant was injured. The claimant attempted to sue his co-burglar for the injury, but the court held that the defence of illegality could apply to prevent the claim. Similarly, in **Pitts** *v* **Hunt** (1991) (see p. 126), the claimant was prevented from claiming for injuries caused when the defendant's drunken driving caused an accident, because he had encouraged the defendant to drive dangerously.

The defence will not apply in every case where the claimant happens to have committed an illegal act; it will only apply where there is a causal link between the illegal act and the tort. This was explained in **National Coal Board** *v* **England** (1954):

> If two burglars, A and B, agree to open a safe by means of explosives, and A so negligently handles the explosive charge as to injure B, B might find some difficulty in maintaining an action for negligence against A. But if A and B are proceeding to the premises which they intend burglariously to enter, and before they enter them, B picks A's pocket and steals A's watch, I cannot prevail upon myself to believe that A could not sue in tort.

This issue arose in **Delaney** *v* **Pickett** (2011), where the claimant was a passenger in a car driven by the defendant, which was involved in a serious crash, injuring the claimant. The claimant was found to be in possession of cannabis, and the trial judge found that the car journey was for the purpose of fetching drugs in order to sell them, and therefore that the defence of illegality applied. The Court of Appeal was divided on whether the judge's conclusion about the purpose of the journey was factually correct, but said that, regardless of whether it was or not, the defence could not apply. If the judge was wrong, and the claimant was only in possession of drugs and not on a journey involved with supplying them, his possession of the drugs had no effect on the defendant's driving, which caused the accident. If the judge was right, and the pair were going to fetch drugs in order to sell them, the defence could still not apply because, although the accident would not have happened if they had not gone to buy drugs, it was not caused by the criminal activity, but by the defendant's negligent driving.

The Court of Appeal said that the question to ask was:

> whether the injury was truly a consequence of the unlawful act, or whether it was a consequence of the unlawful act only in the sense that it would not have happened if the claimant had not been committing an unlawful act. In other words, could one say that, although the damage would not have happened but for the tortious conduct of the defendant, it was caused by the criminal act of the claimant [rather than the tort] or was the position, rather, that, although the damage would not have happened without the criminal act of the claimant, it was caused by the tortious act of the defendant?

In other words, for the defence to apply, the illegal act must have played some specific part in causing the injury. If the injury merely happened at the time or in the place where the illegal act was committed, or on the way to or from it, but was caused by something other than the illegal act, the defence will not apply.

In **Clunis** *v* **Camden and Islington Health Authority** (1998), the case resulted from the murder of a young man, Jonathon Zito, by Christopher Clunis, who was mentally ill. Clunis, the claimant in this case, was supposed to have had psychiatric care from the health authority, and claimed that the authority had been negligent in not providing this, the implication being that he would not have killed if he had been receiving the proper treatment. The Court of Appeal said he could not use his own illegal act to form the basis of a claim.

In **Vellino** *v* **Chief Constable of Greater Manchester Police** (2001), the case (discussed on p. 55) where the criminal jumped out of a window to avoid arrest, then sued the police for letting him do so, the Court of Appeal held that the defence of illegality applied because the very act that caused the claimant's injuries was the act of escaping from police custody, which is a crime.

In **Gray** *v* **Thames Trains Ltd** (2009), the claimant had been involved in a serious train crash caused by the defendants' admitted negligence, and had suffered post-traumatic stress disorder as a result. As a result of this condition, he killed someone, and, when he was found guilty of the killing, the criminal court imposed a hospital order, which meant he was detained in a mental hospital for treatment. It was accepted that up until the train accident, the claimant had been, in Lord Brown's words, 'a decent and law-abiding citizen', and that had it not been for the post-traumatic stress disorder, it was impossible to believe he would ever have killed anyone.

Mr Gray sued the train authority in negligence for causing the post-traumatic stress disorder, and part of his claim included a sum for loss of earnings while he was detained in hospital, and for damages for the remorse and shame he felt over the killing. Despite expressing sympathy for the claimant's situation, the Court of Appeal refused to allow either of these parts of the claim. They said that *ex turpi causa* applied because, even though the claimant's responsibility for the killing was reduced by the mental problems that he was suffering from, it was still clear that he knew what he was doing and was responsible for what he did. It would be offensive to public opinion about the fair distribution of resources to compensate him for the consequences of killing someone. In addition, in imposing the hospital order on him, the criminal court had removed his earning capacity for as long as the order was in force. It would be contrary to public policy for a civil court to undermine the order by allowing him to claim back the lost earnings from the defendants.

A case where the illegality defence was held not to apply is **Revill** *v* **Newbery** (1996). The case (referred to on p. 123), concerned an occupier who shot a burglar. The defendant argued that the defence should apply because the claimant was clearly committed an illegal act, but the Court of Appeal disagreed. They pointed out the the Occupiers' Liability Act 1984, under which the claim was brought, created a duty for occupiers regarding the safety of trespassers, and allowing the defence would go against that. This created the slightly bizarre situation that, had the defendant been injured by a fellow burglar, he may have been prevented from suing, but the legal occupant, and victim of the crime, had no such protection.

Illegality and human rights law

It now appears that, in some circumstances, claimants whose actions in tort would have failed because of the defence of illegality may nevertheless succeed if they can sue under the Human Rights Act instead. This was the case in **Al Hassan-Daniel** *v* **Revenue and Customs Commissioner** (2010). The defendant was an experienced drug smuggler, who was arrested and detained at Heathrow Airport after being found to have traces of cocaine on his body. On further examination, he was discovered to have swallowed 16 small packets of the drug. The usual practice in these cases is to wait for the evidence to take the usual course out of the defendant's body, but, in an attempt to prevent this, the defendant refused to take any food or drink for a week, despite being warned of the risks of doing so by two separate doctors. After seven days, he died of cocaine poisoning. His family sued, arguing that his treatment breached the right to life under Art. 2 of the European Convention on Human Rights, because if Customs had had a better policy for handling such cases, and treated him with more care, his life could have been saved.

Customs argued that the defence of illegality should apply, because the defendant's death arose from his own illegal act, but his family responded that human rights apply to everyone, not just those who behave well. The Court of Appeal ruled that the defence could not bar a claim in Convention law, and the claim was allowed to go forward to trial, though the court stressed that this should not be taken as suggesting that it would definitely succeed.

Statutory authority

If a statute entitles a person or body to do something which would normally be considered a tort, the person committing the act cannot be sued, and anyone who suffers damage as a result will be unable to get compensation unless the statute provides that they should. The defence is most commonly used in nuisance, but it can apply in negligence too. In **X** *v* **Bedfordshire County Council** (1995) (see p. 68), the House of Lords stated that where a public body is given a discretion to act, they will have the defence of statutory authority when exercising that discretion, unless the choice they make is completely unreasonable. The House explained:

> Most statutes which impose a statutory duty on local authorities confer on the authority a discretion as to the extent to which, and the methods by which, such statutory duty is to be performed. It is clear both in principle and from the decided cases that the local authority cannot be liable in damages for doing that which Parliament has authorised. Therefore if the decisions complained of fall within the ambit of such statutory discretion they cannot be actionable in common law. However, if the decision complained of is so unreasonable that it falls outside the ambit of the discretion conferred upon the local authority, there is no *a priori* reason for excluding all common law liability.

The House stated that the reason for the defence is that in reaching such decisions the public body would take into account policy issues such as the allocation of resources and the best balance between competing social aims, and it was not appropriate for the courts to second-guess such decisions. They also made it clear that the defence only applies to the use of discretion; it will not excuse negligent carrying out of a decision once made. For example, a council which has discretion over the issue of how to provide special teaching help for dyslexic students is protected by the defence when it decides whether to provide special classes once a week or every day, and, unless it makes a completely unreasonable decision, the courts will not allow a claimant to sue in negligence on the basis that the wrong option was chosen. However, once the council has settled on, for example, one class a week, the defence of statutory authority would not protect it if it then negligently fails to provide that service.

Equally, the defence will not apply if the decision made goes outside the discretion permitted by the statute. In the previous example, if the statute had allowed a discretion on the number and timing of classes, but stipulated that they must be held in schools, the council could not rely on statutory authority as a defence if it was sued because it held the classes somewhere else.

Inapplicable defences

Necessity

This is a defence which applies where a defendant intentionally causes damage in the course of preventing some other, worse, damage. An example might be a motorist knocking down a wall at the side of a road while swerving to avoid a head-on collision with another car. Because it only applies to intentional damage, it is not used in negligence cases (**Rigby** *v* **Chief Constable of Northamptonshire** (1985)).

Mistake

Mistake is generally not a defence in negligence, because of the emphasis on the standards of the reasonable person. For example, if a doctor says that their incorrect diagnosis or treatment was the result of a mistake, there are two possible outcomes. First, the mistake might be one which the court believes a reasonable doctor could make; in that case, the defendant has not fallen below the required standard of care, and so needs no defence because they have not been negligent. An example would be **Roe** *v* **Minister of Health** (1954) (see p. 84), where storing the ampoules of anaesthetic in disinfectant was, with hindsight, a mistake, but, given the state of knowledge at the time, it was a reasonable one. Or, alternatively, the mistake might be one which no reasonable doctor could make, in which case the doctor has fallen below the standard of care and the mistake, far from offering a defence, is the thing which makes them negligent.

Inevitable accident

An inevitable accident is one which the defendant could not possibly have avoided, no matter how much care they took. Like mistake, it has no real application in negligence, because if the claimant fails to prove that the defendant could have avoided the accident if they had taken more care, there is no negligence anyway so no defence is needed.

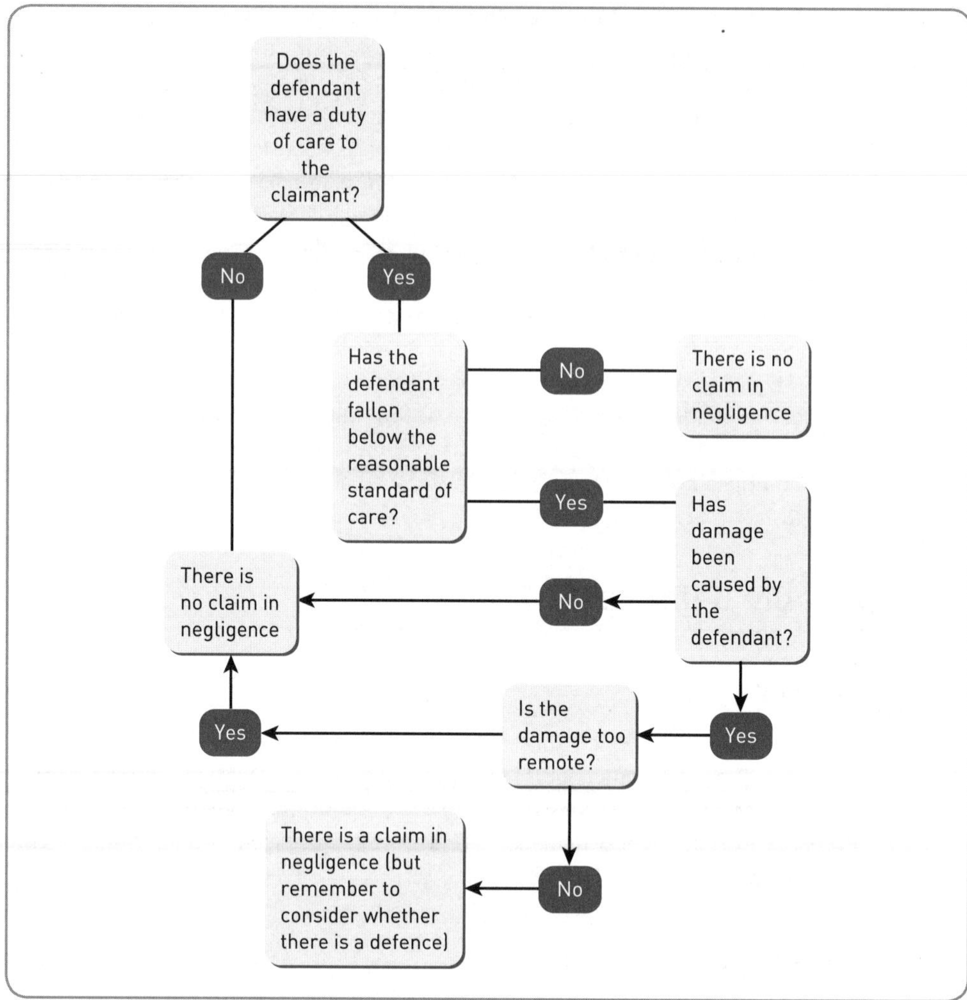

Figure 3.2 Is there liability in negligence?

Time limits

The law recognises that it would be unfair to defendants if claimants could bring an action against them at any time in the years after a wrong has taken place, and so there are time limits within which an action must be brought. The courts were always able to hold that a particular claimant had delayed too long in bringing an action, but in 1980 the Limitation Act for the first time laid down specific time limits for different types of court case.

The general limitation period for an action in tort is six years, which means that an action must be begun within six years of the date on which the cause of action came into existence (different rules apply to defamation, discussed in Chapter 9, product liability, discussed in Chapter 6, and personal injury cases, which are discussed below). For torts which are actionable *per se* (without proof of damage), the cause of action comes into existence when the defendant commits the tort;

for torts where damage must be proved, including negligence, the cause of action comes into existence when the claimant suffers the damage.

Although these rules sound straightforward, the issue of when damage has occurred is not always as clear as you might imagine, and this can lead to difficult distinctions in apparently similar cases. In **Law Society** *v* **Sephton & Co** (2006), the House of Lords stated that the relevant date is when damage actually occurs, and not when it becomes a possibility. The case arose after a solicitor in the defendants' firm misappropriated money from a client. The solicitors' ruling body, the Law Society, runs a scheme to compensate clients in cases like this, and such a claim was made in this case. The Law Society believed that the firm's negligence had allowed the solicitor to take the money, and so they sued the firm to get back the compensation they had paid out. The defendants argued that, as the money had been taken more than three years before the Society sued, the action was outside the time limits. However, the Society argued that the relevant date was not when the money was taken, but when the client claimed against them. The House of Lords agreed: when the money was taken it became a possibility that the Society would suffer loss if a claim was made to their compensation scheme, but at that point there was no actual loss: the money might have been repaid some other way, or the client might not have claimed anyway. The time limit only began to run when an actual loss occurred, which was when the client made the claim to the compensation scheme.

In the apparently similar case of **Watkins** *v* **Jones Maidment Wilson** (2008), however, the Court of Appeal took a more restrictive view. The claimants, the Watkins, contracted to buy land and have a house built on it. The original contract contained an option to take the house before it was finished, at a reduced price, if the developers failed to finish it by a set date. On advice from the defendants, their solicitors, the Watkins turned down this option. This proved to be a mistake, as the building later ran into problems, which caused delay and cost the Watkins a lot of money. They sued the solicitors for giving negligent advice, but by that time more than six years had passed since they turned down the option in the contract. On the basis of **Sephton**, they argued that the point at which damage occurred was not when they refused the option, but much later, when the problems with the building happened. The point at which they refused the option, they claimed, was merely when the risk of damage occurred, as in **Sephton**. The Court of Appeal disagreed. It said that the option in the contract was itself a valuable right, and letting it go meant losing something of value, so that was the point at which damage occurred. The fact that that loss also exposed them to the risk of further loss later made no difference. Therefore, too much time had passed since the damage occurred, and the case was out of time.

In some cases, damage or loss may not occur until some time after the event which caused it, and then may not be discovered until some time after that. An example of such a situation can be seen in **Pirelli General Cable Works** *v* **Oscar Faber & Partners** (1983). The defendant in the case had designed a chimney for the claimants in 1969. By April 1977, cracks could be seen around the top of the chimney, and in 1978 the claimants began an action against the defendant for negligence, but technical evidence revealed that the cracks had actually begun forming in 1970, even though they were not visible from the ground until later. The House of Lords held that the case was outside the six-year time limit, which began to run when the cracks occurred, and not when they were discovered.

In recognition of problems like these, the Latent Damage Act 1986 amends the Limitation Act 1980 by adding a new s. 14A, which applies to all negligence claims, except those for personal injury. It provides that where damage is not apparent when it first occurs, the time limit is either six years from the time when the damage occurred, or three years from the time when the claimant knew, or ought to have known, of the damage (whichever is the later) up to a final limit of 15 years from the time the damage occurred. A claimant who ought to have known of damage is said to have 'constructive knowledge': even if the claimant does not actually know of the damage, the limitation period will begin to run when they are in possession of such facts as would enable a reasonable person to realise there might be damage.

Personal injury cases

The problems time limits may cause can be even more serious in personal injury cases, as the example of **Cartledge** *v* **Jopling** (1963) shows. The claimant's husband had died from a lung disease caused by the defendant's negligence, but the nature of the illness was such that it did not show symptoms until decades after the damage was done. As a result, his widow was unable to claim damages from those responsible for his illness and premature death.

In recognition of the specific problems faced by personal injury claimants, the Limitation Act 1980 lays down separate provisions for cases involving personal injury caused by negligence, nuisance or breach of a duty imposed by statute and, since the case of **A** *v* **Hoare** (2008), these also apply to trespass to the person (see p. 346).

The Limitation Act 1980 sets down a time limit of three years for personal injury cases, and s. 4 states that this limit begins to run either from when the damage was done, or from the point at which the claimant first had knowledge of the following facts, whichever is the later:

- that the injury was significant;
- that it was wholly or partly caused by the act or omission which is alleged to constitute negligence, nuisance or breach of statutory duty;
- the identity of the defendant;
- where the allegation is that someone other than the defendant committed the relevant act or omission, the identity of that person, and the additional facts which suggest that the defendant should be held liable.

Obviously, there will be many cases where the court cannot possibly know when the claimant had knowledge of the relevant facts, since they cannot look inside the claimant's mind. For that reason, a claimant can be deemed to have 'knowledge' of the above issues where they might reasonably be expected to have acquired it from facts which could be seen, or which could have been found out, with or without the help of medical or other experts. This is known as 'construction knowledge'.

In **Adams** *v* **Bracknell Forest Borough Council** (2004), the claimant was suing his local education authority for their failure to diagnose his dyslexia. He had had serious problems with reading and writing ever since he was at school, and, as well as making it more difficult for him to get a job, these problems had led to psychological problems such as depression. He argued that, had the education authority diagnosed the dyslexia, steps could have been taken to help him.

By the time of the case, the claimant was grown up, but he had not brought an action earlier because he had only recently learned that he was dyslexic through a chance meeting with an educational psychologist. The House of Lords held that the neglect of his dyslexia could be treated as a personal injury for the purposes of the case, which meant that the limitation period would be three years from the time at which he had knowledge of the facts. The meeting with the educational psychologist was within that period, but the House of Lords held that was not the relevant date. Although the claimant had not known that he was dyslexic until that time, he had known for years that he had serious problems with reading and writing, and that those difficulties were the root of his psychological problems. That being the case, he should have sought help, and, if he had done so, he would have been diagnosed as being dyslexic much earlier. He was therefore held to have constructive knowledge of the facts more than three years before bringing the case, and was outside the limitation period.

A similar approach was taken in **AB and others** *v* **Ministry of Defence** (2012), which was heard by the Supreme Court. The claimants in the case had all been soldiers who were exposed to radiation when they were made to take part in tests of nuclear bombs, carried out by the British government in the Pacific area during the 1950s. Around 22,000 soldiers were involved and, in the years since then, many of them began to suffer health problems, including cancer, skin defects and fertility problems. They believe these were caused by the radiation and in 2004, around 1,000 of them issued claims against the Ministry of Defence (MOD). The MOD argued that the claims were out of time, because the claimants had not sued within three years of having knowledge of a possible claim. The question at issue was when they had such knowledge. The MOD said it was when they realised that they had been exposed to radiation, and that they had health problems that could be caused by radiation. But questions had been raised about the health problems suffered by the soldiers since the 1980s, and the MOD had always maintained that they had not been exposed to levels of radiation that could be harmful. The claimants therefore argued that they did not have the required knowledge until later, when independent research was published which showed a link between exposure to the tests and cancer. The Supreme Court rejected the claimants' argument, stating that the limitation period began to run when the men knew that they had been exposed to the radiation, and that there was a real possibility that it could have caused their health problems. The test was 'whether the claimant had such a degree of belief that, objectively considered, it was reasonable for him to commence investigating whether or not he had a viable case'. It was not reasonable to say that knowledge did not exist until evidence was available to suggest that that case could be won.

Extending the limitation period

Section 33 of the Limitation Act 1980 gives the courts a wide discretion to extend the limitation period in personal injury cases. In deciding whether to do so, the court should look at all the circumstances of the case, and, in particular, the following issues:

- the length of the delay and the reason for it;
- the effect of this delay on the evidence;
- the conduct of the defendant after the cause of action arose;
- how long the claimant's disability has lasted;
- whether the claimant acted reasonably once they knew that they might have a claim;
- the steps taken by the claimant to get expert advice, and the nature of that advice.

In **McGhie** *v* **British Telecommunications plc** (2005), the Court of Appeal explained that, in applying s. 33, the courts should consider the 'balance of prejudice' between claimant and defendant; in other words, whether it would be more unfair to the defendant if the time period was extended, or to the claimant if it was not. The claimant in the case had hurt his back in an accident at work, possibly caused by his employers' negligence, but had not realised that he might have a case against them. Later, he had an operation, which greatly improved his condition, and it was only after that that he learnt that he should have been given special training and equipment when doing the job that caused the injury, and that therefore his employers might have been negligent.

The judge at first instance used his discretion under s. 33, on the grounds that the claimant had been devoted to his job, and had acted reasonably in the circumstances, but the Court of Appeal stated that this was the wrong test. The judge should have considered, as part of the balance of prejudice test, what a prudent employer would have been expected to do at the time, and what evidence there was that special training or equipment would have made a difference. Another important factor was that, as the claimant was now better, the size of the claim would have been quite small. Applying these criteria, the Court of Appeal found that this was not a suitable case for extending the limitation period.

In **Cain** *v* **Francis; McKay** *v* **Hamlani** (2008), the Court of Appeal gave further guidance on how the courts should use their discretion in extending the limitation period. They said that it would always be relevant to consider how soon the defendant had known that a claim was possible, and what opportunities they had had to investigate and gather evidence in their defence. If the defendant knew quite early on that there might be a claim against them, the fact that the actual claim was delayed was unlikely to cause them any real prejudice. The delay should only be counted as prejudice to the defendant if it effectively took away or reduced the chance of a fair opportunity to defend him or herself.

An example of a case where the discretion was exercised is **Das** *v* **Ganju** (1999). The claimant had a child who, it was claimed, was injured as a result of medical negligence. She was told by her lawyers that if she did not sue on her daughter's behalf, her daughter could bring an action herself when she was grown up, for which she could claim legal aid. This was incorrect, but the claimant did not discover that until five years after her 'date of knowledge', and so outside the statutory time limit. The court held that it could exercise its discretion under s. 33, because the delay was not the claimant's fault, and she should not be prejudiced because of her lawyer's negligence.

In **A** *v* **Hoare (No 2)** (2008), the court had to consider an unusual reason for delaying a claim. The litigation arose from the case (discussed at p. 346), where the claimant sued the defendant, who had raped her 16 years earlier. The reason for the delay was that the defendant had recently won the National Lottery, and therefore became worth suing; he would not have had any money to pay damages at the time of the attack. The court therefore had to consider whether to exercise its discretion under s. 33 to allow the claim to take place. Coulson J said that the delay had been a very long one, but what mattered most was not the length of the delay but the reasons for it. It was reasonable for the claimant not to have made a claim when the defendant had no prospect of being able to pay damages, and she had acted promptly and reasonably once she became aware of the change in his financial position. The fact that the tort committed had been very serious was also relevant, and, in these exceptional circumstances, the claim should be allowed to proceed.

An example of a case in which the courts refused to extend the limitation period is **Forbes** *v* **Wandsworth Health Authority** (1996). The claimant had had an operation on his leg, which went wrong; a second operation failed, and he had to have his leg amputated in order to save his life. Nine years afterwards, he consulted a solicitor, and discovered that the amputation had only been necessary because the first operation was not done properly. He argued that the limitation period should run from the time when he discovered the truth, but the Court of Appeal disagreed, saying that although he had not known the full facts, he had known that amputation was not the inevitable consequence of the surgery he had had, and that a reasonable person who suffered such a major injury after surgery would have taken advice within at most 18 months of the operation. The limitation period could therefore be said to run from then, so he was out of time. The court refused to use its discretion to extend the period on the grounds that the claimant had not acted reasonably, and the delay was so long that it would seriously prejudice the defendants' chances of fighting the case.

Where negligent personal injury results in a death within three years of the date on which the cause of action came into existence, a fresh limitation period of three years begins to run for the personal representatives or dependants of the dead person.

Reform of limitation periods

The current law on limitation periods was recently examined by the Law Commission, which concluded that it was complex, outdated and sometimes unfair. It criticised the fact that the Limitation Act 1980 contains different provisions for different causes of action, explaining that this creates uncertainty and lack of clarity, as it is not always clear which category a cause of action falls into, and therefore how it should be treated for limitation purposes. In addition, the Commission said, the date on which the limitation period starts to run does not always take account of the claimant's knowledge of the relevant facts, which in some cases leads to unfairness.

The Law Commission therefore proposed that the 1980 Act should be repealed and replaced with a new Act. The recommendations would apply a core limitation regime to the majority of tort claims. The primary limitation period would be three years, which would run from the date on which a claimant knows (or ought reasonably to know) the facts giving rise to the cause of action, the identity of the defendant and that any injury, loss, or damage (or benefit received by the defendant) was significant. No claim could be brought after the expiry of a 10-year long-stop period, which would normally run from the date on which the cause of action arose. In personal injury cases the long-stop period would not apply, and the court would have a discretion to permit a claim to be brought outside the primary period. Claims in relation to land would only be subject to a 10-year limitation period.

In July 2002, the then Lord Chancellor stated that the government had in principle accepted the proposals, but no timescale was suggested for the legislation. The reforms were planned to be included in a new Civil Law Reform Act, but in 2009 it was announced that reforms of limitation periods would not be part of this legislation, and no further plans appear to have been made to change the law in this area.

Criticisms of negligence law

In order to highlight the general problems with the law of negligence, we need to look first at what the aims of this area of the law are, so as to provide a gauge by which its success can be measured. The law of negligence has several aims, not all of which are necessarily consistent with each other:

- to compensate victims of harm caused by others;
- to mark the fault of those who cause harm;
- to deter carelessness;
- to spread the financial costs of harm caused by carelessness;
- to do all these things quickly and fairly.

To judge how well it achieves these aims, we need to look at both the law itself, and the context in which it operates.

Compensating victims of harm

Considering that compensation is generally seen to be its most important function, the law of negligence is remarkably inefficient in this area and, in practice, only a small proportion of victims of harm get compensation through it.

The first reason for this is that, if we take a wide view of harm, many people are caused harm by circumstances in which nobody can be blamed, for example those with genetic illnesses or those who suffer damage of any kind in accidents which are genuinely nobody's fault. You might well ask why they should be compensated, but the wider picture is that, as we shall see, society as a whole spends a lot of money on negligence cases, yet the result is that a few people get large amounts of money in damages, while many other people whose needs are the same, but result from different causes, do not. The question is therefore whether the system we currently have gives good value for our money.

Added to those people who cannot prove fault in anyone are those who possibly could, but who the law of negligence will not compensate. Examples include those victims of psychiatric injury and economic loss who fall outside the rules on compensating these types of damage and those whose damage is the result of carelessness by categories of defendant to whom the law gives special protection in certain circumstances, such as the police and local authorities.

Even among those who have suffered damage in circumstances where someone else might be liable, only a small proportion take legal action. This might come as a surprise, given that most of the media seems to be convinced that suing is the most popular hobby in Britain. However, as we saw earlier, the government's own taskforce found that the compensation culture was a myth, and this view was echoed by the Constitutional Affairs Select Committee, which scrutinised the Compensation Bill as it made its way through Parliament. The Committee suggested that part of the reason why the myth of the compensation culture has grown up is that organisations have begun to use alleged fears about being sued as an excuse to ban activities that they don't want to provide for purely financial reasons. Research published by Warwick University in 2007 found that claims were in fact going down, not up, and, despite the availability of no win, no fee services, it is still the case that the vast majority of people injured through negligence never make a claim, let alone win one. With regard to workplace accidents, for example, the TUC's 2005 report, *A Little Compensation*, found that only one in ten people injured or caused illness by their jobs ever get compensation.

The reasons for this will be well known to those of you who have studied access to justice on English Legal System courses: people are often unaware of the possibility of legal action, or are put off by the inaccessible image of the legal world, and the cost of legal action is extremely expensive. In recent years, 'no win, no fee' actions, and more accessible legal advice (from, for example, accident management companies, who advertise widely and lack the sometimes forbidding image of solicitors) have probably eased these problems to some extent, but a survey by MORI in 2000 suggests that such barriers still play an important part. The survey found that almost 72 per cent of people would consider making a claim if they were injured through someone else's negligence – but the likelihood of this actually translating into a similar proportion of actual claims seems slim, given that over 60 per cent thought they would probably not be able to afford legal action, and almost 70 per cent said they knew little or nothing about how to go about making a claim.

Among those who do bring cases, the chances of success are sometimes slim. This is particularly the case in medical negligence, where the **Bolam** ruling has traditionally meant that if doctors stick together, it is extremely difficult to prove them negligent, and the judgment in **Bolitho** still leaves plenty of room to keep the old standard in all but exceptional cases. Yet there seems no compelling reason why medical negligence should be treated so differently from other areas of negligence, and English law is alone among the major common law jurisdictions in giving doctors this privileged status.

In practice the vast majority of negligence cases are settled without going to court – sometimes early on, but often almost literally at the door of the court. This saves a lot of money for the side which would have lost the case, since a trial can drastically raise the costs, and the loser must pay those of the winner as well as their own. From the point of view of adequately compensating those injured though, out-of-court settlements can be problematic. Hazel Genn's 1984 study, *Hard Bargaining*, showed that in cases where the defendant is an insurance company (which is the case in the vast majority of accident and professional negligence claims, for example) and the claimant an ordinary member of the public, the insurance companies, with their vast experience of these cases, are able to manipulate the pre-trial process in order to achieve not a fair settlement but the lowest offer they can get away with. What seems to happen is that small claims are over-compensated because it is not cost-effective for insurance companies to fight them, while very big claims (such as, for example, those brought by parents of children damaged by negligence at birth, who will need care throughout their lives) are often undercompensated because the claimants need compensation quickly, and cannot afford to take the risk that they might lose in court and so can effectively be forced to accept a lower settlement than they might get if they went to court.

Because the law on negligence is complicated, cases can be long and involved. Specialist legal representation is usually required, and the expert witnesses often needed to prove fault add to the cost. The result in practice is that only a fraction of the money spent on negligence cases actually goes to the victims of harm. For example, in 2007, a report from the insurance industry calculated that lawyers' fees took 43p of every £1 paid in personal injury damages for motor accidents, although the Association of Personal Injury Lawyers claimed the true figure was nearer 33p.

Marking fault

The original basis of the law of negligence was claimed to be essentially moral: those who carelessly cause harm to others should bear the responsibility for that harm. In fact this was always debatable; for example, the direct consequence test for remoteness of damage, laid down in **Re Polemis** (1921), created cases where the damage the defendant was required to compensate could be violently out of proportion to their fault, and, even though this test has been superseded, the 'eggshell-skull' rule can have a similar effect.

What makes the shift away from a moral basis much clearer, though, are the cases on economic loss and psychiatric injury. They show that where new sources of potential liability arise, what the courts look at now is not the rights and wrongs of the situation, but what the economic effects of such liability would be. In **Alcock** *v* **Chief Constable of South Yorkshire** (1992), the lines drawn with regard to closeness of relationship take no account of the degree of carelessness involved in the police decision that caused the tragedy: the decision was no more or less careless because the relationship between some of the deceased victims and their relatives was or was not factually close. What the court was looking for was a way to limit liability, and it based its decision not on degree of fault, but essentially on the effect it would have on insurance premiums for the police and others.

The very existence of insurance is a double-edged sword for the law of negligence. Without it, far fewer claims would be brought, because the majority of defendants would not have the money to pay damages, and in terms of compensation this would make the law even more inadequate. But in terms of fault, insurance causes a problem because the damages are usually paid by insurance companies, and not by the party whose carelessness has caused harm. Insurance premiums may rise slightly as a result of a claim, but not usually by anything like the cost of that claim, and in many cases premiums are indirectly paid for by all of us, rather than the individual policyholder: employers' insurance is paid for in higher prices to customers, for example; insurance for health authorities is paid for by our taxes; and the damages paid out by motor insurance companies are funded by all of us who have motor insurance, whether we claim or not. As a result, it is rarely the case that damages are actually paid by the party who has been careless.

Deterring carelessness

The argument here seems obvious: the tort system means that people and organisations know they are liable to be sued if their carelessness causes damage, and therefore its existence should mean that they are more likely to take care to avoid causing harm. In practice, however, the deterrence issue is not so straightforward.

First, the possibility of being sued for negligence can only really act as a deterrent if it is clear that everybody who suffers damage through negligence will sue, and, as we have seen, that is not the case. Secondly, the presence of insurance means that even if you are sued, your carelessness is quite likely not to cost you anything, giving you little incentive to be careful.

Thirdly, the market system on which our society is run actually makes it much more difficult for businesses to take sufficient care, where such care costs (and it usually does). This is because in a market system companies have to keep their costs in line with those of other competing firms. Any company which went out on a limb and spent a lot more money on safety precautions than its competitors were spending would soon be put out of business (a fact which was implicitly acknowledged by the courts in **Thompson** *v* **Smith Shiprepairers (North Shields)** (1984) (see p. 86).

A fourth problem is that in many cases the objective approach can mean that it is actually impossible for the tortfeasor to reach the required standard; in **Nettleship** *v* **Weston** (1971), and **Djemal** *v* **Bexley Heath Health Authority** (1995) (see pp. 76 and 82), the defendants were judged by standards that in reality they could not have been expected to attain. The decisions may have been right, given that both defendants would have been protected by insurance, but, as far as deterrence is concerned, they were meaningless.

Similarly, in many cases the standard of care imposed is too vague to be of much use in deterring careless behaviour. In practice, most tortfeasors do not sit and balance the magnitude of the risk against its seriousness, while taking into account their own special characteristics and those of the potential claimant, and contemplating the possible benefits to society of what they are about to do. So, in practice, what the law of negligence really does is not so much deter carelessness as attempt to mop up the mess that carelessness leaves behind.

Spreading risk

This is one area where the law of negligence can be seen to work very well at times; rather than leaving loss to lie where it falls, it can pass it on to those most able to bear it financially. The fine judgements needed to do this are not always easy, but there are many cases where the courts have shown obvious good sense in this area. An example is the case of **Smith** *v* **Eric Bush** (1990) (see p. 32), where the courts explicitly considered who was best able to bear the loss, and concluded that it was the surveyors, since they were insured, and their liability was in any case limited to the value of the house.

Having said that, it is worth bearing in mind that, as we have explained, when loss is shifted to insurers, in practice it is actually shifted from them to all of us. This is not necessarily a bad thing, since it spreads the costs of harm thinly – but if this is what society wants to do, it might be more efficiently done by compensating all victims of harm, however caused, through welfare systems based on need and paid for by taxes. In this way much more of the money spent would go to victims of harm, because there would be no need to take out the element of profit for insurance companies, nor the costs of legal actions. It would also mean that money would go to all those who need it to cope with their injury or illness, and not just those who can prove that someone else was to blame.

Individualism and negligence

Supporters of the school of thought known as critical legal theory criticise negligence law for the way it focuses almost exclusively on individual fault, when in fact there may be wider issues involved. For example, many of the activities which crop up in negligence cases – transport, industry and medicine, for example – are activities which benefit society as a whole, but also necessarily carry risks. As the judge in **Duborn** *v* **Bath Tramways** (1946) put it:

> If all the trains in this country were restricted to a speed of five miles per hour, there would be fewer accidents, but our national life would be intolerably slowed down.

It can be argued then that those people who are injured as a result of such risks bear the brunt of the convenience and other benefits which the relevant activities provide for all members of society, and that it might therefore be appropriate for society to compensate such victims automatically, rather than making them jump through the hoops of negligence law.

This argument becomes even stronger when the harm suffered by the claimant itself results in a benefit to society, through better knowledge of possible risks. For example, in **Roe** *v* **Minister of Health** (1954) (see p. 84), it was only the injury caused to the claimant that revealed the danger of keeping ampoules of anaesthetic in disinfectant. Because the hospital could not have known of the risk beforehand, they were not liable. As a direct result of what happened, they had changed their procedures so that it could not happen to any future patients, but the patient whose suffering had allowed this progress went uncompensated.

Critical theorists argue that since society benefits in all these cases, society should pay; this would require an acceptance that we have social, as well as individual responsibilities.

An economic solution?

It has been suggested that negligence should be assessed on the basis of an economic formula: if the likelihood of the injury, multiplied by its seriousness, exceeds the cost to the defendant of taking adequate precautions, they would be liable. The rationale behind this approach is that finding negligence effectively transfers the loss from the claimant to the defendant and, for economic reasons, this should only happen where the cost of avoiding the accident is less than paying compensation for it.

While this approach may have practical attractions, it lacks any concept of disapproving the wrongdoer's conduct, and could also raise difficulties when it came to calculating (or guessing) the cost of preventing an accident.

Answering questions

Adam is driving his car through a residential area. He suddenly realises that he is going to be late for an appointment. He increases his speed. Suddenly Ben, a ten-year-old boy, runs out into the road without looking, and because Adam is going too fast, he hits Ben and crashes into the front garden of a house owned by Bill. Ben is severely injured. Bill's garden wall and front gates are destroyed.

Bill is cutting the grass in his front garden at the time of the accident. He is unhurt but he is stunned when he witnesses the crash and sees the extent of Ben's injuries. He is subsequently diagnosed as suffering from post-traumatic stress disorder.

Ben's mother, Elizabeth, who is at work when the accident happens, is contacted by telephone by the child minder and informed that Ben has been taken to hospital for treatment following an accident. She visits him in hospital that evening. A few weeks later, Elizabeth suffers a nervous breakdown.

Advise Adam as to who he might be liable to in negligence.

In a problem question like this, your answer will be clearest if you take each potential claim in turn, and work through the elements of negligence (duty of care, breach, and damage, plus causation, remoteness and any defences) as they apply to that claim. Ben's case is fairly straightforward: it is well established that motorists owe a duty of care to other road users, and that, in going too fast, Adam was falling below the standard of a reasonable driver, and therefore in breach of that duty. Damage is also clear as we know Ben was seriously injured, and clearly Adam caused this. The main issue here then is whether Adam may have a defence, because Ben could be considered contributorily negligent in not looking as he crossed the road. You should refer to the case of **Gough** *v* **Thorne** on contributory negligence by children.

Regarding Bill, there are two possible claims, one for the damage to his property and the other for his post-traumatic stress disorder. With regard to the property, do not be tempted to think that this is a case of economic loss. Although it will cost money to repair the wall and gates, this is a straightforward case of property damage, which falls under the same test for a duty of care as personal injury, the **Caparo** test (see p. 21). You need to consider the issue of remoteness of damage here, and explain that the test is whether the damage was a reasonably foreseeable result of Adam's breach of duty.

Bill's post-traumatic stress disorder would be considered a recognisable psychiatric injury, so the test of duty of care here is the one established in **White**. Applying this test to Bill, and referring also to **Bourhill** *v* **Young**, you can explain that there will be no duty of care because he was merely a bystander to the accident, and, if there is no duty of care, there is no liability.

Elizabeth's claim is also for psychiatric injury, so, again, the test is the one laid down in **White**. You need to apply the three **White** elements (nature and cause of the injury, class of person, proximity to the accident) to her situation, referring to the cases of **McLoughlin**, **Alcock** and **Tan** *v* **East London and City Health Authority**.

Summary of Chapter 3

Causation

The claimant must prove that the defendant's negligence caused the damage. The rules on causation apply to all torts which require proof of damage.

The basic test is the 'but for' test: would the damage have happened if the defendant had not been negligent?

More complex rules apply in cases where:

- the damage has more than one cause;
- the negligence causes 'loss of a chance';
- there are multiple tortfeasors;
- there is an intervening event after the negligence which contributes to the damage.

Remoteness of damage

The claimant must also prove that the defendant's negligence is not too remote from the damage: a legal, rather than factual, test.

The remoteness test in negligence is reasonable foreseeability; was the kind of damage suffered reasonably foreseeable at the time the duty was breached?

So long as the type of damage is reasonably foreseeable, it does not matter that it is more serious than the defendant could have foreseen.

Proving negligence

The claimant has the burden of proof except where:

- the defendant has a criminal conviction based on the same facts;
- the principle *res ipsa loquitur* applies.

Defences

The main defences are:

- Contributory negligence, which applies when the claimant is partly to blame for the damage, or its extent.
- *Volenti*, which applies when the claimant has consented to what was done by the defendant.
- Illegality, which applies where the claimant's case is connected with their own criminal act.
- Statutory authority, which applies where a statute entitles the defendant to something which would normally be a tort.

→

These defences apply to most other torts as well as negligence.

Defences which do not apply to negligence are:

- necessity;
- mistake;
- inevitable accident.

Time limits

Negligence claims (other than personal injury) must be brought within six years from damage occurring, or three years from when the claimant knew/ought to have known of it.

Personal injury claims must be brought within three years of the damage, or of the claimant knowing they might have a claim. The courts have discretion to extend this limit.

Criticisms of negligence law

Problems with the law on negligence arise in each one of its aims:

- compensating victims of harm;
- marking fault;
- deterring carelessness;
- spreading the costs of harm caused by carelessness;
- fulfilling these tasks quickly and fairly.

Reading list

Text resources

Amirthalingam, K (2005) 'Causation and the gist of negligence' 64 *Cambridge Law Journal* 32

Atiyah, P (1972) '*Res ipsa loquitur* in England and Australia' 35 *Modern Law Review* 337

Clarke, J (2008) 'Fatal accident claims: victory in suicide case' *Solicitors Journal* 10

Conaghan, J and Mansell, W (1998) *The Wrongs of Tort*, 2nd edn, Chapter 2. Pluto

Dias, R M W (1962) 'Remoteness of liability and legal policy' *Cambridge Law Journal* 178

Dias, R M W (1967) 'Trouble on oiled waters: problems of the Wagon Mound (No 2)' *Cambridge Law Journal* 62

Foster, C (2005) 'Police duty of care' *Solicitors Journal* 620

Glofcheski, R (1999) 'Plaintiff's illegality as a bar to recovery of personal injury damages' 19 *Legal Studies* 6

Hickman, T (2002) 'Negligence and Article 6: the great escape?' 61 *Cambridge Law Journal* 1

Hill, M (1991) 'A lost chance for compensation in the tort of negligence by the House of Lords' 54 *Modern Law Review* 511

Hoffmann, Lord (2005) 'Causation' 121 *Law Quarterly Review* 592

Jaffey, A J E (1985) '*Volenti non fit injuria*' *Cambridge Law Journal* 87

Kidner, R (1991) 'The variable standard of care, contributory negligence and volenti' 11 *Legal Studies* 1

Law Commission, *The Illegality Defence in Tort* (2001) Law Commission Report No 160

Morgan, J (2003) 'Lost causes in the House of Lords: Fairchild *v* Glenhaven Funeral Services' 66 *Modern Law Review* 277

Peel, E (2005) 'Loss of a chance in medical negligence' 121 *Law Quarterly Review* 364
Reece, H (1996) 'Losses of chances in the law' 59 *Modern Law Review* 188
Robertson, D (2003) 'An American perspective on negligence law' in Deakin, S *Tort Law*, 5th edn. OUP
Scorer, R (2007) 'Out of time' *New Law Journal* 1596
Stapleton, J (1988) 'Law, causation and common sense' 8 *Oxford Journal of Legal Studies* 111
Stapleton, J (1988) 'The gist of negligence, Part II' 104 *Law Quarterly Review* 389
Stapleton, J (1997) 'Negligence valuers and falls in the property market' 113 *Law Quarterly Review* 1
Stapleton, J (2003) 'Lords a'leaping evidentiary gaps' 10 *Tort Law Review* 276
Stapleton, J (2003) 'Cause-in-fact and the scope of liability for consequences' 119 *Law Quarterly Review* 388
Stapleton, J (2006) 'Occam's Razor reveals an orthodox basis for Chester *v* Afzar' 122 *Law Quarterly Review* 426
Tan, C (1995) '*Volenti Non Fit Injuria*: an alternative framework' *Tort Law Review* 208
Weir, T (2002) 'Making it more likely v making it happen' 61 *Cambridge Law Journal* 499

Reading on the Internet

The Law Commission's 2001 report on limitation periods can be read at:
http://www.lawcom.gov.uk/lc_reports.htm

The House of Lords judgment in **Barker** *v* **Corus** (2006) can be read at:
http://www.publications.parliament.uk/pa/ld200506/ldjudgmt/jd060503/barker-1.htm

The House of Lords judgment in **Reeves** *v* **Commissioner of Police for the Metropolis** (1999) can be read at:
http://www.parliament.the-stationery-office.co.uk/pa/ld199899/ldjudgmt/jd990715/reeves01.htm

The House of Lords judgment in **Corr** *v* **IBC** (2008) can be read at:
http://www.publications.parliament.uk/pa/ld200708/ldjudgmt/jd080227a/corr-1.htm

Visit **www.mylawchamber.co.uk** to access tools to help you develop and test your knowledge of tort law, including interactive multiple choice questions, practice exam questions with guidance, weblinks, glossary flashcards, legal newsfeed and legal updates.

Use Case Navigator to read in full some of the key cases referenced in this chapter with commentary and questions:

Fairchild *v* **Glenhaven Funeral Services Ltd and others** (2002)
Gregg *v* **Scott** (2005)

Chapter 4
Employers' liability

This chapter discusses:

- Employers' duty to their employees in tort
- Types of harm for which an employer may be liable
- Precautions employers must take to avoid liability.

In addition to the general common law rules of negligence, there are some areas where the law has created special rules – including statutory ones – about the way in which carelessness that damages others should be treated. This chapter deals with the duty of care owed by employers to their employees: other examples of special liability regimes are occupiers' liability, discussed in the following chapter; and liability for harm caused by defective products, considered in Chapter 6.

As far as employers are concerned there are three main ways in which they can incur liability for harm done to an employee. The first is vicarious liability, which can arise when one employee injures another and the law requires the employer to take responsibility; this is the subject of Chapter 17. The second arises where an employer has a statutory duty to protect the safety of employees, as a result of legislation such as the Health and Safety at Work Act 1974; the rules concerning breach of a statutory duty are examined in Chapter 6. The third type of liability comes from the common law rules which impose on employers a personal duty to take reasonable care of their employees' safety with regard to work. This type of liability is the subject of this chapter.

Employers' liability: the historical position

Before we look at the current law on employers' liability, it is worth knowing a little about how this area of the law first developed, as that will help you put the current law in its practical context. Specific legal protection for employees really only started to come into English law from the nineteenth century onwards. Before that, three legal principles existed which, between them, meant it was extremely difficult for injured employees to make a claim against their employers, even where they had clearly suffered injuries that were caused by the employer failing to take even basic safety precautions. These principles have become known as the 'unholy trinity', and consist of the following:

- The doctrine of 'common employment'
- The defence of contributory negligence
- The defence of *volenti non fit injuria*.

The doctrine of common employment, established in **Priestly** *v* **Fowler** (1837), meant that if an employee suffered harm where the direct cause was the actions of another employee, the employer would not be liable, even if the ultimate cause was the employer's failure to take adequate safety precautions. The only exception was if the employer had failed to make sure that employee who did the harm was competent, which was was very difficult to prove. The theory behind the doctrine was that every contract of employment had in it an implied term stating that the employee accepted the risk of negligence by a fellow employee, and so workers were voluntarily accepting this risk. In practice, of course, this was nonsense, as most workers in those days were not in a position to accept or reject any terms or conditions, but had to take what the employer offered or find another job. There were no trade unions to fight for fair terms, and individual workers had little, if any, say in their working conditions.

The second element of the 'unholy trinity', the defence of contributory negligence, is one we looked at earlier (in Chapter 3). You will remember that, in modern law, it applies where the claimant was partly to blame for the accident or injury, and reduces the damages to reflect that. However, this has only been the case since the passing of the Law Reform (Contributory Negligence) Act 1945. Until then, common law provided that anyone who was partly responsible for damage done to them could not sue at all. The result of this principle was that that if the employee was in any way at fault, they had no claim.

The third element of the trinity, the defence of *volenti*, is also one we came across earlier (in Chapter 3), and which applies where the claimant has voluntarily taken the risk of being harmed. The modern courts are aware that doing work which carries risks may not be a genuinely voluntary choice, given that many people are not in a position to challenge their employers' orders. Back in the nineteenth century, however, the courts did not take this view, and it was easy for an employer to claim that if an employee had chosen to do a job that was dangerous, the defence of *volenti* applied.

Taken together, these three doctrines meant that nineteenth-century employers could, and did, impose extremely dangerous conditions and practices on their employees, with practically no risk of being sued. This was a time when Britain was industrialising, and many employees worked in factories, mills and mines where the machinery was highly dangerous, safety precautions were scarce, and hours were long. Accidents were common and, if someone was seriously injured, there was no NHS to look after them, and no welfare benefits to support them if they were unable to work again. But the growth in industry was making Britain prosperous, and the courts were reluctant to disturb this by exposing employers to the costs of either taking safety precautions, or paying compensation for the harm done by not taking safety precautions. The courts therefore largely took the view that it was up to employees to look after their own safety, and if they failed to do so, they could not expect to make the employer liable.

Changes in the law

Towards the end of the nineteenth century, this situation started to change, for three main reasons. First, as the amount of industry increased, there was greater awareness of the numbers of serious accidents being caused to workers, and the harshness of the law regarding them. Secondly, workers were beginning to organise into trade unions, and together, they were able to fight for better treatment in a way that individuals had never been able to do for themselves. Thirdly, the beginnings of a market in insurance cover for business owners was developing, and this meant that if an employer was sued, they would not have to pay the costs themselves.

As a result of these developments, both the courts and Parliament began to offer more protection to injured employees, though it took some time. The first major development came in **Smith** *v* **Baker** (1891) (the case we looked at in Chapter 3), where a worker was injured when a large stone fell on him. As you may remember, the claimant worked in the defendant's quarry, and while he was working, a crane was being operated above his head, swinging huge rocks. The claimant had frequently complained that there was a risk of one of the stones falling on him, but when that happened, and he sued, his employer pleaded *volenti*, arguing that, since he knew of the risk and carried on working, he was accepting it. The House of Lords disagreed. They said that if a person took on work that would have been dangerous even if their employers took proper precautions, they might be said to be accepting the risks involved in that work. But in this case, the work itself was not dangerous, but was made so by the defendant's negligence. Therefore, merely continuing to do the work when he knew of the risk did not mean the claimant consented to it and *volenti* did not apply. This made it much more difficult for employers to use the *volenti* defence in cases where the only acceptance of the risk was taking the job, or carrying on doing it.

The other major developments took a little longer but, by the 1930s, the key case of **Wilsons and Clyde Coal** *v* **English** (1938) established that employers had a duty towards the safety of their employees, and this case remains a cornerstone of common law liability on employers today. Finally, during the 1940s, the remains of the 'unholy trinity' were dismantled. As we saw earlier, the 1945 Law Reform (Contributory Negligence) Act altered the contributory negligence defence so that it could only reduce damages and not prevent a claim completely. Three years later, the Law Reform (Personal Injury) Act 1948 abolished the doctrine of common employment, making it possible to sue employers for torts committed by their employees (we will look at why this is so important in the next chapter, when we look at vicarious liability). Further protection for employees came in 1969, when the Employers' Liability (Compulsory Insurance) Act provided that employers must take out insurance against workplace accidents. In practical terms, this was very important, as it made it much more likely that employers would be able to pay damages if they were sued.

The employer's personal duty

The duty of employers regarding the safety of their workers was first defined in **Wilsons and Clyde Coal Co Ltd** *v* **English** (1938). The claimant was a miner at the defendant's coal mine. As he was leaving the mine at the end of his shift, some machinery that should have been switched off was turned on, and he was crushed. The defendants said that they had employed a competent manager, whose job it was to look after the technical operations of the mine, and since they had done that, they should not be liable. The House of Lords disagreed. They stated that employers had a duty to provide a competent staff, adequate materials and a proper system of work. Later cases have added a requirement for a safe place of work. Essentially, the duty requires the employer to take reasonable care to keep employees safe, and so is very similar to the general common law standard in negligence.

In **Wilsons and Clyde Coal**, the court stated that this duty was 'non-delegable'. That meant that, although an employer could delegate the task of doing those things to someone such as a manager, they could not delegate the legal liability for them. The duty is owed to employees only, and not to people who may be in the workplace but are not employed there, such as visitors, or people who come to do work there but are self-employed or employed by someone else (such as, for example, a window cleaner who comes to clean the windows of a factory; he or she would be working there, but would not be an employee of the factory owner). In employer's liability cases, people in this situation are referred to as independent contractors. They may be owed a duty under the normal laws of negligence, or under the Occupiers' Liability Acts, or by their own employer.

Competent staff

Where an employer takes on someone without sufficient experience or training for a particular job, and as a result another worker is injured, the employer may be in breach of their personal duty of care towards employees. The practical importance of this principle is limited by the fact that in most such cases the injured employee will be able to sue the employer vicariously for the wrong-doing of their colleague, but it is still valuable in situations where vicarious liability does not apply, such as where the injury was not caused by any specific employee, or where the employee causing the injury was acting outside the course of employment (this concept is explained in Chapter 17). An example of such liability occurred in **Hudson** *v* **Ridge Manufacturing Co Ltd** (1957), where injury was caused by an employee playing a practical joke. While playing jokes was obviously not within the course of his employment, making the imposition of vicarious liability impossible, the employee concerned had a reputation for persistently engaging in practical jokes, and his employers were held liable for not taking any steps to curb this habit.

An employer's duty also includes protecting employees from harassment, bullying or victimisation by other employees. In **Waters** *v* **Commissioner of Police of the Metropolis** (2000), the claimant was a police officer who claimed that the police force were negligent in failing to protect her from harassment by her colleagues, which happened after she alleged that one of them had raped her (strictly speaking, a police officer is not an 'employee' of the police force, for historical reasons that are not important here, but in such cases the courts will often assume that the relationship is one of employer–employee). The House of Lords confirmed that an employer who knows, or can foresee, that acts done to an employee by their colleagues may cause physical or mental harm, and does nothing to prevent such harm, may be in breach of their duty to the injured employee. A breach can also arise when harm was not foreseeable from the start, but becomes foreseeable while the harassment is going on, and the employer fails to take steps to prevent it. In this case the court held that harassment was a foreseeable result of the claimant's complaint about a fellow officer, and that therefore she had an arguable case.

Adequate equipment

Employers have a duty to take reasonable care to provide their workers with adequate equipment, including protective devices and clothing, and to maintain it all properly. In some cases, this duty will include a responsibility to warn employees that protective equipment should be used. In **Bux** *v* **Slough Metals** (1973), the claimant was a foundry worker, who was splashed with molten metal and lost the sight of one eye. His employer was bound by statute to provide protective goggles, and had complied with this duty, but the court held that his personal duty at common law went further than the statutory duty, and required him to encourage or even insist on the use of protective equipment. Having failed to do so, he was in breach of his duty towards the injured employee.

Where, however, employees object to or even refuse to use safety equipment, an employer may not be negligent for failing to make them do so. In **Yorkshire Traction Co Ltd** *v* **Walter Searby** (2003), the claimant was a bus driver who had been stabbed by a passenger. He claimed that the bus company had been negligent in not placing protective screens between drivers and passengers. However, the court heard that the company had bought some buses with screens, but their drivers had objected to them, and in some cases had even removed them, because they said the screens reflected light at night and were therefore potentially dangerous. In addition, evidence was given that the risk of assault from passengers was very low in that area. The Court of Appeal held that, although there were situations where an employer might be obliged to put certain safety precautions in place even if the workforce objected to them, in this case it was reasonable for the employer to take notice of the objections, given that they referred to health and safety, and that the risk to be protected against was actually very low. Balancing these factors against each other, the bus company was not negligent in failing to put up the screens.

This common law liability will not apply if an injury is caused by some latent defect in equipment, which could not have been discovered by the employee concerned using reasonable care. However, under the Employers' Liability (Defective Equipment) Act 1969, s. 1(1), if employees are injured in the course of their employment as a result of defective equipment provided by their employer, and the defect is due to the fault of a third party, the employer may be held liable, even if they are in no way to blame. This means that if an employee injured by a defective tool or other equipment can show that, on a balance of probabilities, the defect resulted from negligence or other fault in the tool's manufacture, and that the injury was caused by that defect, then both the employer and the manufacturer will be liable. The main advantage of this for employees is that they do not need to track down the manufacturer of the defective equipment, which may prove difficult, while employers are entitled to an indemnity from the manufacturer. In practice, however, employers are rarely found liable under the Act because of the problems of proving third-party fault and causation.

A safe place of work

Employers must take reasonable steps to ensure a safe place of work; but this does not mean that every foreseeable risk must be eliminated, if doing so would be unreasonably onerous. This principle can be seen in the case of **Latimer** *v* **AEC** (discussed on p. 86).

Where a place of work is in the occupation or control of the employer, this poses no major problems, but in some cases employees may be working on premises controlled by a third party – an obvious example would be a painter sent out to a private house. At one time it was thought that an employer owed no duty to provide a safe place of work in such cases, but in the case of **Wilson** *v* **Tyneside Window Cleaning Co** (1958) it was established that the duty of care remains, although the standard of care required may be lower where the place of work is not under the employer's control:

> The master's own premises are under his control: if they are dangerously in need of repair he can and must rectify the fault at once if he is to escape the censure of negligence. But if a master sends his plumber to mend a leak in a private house, no one could hold him negligent for not visiting the house himself to see if the carpet in the hall creates a trap.

The nature of the duty was further explained in **Cook** *v* **Square D Ltd** (1992), which concerned an employee sent to Saudi Arabia on a two-month contract. The court said that as the employers had satisfied themselves that the site occupiers and the general contractors were both reliable companies and aware of their responsibility for the safety of workers on the site, they could not be expected to be held responsible for daily events on the site; however, if several employees had been sent out there, or if one or two had been sent for a considerable period of time, the employer's duty might include a responsibility to inspect the site and ensure that the occupiers were conscious of their safety obligations. Again, what the courts seem to be suggesting is that the possible risks must be balanced against the onerousness of the employer's task.

A safe system of working

This duty includes such matters as organisation of work, the manner and order in which it is to be carried out, the number of employees needed for specific tasks and what each person is actually to do, safety precautions and special instructions, warnings and notices, particularly to inexperienced employees. In **Johnstone** *v* **Bloomsbury Health Authority** (1991), for example, it was held that a breach of duty might occur if the claimant was obliged to work such long hours as might foreseeably injure his health.

As with safety equipment, it is not necessarily enough simply to tell employees what the safety procedures are; employers may be required to make sure they are followed. In **Pape** *v* **Cumbria County Council** (1992), the claimant developed dermatitis as a result of contact with cleaning products. His employers had provided protective gloves, but were nevertheless held liable for breach of their duty towards the employee because they had failed to warn cleaning staff about the dangers of exposing the skin to chemicals, or to tell them to wear protective gloves at all times.

The degree of care required will vary in different circumstances; where a worker is skilled and experienced, for example, it may be reasonable to expect them to guard against obvious dangers which a less experienced worker might not recognise. In **Fraser** *v* **Winchester Health Authority** (1999), the claimant was a 21-year-old support worker employed by the health authority, who was sent on a camping trip with a patient. She was burnt when she attempted to change a gas cylinder near a lit candle; she had not been given any training in using the camping equipment, or instructions on how to use it. The health authority argued that they were not negligent, because the risks involved in what the claimant had done were so obvious that she must have seen them, and therefore there was no need for them to have given any warnings or instruction. The Court of Appeal disagreed: the claimant's inexperience and the importance of her responsibilities meant that she should have been given some instruction. They agreed that she must have seen the risk, but held that this amounted to contributory negligence rather than to a complete lack of liability on the health authority's part; they were held to be negligent but damages were reduced by one-third for the contributory negligence.

Where an employer's practice is in line with that generally followed in their trade or industry, the claimant is unlikely to succeed in a claim that such a practice is negligent unless it displays serious lack of concern for employees' health and safety: see **Thompson** *v* **Smiths Shiprepairers (North Shields)** (1984) (p. 86).

Types of harm

In the majority of employers' liability cases, the harm complained of will be some kind of physical injury or illness and it is clear that employers have a duty to take precautions to prevent this. However, employers also have a duty not to cause psychiatric injury to their employees and, to a much more limited extent, not to cause them economic loss.

Psychiatric injury

Key Case **Walker** *v* **Northumberland County Council (1995)**

The case of **Walker** *v* **Northumberland County Council** (1995) established that the employers' duty to take reasonable steps to ensure employees' safety could include a duty not to cause psychiatric damage. The claimant was employed by the council to manage four teams of social workers in an area with a high proportion of children at risk, which created a huge caseload for his department. In 1986, because of the stress and pressure of work, he had a nervous breakdown and was off sick for three months. When he went back to work, the council agreed to provide assistance to reduce his workload, but this was never properly done, and six months later he had another breakdown and was unable to carry on working. He sued for negligence and it was held that the council were liable for the second breakdown; once the first breakdown had happened, it was foreseeable that a continuation of the stress he was under would damage his mental health, and they were negligent in failing to take reasonable steps to prevent that.

Legal Principle

The employer's duty of care to employees can include a duty not to cause psychiatric injury.

The issue of workplace stress was re-examined in **Hatton** *v* **Sutherland**; **Barber** *v* **Somerset County Council**; **Jones** *v* **Sandwell Metropolitan Borough Council**; **Bishop** *v* **Baker Refractories Ltd** (2002), a decision which put fairly strict limits on such claims (although an appeal by one of the parties later loosened these limits a little). The Court of Appeal heard four cases together. Three of the claimants – Ms Hatton, Mr Barber and Ms Jones – were arguing that overwork and lack of help had caused them to suffer clinical depression. The fourth, Mr Bishop, had had a nervous breakdown after his company reorganised and changed his job, requiring him to fulfil a wider variety of roles, which he could not cope with.

In Mr Bishop's case, the court focused on what his employer could have done to prevent the problem. They could not be under a duty to give him his old job back, because it simply no longer existed. The only other possible duty was to sack him for his own good, but, as Mr Bishop had said he did not want to leave, and would try to carry on, the court held that they could not be said to owe him that duty either. His claim was rejected.

With regard to the other three claimants, the court's main interest was whether the employers could reasonably have been expected to foresee the damage, and in this they focused on what the claimants had done to make them aware of the problem. Ms Hatton had not told her employers that she felt she was in danger of a breakdown if she did not get help with her workload; she had suffered periods of illness during her employment, which might have alerted her employers to a problem, but the court held that these were readily attributable to 'causes other than stress at work', and so did not put the school on notice that she was struggling to cope. Mr Barber only complained about his workload once, and that was just at the end of the summer term, so, the court held, his employers were entitled to think that after the school summer holidays he would be rested, so it was not foreseeable that, if they failed to give him any help when he returned in September, psychiatric injury might result. Both these claims were therefore rejected.

The only one of the four claims that was accepted – and that rather reluctantly – was that of Ms Jones. The difference in her case was that she had complained about her workload from an early stage, and the court accepted 'with some hesitation' that she had done enough to make it foreseeable that, if she was not given some assistance, she might suffer psychiatric injury.

The judgment in the case laid down a number of principles to be applied to workplace stress cases. It said that there are no special control mechanisms applying to claims for psychiatric illnesses arising from doing the work that the employee is required to do. The test is the normal one for employers' liability: was the kind of harm suffered reasonably foreseeable? The answer in each case would depend on what the employer knew (or reasonably ought to know) about the individual employee.

The court pointed out that the potential for psychiatric injury may be harder to foresee than that of physical injury. An employer would usually be entitled to assume that an employee can withstand the normal pressures of the job, unless they are aware of some special vulnerability.

A number of facts would need to be considered when deciding whether the injury was foreseeable. With regard to the job itself, important questions would include:

- whether the workload was much more than would normally be expected in that job;
- whether the demands made on that employee were unreasonable compared with those made on others in comparable jobs; and
- whether there were signs that others doing that job were suffering from stress, such as an abnormal level of staff sickness in that department.

Courts would also need to look at employees:

- did they have a particular vulnerability, or previous sickness resulting from stress at work?
- had they been off sick to an uncharacteristic degree?
- had they or others warned the employer of a potential problem?

The court stated that an employer was entitled to take what they were told by an employee at face value, unless there was good reason not to, and, if the employee said they were coping, there was no duty on the employer to make sure that was true.

As in all employers' liability cases, the employer is only expected to take such steps to prevent psychiatric harm as are reasonable in all the circumstances, bearing in mind the size and seriousness of the risk, the costs and practicability of preventing it, and the justifications for running that risk. The size and resources of the firm will have a bearing on that, as will the need to treat other employees fairly, for example in redistributing duties. The court specified that an employer who offers a confidential advice service, with referral to appropriate counselling services, will in most cases be deemed to have taken reasonable steps to prevent psychiatric injury. An employer is only expected to take steps which are likely to do some good, and, if the only reasonable and effective precaution would be to sack or demote the employee, an employer will not be in breach of duty if they fail to do that because the employee does not wish it.

These strictures will clearly make it difficult for claimants now to succeed, but the court went further. Where a claimant could prove that the employer's breach of duty had materially contributed to their psychiatric injury, but there were also other causes for that injury (such as, for example, a marriage break-up), then 'a sensible attempt should be made to apportion liability accordingly'. Similarly, if the breach of duty has made an existing vulnerability or mental injury worse, rather than caused it in the first place, the employer is only liable for the increase in the problem, and not the whole of the damage.

Case Navigator

The rules laid down in **Hatton** *v* **Sutherland** were considered by the House of Lords in **Barber** *v* **Somerset County Council** (2004), which was an appeal by the Mr Barber who had been one of the claimants in **Hatton**. He had won his case at first instance, and the House of Lords reinstated his victory. The issue in question was whether the school had had a duty to spot the problems that Mr Barber was having and do something about them, or whether they only had such a duty if he drew the problems to their attention. The Court of Appeal's view, as stated above, was that employers were entitled to assume an employee was up to the job, unless there was something about the job or the employee that might suggest a risk of increased stress. Even in that case, the employer only had to be aware of the risk, and was not obliged to make 'searching or intrusive enquiries'.

The House of Lords confirmed that this was 'useful practical guidance', but said it should not be seen as a strict and inflexible rule – the real test was simply whether the employer had acted reasonably in the light of what they knew or ought to know, and had weighed up the risk of the injury, and the probable effectiveness, cost and inconvenience of any precautions that could be taken. In this case, the very fact that an obviously dedicated and hard-working teacher had on three occasions taken time off because of stress meant the school should have realised there was a problem, and should have taken steps to help Mr Barber cope with the pressures of the job. The case by no means cancels out the strict limitations placed on workplace stress claims in **Hatton** – in fact the House of Lords broadly supported the approach taken in the Court of Appeal – but it does confirm the principle that there will be situations where an employer has a duty to notice a problem without necessarily having it pointed out by the employee, and to take positive steps to prevent workplace stress from developing into a full-blown psychiatric illness.

In **Hatton**, the House of Lords said that employers who provided a counselling service would usually be considered to have taken reasonable steps to protect employees from excessive stress. In **Daw** *v* **Intel Corporation** (2007), the Court of Appeal emphasised that this still allowed room for cases where providing counselling would not be enough. Ms Daw worked for the defendants for many years, and was highly thought of, and considered to be a hard worker. Over the years, however, her workload became heavier and heavier, in part because she worked for several different bosses at once, all making conflicting demands on her time. By 2001, she was having to work excessive hours to get the job done, and had told her bosses about the problem at least 14 times. After sending a detailed e-mail about the problem, she was promised help with her work, but this was not provided; shortly afterwards, she suffered a breakdown and chronic depression, and became unable to work at all. The defendants had a confidential counselling service for employees, which they claimed meant they had taken reasonable steps to carry out their duty of care regarding workplace stress. The Court of Appeal rejected this argument, stating that, in this case, the counselling service would not have been able to help, as the problem arose from Ms Daw's workload. It upheld the trial judge's finding that, in order to fulfil their duty of care, Intel should have taken urgent action to deal with the problem when they received Ms Daw's memo in 2001, at the latest.

Interestingly, a recent case has revealed a way in which employees who are caused stress at work may be able to avoid the restrictions described above, at least in some circumstances. In **Majrowski** *v* **Guy's and St Thomas' NHS Trust** (2006), the claimant said he had been bullied by his department manager, and that the manager's behaviour amounted to harassment under the Protection from Harassment Act 1997 (see p. 352). He sued the NHS Trust on the basis that it was vicariously liable for the manager's behaviour. At first instance, the judge struck out the claim, stating that the Act was designed primarily to punish those who committed harassment, and so vicarious liability could not apply. The House of Lords, however, ruled that there was nothing in the legislation to say this, and that it was therefore possible for an employer to be vicariously liable for harassment by an employee. This has important implications for stress at work cases, not least because the Act does not require claimants to have suffered a recognised psychiatric illness, so employees who could not claim under the normal principles of employers' liability may be able to sue under the Act, if they can show that another employee has subjected them to a course of conduct which amounts to harassment. It would not, however, be of use where the complaint concerns too heavy a workload, or general workplace stress.

Psychiatric injury at work and secondary victims

The cases referred to above all feature stress caused directly by pressure of work, but there is another set of cases concerning psychiatric injury caused by workplace activities, which is treated differently. These are the so-called 'secondary victims', who suffer psychiatric injury because of witnessing horrific injury to others, such as members of the emergency services who attend terrible accidents. These cases are discussed fully earlier (see Chapter 2), but essentially the principle is that employees cannot sue employers for psychiatric injury caused in this way, unless they themselves were in danger of physical injury, or had a close relationship with the actual victims of the accident.

If employees are themselves at risk of reasonably foreseeable physical injury, however, the employer will be liable for any psychiatric injury caused by that risk, as well as any physical injury, under the normal principles of causation (explained on p. 102). This was confirmed in **Simmons** *v* **British Steel plc** (2004), the case (discussed on p. 40) where an employee's anger at an accident which caused him a head injury led to a severe skin disease, and the stress of that eventually resulted in a severe depressive illness. The House of Lords held that his employer was liable for the mental illness, even though only the physical injury (the head injury) could have been foreseen.

In **Donachie** *v* **Chief Constable of Greater Manchester Police** (2004), the claimant was a police officer who had had to attach a tagging device to a car used by a dangerous criminal gang, while the gang members were in a nearby pub. The situation was clearly stressful in itself, but was made much more so by the fact that the equipment supplied was defective, and the police officer had to go back, crawl under the car and reattach the device eight times, because the batteries kept turning out to be faulty. Not surprisingly, he became increasingly frightened, and two days later he had a stroke, which medical evidence suggested was a result of the stress. His employers had argued that, under the principles set down in **Hatton**, they were not liable because they had no reason to believe that he was particularly vulnerable to stress or likely to suffer a stroke. The Court of Appeal held that the **Hatton** test did not apply here, because it was reasonably foreseeable that the claimant might suffer physical injury in the situation the claimant was in, and the employer was therefore liable for any physical or psychiatric injury arising from that risk.

Economic loss

The courts have also stated that, in exceptional cases, employers may have a duty not to cause economic loss to employees. This was the case in **Spring** *v* **Guardian Assurance plc** (1995), where an employer was successfully sued for negligence after giving a bad reference, and in **Scally** *v* **Southern Health and Social Services Board** (1992), where the employer was found negligent in failing to advise the employee that he was entitled to exercise valuable pension options. However, it was made clear in **Crossley** *v* **Faithfull and Gould Holdings Ltd** (2004) that although there are specific circumstances where an employer has a duty not to cause economic loss to an employee, that did not amount to a blanket duty on employers to look after the well-being of their employees. The claimant in the case had lost out on certain benefits available under his employer's insurance scheme, because he had resigned. He had not known that resigning would have this effect, but his employer had known, and had still advised him to resign. He argued that employers had a duty to take reasonable care for the economic well-being of their employees, but the Court of Appeal rejected this idea. They said that if an employer assumed the responsibility of giving financial advice to an employee, they had a duty to take reasonable care in giving that advice, under the principles laid down in **Hedley Byrne** (see p. 28), but they did not have a duty to give such advice in the first place, or to generally safeguard the employee's financial situation.

Table 4.1 Employers' responsibility for different types of harm

Physical harm	The duty is essentially the same as in negligence; employers must take reasonable steps to prevent foreseeable physical harm.
Psychiatric harm	Employers have a duty to take reasonable steps to protect against foreseeable psychiatric injury, but the courts accept that psychiatric injury may be harder to foresee. The employer is entitled to assume the employee can withstand normal pressures unless there are indications that they are not.
Economic loss	Employers only have a duty in exceptional circumstances, primarily where they have assumed responsibility under the principles in **Hedley Byrne** *v* **Heller**.

The scope of the employer's duty

An employer's personal duty to employees, under any of the above heads, can be discharged by taking reasonable care; it is not an absolute duty to eliminate all risks. This is highlighted by the case of **Withers** *v* **Perry Chain** (1961). The claimant had in the past suffered from dermatitis because of contact with grease while at work, so her employers gave her the driest work that they could offer. However, she developed dermatitis once more, and sued her employers on the basis that as they were aware that she was susceptible to the illness, they ought not to have allowed her to do work involving any risk of activating it. The Court of Appeal rejected her claim: the employers had done everything reasonable for her protection.

This approach was confirmed in **Henderson** *v* **Wakefield Shirt Co Ltd** (1997). Here the employee's job was to press garments, but she had a back condition which made such work painful. She claimed that her employers' failure to take steps to alleviate this problem – by altering the equipment she used or her work routine – was in breach of their duty regarding her safety at work. The Court of Appeal disagreed, finding that, as the work conditions and equipment were not actually unsafe, the employers were not in breach of their duty.

The personal duty is owed individually to each employee, so any characteristics of the particular worker which are known or which ought to be known to the employer will affect the precautions which the employer must take in order to fulfil the duty. In **Paris** *v* **Stepney Borough Council** (1951), the claimant, who worked in a garage, had only one eye; his employer was aware of this. The claimant did work which involved a risk of injury to his remaining eye, and his eye was in fact injured. It was held that although the risk was not so great as to require protective goggles to be issued to other workers doing the same job, the fact that if the claimant's eye was injured he might lose his sight completely meant that better precautions should have been taken, and the employer's failure to issue goggles was a breach of their duty to him.

Delegating the employer's duty

Clearly there will be many situations where the employer hands over day-to-day responsibility for safety procedures to certain employees. If those employees do not take the reasonable care expected by the law, it is the employer who remains liable. The employer's duty is therefore known as non-delegable: an employer can delegate the performance of the duty, but not the liability for that performance. An example of this principle in action would be if an employer delegated a manager to organise a safe system of working, but an accident occurred. The courts would then look at whether the employer's conduct, in delegating the job to that person, amounted to reasonable care.

In **Mullaney** *v* **Chief Constable of West Midlands Police** (2001), the claimant was one of a group of police officers sent to deal with a group of men who were thought to be importuning (approaching other men for sex) in local public toilets. The claimant was one of a group of three assigned to monitor one of the toilets; a fourth officer, PC McKirdy, was left behind at the police station to monitor calls from the officers keeping watch and respond if any of them called for help. At one point during the exercise, the claimant's two colleagues took a break, leaving him alone. Unluckily for him, it was after they had left that an importuning incident took place, involving a Mr Corbett. The claimant called for help, but PC McKirdy had, apparently for no good reason, left his post, and failed to hear the call. The claimant tried to arrest Mr Corbett, and ended up being kicked in the head and sustaining very serious injuries, which eventually led to him having to leave the police force.

He sued the police as his employer, and the Court of Appeal held that the Chief Constable had breached his personal duty to the claimant. The Chief Constable had entrusted the job of ensuring a safe system of working to PC McKirdy, and, in failing to take reasonable steps to ensure safety, PC McKirdy had put the Chief Constable in breach of that duty.

Defences

The general defences of contributory negligence and *volenti non fit injuria* are available in actions for breach of the employer's duty, but you can see from the case of **Smith** *v* **Baker** (1891) (described on p. 125), that the courts are aware that in many employment cases what looks like a voluntary choice may in reality be nothing of the kind, and they will bear this in mind when considering such cases.

Answering questions

Siobhan and Brian are mechanics who work in a garage owned by Krafty Kars. The business has grown over the past year, and Siobhan and Brian's workload has increased. Brian also has to do a large amount of the firm's paperwork. Six months ago, he felt that the workload was becoming too much for him: he had not been sleeping well and was feeling very stressed at the long hours he was having to work. At the same time, his marriage was breaking up. He spoke to the garage owner about his workload, and asked if they could recruit a third mechanic, or take on someone to do the paperwork. The owner refused, saying that they could not afford extra help.

Last week Brian phoned in sick and his doctor has diagnosed a nervous breakdown. Siobhan was left to cope on her own and, during the day, she needed to lift a very heavy piece of machinery. Krafty Kars had instructed Siobhan and Brian that the machinery should only be lifted by two people, but Siobhan lifted it anyway. It fell, trapping her leg. Before passing out with the pain, she was able to grab her mobile phone and call the fire brigade to rescue her.

Siobhan's husband Tim is a firefighter, and he was among the group who came to her rescue, along with a close friend of theirs, Jennifer. Both Tim and Jennifer saw Siobhan trapped, unconscious and in terrible pain, and have since suffered nightmares and terrible flashbacks to the scene. Siobhan's leg was badly broken and she had to have six months off work.

Advise Brian, Siobhan, Tim and Jennifer as to any claims they may have against their employers.

Beginning with Brian, the claim here is for psychiatric injury, and we know from **Walker** that the general duty to provide a safe place and system of work includes a duty not to cause psychiatric injury. You should apply the principles laid down in **Hatton** *v* **Sutherland** and clarified in **Barber** and **Daw**, discussing the foreseeability of psychiatric injury, bearing in mind that Brian mentioned his workload problems to his boss, and the issue of whether it was reasonable for the firm to take no action in the circumstances. You should also address the issue of whether his nervous breakdown was entirely due to the stress at work, or partially caused by his marriage break-up, and consider how this might affect Krafty Kars' liability.

With regard to Siobhan, the issue is straightforward physical injury, which the employers' duty clearly covers. What you need to consider is whether Krafty Kars did or failed to do something which put them in breach of their duty to Siobhan, and whether that breach caused her injury. Remember that the employers' duty to provide a safe system of working includes having sufficient staff to do a job safely; the courts will look at whether it was reasonable to have left Siobhan to work alone. However, you also need to consider whether the fact that Siobhan was warned not to lift the machinery alone makes a difference. It could potentially allow Krafty Kars to put forward the defences of contributory negligence and *volenti*, so you need to explain how these work, and discuss the case of **Smith** *v* **Baker** on whether an action is truly voluntary in a work situation.

Tim and Jennifer will be seeking to sue their own employer for psychiatric injury. You should point out that they will only have a claim if they can prove that their mental problems amount to a recognised psychiatric illness. Assuming this is proved, you then need to consider the principles explained in **White**. Both Tim and Jennifer would be considered secondary victims, so, as explained in **White**, this means that, despite the employer–employee relationship, they are subject to the normal rules of negligence. You therefore need to look at each person's relationship to Siobhan and their proximity to the accident, applying the principles stated in **White**.

Summary of Chapter 4

Common law rules impose a duty on employers to take reasonable care of their employees' safety. The duty is only owed to staff, not independent contractors.

The employer must take reasonable steps to ensure:

- a competent staff;
- adequate equipment;
- a safe place of work;
- a safe system of working.

The duty can apply to:

- physical harm;
- psychiatric harm, if:
  - reasonably foreseeable and caused by workplace stress;
  - caused by a sudden shock, and the employee was in physical danger (but not if the employee only witnessed another in danger);
- economic loss (but only in exceptional cases).

Scope of the duty

The duty is to take reasonable care, not to eliminate all possible risks. It is owed to each individual, so special characteristics of the individual must be taken into account.

Delegating the duty

Employers can delegate performance of the duty (for example to a manager), but not liability for it.

Defences

The available defences are:

- Contributory negligence
- *Volenti*.

Reading list

Text resources

Barrett, B (2000) 'Harassment at work: a matter of health and safety' *Journal of Business Law* 343

Conaghan, J and Mansell, W (1998) *The Wrongs of Tort*, 2nd edn, Chapter 4. Pluto

Freidman, L M and Ladinsky, J (1967) 'Social change and the law of industrial accidents' 67 *Columbia Law Review* 50

Harlow, C (2005) *Understanding Tort Law*, 3rd edn, Chapter 3. Sweet & Maxwell

Harris, P (2006) *An Introduction to Law*, 7th edn, Chapter 9. Cambridge University Press

McKendrick, E (1990) 'Vicarious liability and independent contractors – a re-examination' 53 *Modern Law Review* 770

Marnham, M (2007) 'Stressed out' *New Law Journal* 309

Mullany, N J (2002) 'Containing claims for workplace mental illness' 118 *Law Quarterly Review* 373

Mullender, R (1996) 'Law, labour and mental harm' 59 *Modern Law Review* 296

Newark, F H (1966) 'Bad law' 17 *Northern Ireland Legal Quarterly* 469

Williams, G (1960) 'The effects of penal legislation in the law of tort' 23 *Modern Law Review* 233

Reading on the Internet

The Court of Appeal judgment in **Hatton** *v* **Sutherland** (2002) can be read at:
http://www.bailii.org/cgi-bin/markup.cgi?doc=/ew/cases/EWCA/Civ/2002/76.html

The House of Lords judgment in **Barber** *v* **Somerset County Council** (2004) can be read at:
http://www.publications.parliament.uk/pa/ld200304/ldjudgmt/jd040401/barber-1.htm

The House of Lords judgment in **Majrowski** *v* **Guy's** (2006) can be read at:
http://www.parliament.the-stationery-office.com/pa/ld200506/ldjudgmt/jd060712/majro.pdf

Visit **www.mylawchamber.co.uk** to access tools to help you develop and test your knowledge of tort law, including interactive multiple choice questions, practice exam questions with guidance, weblinks, glossary flashcards, legal newsfeed and legal updates.

Use Case Navigator to read in full some of the key cases referenced in this chapter with commentary and questions:
Barber *v* **Somerset County Council** (2004)

Chapter 5
Occupiers' liability

This chapter discusses:

- Occupiers' duty to people who come onto their land
- Differences in liability between authorised visitors and trespassers
- Defences to occupiers' liability.

For well over a century, the law has recognised that people who occupy land (including buildings on land) have a duty towards the safety of others who come onto the land. This duty developed through the common law, but in 1957 it began to be regulated by statute with the introduction of the Occupiers' Liability Act, which laid down rules about the duty of occupiers towards people who come onto their land with permission. This was followed by the Occupiers' Liability Act 1984, which set out the duty owed by occupiers towards those who enter their land without permission, known as trespassers. The modern duty of occupiers of land is now contained in these two pieces of legislation; both of them incorporated some concepts from the previous common law, which is why this chapter refers to some pre-1957 cases which remain good law.

The law before the Occupiers' Liability Acts

Before we look at the current law on occupiers' liability, it is useful to have a quick look at what the law was like before the first Occupiers' Liability Act was passed in 1957, because this will help explain what the Acts were designed to do. Before 1957, liability for harm caused by dangerous premises was covered by the ordinary law of negligence. However, case law had developed different levels of protection for different categories of people. Someone who entered the premises as part of a contract (such as a plumber coming to fix a pipe, or a guest at a hotel) was covered by a higher standard of care than someone who was invited in for business purposes (such as a customer browsing in a shop), while a third standard, lower still, covered anyone who was just a guest on the premises (such as a friend coming round for dinner). Someone who did not have permission to be on the premises had very little protection at all; if they were injured, the occupier could only be liable for deliberately or recklessly causing them harm, and not for negligence. Bear in mind that this category would not just include people who deliberately entered premises knowing they should not be there, but also someone who got lost, or a child who was too young to understand that they needed permission to enter, and you can see that there was potential for injustice in the law, as well as over-complexity and confusion, which gave rise to a huge amount of litigation.

The situation was widely criticised, and in 1954, a report by the Law Reform Committee recommended legislation to clarify the law. The result was the Occupiers' Liability Act 1957, which established one standard of care to cover all the different categories of people who enter premises with permission. This made the law much less complex and more consistent. However, it still left one problem unsolved, in that people who did not have permission to enter premises were not covered by the Act, and so had very little protection. Over the years, this was increasingly seen as unjust. There were, for example, a number of cases where children had strayed onto land without permission and been injured, as well as adults hurt in situations where, although they did not have permission to be there, they would not generally be seen as having done anything wrong, yet it was difficult for them to make a claim. In response to this problem, the Occupiers' Liability Act 1984 was passed, which establishes that occupiers do have a duty of care for the safety of people who enter the land without permission, although it is more limited than the duty they owe to people who do have permission to enter, under the 1957 Act.

Who is an occupier?

Neither of the Acts defines 'occupier'; they state that an occupier is a person who would be treated as such under common law. Under common law an occupier is the person who controls the premises. They do not have to be the physical occupier, nor the owner; the critical issue is whether they exercise a sufficient degree of control to allow or prevent other people entering. In each case, whether this level of control is exercised will be a question of fact.

In **Harris** *v* **Birkenhead Corporation** (1976) a compulsory purchase order had been served on a house by a local council, with a notice of entry which allowed the council to take over the premises 14 days later. After the residents had moved out, the council failed to board up the house. The claimant, a four-year-old child, got into the house through an unsecured door, and ended up falling from a second-floor window. The Court of Appeal held that the fact that the local authority had the legal right to control the premises made them the occupiers, and excluded the previous owners from any liability; the local authority was in the best position to prevent any accidents.

In some situations, there may be more than one occupier, in which case both or all can be liable in respect of the same damage. For example, if a landlord rents a whole building to one tenant, the tenant is the occupier, not the landlord. However, if the landlord retains possession of part of the building, such as a common staircase, or has a right to enter the premises to do repairs, both the tenant and the landlord will be occupiers at the same time.

In **Wheat** *v* **E Lacon & Co** (1966) the defendants owned a public house. It was run by a manager and his wife, who lived on the first floor, and were allowed to take in paying guests. A paying guest was killed when he fell on the emergency staircase, while trying to get to the bar on the first floor. The House of Lords held that both the manager and the owners were occupiers (but on the facts, neither was held to be in breach of duty – the bad lighting on the staircase was caused by a stranger removing the bulb, and they were not responsible for the stranger's actions).

Key Case **Revill** *v* **Newbery (1996)**

In **Revill** *v* **Newbery** (1996) it was made clear that the legislation does not apply to every situation where the defendant happens to be an occupier of the land in which the incident complained of occurred. The claimant and an accomplice had sneaked onto the defendant's land, intending to steal from his shed. The defendant, an elderly man, had taken to sleeping in his shed with a shotgun, as his property had frequently suffered the attentions of vandals and thieves. Hearing movement outside, he poked his gun through a little hole in the shed door, and fired, hitting the claimant in the arm. The Court of Appeal held that the situation was covered by the general law of negligence, and not statutory occupiers' liability, because the fact that he was the occupier of the land was not relevant to his liability – he was liable in just the same way as he would have been if he had been, for example, a friend of the occupier staying in the shed.

Legal Principle

Occupiers' liability only applies where the fact that the defendant is the occupier of the land is in some way relevant to their liability. Where the damage could equally have been done by someone who was not the occupier, the normal rules of negligence apply.

This seems to suggest that the Acts will only be applied to situations where harm is caused by dangerous conditions on land, or dangerous conduct which resembles a dangerous condition in that it is a continuing source of danger on the land. It seems not to be applicable where the harm arises from an isolated action of the occupier which could equally have been the action of someone who was not the occupier.

What must they occupy?

The Acts impose liability on 'occupiers of premises', and premises are defined in s. 1(3) of the 1957 Act as including land, buildings and 'any fixed or movable structure, including any vessel, vehicle or aircraft'.

Liability to visitors: Occupiers' Liability Act 1957

The central provision of the 1957 Act is s. 2(1), which provides that an occupier of premises owes a common duty of care to visitors to those premises.

Who is a visitor?

A visitor is someone who has express or implied permission from the occupier to enter the premises. Anyone who enters the property without such permission is a trespasser, whose rights are governed not by the Act of 1957 but by the Occupiers' Liability Act 1984 (discussed on p. 170).

Where permission to enter has been given but is then withdrawn while the entrant is still on the property, they are allowed a reasonable time in which to leave; once that expires, the person becomes a trespasser.

Implied permission

Permission can be implied from conduct or circumstances. Occupiers are treated as having given implied permission to people such as meter readers, people delivering goods, and even door-to-door salespeople, and all of these will be legally classed as visitors.

Legal rights of entry

The 1957 Act includes in the definition of a visitor anyone who enters premises under a right conferred by law (s. 2(6)) with or without the occupier's express permission. Examples would be police officers and firefighters carrying out their legal duties.

Rights of way

A person using a public right of way (walking down an ordinary street, for example) is not considered to be a visitor, and is therefore not owed a duty of care under the 1957 Act by the people over whose land the right of way passes. This rule was laid down in the old case of **Gautret** *v* **Egerton** (1867) and confirmed by the House of Lords in **McGeown** *v* **Northern Ireland Housing Executive** (1994). The appellant was walking along a public footpath which ran over the defendants' land. She tripped in a hole and was injured and sued the defendants. Her case was rejected. The House of Lords confirmed that people who used rights of way were neither visitors nor trespassers and were therefore owed no duty. Lord Keith justified this conclusion on the basis that:

> Rights of way pass over many different types of terrain, and it would place an impossible burden on landowners if they not only had to submit to the passage over them of anyone who might choose to exercise them but also were under a duty to maintain them in a safe condition. Persons using rights of way do so not with the permission of the owner . . . but in the exercise of a right.

This exception can be criticised, particularly in the light of the greater protection now afforded trespassers.

Walkers and ramblers

The Countryside and Rights of Way Act 2000 gives a general right to walk over open land which falls within the description of 'mountain, moor, heath or down'. This right has become known as 'the right to roam'. The 2000 Act provides that people exercising this right are not 'visitors' within the meaning of the 1957 Occupiers' Liability Act, but are covered by the 1984 Act, with some restrictions (see p. 172).

Requirements of the 1957 Act

Section 2(2) of the 1957 Act provides that 'occupiers have a duty towards visitors to take such care as in all the circumstances of the case is reasonable to see that the visitor will be reasonably safe in using the premises for the purposes for which he is invited or permitted to be there'. (This is known as the 'common duty of care'.) As with negligence, this will always be a balancing act: defendants are not required to provide absolute safety, only to take reasonable care. Note too that the Act does not require the occupier to take reasonable care to make the premises safe, but to make the visitor safe, and this could be done by, for example, giving reasonable warning of a danger.

In **Ward** *v* **The Ritz Hotel** (1992), the claimant was injured when he fell over a balcony in the defendants' hotel. The balcony had a rail around it, but evidence showed it was about six inches lower than the British Standards Institution (which sets safety standards) recommended that a rail in such a situation should be. These standards are not legally binding, but the Court of Appeal said that they showed there was a need for strict safety standards in this kind of area, and the fact that the hotel had not complied with them was strong evidence that they had not taken the reasonable care required by the Act. The hotel was found liable.

In **Horton** *v* **Jackson** (1996), the claimant was a golfer who had lost the sight in one eye after being hit by a ball. He successfully sued the golfer who had hit the ball, who then claimed that the accident was partly the fault of the golf club where they were playing. He argued that the club was in breach of its duty under the 1957 Act, because they should have erected a screen between two particular tees to prevent balls hit at one from hitting people playing at the other; there was a sign asking players at the second tee to wait until those at the first had moved on, but he argued that this rule was not enforced. The Court of Appeal disagreed: there was expert evidence that a screen would not have prevented the accident, and the fact that in 800,000 rounds of golf played at the club only two accidents had ever occurred in that spot entitled the judge to conclude that the existing precautions were reasonable and there was no breach of duty.

Darby *v* **National Trust** (2001) concerned a man who drowned while swimming in a pond at a National Trust property. His widow sued under the 1957 Act, claiming that as there had been no warnings about the danger of drowning, the National Trust had not taken reasonable care. The Court of Appeal disagreed: drowning was an obvious risk, even if a small one, so there was no need to warn against it.

In **Clare** *v* **Perry** (2005), the claimant and her partner had visited the defendant's hotel. The couple were leaving the premises at night and, instead of taking the designated exit, decided to go over the wall which ran round the edge of the property. Ms Clare's partner successfully climbed over the wall and down onto the road, but because it was dark Ms Clare did not realise that the section she was trying to climb over had a six-foot drop down to the road. She fell, and was seriously injured. She sued the hotel, claiming that it was reasonable to expect the area to be fenced off. At first instance, the judge agreed, stating that it was reasonable to expect a fence to be put up to prevent accidental falls from the wall, and taking that precaution would also have prevented an accident caused by deliberately climbing over the wall. However, the Court of Appeal rejected this reasoning. The risk of an accidental fall was different from the risk of someone deliberately climbing over the wall, and the fact that the occupier had a duty to take precautions against the first type of risk did not mean they also had a duty with regard to the second. In assessing whether precautions were reasonably required, the court could take account of the behaviour reasonably to be expected of a visitor, and, in this case, the claimant's behaviour was both unexpected and foolish. The defendant had not, therefore, fallen below the required standard in failing to take precautions to prevent her climbing the wall.

The Act gives specific guidance on particular issues concerning the statutory common duty of care.

Children

Section 2(3)(a) of the 1957 Act states: 'An occupier must be prepared for children to be less careful than adults. If the occupier allows a child to enter the premises then the premises must be reasonably safe for a child of that age.'

In **Perry** *v* **Butlins Holiday World** (1997), the claimant was a three-year-old who badly cut his ear when he fell onto a brick wall at the defendants' holiday camp. The wall was a low one built of very sharp bricks, and was near an open area where children's shows were regularly performed. The Court of Appeal held that the case was borderline, but the design of the wall, coupled with its position where children were obviously likely to be, meant that the defendants had breached their duty under the Act.

In the tragic case of **Jolley** *v* **London Borough of Sutton** (2000), the claimant was a 14-year-old boy. He and a friend had found an old boat abandoned on the council estate where they lived, and had decided to try to repair it. They had propped it up with a car jack, but this collapsed; the boat fell on the claimant, injuring him so badly that he was left paralysed. The council admitted that they should have moved the boat, because it was reasonably foreseeable that children would be attracted to it; however, they argued, what was foreseeable was that children would get into it to play, and possibly fall through the rotten floor. They claimed that what the claimant and his friend had done was an unusual use of the boat and so the accident he had was not foreseeable.

The Court of Appeal had agreed with that view, but the House of Lords held that this approach was too narrow. What was foreseeable was that children would meddle with the boat; it was not necessary for the council to be able to foresee exactly what they would do with it. The Lords made the point that children typically show considerable ingenuity in finding ways to put themselves in danger, and said that this needed to be taken into account when assessing the precautions needed to keep them safe. They also pointed out that the council had admitted that the risk of children playing in the boat was foreseeable, and that they should therefore have removed the boat; preventing the wider risk would have involved exactly the same action, and would therefore not have involved any more effort or expense.

In **Glasgow Corporation** *v* **Taylor** (1922), a seven-year-old child had died from eating poisonous berries that he had picked from a bush in a park, which was under the control of the corporation. The corporation knew the berries were poisonous, but had neither fenced off the shrub, nor put up any warning notice. They were held liable. It was accepted that the child had no right to take the berries and that an adult doing the same thing might well have been considered a trespasser. However, the berries, which looked like cherries, were obviously tempting to children, and the court held that that constituted an 'allurement' to the child. Simply by leaving the berries there the corporation had breached their duty of care to the child, though this would not have been the case if the victim had been an adult. This case was obviously decided well before either of the Occupiers' Liability Acts existed; were the same circumstances to arise today, it would probably be decided on the basis of the 1984 Act, although the result might well be the same given the allowances made for children in the legislation.

An occupier is entitled to assume that very young children will be accompanied by someone looking after them, and that may reduce the degree of care expected from the occupier. In **Phipps** *v* **Rochester Corporation** (1955) the claimant was a boy aged five, who was picking blackberries with his seven-year-old sister. They crossed some open land where the defendants were building houses. The land was commonly used by local children as a play area, and although the defendants knew this, they made no attempt to keep the children out. In the centre of the land, the defendants had dug a long, deep trench, and the claimant fell into this, breaking his leg. An adult would have seen the danger immediately. The defendants were held not liable, because they could presume that no sensible parent would allow such young children to enter the area in question alone, without at least checking first for danger themselves. Although the defendants' failure to try to keep children out meant that the claimant had implied permission to be on the land, giving rise to a duty of care, the defendants were not in breach of that duty.

The same approach was applied in the tragic case of **Bourne Leisure** *v* **Marsden** (2009), which involved the death of a two-year-old boy. The Marsden family were staying at a caravan park operated by Bourne Leisure, and, while Mrs Marsden was talking to another camper, her son Matthew wandered away without her noticing. After a frantic search, he was found drowned in a pond on the site. The Marsdens sued Bourne Leisure, claiming that the pond should have been fenced off to prevent danger to children, but the Court of Appeal disagreed. It found that the park owners did not have a duty to fence off the site because guests at the park were made aware of the existence of this and two other ponds, and it would have been clear to any parent that these ponds would have presented a danger to any small child who wandered off on their own. The Court of Appeal pointed out that this decision did not mean that the Marsdens, who were described as 'responsible, attentive and caring' parents, were at fault, because it was well known that children could 'disappear in an instant'. But the fact that they were not at fault in losing sight of Matthew did not mean that the park was liable for his death.

Persons exercising a calling

Section 2(3)(b) of the 1957 Act states: 'An occupier may expect that a person, in the exercise of his calling, will appreciate and guard against any special risks ordinarily incident to it, so far as the occupier leaves him free to do so.' The term 'exercising a calling' simply means the person is on the land for the purpose of their job. Section 2(3)(b) means that where a risk normally arises in the course of a person's work, the occupier need not take special precautions to protect that person against such a risk, so long as they allow the person to take their own precautions.

In **Roles** *v* **Nathan** (1963) two chimney sweeps were killed by carbon monoxide gas while working on the chimney of a coke-fired boiler, which was alight at the time. The occupiers were held not liable, because they could expect sweeps to be aware of this particular danger and these sweeps had in fact also been warned of the danger. As Lord Denning pointed out, the result would have been different if the sweeps had been killed because the stairs leading to the basement had given way; only a risk relevant to the trade in question can allow the occupier to escape liability.

This section does not mean that the occupier owes no duty to the skilled professional. In **Ogwo** *v* **Taylor** (1988) the defendant negligently set fire to his house. The claimant was a firefighter who was called to the house to put out the fire and he was injured while doing so. The blaze was such that no amount of care by the claimant could have protected him so the defendant could not rely on s. 2(3)(b) to avoid liability.

Independent contractors

Section 2(4)(b) of the 1957 Act provides that:

> Where damage is caused to a visitor by a danger due to the faulty execution of any work of construction, maintenance or repair by an independent contractor employed by the occupier, the occupier is not to be treated without more as answerable for the danger if in all the circumstances he had acted reasonably in entrusting the work to an independent contractor and had taken such steps (if any) as he reasonably ought in order to satisfy himself that the contractor was competent and that the work had been properly done.

This essentially means that occupiers employing independent contractors will be found liable when their independent contractor's activities fall below the common duty of care, unless they take reasonable steps to satisfy themselves that the contractor is competent; and, if the nature of the work allows, to make sure that the work has been properly done. What amounts to reasonable steps will depend on the nature of the work: in a large-scale, complex project such as the construction of a large building, it may involve employing an architect or other expert to supervise the work, whereas in a small job such as installing a central heating system in a house, the occupier is entitled to rely solely on the contractor.

In **Haseldine** *v* **Daw** (1941), the claimant was killed when a lift plunged to the bottom of its shaft. It was held that the building's occupiers were not liable for the death; they had fulfilled their duty of care by appointing an apparently competent firm to maintain the lift, and the highly technical nature of the work meant that they could not be expected to check whether it had been done properly.

In **Woodward** *v* **Mayor of Hastings** (1945), the claimant, a child, slipped at school on a step covered in snow. The step had been negligently cleaned, and, although there was some doubt as to whether the cleaner was an employee, the occupiers were held liable for failing to take reasonable steps to check that the work had been done properly, because the nature of the work was such that this could be easily checked.

Most cases involving independent contractors concern people who have negligently done maintenance, construction or repairs on the occupier's land, but the same principles can apply to anyone that the occupier allows onto the land to provide a service. In **Bottomley** *v* **Todmorden**

Cricket Club (2003), the cricket club held a firework display, during which Mr Bottomley, who was helping out as a volunteer, was injured. Evidence showed that the fireworks firm were not insured and did not have sufficient experience for the type of show they were putting on. Mr Bottomley sued the cricket club as occupiers of the land (as well as the firm which put on the display), but the club argued that they could not owe a duty to someone who was effectively an employee of the fireworks firm; the only duty owed to him was the firm's. The Court of Appeal disagreed; the club could be liable because they had not taken sufficient care to make sure that the contractors were capable of doing the work and had adequate insurance.

A contractor will often also be liable to the claimant, either by being regarded as an occupier, or under the general principles of negligence.

Contractual rights of entry

Under s. 5(1) of the 1957 Act, a person entering premises under a contractual right is in the same position as any other visitor, unless the contract expressly provides for a higher standard of care than the statutory common duty of care.

Defences under the 1957 Act

The two general defences of contributory negligence and *volenti* are available for actions concerning breach of the 1957 Act; in addition, occupiers can protect themselves from liability by the use of warnings and exclusion notices, subject to the rules explained below.

Contributory negligence

Section 2(3) of the 1957 Act specifies that in considering whether an occupier has breached the common duty of care, the courts may take into account the degree of care a reasonable visitor can be expected to show for their own safety.

Volenti

Section 2(5) of the 1957 Act states that 'The common duty of care does not impose on an occupier any obligation willingly accepted as his by the visitor', thus allowing for the application of *volenti*. However, a visitor will not be deemed to have accepted a risk merely because the occupier displays a notice to that effect (see below).

Warnings

Under s. 2(4)(a) of the 1957 Act, if an occupier gives a visitor sufficient warning of a danger to render a visitor reasonably safe, the occupier will not be liable for any damage suffered by the visitor as a result of that danger. Lord Denning gave an illustration of such a situation in **Roles** *v* **Nathan** (1963). If a house has a river in front of it, and the sole means of access to the house is by crossing a dangerous bridge, the occupier will not secure a defence by simply affixing a sign stating that the bridge is dangerous. The sign would not make visitors safe, since they would have to use the bridge anyway. If, however, there were two bridges and a notice on the dangerous one warned visitors to use the other, the occupier would bear no liability for injury caused to a visitor who was injured through ignoring the warning and using the dangerous bridge.

However, if a danger is very serious, or unusual, a warning may not be enough. In **Rae** *v* **Mars** (1990), the claimant was a surveyor visiting a factory, which was empty. Just inside the entrance was a deep pit, and he fell into it before he had a chance to switch on his torch and see it. There was disputed evidence about whether he had been warned about the pit, but the court found that, even if he had, the danger was such that a warning was not sufficient to keep a visitor safe, and the occupiers had a duty to go further and provide some sort of barrier around the pit. By contrast, if a danger is really obvious, there may be no need even for a warning sign. In **Staples** *v* **West Dorset District Council** (1995), the claimant slipped on algae-covered rocks at the seaside. He claimed there should have been a warning notice in place, but the court found that the danger was obvious and a visitor should have been aware of it.

Exclusion of the common duty of care

Section 2(1) of the 1957 Act states that 'An occupier of premises owes the same duty, the "common duty of care", to all his visitors, except in so far as he is free to and does extend, restrict, modify or exclude his duty to any visitor or visitors by agreement or otherwise.'

This means that an exclusion notice or clause may be used to impose a lesser duty of care, or even none at all. However, this provision is subject to the Unfair Contract Terms Act 1977 (UCTA). Section 2(1) of UCTA prevents an occupier from excluding liability for death or personal injury caused by negligence (defined as including the common duty of care). Where an occupier is acting in the course of a business, or from premises used for business purposes, liability for damage to property can only be excluded if it is reasonable to do so (1957 Act, s. 2(2)).

Section 3(1) of UCTA states that an occupier cannot use a contract to reduce their obligations to less than those required by the common duty of care, for visitors who are not parties to the contract.

These provisions of UCTA do not apply where visitors enter premises for recreational or educational purposes, unless that access is itself allowed for business purposes (Occupiers' Liability Act 1984, s. 2). So a church which allows the local badminton club to play in its hall may exclude all liability as an occupier, but a leisure centre doing the same could not.

Section 2(3) of the 1957 Act provides that a visitor will not be considered to have voluntarily accepted a risk just because the occupier has displayed a notice excluding liability for that risk, and the visitor is aware of that. There must be evidence of voluntary acceptance of the risk.

Damage under the 1957 Act

Section 1(3) of the 1957 Act provides that a claim can be made for personal injuries and damage to property, including subsequent financial loss that is not too remote, but not for pure economic loss.

Liability to trespassers: Occupiers' Liability Act 1984

The 1984 Act sets out the duties which occupiers have towards people who come onto their land without permission. It provides that there is a duty to take such care as is reasonable in the circumstances to see that they do not suffer injury on the premises 'by reason of any danger due to the state of the premises or to things done or omitted to be done on them'. The meaning of this phrase was examined in **Keown** *v* **Coventry Healthcare NHS Trust** (2006). The claimant had been 11 years old at the time of the accident which gave rise to the case. He was climbing on an external fire escape, attached to a building at one of the Trust's hospitals, when he fell, hitting his head and suffering brain damage. It was accepted by both sides that he was trespassing on the site. At first instance, the judge found that the Trust was liable, but reduced the damages by two-thirds for contributory negligence, but the Trust appealed, arguing that there was nothing about the state of the fire escape itself that made it dangerous; as a fire escape, there was nothing wrong with it at all. What had caused the risk was the claimant's decision to climb on it. Therefore, the danger was not caused by the state of the premises, or by something the occupiers had done or not done. The Court of Appeal upheld this reasoning and the claimant lost.

A similar approach was taken in **Siddorn** *v* **Patel** (2007), where the claimant was injured when she fell through a perspex skylight, while dancing on a flat garage roof at a party. She lived in a rented flat next door, and had got onto the roof through a window in her flat. Her landlords also owned the garage, and she claimed they were in breach of their duty under the 1984 Act, for not making sure the skylight was safe, failing to warn her about the unsafe condition of the roof, and failing to warn her not to go out onto the garage roof. The judge rejected her claim, stating that the Act only applied to dangers 'due to the state of the premises', and in this case the state of the premises was not in itself dangerous. The cover of the skylight was not unsuitable or unsafe for its usual purpose; what had caused the danger was the claimant choosing to go and dance on the roof. She was an educated and sensible person, and the landlords had no reason to suspect she would go onto the roof; they were not liable for the fact that she had undertaken a dangerous activity which happened to take place on their premises.

When will the duty exist?

The duty to trespassers only exists if the following conditions, stated in s. 1(3), are met:

(a) [the occupier] is aware of the danger or has reasonable grounds to believe that it exists;
(b) he knows or has reasonable grounds to believe that the other [i.e. the trespasser] is in the vicinity of the danger concerned or that he may come into the vicinity of the danger . . . ; and
(c) the risk is one which in all the circumstances of the case, [the occupier] may reasonably be expected to offer the other some protection from.

Where a defendant actually knows of a risk, or actually knows that trespassers are or may come within the vicinity of it, there is little problem; what tends to arise in the cases are the issues of what will amount to 'reasonable grounds to believe' that a risk exists and 'reasonable grounds to believe' that a trespasser will or may be in the vicinity.

In **Swain** *v* **Natui Ram Puri** (1996), the claimant was a nine-year-old boy who was injured when he fell from the defendant's factory roof, where he was trespassing. His case was that there was reason to believe that children would climb the roof, and the defendants were therefore in breach of their duty because they had not made sufficient efforts to keep children away. The Court of Appeal disagreed; there was no evidence of previous trespass, and while the factory fences were not completely intruder-proof, they were substantial, so there were no reasonable grounds to suspect that trespassers might enter and try to scale the roof. The court held that the phrase 'reasonable grounds to believe' in s. 1(3) meant that it was necessary to show that the defendants had actual knowledge of relevant facts which provided grounds for such a belief; it did not mean 'ought to have known'.

In **Higgs** *v* **Foster** (2004), the claimant, a police officer, went into the defendants' yard, looking for a stolen trailer. He fell into an uncovered inspection pit and was injured. For reasons of law which are not important here, the police officer was judged to be a trespasser, so his claim was covered by the 1984 Act. The judge found that although the defendants knew that the pit was a potential danger to trespassers, it could not be said that they had reasonable grounds to suspect that a trespasser might come within the vicinity of the danger. The only reason they had to suspect that someone might enter the yard was that the yard was only partially fenced in, and, even then, they had no reason to think that someone who got in would go into the area around the pit at the back of the yard, since there was nothing to draw anyone to that area.

An example of a case where this requirement was satisfied is **Scott** *v* **Associated British Ports** (2000). The defendants owned land on which there was a railway line. In separate accidents, four years apart, two boys had lost limbs when they had played on the land and attempted to get onto moving trains. The court held that the defendants owed no duty under the 1984 Act for the first accident because they had been unaware of the risk. However, their knowledge of the first accident, along with newspaper coverage and complaints made to them later, meant that they did owe a duty under the Act with regard to the second accident (they were, however, not liable because the court found that fencing off the area would not have prevented the boys getting in, and therefore causation was not proved).

Who is a trespasser?

A trespasser is someone who goes onto land without any kind of permission, and whose presence there is either not known to the occupier, or, if known, is objected to. This means that trespassers can include not only burglars and squatters, but also anyone who, for example, innocently wanders onto land because the boundaries are not marked, or because they are lost.

Case Navigator

It is possible to become a trespasser in specific parts of a building or land, even though you are legally a visitor to the place as a whole. In **Tomlinson** *v* **Congleton Borough Council** (2003), Mr Tomlinson visited a lake in a public park on which yachting and other activities were permitted. Swimming, however, was forbidden, and the defendant council, which owned the park, had put up notices saying 'Dangerous water; no swimming'. Mr Tomlinson swam anyway, and injured himself by diving in too shallow a part of the water. The House of Lords held that his claim should be judged under the 1984 Act because, although he was a visitor to the park, he became a trespasser when he ignored the signs and got into the water.

The Countryside and Rights of Way Act 2000 states that people exercising the 'right to roam' are also to be covered by the 1984 Act, although they are owed a more limited duty than other 'trespassers'. The Act provides that an occupier cannot be liable to people exercising the right to roam for injuries caused by natural features of the landscape, or while crossing fences or walls except by means of gates or stiles, unless the occupier has intentionally or recklessly created a danger. When assessing cases involving injuries caused while exercising the right to roam, the courts should not allow the right to put an undue burden on occupiers, and should take into account the importance of maintaining the character of the countryside.

The duty of care

In practice, the appropriate precautions for avoiding injury to trespassers are often obvious, and the presence of trespassers not significantly less foreseeable than that of lawful visitors, so that there is little effective difference between when a duty is owed to lawful visitors under the

1957 Act and when it is owed to trespassers under the 1984 Act (but see the section on 'Damage' below).

According to the Lord Chancellor of the time, the standard of the duty of care imposed by the 1984 Act was intended to be pitched at a similar level to that which had previously existed under the old common law in **British Railways Board** *v* **Herrington** (1972), so while the old common law has been specifically abolished by the 1984 Act it can still be of assistance in understanding the duty imposed under the Act. The case involved a six-year-old claimant who passed through a gap in a fence and was electrocuted on the defendants' railway line. The fence had been in need of repair for some time but the stationmaster had done nothing about it, despite the fact that he was aware both that it needed repair and that children had the habit of passing through it. The House of Lords found on these facts that the defendants were in breach of the duty they owed to a trespasser, known as the duty of 'common humanity'. This duty was less demanding than that owed to a legitimate visitor.

The Act was applied in **White** *v* **St Albans City** (1990). The claimant was taking a short cut across the council's land to a car park, when he fell down a 12-foot trench and injured himself. The land was clearly private, and surrounded by a fence, and there was no evidence that the council were aware of it being used as a short cut to the car park. The Court of Appeal concluded that this made the claimant a trespasser. According to the provisions of the 1984 Act, the council had taken reasonable care in the circumstances and so were not liable for his injury. The common duty of humanity was less onerous than the usual duty of care owed to visitors as opposed to trespassers.

Key Case **Tomlinson** *v* **Congleton Borough Council (2003)**

A key House of Lords case on just how much responsibility occupiers have for adult trespassers is **Tomlinson** *v* **Congleton Borough Council** (2003). As explained earlier (on p. 172), Mr Tomlinson injured himself while swimming in a boating lake, after ignoring notices prohibiting swimming because the lake was dangerous. The court heard that it was common for people to swim in the lake despite the signs. The defendant council were very conscious of this and, as well as putting up the signs, they had recently begun work to cover the areas around the lake with plants, to make it more difficult to get into the water.

The Court of Appeal found in favour of Mr Tomlinson, stating that the seriousness of the risk the lake posed meant that the council should in fact have made the beaches completely unusable, by turning them into marshland, so that no one could get into the water. The House of Lords, however, rejected this approach. They said that in order to be liable under the 1984 Act, there had to have been a danger on the council's premises that was 'due to the state of the premises or to things done or omitted to be done on them'. In this case, however, the danger arose not because the lake was in a dangerous condition – it was no more dangerous than any other lake – but because the claimant had made a misjudgement in diving into the water. The risk was obvious to any adult, and he was free to make his own decision about whether to take it.

Furthermore, even if the council had owed him a duty to discourage him from swimming in the lake, they had fulfilled that duty in putting up clear warning signs. It was not reasonable to expect them to turn the beaches into marshland, which would not only cost money, but would disadvantage the thousands of people who enjoyed using the beaches safely.

Legal Principle

A defendant will only be liable under the 1984 Act for damages caused by dangers 'due to the state of the premises or things done or omitted to be done on them', and not for injuries caused as a result of adults voluntarily taking an obvious risk.

The issue of what it is reasonable to expect occupiers to do to protect people under the 1984 Act was also addressed in another swimming case, **Donoghue** *v* **Folkestone Properties Ltd** (2003). Here the defendant owned a harbour, and the claimant, a professional diver, was seriously injured when he jumped into the water and hit a 'grid pile', which was used for mooring boats, and would have been visible at low tide. The accident happened during the middle of winter, and though there were a few signs forbidding swimming in the harbour, none was near the place where the claimant jumped in. He argued that the harbour owner owed him a duty to protect him from being injured by the grid pile, and had failed in this duty by not putting up enough notices. The Court of Appeal disagreed and said that, under the 1984 Act, it had to be shown that the defendant knew or ought to have known that someone would come into the vicinity of the danger. Given that it was the middle of winter, the defendant had no reason to think that anyone would jump into the harbour.

As with the duty under the 1957 Act, allowances are made for children. In **Keown** *v* **Coventry Healthcare NHS Trust** (see above), the Court of Appeal confirmed that a place considered reasonably safe for adults might still be dangerous for a child. However, they pointed out that where a child decided to take a risk, that decision could not be ignored simply because the claimant was a child; the key issue was whether the child realised the risk. In **Keown**, it was admitted that the boy knew that there was a risk of falling from the fire escape, and knew he should not climb on it, so it could not be said that he did not recognise the danger.

Defences under the 1984 Act

The general defences of contributory negligence and *volenti* are available for actions under the 1984 Act, and occupiers may also protect themselves from liability by using warnings and (probably) exclusion notices.

Contributory negligence

The case of **Revill** *v* **Newbery** (1996) (discussed on p. 163) suggests that contributory negligence is also a defence to actions against trespassers. In that case, the claimant's damages were reduced by two-thirds because of the claimant's contributory negligence in coming onto someone's land in the middle of the night and acting in a manner that was likely to make the occupier suspect wrongdoing. (You may recall that in **Revill** the Court of Appeal decided the case on the basis of general negligence, rather than statutory occupiers' liability; however, they used the 1984 Act to determine the scope of the duty owed, and so their findings on defences are likely to be relevant to cases of true occupiers' liability.)

Volenti

Section 1(6) of the 1984 Act provides that 'No duty is owed by virtue of this section to any person in respect of risks willingly accepted as his by that person (the question of whether a risk was so accepted to be decided on the same principles as in other cases in which one person owes a duty of care to another).'

In **Titchener** *v* **British Railways Board** (1983), it was stated that adult claimants are regarded as accepting any risk which they knew about when entering the land. Should this principle apply to the 1984 Act, the defence of *volenti* provides greater protection for occupiers with regard to trespassers than it does with regard to visitors, where the defence only applies if the visitor knows enough to be reasonably safe.

Warnings

Section 1(5) of the 1984 Act provides that an occupier of premises discharges their duty to a trespasser 'by taking such steps as are reasonable in all the circumstances of the case to give warning of the danger concerned or to discourage persons from incurring the risk'. As a general rule, the existence of a warning sign is not enough; it must be sufficiently clear to ensure that the risk is obvious.

Exclusion

The 1984 Act does not state whether the duty under it can be excluded by the occupier. It is sometimes suggested that this implies exclusion is possible, since it is not forbidden nor made subject to any special rules under the Act. If exclusion is possible, then such exclusions would not be subject to the Unfair Contract Terms Act 1977, which is stated to apply only to the old common law and the 1957 Act; the result would be that occupiers would have a wide opportunity to exclude their liability, thus weakening the Act considerably.

An alternative view is that the duty imposed by the 1984 Act cannot be excluded, because it was designed to uphold the old common law 'duty of common humanity', which was unexcludable because it was a minimum standard below which the law would not allow occupiers to fall, no matter how unwelcome the visitor. Unfortunately there is no authority on the point; should it come up in an exam problem question, you will need to explain this, and examine what the implications in the situation described would be if the duty is excludable, and then what they would be if it is not.

Damage under the 1984 Act

One major difference between the 1957 and 1984 Acts is that the latter only allows claims for death or personal injury; unlike visitors, trespassers cannot claim for damage to property. Take, for example, a situation where A has gone out for a drive in the country in her brand-new car. She becomes lost and accidentally ends up on B's land, where there is a dangerous bridge. She drives across the bridge, which collapses, depositing her and the car in the river. She may be able to claim for her own injuries, but not for the damage to her car.

Table 5.1 The Occupiers' Liability Acts 1957 and 1984 at a glance

	The Occupiers' Liability Act 1957	The Occupiers' Liability Act 1984
What type of claimant is covered?	Visitors – people who have permission to enter	Non-visitors/trespassers – people who do not have permission to enter
What type of damage is covered?	Personal injury and damage to property	Only personal injury
What is the duty?	The occupier must take 'such care that the visitor is reasonably safe'	The occupier must take 'such care as is reasonable in all the circumstances of the case'
When does the duty apply?	It applies automatically to anyone who is a visitor.	It only applies if the occupier • knew or had reasonable grounds to suspect the danger existed; and • knew or had reasonable grounds to suspect a non-visitor was near or might go near the danger; and • the risk was one that it was reasonable to expect them to provide protection from
Can the duty be satisfied by using warnings?	Yes, if the warning enables the visitor to be 'reasonably safe'.	Yes, if reasonable steps are taken to warn the non-visitor of the danger (so no need for warning to make non-visitor 'reasonably safe')
What defences apply?	Contributory negligence and *volenti*	*Volenti*
Can the duty be restricted or excluded?	Yes, but subject to the provisions of the Unfair Contract Terms Act 1977	Not clear from the words of the legislation

Answering questions

Chez Col is an exclusive hairdressing salon. It is owned by Chez Col Ltd and managed by Roland. Near the entrance there is a notice which says that no responsibility can be taken for any injury, loss or damage suffered on the premises.

Mary is a regular customer. She visits the salon with her daughter Jemima who is nine years old. The floor has not been properly cleaned and Mary steps on a small pool of shampoo. She slips and falls. She breaks her ankle, and the heel of one of her expensive designer shoes snaps off.

In the excitement, nobody notices that Jemima has wandered off. At the rear of the salon, there is a door marked 'Private'. She pushes the door open and falls down a flight of steps leading to the salon's store room. She is injured, and the watch she got for her birthday is smashed.

Advise Chez Col Ltd and Roland as to their liability to Mary and Jemima under the Occupiers' Liability Acts 1957 and 1984 and as to whether they can successfully exclude liability.

The first thing to consider here is who may be liable under either of the Acts: is the occupier Chez Col, Roland, or both? The issue is which of them has sufficient control over the salon, and you should consider the case of **Wheat** *v* **Lacon**. Regarding Mary, as a regular customer she clearly has permission to be on the premises, and so the relevant Act is the 1957 Act. You should explain that the test will therefore be the one in s. 2(2) of the Act (see p. 164). If the occupier is liable, the Act allows claims for both personal injury and damage to property, so cover both Mary's injury and the damage to her shoes. You then need to look at whether the sign outside allows the occupier to exclude liability, and here the Unfair Contract Terms Act is relevant (see p. 170). Remember that there may be a difference between excluding liability for personal injury and that for property damage.

With Jemima, you need to consider whether she is a visitor or a trespasser. She would appear to have implied permission to be in the salon with her mother, but she doesn't have permission to go through the door marked 'Private', and this is likely to make her a trespasser, following the reasoning in **Tomlinson**. Therefore her accident is covered by the 1984 Act, so you should explain the test imposed by this Act, and then apply it to Jemima's situation. Was the occupier aware of the danger? Did the occupier have reasonable grounds to expect that Jemima might come into the vicinity of that danger? Could they reasonably have been expected to offer protection from the harm and, if so, did they take such care as was reasonable? Consider also the fact that allowances are made for children, referring to the case of **Keown**. You should point out that it is not clear whether the duty under the 1984 Act can be excluded, and explain the two views on this point. Remember to point out that if the occupier is in breach of the 1984 Act, there will only be a claim for the injury to Jemima, and not her watch (see above).

Summary of Chapter 5

Occupiers of land owe a duty to people who come onto the land, under two Acts:

- the Occupiers' Liability Act 1957 covers their duty to visitors;
- the Occupiers' Liability Act 1984 covers their duty to trespassers.

An occupier is the person who controls the land or premises, and need not be the owner. The key question is whether a person exercises a sufficient degree of control to allow or prevent others entering.

The Acts apply to land, buildings and any fixed or movable structure.

Liability to visitors

A visitor is someone with express or implied permission to enter. People using rights of way or the right to roam under the Countryside and Rights of Way Act 2000 are not visitors.

The 1957 Act:

- imposes a duty to 'take such care as in all the circumstances of the case is reasonable to see that the visitor will be reasonably safe';
- requires occupiers to be prepared for children to be less careful than adults;

- entitles occupiers to expect that people entering for work purposes will be aware of any risks that normally arise from their work;
- provides that occupiers are not liable for risks caused by independent contractors, if it was reasonable to entrust the work to them, and reasonable steps were taken to check their competence and the work done;
- provides that people entering under a contractual right are in the same position as others, unless the contract provides for a higher standard than the statutory duty.

Defences under the 1957 Act:

- Contributory negligence
- *Volenti*
- Use of warnings
- Exclusion of the duty of care (subject to the Unfair Contract Terms Act 1977).

Damages can be claimed for personal injury or damage to property, but not economic loss.

Liability to trespassers

The 1984 Act imposes a duty to take such care as is reasonable in the circumstances to see that trespassers do not suffer injury on the premises 'by reason of any danger due to the state of the premises or to things done or omitted to be done on them'. In practice this is very similar to the duty owed to visitors.

However, the duty only applies where:

- the occupier knows about or has reason to believe a danger exists;
- the occupier knows or has reason to believe that the trespasser is or may come within the vicinity of the danger; and
- the risk is one which the occupier can reasonably be expected to offer protection from, considering all the circumstances.

A trespasser is anyone who goes onto land without permission, where the occupier objects to, or does not know of, their presence there.

Defences under the 1984 Act:

- Contributory negligence
- *Volenti*
- Use of warnings.

It is unclear whether the duty can be excluded.

Damages can only be claimed for personal injury, not damage to property.

Reading list

Text resources

Bragg, R J and Brazier, M R (1986) 'Occupiers and exclusion of liability' 130 *Solicitors Journal* 251

Hopkins, C (2002) 'Occupiers' liability: unheeded warnings' 61 *Cambridge Law Journal* 499

Jones, M A (1984) 'The Occupiers' Liability Act – the wheels of law reform turn slowly' 47 *Modern Law Review* 713

Law Commission (1976) *Liability for Damage or Injury to Trespassers and Related Questions of Occupiers' Liability*, No 75, Cmnd 6428

McMahon, B M E (1975) 'Conclusions on judicial behaviour from a comparative study of occupiers' liability' 38 *Modern Law Review* 39

Mesher, J (1979) 'Occupiers, trespassers and the Unfair Contract Terms Act 1977' *Conveyancer* 58.

Reading on the Internet

The House of Lords judgment in **Tomlinson** *v* **Congleton** (2003) can be read at:
http://www.publications.parliament.uk/pa/ld200203/ldjudgmt/jd030731/tomlin-1.htm

The Court of Appeal judgment in **Donoghue** *v* **Folkestone Properties** (2003) can be read at:
http://www.bailii.org/cgi-bin/markup.cgi?doc=/ew/cases/EWCA/Civ/2003/231.html&query=Donoghue&method=all

The Court of Appeal judgment in **Clare** *v* **Perry** (2005) can be read at:
http://alpha.bailii.org/ew/cases/EWCA/Civ/2005/39.html

The Court of Appeal judgment in **Keown** *v* **Conventry** (2006) can be read at:
http://www.bailii.org/ew/cases/EWCA/Civ/2006/39.html

Visit **www.mylawchamber.co.uk** to access tools to help you develop and test your knowledge of tort law, including interactive multiple choice questions, practice exam questions with guidance, weblinks, glossary flashcards, legal newsfeed and legal updates.

Use Case Navigator to read in full some of the key cases referenced in this chapter with commentary and questions:

Tomlinson *v* **Congleton Borough Council** (2003)

Chapter 6
Product liability

This chapter discusses:

- Liability for defective products under contract law
- Liability for defective products in negligence
- Liability under the Consumer Protection Act 1987.

During the summer of 2006, thousands of buyers of leather sofas found themselves getting a little extra with their furniture that they neither expected nor wished for. Imported from China, the sofas were treated with an anti-mould chemical which caused serious skin and breathing problems. While the effects were unpleasant and painful, the victims did have one thing in their favour: thanks to the Consumer Protection Act 1987, it was relatively straightforward for them to claim compensation for their injuries, and between them, they won over £17 million in damages. In this chapter, we will look at how the Act works, and also at the two other ways to claim for problems caused by products: contract and negligence.

Product liability in contract

In Chapter 2, you will have read the story of the unfortunate Mrs Donoghue, whose encounter with a decomposing snail not only spoilt what she thought was going to be a quiet drink with a friend, but also went on to form the basis of the case which is credited with giving birth to the modern law of negligence, **Donoghue** *v* **Stevenson** (1932).

Before Mrs Donoghue's snail popped out of her ginger beer bottle and started a legal revolution, the only real remedy for users of defective goods was the law of contract. This provided that someone who bought a product that was defective could sue the person they bought it from for breach of contract. The protection that this offered was increased by a line of statutes, beginning with the Sale of Goods Act 1893, which stated that certain terms regarding the quality of the goods sold should be implied into sales contracts, even though the parties themselves had not specifically mentioned them, and therefore giving the buyer a remedy if the goods were not up to the standard implied by the Act. Since 1893, the Sale of Goods Act has been regularly updated and extended by further statutes (see below).

Today, contract law is still a very important source of claims for defective products, and has both advantages and disadvantages over other types of claim, in terms of who can sue and be sued, what type of damage can be the subject of a claim, and what must be proved.

Who can sue?

Until 1999, with very few exceptions, only the person who actually bought the defective product could bring an action for breach of contract. This rule is known as the doctrine of privity, and meant that there was no contract claim available, for example, to anyone who received a defective product as a gift, or who used something belonging to another member of the family or an employer. This is why Mrs Donoghue could not have brought a claim in contract, as it was not her but a friend who had bought the drink.

The Contracts (Rights of Third Parties) Act 1999 changed this position. It states that a third party can enforce a contractual term where the contract either expressly states that that term (or the whole contract) should give rights to a third party, or where the particular term purports to confer a benefit on the third party. For example, a shopper buying a gift for someone else can write on the receipt that the recipient should have rights under the contract of sale, and get the retailer to sign it. If the product then turns out to be defective, the recipient can sue in their own right. Where a contract does not state whether it should give rights to third parties, a court will look at whether there is other evidence that suggests the relevant term purports to confer a benefit on a third party. However, liability in contract does not extend to anyone other than the buyer or someone who has the benefit of the contract under the Contracts (Rights of Third Parties) Act. This means it would not offer a claim to, for example, a bystander who was injured by a dangerous product which exploded or fell on them.

Who can be sued?

The other side of the privity rule is that only the person (or company) who actually sold the product can be sued, and this part of the rule remains. If the seller cannot be traced, is bankrupt or otherwise unable to pay damages, the consumer has no claim in contract against anyone else involved in the product's supply.

This rule can also cause hardship to the seller, since it applies even if it was not the seller but the manufacturer who caused the defect. To make a manufacturer responsible for a defective product in contract, the consumer must sue the seller, who in turn sues their supplier, and so on back up the chain to the manufacturer. If at any point the next person in line turns out to be bankrupt, to have disappeared or to be insufficiently well-off or insured to be worth suing, there is no way for the last party sued to leap-frog over them to their supplier, and so the chain breaks and the loss lies with the last party sued.

Types of product covered

A breach of contract action can be brought regarding the sale of any type of product or commodity.

Defects and damage

There are two ways in which a product can be considered defective: first, it may simply fail to perform as expected, or to be of adequate quality; secondly, it may be dangerous, which includes having the potential to damage other property as well as to injure people. Either (or both) of these types of defect can give rise to a claim for breach of contract.

Of the three main types of product liability claim, contract is the least restrictive in terms of the type of damage that can be compensated: damages for breach of contract can cover personal injury, damage to property, pure economic loss and even, in limited cases, anxiety, distress and loss of recreational enjoyment.

What must be proved?

A claimant claiming breach of contract does not need to prove that the product was defective because of something that the seller did or failed to do; in other words, there is no need to prove fault. What has to be proved is that there was a term in the contract which stated that the product would be of a certain quality, and that the defect concerned means that this term has not been fulfilled. The term may be something agreed specifically between buyer and seller, but more commonly, in consumer disputes, it will be one of the terms implied into contracts by the Sale of Goods Act 1979. The main terms implied by the Act are that goods sold are 'of satisfactory quality' and reasonably fit for their purpose.

Defences

There are a number of defences available to a breach of contract action; these are outside the scope of this book as they are usually taught on a contract law course.

Evaluating product liability in contract

In many ways, contract offers a very effective method of compensation for defective products. It covers all kinds of defects, not just those which make a product dangerous, and a claimant need only prove that a term of the contract has been breached; there is no need to prove fault, which, as we shall see when we look at negligence claims for product liability, can be a huge hurdle, especially for an individual claimant suing a big manufacturer.

In the past, the major drawback to contract as a cause of action for product liability claims was the privity rule, because it severely limited the class of people who could sue in contract. The Contracts (Rights of Third Parties) Act was designed to address this problem.

Product liability in negligence

As we have seen, **Donoghue** *v* **Stevenson** established for the first time that the producers of defective products can owe a duty to the end consumer of that product. Over the 70 years since it was decided, the tort of negligence has played an extremely significant role in consumer protection, and remains important even since the passing of consumer protection legislation.

Who can sue?

Anyone injured or caused loss by a defective product can bring an action in negligence (although there are restrictions on the type of damage covered; see Chapter 2). Unlike contract, this allows a remedy for people given a defective product and for users of something belonging to someone else. It also applies to someone who, while not actually using the product, is injured as a result of the defect in it. Two examples of this are **Brown** *v* **Cotterill** (1934), where a tombstone fell on a child, and **Stennett** *v* **Hancock** (1939), where a pedestrian was hit by part of a defective wheel on a passing lorry.

Who can be sued?

In **Donoghue**, Lord Atkin spoke of a duty owed by manufacturers to the end consumers of their products. This duty was very quickly widened; in less than 10 years after **Donoghue**, it had come to include repairers (**Stennett** *v* **Hancock**, above); erectors (**Brown** *v* **Cotterill**, above); assemblers (**Howard** *v* **Furness, Houlder Ltd** (1936)); and distributors (**Watson** *v* **Buckley, Osborne, Garrett & Co** (1940)).

It now seems that anyone involved in the supply chain of a defective product can potentially be sued in negligence, including sellers. In **Andrews** *v* **Hopkinson** (1957), the defendant, a second-hand car dealer, sold an 18-year-old car to the claimant without checking whether it was in a roadworthy condition. In fact the car had a dangerous steering defect; a week after buying it, the steering failed and the claimant was injured. Expert evidence suggested that the steering mechanism is a well-known danger spot in very old cars, and that the defect could quite easily have been discovered by a competent mechanic. The court held that, given the serious risk involved, the supplier owed a duty to have the car examined, or at least to have warned the buyer if no examination had been made.

Whether a seller will be found negligent will, however, depend on the circumstances of the case; as always in negligence, the standard is what the reasonable person could be expected to do. In **Andrews**, it was emphasised that the defect posed a very great danger, and also that it would have been very easy to discover it.

Types of product covered

Donoghue could have been read as applying a duty only to manufacturers of food and drink, but the courts soon extended it beyond this to any type of product; decided cases have covered products ranging from underpants to tombstones, and also packaging (**Barnes** *v* **Irwell Valley Water Board** (1938)), and labels or instructions for use (**Watson** *v* **Buckley** (1940)).

Defects and damage

A product liability action in negligence can only be brought in respect of products which are dangerous; defects which make a product work less well, or products which are simply low quality, are not covered. As you will remember from the first chapter, an action for negligence requires proof of damage, so the product must not only be dangerous, but must actually have caused some harm as a result; a claimant cannot bring a negligence claim on the basis that a product could cause harm, if that harm has not actually happened. This was confirmed in **D & F Estates** *v* **Church Commissioners** (1998).

In terms of the type of damage which a negligence claim will compensate, it is clear that both personal injury and damage to other property is covered. However, damage to the defective product itself is classified as pure economic loss, and is not recoverable in negligence. This means that if, for example, a defective television blows up and causes a fire in the claimant's living room, they can sue in tort for the value of all the property damaged by the fire, but not for the cost of the television itself.

Components and packaging

Difficulties arise where the defect is in a component part of a bigger product – the tyres of a car, for example, or the heating system of a house. Where the defective component is a replacement for an earlier component (such as a new tyre on a car when an old one has worn out), any damage which it causes to the bigger product (the car) can be compensated. Take, for example, a claimant who buys a car and, three years later, has new tyres fitted. If the tyres prove to be defective and cause an accident which damages the car, the claimant can claim for the damage to the car (although not the tyres themselves). The same is likely to apply if the tyres are the original ones fitted by the manufacturer, but supplied by another firm.

At the other end of the spectrum, where a component is made and assembled by the same firm as that which makes the rest of the car, the component will probably not be treated as a separate product – so, for example, a claimant who buys a Ford car, with an engine made and fitted by Ford, will not be able to claim for damage to either the car or the engine if that engine proves defective (although they would be able to claim for any damage caused to other property, such as nearby property burnt if the car caught fire, and of course for personal injury). As you can imagine, between these two situations lie a mass of grey areas, given that complex products can contain components from many different manufacturers. For example, if one company produces a car with an engine component manufactured by another firm, and a defect in that component leads to a fire that destroys the car, can the claimant claim for damage to the engine, to the rest of the car, or to neither?

Similar issues arise when a defect in packaging causes damage to the contents of that packaging. In **M/S Aswan Engineering Establishment Co** *v* **Lupdine Ltd** (1987), the claimants, a building company, bought some waterproofing compound, called Lupguard, from the first defendants. The Lupguard was packed in strong plastic buckets, which were made by the second defendants. The claimants had ordered the Lupguard for use on a project in Kuwait, and, when the consignment arrived there by ship and was unloaded and stacked on the quayside, the extremely high temperatures there melted the plastic buckets and the Lupguard spilled away. The action in tort failed because the damage was held not to be reasonably foreseeable, but the court also discussed the issue of whether, if there had been liability, the Lupguard should be considered a separate product from the buckets; if it could, the loss of it would be considered damage to property; if it could not, the damage would be pure economic loss and so not recoverable in tort. The majority held that it was 'other property' and therefore a recoverable loss.

What must be proved?

Product liability cases in tort are subject to the ordinary rules of negligence. As you will remember from Chapters 2 and 3, negligence requires proof of fault, and of causation; the claimant must prove that the defendant's failure to take reasonable care caused the defect that made the product dangerous. We also saw in Chapter 2 that in deciding whether a defendant has taken reasonable care, the court will seek to balance a variety of factors, including the seriousness of the danger, and how practical it would have been for the defendant to prevent it. As the leading tort academics Winfield and Jolowicz put it, 'the law expects a great deal more care in the handling of a pound of dynamite than a pound of butter' (*Winfield and Jolowicz on Tort*, 16th edn by W V H Rogers, Sweet & Maxwell 2002, p. 342).

Although a claimant must prove that the defect was due to the defendant's lack of reasonable care, they need not show exactly what it was that the defendant did wrong. In **Mason** *v* **Williams & Williams Ltd** (1955), the claimant was injured through using a chisel that was too hard for its purpose. He could not point to anything that was done wrong in its manufacture, but he could prove that nothing had happened to it since it left the defendant's factory that could have caused the excessive hardness. The court held that this was enough to establish that the defendant had been negligent.

Key Case **Carroll** *v* **Fearon (1998)**

This approach was challenged in **Carroll** *v* **Fearon** (1998), but the courts stood firmly behind it. The case concerned a car crash in which a little girl was killed, a woman blinded and six other people seriously injured. The crash was caused by faulty tyres, made by Dunlop, and there was overwhelming evidence that the manufacturing process had been defective (in fact it was stated that the company had already known that there was a problem with the tyres, but had decided to conceal the risk rather than alert the public and recall the tyres).

The trial judge found that Dunlop had been negligent, and Dunlop appealed, on the ground that the judge had not been able to identify any particular negligent act or omission by anyone involved in their manufacturing process. The Court of Appeal held that it was not necessary to do so: it had been established overwhelmingly that the tyres were defective because of a fault in the manufacturing process, and, since the manufacturer could not explain how the defects could have been caused without negligence, it was open to the judge to conclude that, on the facts, there was negligence.

Legal Principle

Where it is established that damage has been caused by a defect in the manufacturing process of goods, it is not necessary to show exactly what was wrong with the process.

In some cases this approach can look very like strict liability. In the famous case of **Grant** *v* **Australian Knitting Mills** (1936), the claimant suffered a painful skin condition after wearing some new underpants. Tests showed that the fabric of the pants contained high residues of a chemical which was used in the manufacturing process, and that this had caused the problem. The claimant could not point to a specific defect in the manufacturing process, and the manufacturers argued that they had taken reasonable care to prevent the risk, by putting in place a quality control system which complied with industry standards. However, the court held that this was not only insufficient to prove reasonable care had been taken, but in fact could be taken as evidence of negligence – in that if there was such a system in place, the problem could only have arisen if one of the company's employees had been careless and prevented the quality control system from operating properly. The manufacturers were vicariously liable for the acts of their employees, and therefore the claimant won his case.

One factor that will make a difference is whether there is sufficient evidence that the defect existed when the product left the defendant's hands. In **Evans** *v* **Triplex Safety Glass Co Ltd** (1936), the claimant bought a car with a windscreen made of what was described as 'toughened safety glass', manufactured by Triplex. A year later, he was driving along in the car when the windscreen suddenly shattered, for no apparent reason, injuring the claimant and his wife and son. He sued Triplex, but the court held that the defect could have been caused after the glass left the defendant's factory; there had been a long period of time between the sale and the accident, and it was known that the glass could be strained during installation.

An important factor in the **Triplex** decision was that it was possible to examine the glass for defects in the time between it leaving the manufacturer and the car journey during which it shattered. This factor was emphasised by Lord Atkin in **Donoghue**, and is taken into account in deciding whether the damage to the ultimate consumer was foreseeable – if goods are likely to be examined by someone other than the defendant before they reach the ultimate consumer, there is obviously reason to believe that any defects will be spotted, preventing the product from reaching the consumer and injuring them.

However, the possibility of intermediate examination will only affect foreseeability if it gives the defendant reason to expect that it would reveal the defect and that, as a result, the product will be made safe or not allowed to reach an ultimate consumer, or the consumer would be warned about it in such a way as to allow them to avoid the danger. In **Griffiths** *v* **Arch Engineering Co** (1968), the claimant borrowed a tool from the first defendants, which had been lent to them by the second defendants. The tool was dangerous because the second defendants had repaired it badly, and the claimant was injured as a result. The second defendants claimed that they were not liable, because the first defendants had had time to examine the tool before they lent it out, but the court disagreed; although it was true that the first defendants had the chance to look at the tool and spot the danger, there was no evidence that the second defendants had any reason to think that such an examination would be carried out. Both sets of defendants were held liable, and damages apportioned between them (this is a case of several liability) (see Chapter 16).

Similarly, a defendant can in some cases avoid liability by warning of a risk. This was the case in **Kubach** *v* **Hollands** (1937). In this case a schoolgirl was injured when chemicals used in a science lesson exploded. The manufacturer had sold the chemicals to a retailer, with a warning that they should be tested before resale; the retailers ignored the warning and sold the chemicals to the school without testing them, and without passing on any warnings. The court held that the retailers were liable, but the manufacturers were not.

Defences

The usual defences to negligence apply (see Chapter 3), the most important in practice being *volenti* and contributory negligence.

Evaluating product liability in tort

Types of defect

Tortious liability does not cover defects which are not dangerous so it is of no use in cases where a product does not work, is of poor quality, or does not last, but is not actually harmful.

The need to prove fault

The main drawback with negligence as a means of compensating users of dangerous products is the need to prove fault; unless the claimant proves that a defendant has failed to take reasonable care, the defendant will not be liable for any risks caused by their products. To many people, all this will seem perfectly reasonable: why should a producer be sued when they have not done anything wrong? Accidents happen, after all.

The first point to bear in mind in response to this argument is that tort law does not just require that the defendant was at fault, but that the claimant can prove it. You will remember from the chapter on negligence that this can be a difficult process in any negligence action. Given that in many product liability cases, the claimant will be an individual consumer and the defendant a large and wealthy company, with access to the very best legal advice, you can see that already the chances may be tipped in favour of the defendant. Add to that the fact that the most convincing evidence of negligence in a manufacturing or quality control process is likely to come from someone involved in that process, and the problems increase: employees are unlikely to be keen to testify against their employer. In addition, in many cases processes will be highly specialised and technical, so that only those with a detailed knowledge of them would be able to spot a problem. Of course claimants can use expert witnesses, but this all adds to the expense of a case and makes the prospect of litigation more off-putting. What this all adds up to is that it may be all too easy for manufacturers to get away with negligence in relation to their products.

Over and above the problems of proving negligence where it exists, there is an argument that product liability should not even depend on the existence of negligence, and that instead manufacturers should be liable for any injury caused by their products, whether or not they were to blame for it. The reasons why this should be the case are well expressed in the US case of **Escola** *v* **Coca-Cola Bottling Co of Fresno** (1944). The judge, Traynor J, argued that the manufacturer of a dangerous product should be held liable, regardless of whether they were negligent or not, because:

> public policy demands that responsibility be fixed wherever it will most effectively reduce the hazards to life and health inherent in defective products that reach the market. It is evident that the manufacturer can anticipate some hazards and guard against the recurrence of others, as the public cannot. Those who suffer injury from defective products are unprepared to meet its consequences. The cost of injury and the loss of time and health may be an overwhelming misfortune to the person injured, and a needless one, for the risk of injury can be insured by the manufacturer and distributed among the public as the cost of doing business. It is to the public interest to discourage the marketing of products having defects that are a menace to the public. If such products nevertheless reach the market, it is to the public interest to place the responsibility for whatever injury they may cause upon the manufacturer, who, even if he is not negligent in the manufacture of the product, is responsible for its reaching the market.

Another reason for strict liability is that manufacturers stand to benefit financially from launching products onto the market, so they should bear the cost of any injury caused by those products.

There are, however, other arguments against the imposition of strict liability (these are discussed at p. 5).

Are decisions suitable for the courts?

As we saw in the negligence chapter, deciding whether a defendant has taken reasonable care involves balancing up a number of different factors, including the usefulness of the activity which caused the damage, the practicality of preventing the damage, and the seriousness of the risk, in terms of both the likelihood of causing harm, and the seriousness of the harm if it happens. These are often difficult choices and in product liability cases they can very easily involve choices that the courts are ill-equipped to make. Take, for example, the situation where a company discovers a cure for heart disease, but subsequently the drug is found to cause side-effects which can kill some patients, although it cures the majority. Is a tort action really the place to decide whether that drug should have been put on the market? Are judges qualified to decide whether the risk to some people outweighs the chance of life to the others? Or should this kind of decision be made somewhere else, where it is not linked to individuals' claims for compensation, and where the whole social context can be examined?

The Consumer Protection Act 1987

The Consumer Protection Act was passed against a background of concern about the inability of the law of negligence to protect consumers against dangerous products and, in particular, the Thalidomide scandal, which arose when it was discovered that Thalidomide, a drug widely given to pregnant women during the 1960s (for morning sickness), had caused severe damage to their babies during pregnancy. The parents, and later the children themselves, had to fight for years to prove that the drug had caused their injuries and receive compensation. However, the actual trigger for the new law was the drive towards establishing a single market across the countries of the EEC (for those who have not studied European Law, this was the original name for the community which evolved into what we now call the European Union, or EU). To make this possible, it was necessary to harmonise laws affecting trade in the different countries, so that firms in one country would not have an advantage over those in another – as would be the case if, for example, manufacturers in one country faced strict liability for dangerous products, while, in another, consumers had to prove negligence.

In 1985, the EEC issued a Directive laying down its requirements; the Consumer Protection Act 1987 was passed to give effect to these requirements. The Directive, and the Act, are often described as imposing strict liability, but there is considerable debate about whether this has been the result. There is also some debate about what exactly some of the provisions mean, because so far very few cases under the Act have been brought to court, so there has been little opportunity to clarify the terms.

Who can sue?

Anyone who suffers personal injury or property damage caused by a defective product can sue under the Act; as with a claim in tort, this includes bystanders as well as actual users of the product.

Who can be sued?

The Act imposes liability on the 'producer' of the defective product, and gives this term a wide definition. It is stated to include the manufacturer of the product and the person who 'wins or abstracts' it (this applies to, for example, products that are mined or excavated). It also applies to anyone who is responsible for a process which adds 'essential characteristics' to the product; this might include, for example, cleaning, peeling and slicing vegetables to be sold in ready-to-cook packs.

Retailers can also be liable for products made by other companies which are sold under the retailer's 'own brand'. This is an important provision when you realise that it applies not only to the 'own brand' goods sold by supermarkets alongside other brands, but also, for example, to most, if not all, of the products sold by chain stores such as Marks & Spencer, Bhs and Next, which tend not to manufacture goods themselves, but nevertheless sell everything under their own labels. However, a retailer will only be liable for defects in 'own brand' goods where it can be said that they 'hold themselves out' as being the producer, so a retailer who uses a label clearly stating that a product is made *for* the store, rather than *by* it, will almost certainly escape liability. In theory it could even be found that a retailer such as Marks & Spencer is not 'holding themselves out' to be the producer simply by attaching their branding to a product, since they make no secret of the fact that they use outside suppliers, but this question has not been tested so far.

Where goods originate outside the EU, a further category imposes liability on the person who first imported the goods into the EU, but not on anyone who imports it from one European country to another (unless they fall within one of the other categories of liability, by, for example, being responsible for a process which adds essential characteristics, or selling it under an 'own brand'). So if, for example, a toy made in China was imported into Sweden by firm A, and then exported by firm B to Britain, firm A could be liable if someone in Britain was injured by it, but not firm B.

Someone who merely supplies the goods is generally not liable under the Act. However, they may become liable if a claimant uses s. 2(3). This states that a claimant who does not know who the 'producer' is can ask the supplier of the goods to identify the producer. If the supplier fails to identify either the producer or their own supplier within a reasonable time, they will be liable as if they were the producer. The idea of this provision is to enable the claimant to trace goods back along the supply chain to the actual producer, with the risk of being sued themselves acting as an encouragement for suppliers to keep accurate records of their suppliers, and to divulge that information when required. Whoever breaks the chain by failing to identify their own supplier can be liable.

Types of product covered

A 'product' is defined in s. 2(1) of the Act as 'any goods or electricity', and 'goods' is further explained as including 'substances, growing crops, and things comprised in land by virtue of being attached to it, and any ship, aircraft or vehicle' (the reference to electricity applies only to defects in the generation of electricity, and not breaks in the supply of it). The term 'product' also includes 'a product which is comprised in other products, whether by virtue of being a component part, raw material or otherwise'.

The Act lists a number of types of item which do not fall within the term 'product'. 'Immovables', which essentially means buildings, are not covered by the Act, but building materials are. This means that a house which was dangerous through defects in construction or design would not be covered, but one made dangerous through defects in the materials used to build it could be.

Another grey area is whether information can count as a product. If, for example, you buy a book on DIY which gives you incorrect instructions on how to wire a plug, can you sue the publisher if the plug blows up and injures you? Common sense would suggest the answer should be yes, since the book is clearly a product and a defect in it has caused you injury.

In **A and others** *v* **National Blood Authority** (2001), it was accepted that blood for transfusions was a product for the purposes of the Act (see below for more on this case).

Defects and damage

The Act only covers defects which are dangerous, and not those which merely make the product perform less well or become less valuable. Section 3 states that a product will be held to be defective under the Act if 'the safety of the product is not such as persons generally are entitled to expect'. It is important to note the word 'entitled': essentially, this means that the courts can set the standard according to what it is reasonable to expect from a particular type of product; the fact that the claimant personally might have expected a higher standard is not relevant.

In assessing the standard of safety, the Act directs the courts to take into account 'all the circumstances', and it mentions three different types of factor which are considered relevant.

- **The way the product is marketed, including any advertising claims, instructions or warnings that come with the product.** Clearly, the way a product is advertised can affect the standard of safety which people are entitled to expect from it: a skin cream marketed as hypo-allergenic, for example, might legitimately be expected to be less likely than other skin creams to cause a rash. Similarly, products which are inherently dangerous can be brought within the standard of safety by their instructions or warnings; an obvious example is a medicine which would be dangerous if taken in large amounts but is safe when taken at the dosage recommended on the labels, and is also clearly labelled with warnings of the risk of overdosing.
- **'What might reasonably be expected to be done with or in relation to the product.'** For example, a bed should be safe to sleep on, and possibly for children to jump up and down on, but would probably not be expected to protect from injury a consumer who chooses to hide under it during a hurricane. The provision is not restricted to the way a product is actually used, however, but also covers, for example, whether it might be expected to fall into the hands of children.

- **When the product was supplied by the producer to another.** Essentially, this provision refers to the fact that as manufacturers develop their products, they often add new safety features. The section goes on to explain that the mere fact that products supplied after the one in question are safer than it does not establish that the earlier product is defective.

During the last decade, the first crop of cases brought under the Act have been heard, and these shed some light on how the courts will treat the factors discussed above. In **Bogle** *v* **McDonald's** (2002), the claimants were McDonald's customers who had been scalded after spilling coffee on themselves. They argued that the coffee was defective because it was too hot, and also because the cups it was sold in had lids which came off easily. The court found that the temperature at which the coffee was sold was acceptable, given that customers would not have wanted to drink it at lower temperatures, and the design of the cups was also reasonable, because the lids had to be easily removable so that the customer could add milk and sugar. This looks suspiciously like the same approach the courts use for negligence (and in fact the same arguments were used to dismiss the claimants' case in negligence), but it could be argued that the reasoning with regard to the Act was that the standard of safety was such as 'persons generally are entitled to expect', because no one would expect McDonald's to sell cold coffee in order to prevent a risk of scalding.

In **Richardson** *v* **LRC Products Ltd** (2000), the product concerned was a condom. Its tip had broken off at a fairly crucial moment, with the result that Mrs Richardson became pregnant. She sued for the costs of bringing up the baby. The court held that it was in the nature of condoms that they would occasionally fail, and so the fact that this one had broken did not necessarily mean it was defective under the Act. However, the main reasons why the action failed were that, following **McFarlane** *v* **Tayside** (see p. 90), there is no claim for the costs of bringing up a healthy baby, and also that the claimant could have mitigated her loss by taking the 'morning-after' pill when she realised the condom had broken.

In **Abouzaid** *v* **Mothercare** (2000), the claimant, who was 12 at the time he was injured, had been helping his mother to get a baby sleeping bag known as a 'cosytoes' attached to his little brother's pushchair. It was designed to be attached by two elastic straps, which went round the back of the pushchair and clipped together with a metal buckle attached to the end of one of the straps. As the claimant tried to fix them, one of the straps slipped from his grasp, and the buckle flew back and hit him in the eye. It damaged his retina, leaving him with severely reduced vision in that eye.

The defendants' main argument was that, in 1990, when the sleeping bag was sold, they did not know that there was a danger of injury from the straps. No similar accident had been reported to them, nor recorded in the database kept by the Department of Trade and Industry. However, the Court of Appeal referred back to the fact that the test for a defect under the Act is simply that the level of safety is less than that which persons generally are entitled to expect under all the circumstances. It held that expectations were no lower in 1990 than they are now, so the time gap was not relevant. The risk was one which the defendants could have prevented, by using a different method of attaching the straps, and/or providing a warning of the risk.

In **A and others** *v* **National Blood Authority** (2001), the claimants were all people who had been infected with hepatitis C virus through having transfusions of contaminated blood. The blood had been taken from donors who were infected with the virus. At the time of the transfusions it was known within the medical profession (but not the wider public) that there was a risk of passing on the virus that way, although there was no way of testing the blood to make sure it was not contaminated.

The defendants argued that the words 'under all the circumstances' in the Act's definition of a defect meant that issues such as what could have been done to prevent the risk were relevant. They claimed that this meant the blood was not 'defective' under the Act, because the public were only entitled to expect such a level of safety as would have been acheived if reasonable precautions were taken, and in this case there were no precautions they could have taken.

The court roundly rejected this argument. It stressed that the point of the original directive had been to make it easier for injured consumers to receive compensation, by removing the concept of negligence as an element of liability; to bring in the issue of reasonable precaution would be to reintroduce the concept of negligence. The infected blood was a 'non-standard product', in that it differed from the usual product because it contained a harmful virus. This made it comparable to a defective product. The public expected, and had legitimate reason to expect, that blood supplied for transfusion was uncontaminated. The contaminated blood was therefore defective within the meaning of the Act. A 'non-standard' product might not be defective where it was clear that the public at large accepted that a proportion of such products would be flawed (as with the condom in **Richardson**), but here, there had been no warnings about infected blood and the public had no reason to suspect the possibility of infection.

In **Worsley** *v* **Tambrands** (2000), the claimant suffered a condition called toxic shock syndrome (TSS), which is known to be associated with the use of tampons. The tampon brand she bought carried warnings about TSS on leaflets inside the boxes, which included advice about what to do if the symptoms of TSS appeared, but the claimant's husband had thrown away the leaflet from the box she was using at the time. She argued that given the seriousness of the disease, the warnings should have been printed on the boxes, or the warnings in the leaflet (which she could have seen every month) should have been more strongly presented so as to make an impact on her memory. The court held that her claim failed: the presence of the leaflet was mentioned on the box, the leaflet itself was clear and easy to read, and the manufacturers could not be expected to take precautions against people losing the leaflet or throwing it away.

In **Pollard** *v* **Tesco Stores Ltd** (2006), the case involved a boy just over a year old, who had become seriously ill after eating some dishwasher powder. He had opened the cap of the bottle himself, despite the fact that the cap was supposed to be child-resistant. His claim alleged that the cap was defective. Scientific evidence was produced which showed that it could be opened using a degree of force measured as 10 to 18 inches per pound torque. There was a British Standard for childproof caps of the type used, which said that they should be able to resist a force up to 33 inches per pound, but manufacturers are not required by law to meet that standard, nor is there any legal requirement for dishwasher powder bottles to be fitted with childproof caps at all. The Court of Appeal found that a customer buying a bottle fitted with a childproof cap was only entitled to expect that it would be more difficult to open than an ordinary screw top. They could not be entitled to expect that it would meet the British Standard, since members of the public were unlikely to have any idea what that standard would be. The cap was more difficult to open than a non-childproof one, and therefore the company had not fallen below the required standard. This decision appears to suggest that careless manufacturers might be able to rely on public ignorance about safety standards, which hardly seems to be within the spirit of the legislation.

The Act only covers personal injury and damage to property worth more than £275; property damage worth less is not covered, and nor is economic loss, including damage to the defective product itself. There is also another important restriction in that the Act does not cover damage to business property, which is defined as property which is not ordinarily intended for private use, occupation or consumption, and not intended by the person who suffers the loss for their own private use, occupation or consumption. This means that, for example, if a computer which was used purely for private purposes, in a private house, blew up and burnt the house down, the house owner could claim under the Act, but the Act would not apply if the computer was in a commercial office.

What must be proved

The key difference between a claim under the Act and a product liability claim in negligence is that the Act is said to impose strict liability. All a claimant has to prove is that the product is defective under the terms of the Act, and that this defect caused them personal injury or damaged property worth more than £275. They do not have to prove that any of this was the defendant's fault. However, it is important to note that liability may be strict, but it is not absolute: there are a number of defences, discussed below, that can place considerable hurdles in the way of claimants. Moreover, it has been argued that the assessment which the court is required to make in deciding whether a product is defective under the terms of the Act can come very close to a requirement for negligence; we will look at this issue towards the end of this chapter when we examine the problems with the Act.

Topical issue

Products

In 2010, one of the biggest group actions under the Consumer Protection Act was resolved, after over 2,000 people sued a number of furniture retailers over injuries caused by sitting on leather sofas. The sofas were imported from China by stores including Argos and Homebase, and had been stuffed with sachets of a chemical called dimethyl fumarate (DML), which was intended to stop the leather going mouldy during the long journey by ship from China. DML is highly toxic, and once the sofas were in people's homes, the originally solid chemical turned into a gas, which came through the leather, and people who bought the sofas developed severe and painful skin rashes and breathing problems as a result.

The retailers did not know that the sofas contained an unsafe chemical, but because the Consumer Protection Act imposes strict liability, the people who bought the sofas were not required to prove that the retailers were at fault. The retailers therefore admitted liability, and paid damages of around £17 million.

Defences

The ordinary defence of contributory negligence applies under the Act, and can be applied where the claimant has been caused damage partly as a result of a defective product, and partly by their own fault (for example, by using the product in an unsafe way).

Section 4 of the Act also sets down the following six specific defences, which a defendant can put forward to avoid liability once the claimant has established that they have been caused damage by a defect in a product for which the defendant is responsible under the Act.

Compliance with the law

A defendant can avoid liability by proving that the defect is 'attributable to compliance with any requirement imposed by law'. If, for example, the law required that bread had to contain a certain type of preservative, and this preservative was later found to be harmful – either to people generally, or to a particular claimant – the producer of the bread would have a defence.

This defence can only apply where the law actually requires whatever caused the defect, and not where it merely permits it. So, in the bread example above, there would be no defence if the law merely allowed manufacturers to add the preservative, but did not insist on it. In such a case, the fact that the ingredient is legally permitted will be relevant to the question of whether the product should be considered defective, but it is not a complete defence.

Product not supplied

Where a supplier is sued under the Act, they will have a defence if they can prove that they did not actually supply the product. Supply is widely defined and includes hiring out and lending as well as selling goods, but it would not apply where a product is simply given to someone to use – for example, if an employer gives an employee a tool to use at work (although obviously in this case there would be other remedies for the employee to use – see Chapter 4).

Non-commercial supply

The Consumer Protection Act was designed to impose liability on businesses rather than individuals, so it does not apply to goods which have not been supplied in the course of business, or with a view to making a profit. Examples would be home-made products sold at village fairs, or cakes sold at a school fête.

Defects arising later

Producers will not be liable for defects that arise after they release a product. This defence applies to cases where a product has been interfered with or misused after it leaves the producer, or where the defect is the result of wear and tear. It can also be of use where goods are perishable, or need regular servicing, or a chain of suppliers is involved; anyone in the chain who can prove that the defect did not exist when the product left their hands will have a defence. The product must have left the hands of the relevant defendant when the defect occurs, so there is no defence where, for example, a product is deliberately sabotaged before it leaves the factory or warehouse, whether by an employee of the producer or someone else; in that case strict liability still applies.

It is for the defendant to prove that a defect occurred after the product had left their control; where it is not clear whether the defect existed before the producers released it or happened later, the defence will fail and the claimant should win their case.

The development risks defence

This is the most controversial part of the Act. It is similar to the 'state of the art' argument developed in negligence from the case of **Roe** *v* **Minister of Health** (see p. 84), and allows a defence where:

> the state of scientific and technical knowledge at the relevant time was not such that a producer of products of the same description as the product in question might be expected to have discovered the defect if it had existed in his products while they were under his control.

This defence can apply where, for example, a drug turns out to have harmful side-effects, but at the time when it was launched, no one in the drug industry would have been able to spot the risk.

The wording of the development risks defence in the Act differs from that used in the Directive, which states that the defence will only allow a producer to avoid liability where 'the state of scientific and technical knowledge at the time when he put the product into circulation was not such as to enable the existence of the defect to be discovered'. The difference here is that the

Directive refers to the general state of scientific and technical knowledge, whereas the Act appears to narrow the standard to what the members of a particular industry could be expected to know. Take, for example, a situation where, at the time a product was put into circulation, the possibility of a risk had been suggested in a handful of scientific journals, but had not filtered down to become known in the relevant industry. The wording of the defence in the Act seems to suggest that the producer could avoid liability, but the wording of the Directive would seem to suggest that the development risks defence should not apply, because the state of scientific knowledge was such that the risk could have been discovered.

As students of EU law will know, the European Commission can bring a case before the European Court of Justice (ECJ) against any EU country which it claims has failed to apply EU law properly, and, in **European Commission** *v* **United Kingdom** (1997), it challenged the part of the Act which contains the defence, s. 4(1)(e), on the grounds described above. In its judgment, the ECJ clarified how the development risks defence should apply. It acknowledged that the 'state of scientific and technical knowledge' could be a fairly fluid concept; for example, when a risk was first suggested, the idea might be criticised and rejected by other experts, but then over time, as evidence built up, could come to be accepted. The issue for the application of the development risks defence was at what point in that process it could be said that the state of knowledge was such that the risk could be discovered.

The court said that it was not acceptable to wait until a risk was widely recognised: the standard was that of the most advanced research, and once even one isolated opinion suggests there may be a risk, the risk cannot be said to be unforeseeable. However, the ECJ acknowledged that the availability of information could be taken into account. It gave the example of two pieces of research, one undertaken by a researcher at an American university and published in an English language journal, and the other carried out by an academic in Manchuria and published in Chinese in a local scientific journal. Clearly it would be more reasonable to expect an EU producer to know about the former than the latter, and the ECJ stated that a producer should not be held liable on the ground that when the product was put into circulation, one brilliant researcher in Manchuria had spotted a problem with it. Therefore, the ECJ concluded:

> the state of knowledge must be construed so as to include all data in the information circuit of the scientific community as a whole, bearing in mind, however, on the basis of a reasonableness test, the actual opportunities for the information to circulate.

Interestingly, the ECJ found that the Act did not fail to achieve the effects laid down in the Directive. It acknowledged that there was a potential ambiguity, and that the narrow interpretation of the defence described earlier in this section would not properly put into effect the aims of the Directive. But, it said, the words of the Act were also open to an interpretation which did fulfil the requirements of the Directive, and there was no evidence that the English courts would interpret the Act in a way that would not do so. The effect of this judgment is that the English courts are now likely to interpret the defence in line with the guidance offered by the ECJ, rather than in the narrower way.

This has certainly been the case in the two recent actions which have raised the defence. In **Abouzaid** *v* **Mothercare** (see above), the defendant argued that, given the lack of any previous report of a similar accident, the state of scientific and technical knowledge in 1990 was not such that a producer of a similar product would have been expected to discover the defect. The Court of Appeal rejected this view. They said that this was not the kind of knowledge covered by the defence. The defence concerned scientific and technical advances, not information on previous accidents.

In **A** *v* **National Blood Authority** (also detailed above), the defendants argued that they were covered by the defence because, at the time of the transfusions, it was not possible to discover whether a specific batch of blood was infected, even though it was known that there was a general risk that any batch might be. The court disagreed: where there is a known risk, the defence cannot apply, and if the producer chooses to supply the products, knowing of the risk, they must take the consequences if injury results. Any other result, the court said, would be inconsistent with the purpose of the Directive.

Component products not defective

The Act also allows a defence where the defendant has supplied a component which is made up into a product (referred to as the 'subsequent product'), and they can prove that the defect complained of is in the subsequent product rather than the component, and is completely due to the design of the subsequent product, or to the producer of the component complying with instructions given by the producer of the subsequent product. This would apply where, for example, a tyre manufacturer sells ordinary tyres to a car manufacturer, who fits them to a racing car; if the tyres exploded, the tyre manufacturers could use the defence to argue that the defect was in the car, not the tyres.

Limitation periods

Cases brought under the Consumer Protection Act are subject to a special limitation period, which states that the right to bring a case is lost after ten years from the date on which the defendant supplied the product. Subject to this, claimants must begin proceedings within three years of discovering the defect, the damage, or the identity of the defendant, or, if the damage is latent (meaning that it takes a long time to appear), within three years of the date of knowledge (see p. 132). Where the case concerns personal injury, the courts have a discretion to override the three-year rule, but not the ten-year limitation.

Evaluating the Consumer Protection Act

Is liability really strict?

As we have seen, there are powerful arguments for the imposition of strict liability in the area of product liability, and the Consumer Protection Act is generally described as imposing such liability. Looked at closely, however, clearly it falls short of strict liability, and some academics have suggested that it actually offers little more than a standard of negligence, with the burden of proof reversed. Take, for example, the issues which a court will take into account when deciding whether a product should be considered defective under the Act. As we have seen, s. 3 states that a product will be held to be defective under the Act if 'the safety of the product is not such as persons generally are entitled to expect', and this means that the courts can set the standard according to what it is reasonable to expect from a particular type of product. In deciding this, the courts can look at all the circumstances, and in practice these are likely to include many of the same factors that they would look at in a negligence claim when deciding whether reasonable care was taken. What is being judged is still a standard of reasonableness, albeit looked at from a slightly different angle. However, recent cases, namely **Abouzaid** and **A** *v* **National Blood Authority**, suggest that the courts are prepared to resist the temptation to dilute strict liability with too wide a concept of reasonableness.

A further consideration is that of causation. The Act states that a causal link between the defect and the damage must be established, apparently by the claimant, but does not give explicit rules on what will and will not amount to causation. The courts are therefore likely to apply the rules of causation used in negligence and, as we have seen in Chapter 2, this can be a formidable hurdle for the claimant, and could considerably weaken the concept of strict liability. However, s. 2 does provide that where damage is caused partly by the defective product and partly by something else, the producer will still be liable.

Should liability be strict?

In contrast to the argument above, some believe that strict liability for defective products is not a good idea. This has not just been an academic debate; fuelled by bizarre-sounding cases (usually from the USA) the British press have criticised the willingness to sue over injuries caused by defective products. The main argument used is that the threat of strict liability strangles innovation and enterprise. Manufacturers, it is argued, will be less likely to launch ground-breaking new products if they are afraid of being sued if those products turn out to be dangerous, through no fault of the manufacturer; or the threat of strict liability might lead to manufacturers taking excessive care, so that the costs of the product are pushed up so high that they are priced out of the market. A study reported in the *Financial Times* (9 February 1993) suggested that this was already happening, just six years after the introduction of the Act.

A further argument refutes the suggestion that producers are in the best position to insure against injury from defective products. As far as injury to property is concerned, that may be true – since many people have insurance for cars and household contents, strict liability for damage to such property may be nothing more than double insurance. However, the argument is much weaker when it comes to personal injury. It can be argued that since the risks of product innovation come with the potential for huge social benefits, society, rather than individual producers, should pay when the risks cause harm, in the form of welfare benefits rather than tort damages. The argument for this as a reason for abolishing personal injury actions in negligence is a strong one (we discuss it on p. 139), but it would require much better welfare provision than we have today. The suggestion that within the current system, product liability actions should be scrapped because people can claim benefits as a result of their injuries would be a recipe for lowering safety standards.

The apparent watering-down of liability would appear to be the result of massive lobbying by industry during the passing of both the Directive and the Act. Farmers were successful in removing agricultural products from their scope (although these have since been added), while the development risks defence was demanded largely by drugs companies, and backed up by a Conservative government which was keen to make sure that British industry was not weakened by higher costs.

The development risks defence

This is perhaps the most criticised part of the Act. Many of the earlier criticisms of the defence centred around the accusation that its expression in the Act was weaker than that intended by the Directive. However, as we saw earlier, the ECJ has clarified that the words of the Act can, and should, be read in a way that is in line with the intention of the Directive, and the courts have responded. Even so, some critics have argued that the whole idea of the defence is mistaken, and too serious a compromise of the idea of strict liability – it is argued that in practice it is really no more than an application of the foreseeability rule from negligence, and that essentially it means that a supplier that can prove that their lack of knowledge was not negligent can escape liability. In recognition of these concerns, several EU states do not include the defence in the legislation they put in place to enact the Directive.

However, the development risks defence does compare favourably with its counterpart in negligence, the 'state of the art' argument laid down in **Roe** *v* **Minister of Health** (1954). Whereas **Roe** seems to set a minimal standard, in that the defendant's practices must be no worse than what another person in the same field would do, but need not be as good as the best, the development risks defence, as explained by the ECJ, imposes a much higher standard, requiring producers to be aware of the latest knowledge, provided it is accessible.

The Act in practice

Since the Act was passed, there have been a relatively small number of reported judgments under it. Some critics have seen this as a criticism of the Act, suggesting that it adds little to the remedies previously available, but this may be misleading. In the first place, a reported case frequently suggests a problem with a statute, in that the parties disagree over its interpretation or application. A lack of such disputes can be a sign that a statute is clear and well expressed.

Secondly, many cases are settled out of court, and we have no way of knowing how many of these have been successfully settled because of the Act; it may be that the threat of strict liability (even if not as strict as it could be) encourages suppliers to settle. Nor do we know how far the existence of the Act has encouraged manufacturers and suppliers to take more care, although it should probably be assumed to have had at least some threatening effect, given the degree to which industry lobbied against it being passed in the first place.

Other remedies for defective products

The Consumer Credit Act 1974

This is an important, though surprisingly little-known, remedy available to consumers of defective products (see Table 6.1). The Consumer Credit Act 1974 states that if goods are bought using a credit card and prove to be defective, the buyer can sue the credit card company. The action applies to any goods which cost more than £100 and less than £30,000, and covers defects in quality or performance as well as dangerous defects. It can provide a useful remedy where the seller is bankrupt or impossible to find.

Safety regulations

The Consumer Protection Act 1961 gave the Secretary of State powers to make regulations which impose safety requirements on particular types of product, and to make orders prohibiting the supply of goods which are not safe. These powers are now contained in Part II of the Consumer Protection Act 1987, and anyone affected by breach of such regulations can sue as a breach of statutory duty. Part II also allows the enforcement of safety rules by criminal sanctions.

Table 6.1 Liability for defective products

	Liability in contract	Liability in tort	Liability under the CPA 1987
Who can sue?	The buyer and the person benefitting from the contract	Anyone who is injured or whose property is damaged by a defective product	Anyone who is injured or whose property is damaged by a defective product
Who can be sued?	Only the seller	Anyone involved in the supply chain of a defective product	The producer; the retailer of own brand goods; other suppliers in the chain if they do not identify the producer or their supplier
What kinds of product are covered?	Any type of product	Any type of product	Most products, but not buildings
What kinds of defect are covered?	Any defect which amounts to a breach of the contract	Defects which make the product dangerous or cause damage to other property	Defects which make the product dangerous or cause damage to other property
What kind of damage is covered?	Personal injury, property damage, economic loss and (in limited cases) anxiety, distress and loss of enjoyment	Personal injury and damage to property	Personal injury and damage to property worth over £275
Must fault be proved?	No	Yes	No

Answering questions

Frida is out shopping for a birthday present for her husband Benny. He wants an electric drill, and she sees one at what she thinks is a bargain price. The shop assistant explains that the drill is cheap because the manufacturer has gone bankrupt and all their stock has to be sold off as quickly as possible. Frida buys it and, pleased at having saved money, she buys him a little radio as well. Later, she calls in at their daughter's school, where the parent teacher association is running a fair, and she buys some cakes.

Benny is delighted with his presents, but when he switches on the radio, he finds that it does not work. He decides to try out his drill, but, within a couple of minutes, it gets very hot, and then explodes, injuring him and burning a section of the wall. When they eventually get back from the local casualty department, Benny and Frida settle down in front of the TV with their cakes. Unfortunately, when Frida takes a bite of one of them, she cracks a tooth on a stone.

Four weeks later, they read a newspaper report which says that the drill manufacturers are recalling the model of drill that Frida bought because of a scientific report stating that the material that the casing is made from is potentially dangerous. The newspaper story says that the manufacturers had no idea of this before the report was published.

Advise Benny and Frida.

The clearest way to answer this question is to take the potential claims raised by each product in turn, and look at whether a claim might lie in contract, in negligence, or under the Consumer Protection Act; important issues in deciding this will be who bought the product and what type of damage it causes.

Beginning with the radio, the important issue here is that the product is defective but, as far as we know, not dangerous. As a result, the only claim is in contract. Benny has no contract with the retailer, since Frida bought the radio, so you will need to look at whether he can claim as a result of the Contracts (Rights of Third Parties) Act 1999.

The drill offers more possibilities because it has caused physical harm to Benny, as well as damage to property. He may therefore be able to claim under both the common law of negligence and the Consumer Protection Act, but you will need to consider who he can sue, given that the manufacturer has apparently gone bankrupt. One possibility is the manufacturer of the casing material; this is possible in negligence and under the Act, but, in an action under the Act, they may argue that the drill manufacturer caused the danger by the way they used the casing material. An alternative is suing the retailer, and, again, you should discuss what would need to be proved in each type of case. You should take into account the potential effect of the information contained in the newspaper report, if it is true – the case of **Roe** will be relevant in an action for negligence, and the development risks defence for an action under the Consumer Protection Act. You should be in a position to say which action gives Benny the best chance of success, although he can of course bring both.

It is also worth pointing out that he may also be able to bring an action in contract, if the Contracts (Rights of Third Parties) Act 1999 applies, and this may be advantageous since it does not require proof of fault. Note that if you discussed what would decide whether the 1999 Act applies when looking at the issue of the radio, you should not repeat the same material: it is quite sufficient to say that if, on the rules you have discussed previously, the Act does apply, Benny will have a claim, and if it does not apply, he will not.

Finally, consider Frida's potential claim with regard to the cakes, and here you should discuss both contract and negligence. Note that the Consumer Protection Act is unlikely to apply, because the cakes were not sold in the course of a business.

How far has the Consumer Protection Act 1987 improved the law on defective products?

For this essay, you need to begin by looking at what actions were available for defective products before the 1987 Act was passed. Discuss contract and tort in turn, highlighting any problems and gaps: these will include the doctrine of privity for contract, and for tort, the need to prove fault and the lack of cover for non-dangerous defects. You should discuss the issue of whether liability for defective products should be strict.

You can go on to outline what the 1987 Act brings to the law, and then to look at the problems with it. You need to discuss the issue of how far the Act really introduces strict liability, and how it compares to negligence, and also look at the suggestion that it has stifled manufacturing innovation, and whether you feel this is a valid criticism.

You could also briefly mention that the situation has also been improved by other measures, notably the Contracts (Rights of Third Parties) Act 1999, and the Consumer Credit Act.

Summary of Chapter 6

There are three main ways to claim compensation for defective products:

- Breach of contract
- Negligence
- The Consumer Protection Act 1987.

Product liability in contract

The buyer of a defective product can sue the seller for breach of contract; this protection is strengthened by the terms implied into contracts by the Sale of Goods Acts.

- Only the buyer and third parties given the benefit of the contract can sue.
- Only the seller can be sued.
- All types of product are covered.
- Claims can be made for any type of defect, not just dangerous ones.
- The claimant must prove breach of a contractual term but need not prove fault.

Contract law includes a range of defences, detailed in contract law texts.

Evaluating product liability in contract

Key issues are:

- wide range of defects covered;
- no need to prove fault;
- limits on who can sue.

Product liability in tort

- Producers of defective products owe a duty of care in negligence to the buyers and users of the products.
- Anyone injured or caused loss may sue.
- Anyone involved in the supply chain from manufacturer to seller can be sued.
- All types of product are covered.
- Claims can only be made for defects which cause injury or property damage, not defects which only affect performance or quality.
- The claimant must prove the defendant's failure to take reasonable care caused the danger.

The usual defences to negligence apply.

Evaluating product liability in negligence

Key issues are:

- the types of defect covered;
- the need to prove fault;
- whether decisions are suitable for the courts.

→

Product liability under the Consumer Protection Act

The Act imposes strict liability for defective products which are dangerous.

- Anyone who suffers injury or property damage can sue.
- The 'producer' of the product can be sued, as can suppliers if they cannot identify the producer, and retailers of own brand goods.
- Most types of product are covered, but not buildings.
- The claimant must prove that the safety of the product is 'not such as persons generally are entitled to expect'; fault need not be proved.

Defences under the Act are:

- contributory negligence;
- compliance with the law;
- product not supplied;
- non-commercial supply;
- defects arising later;
- development risks;
- component products not defective.

Cases are subject to special limitation period of:

- ten years from the time the defendant began supplying the product; and
- three years from the time the defect, damage, or defendant's identity was known; or
- three years from the date of knowledge in latent damage cases.

Evaluating the Act

Key issues are:

- Is liability really strict?
- Should liability be strict?
- Use of the development risks defence.

Other remedies for defective products

- The Consumer Credit Act 1974
- Safety regulations under the Consumer Protection Act 1987.

Reading list

Text resources

Albanese, F and Del Duca, L (1987) 'Developments in European product liability' 5 *Dickinson Journal of International Law* 193

Borrie, G (1987) 'Product liability in the EEC' 9 *Dublin University Law Journal* 82

Conaghan, J and Mansell, W (1998) *The Wrongs of Tort*, 2nd edn, Chapter 5. Pluto

Deards, E and Twigg-Fiesner, C (2001) 'The Consumer Protection Act 1987: proof at last that it is protecting the consumer?' 10 *Nottingham Law Journal* 1

Griffiths, Lord, De Val, P and Dormer, R J (1988) 'Developments in English product liability law: a comparison with the American System' 62 *Tulane Law Review* 353

Guide to the Consumer Protection Act 1987 (2001) HMSO

Harris, P (2006) *An Introduction to Law*, 7th edn, pp. 212–14. Cambridge University Press

Hodges, C (1998) 'Development risks: unanswered questions' 61 *Modern Law Review* 560

Hodges, C (2001) 'A *v* National Blood Authority' 117 *Law Quarterly Review* 528

Law Commission Report No 82 (1977) Cmnd 6831

Newdick, C (1985) 'Liability for defective drugs' 101 *Law Quarterly Review* 405

Newdick, C (1987) 'The future of negligence in product liability' 103 *Law Quarterly Review* 288

Newdick, C (1988) 'The development risk defence of the Consumer Protection Act 1987' 47 *Cambridge Law Journal* 455

Stapleton, J (1986) 'Products liability reform – real or illusory?' 6 *Oxford Journal of Legal Studies* 392

Stapleton, J (1991) 'Three problems with the new product liability' in Cane, P and Stapleton, J (eds) *Essays for Patrick Atiyah*. Clarendon Press

Whittaker, S (1989) 'European product liability and intellectual products' 105 *Law Quarterly Review* 125

Reading on the Internet

The Department for Business, Innovation and Skills' (formerly DTI's then Department for Business, Enterprise & Regulatory Reform's) guide to the Consumer Protection Act can be read at:
http://www.bis.gov.uk/files/file22866.pdf

The Court of Appeal judgment in **Carroll** *v* **Fearon** (1998) can be read at:
http://alpha.bailii.org/ew/cases/EWCA/Civ/1998/40.html

Visit **www.mylawchamber.co.uk** to access tools to help you develop and test your knowledge of tort law, including interactive multiple choice questions, practice exam questions with guidance, weblinks, glossary flashcards, legal newsfeed and legal updates.

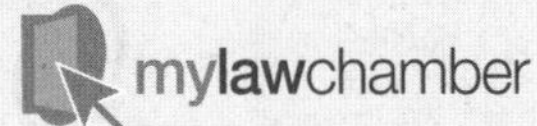

Chapter 7
Breach of statutory duty

This chapter discusses:

- When a statute will create a right to sue in tort
- How the courts decide whether a statutory duty has been breached
- Problems with statutory torts.

Among the many statutes enacted by Parliament, a high proportion will impose duties – some on public bodies, some on companies or private individuals. The issue discussed in this chapter concerns what happens when those duties are not performed (or not performed properly): namely, can those affected by the non-performance sue those who should be performing the duty? The answer, unfortunately for students but fortunately for lawyers, is that sometimes they can, and sometimes not.

Some statutes expressly state that failure to perform a specified duty will give rise to a right to sue, and some expressly state that it will not. The Race Relations Act 1976 and the Sex Discrimination Act 1975 are examples of statutes that make it plain that they do give rise to liability in tort, while the Health and Safety at Work etc. Act 1974 and the Safety of Sports Grounds Act 1975 are among those which state that they do not. However, the reason why this chapter exists is that a great many statutes simply say nothing on the subject, leaving the courts to decide whether a right to sue should exist, and it is the rules they have developed to do this which are discussed here.

It might be thought that, in a modern, sophisticated democracy, where statute is the highest form of domestic law, Parliament would make a point of deciding this important issue during the passage of a piece of legislation. The fact that there are so many statutes where this is not done suggests it may be more than the result of an oversight or lack of time. In **M** *v* **Newham Borough Council**, Staughton LJ suggested that in some cases the reason may be that it is politically embarrassing to state specifically that people will not be entitled to a common law remedy where a public authority fails in its duty.

Scope of the tort

Key Case **X** *v* **Bedfordshire County Council (1995)**

The general rule, confirmed in the key House of Lords judgment, **X** *v* **Bedfordshire County Council** (1995), is that breach of a statutory duty does not give rise to a right to sue in tort, unless the statute concerned makes it clear that Parliament intended to create such a right. In order to decide whether this is the case, the courts look at the words of the relevant statute, and consider a number of factors, including:

- who the statute was intended to benefit;
- whether any other remedies for breach are available;
- the degree of detail with which the duty is set out;
- the background to the legislation;
- the type of harm involved.

Legal Principle
Breach of a duty laid down in statute does not give those affected a right to sue, unless the statute makes it clear that Parliament intended to create such a right.

No single one will be treated as conclusive proof that tortious liability was intended; the courts tend to use them as starting points for their reasoning, but may include other factors as well.

Who is the statute intended to benefit?

The courts will consider whether the Act was aimed merely to confer a general public benefit, or whether it was actually designed to create individual rights against the party supposed to provide the benefit. Only in the latter case will any tortious liability arise. **X** *v* **Bedfordshire County Council** was concerned with legislation instructing local authorities to provide protection for children at risk of abuse and to provide education services for children with special needs. Lord Browne-Wilkinson said:

> Although regulatory or welfare legislation affecting a particular area of activity does in fact provide protection to those individuals particularly affected by that activity, the legislation is not to be treated as being passed for the benefit of those individuals but for the benefit of society in general.

The House of Lords concluded that the relevant statutes did not create liability in tort if the statutory duty was breached.

The approach taken in **X** *v* **Bedfordshire County Council** confirms the earlier case of **Lonrho** *v* **Shell Petroleum (No 2)** (1982). Shell had contracted to use Lonrho's pipeline for transporting their petroleum products into Rhodesia, but when Rhodesia unilaterally declared independence, exporting oil to it became illegal under the Southern Rhodesia (Petroleum) Order 1965, part of legislation designed to undermine the illegal government by means of economic sanctions. Shell in fact continued to supply oil by different means, in contravention of the Order, and Lonrho sued for the loss this caused them by prolonging the illegal government. The House of Lords held that they had no right of action; the clear intention of the legislation was to undermine the Rhodesian government, and not to create individual legal rights for those caused loss by its continuance.

The courts are more likely to allow tortious liability where a statute is aimed at protecting a particular class of individuals. In **Ex parte Island Records Ltd** (1978), the statute in question provided that it was an offence to record a live musical performance without the performers' consent. The Court of Appeal found that such a provision was clearly for the benefit of a specific class of individuals, namely musicians, and that they should have a right of action under it, in addition to the imposition of criminal sanctions.

Availability of alternative remedies

Where a statute provides for some other way to penalise breach of the duty, the courts will generally presume that Parliament meant this to be the only way, and will not impose liability in tort as well. The fact that the common law provides sufficient remedies for the individual may also be taken to suggest that the legislature did not intend to provide a further cause of action when passing a relevant statute.

In **Olotu** *v* **Home Office** (1997), the claimant had been charged with various criminal offences and detained in custody awaiting trial. Under statute, there was a limit on the length of time she could lawfully be detained in such circumstances, and regulations made under the Prosecution of Offenders Act 1985 imposed a duty on the Crown Prosecution Service (CPS) to ensure that accused persons did not spend longer than the lawful period in custody. The claimant brought an action against the CPS for breach of this statutory duty. In the Court of Appeal, Lord Bingham CJ explained that the approach laid down in **X** *v* **Bedfordshire County Council** required them to discern the intention of Parliament by looking at 'the object and scope of the provisions, the class (if any) intended to be protected by them, and the means of redress open to such a class if the statutory duty is not performed'. In this case, the court held that no tortious liability was incurred: there were several other remedies available to people in the claimant's situation, including an application for bail and certain public law actions. In addition, there was no sign in the words of the 1985 Act that the Secretary of State, who made the regulations, had power to confer a private right of action in such cases, and, in policy terms, the existence of a private right to sue might adversely influence the way prosecutors conducted their work, and could open the floodgates to a vast amount of litigation.

In **Todd** *v* **Adams** (2001), the families of four fishermen killed when their boat sank sued the owner of the vessel, claiming that the accident had been caused by the boat being unsafe, which they said was a breach of his statutory duty under the Fishing Vessel (Safety Provisions) Rules 1975. The court noted that the relevant legislation allowed for prosecution of the vessel owner, and concluded that Parliament had not intended to allow owners to be sued in addition to being fined if convicted. Similarly, in **Phelps** *v* **Hillingdon Borough Council** (2000), the case of misdiagnosed dyslexia (discussed on p. 70), an action for breach of statutory duty was rejected because there were alternative remedies, such as appeal procedures and judicial review, and the court held that the existence of these meant that if Parliament had intended to create additional remedies, it would have said so.

Case Navigator

However, there is a handful of cases where the courts have not treated the existence of an alternative remedy as decisive, and they give an interesting insight into the way policy, and the judges' view of the justice of a particular case, have affected the law in this area. In **Groves** *v* **Wimbourne** (1898) a 15-year-old factory employee had to have his arm amputated after catching his hand in an unfenced machine. A statute provided that such machines should be fenced, that factory owners who failed to do this could be fined £100, and that all or part of that fine could be used for the benefit of someone injured by the breach, at the Secretary of State's discretion. Following the general presumption, this provision should have meant that this was the only penalty for the breach, and no tortious liability existed. However, the courts interpreted the provision as suggesting that there should be tortious liability by arguing that it clearly intended that compensation to the victim should be possible, and since there was no certainty that all or any of the fine would go to the victim, and even if it did, £100 would be insufficient compensation for a serious injury, they must have meant further compensation to be possible. Therefore the court allowed the boy to sue in tort.

It is not hard to see that the convoluted reasoning which allowed the claim actually owes very little to the provisions of the statute; the case took place at a time when there was increasing concern about the danger to employees from industrial work, and a growing amount of legislation on the subject, and against this background the courts seem to have consulted their own sense of justice first, and constructed support from the statute afterwards.

A similar approach can be seen in **Monk** *v* **Warbey** (1935). The claimant was injured when riding in a car owned by the defendant; the driver was a third party who had borrowed the car. The driver was not covered by insurance, and the Road Traffic Act 1930 made it a criminal offence for an owner to allow an uninsured person to drive their car. However, the Court of Appeal held that the existence of criminal penalties did not mean that there could not be civil liability; the provision was clearly there for the very purpose of making sure that people injured in such circumstances could be compensated, yet without the possibility of civil liability it could not offer them that protection as the imposition of criminal sanctions would not compensate the claimant.

The Court of Appeal recently declined to apply **Monk** *v* **Warbey** in the case of **Richardson** *v* **Pitt-Stanley** (1995), which involved an employer who was in breach of a statutory requirement to have insurance cover for the possibility of injury to employees. The facts of the case were very similar to those in **Monk** *v* **Warbey**, and the result may therefore suggest that the approach taken in that case and in **Groves** is less likely to find favour now.

Degree of detail

The more detailed and specific the statutory provisions concerning a duty, the more likely it is that the courts will find civil liability in respect of that duty. In **X** *v* **Bedfordshire County Council**, discussed above, Lord Browne-Wilkinson said:

> The cases where a private right of action for breach of statutory duty have been held to arise are all cases in which the statutory duty has been very limited and specific as opposed to a general administrative function imposed on public bodies and involving the exercise of administrative discretion.

In that case the House of Lords concluded that Parliament was unlikely to have intended to create a private right of action under the relevant statutes because of the very general nature of the duties imposed on the authorities (such as to 'safeguard and protect the welfare of the children within [the area] who are in need') and the wide discretion granted to the authorities in carrying out these duties.

In **Danns** *v* **Department of Health** (1998), the relevant statute was the Ministry of Health Act 1919, which provides that the Minister of Health has a duty, among other things, to give out such information as is desirable for the health of people in the country. The claimant alleged that this duty had been breached, because the department had not warned the public after a medical research paper suggested that in men who had had a vasectomy there remained a 1 in 2,000 chance that the operation might reverse itself, and, where this happened, the man would no longer be sterile. The claimant had had exactly this experience, with the result that his wife had become pregnant. The Court of Appeal rejected his claim, stating that the statute clearly gave the Ministry a wide discretion as to how it performed the duty, and warning the public was not the only reasonable way to act.

The background to the legislation

In a case involving breach of statutory duty, the courts are essentially trying to work out whether Parliament, when passing the legislation, intended to give individuals the right to sue under it, and the background to the legislation can be a clue to this intention. In **Ziemniak** *v* **ETPM Deep Sea Ltd** (2003), the claimant was a seaman who had been seriously injured when the chain holding up a lifeboat he was testing on the defendants' ship gave way. The Merchant Shipping (Life Saving Appliances) Regulations 1980 provided that the defendants had to ensure that such chains were of 'adequate strength' to hold the lifeboat in place. They admitted that they had breached this duty, but argued that the legislation did not give a right for individuals to sue.

To decide whether this was the case, the Court of Appeal looked at the background to the legislation. The Regulations had been made under the Merchant Shipping Act 1979, which built on an earlier Act, the Merchant Shipping Act 1970. The 1970 Act was the first real attempt to address the issue of workplace safety for seamen, and the notes to that Act explained that its purpose was to bring safety for workers at sea in line with that of those on land. The court said that this purpose had been carried over into the modern legislation. They pointed out that it is an accepted principle that most legislation concerning safety at work on land allows a right to sue for breach of the duties contained in it, so legislation that was designed to give seamen the same protection as land-based workers should allow the same rights. The claimant was therefore entitled to sue for breach of statutory duty.

The type of harm involved

In **Cullen** *v* **Chief Constable of the Royal Ulster Constabulary** (2003), the House of Lords included the type of harm caused as a factor influencing whether a statute should give rise to an individual right to sue for breach of statutory duty. The claimant had been arrested, and had asked to see a solicitor. Section 15 of the Northern Ireland (Emergency Provisions) Act 1987 allowed the police to delay a suspect's access to a solicitor, and they did so; however, the Act required them to give the suspect reasons for the delay, and the police did not do this. On that basis, the claimant sued for breach of statutory duty.

The House of Lords refused his claim, and pointed to two reasons why the statute should not be held to create liability to individuals. The first was that the claimant had other means of redress (namely judicial review), and the second was that a breach of this particular duty was not likely to lead to any of the types of harm that tort law usually concerns itself with, such as personal injury, property damage or economic loss. The House was also influenced by the fact that, since he had eventually been able to consult a solicitor, the claimant had not in fact suffered damage of any kind.

Elements of the tort

Once the court has decided that breach of a particular statutory provision does give rise to liability in tort, it must then decide whether, in the case before it, there has actually been a breach, and whether the damage suffered by the claimant is of a kind that falls within the tortious liability arising from that statute.

Breach of duty

In order to decide whether there has been a breach, the court must decide precisely what the duty imposed by the statute consists of, and whether the situation complained of conforms with it or not. This is done by looking closely at the words of the statute. In **R** *v* **East Sussex County Council, ex parte T** (1998), the council had been supplying five hours a week of home tuition to a child who was unable to attend school through illness. When it reduced those hours in order to save money, it was sued on the grounds that the reduction was in breach of the statutory duty under the Education Act 1993 to provide suitable education for children who could not attend school because of illness.

The House of Lords held that the statute imposed a duty on the council to decide what was suitable education, and to do so on educational grounds, not financial ones. It came to this conclusion on the basis that other parts of the Act made reference to taking into account financial considerations, but the section in question did not; if Parliament had intended finance to be an issue in the decision it would have said so, as it had elsewhere. Therefore Parliament could not have intended that such considerations should affect the council's assessment of what was suitable education for the claimant, and the council was in breach of its duty.

In **Gorringe** *v* **Calderdale Metropolitan Borough Council** (2004), the claimant was injured when she crashed into a bus which had been hidden from her view over the crest of a hill. She argued that the council should have painted warning signs on the road to encourage drivers to slow down, and that its failure to do so was in breach of its statutory duty under the Highways Act 1980 to 'maintain the highway'. The House of Lords disagreed: the provision of information and warnings, whether by street signs or road markings, was a different thing from keeping the highway in good repair, and failure to provide such information was therefore not a breach of that duty.

As well as looking at precisely what the statute requires the defendant to do, the courts have to look at the degree of fault required to constitute a breach of duty. Some statutes impose absolute duties, which means that where a court finds that tortious liability can be imposed, that liability will be strict, and a defendant may be in breach even if they could not have prevented the harm. Such cases are rare, but one example is **Galashiels Gas Co Ltd** *v* **Millar** (1949). Here the relevant statute was the Factories Act 1937, which provided that 'every hoist or lift shall be properly maintained'. The House of Lords held that this could only be read as imposing an absolute duty to maintain a lift in perfect working order; not a duty to do so where it was reasonably practical, or to take reasonable steps to do so. Therefore any failure in a lift mechanism meant there had been a breach of the duty, regardless of whether the failure or the harm caused by it was foreseeable, or could have been prevented.

The majority of statutes, however, impose qualified duties, which create a fault requirement similar to that of negligence, in that it is based on a standard of reasonableness. In these cases the courts apply the same balancing exercise as they would in a negligence case. An example of this is **McCarthy** *v* **Coldair Ltd** (1951), where the relevant statute stated that 'there shall, as far as is reasonably practicable, be provided and maintained safe means of access to every place at which any person has at any time to work'. The claimant in the case had been injured when he fell from a short ladder, which slipped on a shiny floor that had been splashed with paint. He alleged that his employer was in breach of the duty imposed by the Act, because it would have been 'reasonably practicable' to have another employee standing by to keep the ladder in place, but the employer had not done this. The court said that the risk of harm from falling from a ladder of this length was not great and, ordinarily, placing an extra employee at the foot of the ladder would be a disproportionately expensive way of avoiding a small risk; however, the slipperiness of the floor increased the risk, and so meant that the precaution suggested would have been reasonably practicable, and by not taking it the employer was in breach. Had the floor not been slippery, there would have been no breach.

Damage

The claimant can only recover for damage which is of the kind that the statutory provision is intended to prevent. Again, in deciding this, the courts will look closely at the words of the statute, and its purpose.

Key Case **Gorris** *v* **Scott (1874)**

The leading case on this issue is **Gorris** *v* **Scott** (1874). The defendant was a shipowner, who was transporting some of the claimant's sheep. The Contagious Diseases (Animals) Act 1869 required that cattle or sheep being transported by ship to Great Britain from abroad had to be kept in special pens on board. The defendant failed to do this, and the claimant's sheep were washed overboard. However, the court held that he could not succeed in his action for breach of the duty, because the statute had been passed to prevent disease spreading between different groups of animals on the ship, and not to prevent the animals from being washed overboard and drowning. The defendant had been in breach of the duty, but the damage caused as a result was not the kind for which the statute could allow a remedy.

Legal Principle
A claimant can only claim for damage of a kind which the statute was designed to prevent.

A more difficult issue is what happens when the damage caused by the breach is the kind that the statute aims to prevent, but it happens in a different way from that referred to in the statute. In **Donaghey** *v* **Bolton & Paul** (1968), regulations made under a statute required that special safety equipment should be used where employees had to climb on 'roofs . . . covered with fragile materials through which a person is likely to fall a distance of more than ten feet'. The claimant was injured by falling through a hole in a roof, rather than through fragile material, but the House of Lords held that he could recover compensation under the statute: the damage caused to him by failure to provide the safety equipment was exactly the kind which the statute sought to prevent, and it did not matter that it had happened in a way that the makers of the regulation had not considered.

However, in other cases, the House of Lords has taken a more restrictive approach. **Close** *v* **Steel Co of Wales** (1962) is one of a number of 'flying part' cases, where the courts have held that legislation imposing a duty on factory owners to fence off the moving parts of dangerous machinery was intended to prevent employees being injured by being caught in the machines; employees who had been injured when parts of the machine came loose and flew out could not recover compensation for breach of such provisions.

Defences

Contributory negligence is available as a defence to breach of statutory duty. This was stated to be the case in **ICI** *v* **Shatwell** (1965) (discussed on p. 125). The defence of *volenti* may be available, but its use is limited by the need to prove genuine consent. Where the claimant has had no real choice in the matter, as in many cases where the statutory duty is one imposed on employers for the benefit of employees, *volenti* will not apply.

Problems with statutory torts

As we have seen, there is a lot of uncertainty in this area of law and the courts' view, that the existence or not of tortious liability is merely a question of statutory interpretation, conceals (as emphasis on statutory interpretation normally does) the exercise of some discretion, as the

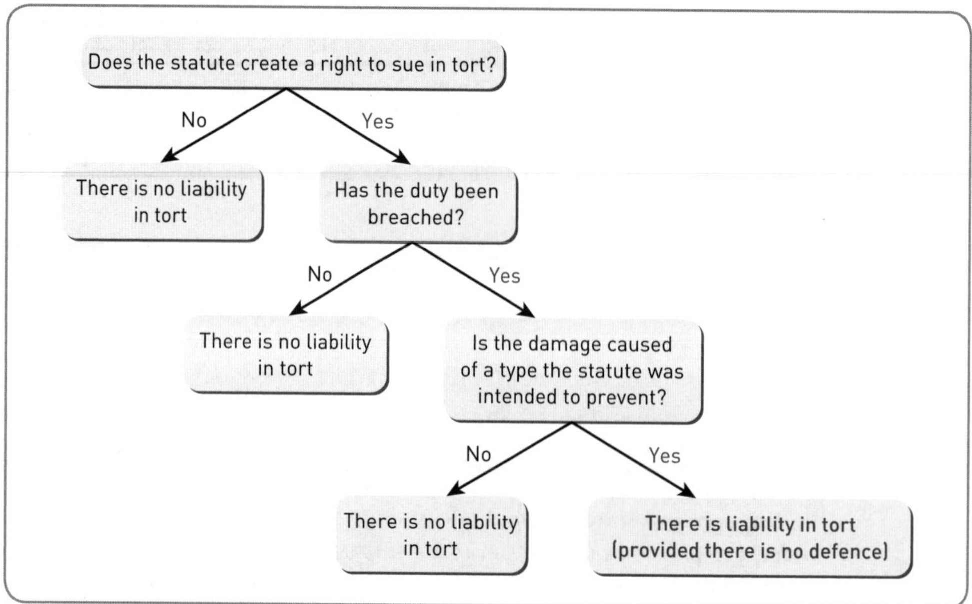

Figure 7.1 Liability for breach of statutory duty

contrast between, for example, **Atkinson** *v* **Newcastle and Gateshead Waterworks Co** (1877) and **Groves** *v* **Wimbourne** (1898) shows.

It has been suggested that Parliament's intentions would be better known if statutes expressly stated whether or not civil liability should be incurred for breach, and moves towards this are visible in modern legislation. The Sex Discrimination Act 1975, s. 66(1) and the Race Relations Act 1976, s. 57(1), for example, provide that discriminatory acts 'may be made the subject of civil proceedings in like manner as any other claim in tort . . . for breach of statutory duty'.

Breach of EU legislation

Duties imposed on government bodies by European Union legislation can give rise to a right to sue for breach. In the joined cases of **Brasserie du Pêcheur SA** *v* **Federation of Republic of Germany** and **R** *v* **Secretary of State for Transport, ex parte Factortame Ltd (No 4)** (1996), the European Court of Justice held that governments were liable for financial loss suffered as a result of their breach of EU law.

The ECJ said there would be a right to compensation where three conditions were met:

- the rule of Community law infringed must be intended to confer rights on individuals;
- the breach must be sufficiently serious; and
- there must be a direct causal link between the breach of the obligation and the damage sustained by the injured parties.

In some cases this will give claimants an alternative way to claim for breach of a duty by official bodies.

Answering questions

The issue of breach of statutory duty rarely arises as the sole topic of an exam question, but you should look out for it as an element of problem questions, especially those involving public bodies.

Summary of Chapter 7

Many statutes impose duties, but this does not always mean that failure to perform the duty gives rise to a right to sue in tort.

Scope of the tort

To decide whether a right to sue exists, the courts look at the wording of the statute, and at other factors which can indicate Parliament's intention to create a cause of action.

Who the statute is intended to benefit

Tortious liability only arises where an act is designed to create individual rights against the party which has the duty, not where the intention is a general public benefit.

Availability of alternative remedies

Where an alternative way to penalise breach of the duty exists, there is a presumption that no right to sue in tort exists.

Degree of detail

The more detailed and specific the provisions creating the duty are, the more likely that the courts will find there is civil liability for its breach.

Background to the legislation

The courts look at the background to determine what Parliament's intention was when creating the legislation.

The type of harm

Where a statute protects against a type of harm not covered by tort law, it is unlikely to create a right to claim in tort.

Elements of the tort

If there is civil liability, the courts look at the wording of the statute to determine what the duty is, and whether it has been breached.

The claimant can only recover for damage of the kind the statute was designed to prevent.

Defences

Volenti and contributory negligence apply as defences.

Reading list

Text resources

Buckley, R A (1984) 'Liability in tort for breach of statutory duty' 100 *Law Quarterly Review* 204

Davis, J L R (1998) 'Farewell to the action for breach of statutory duty?' in Mullany, N and Linden, A M (eds) *Torts Tomorrow: A Tribute to John Fleming*, LBC Information Services

Harlow, C (2005) *Understanding Tort Law*, 3rd edn, Chapter 8. Sweet & Maxwell

Law Commission (1969) *The Interpretation of Statutes: Report by the Two Commissions*, Scot Law Commission Report No 11 (NC 256)

Morris, C (1949) 'The role of criminal statutes in negligence actions' 49 *Columbia Law Review* 21

Stanton, K (2004) 'New forms of the tort of breach of statutory duty' 120 *Law Quarterly Review* 324

Thayer, E R (1914) 'Public wrong and private action' 27 *Harvard Law Review* 317

Williams, G (1960) 'The effects of penal legislation in the law of tort' 23 *Modern Law Review* 233

Reading on the Internet

The Court of Appeal judgment in **Olutu** *v* **Home Office** (1997) can be read at:
http://www.bailii.org/ew/cases/EWCA/Civ/1996/1070.html

The Court of Appeal judgment in **Danns** *v* **Department of Health** (1998) can be read at:
http://alpha.bailii.org/ew/cases/EWCA/Civ/1997/1168.html

The House of Lords judgment in **Phelps** *v* **Hillingdon** (2000) can be read at:
http://www.publications.parliament.uk/pa/ld199900/ldjudgmt/jd000727/phelp-1.htm

The Court of Appeal decision in **Ziemniak** *v* **ETPM** (2003) can be read at:
http://alpha.bailii.org/ew/cases/EWCA/Civ/2003/636.html

The House of Lords decision in **Cullen** *v* **Chief Constable of the Royal Ulster Constabulary** (2003) can be read at:
http://www.publications.parliament.uk/pa/ld200203/ldjudgmt/jd030710/cull-1.htm

The House of Lords decision in **Gorringe** *v* **Calderdale** (2004) can be read at:
http://www.publications.parliament.uk/pa/ld200304/ldjudgmt/jd040401/gorr-1.htm

Visit **www.mylawchamber.co.uk** to access tools to help you develop and test your knowledge of tort law, including interactive multiple choice questions, practice exam questions with guidance, weblinks, glossary flashcards, legal newsfeed and legal updates.

Use Case Navigator to read in full some of the key cases referenced in this chapter with commentary and questions:
Phelps *v* **Hillingdon Borough Council** (2000)

Chapter 8
Deceit

This chapter discusses:

- How the tort of deceit is committed
- How damages for deceit are calculated
- Differences between negligent misstatement and deceit.

As we saw in Chapter 2, under the principle established in **Hedley Byrne** *v* **Heller**, someone who negligently makes a misleading statement can be liable for economic loss caused to another as a result. The action for deceit also concerns misleading statements, but applies where the person making the statement knew it was untrue, or was reckless about whether it was true or not. Also known as fraud, it is a much older tort than negligent misstatement, and was first established in the case of **Pasley** *v* **Freeman** (1789), but, even though most of the principles come from old cases, it is still very much a part of modern tort law.

Elements of the tort

A claimant in deceit must prove six things:

- that the defendant made a false representation (in other words, that he or she lied);
- that the representation was one of fact;
- that the defendant knew that the representation was false, or at least had no genuine belief that it was true;
- that the defendant intended the claimant, or a group of people which included the claimant, to act on the false representation;
- that the claimant acted on the representation;
- that acting on the representation caused the claimant damage.

A false representation

A 'representation' will often be a statement, which can be either written or spoken. However, it need not be made in words, but can also be suggested by the way the defendant acts. In **R** *v* **Barnard** (1837), the defendant wore an academic cap and gown when he went into a shop to try to obtain goods on credit, giving the impression that he was a member of the university and therefore likely to be able to pay the bill. As he was not a member of the university, this was an example of making a false representation by conduct, rather than words. Similarly, in **Legh** *v* **Legh** (1930), it was held that a man who has agreed to pay his wife half his income would be making a false representation if he sent her £30,000 when his income was £80,000; even without words, he would be implying that his income was £60,000.

The effect of silence

Simply remaining silent about something will not usually amount to a false representation, but there are exceptions to this rule:

- Half-truths: a statement which tells only part of the truth can be a false representation if leaving out part of the picture makes what is said misleading.
- Deliberate concealment: actively concealing information can amount to a false representation (for example, if when selling something you actively conceal a fault which the buyer would otherwise have easily been able to see, you are making a false representation that the fault does not exist).
- Failure to meet statutory requirements: in some circumstances, there is a statutory duty to reveal particular information and, in these cases, failure to do so can amount to a false representation.

An example would be that, under the Companies Act 2006, certain information must be included in a company prospectus (a document issued to people who may want to buy shares in the company). Failing to include that information could give rise to an action in deceit.

Silence can also amount to a false representation where a situation changes after the initial representation is made. In **Incledon** *v* **Watson** (1862), it was held that if a defendant makes a statement which is true at the time, but it later becomes untrue and the defendant knows this and chooses to stay silent, he or she may be liable in deceit.

A representation of fact

The lie told by the defendant (whether in words or by conduct) must be about a matter of fact. So, for example, if the seller of a racehorse were to (falsely) say 'He is the son of a Derby winner', that would be a false representation of fact, and could give rise to liability in deceit. However, if the seller said 'This horse is going to win the Derby', that could only be a statement of his or her opinion; he or she could not know that as a fact and so the statement could not lead to liability in deceit.

However, there are two situations where an apparent statement of opinion may be taken as a false representation of fact. The first is where the defendant falsely gives the impression that he or she holds an opinion, but actually does not, and the second is where a defendant makes a statement of opinion, and falsely implies that there are reasonable grounds for that opinion, when there are no such grounds.

When assessing cases involving statements of opinion, the courts will allow a certain amount of leeway for what they call 'sales talk', so a salesman who tells you that 'This is the best DVD player you'll find', for example, would not usually be liable in deceit, unless specific false claims are made as well.

Promises and intentions

Promises and statements of intention are not usually considered representations of fact, but they may be if they can be taken to mean that a certain situation does or will exist.

Key Case **Edgington** *v* **Fitzmaurice (1885)**

In **Edgington** *v* **Fitzmaurice** (1885), the directors of a company tried to attract people to invest in their company by saying that the money invested was to be used to finish off company buildings, buy equipment, and generally develop the company. In fact, the company was in debt, and the money was to be used to pay some of what it owed. The defendants argued that they were making a statement of intention and this could not be considered a representation of fact, but Bowen LJ rejected this idea, famously stating that 'the state of a man's mind is as much a fact as the state of his digestion'. In other words, the defendants had been stating as a fact that they intended to spend the money as they described.

Legal Principle

A promise or statement of intention can be considered a statement of fact, if it can be taken to mean that a certain situation does or will exist.

By contrast, in **Wales** *v* **Wadham** (1977), a woman's statement that she did not intend to remarry after her divorce was held to be a statement of opinion, not fact. The deciding factor in **Edgington** was that when they issued the prospectus, the defendants did not genuinely intend to use the money as they said. However, a promise which goes on to be broken will not create liability in deceit where, at the time the promise was made, the defendant intended to keep it.

Knowledge or recklessness

Key Case **Derry** *v* **Peek (1889)**

Making a false representation through carelessness or stupidity is not enough to create liability in deceit. The case of **Derry** *v* **Peek** (1889) established that the defendant must either know that the representation is false, or be reckless about whether it is true or not. In this context, to be reckless means to be indifferent about whether the representation was true or not.

The facts of **Derry** were that the defendants were directors of a tram company, who issued a prospectus stating, among other things, that they were going to run steam-driven trams. They needed permission from the Board of Trade to do this and, although they did not have this permission when they issued the prospectus, they honestly believed they would have no problem in getting it. This turned out not to be true, and permission was refused, which meant that the shareholders lost money. The House of Lords held that where defendants honestly believe they are telling the truth, there can be no liability for deceit, even if they have been careless in not making sure of the truth.

Legal Principle

A defendant in deceit will only be liable if they know their statement was false, or are reckless as to whether it was true or not.

Intention that the claimant should act

To be liable, the defendant must have made the false representation with the intention that the claimant should act on it. So, for example, if a statement is put into a company prospectus, there is a clear intention that it should be acted on by people reading the prospectus, who will be potential investors in the company. However, if a director of the company were to make the same statement to someone he or she happened to meet at a party, and who, as far as the speaker knows, has no intention of buying shares in anything, it would be harder to prove intention.

The false representation does not necessarily have to be made to the claimant, so long as the defendant intends the claimant, or a group of which the claimant is part, to act on it. In **Langridge** *v* **Levy** (1837), the defendant sold a defective gun to a man, who made it clear that the gun would be used by his sons. The seller falsely (and knowingly) claimed that the gun was sound, but in fact it was defective, and one of the man's sons was injured while using it. He was able to claim for deceit.

Where the false representation is aimed at a particular group, anyone in that group who is caused damage may sue, but someone outside the group which was intended to act on the representation may not. In **Peek** *v* **Gurney** (1873), the court pointed out that a company prospectus was aimed at people buying shares in a company when they were first put on sale, and so those people could sue over the false statements made in it, but if they later sold on their shares, the people who bought from them could not sue.

Ambiguous representations

What is the situation where the representation made is capable of being understood in two different ways, one of which is true, and the other not? In **Smith** *v* **Chadwick** (1884), the defendants issued a company prospectus saying that 'the present value of the turnover or output of the entire works is over £1,000,000 per annum'. This could have been taken to mean that the business was capable of making that amount of money (which was true), or that it had actually made that amount in a specific year (which was not true). The court held that, in order to make a claim based on the untrue meaning, claimants had to prove that the defendant had intended them to act on that meaning, or had deliberately used the ambiguity to deceive the claimants. If, however, the defendant had not realised there was another meaning, or intended an untrue meaning to influence the claimant, there was no liability.

To be liable, the defendant only needs to intend the claimant to act on the representation; he or she does not have to intend that the claimant should suffer damage as a result.

Acting on the representation

Someone who suffers damage as a result of a false representation can only sue if the representation actually influenced them to act as they did. However, in **Edgington** *v* **Fitzmaurice** (see above), it was established that the false representation need not be the only reason for acting, as long as it is one of them. Nor is it necessary for the claimant to prove that, had it not been for the statement, they would not have acted as they did.

If the false representation is one of the factors that made the claimant act in the way which caused damage, it does not matter that he or she could have avoided the damage if they had made checks or sought further information, even if it can be argued that a reasonable person would have checked up. In **Central Rly of Venezuela** *v* **Kisch** (1867), the defendants made false statements in a prospectus, with the result that a shareholder lost money. The prospectus listed some documents which it said could be inspected at the company offices, and the defendants argued that, if the claimant had checked these, the fraud would have been noticed. The court rejected this argument, and the defendants were held liable. Similarly, in **S Pearson & Son Ltd** *v* **Dublin Corp** (1907), it was held that inserting a clause in a contract, stating that the claimant should check all representations that had been made and not assume them to be accurate, did not prevent liability for fraud if the claimant did not make those checks.

Damage to the claimant

The claimant's reliance on the false representation must cause them damage. In most deceit cases, this damage will be financial loss, but the courts have established that claims in deceit can be brought where reliance on false representations causes damage to property, personal injury (**Langridge** *v* **Levy**; see above) or mental distress (**Shelley** *v* **Paddock** (1979)).

The rule on causation is that the defendant is liable for all losses which directly flow from the claimant acting on the false representation (and not, as in negligent misstatement, only those which are reasonably foreseeable).

Topical issue

Claims about paternity

As you might expect, most deceit claims involve business transactions. But, in 2007, the courts were asked to look at whether a claim for deceit could be made in a quite different situation: namely, where a woman was alleged to have lied to her (by then former) partner by saying that he was the father of her child. The case, **A** *v* **B** (2007), was brought by a man who had believed that he had a son, whom he loved very much, with his girlfriend. When the boy was five years old, the claimant found out that he was not his son, but the son of someone his girlfriend had had an affair with. He sued for deceit. Evidence was given that his girlfriend had not been certain that the boy was not his, but knew there was a possibility because she had had unprotected sex with the other man at the relevant time. Mr A had known at that time that his partner had slept with someone else, and so had asked her whether he was the father of the child. She repeatedly said yes. The fact that she did not know whether this was true, but ignored the possibility that it was not true, was clearly enough to establish recklessness. Mr A successfully claimed damages for the distress caused by finding out that the child, whom he loved as his own, was not in fact his.

The decision was a controversial one, which was widely reported in the press. While some argued that a man in Mr A's situation had a right to know the truth, it was also suggested that the case effectively meant women had a legal duty to 'spill the beans' if they had doubts about who had fathered their child, and that this could lead to many more families breaking up, with consequent harm to the child, even if the doubts proved to be wrong. Mr A was also criticised for taking the case to court, because of the effect this would have on the child who, like Mr A, was an innocent victim. The main question raised was whether this was an area where an action that was designed for commercial disputes was really appropriate, even though, in the case of **A** *v* **B**, it proved quite straightforward to frame the facts into a claim for deceit.

Calculating damages for deceit

The claimant is entitled to be put back into the position he or she would have been in if the deceit had not taken place. This means that if, for example, a claimant was led to believe they were buying property worth £100,000, but the defendant knew that it was only worth £50,000, the claimant is entitled to damages of £50,000.

As stated above, the defendant is liable for all losses directly flowing from their wrongdoing. The effect of this can be seen in **Smith New Court Securities** *v* **Scrimgeour Vickers** (1997). The claimant was persuaded to buy 28 million shares in a company called Ferranti, at the price of 82p each, after the defendant falsely stated that there were other buyers who wanted them. The shares were in fact worth only 78p each. Unknown to the defendant, Ferranti had itself been the subject of a major fraud, and when this fraud was made public the shares dropped to 44p each. When the claimant succeeded in an action for deceit, the defendant argued that the damages should be the difference between the cost of 28 million shares at 82p and the cost at 78p. The House of Lords disagreed; the fraud on Ferranti had already happened when the defendant made the false representation, so, as a direct result of the defendant's deceit, the claimant had ended up with 28 million shares which were only going to be worth 44p and therefore the damages were the difference between that and the price paid. The situation would have been different if the fraud had happened after the claimant bought the shares.

In **Eng Ltd** *v* **Harper and another** (2008), the defendants made false claims which persuaded the claimant to buy their company, Excel. The claimant said that if he had not bought Excel, he would have bought a different company, and he claimed that had he done so, he would have made a considerable profit. He therefore claimed that their deceit had caused him to lose the money he would have earned from the other company, and that his damages for deceit should reflect that. This kind of award is known as damages for loss of a chance, and is allowed in negligence. Loss of a chance awards had not previously been given in deceit but the court found that there was no reason why they should not be.

Once a claimant becomes aware of the fraud, they are required to take reasonable steps to mitigate their loss (as explained in Chapter 2). The differences between negligent misstatement and deceit are outlined in Table 8.1.

Table 8.1 Differences between negligent misstatement and deceit

	Negligent misstatement	Deceit
Special relationship between parties required	Yes	No
Must be reasonable for claimant to rely on statement	Yes	No
Defendant's state of mind	Negligence	Knowledge/recklessness
Test for causation	Reasonable foreseeability	Direct consequence

Answering questions

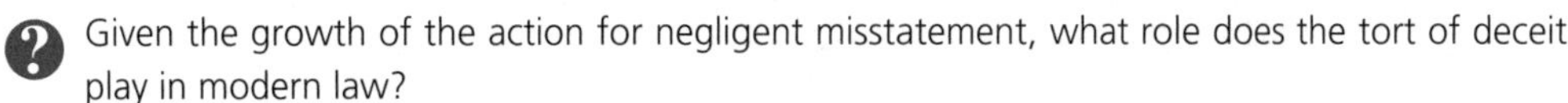

Given the growth of the action for negligent misstatement, what role does the tort of deceit play in modern law?

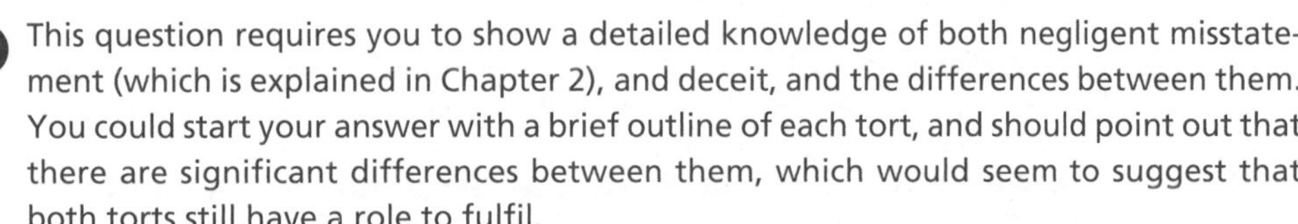

This question requires you to show a detailed knowledge of both negligent misstatement (which is explained in Chapter 2), and deceit, and the differences between them. You could start your answer with a brief outline of each tort, and should point out that there are significant differences between them, which would seem to suggest that both torts still have a role to fulfil.

You could then go through each of the major differences in turn, explaining how these equate to a need for both torts. A sensible place to start would be with the different states of mind required for each tort, as these to some extent explain the other differences; the intention or recklessness of deceit is seen as more blameworthy than negligence and so some of the restrictions on liability in negligent misstatement do not apply in deceit.

You should look at the fact that negligent misstatement will only apply where there is some kind of existing relationship between the parties, and explain the justification for this. The cases of **Esso** *v* **Mardon** and **Lennon** explain that a key ground of the tort is that where it is clear that the claimant is trusting the defendant's advice, the defendant should take care when giving it. In deceit, by contrast, we are talking about deliberate wrongdoing, so the courts do not apply the same restrictions on liability. Similar arguments will apply to the fact that in negligent misstatement the claimant must have acted reasonably, whereas in deceit the claimant could have avoided damage by making their own checks, and here you could talk about the cases of **Caparo** *v* **Dickman, Reeman** and **Smith** *v* **Eric Bush**, as compared to **Central Rly of Venezuela** *v* **Kisch** and **S Pearson & Son Ltd** *v* **Dublin Corp**.

Finally, discuss the different rules on causation, and the effects these can have on what a claimant can receive in damages. You should end with a conclusion that sums up the different roles played by each tort.

Summary of Chapter 8

The action for deceit compensates for loss caused by deliberate false representations.

Elements of the tort

A false representation

A representation may be written, spoken or in the form of conduct. Silence is not usually sufficient, but may be if it takes the form of half-truths or deliberate concealment, or where there is a statutory duty to reveal information.

A representation of fact

The representation must concern fact, not opinion; the exceptions are where a defendant falsely suggests they hold an opinion, or have grounds for doing so. Promises or statements of intention do not suffice, unless they suggest that a situation does or will exist.

Knowledge or recklessness

The defendant must know the statement is false, or be indifferent as to whether it is true. An honest belief in an untrue statement cannot give rise to liability.

Intention for the claimant to act

The statement need not be made to the claimant, but the defendant must make it with the intent that the claimant or a group of which they are a part should act on it. If a statement is ambiguous, the defendant is only liable if they intended the claimant to act on an untrue meaning.

Acting on the representation

The claimant must have been influenced to act by the representation, but it need not be the only reason. The fact that a claimant could have avoided damage by making checks does not prevent liability.

Damage to the claimant

Damages can be claimed for financial loss, property damage, personal injury and mental distress. The defendant is liable for all damage which flows directly from the claimant's reliance on the false representation.

Calculating damages

The claimant can claim the cost of being put back in the position they would have been in had the deceit not happened. This includes the cost of any damage which is a direct result of the deceit. The claimant must mitigate their loss from the time they become aware of the deceit.

Reading list

Text resources

Fox, D (2002) 'Enforcing a possessory title to a stolen car' 61 *Cambridge Law Journal* 1
Fullager, W K (1951) 'Liability for representations at common law' 25 *Australian Law Journal* 278
Keeton, R E (1937) 'Fraud: misrepresentations of law' 15 *Texas Law Review* 409

Reading on the Internet

The House of Lords judgment in **Smith New Court Securities** *v* **Scrimgeour** (1996) can be read at:

http://www.parliament.the-stationery-office.co.uk/pa/ld199697/ldjudgmt/jd961121/smith01.htm

Chapter 9
Defamation

This chapter discusses:

- How the tort of defamation is committed
- Who can sue or be sued for defamation
- Defences to a defamation action
- Remedies for defamation
- Problems with the law on defamation.

Defamation is a tort which protects against damage to reputation. If someone says, or writes, something about someone else that could cause harm to that person's reputation, that person can sue for damages. Although anyone can sue for defamation, cases are most often brought by famous people, for the simple reason that damaging remarks about them are more likely to be reported to a wide audience. As an example, in 1997, the Hollywood actress Nicole Kidman sued the *Express on Sunday* after it reported that she had instructed builders working at her home to face the wall whenever she walked past, and not to look at her. This clearly made her look arrogant and unpleasant, and the Court of Appeal upheld her claim that the words were capable of being defamatory (the case was then settled out of court).

One important thing to know about defamation before we look at the tort in detail is that cases almost always require a court to balance two competing rights: the right of the claimant to protect their reputation, and the right of the defendant to freedom of expression, meaning the right to freely communicate thoughts, ideas and opinions. This right is considered very important in democratic societies (a democratic vote is, after all, a form of freedom of expression), and is protected under Art. 10 of the Universal Declaration of Human Rights. In most democratic societies, including ours, it is viewed as especially important for the media to be able to report freely, and as the vast majority (though not all) of defamation cases involve the media, courts almost invariably have to consider this issue.

Over the past 20 years or so, the English law of defamation has come under increasing criticism from academics, campaigners for freedom of expression and the media, who have argued that it tipped the balance too far in favour of protecting a claimant's reputation, while not giving enough protection to the right of freedom of expression. To address these issues, the Government introduced new legislation. The Defamation Bill was going through Parliament when this book went to press, and was thought likely to become law, as the Defamation Act, in 2013. As it was unclear when the changes would come into force, in this chapter we include both the old law, and the changes which were planned at the time of going to press; check this book's websites for updates.

Defamation used to be one of the few torts which was usually heard by a judge and jury, unless a judge decided that it was more suitable for hearing by a judge alone, for example because it raised particularly complex issues that a jury might not understand. Section 11 of the Defamation Act 2013 reverses this situation, stating that defamation cases are to be heard without a jury, unless a court orders otherwise.

Elements of defamation

Defamation is committed by publishing a statement which lowers the reputation of the person referred to. To succeed in an action for defamation, the claimant must therefore prove three things:

- the statement complained of was defamatory;
- the statement referred to the claimant;
- the statement was published.

The Defamation Act 2013 is likely to add a fourth requirement, that publication of the statement has caused or is likely to cause serious harm to the claimant's reputation. This requirement may not yet be in force (see the companion website for updates).

There are a number of defences to defamation, which are discussed later in this chapter, but it is worth knowing at this stage (because it will help explain some of the cases in this chapter) that a defendant who can prove their statement was true will have a complete defence. This defence is known as justification.

There are two types of defamation: libel and slander.

- Libel covers statements made in some permanent form. This includes written or printed words, online material, film and pictures. The Defamation Act 1952 provides that it also covers radio broadcasts, and the Theatres Act 1968 states that it covers plays performed to an audience.
- Slander applies to defamation committed in some kind of transitory or temporary form, such as spoken words or gestures.

In the case of libel, merely committing the tort without a defence is sufficient for liability, but with slander, a defendant will usually only be liable if the defamation has caused the claimant special damage, usually in the form of financial loss, over and above the injury to the claimant's reputation. There are some exceptions to this rule (see p. 233).

Defamatory statements

Most of the original law on defamation comes from case law, rather than statute, so there is no single definition of what 'defamatory' means. Traditional definitions are that a statement will be defamatory if it 'tends to lower the person in the estimation of right-thinking members of society', or exposes the person to 'hatred, contempt or ridicule'. Both of these are still accurate, but a more comprehensive definition, in line with modern legal thinking, is given by the legal academics McBride and Bagshaw in their textbook *Tort Law* (Longman, 2008). They say that a statement is defamatory if reading or hearing it would make an ordinary, reasonable person tend to:

- think less well as a person of the individual referred to;
- think that the person referred to lacked the ability to do their job effectively;
- shun or avoid the person referred to; or
- treat the person referred to as a figure of fun or an object of ridicule.

Their definition makes it clear that the important issue is not how the defamatory statement makes the person referred to feel, but the impression it is likely to make on those reading it. The person defamed does not have to prove that the words actually had any of these effects on any particular people or the public in general, only that the statement could tend to have that effect on an ordinary, reasonable listener or reader. Nor does the claimant need to prove that they have lost money, or suffered any other kind of loss or damage (except in some cases of slander).

Examples of defamatory statements

Obvious examples of defamatory statements would be saying (falsely) that someone was a thief, had been violent, or was corrupt, but over the years the courts have had to deal with a very wide range of statements alleged to be defamatory. In **Byrne** *v* **Deane** (1937), the claimant was a member of a golf club, whose owners illegally kept gambling machines on the premises. Someone reported them to the police, and afterwards a poem was posted up in the club, implying that the claimant had been the informant. He sued, and won the original case, but on appeal the courts held that the suggestion was not defamatory, because a right-thinking member of society (or as it might be expressed today, an ordinary, reasonable person) would not think less well of someone for telling the police about criminal activity.

In **Mitchell** *v* **Faber & Faber** (1998), the claimant was a musician who had worked with the rock star Jimi Hendrix during the 1960s. The defendants were the publishers of a book about Hendrix, in which the author said that the claimant had a 'strange contempt' for Hendrix and routinely used words like 'nigger' and 'coon' in everyday conversation. However, he said that the claimant had no idea that what he said might offend anyone, and did not intend any harm. The claimant sued on the basis that the book made him appear to be racist. The defendant argued that the book was not defamatory, in that it made clear that the claimant had not intended to offend Hendrix, and that his attitude was simply typical of many people in the UK 30 years ago. The Court of Appeal said that although it was true that those attitudes were widely held at that time, it was necessary to consider what impression the book would have on people reading it now, and therefore the words could be defamatory.

In **Jason Donovan** *v* **The Face** (1998), the singer Jason Donovan successfully sued *The Face* magazine for saying he was gay. He based his argument on the fact that he had always presented himself as being heterosexual, and that *The Face* was therefore defaming him by suggesting he had deceived the public about his sexuality. The case did not, therefore, test whether it is defamatory merely to say someone is gay.

In many cases, allegations which might, on the face of them, not seem to be damaging, can be considered defamatory when taken against the background of factors about the claimant, such as their work, or even their relationship status. In **Berkoff** *v* **Burchill** (1996), the journalist Julie Burchill described the actor Steven Berkoff as 'hideous-looking' and compared him to Frankenstein's monster. Although upsetting, these kinds of remarks would not usually be considered defamatory, but in this case the court said that the fact that the claimant earned his living as an actor meant the words made him an object of ridicule.

In **Thornton** *v* **Daily Telegraph Media Group** (2011), the *Telegraph* was successfully sued by Dr Sarah Thornton, an academic, over a review of one of her books. The case is thought to be the first successful libel claim over a book review in several decades. The review was of a book about the art world, and it contained quotes from Lynn Barber, a *Telegraph* journalist who was interviewed for the book because she was a member of the jury for a prestigious art prize. The review was written by Ms Barber, and in it, she claimed that Dr Thornton had never interviewed her for the book, which was untrue. The review also said that Dr Thornton allowed people she interviewed to have copy approval. Dr Thornton said these allegations were defamatory because it is generally considered bad form for writers to compromise their independence by allowing subjects copy approval, and so the claims reflected badly on her integrity as a writer and academic. She was awarded £65,000.

In 1997, a columnist on the *Express on Sunday*'s magazine mentioned a newspaper story which had stated that the film star Nicole Kidman has insisted that builders working on her house should face the wall whenever she walked past. A judge initially found that the story, although unpleasant, was not capable of being defamatory, but Ms Kidman appealed. The Court of Appeal agreed with her that the statement was capable of being defamatory. In the event the case was settled out of court. In **Cruise** *v* **Express Newspapers** (1999) Ms Kidman and her then husband Tom Cruise won damages, said to be a six-figure sum, from the *Express*, after the paper falsely claimed that their marriage was a sham, designed to cover up the fact that they were both gay.

In **Bowman** *v* **MGN Ltd** (2010) a West End actor called Simon Bowman won damages of £4,250, after the *Daily Mirror*'s website described him as former *Eastenders* actress Hannah Waterman's 'new man'. While the words in themselves would not be considered defamatory, Mr Bowman had been in a serious relationship with someone else for 20 years, and so the words could be taken to imply that he was being unfaithful to that person.

Remember that the defence of justification provides a complete defence where the statement complained of is true. A statement which can be proved to be true cannot give rise to a successful claim in defamation, no matter how damaging it is to the claimant's reputation.

Indirect criticisms

Key Case **Tolley *v* J S Fry & Sons Ltd (1931)**

A statement need not directly criticise the claimant; it may do so by implication, known as an 'innuendo'. In **Tolley *v* J S Fry & Sons Ltd** (1931) the claimant was an amateur golfer, and his amateur status meant that he was not allowed to accept money to advertise products. Without his knowledge the defendants published an advertisement containing a cartoon of him, with a rhyme praising the chocolate. He succeeded in proving that the advertisement amounted to a defamatory statement by way of innuendo, because readers seeing the advertisement were likely to assume that Tolley had been paid to lend his name to it and therefore compromised his amateur status.

Legal Principles

A defamatory statement need not directly criticise the claimant. An implied criticism, known as innuendo, can be sufficient.

In **Dwek *v* Macmillan Publishers** (1999), the 'statement' complained of arose from a picture and its caption, which did not even name the claimant. The picture, taken 20 years earlier, appeared in a book and showed the claimant, who was not the subject of the book, and was not named anywhere in it, sitting next to a woman who was (correctly) identified as a prostitute. The claimant argued that readers would understand the words and photograph as suggesting that he was a client of the prostitute. The defendant applied to have the action struck out, claiming that the words and picture were not capable of bearing this defamatory meaning because they made no reference to the claimant, there was nothing in the picture or anywhere else in the book to suggest that he even knew the woman was a prostitute, and he had not produced any readers who had recognised him in the photo. The Court of Appeal said that the action should not be struck out; taken together, the words and photo were capable of carrying the alleged meaning, and it should therefore be left to a jury to decide whether they were actually defamatory. The claimant was not required to prove that identified individuals had recognised him in the photograph.

In assessing whether a statement is defamatory, a court will look at the whole context in which it was made. In **Norman *v* Future Publishing** (1998), the claimant was the famous opera singer, Jessie Norman. She was interviewed by a classical music magazine, and in the article was quoted as saying, with apparent reference to her size, that she never went through doorways sideways because 'Honey, I ain't got no sideways'. Ms Norman denied making the remark, and claimed that it suggested she was vulgar and undignified, and 'conformed to a degrading racist stereotype of a person of African-American heritage'. The Court of Appeal dismissed her appeal against a strike out application, on the grounds that the words had to be read within the context of the article as a whole, which portrayed her as a person of high standing and impeccable dignity.

The case also makes the point that the fact that Ms Norman claimed she had never made the remarks was irrelevant if the remark itself was not defamatory; there is no liability in defamation simply for making up a quote from someone and publishing it, unless the alleged quote is defamatory.

Changes over time

In deciding whether a statement could lower its subject in the eyes of others, the court is asked to consider how an ordinary, reasonable person (referred to in some cases as a 'right-thinking person') would read and understand it. This person is often referred to by judges as 'the reasonable man', and one of the things that makes defamation claims so unpredictable is that, clearly, the views of the 'reasonable man' will change over time. At one time, for example, it would certainly have been defamatory to say of an unmarried woman that she spent the night with her boyfriend; this would not be the case today, unless, for example, that particular woman had presented herself as being against extra-marital sex, in which case she might be able to argue that the claim made her appear to be a liar and a hypocrite.

Statement must refer to the claimant

As well as proving that the statement in question is defamatory, the claimant has to show that an ordinary, reasonable reader or listener, including acquaintances of the claimant, would take the statement as referring to him or her (or it, in the case of companies). That means that if people who know the claimant would assume that the statement referred to him or her, the statement can be said to refer to the claimant; it does not matter that the public at large might not make the same assumption.

Where the claimant is named (or, as in **Dwek**, actually pictured) in the statement, this is not a problem, but there are cases where the person referred to in a defamatory statement is not named. This can still be defamatory if a reasonable person knowing the claimant would have thought the claimant was referred to. For example, in **J'Anson** *v* **Stuart** (1787) a newspaper referred to 'a swindler', describing the person meant in the words 'his diabolical character, . . . has but one eye, and is well known to all persons acquainted with the name of a certain noble circumnavigator'. The claimant had only one eye, and his name was very similar to the name of a famous admiral; he was able to prove that the statement referred to him, even though his name was never mentioned.

Where a defamatory statement was intended to refer to a fictitious character, or to someone other than the claimant, the defendant will be liable for defamation of the claimant if a reasonable person would think the statement referred to the claimant. An example of a case where the defamatory statement referred to a fictitious character is **Hulton** *v* **Jones** (1910). The defendants published a humorous newspaper story of the discreditable behaviour in Dieppe of a fictitious character called Artemus Jones. He was said to be a churchwarden in Peckham. Unknown to the author or editor, the claimant was also known as Artemus Jones, although he had actually been baptised Thomas Jones. He was a barrister not a churchwarden, did not live in Peckham and had never visited Dieppe. But he had contributed articles to the newspaper in the past and some of his friends thought that the article referred to him. He sued the owners of the newspaper for libel and was awarded £1,750, a decision that was upheld by the House of Lords. It did not matter that the defendants did not intend to defame him; all that mattered was what a reasonable person would understand the words to mean.

The publisher can also be liable where the statement was intended to refer to someone else, and was true of that person, but could be taken to refer to the claimant and was not true of them. This was the case in **Newstead** *v* **London Express Newspapers Ltd** (1940). The newspaper had printed a story saying that a Harold Newstead, described as a 30-year-old Camberwell man, had been convicted of bigamy. This was in fact true of the Harold Newstead the paper was talking about, but there was also another Harold Newstead living in Camberwell, who was not a bigamist. In fact the newspaper had been given the bigamist's exact address and occupation, which would have distinguished him from the innocent Harold Newstead, but this was left out of the published report due to lack of space. The defendants were held liable. However, in such cases of unintentional defamation, a special defence of offer of amends may be available under the Defamation Act 1996 (see p. 253).

The case of **O'Shea** *v* **MGN Ltd** (2001) displays a rather less strict approach to liability for unintended references and, in its reference to the Human Rights Act, suggests that the courts may in future be less willing to find against publishers for inadvertently referring to someone who has nothing to do with the story they publish. The defendant newspaper company published an advert for a pornographic website. The advert contained a picture of a woman, whom we can call X, which had been published with her full permission. However, the claimant was a woman who looked very like X, and certain details in the advert might also have been taken as referring to her by those who knew her. She sued, claiming that people who knew her would have reasonably thought that it was her, and that it was defamatory to suggest she would allow her picture to be used in such a context. On an application to have the case struck out, the court found that the 'ordinary sensible reader', who knew the claimant, could well think that it was her in the picture.

However, the court then looked at whether it was right to impose strict liability on the publishers. Referring back to **Hulton** *v* **Jones**, they held that following that case would require that the defendants could be liable, despite the fact that they had not intended to refer to the claimant. However, they then addressed the issue of the Human Rights Act 1998, which in Art. 10 provides that 'Everyone has the right to freedom of expression'. Article 10 accepts that this right may be restricted by such measures as are prescribed by law and necessary in a democratic society. The court accepted that advertising is a form of expression, and said that a decision for the claimant would require a restriction on the right of free expression that would go beyond what was necessary in a democratic society to protect people's reputations. Where a 'lookalike' was used deliberately, people in the claimant's position would have a claim under a different tort, called malicious falsehood, and that was sufficent protection. Where the use of a similar-looking person was innocent, it would impose an 'impossible burden' to expect publishers to check whether every picture they published resembled someone else, who might, in the context, claim defamation, and that would be an unreasonable interference with the right of free expression. Therefore the case was struck out.

Defaming a group

Where a defamatory statement refers to a class or group of people (such as 'All footballers are greedy' or 'British politicians are corrupt'), it is not usually possible for that group of people to sue for defamation as a group, nor for one member of a group to sue on the grounds that the remark libels them personally. So, for example, if you were to say that plumber John Bloggs was useless at his job, he might be able to sue, but if you were to say that all plumbers are useless, neither John Bloggs alone nor the whole plumbing trade could sue. In **Knupffer** *v* **London Express Newspapers**

Ltd (1944), the defendants published an article describing the Young Russia party, a group of Russian émigrés, as a Fascist organisation. The group had approximately 2,000 members, 24 of whom were based in the UK. The claimant, a Russian emigrant living in London, sued on the basis that, as a member of the group, the statement defamed him personally. The House of Lords refused his claim, on the grounds that the statement was aimed at a large class of people, and nothing in it singled him out.

However, where the group referred to is so small that the statement could be taken to refer to each and every one of them, one or all of them may be able to successfully sue. So while it is not dangerous to say 'All lawyers are useless', it may be a different story to say 'All lawyers employed at Bodgit, Snatch and Run are useless'.

There is no set number above which a class of people will be considered too big for one of the members to be able to sue for a remark aimed at all of them. Each case will depend on the facts and, in particular, how large the potential group is, and how closely the individuals in that group were associated with the defamatory statement. In **Aspro Travel** *v* **Owners Abroad Group** (1995), the defendants made a defamatory statement about the claimants' business, which was a family firm run by four members of the same family. They successfully argued that the statement could be taken to refer to any or all of them, and so were each able to sue. In **Riches** *v* **News Group** (1986), the *News of the World* published a letter from a man who was holding his own children hostage at gunpoint, which made serious allegations against the 'Banbury CID', although without mentioning specific officers by name. Ten members of the Banbury CID successfully sued the paper for damages.

The statement must be published

Most high-profile defamation cases involve publication of untrue statements in newspapers, magazines or books, or sometimes on radio or television. However, the law covers much more than this. For the purposes of establishing a case for defamation, a statement is considered to have been published when the defendant communicates it to anyone other than the claimant, or the defendant's husband or wife.

A defendant may escape liability if they can prove that it was not possible to foresee that publication would occur. In **Huth** *v* **Huth** (1915), a letter was sent in an unsealed envelope by the defendant to the claimant. The butler secretly read the letter without the claimant's permission. This was not treated as a publication, as the defendant could not have foreseen the butler's behaviour, so he was not liable for defamation.

By contrast, in **Theaker** *v* **Richardson** (1962), communication to a third party was foreseen by the defendant and therefore amounted to publication. The defendant had written a letter stating that the claimant was 'a lying, low down brothel keeping whore and thief'. He put the letter in a sealed envelope and posted it through the claimant's door. The claimant's husband opened the envelope and the defendant was held liable for defamation as he had foreseen that the letter might be opened by some person other than the claimant.

In **Godfrey** *v* **Demon Internet** (1999), it was stated that an Internet service provider could be said to have 'published' messages posted on its server by users. However, this will only apply in situations where an Internet service provider's part in publishing the words is, broadly speaking, comparable to the role of a book or newspaper publisher. In **Bunt** *v* **Tilley** (2006) a number of Internet service providers were sued over defamatory remarks published online. However, unlike **Demon**, they did not host the websites complained of, but merely provided the system by which the messages were conveyed from the writer to the websites. This made them more like a telephone or postal service than a publisher, and so it was held that they could not be liable.

In **Metropolitan International Schools Ltd** *v* **Designtechnica Corp, Google UK Ltd, Google Inc** (2009), the court considered whether an Internet search engine could be said to have published material that was located via an Internet search, including the 'snippets' from each website that appear in the search list. Eady J ruled that the search engine was not the publisher of any defamatory material that appeared on the websites searched for or the snippets from them. The search engine merely made it possible to find the defamatory material, and, even if it was told that the material was defamatory, it could not remove it but could only block the relevant addresses, and in this case the search engine had been trying to do that.

It was traditionally the law that every repetition of a defamatory statement created a fresh cause of action. However, this principle had in recent years caused problems for publishers who put material on the Internet, because it had been held that the moment of publication was every time a defamatory statement was downloaded (rather than, as might have seemed more sensible, when it was actually placed on the Internet). A claim for defamation has to be brought within a year of publication, but because publication was considered to take place when online material was downloaded by a claimant, publishers could be sued for something which was actually written years before.

This situation is addressed in s. 8 of the Defamation Act 2013, which introduces what it calls a 'single publication rule'. This provides that where someone publishes a defamatory statement, and then later publishes the same statement again, or publishes one which is substantially the same, the limitation period for any claim will run from publication of the first statement, so there will not be a fresh time limit starting at the time of the later publication. This means that if, for example, a newspaper publishes a story that is defamatory, and then puts that story on their website, a claimant will only be able to bring a claim within a year of the first publication in the newspaper, and not, as was the case previously, to bring a claim years later because the story has been downloaded from an online archive. However, a court can still use its discretion to waive the limitation period, under s. 32A of the Limitation Act 1980 (see p. 135).

The single publication rule only applies when the republished statement is the same or 'substantially the same' as the first one. Section 8(4) provides that where the 'manner of publication' of the later statement is 'materially different' from the first publication, the rule does not apply and so a new cause of action can arise from the time of the later publication. Whether the manner of publication is 'materially different' is a matter for the judge to assess, and s. 8(5) provides that, in deciding this, the court may take into account, among other things, the level of prominence that the defamatory statement is given, and the extent of the subsequent publication. The explanatory notes to the Act state that a possible example of the manner of publication being 'materially different' might be where a story was initially published in a section of a website where a reader would have to click through several links to get to it, and was later moved to a position where it could be directly accessed through the home page, which would almost certainly increase the number of hits it receives.

Note that the single publication rule only applies to re-publication by the same publisher. Where a defamatory statement is republished by a different party, a new cause of action still arises from that later publication. Examples would include where a newspaper reports a defamatory statement that someone else has made, or where one newspaper or broadcasting organisation repeats a defamatory statement made in another.

The single publication rule may not yet be in force (check the companion website for updates).

Serious damage to reputation

Before the passing of the Defamation Act 2013, a claimant in a libel action only had to prove that a statement was defamatory, under the definition we looked at earlier (see p. 226); if it was, the court would assume that there had been damage to their reputation. This will change under the Defamation Act 2013, which requires a claimant to prove that the defamatory statement has caused or is likely to cause serious damage to their reputation.

With slander, the situation is slightly different. In a slander action, the claimant will usually have to prove what is called 'special damage', which essentially means some kind of financial loss has been caused as a result of the defamation. However, under the law before the Defamation Act 2013, there are two situations where a slander claim can succeed without proof of special damage. These are where the slanderous statement suggests that:

- That the claimant has committed an imprisonable offence.
- That the claimant is unfit for their trade, profession or business, or any appointment they hold: the Defamation Act 1952, s. 2. Examples would be saying that a particular cook could not boil an egg, or that the local mayor was corrupt.
- That the claimant has a contagious disease of a kind that could lead to them being excluded from society.
- That, in the case of a female claimant, she is not chaste, which effectively means she has had sex outside marriage.

However, the Defamation Act 2013 abolishes the last two exceptions, so once it is in force, special damage would be required in claims involving such statements (though, in fact, a claim that a woman was not chaste would be unlikely to be considered defamatory these days, unless the woman concerned was a nun or was known for her objections to extra-marital sex). Slander claims will also be subject to the requirement that the defamatory statement has caused or is likely to cause serious damage to their reputation.

A case which raised the issue of causation of damage in slander was **McManus** *v* **Beckham** (2002). The defendant in this case was the former pop star Victoria Beckham, and the claimant was the owner of a shop which sold autographed memorabilia. Mrs Beckham was in the shopping centre where the shop was situated, when she spotted a display of photographs of her husband, David Beckham. According to the claimant, she loudly declared the autographs on them to be a fake, and told three customers that the claimant was in the habit of selling fakes, advising them not to buy anything from the shop. The incident was later reported by the newspapers, and the claimant sued Mrs Beckham for slander, alleging that her words had done severe damage to his business. Mrs Beckham argued that this claim should be struck out, because most of the damage had been done by the newspaper reports, and these broke the chain of causation so she could not be held responsible for damage done by third parties.

The Court of Appeal rejected this argument, and said that she could be liable if she realised that the 'sting' (in other words, the main message) of her remarks was likely to be reported in the papers, or if a reasonable person in her position would have seen that risk, and that the result would be damage to the claimant's business. The dispute was eventually settled out of court.

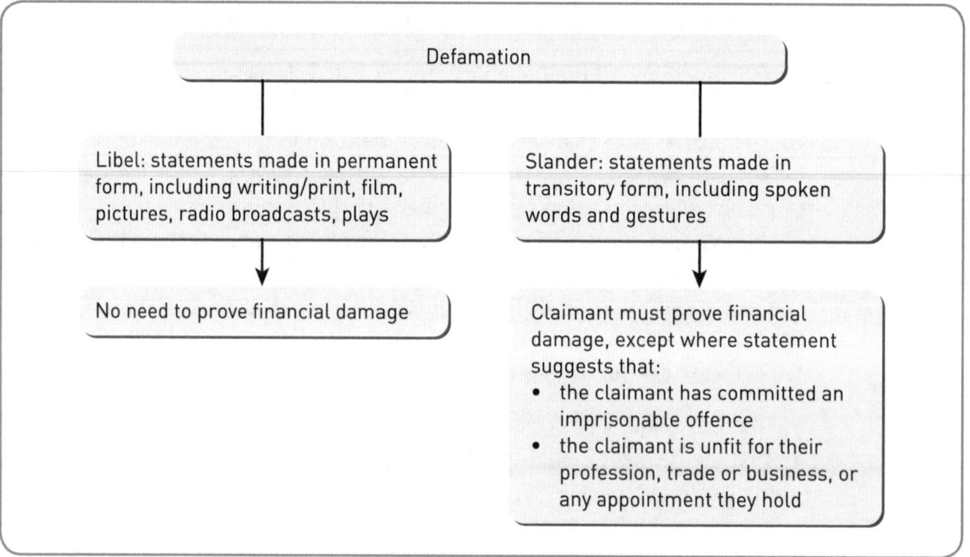

Figure 9.1 Libel and slander

Parties to a defamation action

Who can be sued?

A claimant in defamation can sue the person or organisation who published the statement. In media cases, under the law before the Defamation Act 2013, this could include any or all of the following:

- the journalist who wrote the story or presented it in a broadcast;
- the editor of the publication;
- the publishing or broadcasting company which owns the publication or programme which ran the story, and anyone involved in distributing it, such as wholesalers and newsagents.

The defence of innocent dissemination gave some protection to those who were only involved in distribution where they essentially had no means of control over the publication of defamatory material. This protection increases under the Defamation Act 2013, which provides, in s. 10, that it is no longer possible to bring an action against anyone who is not the author, editor or publisher of the statement, unless the court is satisfied that it is not reasonably practicable to sue the author, editor or publisher.

If a media story repeats an allegation made by someone else, rather than making the allegation themselves, the media organisation and personnel responsible can still be sued. So if, for example, a newspaper writes that 'Actress Jane Lovey says that reality TV star Chanel Hoggsbottom broke up her marriage by having an affair with her husband', it is no defence for the newspaper to say that they were not making the accusation, but simply reporting what Jane Lovey said. The only exception to this is for neutral reports of disputes regarding issues of public interest, which are covered by the neutral reportage defence (see p. 251). The person making the original allegation who was quoted in the media – in our example Jane Lovey – could also be sued but it is usually the media who find themselves on the receiving end of a claim, because they have the money to pay.

Internet publications

In recent years, the courts have had to address the issue of who can be sued when material is published online. In **Godfrey** *v* **Demon Internet** (1999), it was decided that an Internet service provider (ISP) can be liable for material posted on its server by users. However, this only applies where their role in doing so can be said to be comparable to that of a newspaper publisher with regard to material in its newspapers. In **Bunt** *v* **Tilley** (2006), a number of ISPs were sued over defamatory remarks published online, but the court held that their role in the publication was not like that of a newspaper publisher, but more like that of a telephone company, which has no control over what is said during conversations made on its lines. They were therefore not liable.

The Defamation Act 2013 introduces special rules for the operators of websites. The reason for these is obvious if you look at the comments left at the end of many online news stories, YouTube videos or blogs, or on public forums and social networking sites, which are frequently highly defamatory, but posted anonymously by members of the public who, even if they were identified, would not have the money to pay libel damages. Because of this problem, known as 'trolling', there have been attempts to sue the operators of websites where defamatory material was posted, instead of the people making the defamatory allegations, and s. 5 of the 2013 Act seeks to establish rules for when website operators will and will not be liable, by looking at what control or responsibility they actually have for defamatory postings.

The Act provides, in s. 5(2), that a website operator will not be liable for defamatory statements posted on their site where they can show that they did not post the statement, or in other words that they were hosting the content rather than putting it out themselves. However, this defence will not apply where the claimant can show that:

- it is not possible for the claimant to identify the person who posted the statement;
- the claimant gave the operator a notice of complaint about the statement; and
- the operator has failed to respond to the complaint.

How much protection this gives to claimants will very much depend on how the courts interpret the first of the three factors. If it applies, for example, merely when the person posting uses an online name instead of their own, there may well be many cases where a claim can be brought. But the words 'it is not possible' could equally mean that the claimant is expected to try quite hard to find out the identity of the person posting, perhaps going as far as trying to get a court order requiring the website to identify them, and in that case very many people would be put off trying. Check this book's website for when this comes into force.

Defendants from other countries

In recent years there has been concern about the practice of 'libel tourism', where claimants choose to sue in London, even if a defamatory statement has been published in a newspaper or magazine with a largely overseas circulation, because our libel laws make it easier for a claim to succeed here than in their own countries (see 'Topical Issues: Libel tourism' box, below). The Defamation Act 2013 addresses this problem by stating when a court can hear a case brought by a claimant who is not domiciled in the UK, another member state, or a state which is a contracting party to the Lugano Convention (these are Iceland, Norway and Switzerland). 'Domiciled' is a legal term which essentially means the place where someone has their permanent residence, or if a company, their main headquarters.

Section 9 of the Act provides that cases brought by claimants from outside the countries stated may not be heard here, unless the court is satisfied that, of all the places where the defamatory statement has been published, England and Wales is 'clearly the most appropriate place in which to bring an action'. This is quite a wide and flexible test, so how far it restricts libel tourism will depend very much on how the courts interpret the test: there might be difficult judgements to make where, for example, a defamatory statement was published more widely abroad than in the UK, but the claimant lives here for much of the time, or has important business interests here. Check this book's website to see when this comes into force.

Topical issues

Libel tourism

Compared to most other countries, our defamation laws give far more protection to reputation than to freedom of speech, which makes it easier for a claimant to win here than in most other countries. In addition, the cost of a libel action is much higher here than elsewhere, so there is pressure on defendants to settle a claim, even if there is a chance they could have won it, rather than risk the huge cost of going to court. As a result, in recent years, increasing numbers of claimants from abroad have brought libel cases here, even if the defamatory statements were made in newspapers or magazines that are primarily published in a different country. Known as 'libel tourism', this practice has earned London the nickname of 'the libel capital of the world'.

Claimants have been able to do this because the UK courts have traditionally imposed very few restrictions in cases from abroad. Until the Defamation Act 2013 was passed, claimants from abroad only had to show two things in order to be able to sue under English law:

- They have a reputation in this country. This effectively means little more than that a number of people in this country know who they are.
- The defamatory statement was circulated here. The arrival of the Internet means that the second requirement is also very easy to satisfy, since material published all over the world can be downloaded here.

By contrast, defamation claims in the USA can only be heard if the publication was 'expressly aimed' at readers/listeners in that country.

As a result of these lax rules, cases were accepted by the English courts even where, in common-sense terms, there was no real link to the UK. In **Mahfouz** *v* **Ehrenfeld** (2004), for example, a Saudi Arabian billionaire sued an American academic in London, over a book which was not published in the UK, but was only available if bought from America via the Internet. Only 23 copies were bought by UK buyers. Similarly, in **Mardas** *v* **New York Times** (2008), the claimant was a Greek citizen, suing two American newspapers. One of the papers has a UK edition but did not publish the article there, the other only sold 177 copies in the UK, and only 31 people in the UK read the article on the Internet. Mr Mardas did not pursue a claim in the US courts, where he would have been unlikely to win.

The UK courts were increasingly criticised for allowing libel tourism, because it effectively means that claimants can bypass the laws in their own countries, and avoid any protection for free speech that those laws may give. In response, some US states passed new laws, providing that libel judgments won in the UK are unenforceable.

There has also been concern that the libel tourism trend was spreading beyond claims against the media. Mark Stephens, a media lawyer who frequently acts for defendants in libel cases, told *The Times* in November 2009 that threats of libel action in London are regularly made against human rights and anti-corruption organisations, by those they criticise: 'We have threats against just about every reputable organisation you can think of, from Human Rights Watch to Greenpeace', he said. 'The organisations know that even if they are right, they may still be sued, and the cost of defending themselves [in London] will be huge.'

It was for all these reasons that the government introduced provisions against libel tourism in the Defamation Act 2013, though, as we saw above, it remains to be seen how far they will prevent the problem.

Who can sue?

Only living persons can sue for defamation – it is not possible to sue for damage to the reputation of a dead relative, for example, unless the claimant can prove that the alleged defamation of their relative affected the claimant's own reputation.

As stated earlier, the law of defamation is a curb on the general right of free speech, and, in an attempt to preserve a balance between free speech and the protection of reputation that is in the public interest, the courts have developed some limitations on libel actions brought by certain types of public body.

Key Case **Derbyshire County Council** *v* **Times Newspapers (1992)**

In **Derbyshire County Council** *v* **Times Newspapers** (1992), the Court of Appeal held that local authorities may not sue for libel; to allow such actions to be brought by democratically elected bodies, or any government body, would be against the public interest in free debate about the actions of elected authorities. Individual members of a council may still sue for libels against them personally.

Legal Principle
Elected bodies may not sue for defamation.

In **Goldsmith** *v* **Bhoyrul** (1998), Buckley J built on the **Derbyshire** decision in holding that political parties were unable to sue for libel because of the public interest in free speech concerning those who put themselves forward for public office.

Commercial companies can – and frequently do – sue for libel. In the long-running and much-publicised litigation popularly known as the McLibel case, when two environmental campaigners were sued for statements they made about McDonald's, the defendants attempted to argue that there was a public interest in free speech concerning the activities of huge multi-national corporations such as McDonald's, and that therefore such companies should be unable to sue for libel, but the argument was unsuccessful (**Steel** *v* **McDonald's Corp (Locus Standi)** (1999)).

Defences

The general defences described in Chapter 3 technically apply here, though in practice only *volenti* is likely to be of much practical use; it applies where the claimant has consented to the information being published. Of much more importance are a number of defences specific to defamation, which are covered in the following section.

Justification

This defence applies where the defendant can prove the defamatory remark is true. It is not necessary that every single detail is true, as long as overall, the statement is accurate. In **Alexander** *v* **North Eastern Railway** (1865) , the defendants successfully pleaded justification after saying that the claimant had been sentenced to three weeks imprisonment, when in fact it was two.

Section 5 of the Defamation Act 1996 states that where two or more accusations are made, it is not necessary to prove all of them, provided that those not proved do not materially damage the claimant's reputation, when considered with what is proved. In **Gecas** *v* **Scottish Television** (1992), Scottish Television was sued for accusing the defendant of the murder of thousands of Jews during the war, when he was head of a police battalion. Their programme included an allegation that he personally 'finished off' people who had been thrown into a burial pit but were still alive. Scottish TV could prove that he was involved in the murders, but not the specific allegation about the burial pits. They successfully pleaded justification, as that allegation did not materially injure the claimant's reputation, given what they could prove he had done.

Changes under the Defamation Act 2013: truth

Under the Defamation Act 2013, the defence of 'justification' changes its name to the more accurate and simple 'truth'. The Act follows the old law in providing, in s. 2(1), that the defence will apply where the words complained of are 'substantially true', so minor inaccuracies will not prevent the defence applying, and a statement can be covered even if not every word is literally true, so long as, as a whole, it is broadly accurate. This means that a case like **Alexander** *v* **North Eastern Railway** (1865) would be decided in the same way under the new law.

The Defamation Act 2013 abolishes the s. 5 defence from the Defamation Act 1996, but replaces it with a similar provision. Section 1(2) provides that where a statement contains two or more allegations about the claimant, the defendant does not necessarily have to prove all of them. If they can only prove one or some of the allegations, s. 1(2) provides that the defence can still apply, providing that anything that is not proved to be substantially true does not materially injure the claimant's reputation, given what was proved to be substantially true. So again, a case like **Gecas** would be decided in the same way under s. 1(2). (The change may not yet be in force; check the companion website for updates.)

Honest comment

The defence of honest comment provides protection for statements of opinion (rather than fact) on matters of public interest. These traditionally include subjects like politics and the behaviour of official bodies, but also reviews of everything from plays to restaurants. The defence was originally called fair comment, but its name was changed by the Supreme Court in **Joseph** *v* **Spiller** (2010), to better reflect what the defence is about (we will look at this case later in the chapter). In **Cornwell** *v* **Sunday People** (1983), the actress and singer Charlotte Cornwell sued the *Sunday People* over an article written by its television critic Nina Myskow. The article said of Ms Cornwell that she couldn't sing or act, and had 'the kind of stage presence that jams lavatories'. The *News of the World* argued that these were comments on Ms Cornwell's performance, rather than assertions of fact, but the jury disagreed and found for Ms Cornwell. In **Burstein** *v* **Associated Newspapers** (2007), the case concerned a review in the *London Evening Standard* of an opera about suicide bombers. The reviewer described the opera as 'horribly leaden and un-musical' and concluded 'I found the tone depressingly anti-American, and the idea that there is anything heroic about suicide bombers is, frankly, a grievous insult.' The composer sued for defamation, claiming that the review implied that he sympathised with terrorist causes, and considered suicide bombers to be heroes. The Court of Appeal threw the case out, saying that it was very clear that the review was a comment and not a statement of fact, and the fact that it might imply anything about Mr Burstein's motives did not mean it ceased to become a comment. The facts referred to in the review were accurate, and the opinions the reviewer formed on the basis of those facts were ones which could be honestly held. In **Keays** *v* **Guardian Newspapers** (2003) *The Guardian* published a story about Sarah Keays, who was known as the former mistress of a Cabinet Minister and mother of his child. After long refusing to talk to the press, Ms Keays had recently decided to publish her story, and the *Guardian* article speculated about her motives. The judge held that the article could only be read as comment, since the writer could not know as a fact what was in Ms Keays' mind.

In **British Chiropractic Association** *v* **Singh** (2010), the British Chiropractic Association (BCA) sued science journalist Simon Singh over a story in *The Guardian*, which said that BCA members' claims about the medical problems their treatments could treat were made 'without a jot of evidence', and that the BCA 'happily promotes bogus treatments'. The BCA argued that the words were intended as statement of fact, and therefore could not be covered by the fair comment defence. The Court of Appeal disagreed. They pointed out that in the evidence supplied to the court, Mr Singh had set out his reasons for believing that there was no reliable evidence that the treatments worked, while the BCA in their evidence had been able to make an equally detailed case arguing that there was evidence that the treatments worked. This showed, they said, that the original article had not been intended as a statement of fact, but as an evaluation of the available evidence about the treatments. The word 'bogus' was used to emphasise Mr Singh's opinion of the evidence, rather than a factual assertion. That made the article a statement of opinion, not fact, and so the defence was available. The Court of Appeal case was purely to decide whether fair comment was available (not to try the libel claim itself) and the effect of the decision was that, had the case gone to trial, Mr Singh would have been able to argue the fair comment defence. Whether it would have succeeded must remain a mystery, as the BCA dropped their claim after the Court of Appeal decision on fair comment.

In most cases, an opinion will have some kind of factual basis. If you say someone is a thief, or a liar, or a womaniser, for example, that will usually be because of something that you know, or believe, they have done. The honest comment defence will usually not apply where the facts on which a comment is based turn out not to be true. The exception is where the comment is based on material that is privileged, which means where it is covered by the defence of absolute or qualified privilege. We will look at these defences later in the chapter, but as an example, anything said in Parliament is privileged, so if an MP were to say in the House of Commons that the Prime Minister had had an affair, despite constantly expressing his belief in family values, and a journalist were to write that that made him a hypocrite, they would be covered by the honest comment defence, even if it turned out not to be true that he had had an affair.

Traditionally, it was considered that, to be covered by the defence, the facts on which the opinion was based had to be stated at the same time. This aspect of the defence was loosened in **Joseph** *v* **Spiller** (2010), where the Supreme Court stated that, in order to be covered by fair comment, the defendant only had to have identified 'in general terms what it is that has led the commentator to make the comment, so that the reader can understand what the comment is about'. It was not necessary, the court said, to specify the facts in such a degree of detail that the reader could judge whether the comment was accurate. The claimants were a Motown tribute band called the Gillettes, who had a contract with the defendants, a booking agency. The contract included a 're-engagement clause', which stated that if the Gillettes were asked to perform again at any of the venues the agency had booked for them, within a year, that booking had to be arranged through the agency, which would then receive a fee. However, after performing at one venue booked by the agency, the group accepted a further booking direct from the venue, which was a breach of their contract. The agency complained and the group sent an email saying, among other things, that the contract was just a formality and 'holds no water in legal terms'. The agency then posted a notice on its website, which said they would not be accepting further bookings for the Gillettes, because the band were unprofessional and unable to stick to their contract. It said that Mr Joseph, who ran the Gillettes, had advised the agency that 'the terms and conditions of . . . contracts hold no water in legal terms', and suggested that this meant it would be unwise for anyone to book them as they might not meet their commitments.

The band sued for defamation but the agency argued that the notice was fair comment, and that the facts it was based on were the email that said the contract held no water, and the fact that the Gillettes had breached their contract by accepting a direct booking. The claimants argued that the defence could not apply, because the notice had not specified what the breach of contract related to, and had misquoted their email by suggesting that they considered 'contracts' generally not to be legally binding, when what they had said was specific to the contract with the agency. This, they argued, meant the facts on which the comments were based were not sufficiently clear. The Supreme Court rejected this argument. Giving the leading judgment, Lord Philips said that it was necessary to 'identify in general terms what it is that has led the commentator to make the comment, so that the reader can understand what the comment is about'. But it was not necessary to detail the facts so specifically as to allow the reader to judge whether the comment was accurate. Part of the reason for making this change, Lord Philips said, was that the Internet had made it possible for people to make public comment about others in a way that did not exist when the defence of fair comment was developed. It would often be impossible for readers to assess these comments without detailed information about the facts, and if fair comment was only to apply where readers were able to do this, the defence of fair comment would lose much of its point.

Applying this approach to the **Spiller** case, the court held that the defendant was entitled to plead the defence of honest comment. The two facts relied on as the basis of the comment were the email, and the breach of contract. The Supreme Court said the email did show a careless disregard for the band's contractual obligations, which was what the website notice had alleged, and the misquoting did not appear to make much difference to that. In addition, it was sufficient that the notice had referred to a breach of contract; they did not have to go into detail about what the breach was.

Changes under the Defamation Act 2013: honest opinion

The Defamation Act 2013 replaces the honest comment defence with a new defence of honest opinion, introduced in s. 3 of the Act. It is in some respects based on the old law, but contains some key changes, in an attempt to widen the protection given to expressions of opinion, and also clarify the law. Perhaps the most important difference is that the old defence only applied when the material complained of was about a matter public interest. This requirement is not included in the new defence, which means that the new law gives much wider protection to statements of opinion, whether they are about important matters, such as the behaviour of government, or much more trivial issues. As well as statements of opinion on serious public interest, the old defence was traditionally used to cover reviews, such as those on books, plays, films and restaurants, and these clearly still come within the new defence.

The defence of honest opinion will apply when three conditions, listed in s. 3, are satisfied:

- The statement complained of was a statement of opinion.
- The statement complained of indicated, whether in general or specific terms, the basis of the opinion.
- An honest person could have held the opinion on the basis of:
  - any fact which existed at the time the statement complained of was published, or
  - anything claimed to be a fact in a privileged statement that was published before the statement complained of.

We will now look at each of these requirements in turn.

- **The statement must be a statement of opinion.** This simply restates the former law under the fair comment defence, and it is likely that the cases we looked at above on this issue will still provide useful guidance.
- **The statement must indicate what the opinion was based on.** Again, this is a restatement of the previous law under the fair comment defence, as explained by the Supreme Court in **Joseph** *v* **Spiller** (2010). It basically means that, to be covered by the honest opinion defence, a statement must give some idea of what facts or other material led the maker of the statement to form the opinion they have put forward.
- **An honest person could have held the opinion based on existing facts or previously published privileged material which asserts a fact.** This is a change to the previous law. The old fair comment defence used the concept of malice to try to ensure that only honestly held opinions were protected. If it could be shown that the claimant did not honestly believe what they said, they were said to have made the comment 'with malice', and the defence would not apply. The new defence changes the law in that the test is not the subjective one of what the defendant actually believed (which of course is always hard to assess), but the objective test of whether an honest person could have formed the opinion that was expressed, on the basis of the facts that existed, or privileged material on the relevant issue. This is in some ways more of a restriction on freedom of expression than the old law, because it effectively means the opinion must be a reasonable one; if the jury come to the conclusion that no one could honestly hold the opinion expressed, the defence will fail, even if in fact the defendant did honestly hold that opinion. This contrasts with the old fair comment defence, about which Nicholls LJ said in **Cheng** *v* **Paul** (2000): 'the basis of our public life is that the crank, the enthusiast, may say what he honestly thinks as much as the reasonable person who sits on a jury.' In addition to this provision, s. 3(5) states that the defence will not apply where the claimant can show that the defendant did not honestly hold the opinion they expressed (even if it was an opinion that an honest person could have come to). If you are wondering how the claimant could possibly prove that the defendant did not hold a particular opinion, the answer is that they will simply bring evidence that suggests this; for example, if someone publishes a very bad review of a restaurant, and there is evidence that the journalist and the restaurant owner have a history of falling out, that might suggest that the journalist did not honestly think the food was terrible, but simply wanted to annoy the restaurant owner and damage their reputation. It is then up to the jury to

decide whether, despite that evidence, they believe the defendant's claim that he or she did hold the opinion that was published, or whether the claimant's evidence leads them to believe that that is a lie.

Note that the comment need not necessarily be based on facts; it can also be based 'a privileged statement' that was already published. The Act defines 'a privileged statement' in s. 3(7) as a statement which would be covered by any one of four defences listed in the Act:

- responsible publication on matter of public interest;
- peer-reviewed statement in a scientific or academic journal;
- absolute privilege applying to a report of court proceedings; or
- qualified privilege under s.15 of the Defamation Act 1996.

We will look at all these defences below, but the key thing to note at this stage is that all of them can apply to material which is not factually true or accurate. This means that the honest opinion defence can apply where someone makes a comment or states an opinion, even where that opinion turns out to be based on an untruth.

The Act also adds a new provision applying to anyone who has published the comment, but was not the author of it. Under s. 3(6), someone is this position is unable to use the defence if the claimant can show that they knew or ought to have known that the author did not hold the opinion they expressed. Check this book's website to see when this change is in force.

Absolute privilege

This defence protects the makers of certain defamatory statements because the law considers that, in the circumstances covered by the defence, free expression is more important than protection of reputation. The defence makes it impossible to sue the person who makes a defamatory statement in any of the following circumstances:

- Any statement made in Parliament by a member of either House, or in any report published by either House (such as Hansard).
- Any report published by either House (such as Hansard), or such a report when republished in full by someone else (Parliamentary Papers Act 1840, s. 1).
- Any statement made by one officer of state to another in the course of the officer's duty. Secretaries of State and Ministers are officers of state, but it is not clear how far below that rank absolute privilege extends.
- Any statement made by one spouse to another.
- Statements made by officials and other servants of the EU in the exercise of their functions.
- Statements made in the course of judicial proceedings, by judge, jury, witnesses, lawyers or the parties themselves.
- Fair, accurate and contemporaneous reports of court proceedings which are held in public. Under the Defamation Act 2013, this provision covers reports of any UK court, any court established legally in another country, and any court or tribunal established by the Security Council of the United Nations, or by an international agreement. The requirement for reports to be contemporaneous means they must usually be published while the court proceedings are going on, or as they finish. In some cases, the media will be prevented from reporting a case for a certain period (for example, if the accused is also facing charges in another case, the result of the first one will not be published to avoid influencing the jury in the second one). In this situation, reports will be considered to be contemporaneous if they are published as soon as practicable after publication is allowed.

Note that absolute privilege covers the person making the statement, in the situation described; with one exception, it does not cover subsequent reports of those statements. So while an MP may make a defamatory statement about someone in Parliament and be covered by absolute privilege, a newspaper which reports that statement would not be covered by the same defence (though they may be covered by qualified privilege; see below). The exception is the last item on the above list: fair and accurate media reports of court proceedings in public, where the media, as well as the individuals making defamatory statements, can be covered by absolute privilege. The reason for this is fairly obvious: by their nature, court proceedings tend to involve people making serious allegations against others, some of which may be untrue. It would not be possible for papers to report court proceedings if they could be sued for repeating those allegations, and since there is clearly a public interest in people knowing what goes on in the courts, absolute privilege makes this possible.

Qualified privilege

Like absolute privilege, qualified privilege is a defence that protects statements made in certain specified circumstances. There are two types of qualified privilege: qualified privilege under statute, and qualified privilege in common law, which has been built up by the decisions in cases over the years. Both types cover a number of situations where free speech is considered to be important, but where the right to free speech is not unrestricted as it is for the situations protected under absolute privilege. One key restriction applies to both types of qualified privilege: the defence will not apply where the defamatory statement was made with malice, which for the purposes of this defence means where it was made with a bad motive, or if the person making the statement did not honestly believe it was true (we will look at this in more detail below). Each of the two types of qualified privilege also has other restrictions which we will now look at.

Qualified privilege under statute

The rules of statutory privilege are contained in the Defamation Act 1996, as amended by the Defamation Act 2013, with an additional provision in s. 6 of the Defamation Act 2013, which introduces a new qualified privilege for statements made in scientific and academic journals.

The 1996 Act provides protection for statements made about or in connection with a list of certain types of occasion and material, largely covering the behaviour and publications of official and public bodies. It is made clear in s. 15(3), that the defence will only apply where the material published is of public concern, and the publication of it is in the public interest.

The situations in which statutory qualified privilege will apply are divided into two groups. The first group, listed in Part 1 of Sched. 1 to the 1996 Act, are described as being covered by qualified privilege 'without explanation or contradiction'. This means that statements made in the situations listed will be covered by the defence, unless made with malice. They are:

- Fair and accurate reports of the proceedings of legislatures, courts, governmental inquiries and international organisations held in public anywhere in the world.
- Fair and accurate copies of, or extracts from, material published by or on the authority of any government, legislature, international organisation or international conference, anywhere in the world.

Part II or Part V lists the second group, which the Act describes as 'privileged subject to explanation or contradiction'. This means that a person who makes a defamatory statement in one of the situations listed in Part V cannot normally be sued unless they have made the statement with malice; but they can lose this protection if the person they made the statement about attempts to put their side of the story, and the publisher of the statement does not give them a reasonable opportunity to do so. So if, for example, a newspaper reports that a local politician was accused of fraud at a public meeting (one of the situations covered by Part II), and does so without malice, they cannot normally be sued for defamation. However, if the politician then writes to the paper to give his or her side of the story, and asks for that letter to be published, the newspaper may lose the protection of qualified privilege if they refuse to publish it. The Act makes it clear that explanations or contradictions must be published in 'a suitable manner', and s. 8(3) states that this means they must be published 'in the same manner as the publication complained of' or 'in a manner that is adequate and reasonable in the circumstances'. This provision is aimed at preventing the common practice among newspapers of printing corrections as a small story, often tucked away at the bottom of a page, when the original story was given much more prominence, with the result that a proportion of readers who read the original, incorrect story may never notice the correction.

The most important types of statement listed in Sch. II are the following:

- Fair and accurate copies of, extracts from or summaries of material issued for the information of the public by or on behalf of:
  - legislatures and governments anywhere in the world;
  - any authority in the world exercising governmental functions, which includes police functions;
  - any international organisation or conference;
  - any document made available by a court anywhere in the world;
  - certain documents circulated to members of a listed company;
  - material published by a scientific or academic conference anywhere in the world.
- Fair and accurate reports of:
  - public meetings of a local authority or local authority committee;
  - public hearings of any enquiries set up by statute, the Crown or Ministers;
  - local inquiries set up under statute;
  - public hearings of any other tribunal, board or committee acting under statutory authority;
  - proceedings in a scientific conference anywhere in the world;
  - press conferences held anywhere in the world for the discussion of a matter of public interest.
  - any public meetings held anywhere in the world to discuss a matter of public interest;
  - general meetings of a UK listed company.

The above is not the entire list, but what you can see from it is that the aim is to protect discussion of the acts, decisions and publications of bodies which have an impact on the public and of matters of scientific and academic interest.

Changes under the Defamation Act 2013: statutory qualified privilege

The Defamation Act 2013 widens the list of occasions and types of material that is covered, among them press conferences, thus confirming the decision on **McCarten Turkington Brean** *v* **Times Newspapers** (2000).

Qualified privilege for scientific and academic writing

The Defamation Act 2013 also creates a new form of statutory qualified privilege, designed to provide protection for free and open discussion of scientific and academic issues. It was introduced in response to controversy about a number of claims brought in recent years, which were seen as attempts by business and large organisations to silence criticism of their products. An example was the case of **NMT** *v* **Wilmshurst** (2010), where a British cardiac surgeon was sued by an American manufacturer of medical devices, after he made comments at a medical conference about the way they had conducted clinical trials of one of their products. Dr Wilmshurst argued that he was engaging in a scientific argument about the trials, and that the company was using the libel action – with the associated threat of how much it would cost him to defend himself – to stifle debate about legitimate concerns that affected patients in the UK. The claim was eventually dropped, but only after four years of attempts to pursue Dr Wilmshurst through the courts. He told the BBC that a number of medical colleagues had told him they had become reluctant to raise concerns about medical trials because of what had happened to him. Similar issues were raised in **British Chiropractic Association** *v* **Singh** (2010), where journalist Simon Singh was sued for a critical article on chiropractic, a form of alternative medicine, which among other things said that there was no evidence to support chiropractors' claims to be able to cure certain ailments.

The new defence, defined in s. 6, aims to address this problem, by providing protection for serious discussion of scientific and academic matters. The defence will apply to statements published in scientific or academic journals, where:

- the statement relates to a scientific or academic matter; and
- before it was published, an independent review of the statement's scientific or academic merit was carried out by the editor of the journal, and at least one person with expertise in the subject concerned (this is a process known as 'peer review', which is used by all serious academic and scientific journals, and is designed to make sure that any research has been done properly and conclusions reached are valid).

The defence not only protects the original statement published in a scientific or academic journal, but also offers the same protection to two further types of publication related to it:

- an assessment of the statement's scientific or academic merit, if written by one or more of the people who carried out the independent review of it, and written in the course of that review; and
- publication of a fair and accurate copy of, extract from or summary of the statement, or the above-mentioned assessment of it.

As with all types of qualified privilege, this defence does not apply if any of the above types of statement were made with malice. (The defence may not yet be in force; see the companion website for updates.)

Qualified privilege under common law

Key Case **Adam** *v* **Ward (1917)**

At common law, the traditional definition of where qualified privilege will apply comes from **Adam** *v* **Ward** (1917), in which Lord Atkinson explained that

> a privileged occasion is . . . an occasion where the person who makes a communication has an interest or a duty, legal, social or moral, to make it to the person to whom it is made, and the person to whom it is so made has a corresponding interest or duty to receive it. This reciprocity is essential.

Legal Principle

Where information is communicated by someone who has an interest, or a moral, social or legal duty in communicating it, to someone who has a corresponding duty or interest in receiving it, it can be covered by the defence of qualified privilege.

Cases have established a number of categories in which these mutual duties and/or interests can be found, among them the following:

- **Protection of an interest**. In **Bryanston Finance** *v* **De Vries** (1975), the defendant was found to be covered by qualified privilege when he made defamatory statements which were concerned with protecting his business interests in a memo to a secretary. Similarly, in **Adam** *v* **Ward**, the claimant had severely criticised an army general. These criticisms were protected by absolute privilege because they were made within Parliament, but after the army investigated his allegations and announced that they were totally unfounded, the claimant wrote to a newspaper defending his position, and again criticising the general. The House of Lords held that the letter was covered by qualified privilege as the claimant was protecting his own reputation.
- In **Thour** *v* **Royal Free Hampstead NHS Trust** (2012), the court accepted that qualified privilege applied where one NHS trust gave another NHS trust an inaccurate employment reference for the claimant, who had worked at the first trust and been offered a new job at the second. Tugenhat J said that, as the organisations were both members of the NHS, they had an obvious mutual interest in exchanging information about a potential employee of one of them.
- **Communications between officers of a company**. In **Watt** *v* **Longsdon** (1930), the claimant was working abroad for the company of which the defendant was director. While the claimant was away, the defendant received a letter saying that the claimant was, among other things, 'a blackguard, a thief and a liar' who 'lived exclusively to satisfy his own passions and lust'. None of this was true. The defendant showed the letter to the chairman of the board of directors, and also to the claimant's wife, who decided to get a divorce as a result. When the claimant sued for defamation, it was held that showing the letter to the board was covered by qualified privilege because they had an interest in seeing it, and as a fellow officer of the company the defendant had a duty to show it to them. However, showing the letter to the claimant's wife was not covered by the privilege; although she had an interest in receiving the information, he had no duty to give it to her.
- **Information given to the police where a crime is suspected**. In **Croucher** *v* **Inglis** (1889), it was stated that 'when a person suspects that a crime has been committed, it is his right and his duty to inform the police'.

As stated in **Adam** *v* **Ward**, a key factor in deciding whether qualified privilege will apply is reciprocity, meaning that it is not enough for one party to have an interest in communicating certain information – the other party must have a legitimate interest in receiving it. This was stressed in **Downtex** *v* **Flatley** (2003). The claimant and defendant had entered into a business contract which eventually broke down, with each party claiming that they were owed money by the other. The defendant, Mr Flatley, received an anonymous letter claiming that Downtex were in financial difficulties; it was never proved where this letter had come from. He then obtained the addresses of a number of other companies supplying goods to Downtex, and wrote to them, suggesting that Downtex might be unable to pay their debts. The content of these letters was accepted to be defamatory, but Mr Flatley pleaded qualified privilege, saying that there was a mutual interest in those people who might be affected by Downtex's alleged financial difficulties finding out about them.

The Court of Appeal rejected this argument, saying that there was in fact no reciprocity of interest. Mr Flatley had no relevant interest in communicating the letters to Downtex's suppliers, nor did those suppliers have an interest in receiving them. Downtex had not actually failed to pay Mr Flatley any debt about which there was no dispute, and it was not reasonably necessary for Mr Flatley to seek the assistance of other potential creditors (let alone 'suppliers', who might not be creditors at all) in order to protect the defendant's interest. Nor was there any evidence that Downtex had failed to pay, or were contemplating failing to pay, any of its suppliers or creditors.

Malice

Where a statement is made with malice, the defence of qualified privilege cannot apply (and nor can that of fair comment). In everyday language, malice means spite or ill-will, and in some cases it will be precisely this that deprives the defendant of qualified privilege. This was the situation in **Angel** *v* **H H Bushell & Co** (1968). The claimant and defendant had started to do business together, but relations between them soured, and the defendant wrote a letter to the mutual friend who had introduced them saying that the claimant 'did not know normal business ethics'. He claimed qualified privilege, but the court held that it did not apply because the letter had clearly been motivated by anger, rather than any duty to inform the friend of what had happened.

However, the legal definition also goes wider than ordinary spite or ill-will. In **Halpin** *v* **Oxford Brookes University** (1995), the claimant was a lecturer who had been the subject of a number of memos making untrue allegations about him, which were circulated to other members of staff. The Court of Appeal stated that malice could be proved if it could be shown that the writer knew what he was publishing was untrue, or was reckless as to whether it was true or not. In **Lillie and Reed** *v* **Newcastle City Council** (2002), the claimants were nursery nurses, who were accused of abusing very young children in their care in a report prepared by a Review Team employed by Newcastle City Council. The accusations were completely false, and they sued the council for libel. The court agreed that there was a public interest in publishing allegations of child abuse, which would normally have meant that the Review Team was covered by qualified privilege, but this protection was lost because the statements in the report had been made with malice. The authors of the report had made statements that they must have known were not true, and had misrepresented the 'evidence' they claimed to have against the claimants, in order to support their subjective belief that the claimants were guilty.

What happens when a defendant is motivated by ill-will, but nevertheless honestly believes that what they are saying is true? This was the case in **Horrocks** *v* **Lowe** (1975). The claimant and the defendant were both local councillors in Bolton. The claimant had interests in a large amount of property in the town, and it was accepted that the defendant felt this made him unsuitable to sit on the council because of the potential for conflicts of interest. During a council meeting, the defendant accused the claimant of misleading the council over a property-related dispute, and the claimant sued for slander. It was accepted that the council meeting was a privileged occasion, but the claimant claimed that the defendant's personal prejudice against him amounted to malice and should prevent the defendant being protected by privilege. The trial judge had found that, on the evidence, the defendant believed that what he had said was true, but his motivation in saying it was his prejudice against the claimant, and so qualified privilege could not apply. The House of Lords disagreed, and held that on these facts the defence could apply; if a defendant, however prejudiced, honestly believed in the truth of the allegations made, there was no malice.

The Reynolds defence

The Reynolds defence was created to give protection to the media when they report matters of public interest in a responsible way, even if the reports turn out to be untrue. You might wonder why there should be protection for untrue statements; the reason is that it can be very difficult, especially when dealing with powerful people and organisations, to prove a story is true, especially where there is time pressure because the issue is newsworthy, and without the protection of this kind of defence, some important – and true – stories might simply never come out. The Reynolds defence protects freedom of expression by allowing that it is better that some untrue stories are published, if that means that important and true stories are not suppressed because they might not be provable.

Key Case **Reynolds *v* Times Newspapers (1999)**

The Reynolds case arose from a news story published by *The Times* about the former Taoiseach (Irish prime minister), Albert Reynolds, and the circumstances leading up to his resignation. Mr Reynolds claimed that the article suggested that he had deliberately misled the Irish parliament. The Times argued that there should be protection for all stories on matters of public interest, of which this was one. The House of Lords refused to go that far, but adapted the traditional qualified privilege defence into a new one which would apply, they said, where information in the public interest was reported in a responsible way. The judgment listed a number of factors which would help decide whether reporting was responsible, including the seriousness of the allegation; the nature of the information and how far it was of public concern; how reliable and authoritative the source was; the steps taken to check the information; how urgent it was to publish the story; whether the claimant had a chance to comment, and whether their side of the story was included; and the tone of the article, meaning whether it presented a balanced view or raised questions, or whether it assumed the information was true, or presented it in a sensationalised way.

In the Reynolds case itself, the House of Lords agreed the subject was one of public interest, but said the paper was not covered by the defence because they had not mentioned Mr Reynold's explanation for the events, even though it was available to them.

Legal Principle

Information that is in the public interest, and is published in a fair and responsible manner, is covered by the defence of qualified privilege.

Reynolds was applied in **Bonnick *v* Morris** (2002), a Privy Council case. The defendant paper had published a story about a state-owned Jamaican company, JCTC, entering into two contracts with another company, Prolacto. The claimant worked for JCTC, but had left shortly after the second contract was agreed. The newspaper report stated that the contracts were unusually advantageous to Prolacto, and that the claimant had left JCTC just after the second contract had been arranged. The claimant argued that this was defamatory of him, in that a reasonable person would think he had acted improperly in arranging the contracts and had had to leave as a result. The newspaper pointed out that they had approached JCTC for comments and they had been unwilling to answer, and they had also approached the claimant, who had explained that there was nothing suspicious about the contracts and there was no connection between them and his leaving the company.

The Privy Council agreed that the article was defamatory, but allowed the defence of qualified privilege because the subject was a matter of public interest; the newspaper had acted responsibly in publishing the story, and the story was not one which was obviously defamatory, so the newspaper might not have thought, at the time it published, that the story could be defamatory. This is a straightforward application of the **Reynolds** principle that qualified privilege will apply where the article is on a matter of public concern or interest, and the newspaper was justified in going ahead and publishing it when they did and in the form they did.

In **Grobbelaar** *v* **News Group Newspapers** (2001), the footballer Bruce Grobbelaar sued the *Sun* over reports that he had been paid to fix the results of matches he played in. The paper had been given a tip-off that Mr Grobbelaar had been involved in match-fixing, and had arranged for the source to tape a conversation in which he accepted money to fix a match, and admitted to doing so in the past. The resulting story took up several pages, with headlines screaming 'World exclusive – Grobbelaar took bribes to fix games' and 'I saved goal by mistake and lost £125,000'. Before the case came to court, Mr Grobbelaar was charged with two criminal offences related to match-fixing, but was acquitted. The Court of Appeal rejected the *Sun*'s defence. Among the factors which the court said led to this decision included the facts that the main witness against the claimant was thoroughly unreliable, the newspaper had evidence from a world-class goalkeeper that suggested Mr Grobbelaar's performance on the pitch showed no signs of match-fixing, and that there was no real urgency for the paper to publish when they did. But the main factor was the tone and weight of the story, which appeared over several pages, for seven days, and asserted Mr Grobbelaar's guilt as a fact, rather than, for example, raising questions or asking for an investigation (however, the result of the case was less of a disappointment for the paper; although Mr Grobbelaar won, the House of Lords reduced the £85,000 damages to £1, in recognition of the fact that, although it was not proved that he fixed matches, he had admitted that he took bribes).

In **Loutchansky** *v* **Times Newspapers** (2001), where *The Times* accused Russian businessman Grigori Loutchansky of being involved in serious crime, the paper claimed qualified privilege because, it said, the subject was one of public concern, and the story was based on authoritative sources, including reports by the CIA and British intelligence services. *The Times* initially lost and appealed, and the resulting series of appeals culminated in the Court of Appeal sending it back to the original judge to reconsider in the light of their clarifications of the **Reynolds** defence. Second time around, the judge still found against the newspaper. Summarising the **Reynolds** defence, he said the question was whether the paper had behaved responsibly in publishing the articles. He agreed that the matter was one of public concern, but said that that the allegations made were very serious and potentially very damaging to Mr Loutchansky's reputation, and therefore demanded a high degree of care on the paper's part before publishing them. This standard had not been met: some of the sources were unsafe, while the allegations were vague and the paper had not made enough effort to check them. The paper had tried to contact Mr Loutchansky, but, the judge said, they should have tried harder, and although the story stated that Mr Loutchansky had repeatedly denied the allegations, this did not amount to giving his side of the story.

In **Flood** *v* **Times Newspapers** (2012), the claimant was a police officer who, *The Times* reported, was being investigated over allegations that he had taken bribes from suspected Russian criminals, in exchange for information about Home Office attempts to extradite them. The background to the story was that an informant had reported the allegations to the paper, and to the police, and when the journalists looked into the claims, they found reason to believe that the police were not investigating them. They then approached the claimant and others with the allegations, which caused a police investigation to begin. The paper reported both the allegations and the investigation. The investigation eventually found that there was no evidence for the allegations.

The Times claimed the **Reynolds** defence, arguing that it was in the public interest to publish the fact that a senior police officer was being investigated for corruption. The claimant argued that, although the subject matter of the story was of public interest, publishing details of the actual allegations against him, without checking whether they were true, took the story outside the defence, because those matters were not in the public interest. The Supreme Court rejected this argument. They said that the story was of serious public importance, and the allegations were an essential part of the story. They were published with the legitimate aim of getting the allegations investigated, where there was good reason to believe this was not happening. Lord Philips said that, as the police officer was not a public figure, it could be argued that it was not in the public interest to name him but, on the facts, it would not have been possible to report the story without doing so, so the defence was not lost for that part.

Summing up the reasons for allowing the defence, Lord Mance said:

> The starting point is that the investigation into possible police corruption in the area of extradition of a Russian oligarch to Russia informed the public on a matter of great public interest and sensitivity. TNL journalists were motivated by a concern to ensure that the investigation was being or would be properly pursued. They had themselves investigated the sources and nature of the allegations exhaustively over a substantial period as far as they could. The article would have been unlikely to be publishable at all without details of the names and transactions involved in the alleged corruption. The facts regarding such transactions were accurately stated.

Changes under the Defamation Act 2013: responsible publication on matters of public interest

Under the Defamation Act 2013, the **Reynolds** defence is replaced by a new statutory defence called responsible publication on matters of public interest. This new defence is very clearly based on the **Reynolds** defence, and has the same purpose: to give protection to the media, when they report matters of public interest in a responsible way, even if what is said actually turns out to be untrue. The defence is contained in s. 4 of the Act, which provides that there is a defence where a defendant can show that:

- the statement complained of was, or was part of, a statement on a matter of public interest; and
- the defendant acted responsibly in publishing it.

The defence can apply to reports that are purely allegations of fact, or are expressions of opinion, or a mixture of both (s. 4(5)). The Act does not define 'matters of public interest', but it is generally recognised that this description applies to serious issues, such as the behaviour of elected or official bodies and commercial companies, and the people who work in or represent them, but not to things like the private lives of celebrities.

If the defamatory remarks are considered a matter of public interest, the courts must then decide whether the media acted responsibly in publishing them. In deciding this, s. 4(2) states that a court may take into account the following circumstances:

- the nature of the publication and its context;
- the seriousness of what is said or implied about the defendant;
- the relevance of the allegation against the defendant to the matter of public interest which the statement is about;
- the importance of the matter of public interest;
- what information the defendant had before publication, and what they knew about how reliable that information was;

- whether the defendant tried to get the claimant's view on the statement before publishing it, and if so, whether the published statement included the views that the claimant expressed;
- whether the defendant took any other steps to check whether the statement was true;
- the timing of the publication;
- the tone of the statement.

The explanatory notes to the Defamation Bill make it clear that the above list is not intended to be a checklist, or a series of hurdles which a defendant must get over. It is merely a list of the kind of factors which a court could take into account, depending on the circumstances of the case, and it may also take other factors into account as well. This is backed up by the wording of s. 1(4), which introduces the list of factors with the words: 'These circumstances may include (among other things).'

The Explanatory Notes also state that, although the new statutory defence is intended to replace the old **Reynolds** defence, it is based on that defence, and so the courts will be expected to take previous case law on the **Reynolds** defence into consideration when applying the new statutory defence, though it will not be binding.

(This change may not yet be in force; check the companion website for updates.)

Neutral reportage

In 2006, although the **Reynolds** defence continued to be available, the courts began to develop what has been described as a 'sub-species' of the **Reynolds** defence, known as 'neutral reportage'. It applied to reports on matters of public interest, where defamatory allegations were presented in a completely neutral manner, rather than making any attempt to suggest that they were true, and the courts held that in such cases, it was not necessary to check whether the allegations were true. The case which is generally thought to have given birth to the defence is **Jameel** *v* **Wall Street Journal** (2006), where a wealthy Saudi Arabian businessman sued the *Wall Street Journal* after it published a story stating that the Saudi Arabian government had monitored the bank accounts of a number of prominent Saudi citizens, including Mr Jameel, at the request of the United States government, to ensure that they were not providing money to terrorist groups, either knowingly or unknowingly. Mr Jameel claimed that the article was defamatory because it implied there were reasonable grounds to suspect he was involved in funding terrorism. The paper could not satisfy all ten of the **Reynolds** criteria, but the House of Lords held that these criteria were merely intended to be used as guidelines for judging whether a story should be protected by the defence; they were not specific tests that the media had to pass in order to claim the defence. In this case, the story was presented in a measured, balanced tone and was a serious contribution to a matter of very considerable public interest, and that was exactly the kind of reporting that the **Reynolds** defence should protect.

Case Navigator

In **Roberts** *v* **Gable** (2007), the case concerned a report in the anti-fascist newspaper *Searchlight*, about a feud between different factions in the British National Party, in which the two sides were making allegations about threats of violence, and a theft. The claimants were among those named in the article, and had not been given a chance to comment on the accusations in it; in fact no real attempt had been made to verify the story. They therefore claimed that qualified privilege should not be available as a defence, but the Court of Appeal disagreed. It said that this was a case of neutral reportage, where the paper had simply reported the allegations, without commenting on them or suggesting they were true. In this situation, it said, the journalist did not need to verify that the allegations reported were true. This approach then developed in later cases into the 'neutral reportage' defence.

Changes under the Defamation Act 2013: neutral reportage

The neutral reportage defence is put into statutory form in the Defamation Act 2013, as part of the defence now known as responsible publication on matters of public interest. The Act provides, in s. 4(3) and (4), that where the statement complained of was, or formed part of, an accurate and impartial account of a dispute involving the claimant, a court has to disregard any failure by the defendant to take steps to verify the truth of the allegations contained in the statement. The Explanatory Notes to the Act state that this means that, where a report fits within the category of neutral reportage, in that it gives a balanced picture and reports allegations without suggesting that they are definitely true, the defence can apply even if the defendant did not attempt to check that the information was true.

Apology

Apology is not a true defence, but it can be used to reduce the damages payable if the claimant wins. Section 1 of the Libel Act 1843, as amended by the Libel Act 1845, provides that if the

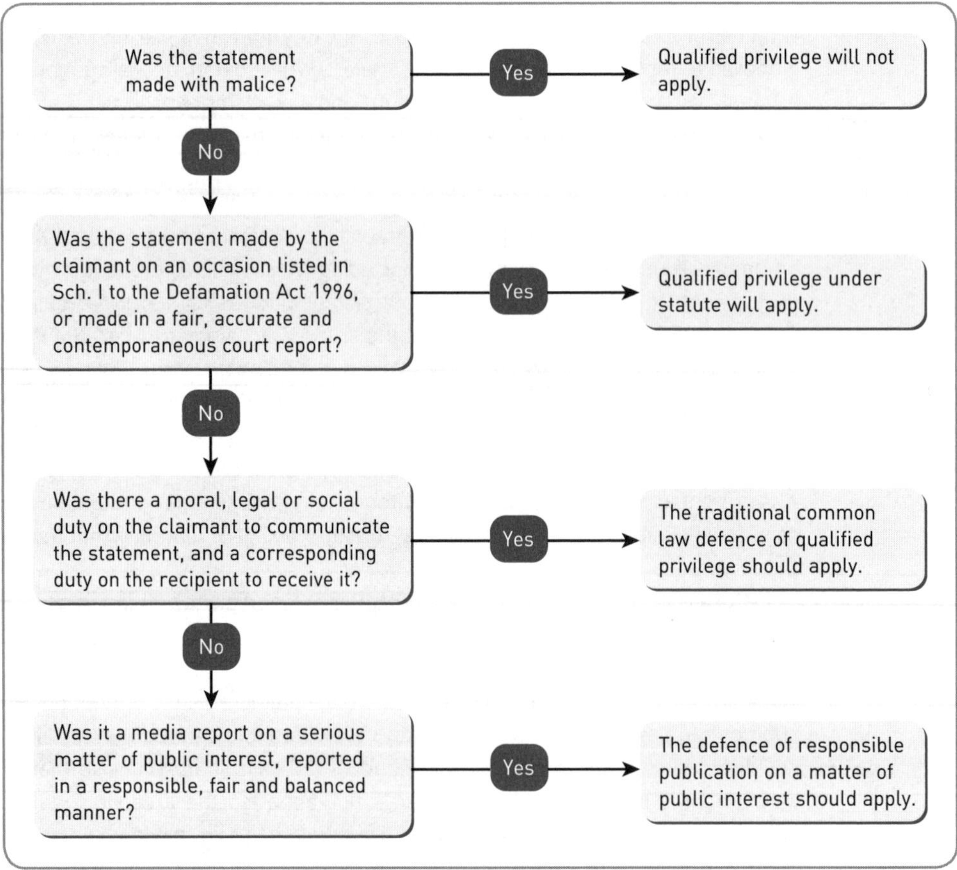

Figure 9.2 The defence of qualified privilege when the 2013 Defamation Act is in force

defendant gives notice to the claimant at the time they serve their defence, they can offer evidence that an apology was offered before the action began, or as soon as possible afterwards, and this evidence may reduce the damages awarded.

Under s. 2 of the Libel Act 1843, a defendant newspaper may plead that the libel was published in the newspaper without malice or gross negligence, and that before the legal action was brought, or as soon as possible after it, a full apology was published in the newspaper. If the newspaper is published less frequently than weekly, the defendant must have offered to publish the apology in any newspaper of the claimant's choice. The plea must be accompanied by payment of money into court by way of amends. However, in practice this provision is rarely, if ever, used, as it is more advantageous to the defendant to use the standard arrangements for payments into court. These provide that a defendant can pay an amount of money into court, and if the claimant wins, but the damages awarded are the same as or less than that amount, the defendant can claim costs from the date of the paying in (the jury is not told about the payment in before they make their decision on damages).

Offer of amends

The Defamation Act 1996 provides a way for claimants to get an apology and compensation at an early stage, while saving the costs of going to trial. Called the offer of amends procedure, it requires the defendant to make a written offer to publish an apology or correction and pay damages, which the claimant can choose whether or not to accept. If a defendant wishes to choose this defence, they must make the offer before putting forward any other defence – it is not possible, for example, to enter another defence and then decide to make an offer of amends later if you think that your original defence might not succeed after all. The offer of amends procedure is designed to be a way for defendants to put right the damage they have done at an early stage, rather than a 'get out of jail card' to have up their sleeves if the case starts to look shaky.

The offer can be in relation to a statement generally, or to a specific defamatory meaning, in which case it is called a qualified offer. A qualified offer might be used, for example, where the statement made is true, but it carries an implication that is not true and is defamatory.

If the claimant accepts the offer, then the parties settle between themselves, although the court can decide the appropriate compensation or the nature of the apology if the parties cannot agree. Accepting an offer of amends puts an end to the action for defamation against that particular publication.

If the claimant does not accept the offer, the defendant can withdraw it and make a new offer, withdraw it and choose to put forward a new defence, or let the offer stand. If they let the offer stand, and the claimant wins the case, the court is likely to reduce the damages payable in recognition of the fact that the defendant had attempted to make amends. This happened in **Nail** *v* **HarperCollins and News Group** (2004). HarperCollins had published an unauthorised biography of the actor Jimmy Nail, which made lurid allegations about his sexual behaviour. Mr Nail decided not to sue because he believed this would have the effect of giving the book and its allegations publicity, but he changed his mind when stories based on the allegations in the book appeared in the high-circulation *News of the World* newspaper. He claimed damages of £70,000–£100,000, and rejected an offer of amends, which included damages of £37,500. Although he won his case, the judge awarded only £30,000, and said that defendants who tried to make amends were entitled to expect that the court would acknowledge that effort by reducing the damages. The Court of Appeal approved this view.

Liability of distributors

The Defamation Act 2013 gives protection to distributors of defamatory material. It provides that the courts will no longer have jurisdiction to hear claims against anyone who is not the author or the publisher, unless the court is satisfied that it would be inpracticable to sue the author or the publisher.

Remedies for defamation

Damages

Damages for defamation may simply compensate for the claimant's loss, or may be exemplary, designed to punish the publisher. In mitigation of damages, the court may take into account the following:

- whether the defendant apologised as quickly as possible;
- whether the claimant already had a bad reputation;
- whether there was provocation by counter-libels;
- whether the claimant has already received damages for the publication of approximately the same defamation;
- the remoteness of damage done to the claimant.

In the past there has been much concern at the size of the awards of damages in defamation cases. The level of damages has been essentially an issue for the jury and, in a string of high-profile cases, juries awarded what appeared to be excessively high damages (see p. 241). Section 8 of the Courts and Legal Services Act 1990 gives the Court of Appeal the right to overturn a jury decision on the amount of damages and substitute 'such sum as appears to the court to be proper'. The Court of Appeal used this power in **John** *v* **Mirror Group Newspapers** (1996), an appeal by the Mirror Group against an award of damages to the singer Elton John. He had initially been awarded £350,000, comprising £275,000 exemplary damages and £75,000 compensation. The award related to an untrue story that the singer-songwriter was hooked on a bizarre diet which was a form of the eating disorder bulimia nervosa.

The initial award was slashed to £75,000, which comprised £50,000 exemplary damages and £25,000 compensation. The Court of Appeal stated that under the old system, juries were like 'sheep loosed on an unfenced common with no shepherd' and commented that it was clearly undesirable for higher compensation to be given for loss of reputation than for many cases of severe mental or physical injury. The court considered that in future judges and lawyers could give clear guidance to juries in valuing damaged reputations, by citing typical awards for victims suffering personal injury and inviting juries to compare the damage a libel claimant has suffered. They might point out, for example, that a paraplegic gets a maximum of £125,000 compensation for the injury, while a lost arm is 'worth' £45,000 and a lost eye £20,000. The Court of Appeal even went as far as suggesting that there should be a £125,000 limit on defamation awards.

Since **John**, the Court of Appeal has continued to be active in levelling down what it considers to be excessive damages. In **McCartan Turkington Breen** *v* **The Times Newspaper** (1998), it reduced an award of £145,000 to £75,000. In **Kiam** *v* **MGN** (2002) the Court of Appeal gave additional guidance on when and how the levelling down power should be used. Mr Kiam, a businessman, had sued the defendants after their newspaper, the *Mirror*, published an article which questioned his business ability and his commitment to his company. There were many aggravating factors surrounding the publication: not only was the article completely untrue but also there was ample evidence that its writer did not much care whether it was true or not. Shortly before the trial the paper published further defamatory articles, without checking with Mr Kiam whether the information in them was true. Neither the writer nor the editor of the paper appeared as witnesses, and the paper did not apologise to Mr Kiam until just before the trial began.

The jury found for Mr Kiam, and the judge suggested that, as a guideline, appropriate damages might be between £40,000 and £80,000, although he stressed that the decision on how much to award was theirs alone. The jury awarded Mr Kiam £105,000 in aggravated compensatory damages. The *Mirror* appealed. The Court of Appeal held that the question that s. 8 of the Courts and Legal Services Act required it to ask was whether a jury could reasonably have thought that the amount awarded was necessary to compensate the claimant. If the answer was yes, the award should stand. If no, the award was excessive and the court should substitute a 'proper award'. A proper award would be the highest sum the jury could reasonably have thought necessary, rather than the sum the court thought appropriate (though it would clearly not be difficult for a court to choose the second and justify it as the first). In this case, the award was not considered excessive and was allowed to stand.

The Defamation Act 2013 provides that defamation cases will now usually be heard by judges without juries, and this is likely to lead to more realistic assessments of damages.

Injunction

A claimant may also seek an injunction, either where a defamatory statement has already been published, to prevent it being published again, or where the claimant knows that the defendant plans to publish a defamatory statement, to prevent this happening. Where the claimant is seeking to prevent initial publication, they will be asking for an interlocutory injunction, which means one that is granted without the issue actually being tried by a court. This clearly has important implications for free speech; it is not difficult to see how wealthy and powerful claimants could effectively freeze all criticism of their activities if these types of injunction were freely granted. For this reason, the courts have always been reluctant to grant interlocutory injunctions in defamation cases; in **Bonnard** *v* **Perryman** (1891), it was stated that they should only do so in the clearest cases, where it was obvious that any reasonable jury would say the statement concerned was libellous.

This traditional principle has been further strengthened by s. 12 of the Human Rights Act 1998, which provides that interim injunctions in cases affecting freedom of expression should not be granted unless the court is satisfied that, if the case does go to trial, the claimant is likely to be able to establish that publication should not be allowed. The Human Rights Act further provides that when considering requests for injunctions on journalistic material, the courts must take into account:

- the importance of freedom of expression;
- the extent to which the material is already, or is about to be, available to the public;
- the extent to which publication would be in the public interest;
- any relevant privacy code.

The result is that interim injunctions in libel cases are likely to be granted only where the claimant can convince the court that the defendant is planning to publish defamatory stories which are obviously untrue, and there is no arguable defence, or a defence put forward is unlikely to succeed.

Time limits

The limitation period for defamation actions is one year, although s. 32A of the Limitation Act 1980 provides that the courts have a discretion to extend this in some circumstances. This discretion was examined in **Steedman** *v* **BBC** (2001). The case concerned a claim for damages by eight police officers from the Metropolitan Police Force, after a local news programme reported on the death in police custody of a Mr Roger Sylvester. The report stated that 'Mr Sylvester died in January, after being restrained by eight police officers'. None of the claimants was identified by name in the report. The report was broadcast on 16 April 1999, but the officers did not start legal proceedings until 26 June 2000, and did not serve particulars of the case until almost four months after that. They had made no complaint to the BBC until June 2000.

The BBC held that the action was time-barred, but the claimants applied to have the primary limitation period disapplied. The judge refused and the claimants appealed. The Court of Appeal found that the manner in which the judge had exercised the discretion given to him under s. 32A was perfectly correct. The principal test laid down in s. 32A involved weighing up whether the disadvantage to the claimants if the limitation period was not extended was greater than the disadvantage to the defendants if it was extended. However, the discretion was a wide one, and the judge was entitled to take all the circumstances into consideration, including the length of and reasons for the delay, and the impact of that delay on the availability of evidence. In addition, in defamation claims an early action was important if the claimant's reputation was to receive any meaningful protection, so the courts should not be too ready to disapply the limitation period.

In this case there were a number of factors which counted against the claimants' application. They had offered no real explanation for the delay in claiming, their claim was not a strong one, and any prejudice they would suffer from not being allowed to carry on with the case could be made up for by the fact that they could claim against their solicitors for negligence.

Issues in defamation

The costs of defamation cases

Bringing or defending a defamation case costs more in the English courts than anywhere else in the world. Even within Europe, the difference in cost is huge: a study by Oxford University looked at costs across 12 different European countries, and found that a defamation case here costs 140 times more than the average across all the other countries, and four times more than the next most expensive, Ireland. Very often, the legal costs are much higher than the damages paid if the claimant wins.

In the past, this was seen as largely a problem for claimants, as it meant that only the wealthy could afford to defend their reputations. The advent of 'no win, no fee' deals has changed this, and now much more concern is directed at the impact of costs on defendants and, in particular, on how far the cost of having to defend a claim stifles free expression.

There are two reasons why the issue of cost can have this effect. First, in most cases, the losing party is ordered to pay the other side's costs, so unless a defendant believes they have an extremely good chance of winning, there is huge pressure on them to settle early and avoid the risk of losing and having to pay not only damages, but also costs. Secondly, even where a defendant wins, they will usually not get back all the money they have spent on legal costs. The claimant can ask the court to look at the costs the winning side is claiming, and decide whether they are reasonable, and it is quite common to find that the court only orders the losing party to pay perhaps 90 per cent of the fees that the defendants have paid to their lawyers. Given that a defamation case can cost hundreds of thousands of pounds to defend, even a defendant who has a very strong case may be put off trying to fight the claim by the knowledge that, even if they win, it could cost them tens of thousands of pounds. Freedom of speech campaigners say that this situation creates a 'freezing effect' on the media, making them more likely to avoid writing about certain subjects, people or organisations altogether; to pull out of a story if a libel claim is threatened; or to agree a quick settlement rather than defending a case.

One recent step which may have an impact on costs is the removal of the presumption that defamation cases will be heard by a jury, under s. 11 of the Defamation Act. One reason why defamation cases are so costly is that jury cases tend to take significantly longer than cases before a judge alone, and if most cases are now heard by a judge, costs should come down.

Cost of a typical defamation trial in England compared to other European countries

Belgium	£28,000
Bulgaria	£600
Cyprus	£5,000
England and Wales (where claimant uses a CFA)	£4,500,000
England and Wales (without a CFA)	£2,750,000
France	£46,000
Germany	£1,250
Ireland	£867,000
Italy	£107,000
Malta	£500
Romania	£4,000
Spain	£2,000
Sweden	£19,000

Source: *A Comparative Study of Costs in Defamation Proceedings Across Europe*, by the Programme in Comparative Media Law and Policy, Centre for Socio-Legal Studies, University of Oxford.

Claimant-friendly rules

English defamation law makes it much easier for a claimant to succeed than the law in many other countries. As long as they can prove that the statement was defamatory (including, once the Defamation Act 2013 is in force, that it caused, or was likely to cause, serious harm to their reputation), that it was published and that it referred to them, they can win their case. They do not have to prove that the statement was untrue; it is up to the defendant to prove this if they want to claim truth as a defence. Nor do they have to show that the defendant was at fault, in the sense of deliberately publishing defamatory material; a defendant can potentially be liable, for example, even if they believed the material was true, or did not realise the statement could be taken to refer to someone other than the person they meant. Campaigners for free speech argue that this aspect of the law compromises freedom of expression, because the fact that the scales seem tipped in favour of the claimant has a similar 'chilling effect' on the media to the problem of cost (and they are of course related, because if the rules make it easier for a claimant to win, they make it more likely that the defendant will have to pay costs and damages).

By contrast, in many other jurisdictions, it is harder to prove a defamation case. In the USA, for example, a claimant has to prove that the statement is false, and has to prove that the defendant was at fault. If the claimant is not a public figure, they must prove that the defendant was careless, but if they are a public figure, they face a harder test, and must show that the defendant knew the statement was false, or had 'serious doubts' about whether it was false or not.

In recent years, we have seen some moves by the English courts to rebalance the law, for example in the case of **O'Shea** *v* **Mirror Group Newspapers Ltd** (2001), where the court said that the media should not be expected to go to unreasonable lengths to ensure that they did not accidentally show a picture that looked like someone else. The defence of responsible publication in the Defamation Act 2013 (and its predecessor the **Reynolds** defence) also focuses on whether the defendant was actually at fault, and provides protection where the defendant has acted responsibly, even if the material published turned out to be untrue. However, it is still easier to succeed in a defamation claim here than in any comparable legal system.

Liability for comment

As far as free speech is concerned, the freedom to express an opinion is just as important as the freedom to publish factual information. Recognising this, the defence of honest comment, and its replacement under the Defamation Act 2013, honest opinion, give some protection for statements which are comments, rather than factual allegations but, as we saw earlier, it can be defeated if the claimant can show that the opinion expressed was not honestly held. This contrasts with the law in the US, and some European countries, where much more of a distinction is made between comment and allegations of fact. In the USA, the Supreme Court has said, in **Milkovich** *v* **Lorain Journal Co** (1990), that statements of opinion about matters of public concern, which do not contain any false factual allegation, cannot be the basis of a defamation action. In some states, the courts have gone further and found that there can be no defamation claim for any kind of comment which does not contain a factual allegation.

Lack of protection for matters of public interest

As we saw earlier, in **Reynolds** *v* **Times Newspapers**, *The Times* argued that the defence of qualified privilege should cover all media coverage of matters on public interest. This, it is argued, would promote free speech, because the media would be free to write about important issues, even if they involved someone wealthy and powerful who might be likely to sue. The courts refused to go this far and, despite calls for an over-arching public interest defence in the Defamation Act 2013, so has Parliament.

We do, of course, have some special protection for material of public interest, in the **Reynolds**/ responsible publication and privilege defences, and the ban on claims by elected organisations and political parties, but even so, the protection in English law for matters of public interest is often compared unfavourably to those in US law. As we saw above, in the USA, a claim made by a public figure, regarding a matter of public interest, can only succeed if the claimant can prove that the defendant published the material knowing it was untrue, or despite having serious doubts about whether it was true. The category of 'public official' includes all politicians, and candidates for public office, appointed public officials, and a wide range of government employees. This rule, known as the ***New York Times*** rules after the case which created it, **New York Times** *v* **Sullivan** (1964), is strictly applied by the courts, and means that it is very difficult for public officials of any kind to prevent discussion of their activities by suing or threatening to sue.

The side-effect of this approach is that there will be times when untrue material is published, and the public official is left without any means of clearing their name. However, supporters of the US approach would argue that this is a price worth paying to make sure that the media is not frightened away from publishing material which the public has an interest in knowing about. Another possible way to shift the balance, which has been suggested both here and in the USA, would be to create a new type of claim where instead of damages, a successful claimant would get a 'declaration of falsity', which would be a statement that what had been said about them was incorrect. This would allow a claimant who has been lied about to defend their reputation, without stifling press investigations with the threat of damages, and for the media, the prospect of having to say their stories were untrue should act as a deterrent to publishing stories without checking properly that they were true. It would, however, also require some action to cut the costs of a defamation action in order to have a real effect.

The distinction between libel and slander

The distinction has been justified on the grounds that libel is more likely to be pre-meditated and is likely to cause greater harm. However, it can cause apparent injustice; a person deliberately making a false and malicious public speech will not be liable for slander if no damage results, but a journalist who honestly reports the speech may be liable for libel. In reviewing this area of the law, in 1975 the Faulks Committee recommended that the distinction should be abolished. Some fear that if the distinction were abolished there would be a rise in petty actions for defamation by words as damage would no longer have to be proved. However, in countries where the distinction does not exist this does not appear to be a problem; the high cost of defamation actions also makes it unlikely.

Problems with remedies

Neither of the remedies for defamation is entirely satisfactory. Damages cannot buy back a reputation; by the time they are awarded, the defamation has not only been published in the first place, but in high-profile cases will also have received a huge amount of media attention during the case. This can mean that, even if the claimant succeeds, doubts may linger in the public's mind, which is after all exactly the effect the claimant is seeking to avoid.

In addition, even though damages can be extremely high, newspapers in particular are often owned by large, wealthy businesses, and a high damages award may simply be set against the increased sales achieved by publishing the libel in the first place and the publicity arising from the court case. Where large and powerful publishing organisations are concerned, alternative (or additional) sanctions, such as being prohibited from publishing at all for a certain period of time, might be more effective. Even losing publication for a day would have a deterrent effect, given the enormous competition between rival publications. After his award of damages was drastically cut in 1995, Elton John said that the result left him £85,000 out of pocket after paying legal fees, and declared that the decision 'has given the press carte blanche to print and be damned, and confirmed to the press that it makes commercial sense to print whatever lies they want and, if sued, just pay what to them is a small fine'.

By contrast, an interim injunction does what the claimant really needs, by preventing the defamation from being published in the first place. However, it amounts to censorship without a jury trial and may therefore be seen as unfair to the defendant and a serious restriction on freedom of the press.

Answering questions

Jack is a reporter on a local paper, the *Waterloo Gazette*. His editor sends him to review a play at the local theatre, and then have a meal at a local pub, and review that as well. The play turns out to star Jack's ex-girlfriend, Jill, and in his review, Jack writes: 'The play as a whole was excellent, but the show was badly let down by Jill Hill, who played Lady Macbeth. She forgot her lines nine times, and her voice was like listening to a parrot on crack. She is a terrible actress.'

As he leaves the theatre, Joe passes the town hall, where a council meeting has just come to an end. He sees a local councillor, Dave Dodgy, arguing with the managing director of a large local building company, and crouches behind a car to listen. He hears the businessman accuse the local councillor of taking bribes to give companies council building work. He writes a story about what he has heard, reporting that 'A local councillor has been accused of taking bribes by the head of Bloggs Building, Joe Honestman. Mr Honestman said that the whole council was corrupt, and that at least one councillor was in the habit of taking bribes from companies seeking contracts from the council. The councillor was heard to shout that Mr Honestman was talking nonsense, before he sped off in his silver Rolls Royce. This is yet another example of the corrupt practices at the local council.' The newspaper can only get hold of one photo of Mr Honestman to illustrate the piece; it shows him talking to a local councillor, Charlie Chatty. The paper uses the picture anyway, with a caption that reads 'Mr Honestman with Councillor Chatty'.

Does anyone have a claim in defamation against the paper? What defences might the paper raise if a claim is made?

The first possible claimant to consider here is Jill. The cases of **Cornwell** and **Berkoff** clearly suggest that what is said about her is defamatory, and she is referred to by name, so the issue is whether the paper might have a defence. Honest comment (or once the Defamation Act 2013 is inforce, honest opinion) is the most obvious candidate, so you need to consider whether the words are comment or statements of fact. Most of what Jack says would seem to be comment, but whether Jill forgot her lines is a matter of fact, so, if this is not true, the defence would not be available for that element of the article. As Jill is Jack's ex-girlfriend, you also need to look at whether, even if he is prejudiced against her, he honestly holds the opinions in the article, referring to **Horrocks** *v* **Lowe**. Remember that you do not necessarily have to know whether Jack was motivated by malice, only how the courts would look at the question.

With regard to the bribery allegations, the first issue is who can sue. Clearly it is defamatory to say that the council is corrupt, but the **Derbyshire** case establishes that local authorities cannot sue in defamation. Individual councillors can sue, however, and it is clearly defamatory to say that a councillor takes bribes. In Mr Dodgy's case, though, the issue will be whether he can show that he was referred to in the article. He is not named, but the description of his car may well be enough to let readers identify him, so you should refer to **J'Anson** *v* **Stuart** here. In this case the paper may put forward the Reynold's defence (or if the Defamation Act 2013 is in force, responsible publication on a matter of public interest), so you should explain how this works, and what will decide whether it can apply here. You should also consider the neutral reportage defence, although it seems the paper has lost any chance of using this as the final sentence of its report assumes the allegations are true. You should also briefly mention the truth defence, since we do not know whether the allegations are true.

Finally, consider the position of Mr Chatty. He may have a case as the use of his photo beside a story about an unnamed councillor taking bribes could be taken to imply that he was that councillor, even though he is not mentioned; the case of **Dwek** *v* **Macmillan** is relevant here.

The law of defamation seeks to strike a balance between protecting reputation and allowing the press to report freely. How far does the Defamation Act 2013 improve the way this balance is achieved?

To start this essay, you could give an introduction explaining why freedom of the press is important, and (briefly) what protections existed before the Defamation Act 2013 was passed.

Then work through the changes made under the Act that affect this balance: the single publication rule, the new defences of honest opinion and innocent publication on a matter of public interest, protection for scientific and academic material, provisions against libel tourism, and the cost-cutting effects of fewer jury trials. For each point, try to highlight what has changed, and how this will (or will not) strike a better balance between freedom of expression and protection for reputation.

To earn yourself some extra marks, you should also point out some of the things that the Act has failed to do, by covering some of the problems that still exist, and comparing our law with the way defamation law works in other jurisdictions (you will find material for this on p. 256–259).

Finish with a conclusion explaining how far you think the new law has improved the balance, and whether you think it should or could have gone futher.

Summary of Chapter 9

Defamation is committed by publishing a statement which lowers the reputation of the person referred to.

Elements of defamation

There are two types:

- libel applies to statements in permanent form;
- slander to statements in temporary or transitory form.

The claimant must prove:

- the statement complained of was defamatory;
- the statement referred to the claimant;
- the statement was published;
- the statement did, or was likely to do, serious damage to the claimant's reputation.

Defamatory statements

- A statement will be defamatory if it 'tends to lower the person in the estimation of right-thinking members of society', or exposes the person to 'hatred, contempt or ridicule'.
- This can include indirect criticisms (innuendoes).
- Changes over time can mean that a statement which was once defamatory would not be now.

The statement must refer to the claimant

- The claimant need not be named; the statement will be taken to refer to them if a reasonable person would think it did.
- Traditionally defendants could be liable even if they did not mean to refer to the claimant, but the Human Rights Act may now prevent this.
- It is not possible to defame a class of people, unless it is so small that the statement could be taken to refer to every individual member.

Proof of damage

- In libel, there is no need to prove damage.
- In slander, damage must be proved, except for claims that the claimant:
  - has committed an imprisonable offence;
  - has certain contagious diseases;
  - is female and 'not chaste';
  - is unfit for their trade, profession or business.

The first two of these exceptions are abolished under the Defamation Act 2013.

Parties to a defamation action

- Under the Defamation Act 2013, it will no longer be possible to sue distributors unless it is impracticable to sue the author or editor.
- Only living people can sue; there is no claim for defamation of someone who is dead.
- Companies and organisations can sue, but not democratically elected bodies or political parties.

Defences

In addition to the general defence of consent, there are defences specific to defamation (plus apology, which can reduce the damages ordered).

Justification/truth

Justification is replaced by the defence of truth under the Defamation Act 2013. Both apply when the defendant can prove the statement is substantially true.

Where there is more than one allegation about the claimant, the defendant need not prove them all true, so long as those they cannot prove do not materially injure the claimant's reputation, in the light of the truth of the others.

Honest comment/honest opinion

Honest comment is replaced by honest opinion under the Defamation Act 2013. Both protect statements of opinion, not fact.

Absolute privilege

Applies to statements made:

- in Parliament by a member, or in parliamentary reports;
- by one officer of state to another;
- by one spouse to another;
- in the course of judical proceedings;
- in fair, accurate and contemporaneous court reports.

Qualified privilege

Qualified privilege arises by statute, and under common law. In both cases statements must be made without malice.

Statutory qualified privilege applies to statements made in a list of circumstances detailed in Sch. I to the Defamation Act 1996, which are in two classes:

- Statements privileged without explanation or contradiction include:
  - reports of courts, legislatures, and government inquiries;
  - reports published by governments, legislatures and international organisations.
- Fair and accurate reports of specified types of public meeting.
- Fair and accurate extracts, copies and summaries of material issued by specified types of organisation.

The Defamation Act 2013 introduces statutory qualified privilege for peer-reviewed articles on matters of scientific or academic interests in scientific and academic journals.

Qualified privilege under common law arises where one party has a legal, social or moral duty to communicate information to another, and that party has a duty to receive it, including:

- where necessary to protect an interest;
- communications between officers of a company;
- information given to the police about crime.

The **Reynolds** defence protects serious, responsible coverage of subjects of public interest, even where the material is untrue.

It is replaced by responsible publication on a matter of public interest under the Defamation Act 2013.

Offer of amends

The offer of amends procedure under the Defamation Act 1996 allows a defence where the defendant offers an apology and damages. If not accepted, and the client wins, damages will be reduced.

→

Remedies

Damages may be compensatory, or, in exceptional cases, exemplary.

Injunctions may be given to prevent initial publication, or prevent repetition. The Human Rights Act puts restrictions on the use of injunctions to prevent initial publication.

Time limits

The limitation period is one year, but the courts have discretion to extend this.

Issues in defamation

Key issues are:

- costs;
- claimant-friendly rules;
- liability for comment;
- lack of protection for matters of public interest;
- the distinction between libel and slander;
- problems with remedies.

Reading list

Text resources

Barendt, E (1993) 'Libel and freedom of speech in English law' *Public Law* 449

Carter-Ruck, P and Starte, H N A (1996) *On Libel and Slander*, 5th edn. Butterworths

Crone, T (2002) *Law and the Media*, 4th edn, Chapter 1. Focal Press

Dadak, R (2005) 'One score draw' *Solicitors Journal* 907

Duncan, C and Neill, B (1983) Defamation, 2nd edn. Lexis Nexis

Fleming, J G (1978) 'Retraction and reply: alternative remedies for defamation' 12 *University of British Columbia Law Review* 15

Gibbons, T (1996) 'Defamation reconsidered' 16 *Oxford Journal of Legal Studies* 587

Harlow, C (2005) *Understanding Tort Law*, 3rd edn, Chapter 7. Sweet & Maxwell

Johnston, I D (1978) 'Uncertainties in the defence of fair comment' 8 *New Zealand Universities Law Review* 359

Kaye, J M (1975) 'Libel or slander: two torts or one?' 91 *Law Quarterly Review* 524

Loveland, I (1994) 'Defamation of government: taking lessons from America' 14 *Legal Studies* 206

Milmo, P, Rogers, W V H and Parkes, R (2008) *Gatley on Libel and Slander*, 11th edn. Sweet & Maxwell

Report of the Faulks Committee on Defamation, Cmnd 5905 (1975)

Robertson, G (1999) *The Justice Game*, Vintage

Robertson, G and Nicol, A (2008) *Media Law*, 5th edn, Chapter 3. Penguin

Rubenstein, M (ed.) (1972) *Wicked, Wicked Libels*. Routledge and Kegan Paul

Sharland, A and Loveland, I (1997) 'The Defamation Act 1996 and Political Speech' *Public Law* 113

Trindade, F (2000) 'Defamatory statements and political discussions' 116 *Law Quarterly Review* 185

Williams, J (1997) 'Reforming defamation law in the United Kingdom' *Tort Law Review* 206

Williams, K (1997) 'Only flattery is safe: political speech and the Defamation Act 1996' 60 *Modern Law Review* 388

Reading on the Internet

The Defamation Act 1996 can be read at:
www.opsi.gov.uk/acts/acts1996/1996031.htm

The Defamation Bill 2010 can be read at:
www.justice.gov.uk

The House of Lords judgment in **Reynolds** *v* **Times Newspapers** (2001) can be read at:
www.parliament.the-stationery-office.co.uk/pa/ld199899/ldjudgmt/jd991028/rey01.htm

The House of Lords judgment in **Jameel** *v* **Wall Street** (2006) can be read at:
http://www.publications.parliament.uk/pa/ld200506/ldjudgmt/jd061011/jamee-1.htm

The House of Lords judgment in **Grobbelaar** *v* **News Group** (2001) can be read at:
http://www.publications.parliament.uk/pa/ld200102/ldjudgmt/jd021024/grobb-1.htm

Visit **www.mylawchamber.co.uk** to access tools to help you develop and test your knowledge of tort law, including interactive multiple choice questions, practice exam questions with guidance, weblinks, glossary flashcards, legal newsfeed and legal updates.

Use Case Navigator to read in full some of the key cases referenced in this chapter with commentary and questions:

Jameel *v* **Wall Street Journal** (2006)

Chapter 10
Privacy

This chapter discusses:

- The background to privacy protection in tort
- How the tort of breach of confidence/misuse of private information is committed
- Remedies for breach of confidence/misuse of private information.

The cases in this chapter are, as the title suggests, all about people who want to keep things private. Very often (though not always) brought by the rich and famous, recent privacy cases have involved the footballers Ryan Giggs and John Terry, who were trying to prevent the press reporting on their extra-marital affairs; the author J.K. Rowling, who was seeking to prevent publication of pictures of her children, taken covertly and without her permission; and a policeman who wrote an anonymous blog about his job, and wanted to stop the press from revealing his name and getting him into trouble at work. These types of case have become increasingly common over the past ten years, so it might surprise you to know that, in English law, there is in fact no tort of 'privacy'. However, as a result of a string cases brought since 2001, there is no doubt that English law does give a degree of protection to privacy that was not part of our law before then. This protection has been based on a combination of two things: the traditional tort of breach of confidence, which has been developed and manipulated to suit the kind of claims now coming before the courts, and the provisions of the Human Rights Act 1998. For this reason, it will help you understand the current law if we look first at how it developed to its current position.

The background to privacy protection

Although English law has never had a tort of privacy, there is a traditional tort that has always protected some types of private information and material. It is called breach of confidence, and its elements were defined in **Coco** *v* **A N Clark** (1969) as:

- there must be information which has 'the necessary element of confidence about it', or, in other words, could be considered private rather than public;
- the defendant must be 'under an obligation of confidence'; and
- the defendant must make 'unauthorised use' of the information.

In other words, the tort of breach of confidence was committed when someone disclosed private information, in circumstances where doing so would be breaking a duty of confidentiality to the owner of the information. The typical case involved a defendant revealing his or her employer's commercial secrets to a rival company, or leaking government information. However, in **Argyll** *v* **Argyll** (1967), it was established that breach of confidence could be used to protect personal information, when the Duke of Argyll was prevented from publishing details of his stormy marriage, on the grounds that married couples owed each other a duty of confidentiality.

However, breach of confidence seemed at this point to offer only very limited protection in cases concerning personal secrets, because it was only available where there was a pre-existing relationship between the parties that suggested they owed each other a duty of confidentiality. This might be, for example, a marriage, or an employer–employee relationship.

Key Case **Attorney-General** *v* **Guardian Newspapers Ltd (No 2) (1990)**

Over the years, however, this requirement was chipped away, until in **Attorney-General** *v* **Guardian Newspapers Ltd (No 2)** (1990), Lord Goff stated categorically that such a relationship was not required, and that:

> a duty of confidence arises when confidential information comes to the knowledge of a person . . . in circumstances where he has notice, or is held to have agreed, that the information is confidential, with the effect that it would be just in all the circumstances that he should be precluded from disclosing the information to others.

This meant that a breach of confidentiality could be found, for example, where obviously private information was stolen, or where someone found a private diary in the street. This still did not amount to complete protection of privacy, but, as we shall see, it did widen the potential usage of the breach of confidence action.

Legal Principle

A duty of confidence arises where someone receives information in circumstances where he or she agrees or has notice that the information is confidential, and it would be just in all the circumstances that they should be prevented from disclosing that information to others.

Outside the limited situations in which a breach of confidence could arise, there was no specific protection for privacy, as the case of **Kaye** *v* **Robertson** (1991) shows. The claimant was Gorden Kaye, an actor who at the time was very well known as the star of a TV sitcom. He was badly injured in an accident, and as he lay semi-conscious in hospital press photographers sneaked in and took pictures of him. Mr Kaye's representative went to court to try to prevent the pictures being published, but, despite admitting that there was probably no situation where someone's privacy deserved protection more than when they were lying half-conscious in a hospital bed, the court said that there simply was no tort of invasion of privacy in English law. The only way that Mr Kaye could succeed was to make a claim in the tort of malicious falsehood, which protects commercial interests, on the basis that the snatched photos compromised his chances of selling his story himself later. This meant that the paper had to make it clear that they had taken the photos without his permission, but it did not prevent them being published.

Until 1998, then, breach of confidence was really the only tort which could be used to prevent disclosure of private information (or pictures) and its use was fairly limited. The first hints of the changes to come appeared in 1998, with the passing of the Human Rights Act, which gives effect to the Art. 8 provision that 'Everyone has the right to respect for his private and family life, his home and his correspondence'. Did this mean that there was now a right to privacy in English law – and if it did, how was this right to be balanced against the Art. 10 provision that 'everyone has the right to freedom of expression'? It was not long before those who had most to gain from a right to privacy began to put these questions before the courts.

The current law on privacy

Case Navigator

It is still the case that there is no English tort of invasion of privacy. This was stated categorically by the Court of Appeal in **Wainwright** *v* **Home Office** (2002) and confirmed in the House of Lords judgment on the subject, **Campbell** *v* **Mirror Group Newspapers** (2004) (see below). **Wainwright** differs from the other 'privacy cases' in that it does not deal with the publication of private information. The claimants were a mother and son who had gone to visit the mother's other son in prison. They were strip-searched, apparently to make sure they were not carrying drugs into the prison, and found the procedure so humiliating and stressful that both developed psychiatric illness as a result. They sued the Home Office for, among other things, invasion of privacy, but the court said that there was no general right to privacy, only existing torts which protected particular aspects of privacy, such as breach of confidence which protected private information, and trespass which protected the privacy of a person's body, home and property.

However, the courts have, since 2001, extended and manipulated the tort of breach of confidence, so that now, while we do not officially have a tort of privacy, the breach of confidence action is certainly able to do some of the work that might be expected of a tort of privacy – and the courts now acknowledge that privacy is the quality that a breach of confidence action is there to protect. In the key House of Lords judgment on the subject, **Campbell** *v* **Mirror Group Newspapers** (2004), Lord Hope used the term 'misuse of private information' to describe this type of confidentiality claim, and it now seems that misuse of private information is becoming a new tort, developed from the old law of breach of confidence, but with its own rules.

The case which is generally seen as kicking off this development is **Douglas, Zeta Jones and Northern & Shell plc** *v* **Hello! Ltd** (2001). The case concerned the star-studded wedding of Hollywood stars Michael Douglas and Catherine Zeta Jones, and was one battle in a long-running circulation war between two magazines, *Hello!* and *OK*, which compete every week for stories about the weddings, babies and lovely homes of celebrities. The happy couple had sold exclusive rights to pictures of their wedding to *OK* magazine. Their contract with the magazine gave them the right to choose which pictures were used, and to have the final say in how they should be 're-touched'. To make sure that no other publication could get pictures, there was heavy security and guests were forbidden to bring cameras. However, one photographer sneaked in, and then sold his pictures to *Hello!* The claimants sought an injunction to prevent publication of the pictures claiming malicious falsehood, interference with contractual relations (both of which protect business interests, and do not concern us here), breach of confidence and breach of laws of privacy, an action which they claimed had been created by the Human Rights Act, and specifically the Art. 8 provision referred to above.

At an interim hearing to decide whether the claimants should be allowed an injunction to prevent publication, the Court of Appeal seemed to give some support to this assertion, but, at the full hearing, the court disagreed. Lindsay J held that the Human Rights Act did not create a specific new tort at all, and that, although the Human Rights Act might require the courts to create new law where existing law did not adequately protect the rights enshrined in the Human Rights Act, there was no reason for them to do so if existing law did provide sufficient protection in the case before them. In this case, he stated, the existing law of breach of confidence provided a remedy.

Looking at the elements specified in **Coco** *v* **A N Clark** (above), he said *Hello!* must have realised that they were 'under an obligation of confidence' with regard to pictures of the wedding, and that their use of them was unauthorised, because the couple had made it very clear that the wedding was a private event, and that they did not want unofficial photographs taken. To many observers in the media, the difficult aspect was whether the wedding pictures could be said to have 'the necessary element of confidence' about them (in other words, to be considered private), given that the Douglases had agreed to sell pictures of the wedding to another magazine. Lindsay J, however, pointed out that it was in fact this that gave the pictures the element of confidentiality – it made them a valuable commercial asset, and it was clear that a breach of confidence action could protect such assets.

Looked at this way, the case was a relatively straightforward application of the traditional law of confidentiality, but it became the springboard for a series of other cases in which celebrities tried to use the breach of confidence action to protect their personal privacy, without the commercial asset argument that won the case for the Douglases. It is the judgments in these cases, along with **Douglas**, that have shaped the current position on breach of confidence as a protector of personal privacy.

Key Case **Campbell *v* Mirror Group Newspapers (2004)**

The latest House of Lords judgment on breach of confidence and privacy is now **Campbell *v* Mirror Group Newspapers** (2004). The case was brought by model Naomi Campbell after the *Daily Mirror* published a series of stories about her treatment for drug addiction, including the fact that she was attending meetings of Narcotics Anonymous (NA), details of the way in which NA was helping her to deal with her addiction, and photos of her leaving an NA meeting.

An early attempt to sue for invasion of privacy was abandoned, and Ms Campbell framed her case specifically in terms of breach of confidence. She accepted that the press had a right to publish the fact that she was a drug addict, given that she had denied this in the past, but said that publishing details of the treatment that she was receiving, and pictures of her at the place where she was receiving it, was a breach of confidence, since these details were clearly the kind of information that any reasonable person must realise was obtained confidentially, just as any detailed information about a person's medical treatment would be.

The House of Lords, by a majority, upheld her claim, and took the opportunity to explain the current relationship between breach of confidence and invasion of privacy. Even the two judges who rejected Ms Campbell's case agreed that there had been a shift in the law on breach of confidence. Lord Nicholls confirmed that, as stated in **Wainwright**, 'there is no over-arching, all-embracing cause of action for "invasion of privacy"'. However, he said, protection of various aspects of privacy was a fast developing area of the law, which had been spurred on by enactment of the Human Rights Act 1998, and the developments in breach of confidence actions were part of this process.

Lord Nicholls stated that once breach of confidence no longer relied on a pre-existing confidential relationship, it 'changed its nature'. As a result, the law now imposed a duty of confidence 'whenever a person receives information he knows or ought to know is fairly and reasonably to be regarded as confidential'. This, he said, effectively meant whenever a person receives information that is private, and the essence of the tort is now 'misuse of private information'. In addition, he said the time had come to recognise that: 'the values enshrined in articles 8 and 10 are now part of the cause of action for breach of confidence'.

Lord Hoffmann agreed, stating that there had been:

> a shift in the centre of gravity of the action for breach of confidence when it is used as a remedy for the unjustified publication of personal information . . . Instead of the cause of action being based upon the duty of good faith applicable to confidential personal information and trade secrets alike, it focuses upon the protection of human autonomy and dignity – the right to control the dissemination of information about one's private life and the right to the esteem and respect of other people.

Legal Principle

The test for misuse of private information is whether the claimant had a reasonable expectation of privacy, and, if they did, whether their right to privacy outweighs the defendant's right to freedom of expression.

Elements of the tort

In **Campbell**, the House of Lords held that in cases involving 'misuse of private information' a two-stage test should be applied (in place of the three-stage test in **Coco** *v* **Clark**). The court should ask:

- did the claimant have a reasonable expectation of privacy with respect to the information disclosed and, if so,
- is the person's right to privacy more important, in the circumstances, than someone else's right to freedom of expression (usually, though not always, the media's right)?

Reasonable expectation of privacy

In deciding whether the claimant had a reasonable expectation of privacy, the courts take account of a range of different factors, which must be weighed up against each other. In **Murray** *v* **Express Newspapers plc** (2008) (which we will look at later), the Court of Appeal said:

> As we see it, the question whether there is a reasonable expectation of privacy is a broad one, which takes account of all the circumstances of the case. They include the attributes of the claimant, the nature of the activity in which the claimant was engaged, the place at which it was happening, the nature and purpose of the intrusion, the absence of consent and whether it was known or could be inferred, the effect on the claimant and the circumstances in which and the purposes for which the information came into the hands of the publisher.

Because so many different factors are considered, privacy cases can be very fact-dependent, making it difficult to predict how later cases will be decided. However, some general principles can be drawn out from the cases the courts have decided.

The effect on the claimant

In **Campbell**, one of the key issues which swayed the court was the effect that the revelations could have had on Ms Campbell. In explaining this, Lord Hope said that it was necessary to take into account the fact that she was recovering from drug addiction which, they said, made her especially vulnerable. Lord Hope stated that the courts should ask:

> whether disclosure of the information about the individual ('A') would give substantial offence to A, assuming that A was placed in similar circumstances and was a person of ordinary sensibilities . . . The mind that has to be examined is that, not of the reader in general, but of the person who is affected by the publicity.

The news stories about Ms Campbell detailed how often she went to Narcotics Anonymous (NA) meetings and what usually happened at them, and the pictures, which were taken without her knowledge, showed her outside the door of the hall where the meeting was held. Before the stories were published, Ms Campbell had talked about the fact that many models were addicted to drugs, but had denied that she was one of them. Because of this, her lawyers agreed that publication of the basic facts of her drug problems, and the fact that she was attending NA, was not a breach of confidence, because it corrected a false image she had previously presented. However, the majority of the judges agreed that revealing the precise details of her treatment was a breach of confidence, for two reasons. First, giving details of the kind of things that would happen at NA meetings, and how frequently Ms Campbell attended them, was essentially the same thing as revealing details of someone's medical treatment, and revealing that kind of information had always been seen as a breach of confidence. Secondly, publishing the details of her treatment could have a harmful effect on Ms Campbell's efforts to beat her addiction, and this too meant she had a reasonable expectation of privacy.

The effect of revelations on the claimant was also an issue in **Terry** *v* **Person Unknown** (2010), though with different results. The case was brought by the footballer John Terry, who was seeking an injunction preventing publication of any stories about his affair with the ex-girlfriend of another England team member. Mr Justice Tugendhat said that the personality and circumstances of the claimant were relevant: 'the less sensitive the information is considered by the applicant to be, and the more robust the personality of the applicant . . . the less a court may find a need to interfere with freedom of expression by means of an injunction.' In this case, he judged that the information was not especially intrusive, and that John Terry appeared to have 'a very robust personality, as one might expect of a leading professional sportsman'. There was no real possibility of him being caused personal distress by the revelations, and it appeared that the real reason for the claim was to protect his commercial interests, because big companies would be less keen to offer him sponsorship or advertising deals if his image was damaged by these kinds of revelations.

Public and private activities

Whether there is a reasonable expectation of privacy will also depend on whether the revelations are about private activities or public ones. Private activities are more likely to give rise to a reasonable expectation of privacy, but public activities usually will not.

The most obvious example of a private activity is sex, and the courts have made it clear that there will usually be a reasonable expectation of privacy for revelations about the details of sexual activity, so long as the activity involves consenting adults. In **Jagger** *v* **Darling** (2005), the model Elizabeth Jagger was awarded an injunction preventing further publication of CCTV images, which showed her and her boyfriend 'engaging in sexual activities' inside the closed door of a nightclub. The court said this was a situation where there was clearly a legitimate expectation of privacy.

This approach was backed up in **Mosley** *v* **News Group Newspapers** (2008). The claimant was Max Mosley, the President of the FIA, which runs Formula 1 motor racing. He had been secretly filmed at a sado-masochistic orgy with five prostitutes, and the *News of the World* published the story. Mr Justice Eady upheld Mr Mosley's claim for misuse of personal information, stating that public figures were entitled to a personal life, and people's sex lives were 'essentially their own business'. He said that there would usually be a reasonable expectation of privacy with regard to sexual activity, especially if it was on private property and between consenting adults, regardless of whether some of them were paid to join in. Similarly, in **CTB** *v* **News Group Newspapers** (2011), where footballer Ryan Giggs tried to prevent revelations of his relationship with the Big Brother contestant Imogen Thomas, Eady J said there was 'no doubt' that there was a reasonable expectation of privacy for 'conduct of an intimate and sexual nature'.

However, although there will usually be a reasonable expectation of privacy with regard to details about sexual activity, the same does not necessarily apply to merely revealing that two people are in a sexual relationship with each other. In **Terry** *v* **Person Unknown** (2010), where footballer John Terry sought a permanent injunction preventing publication of any stories about the fact that he was having an affair, Mr Justice Tugendhat said there was a difference between publishing intrusive details and/or photographs concerning a sexual relationship, and merely publishing the fact that the relationship was going on. He said that if John Terry could have shown that there was a real threat that intrusive details or pictures might be published, he would have been entitled to an injunction preventing that publication, because he would be likely to have been able to prove at trial that the publication was misuse of private information. But the fact that there might be publication of the fact that the relationship existed was not sufficient to justify an injunction.

Examples of activities the courts consider public come less frequently, but in **The Author of a Blog** *v* **Times Newspapers Ltd** (2009), the court ruled that an anonymous blogger did not have a legitimate expectation of privacy regarding his identity, because blogging was a public activity. The claimant was a serving police officer, who writes a blog about his daily life at work, under the pseudonym 'Night Jack'. *The Times* had figured out his real name from things he had said in the blog, and he sought an interim injunction preventing them from publishing any information that would or might lead to his identification, claiming this was misuse of private information. In considering whether he had a reasonable expectation of privacy, Eady J said that the fact that bloggers may take steps to disguise their identity was not sufficient reason to prevent those who work it out from revealing it. Blogging was a public, not a private activity, and there was no reasonable expectation of privacy.

Use of pictures

Photographs, especially if taken without the subject's knowledge, are considered more intrusive than words alone, and so more likely to create an expectation of privacy. In **Douglas**, the court said that this applied even if words could have conveyed exactly the same information, so there might not have been a breach of confidence if *Hello*! had merely reported on the wedding, rather than actually publishing pictures of it.

However, this does not mean that pictures will always be covered by a reasonable expectation of privacy. In **Campbell**, the House of Lords said that this depends on what information they put across, and the context in which they were taken. Baroness Hale said that there was no expectation of privacy with regard to pictures of someone, famous or not, doing ordinary things in a public place, or as she put it, 'popping out for a pint of milk'. Such pictures could only ever reveal trivial information, such as what the person chose to wear when going to the corner shop, and trivial information was not protected by the law of confidence.

However, in the case of the pictures of Ms Campbell leaving her NA meeting, the situation was different. The pictures were taken on a public street, but in the circumstances, their publication could increase the potential harm to Ms Campbell, by making her think she was being followed by photographers, and feel betrayed by whoever told them where the meeting was. This might discourage her from continuing with the meetings, which were important to her recovery from drug addiction. That suggested there was a legitimate expectation of privacy and the pictures should not have been used.

The principle that there is no expectation of privacy regarding pictures of people doing ordinary things in public places was applied in **Sir Elton John** *v* **Associated Newspapers** (2006). The case involved pictures of Elton John, taken when he had just arrived home, which showed him walking from his car, with his driver. He complained that publication of the pictures invaded his privacy because they appeared to show that his baldness was returning (Sir Elton famously had a hair transplant many years ago). He tried to get an injunction preventing the *Daily Mail* from publishing the photos, but his application was refused. Mr Justice Eady said that the pictures did not convey any kind of private information. They were in the same category as a shot of someone 'popping out for a pint of milk', which Baroness Hale had said created no expectation of privacy.

However, a different view has been taken by the European Court of Human Rights, which at some point the UK courts may end up following. In **Von Hannover** *v* **Germany** (2004), Princess Caroline of Monaco tried to sue certain newspapers in the German courts, complaining that she was constantly followed and photographed by paparazzi, even when she was doing ordinary things like shopping or taking her children to school. The German courts refused her claim, saying that, as a public figure, she had to accept that the public had a legitimate interest in knowing about even her ordinary daily life.

Princess Caroline then took her case to the European Court of Human Rights (ECHR), claiming that German law did not protect her right to privacy under Art. 8 of the European Convention on Human Right. The ECHR upheld her claim. They said that the key question when balancing the rights of privacy and freedom of expression was whether the material published contributed to 'a debate of general interest'. If it did, the right of freedom of expression was more likely to win out, but if it did not, the right of privacy was likely to have more importance. In this case, it said, the pictures made no real contribution to a debate of general interest. There was no legitimate public interest in seeing pictures of Princess Caroline when she was not performing her official role, so her right of privacy should take priority over the media's right to freedom of expression.

Usefully, an example of when pictures of someone going about their ordinary business would be considered to contribute to a 'debate of general interest' has come in a subsequent case, also brought by Princess Caroline. In **Von Hannover** *v* **Germany** (2012), the cases involved photos in German magazines of the princess and her family on a skiing holiday. Princess Caroline tried to prevent publication, but although the German courts granted an injunction over two of the pictures, they allowed publication of a third. This picture showed Princess Caroline and her husband taking a walk during the holiday, and was accompanied by a story about the poor health of her father, Prince Rainier, and how his children were dealing with the situation. The German courts found that the Prince's health was a matter of public interest and the press was entitled to report the way in which his children were reconciling their obligations of family solidarity with their need for a private life, including the wish to go on holiday. There was a sufficiently close link between this subject matter and the photograph to justify its publication. They went on to say that where a story on a matter of public interest was just used as a pretext for publication of a photo, the photo would not be a contribution on a matter of public interest and there would be no justification for allowing the public interest in publication to win out over the subject's right to privacy. The Grand Chamber of the European Court of Human Rights approved the German courts' approach, and also noted other factors in favour of allowing publication: that the princess and her husband were public figures, that the photos were not taken surreptitiously or secretly, and that their content was not offensive in any way. As a result, the court said, the decision to allow publication had struck the right balance between freedom of expression and the right to a private life.

Given the ECHR's approach in the Princess Caroline cases, you may be wondering why Elton John lost his case. In the **Elton John** case, Eady J said that the difference between the two cases was that the princess was so constantly followed and photographed that the photographers' behaviour amounted to harassment, and this was not the case for Elton John. Yet although the ECHR's judgment does mention the harassment, with disapproval, the reasons for its decision are clearly more to do with the publication of the pictures than the way in which they were obtained. The Court of Appeal in the **Elton John** case was bound by precedent to follow the decision of the House of Lords in **Campbell**, which included the principle that there was no protection against the revelation of trivial information or pictures of people going about their ordinary business. If a case on the subject were to go before the Supreme Court now, however, they might well fall into line with the ECHR's view that even such ordinary information and pictures should be protected, unless there is something about them that informs public debate on an important subject. Not doing this would mean that the claimant in such a case could potentially bring a claim before the ECHR, for failure to apply the Human Rights Act.

The position of children

It appears that children may have a reasonable expectation of privacy in situations where an adult might not. As we saw in **Campbell** and then in the **Elton John** case, there is no expectation of privacy in English law where an adult is photographed doing ordinary things in a public place. However, in **Murray** *v* **Express Newspapers plc and another** (2008), the Court of Appeal held that it was arguable that a child could have a reasonable expectation of privacy in this situation, which could be breached by a photographer taking pictures of them for publication, when the photographer knew that the child's parents would not have given permission.

The child in the case was David Murray, the 19-month old son of author J.K. Rowling. The Murray family were out walking with David in his buggy when they were photographed by a hidden photographer using a long lens. The claim was initially struck out on the grounds that there was no basis for a claim of privacy regarding pictures of people going about their everyday life, but the Court of Appeal upheld an appeal against the striking out. They said that whether there was a legitimate expectation of privacy would always depend on circumstances, and the position of a child might be different from that of an adult. There was no guarantee of privacy just because the claimant was a child, and the courts would need to balance the right to privacy against the right to freedom of expression, but it was at least arguable that David had a reasonable expectation of privacy, and so the action should not be struck out. The court went on to say that in principle, the courts should protect children from intrusive media attention, at least to the extent of holding that there could be a reasonable expectation that a child would not be targeted for photographs taken for publication, without consent, and which the photographer knew would be objected to.

It is important to note that this was a striking out action and not a full trial. The case establishes that a child in David's situation *may* have a reasonable expectation of privacy, but as the claim has not gone to a full trial, it remains to be seen whether, on the facts, he *did* have an expectation of privacy. The Court of Appeal's finding also emphasised that David's parents had always tried to keep him out of the public eye; it is not clear whether the situation might be different if the claimants were parents who had happily used their children for publicity purposes, but then objected to particular photographs or disclosures.

Where the information comes from

The way in which information was obtained and where it came from are also relevant to whether there is an expectation of privacy. In **Loreena McKennitt** *v* **Niema Ash and Purple Inc Press** (2005), the claimant, Ms McKennitt, was a very successful Canadian folk singer, and the defendant, Ms Ash, had been a close friend of hers. The case arose after Ms Ash wrote a book about her experiences of going on tour with Ms McKennitt, which covered, among other things, Ms McKennitt's personal and sexual relationships; her personal feelings, including how she had reacted to the death of her fiancé some years earlier; her health and diet; her emotional vulnerability; and details of a dispute between her, Ms Ash, and Ms Ash's business partner, concerning a property purchase. In the book, Ms Ash referred to her very close friendship with Ms McKennitt, and said that it was because of this close relationship that she was able to present such a revealing portrait of the singer. In the High Court, Eady J said that the fact that they had a close friendship was a reason why Ms McKennitt had a reasonable expectation that conversations between them, about personal matters, would stay private. He ordered an injunction banning further publication, along with £5,000 damages. This finding was supported by the Court of Appeal.

Information in the public domain

In the traditional tort of breach of confidence, there was a defence where the material complained of was already completely or substantially 'in the public domain', meaning where a number of people already knew about it. The question of whether information is in the public domain is also relevant to a misuse of private information action, but, rather than treating it as a defence, the courts look at how far the information was already known, and who by, as part of the assessment of whether the claimant had a legitimate expectation of privacy.

If information is widely known about, there will be no expectation of privacy, but the fact that some people know about it does not necessarily mean it will be considered to be in the public domain and therefore not given any protection. In **HRH Prince of Wales** *v* **Associated Newspapers** (2006), the case was brought by Prince Charles, after the *Mail on Sunday* published extracts from journals he had written. The prince had been keeping these diaries for a number of years, reporting on his thoughts and views as he went about his official engagements. He routinely sent copies to between 20 and 70 friends and acquaintances, and the newspaper said this meant their content was already in the public domain. The court disagreed, saying they were only ever circulated privately, to specific people, and this did not amount to being in the public domain. Quoting from the judgment in **Douglas** *v* **Hello!** Mr Justice Blackburne said:

> There will generally be an expectation of privacy where information is available to one person (or a group of people) and not generally available to others, provided that the person (or group) who possesses the information does not intend that it should become available to others.

In **ETK** *v* **News Group Newspapers** (2011), the Court of Appeal granted an injunction preventing reporting of a story involving a married man in the entertainment industry who had been having an affair with a colleague. The newspaper argued that there was no reasonable expectation of privacy, because the affair had become common knowledge at the company where the two worked. The court disagreed, saying that the fact that people who worked with them knew about the affair did not mean the information was in the public domain. The claimant was reasonably entitled to expect his colleagues to treat the information as confidential, whether they knew about the affair from their own observations of how the couple behaved, or had heard gossip, or had been told, in confidence, by one of the couple. Therefore, there was a legitimate expectation of privacy.

In **Trimingham** *v* **Associated Newspapers** (2012), the partner of MP Chris Huhne complained about stories in the *Daily Mail* which mentioned the fact that she was bisexual and had previously been in a civil partnership with a woman. Tugendhat J said there could be no legitimate expectation of privacy regarding these issues, as Ms Trimingham was open about her sexuality, and a civil partnership was a public event.

Partial revelations

What is the position where parts of a story are in the public domain, but someone wants to publish other information on the same subject? This was one of the issues in **Loreena McKennitt** *v* **Niema Ash**, the case of the Canadian folk singer and the book written by her friend. Ms McKennitt's fiancé had died in a sailing accident some years earlier, and the book gave a detailed picture of how devastated she had been by his death. Ms McKennitt said she had a legitimate expectation of privacy for this information. But she had in the past given interviews about her fiance's death, as part of a campaign to prevent similar accidents, and Ms Ash claimed that this meant the matter was in the public domain. The court disagreed. It said that where a case involved personal information, the fact that the information had been revealed to one group of readers did not mean that fresh revelations to different groups could not cause grief or distress. For this kind of information, protection should only be lost where the information is so generally accessible that it can no longer be considered confidential.

Privacy *v* freedom of expression

Deciding whether the claimant has a legitimate expectation of privacy is the first part of the two-part test set out in **Campbell**. If the court concludes that there is no legitimate expectation of privacy, then the claimant's case will fail. If there is a legitimate expectation of privacy, the court must then go on to balance the claimant's right to privacy against the defendant's right to freedom of expression. Exactly what factors they take into account varies from case to case, but essentially, what the courts are asking is whether there is a public interest in publishing the information, which might outweigh the claimant's right to privacy.

In **Campbell**, the House of Lords approached the issue by taking apart the various elements of the material published, and asking which parts were in the public interest, and which were not. As we saw earlier, Ms Campbell had previously made a point of denying that she had a drug problem, and their Lordships said it was in the public interest to know that she had been lying about this. Therefore, with regard to the information that she was a drug addict, and was receiving treatment, the paper's freedom of expression outweighed her right to privacy and they were within the law to publish that information.

However, there was not the same public interest in knowing the details of her treatment, such as where and when she attended meetings, and what happened at them. In addition, the photos were particularly intrusive, given that they were taken secretly, when Ms Campbell was at the door of a Narcotics Anonymous meeting. Therefore, with regard to the photos and the detailed information about treatment, Ms Campbell's right to privacy outweighed the paper's right to freedom of expression, and publication should not have taken place.

Contributing to a public debate

One factor which can tip the scales in favour of publication is where the material complained of is relevant to some kind of important debate or discussion which is going on in the news and among members of the public. This was the situation in **Rio Ferdinand** *v* **MGN** (2011), where the footballer Rio Ferdinand sued over a story about an affair he had had. In balancing Mr Ferdinand's right to privacy against the newspaper's right to freedom of expression, Mr Justice Nicol looked first at the effect of the story itself, and found that it did not 'excessively intrude . . . into the claimant's private life'. A picture used with the story showed Mr Ferdinand and the woman concerned in a hotel room, but both of them were fully clothed, they were not embracing or kissing, and the photo had obviously been taken by someone who they both knew was there, so there was no serious intrusion there either. On the other side of the scales, however, there was a genuine public interest in publishing the story. This was because Rio Ferdinand had recently been appointed captain of the England football team, and there had been some debate about whether he was a suitable person to do a job that made him a role model for young boys, because in the past, he had had a 'wild image' and had admitted to being unfaithful to his then partner, now his wife. The story from which the case arose clearly contributed to this debate, especially as Mr Ferdinand had made deliberate attempts to portray himself as a reformed character. Therefore, on balance, the judge concluded 'the balancing exercise favours the defendant's right of freedom of expression over the claimant's right of privacy'.

In **The Author of a Blog** *v* **Times Newspapers Ltd** (2009), the case of the anonymous blog by a police officer (see p. 273), *The Times* argued that there was a public interest in revealing the blogger's identity, given that in the blog, he was revealing information gained during police investigations, which was against police conduct rules. In addition, they argued, the public was entitled to know the blogger's identity, in order to assess how far they should believe what they read on such an important issue. The claimant argued that the public interest was in his favour, because he was contributing to a debate of general interest, which he could only do anonymously and, in addition, if he was identified, he would be disciplined and this would affect his right to freedom of expression. Eady J said that it was not the court's job to protect the claimant from disciplinary action. If the claimant was contributing to a debate of general interest, then *The Times*'s story about him would be doing the same. He therefore refused to order an injunction, on the grounds that even if, at trial, it was found that the claimant did have a right to privacy regarding his identity, this was likely to be outweighed by the public interest in a police officer having made these communications.

Public interest and celebrities

The courts have been very clear that there is a distinction between 'the public interest' and 'things the public are interested in'. This means that there will not, as a rule, be a public interest in publishing stories about the private lives of celebrities, unless they raise an issue which it is in the public interest to know about. In **Mosley** *v* **News Group Newspapers** (2008), the case involving the President of Formula 1 motor racing and his sado-masochistic orgy, the paper claimed that the orgy had had a 'Nazi theme'. They said there was a public interest in knowing that a man in the claimant's public position was indulging in sado-masochistic sex with prostitutes, and doing so within a Nazi-themed setting. Mr Justice Eady found that, on the facts, there was no truth in the allegations of Nazi overtones. That being the case, he said that there was no public interest in revealing the fact that someone in the claimant's position was taking part in sado-masochistic orgies which did not go so far as to break any criminal law. If the claimant had been involved in mocking the Holocaust in such a way as to call into question his role in an organisation to which he was accountable, the defence could apply, but here there was no evidence of this.

After his claim for privacy in the English courts, Max Mosley went on to bring a case at the European Court of Human Rights, claiming that the fact that English law does not oblige the press to give the subjects of intrusive stories notice about what they plan to publish was a breach of the Art. 8 right to privacy. This claim failed.

Conduct of the defendant

The conduct of the defendant may also be relevant in deciding the balance between their freedom of expression and the claimant's privacy. In **CC** *v* **AB** (2006), the claimant was a well-known figure in the sporting world. He had had an affair with a married woman, and her husband had found out. The husband wanted to tell the story to the press, and the claimant applied for an injunction to prevent this. The court agreed to keep the names of the parties secret, since revealing them would obviously have made any injunction pointless. The judge granted the injunction, and said he was influenced in his decision by the fact that the defendant clearly wanted revenge on the claimant, and had in fact behaved threateningly to him. He also took into account the fact that the defendant's wife was said to be very distressed by the thought of publicity, and said that she and their children also had rights to privacy which should be protected, even though it was the claimant who had put that privacy at risk by having the affair.

Correcting a false picture

One situation where there may be a public interest in publishing confidential information about the personal lives of celebrities is where a celebrity has presented a particular image to the public, and the confidential information shows this image to be false. As we saw earlier, in **Campbell**, the House of Lords held that there was a public interest in the *Mirror* revealing that Naomi Campbell was a drug addict, given that she had frequently said that many models had problems with drugs, but that she did not.

This reasoning was also applied in **Beckham** *v* **News Group Newspapers** (2005), where David and Victoria Beckham were refused an injunction to stop their ex-nanny revealing details about the state of their marriage. The newspaper said that there was a public interest in the revelations, because the couple presented themselves as blissfully happily married, and the nanny's stories about blazing rows between them contradicted this. The case was eventually settled out of court.

As we saw earlier, in **Rio Ferdinand** *v* **MGN** (2011), the court accepted that it was in the public interest to publish a story about Mr Ferdinand's extra-marital affair, because he had taken deliberate steps to present himself as a 'family man', who had been unfaithful to his partner in the past but was now reformed. An additional factor was that as captain of the England team, he was supposed to be a role model. Similarly, in **Mosley**, Mr Justice Eady confirmed that publication might have been in the public interest if the information corrected a false image put about by the claimant. This might be the case, for example, if he had promoted himself as someone who was opposed to sex outside marriage. But that was not the situation here, so there was no public interest in publishing the story.

However, this approach will only apply where the story involves serious misbehaviour, and not to more trivial claims about a celebrity not living up to their public image. In **McKennitt**, the author claimed that Ms McKennitt presented herself as holding certain personal values, but these were not always reflected in her behaviour. She said her book corrected this false impression. However, Mr Justice Eady rejected this argument. He said that while revelations of serious misbehaviour by a celebrity might be justified in the public interest, relatively trivial matters would not: 'the mere fact that a celebrity falls short from time to time, like everyone else, could not possibly justify exposure, in the supposed public interest, of every peccadilo or foible cropping up in everyday life.'

The right to tell

Privacy cases often involve weighing the claimant's right to privacy against the media's right to freedom of expression. But where a story involves two people, there may be a second set of clashing rights to consider: the right to freedom of expression by the party wanting to tell the story, against the right to privacy of the party wanting to keep it secret. The courts then have to weigh up one party's right to freedom of expression regarding her own story, against the other's right to privacy. This issue arose in **McKennitt**, where the defendant, Ms Ash, had written a book about the claimant, Ms McKennitt, a well-known folk singer. Part of Ms Ash's claim was that the story was not just Ms McKennitt's but hers as well, because she was a friend of Ms McKennitt and had been involved in a lot of the incidents in the book. She said her right to freedom of expression meant she should be free to tell that story. The court therefore had to weigh Ms Ash's right to freedom of expression with regard to telling the story of her friendship with Ms McKennitt, against Ms McKennitt's right to privacy in wanting to keep parts of what was also her story, private. The court found that if a person wants to publish information about their relationship with someone else, and that information is of a kind that would normally create an expectation of privacy, the material published has to be shaped in such a way as to protect the other person's privacy. Mr Justice Eady commented that: 'It does not follow that, because one can reveal one's own private life, that one can also expose confidential matters in respect of which others are entitled to protection if their consent is not forthcoming.'

This was reiterated in **CTB** *v* **News Group Newspapers** (2011), where the judge said that Miss Thomas was free to exercise her Art. 10 right by selling her life story, but only in so far as she could do so without intruding on the privacy rights of others.

Topical issues

The phone hacking scandal

During 2011, the issue of privacy and the media took a new turn, when it was discovered that reporters at the *News of the World* had been hacking into the voicemails of celebrities and other people in the public eye, in order to get private information which they could use for stories. This had the potential to create liability in both the traditional tort of breach of confidence, since the information was obtained in circumstances where it was clearly confidential, and in misuse of private information, because there is obviously a reasonable expectation of privacy for anyone's private voicemail messages.

Among the people whose voicemails were hacked were two very high-profile victims of crime: Sara Payne, whose daughter Sarah was abducted and murdered by a paedophile, and Milly Dowler, a young girl who was missing for several days before it was discovered that she had been murdered. When this information became known, it caused public outrage, and as a result of this, the proprietors of the *News of the World*, News International, closed down the paper. They settled claims with a number of celebrities, and paid the Dowler family £3 million in compensation, but there are likely to be many more claims to come: one law firm has estimated that there may have been as many as 6,000 victims.

Remedies

Injunction

The main remedy for breach of confidence is an injunction. Claimants can apply for an injunction to prevent publication in the first place, or to prevent further publication if the material has already been published. In either case, the injunction may be an interim one, which is designed to put the situation on hold until the issue is tried, or a permanent one, which is issued if a claimant proves their case at trial (in some cases an interim injunction will be issued before trial, and then, if the claimant wins, it becomes a permanent one).

In media cases, an interim injunction will often be all the claimant needs, because if they can keep the issue out of the news for long enough, the story becomes stale and will not be covered anyway. In this way, an injunction can often effectively kill a story without the defendant needing to prove their case at trial. Injunctions can be issued at very short notice (judges will do this over the phone, even at night), and it is not unusual for an injunction to be ordered just before a paper goes to press, or even after printing has started. On the other hand, in many cases, if the media can successfully fight off an interim injunction, the claimant may not bother taking the matter to trial, because to do so would only give even more publicity to the information.

When considering either type of injunction in a case involving the media, the Human Rights Act 1998 makes it clear that the courts must take into account the potential effect on press freedom. Section 12 of the Act states that if a court is asked to give any order which could affect freedom of expression, with regard to journalistic material, they must take into account the importance of the right to freedom of expression, and must consider the extent to which the material concerned is already in the public domain, and any public interest in publication. Although this merely recognises defences which exist in English law, it makes it clear that the possibility of such defences applying must be considered even in the application for an interim injunction, and not just at trial.

Section 12 also provides that injunctions which restrain publication before trial should only be granted where the claimant can show that they are 'likely' to prove a breach of confidence if the case goes to trial. In **Cream Holdings** *v* **Banerjee** (2004), the House of Lords said this meant that, in most cases, an interim injunction should only be ordered if the claimant could prove that it was more likely than not that they would win at trial. However, an injunction might also be granted in exceptional situations where the claimant could not prove they were likely to win, but where the consequences of disclosing the information would be especially serious for them.

A claimant seeking an injunction to prevent publication before trial must also prove that their loss could not be equally well compensated by damages. This is not usually difficult with confidentiality cases involving secret information, since no amount of money can make the information secret again. There are cases where monetary compensation may be sufficient, however, and there an injunction will be refused. In **Douglas** (see p. 269), the court refused to stop the circulation of *Hello!* on the grounds that, on the facts, the couple's loss could be adequately compensated without suppressing publication. The harm done by *Hello!* was that it had compromised their right to sell pictures of themselves, and this was something that money could compensate for.

If a court imposes an injunction preventing publication, that injunction applies to all media organisations which know about the injunction, and not just the newspaper named in the case.

Damages

Although most breach of confidence cases concern claimants who are trying to get an injunction to prevent publication, there are also cases where confidential information is published before the claimants have a chance to try to prevent it. In this situation, they can go to court to try to get damages (and if necessary an injunction against further publication). However, damages for breach of confidence tend not to be as high as in defamation actions, for example. In **Campbell** *v* **MGN** (2004), the House of Lords upheld an award for £3,500 for model Naomi Campbell, after the *Mirror* published photos and details of her visits to Narcotics Anonymous.

Answering questions

Does English law include a tort of invasion of privacy? Should it?

You could start this essay by explaining that, traditionally, there was no specific tort of invasion of privacy in English law, although other torts, such as trespass and confidentiality protected specific aspects of privacy. As an example of the gap this left in the law, you

could mention the case of **Kaye** *v* **Robertson**. You can then go on to discuss the fact that the Human Rights Act 1998, Art. 8 gives a right of privacy, which led many to believe that a specific tort would be created, but that the House of Lords specifically ruled this out in **Wainwright**. However, the tort of confidentiality has been extended and manipulated to become misuse of private information, so you should spend the main part of your essay considering how far this has, in practice if not in name, become a tort of invasion of privacy. You should discuss the cases in which misuse of private information has provided a remedy for those who claim their privacy has been invaded, such as **Campbell** and **McKennitt**, but also look at the limits on its use, and, in particular, the requirement that the right to privacy be balanced against the right to freedom of expression.

As the question also asks whether there should be a tort of invasion of privacy, you need to consider whether you believe the courts have struck the right balance between privacy and freedom of expression and give some indication of how difficult it is to strike the right balance in this area. Your conclusion and should draw on the points you have made in your essay, to say whether you think there is already a fully-fledged tort of privacy, even if it is without the name, and whether you think there should be.

Mike Newshound is the editor of a daily newspaper which specialises in stories about celebrities. He is contacted by the ex-boyfriend of a TV presenter who has become known for her campaigns against drugs. The ex-boyfriend says he is willing to give an interview about the fact that she frequently took drugs when they were together. He says that she never took drugs in public, but would often smoke cannabis when they were at home alone. Later the same day, Mike gets a call from a freelance photographer, offering him photographs of a well-known politician kissing a woman who is not his wife. The photos were taken without the couple's knowledge; some are taken through the window of the woman's house, the others show them in the street outside. The previous week, a rival paper had run a story alleging that the politician was having an affair.

Can Mike publish the allegations about drug taking? Can he publish the photographs? Discuss these questions with reference to the tort of misuse of private information; do not consider defamation.

Starting with the allegations against the TV presenter, you need to consider, first, whether she had a legitimate expectation of privacy with regard to her drug habits. You should consider **McKennitt** here, as the ex-boyfriend only knows about the drug taking because of their relationship; it was not something she ever did in public. If you find that she did have a legitimate expectation of privacy, you then need to consider whether her right to privacy is outweighed by the newspaper's right to freedom of expression. The main issue here is whether, given that the presenter has portrayed herself publicly as someone who campaigns against drugs, there is a public interest in exposing that image as false. In **McKennitt**, it was made plain that this was only legitimate where the wrongdoing was serious, but **Campbell** suggests that drug taking falls within this definition.

Regarding the photographs of the politician, you need to look at the Princess Caroline case, as well as **Campbell** and the **Elton John** case. Are the photographs taken in a situation where the couple had a reasonable expectation of privacy? It seems fairly clear that there is a reasonable expectation of privacy inside your own house, but outside in the street is more difficult, and you should explain that the difference between the situation in the Elton John case and the Princess Caroline case is a fine one, although clearly one aspect that applies here is that there was no harassment. You should then consider whether the couple's right to privacy outweighs the paper's right to freedom of expression. The case of **Mosley** is relevant here, with its suggestion that people's sex lives are their own business, but bear in mind that the court said there might be a public interest in disclosure if it would prevent the public from being misled about the individual concerned. If the politican were someone who had made a point of portraying himself as happily married, this might apply. As suggestions of an affair have already been published, you should also consider whether the newspaper might argue that the information in the pictures is already in the public domain.

Summary of Chapter 10

There is no specific tort of privacy in English law, but the law of confidentiality has developed to protect privacy.

Background to privacy protection

The traditional tort of breach of confidence protects against the disclosure of confidential information. It applies where:

- the information is private;
- the defendant is under an obligation of confidence;
- the defendant makes unauthorised use of the information.

Outside these rules, there was traditionally no specific protection for personal privacy.

The current law

Since 2001, the courts have developed the law of confidentiality, creating a new type of claim, sometimes called 'misuse of private information'.

It uses a two-stage test:

- Did the claimant have a reasonable expectation of privacy?
- Is that right more important than another's right to freedom of expression?

There is a reasonable expectation of privacy where information was obviously private or disclosure would give substantial offence to someone in the claimant's position.

Remedies

There are two potential remedies for breach of confidence/misuse of public information actions:

- Injunctions
- Damages

Reading list

Text resources

Bingham of Cornhill, Lord (1996) 'Should there be a law to protect rights of personal privacy?' *European Human Rights Law Review* 450

Brazell, L (2005) 'Confidence, privacy and human rights: English law in the 21st century' 27(11) *European Intellectual Property Review* 405

Calcutt, Sir D (1990) *Review of Press Self-Regulation*, Cmnd 1102

Calcutt, Sir D (1993) *Review of Press Self-Regulation*, Cmnd 2135

Crone, T (2002) *Law and the Media*, 4th edn, Chapter 8. Focal Press

Eady, B (1996) 'Opinion: a statutory right to privacy' *European Human Rights Law Review* 266

Feldman, D (1997) 'The developing scope of Article 8 of the European Convention on Human Rights' *European Human Rights Law Review* 266

Fenwick, H and Phillipson, G (2006) *Media Freedom under the Human Rights Act*. Oxford University Press

Markesinis, B (1986) 'The right to be let alone versus free speech' *Public Law* 67

Marshall, G (1975) 'The right to privacy: a sceptical view' 21 *McGill Law Journal* 242

Matrix Media and Information Group (2002) *Privacy and the Media: The Developing Law*

Moreham, N (2006) 'Privacy in public places' 65 *Cambridge Law Journal* 606

Phillipson, G (2003) 'Transforming breach of confidence? Towards a common law right of privacy under the Human Rights Act' 66 *Modern Law Review* 7266

Phillipson, G and Fenwick, H (2000) 'Breach of confidence as a privacy remedy in the Human Rights Act era' 63 *Modern Law Review* 660

Robertson, G and Nicol, A (2008) *Media Law*, 5th edn, Chapter 5. Penguin

Rozenburg, J (2004) *Privacy and the Press*, Oxford University Press

Sanderson, M A (2004) 'Is Von Hannover a step backward' 6 *European Human Rights Law Review* 631

Reading on the Internet

The Human Rights Act 1998 can be read at:
http://www.legislation.gov.uk/ukpga/1998/42

The House of Lords judgment in **Campbell** *v* **MGN** (2004) can be read at:
www.publications.parliament.uk/pa/ld200304/ldjudgmt/jd040506/campbe-1.htm

The European Court of Human Rights judgment in **Von Hannover** *v* **Germany** (2004) can be read at:
www.worldlii.org/eu/cases/ECHR/2004/294.html

The House of Lords judgment in **Wainwright** *v* **Home Office** (2002) can be read at:
http://www.publications.parliament.uk/pa/ld200203/ldjudgmt/jd031016/wain-1.htm

Visit **www.mylawchamber.co.uk** to access tools to help you develop and test your knowledge of tort law, including interactive multiple choice questions, practice exam questions with guidance, weblinks, glossary flashcards, legal newsfeed and legal updates.

Use Case Navigator to read in full some of the key cases referenced in this chapter with commentary and questions:

Wainwright *v* **Home Office** (2002)

Chapter 11
Nuisance

This chapter discusses:

- How the tort of private nuisance is committed
- Who can sue and be sued in nuisance
- Defences in nuisance
- Remedies for nuisance
- Problems with private nuisance
- How the tort of public nuisance is committed.

The tort of nuisance sets out to protect the right to use and enjoy land, without interference from others. There are actually three types of nuisance: private, public and statutory, but this chapter (and this book) deals only with the first two. Private nuisance is a common law tort, and the main subject of this chapter. Public nuisance is a crime, and therefore dealt with through prosecution under the criminal law, but it also comes into the study of tort because there are some cases where parties who have suffered as a result of a public nuisance can sue in tort.

Statutory nuisance is the name given to offences created under various statutes concerning public health and environmental issues – for example, creating excessive noise can be a statutory nuisance under the Control of Pollution Act 1974, and emission of smoke may amount to a statutory nuisance under the Clean Air Act 1956. Statutory nuisances are dealt with by local authorities, who can issue orders to stop the harmful activity. In many cases statutes have given them responsibility for harmful activities that would once have been tackled by tort actions brought by affected individuals, the idea being that these are problems that affect the community as a whole and so should be dealt with by public bodies. Statutory nuisance is not generally considered as part of a tort course and so is not discussed further in this book.

Private nuisance

The tort of private nuisance essentially arises from the fact that, whether we are out in the countryside or in the middle of a city, we all have neighbours, and the way they behave on their land may affect us on ours. The essence of liability for private nuisance is an unreasonable interference with another's use or enjoyment of land and, in assessing what is reasonable, the courts will try to balance each party's right to use the land as they wish.

Elements of the tort

The claimant must prove three elements:

- an indirect interference with the enjoyment of the land;
- that the interference was unreasonable; and
- that this interference caused damage to the claimant.

In addition, there are rules about the parties' relationship to the land, which determine who can sue and who can be sued.

Interference

The claimant must prove that the defendant has caused an interference with the claimant's use or enjoyment of their land. There are many ways that such interference can be caused, but what they have in common is that they must be indirect, and that they will usually (though not always) be the result of a continuing state of affairs, rather than a one-off incident. In some cases there will be a physical invasion of the claimant's land, such as the roots of a neighbour's tree spreading into the claimant's land (**Davey** *v* **Harrow Corporation** (1958)) or water flooding onto land as a result of something done by a neighbour (**Sedleigh-Denfield** *v* **O'Callaghan** (1940)), but often the nuisance is caused by something intangible, such as noise (**Christie** *v* **Davey** (1893)), or smells (**Wheeler** *v* **J J Saunders** (1995)).

The situation complained of must be sufficient to interfere with the claimant's use and enjoyment of their land. Anything which causes actual physical damage to the land fits this requirement, and it is established that things like fumes, noise or smells which make it physically unpleasant to be on the land can be included. The courts have also allowed actions for nuisance caused by situations which cause emotional distress; in **Thompson-Schwab** *v* **Costaki** (1956), the Court of Appeal held that running a brothel in an otherwise respectable residential street could be considered a nuisance.

However, the courts have not allowed the tort to protect what they consider to be recreational facilities, or, as Wray CJ put it in **Bland** *v* **Moseley** (1587), 'things of delight'. That case established that blocking a neighbour's pleasant view could not be considered a nuisance. Similarly, in **Hunter** *v* **Canary Wharf Ltd and London Docklands Development Corporation** (1997) the claimants were people living near the huge tower blocks of Canary Wharf, which was causing interference with their television reception. The Court of Appeal decided that loss of this kind of recreational facility was not sufficient interference to give rise to an action in nuisance.

Case Navigator

Interference may apply directly to the claimant's land, or to a right in land known as a servitude. Examples of servitudes include private rights of way, a right to light through a particular window, or a right to have one's land held in place by adjoining land (called a right of support).

Continuing a nuisance

An occupier of land can also be liable for nuisance caused by naturally arising hazards, providing they are aware of their existence and fail to take reasonable precautions (often known as continuing a nuisance, as opposed to creating one). This was the case in **Leakey** *v* **National Trust** (1980). The defendants occupied land on which there was a large, naturally occurring mound known as Burrow Mump. After one very hot summer, they were aware that the area could be affected by landslides because of the earth drying out, but they took no precautions against this. A landslide did occur, casting earth and tree roots onto neighbouring land, and the defendants refused to remove the debris. The courts held that they were liable for the nuisance, even though they had not actually done anything to cause it, but had merely failed to prevent it. It was made clear, however, that where the defendant has not actually caused the problem, only failed to do something about it, the law will take account of that fact in what it requires the defendant to do, and will take into account the defendant's resources. According to Lord Wilberforce, 'The standard ought to be to require of the occupier what is reasonable to expect of him in his individual circumstances.'

This principle was taken further in **Holbeck Hall Hotel** *v* **Scarborough Borough Council** (2000); **Leakey** involved things falling onto a neighbour's land, but in **Holbeck** the issue was whether allowing physical support for a neighbour's land to fall away could give rise to an action for nuisance. The claimants were the owners of a hotel which collapsed as a result of a landslip on neighbouring land owned by the council. The council had done nothing to cause the landslip, but knew that there was a risk of it happening. However, they had not realised how badly the problem could affect the land where the hotel stood, and could not have known this without ordering very expensive investigations. The Court of Appeal held that a landowner who knows or ought to have known that there is a risk that their property will cease to support a neighbour's may be liable in nuisance if they do not take precautions (although such precautions might be as little as informing the neighbour; it was not necessary to remove the risk of withdrawing the support). However, the council were not liable since they could not have foreseen the damage without an expensive survey.

In **Bybrook Barn Garden Centre** *v* **Kent County Council** (2001), the claimants owned a garden centre, which was badly damaged by flooding when a nearby stream burst its banks. This happened because a culvert which was built and maintained by the defendants had overflowed. The culvert had been adequate when it was built, but changes to the local area meant it was now carrying much more water, and it was not big enough. The claimants sued in nuisance, but the council claimed that they had no responsibility to make the culvert bigger, only to take reasonable steps to maintain it. The Court of Appeal disagreed. Once the council became aware that the culvert was no longer adequate to carry the increased volume of water, the principle in **Leakey** applied, and it had a duty to enlarge the culvert if it was reasonable to do so. On the test of what was reasonable as laid down in **Leakey**, the Court of Appeal stressed that what had to be taken into account was the resources of the particular defendant, rather than any objective standard of what it might be reasonable to spend. On the facts, the court pointed out that if the council had had a statutory notice put on them to do the work, they would have had to do it, so it was safe to assume they could afford to do so.

Unreasonableness

The interference caused by the defendant to the claimant's enjoyment of their land will only amount to nuisance if it can be considered unreasonable. The basic premise is that if we are all to live together there must be give and take, but interference which goes beyond the normal bounds of acceptable behaviour will be unreasonable. This principle can be seen in **Southwark London Borough Council** *v* **Mills** (1999). Here the council had converted a house into flats and the claimant lived in one of them. She sued the council, claiming that the building was poorly sound-proofed and she was troubled by the everyday noise generated by the occupants of other flats. The House of Lords held that the ordinary use of residential premises could not amount to a nuisance; there was nothing unusual about the way the building had been converted and the noise was normal for such a residential building.

In deciding whether an interference is unreasonable, the courts will take into account all the circumstances, and, in particular, the following factors.

Sensitivity

Traditionally, a defendant is not responsible for damage which occurs solely because the claimant, or the claimant's situation, is abnormally sensitive. In **Robinson** *v* **Kilvert** (1889) the claimant occupied the ground floor of the defendant's premises, using it to store brown paper. The defendant's business, carried on in the basement of the same building, involved making paper boxes. This needed a hot, dry atmosphere. The heating used by the defendant in the cellar made the claimant's floor hot too, which dried out the brown paper, reducing its value. The claimant sued in nuisance, but the court found that brown paper was exceptionally delicate. As the heat was not sufficient to damage paper generally and it had not inconvenienced the claimant's workmen, the damage was due more to the sensitivity of the paper than to the defendant's activities, so there was no nuisance.

On the other hand, as soon as the claimant has proved that the defendant has infringed the claimant's right to ordinary enjoyment, they can also claim protection from any extra problems caused by unusual sensitivity. In **McKinnon Industries** *v* **Walker** (1951), the claimant's orchids were damaged and his enjoyment of his land generally affected by fumes and sulphur dioxide gas from the defendant's factory. The defendant claimed that, even if he were liable for the general interference, he should not incur responsibility for the orchids, since growing these was a difficult and delicate operation, and the plants could therefore be considered abnormally sensitive. The

Privy Council rejected this argument, stating that as the right to ordinary enjoyment had been infringed the claimant could also claim protection for his more unusual and sensitive activities.

However, these cases have to be viewed in the light of a recent decision, **Network Rail Infrastructure Ltd** *v* **Morris** (2004), which suggests that the idea of abnormal sensitivity may no longer be relevant to whether interference is reasonable. Mr Morris had a recording studio, and he claimed that electromagnetic interference from a signalling system operated by Network Rail was affecting the sound of electric guitars played in his studio. Network Rail argued that this was an example of abnormal sensitivity, in that Mr Morris was carrying on an unusual business, and most businesses and homes would not have been affected by the magnetic waves that came from the signalling system. The Court of Appeal rejected this argument, though the two judges who gave reasoned judgments both had slightly different reasons for doing so (the third simply said he agreed with the other two). Lord Phillips said that the evidence showed that the interference suffered by Mr Morris was very rare, and that this by itself would suggest this was a case of abnormal sensitivity. But, he went on, the use of complex electronic equipment was a feature of modern life, and there would always be some people wanting to use equipment that caused interference, and some people wanting to use equipment that was affected by interference. The way to strike the balance was simply to decide what was reasonable, and a key part of that decision was whether Network Rail could foresee that the system would cause problems to someone in Mr Morris's position. Buxton LJ agreed with this general approach, but went further and specifically stated that it was no longer appropriate to consider abnormal sensitivity; the correct question was simply whether the damage was foreseeable. On the facts, the damage was not foreseeable so Mr Morris lost his case.

How far this judgment really changes the law is debatable. The courts may no longer wish to use the term 'abnormal sensitivity', but where harm is only caused because of some unusual aspect of the claimant's situation, that will often be relevant to whether the damage was foreseeable. In **Network Rail**, for example, the signalling system did not cause problems to premises other than recording studios, and the evidence showed that the problems it did cause Mr Morris were quite rare, and for that reason, they could not have expected to foresee it.

Locality

Key Case **St Helens Smelting Co** *v* **Tipping Ltd (1865)**

Where the interference takes place will have an important bearing on whether it is reasonable; a landowner in the centre of London cannot reasonably expect the same level of peace and quiet as one in the depths of the country. This point was made in **St Helens Smelting Co** *v* **Tipping Ltd** (1865). The claimant's estate was situated in an industrial area, and, in deciding whether the fumes from the defendant's copper works amounted to nuisance, the House of Lords distinguished between nuisances causing actual injury to property, as in this case, and nuisances causing personal discomfort. In the latter case, claimants should be prepared to put up with the level of discomfort common to the area in which they are situated. However, claimants were not expected to put up with actual damage to their land resulting from the normal activities of the locality, and so an injunction was granted.

Legal Principle

Whether interference with land is reasonable may depend on the locality, and what is a nuisance in a quiet residential area may not be a nuisance in an industrial location.

The result is that interference which would be reasonable in one area may be unreasonable in another. In **Sturges** *v* **Bridgman** (1879), the claimant was a doctor, who sued a confectioner for the noise caused by his industrial equipment. The court took into account the fact that the area in which they both worked consisted mainly of doctors' consulting rooms and concluded that there was a nuisance, explaining that that which would be a nuisance in a quiet residential area would not necessarily be so in a busy industrialised one.

The character of a locality can be changed by decisions on planning permission. In **Gillingham Borough Council** *v* **Medway (Chatham) Dock Co** (1993), the dock company had been granted planning permission for the operation of a commercial port. Access to it was only possible via residential roads, which caused a lot of traffic noise, and so the council sued in nuisance to try to get traffic limited at night. The court held that the fact that planning permission had been granted for a particular activity did not mean that that activity could not give rise to liability in nuisance; however, the existence of planning permission could mean that the character of the neighbourhood had changed (for example, from primarily residential to commercial), which could mean that what might have amounted to a nuisance before the change could now be considered reasonable. It held that that had happened in this case and so the dock authority were not liable in nuisance.

However, planning permission will not, by itself, provide immunity from a nuisance action. In **Wheeler** *v* **J J Saunders** (1995), the defendants had obtained planning permission to build two pig houses close to the claimant's land, resulting in strong smells drifting across the claimant's property. The Court of Appeal confirmed that planning permission could only be taken as authorisation of nuisance if its effect was to alter the character of the neighbourhood so that the nuisance could not be considered unreasonable. The planning permission in this case did not have that effect.

Duration and timing

How long the nuisance goes on for and when it happens, will also affect whether it is considered unreasonable or not. Something noisy may be reasonable if it happens in the middle of the day, for example, but not late at night or early in the morning. In **Halsey** *v* **Esso Petroleum** (1961), the court found that the noise caused by filling petrol tankers was reasonable and so not a nuisance at 10am, but was a nuisance when it happened at 10pm.

In most cases, nuisance is a continuing state of affairs, and generally, the longer it goes on for, the more likely it is to be considered unreasonable. However, the factors relating to unreasonableness overlap, and it is quite possible for a relatively short, one-off incident to be considered a nuisance, if all the factors taken together make it unreasonable. In **Crown River Cruises Ltd** *v* **Kimbolton Fireworks Ltd** (1996), it was held that a 20-minute firework display could amount to nuisance. In this case, the fireworks resulted in sparks and burning debris raining down onto the claimant's boat, so the nuisance was quite a serious one, which counterbalanced the fact that it did not go on for long.

Malice

Malice here means a bad motive. Where a defendant acts with malice, that may be relevant to the question of reasonableness, in that it may make what would have been reasonable conduct unreasonable.

The case of **Christie** *v* **Davey** (1893) illustrates this point. The claimant was a music teacher, and held musical parties in his house. The defendant, his next-door neighbour, deliberately tried to disturb both lessons and parties by blowing whistles, banging trays, shrieking and hammering on the wall. The court held that this malicious motive made the defendant's conduct unreasonable and a nuisance. Had he not been trying to disturb the lessons, he might have had the right to make a noise, just as the claimant did with his lessons and parties.

Another example is **Hollywood Silver Fox Farm Ltd** *v* **Emmett** (1936). The claimant bred foxes on his land. The defendant was a neighbour and, after a disagreement with the claimant, told his son to shoot his gun in the air while standing close to the claimant's land in order to frighten the vixens so that they would not breed. The claimant's action succeeded, for while the claimant was entitled to go shooting for the purposes of hunting game, his malicious motive rendered his activity an unreasonable interference with his neighbour's enjoyment of his land.

Damage

The interference must have caused some sort of damage to the claimant. This can mean physical damage to their land, as in **St Helens Smelting Co** *v* **Tipping** (1865), where the fumes from the copper-smelting works actually damaged trees and shrubs growing on the claimant's neighbouring land. However, physical damage is not essential; discomfort and inconvenience may be enough. In practice the courts tend to treat the type of damage caused as part of the examination of whether the interference was reasonable; interference which causes actual physical damage is more likely to be seen as unreasonable than that which causes mere discomfort or inconvenience.

Case Navigator

The claimant must prove that the interference actually caused the damage complained of, under the rules of causation (described in Chapter 3). The case of **Cambridge Water Co** *v* **Eastern Counties Leather** (1994) establishes that the test for remoteness of damage in nuisance is reasonable foreseeability (see below).

Nuisance and fault

Nuisance was originally a tort of strict liability, in the sense that a defendant who was found to have committed an unreasonable interference with the claimant's land would be liable, regardless of whether they had done so deliberately, carelessly or quite unknowingly. In cases where the claimant is seeking an injunction (an order to stop the defendant from continuing the alleged nuisance), it can be said that strict liability still applies, because, as the House of Lords pointed out in **Cambridge Water Co** *v* **Eastern Counties Leather** (1994), the very fact that the case is being brought means that the defendant knows that their behaviour is alleged to be causing interference with the claimant's enjoyment of land, and is refusing to stop it. If that behaviour is found to amount to nuisance, there is no further fault requirement to be satisfied.

However, where a claimant is seeking damages, and therefore compensation for a past wrong rather than the prevention of a current one, the issue is rather more cloudy. Recent cases have established that strict liability no longer applies, but quite what the fault requirement is has not been made as clear as we, and probably you, would like. The latest House of Lords case on the issue is **Cambridge Water**, which involved the pollution of a water supply by chemicals from a tannery (the full facts are explained on p. 314). The claimants sued in negligence, nuisance and under **Rylands** *v* **Fletcher** (see the following chapter). All three claims failed and, as far as nuisance was concerned, this was because the fault element was not satisfied. Lord Goff explained that if a defendant's use of their land was reasonable, they would not be liable for any damage caused to the claimant's use and enjoyment of their own land. However, if the use was not reasonable, the defendant will be liable, even if they have used reasonable care to avoid damaging the claimant's enjoyment of their land. At this stage of the explanation, what Lord Goff seems to be putting forward is the traditional strict liability view of nuisance. However, he went on to say that 'it by no means follows that the defendant should be liable for damage of a type which he could not reasonably foresee'. This, he argued, was because reasonable foreseeability was required in negligence, and it would be wrong to set a stricter standard for defendants who had interfered with enjoyment of land than that for personal injury.

The outcome seems to be that a defendant who uses land unreasonably and thereby causes damage to the claimant's enjoyment of land will only be liable if such damage was reasonably foreseeable – while a defendant who is found to be using their land reasonably will not be liable, even if damage was foreseeable (although this seems to ignore the effect of malice, which was not mentioned in **Cambridge Water**).

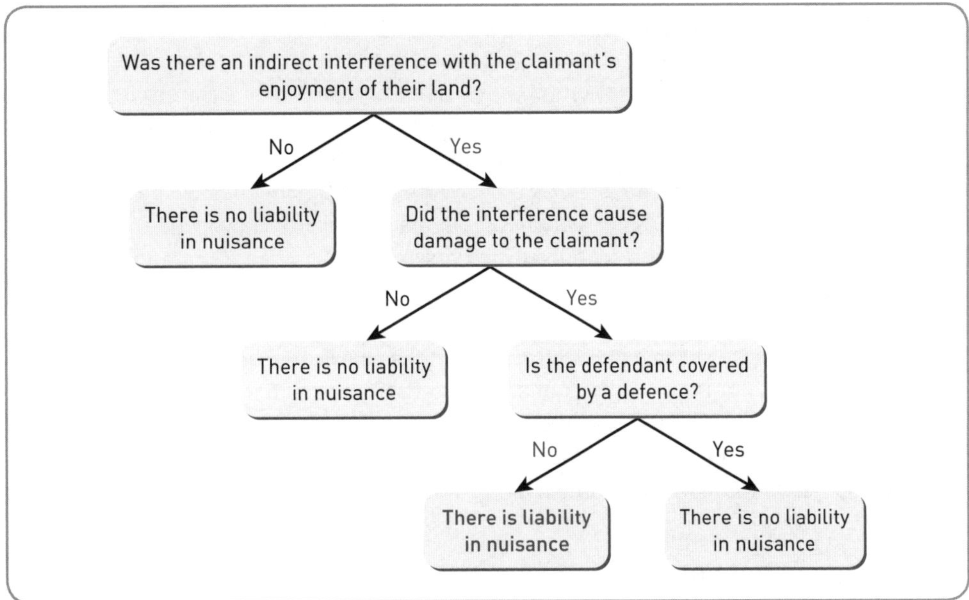

Figure 11.1 Is there a case in nuisance?

Who can be sued?

Depending on the circumstances of the case, a claimant affected by nuisance can sue the owner of the land on which the nuisance originates, the occupier of that land, or the person who created the nuisance.

The creator of the nuisance

Anyone who creates a nuisance by some act (rather than an omission) can be sued for nuisance, regardless of whether that person owns or occupies the land from which the nuisance originates. Nuisance need not necessarily even come from privately owned land; in **Thomas** *v* **National Union of Mineworkers (South Wales Area)** (1985), it was held that striking miners picketing in the road outside a factory could be liable in private nuisance.

The occupier

In the majority of cases, the defendant will be the occupier of the land from which the nuisance comes. An occupier need not be the owner of the land – where land is rented to a tenant, the tenant will usually be considered the occupier, and can be sued for creating a nuisance (in some cases it is also possible to sue the landowner for nuisance caused by the tenant – see below).

An occupier of land is liable for any nuisance caused by themselves, or by their employees, subject to the principles of vicarious liability (see Chapter 17). In an exception to the usual rules of vicarious liability, they may also be liable for nuisance caused by independent contractors, where the activities of the contractors involve 'a special danger of nuisance'. This was established in **Matania** *v* **National Provincial Bank** (1936), where the claimant's flat was affected by noise and dust from work done by independent contractors in the defendant's flat above; the activities were held to involve a special danger of nuisance because it was inevitable that they would interfere with the claimant's use of their flat unless precautions were taken.

Occupiers of land may also be liable for nuisance caused on that land by third parties, such as trespassers or previous occupiers, if the occupier is or ought to be aware of the potential for nuisance to be caused and fails to take steps to prevent it. The leading House of Lords case on this issue is **Sedleigh-Denfield** *v* **O'Callaghan** (1940). The defendants, an order of monks, occupied some land where there was a ditch. The local authority had built a pipe which took water away from the ditch; this was done without the defendants' knowledge and, in legal terms, the workers who built it were considered trespassers. The pipe had a grate to keep out leaves, but it was wrongly placed, and eventually, some three years after the pipe had been laid, it became completely blocked with leaves. As a result, neighbouring land owned by the claimant became flooded. By this time, the defendants knew that the pipe existed because it drained their own land, and the House of Lords held that an occupier who knows of a danger and allows it to continue is liable, even though they have not created the danger in the first place.

As explained earlier, an occupier can also be liable for nuisance caused by naturally occurring hazards on their land (see p. 288).

The owners

Where land is occupied by someone other than the owner, it is generally the occupier rather than the owner who will be liable for nuisance caused by the occupier, but there are three circumstances in which the owners may be held liable:

- where a nuisance already existed when the land was let, and the owners knew or ought to have known about it;
- where the land is let out, but the lease provides that the landlord has an obligation to repair the premises, or the right to enter and do repairs. This was the case in **Wringe** *v* **Cohen** (1940), where the defendant owned a shop that was let out to tenants. The defendant was responsible for keeping the premises repaired but failed to do so, and, as a result, a wall collapsed and damaged the neighbouring shop which belonged to the claimant. The defendant was held liable;
- where the landlord can be said to have authorised the nuisance.

The clearest example of authorising a nuisance is where the purpose for which the tenancy or lease is created is certain to create a nuisance. This applied in **Tetley** *v* **Chitty** (1986), where the local council allowed a go-kart club to use their land, and the noise from it disturbed local residents. The council claimed they were not liable because they had neither created the noise nor permitted it, but the court held that, as such noise was an inevitable result of the activities of a go-karting club, allowing the club to use the land amounted to permitting the nuisance, and the council were liable.

A landlord may be found to have authorised a nuisance if they knew about it and failed to take steps to avoid it. This principle was examined in two recent cases, with contrasting results. In **Lippiatt** *v* **South Gloucestershire Council** (1999), the council had allowed a group of travellers to set up an unofficial encampment on their land. The claimants were farmers on the neighbouring land. They claimed that the travellers had used the land as a 'launching pad' for repeated ventures onto their farm, where they had caused damage, stolen property and behaved aggressively towards them, and they sued the council on the basis that they had authorised the nuisance. The council applied to have the claim struck out, but the Court of Appeal dismissed the application, and held that it was arguable that the council could be said to have authorised the nuisance.

The complaint in **Hussain** *v* **Lancaster City Council** (1999) was essentially similar to that in **Lippiatt**, yet in this case the Court of Appeal reached the opposite conclusion. The claimants owned a small shop and flat on a housing estate owned by the council. They were subjected to continual harassment and abuse by other residents (who were the council's tenants), and had complained many times to the council about this. The council had powers to evict tenants who behaved in this way, but failed to use them, and the claimants argued that this amounted to authorising the nuisance. The Court of Appeal rejected this view, and held that the facts of the case could not give rise to a claim in nuisance, because the harassment did not involve the tenants' use of the land – the fact that they were tenants on the council's land was incidental to what they were doing, whereas in **Lippiatt** it was emphasised that even though the nuisance actually took place off the defendant's land, the land was being used as a 'launching pad' for the nuisance caused to the neighbours.

Who can sue?

The traditional view was that the claimant had to have an interest in the land affected by the private nuisance in order to succeed in an action. This meant that while owners and tenants could sue, a person who only had the use of the land without possession or any other proprietary interest could not. Thus lodgers, guests and spouses of owners or tenants were excluded.

The position appeared to have been changed in **Khorasandjian** *v* **Bush** (1993). Here the claimant was a 16-year-old girl who had been friends with the defendant, a 21-year-old man. After their relationship broke down, he became violent and threatening towards her, making menacing phone calls to her home where she lived with her parents. As a result of his threats to kill her he was jailed in May 1992, and he also received fines under the criminal law for the menacing phone calls. Despite these punishments the phone calls continued and the claimant succeeded in bringing a civil action against the defendant in private nuisance, despite the fact that she had no traditional proprietary interest in the family home. Lord Dillon said in the Court of Appeal:

> To my mind, it is ridiculous if in this present age the law is that the making of deliberately harassing and pestering telephone calls to a person is only actionable in the civil courts if the recipient of the calls happens to have the freehold or a leasehold proprietary interest in the premises in which he or she has received the calls.

Hunter *v* Canary Wharf Ltd and London Docklands Development Corporation (1997)

The view taken in **Khorasandjian** was supported by the Court of Appeal when it considered the case of **Hunter *v* Canary Wharf Ltd and London Docklands Development Corporation** (1995). It stated that there had to be a substantial link between the person enjoying the use of land, and the land itself, but that mere occupation of a home was sufficient to provide this link, and to give the occupant the right to sue for any private nuisance affecting the land. It was no longer right, the Court of Appeal said, to limit the right to sue in nuisance to those who held legal rights in land.

Unfortunately for those without legal rights in land, **Hunter** was appealed in 1997 to the House of Lords, who reverted back to the traditional position. A majority of the House stated that only claimants with a right in land could sue, which (without going into the intricacies of land law) essentially limits the right to sue to those who own or rent land, or for some other reason have exclusive possession of it. The House stated that the change made in **Khorasandjian** had been made for a good reason, as at the time there was no other way to protect the claimant from harassment, but since then the Protection from Harassment Act 1997 had created a new tort to deal with this problem and nuisance was not required to do so.

The House of Lords insisted that there needed to be a clear distinction between nuisance and negligence, and the way to assert this was to maintain nuisance as a tort protecting a claimant's right to use and enjoy land, and negligence as protecting the claimant's bodily security.

In addition, Lord Goff identified practical reasons why the tort should be connected with rights in land. First, in many cases potential claimants and defendants often come to amicable arrangements with each other rather than going to court (for example, those affected by nuisance might agree to it continuing if the party causing it offers payment by way of compensation, or agrees to limit it to certain times). Lord Goff feared that such sensible arrangements would be less likely if the class of potential claimants was made wider. Secondly, it would prove impossible to fix any clear limits if the requirement for rights in land were lifted, and there might be difficult decisions to be made as to the rights of, for example, lodgers, au pairs or employees.

Legal Principle

A claimant in nuisance must have a legal interest in the land which is affected by the nuisance.

In **McKenna *v* British Aluminium** (2002), the High Court considered whether the judgment in **Hunter** might be in breach of the Human Rights Act 1998. Over 30 claimants sued in nuisance over the noise and fumes that were emitted by the defendants' factory. Some of the claimants were children, who had no legal interest in land, and the defendants sought to have their claims struck out on the basis of **Hunter**. However, the court refused the striking out application on the grounds that there was a 'real possibility' that a court hearing the case might decide that the **Hunter** rule was in conflict with Art. 8 of the European Convention on Human Rights, which states that everyone has the right to 'respect for his private and family life, his home and correspondence'.

However, the idea that human rights legislation might provide a remedy for claimants without property rights now seems to have been dismissed by the Court of Appeal. In **Dobson *v* Thames Water** (2009), the claimants sued the water company over foul smells and mosquitoes coming from the company's sewage works. Some of the claimants in the case had property rights in the affected homes, but others, including children who lived there, did not. The Court of Appeal was asked to consider whether the claimants without property rights had a separate claim under Art. 8, in addition to the property owners' claim in nuisance. The Court of Appeal said that this issue had ultimately to be left to the trial judge, but said that it was unlikely that there would be a separate claim because the damages awarded to the property owner would take into account the effects of the nuisance on everyone living at the property. As damages under the Human Rights Act tend to be much lower than those awarded in tort, it was unlikely that any further damages would be awarded on top of those in nuisance.

Defences

The main defences in nuisance are:

- statutory authority;
- prescription.

Defendants may also avoid liability if a statute creates other means of dealing with the problem they are complaining of.

Statutory authority

Where a statute orders something to be done, and doing that thing inevitably creates a nuisance, there will be no liability because the statute is treated as having authorised the nuisance. The leading case on the subject is **Allen** *v* **Gulf Oil Refining Ltd** (1981). Residents in the area where the defendants were operating an oil refinery brought an action claiming that the refinery was causing a nuisance. The company pleaded in their defence that the nuisance was an inevitable result of operating the refinery, which they had power under statute to do. The relevant Act only gave express permission to the company to compulsorily purchase land and to build the refinery but did not expressly give them power to operate it. However, the courts said that it must have been Parliament's intention that they should also operate the refinery, so such a power could be inferred. As Lord Diplock pointed out:

> Parliament can hardly be supposed to have intended the refinery to be nothing more than a visual adornment to the landscape in an area of natural beauty. Clearly the intention of Parliament was that the refinery was to be operated as such . . .

Since the alleged nuisance was an inevitable consequence of the operation of the refinery, arising from its ordinary working, the defence of statutory authority succeeded and an injunction against the operation of the refinery was refused.

In **Barr and others** *v* **Biffa Waste Services** (2012), the claimants lived near a landfill site operated by the defendants. There had been landfill sites in the area before, but this was of a new type, where recyclable material would be removed from the waste before it was delivered to the landfill site. This meant that the rubbish was even more smelly than on a normal landfill site, and the defendants had had to get a special permit from the Environment Agency (the government body that deals with the environment) to operate it. When the claimants sued in nuisance, because of the smell, the defendants argued that the fact that they had got the permit meant they were protected by statutory authority. The Court of Appeal rejected this claim. It pointed out that the permit allowed Biffa to operate the site, but it did not authorise them to create the sort of smell problem that was the subject of the case; in fact it was clear from the terms of the permit that no such problems had been expected.

Biffa also argued that the permit had the effect of changing the nature of the area, which meant it affected the way reasonableness should be judged. The court said this was not the case, as the area was already one in which landfill sites were allowed; this was just a new, smellier version.

If a nuisance can be avoided by the use of reasonable care and skill, statutory authority will not offer a defence. The House of Lords in **Allen** pointed out that if the nuisance caused by the refinery was more than the inevitable consequence of the refining process (if, for example, the owners could have taken reasonable steps to make the works less noisy or smelly), it could not be said to have been authorised by statute.

It has been argued that planning permission acts in the same way as statutory authority. This view was rejected by the courts in **Gillingham Borough Council** *v* **Medway (Chatham) Dock Co** (see p. 291), but it was accepted that planning permission can have a role to play in assessing reasonableness. This issue was raised again in **Watson** *v* **Croft Promo-Sport Ltd** (2009). The Watsons owned a home in the countryside, near a motor racing circuit, and sued the owners of the circuit because of the noise it caused. The circuit owners had planning permission for the circuit and, as part of that permission, had agreed to limit racing to a certain number of days a year. They claimed that the planning permission changed the character of the area, and therefore meant that their activities could not amount to a nuisance. The Court of Appeal disagreed, saying that the area was still largely rural, as it had been before the planning permission was granted. The planning permission could not, therefore, provide a defence to negligence. However, the planning permission was relevant to the question of whether the defendants' use of the land was reasonable. The claimants were awarded damages, but not an injunction.

The effect of planning permission on the nature of a locality was considered again in **Coventry** *v* **Lawrence** (2012). The claimants bought a house near a motor racing track run by the defendants, which was very noisy. The track had been there for many years. When the claimants sued in nuisance, they won at first instance, but the defendants appealed. They said that when the judge had looked at the nature of the locality, as part of the assessment of reasonableness, he had not taken into account the fact that they had planning permission for the track. They said that in this case, the planning permission changed the nature of the locality, and if the true nature of the locality was considered, their use of their land was reasonable. The Court of Appeal agreed. Jackson LJ confirmed that planning permission could not in itself authorise a nuisance. However, in some cases, granting planning permission for particular activities could change the nature of the area, and where this was the case, reasonableness had to be assessed against the background of that changed character. On the facts of this case, the noise from the track was an established part of the character of the locality, and so the appeal was upheld.

Alternative statutory remedies

Key Case **Marcic *v* Thames Water Utilities Ltd (2004)**

The kind of activities that can amount to nuisance (such as pollution) are often regulated by statutes, and the case of **Marcic** *v* **Thames Water Utilities Ltd** (2004) makes it clear that where these statutes provide self-contained systems for dealing with a failure to abide by their requirements, a claimant must use those systems, and cannot choose to sue in nuisance instead. The claimant in the case lived in a house which was frequently flooded with foul water from a sewer belonging to the defendants. The problem had been going on for nine years, and was steadily getting worse; by the time Mr Marcic sued, just 15 minutes of heavy rain or a couple of hours of drizzle were enough to flood his house. Despite Mr Marcic spending £16,000 on a new drainage system, the building was badly affected by damp and would have been impossible to sell.

The cause of the problem was that, since the time when the sewers had been laid, many years before, more and more properties had been built and connected to the water system, and the sewers were no longer adequate to do their job. The water company were well aware of the problem, but they assigned their budget for dealing with such problems according to a strict points system, which balanced the scale of a problem against the cost of putting it right; under this system Mr Marcic's problem did not have sufficient priority for the company to address it.

Mr Marcic sued in nuisance and the House of Lords rejected his claim. It pointed out that the provision of sewerage services was covered by the Water Industry Act 1991, which imposes on the defendants a statutory duty to 'provide, improve and extend such a system of public sewers . . . and so to cleanse and maintain those sewers as to ensure that the area is and continues to be effectually drained'. The Act provides that where a company fails to perform this duty adequately, the Director General of Water Services (the independent regulator of the water industry) can make an enforcement order against them. The Act also expressly provides that customers cannot use a private law action to complain about breach of a statutory duty which the Director General of Water Services can enforce by making an enforcement order. The House of Lords held that to allow a nuisance claim would be inconsistent with the statutory rules, and would conflict with the clear intentions of Parliament.

Legal Principle

Where a statute provides its own system of regulation for the activity alleged to have caused a nuisance, a claimant must use that system, and cannot choose instead to sue in tort.

Prescription

A defendant may be held to have acquired the right to commit a private nuisance by what is called prescription. This applies where it can be shown that the nuisance has been actionable for at least 20 years, and that the claimant was aware of this during the relevant period.

Note that the fact that an activity has been carried on for at least 20 years may not in itself be enough; it must have amounted to a nuisance for at least that long. In **Sturges** *v* **Bridgman** (1879) the defendant confectioner had been running his business for over 20 years, using heavy machinery, before his new neighbour, the doctor, moved in and was disturbed by the noise. The defendant pleaded the defence of prescription, but the court held that this did not apply; although the noise had been going on for more than 20 years, it did not become a nuisance until the claimant's consulting room was built. Therefore the activity must have been a nuisance to the actual claimant (or any predecessors) for at least 20 years; the fact that it may have been a nuisance to people occupying other property is not sufficient to create a prescriptive right.

Inapplicable defences

There are three circumstances which students often think might provide a defence in nuisance, but which in law do not. They are:

- public benefit;
- use of care and skill;
- consent, or coming to the nuisance.

Public benefit

It may seem reasonable that an activity which provides a public benefit should be less vulnerable to nuisance claims, but this is not the case. In **Bellew** *v* **Cement Co Ltd** (1948), Ireland's only cement factory was forced to close down for causing a nuisance, even though new building works were desperately needed at the time.

However, where the nuisance-causing activity has a public benefit, the courts will often try to strike a balance between this and the rights of the claimant, by the remedies they choose to order. Most claimants in nuisance want an injunction, which orders the defendant to stop the activity which is causing the nuisance. In cases of public benefit, the courts may refuse an injunction and order damages instead, or grant only a partial injunction, so that the activity does not have to stop, but the interference with the claimant's rights is reduced. In **Adams** *v* **Ursell** (1913), a fish shop situated in a residential street was held to be a nuisance, even though it was accepted that an injunction forcing it to close would cause hardship to local customers. In this case the court framed the injunction so as to allow the shop to be set up in a different part of the street where the claimant would not be affected by the nuisance.

In **Miller** *v* **Jackson** (1977) the claimants moved into a house beside a cricket club. Cricket balls were frequently hit into their garden, and they attempted to get an injunction against the club to stop play. The Court of Appeal agreed that the cricket club had committed a nuisance, but refused to grant the injunction that the claimants wanted because the usefulness of the club to the local community outweighed the claimants' interest in preventing cricket balls from being hit into their garden.

The issue was addressed from a slightly different angle in the recent case of **Dennis** *v* **Ministry of Defence** (2003), the case concerned aircraft noise from an RAF base. The Ministry of Defence claimed that it was in the public interest that Britain should train jet pilots, and that, as this could not be achieved noiselessly, they had a defence to a claim of nuisance. The High Court agreed that the public interest in this case was so important that it would not be appropriate to stop the flying, but argued that this did not mean that the Ministry should not compensate those affected by the noise. The court held that the principle was that if society benefited from an activity, society (in the form of the Ministry, which is of course funded by taxpayers) should pay to compensate those who suffered as a result of that activity.

Care and skill

The second area which is often wrongly believed to offer a defence in nuisance is that of care and skill. Probably because most students spend the largest part of their course studying negligence, and because it is usually the first tort studied, its principles tend to make a big impression, with the result that students almost instinctively feel that a defendant who has used care and skill to avoid committing a nuisance should not be liable if the nuisance happens anyway. As we have seen when we looked at the fault element in nuisance (p. 292), this is not precisely the case. If a defendant's use of land is unreasonable, and damage to the claimant's enjoyment of their own land was the foreseeable result of that, the fact that they have used care and skill to prevent such damage is not a defence.

'Coming to the nuisance'

As we saw in the chapter on negligence, the defence of *volenti* provides that a claimant cannot sue for injury or loss that he or she consented to. In nuisance, the cases where a type of consent defence has been put forward are those where the nuisance existed when the claimant came to the land, and defendants have sought to argue that this amounted to consenting to the nuisance (the position is usually known as 'coming to the nuisance'). The courts have, however, repeatedly rejected this argument, and stated that the fact that a claimant has voluntarily come into a situation where a nuisance exists does not provide a defence.

The argument was made in **Sturges** *v* **Bridgman**, the case involving the noisy confectioner and his new neighbour the doctor, (discussed on p. 291). The confectioner claimed that the doctor could be considered to have consented to the noise of his business, since it was already in existence when the doctor moved in, but the court held that this was not a defence in private nuisance.

The same view was taken in **Miller** *v* **Jackson** (1977) (see p. 292). The cricket club argued that in moving there, when they were aware of the club, the claimants had 'come to the nuisance', but a majority of the Court of Appeal held that this was not a defence. Lord Denning made a powerful dissenting argument, pointing out that the claimants had come into the situation with their eyes open, and should have had to accept the risks of living beside a cricket ground if that was what they chose to do. This may seem reasonable but, taken to its obvious conclusion, it would mean that a defendant could avoid liability for any activity simply by being there first.

The approach was confirmed in the recent case of **Dennis** *v* **Ministry of Defence** (2003). The claimants were the owners of a country mansion and its surrounding estate in Cambridgeshire. The mansion, Walcot Hall, is about two miles from RAF Wittering, an airbase where young pilots are trained to fly Harrier jets, and the claimants said that the noise of the jets, which flew directly over the Hall, amounted to nuisance. The Ministry of Defence argued that the claimants had no case because the airbase was already operating before they bought the Hall, but the High Court dismissed this argument, confirming that it was no defence that the claimant had 'come to the nuisance'.

Remedies

Injunction

Injunction is the main remedy for nuisance, and it aims to make the defendant stop the activity which is causing the nuisance. An injunction may be perpetual, which orders the activity to stop completely, or it may be partial, and, for example, simply limit the times at which the activity can be performed. As it is a discretionary remedy, an injunction may be refused even though nuisance is proved.

An example of a partial injunction is **Kennaway** *v* **Thompson** (1980). The claimant owned land near Lake Windermere. A motor-boat club had been organising boat races and water-skiing on the lake for several years, and the claimant was aware of this when she started building a house on her land, but believed she would not be disturbed by the noise. However, by the time the house was finished, the club had expanded, and was holding more frequent meetings, involving more powerful and noisier boats. It even began running big national and international competitions.

The claimant sought an injunction to restrain the club from causing or permitting excessive noise to come onto her land. The motor-boat club argued that there was a public interest in the facilities of both racing and observing the sport being made available to a large number of people. The Court of Appeal held that the claimant was entitled to an injunction restraining the club from carrying on those activities which caused a nuisance to her in the enjoyment and use of her land, despite the public interest in those activities. However, they framed the injunction so that it limited, rather than completely stopped, the club's activities.

Damages

Damages can be recovered for damage to the claimant's land, or the enjoyment of it, and also for injury to the claimant which is associated with loss of enjoyment, such as loss of sleep, or discomfort caused by noise or smells.

Abatement

This remedy involves self-help, and allows the claimant to take steps to end the nuisance, for example by trimming back overhanging foliage. Where the claimant needs to enter the defendant's land for this purpose, notice must be given; if it is not, the abator will become a trespasser.

Problems with private nuisance

Types of damage covered

The failure to protect recreational facilities such as views can be criticised. The outcome of the case of **Hunter** *v* **Canary Wharf Ltd and London Docklands Development Corporation** (1997) seems particularly unsatisfactory. The reliance on the old authorities refusing liability for the obstruction of a view is unrealistic. Television forms an important part of many people's lives and it seems extremely unjust to remove that leisure activity without providing any compensation. The reality is that such interference is likely to affect the very value of those people's homes. The type of buildings that are likely to cause this interference are tower blocks, the builders of which are likely to be able to afford to pay compensation. The law as it currently stands seems to provide a green light for large property developers to completely ignore the interests of local residents in the areas under development.

The requirement for rights in land

The House of Lords decision in **Hunter** *v* **Canary Wharf** regarding who can sue for nuisance has been regarded as a backward step by some. In his powerful dissenting judgment, Lord Cooke pointed out that there was no logical reason why those who were actually enjoying the amenities of a home should not be able to sue someone who unreasonably interfered with the enjoyment. The decision was essentially based on policy and, since that was the case, he would have preferred it to uphold justice rather than tidiness.

Certainly some of the arguments of his colleagues seem overstated. There is every reason why people should enjoy special protection when they are inside their homes, whether they own or rent those homes. Cases involving lodgers and au pairs may make for tricky decisions, but not impossible ones: time habitually spent on the land would be one useful criterion by which such cases could sensibly be decided.

This problem may in time be overcome by the increasing use of the Human Rights Act to deal with nuisance-type problems (see below).

Nuisance and human rights

As we have seen in previous chapters, the Human Rights Act 1998 is increasingly being used as an alternative, or supplement, to traditional tort actions, and several recent nuisance cases have also included claims under the Act. The relevant provision in nuisance cases tends to be Art. 8, which sets out the right to respect for private and family life. As with most human rights provisions, however, it is not an unlimited right, and can be restricted on certain public policy grounds, which include the economic well-being of the country and the protection of the rights and freedoms of others.

In other areas of tort, the Human Rights Act has offered remedies where none was available through traditional tort actions, and it has been suggested that the Act might fill some of the gaps in traditional nuisance law – for example, the requirement of a legal interest in land would not exist in a human rights claim. However, recent cases suggest that, if anything, the European Convention on Human Rights may in some cases give more protection to those who cause nuisance, and less to those affected by it, than traditional laws of nuisance.

In **Dennis** (see p. 301), the case concerning the RAF base and the country mansion, the claimants argued that, as well as amounting to nuisance, the noise from the flights was a breach of their rights under Art. 8. The court agreed, but said that this claim would not justify stopping the flights any more than the nuisance claim did, because 'the public interest is greater than the individual private interests [of the claimants]'. Although the court held that the Human Rights Act claim would have justified the claimants getting financial compensation for the nuisance (if they had not already got it through their nuisance claim), this emphasis on the public benefit being more important than the rights of individuals to peaceful enjoyment of their land gives less protection to landowners suffering disruption than traditional principles of nuisance.

A similar approach was taken in **Marcic** (see p. 298), the case where overflowing drains regularly flooded the claimant's house. As well as claiming in nuisance, Mr Marcic argued that the water authority had breached his rights under Art. 8, and also under Art. 1 of the First Protocol, concerning protection of property. The House of Lords disagreed. They referred back to the case of **Hatton** *v* **UK** (2003), in which residents of the area around Heathrow Airport had tried to use Art. 8 to stop night flights. The European Court of Justice in that case held that it was reasonable to assume that night flights contributed to the economic well-being of the country (one of the factors which the Convention allows to limit Art. 8 rights). Given that the residents could move somewhere else if they chose to, the UK government had struck the right balance between their rights and the public interest.

In **Marcic**, the House of Lords followed the approach in **Hatton**, stating that there was a public interest in establishing a system of priorities for building sewers, and that the system adopted included a remedy for anyone who felt that the allocation of priorities was unfair. This meant that a fair balance had been struck between the public interest and Mr Marcic's, and his rights had not been breached.

What we can see in these cases is that when the interests of society are put in the balance against those of individuals suffering disruption to their home life by the type of activities usually classified as nuisance, then the provisions of the European Convention on Human Rights can easily justify upholding the public interest rather than the private one – the opposite to the traditional approach in nuisance.

Public nuisance

Public nuisance, as we said in the introduction to this chapter, is a crime, and those who commit it are generally dealt with by the criminal law, rather than being sued by individuals who are affected by the nuisance. However, there are occasions when a party affected by a public nuisance can sue in tort, and this is the situation that we will be looking at in this section. In some ways it is unfortunate that this crime has been labelled public nuisance, since it is actually quite different from the tort of private nuisance. It need not have any connection with the use of land, either by defendant or claimant, and is as likely to arise from a single act as from a continuing situation.

The leading definition of public nuisance comes from the case of **Attorney-General** *v* **PYA Quarries** (1957). The defendants used a blasting system in their quarry which caused noise and vibrations, and threw out dust, stones and splinters, which affected people living nearby. The Court of Appeal held that this could amount to a public nuisance, which it defined as any nuisance which 'materially affects the reasonable comfort and convenience of a class of her Majesty's subjects'.

This definition has been taken to include a whole range of activities which endanger the public, cause them inconvenience or discomfort, or prevent them exercising their rights. Examples include picketing on a road (**Thomas** *v* **NUM** (1985)); blocking a canal (**Rose** *v* **Miles** (1815)); obstructing a highway by queuing on it (**Lyons** *v* **Gulliver** (1914)); causing noise and disrupting traffic through a badly organised pop festival (**Attorney-General of Ontario** *v* **Orange Productions Ltd** (1971)); and making obscene telephone calls to large numbers of women (**R** *v* **Johnson (Anthony Thomas)** (1996)).

How many people have to be affected in order for them to amount to 'a class of her Majesty's subjects'? This question was examined in **PYA Quarries**, where, as there were only 30 houses nearby, the quarry owners argued that they were too few for the problem to amount to a public nuisance. The court stated that the test was whether the nuisance is 'so widespread in its range or so indiscriminate in its effect that it would not be reasonable to expect one person to take proceedings on his own responsibility to put a stop to it, but that it should be taken on the responsibility of the community at large'. The court explained that this would not be the case where only two or three people were affected by it, but agreed that the 30 householders in the case before them were enough. Beyond that, they declined to give guidelines on numbers and said that the issue of whether the number of people affected by a nuisance amounts to a class is a question of fact, to be examined in each case. The case also establishes that it is not necessary to prove that every member of a class has been affected by the nuisance, so long as it can be shown that a representative cross-section has been affected.

In **R** *v* **Rimmington** (2005), a case of prosecution for public nuisance, it was stated that individual acts of private nuisance committed against several different individuals was not the same thing as a nuisance affecting a section of the public, and could not therefore be a public nuisance.

The defendant had sent 538 packages containing racially offensive material to members of the public, some chosen at random, others selected because of the ethnic group to which they appeared to belong. The House of Lords held that this did not amount to public nuisance because his actions did not cause a common injury to a section of the public.

Tort actions for public nuisance

A defendant whose behaviour comes within the definition of public nuisance can be prosecuted, but they can only be additionally sued in tort for public nuisance if a claimant can prove that they suffered 'special damage' over and above the effects on other members of the affected group. A good example of what is meant by special damage can be found in the old case of **Benjamin** *v* **Storr** (1874). The claimant kept a coffee house in the Covent Garden area of London, and the defendant regularly left his horses and carts outside, obstructing the highway and blocking out light from all the shops in the row. The nuisance affected all the shopkeepers, but as a result of the nature of the claimant's business he was able to prove that he had suffered special damage because the smell of the horses put his customers off.

Special damage may also arise when the nuisance costs the claimants money, though the general public only suffers inconvenience. In **Tate & Lyle Food and Distribution Ltd** *v* **Greater London Council** (1983), the defendant council built some ferry terminals in the River Thames, which caused excessive silting on the riverbed. This caused inconvenience to river users in general, but the claimants were more affected than most as access to their jetty was blocked, and they had to spend a lot of money having the riverbed around it dredged. The House of Lords held that this amounted to special damage.

Defences

The general tort defences discussed in the chapter on negligence apply to public nuisance, and statutory authority is the most important. It was used successfully in **Allen** *v* **Gulf Oil Refining Ltd** (see p. 297) in a claim for public nuisance as well as private.

The defence of prescription, used in private nuisance, does not apply in public nuisance.

Remedies

Both injunctions and damages are available for public nuisance, and, although a tort action for public nuisance may only be brought by those who have suffered special damage, an injunction can obviously also benefit everyone else who has been bothered by the nuisance.

In **Claimants appearing on the Register of the Corby Group Litigation** *v* **Corby Borough Council** (2008), the Court of Appeal confirmed that damages for personal injury can be claimed in a case of public nuisance. It has, however, been suggested that the House of Lords may change this if a suitable future case comes before them.

Differences between private and public nuisance

As we explained earlier, these are separate and in many ways quite different torts, but as they often crop up together in problem questions in exams, it is useful to keep in mind the following specific differences.

Private nuisance	Public nuisance
Creates a cause of action in tort even if only one person is affected	Can only be actionable as a tort if a class of people is affected and at least one of them suffers special damage
Claimant requires an interest in land	No interest in land required
Nuisance must arise from defendant's use of land	Can arise from activities not related to use of land
Prescription is a defence	No defence of prescription

Answering questions

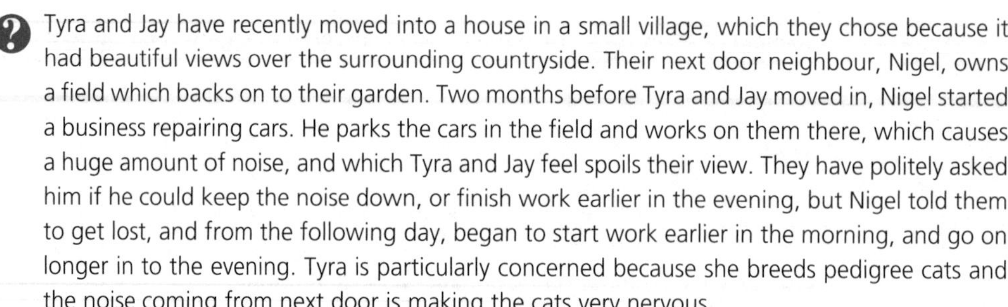

Tyra and Jay have recently moved into a house in a small village, which they chose because it had beautiful views over the surrounding countryside. Their next door neighbour, Nigel, owns a field which backs on to their garden. Two months before Tyra and Jay moved in, Nigel started a business repairing cars. He parks the cars in the field and works on them there, which causes a huge amount of noise, and which Tyra and Jay feel spoils their view. They have politely asked him if he could keep the noise down, or finish work earlier in the evening, but Nigel told them to get lost, and from the following day, began to start work earlier in the morning, and go on longer in to the evening. Tyra is particularly concerned because she breeds pedigree cats and the noise coming from next door is making the cats very nervous.

Tyra and Jay's neighbour on the other side is Paulina, who is a pig farmer and has lived in the village all her life. The smells from her pigs drift across from her farmyard into Tyra and Jay's garden, making it unpleasant for them to sit outside in their garden.

Advise Tyra and Jay as to whether they have a claim against Nigel or Paulina in nuisance.

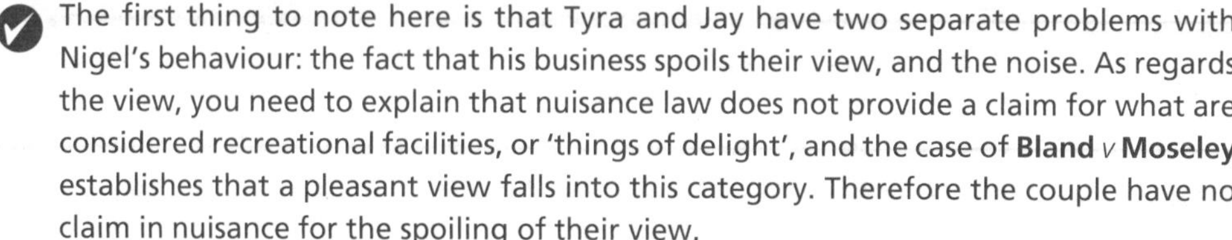

The first thing to note here is that Tyra and Jay have two separate problems with Nigel's behaviour: the fact that his business spoils their view, and the noise. As regards the view, you need to explain that nuisance law does not provide a claim for what are considered recreational facilities, or 'things of delight', and the case of **Bland** *v* **Moseley** establishes that a pleasant view falls into this category. Therefore the couple have no claim in nuisance for the spoiling of their view.

However, it is well established that noise can be considered interference with another's use of land, so there may be a claim for this. You need to consider whether the car repair business is a reasonable use by Nigel of his land, and explain how the courts will balance the various factors in order to decide this. Clearly a relevant issue here will be the location; you should discuss the case of **Sturges** *v* **Bridgeman**, and the fact that a level of noise that would be reasonable in a busy industrial area might not be reasonable in a quiet residential street. We are told that this is a small village, and a court would clearly take this into account when deciding whether Nigel's interference with Tyra and Jay's enjoyment of their land is reasonable.

Nigel's reaction to the couple's polite complaint means you should also consider the question of malice. Referring to the cases of **Hollywood Silver Fox Farm** and **Christie** *v* **Davey**, you should point out that even if Nigel's car repair activities would ordinarily be considered a reasonable use of land, if he is acting maliciously, that can transform his actions into unreasonable interference.

Nigel may wish to argue that as his business was already running when Tyra and Jay moved in, they are 'coming to the nuisance' and this should give him a defence. You should point out that the cases of **Miller** *v* **Jackson** and **Dennis** establish that this is not a defence in nuisance at all.

If the court finds that Nigel's use of the land is unreasonable, and he has no defence, you should point out that there are two elements to Tyra and Jay's claim, the interference with their ordinary enjoyment of their land, and the damage to Tyra's business. Nigel may wish to argue that the damage to the business only occurs because the cat breeding business is abnormally sensitive, following **Robinson** *v* **Kilvert**, but **McKinnon Industries** *v* **Walker** establishes that where the claimant's ordinary enjoyment of their land is damaged, as Tyra and Jay's is, their claim can also cover damage to any more sensitive activities. Consider too the case of **Network Rail** *v* **Morris**.

With regard to Paulina, it is clear that smells can amount to nuisance but, again, the issue will be whether Paulina's use of her land is reasonable in all the circumstances. Location will again be relevant but, in this case, it may be that living in a rural area means farmyard smells are acceptable. As usual in this kind of question, you do not need to say definitely what the court's decision would be, as long as you can explain what factors they would take into account in making that decision.

Again, you need to consider whether Paulina could have a defence, and the most likely one here is prescription, so you should explain how that could apply. Remember to point out that it is not enough for Pauline to have been keeping pigs for 20 years; the smell must have been a nuisance to the occupants of Tyra and Jay's house for all that time as well.

Summary of Chapter 11

Nuisance protects the rights to use and enjoy land, against interference from others.

There are three types:

- Private
- Public
- Statutory (not dealt with by this book).

Private nuisance

Elements of the tort

Claimants must prove:

- interference with their enjoyment of land;
- that the interference was unreasonable;
- damage caused by the interference.

Interference

- must be indirect;
- will usually be a continuing situation rather than a one-off incident;
- must interfere with use of the land, not merely 'things of delight' such as views;
- can result from naturally occurring hazards, if the defendant is aware of them and fails to take reasonable precautions.

Unreasonableness

In judging unreasonableness, the courts balance all the circumstances, and particularly:

- Abnormal sensitivity
- Locality
- Duration and timing
- Malice.

Damage

- Need not be physical damage; inconvenience or discomfort can be enough.
- The claimant must prove the interference caused the damage.

Nuisance and fault

- Where the claimant is seeking an injunction, strict liability applies.
- Where the remedy sought is damages, the fault element is less clear, but reasonable foreseeability appears to be necessary.

Who can be sued?

- The person who creates the nuisance.
- The occupier of the land.
- The owner of the land, if:
  - they knew the nuisance existed when they bought the land; or
  - the land is let but they have the right to enter and repair;
  - they have authorised the nuisance.

Who can sue?

Traditionally only someone with rights in the land affected can sue.

Defences

Contributory negligence may apply, but the key defences are:

- Statutory authority
- Alternative statutory remedies

- Prescription
- Coming to the nuisance.

Neither public benefit nor use of reasonable care and skill provide a defence.

Remedies

- Injunction is the main remedy, and may be complete or partial.
- Damages can be recovered for damage to the land, enjoyment of it, or injury to the claimant.
- Abatement allows the claimant to take steps to end the nuisance.

Problems with private nuisance

Key issues are:

- Types of damage covered
- Requirement for rights in land.

Nuisance and human rights

The Human Rights Act 1998 is increasingly being used to deal with problems that traditionally would fall within nuisance. So far it has tended to uphold the interests of society over those of individuals.

Public nuisance

- Public nuisance is a crime, but also creates a cause of action in tort.
- It applies where a nuisance 'materially affects the reasonable comfort and convenience' of a class of people.
- Claimants must prove they have suffered special damage, other than that suffered by the affected group.

The general tort defences apply; prescription does not.

Injunctions and/or damages may be claimed.

Reading list

Text resources

Buckley, R A (1996) *The Law of Nuisance*. Butterworths

Campbell, D (2000) 'Of coase and corn; a (sort of) defence of private nuisance' 63 *Modern Law Review* 197

Conaghan, J and Mansell, W (1998) *The Wrongs of Tort*, 2nd edn, Chapter 6. Pluto

Davey, M (2002) 'Neighbours in Law' *Conveyancer* 31

English, R (1996) 'The tenant, his wife, the lodger and their telly: a spot of nuisance in Docklands' 59 *Modern Law Review* 726

Gearty, C (1989) 'The place of nuisance in a modern law of torts' *Cambridge Law Journal* 214

Harlow, C (2005) *Understanding Tort Law*, 3rd edn, Chapter 5. Sweet & Maxwell

Hedley, S (1997) 'Nuisance, dust and the right to good TV reception: Canary Wharf in the House of Lords' 3 *Web Journal of Current Legal Issues*

Kidner, R (1989) 'Television reception and the tort of nuisance' *Conveyancer* 279

Kidner, R (1998) 'Nuisance and rights of property' *Conveyancer* 267

Lee, N (2003) 'What is private nuisance?' 119 *Law Quarterly Review* 298

Markesinis, B A (1989) 'Negligence, nuisance and affirmative duties of action' 105 *Law Quarterly Review* 104

Markesinis, B and Tettenborn, A (1981) 'Cricket, power boat racing and nuisance' 131 *New Law Journal* 108

McLaren, J P S (1983) 'Nuisance law and the Industrial Revolution' 3 *Oxford Journal of Legal Studies* 155

Ogus, A I and Richardson, G M (1977) 'Economics and the environment: a study of private nuisance' 36 *Cambridge Law Journal* 284

O'Sullivan, J (2000) 'Nuisance, local authorities and neighbours from hell' 59 *Cambridge Law Journal* 55

O'Sullivan, J (2004) 'Nuisance, human rights and sewage – closing the floodgates' 63 *Cambridge Law Journal* 552

Rodgers, C (2001) 'Nuisance and the unruly tenant' 60 *Cambridge Law Journal* 382

Steele, J (1995) 'Private law and the environment; nuisance in context' 15 *Legal Studies* 236

Tromans, S (1982) 'Nuisance: prevention or payment?' 41 *Cambridge Law Journal* 87

Wightman, J (1998) 'Nuisance – the environmental tort' 61 *Modern Law Review* 870

Reading on the Internet

The House of Lords judgment in **Hunter** *v* **Canary Wharf** (1997) can be read at:
http://www.publications.parliament.uk/pa/ld199697/ldjudgmt/jd970424/hunter01.htm

The House of Lords judgment in **Southwark Borough Council** *v* **Mills** (1999) can be read at:
http://www.publications.parliament.uk/pa/ld199899/ldjudgmt/jd991021/mills-1.htm

The Queen's Bench Division judgment in **Dennis** *v* **Ministry of Defence** (2003) can be read at:
http://www.bailii.org/ew/cases/EWHC/QB/2003/793.html

The House of Lords judgment in **Marcic** *v* **Thames Water** (2004) can be read at:
http://www.publications.parliament.uk/pa/ld200304/ldjudgmt/jd031204/marcic-1.htm

The Human Rights Act 1998 can be read at:
http://www.legislation.gov.uk/ukpga/1998/42

Visit **www.mylawchamber.co.uk** to access tools to help you develop and test your knowledge of tort law, including interactive multiple choice questions, practice exam questions with guidance, weblinks, glossary flashcards, legal newsfeed and legal updates.

Use Case Navigator to read in full some of the key cases referenced in this chapter with commentary and questions:

Cambridge Water Co *v* **Eastern Counties Leather** (1994)
Hunter *v* **Canary Wharf Ltd and London Docklands Development Corporation** (1997)

Chapter 12
The rule in **Rylands** *v* **Fletcher**

This chapter discusses:

- How the tort in **Rylands** *v* **Fletcher** is committed
- Defences to **Rylands** *v* **Fletcher**
- How **Rylands** *v* **Fletcher** relates to other torts
- The role of the tort today.

The tort in **Rylands** *v* **Fletcher** (1868) came into being as a result of the Industrial Revolution which took place during the eighteenth century. Before the Industrial Revolution, Britain was largely an agricultural economy but, with advances in technology, factories and industrial plants began to be set up. These sometimes caused damage to neighbouring land, in the form of fires, floods or escapes of fumes, and in **Rylands** the courts created a new tort to deal with this situation, which attempted to make industrialists strictly liable for any damage they did in this way, regardless of whether or not they could have taken precautions to prevent the damage. **Rylands** was therefore known as a tort of strict liability, but over the years this element of the tort has gradually been worn away, and elements of fault-based liability have been introduced.

Elements of the tort

Key Case **Rylands** *v* **Fletcher** (1868)

In **Rylands** *v* **Fletcher** (1868), the defendant, a mill owner, had paid independent contractors to make a reservoir on his land, which was intended to supply water to the mill. During construction, the contractors discovered the shafts and passages of an old coal mine on the land, some of which joined up with a mine situated on neighbouring land, belonging to the claimant. The contractors could have blocked up these shafts but did not and, as a result, when the reservoir was filled, the water from it burst through the shafts and flooded the claimant's mine, causing damage estimated at £937.

The defendant himself had not been negligent, since there was no way he could have known about the shafts, and nor could he be held vicariously liable for the contractors, who were clearly not his employees for that purpose. An action for trespass (discussed in the next chapter) was unavailable because the damage was not direct and immediate, and at the time of the case the tort of nuisance could not be applied to an isolated escape. Nevertheless, the House of Lords held that the defendant was liable in tort, upholding the judgment delivered in the lower court by Blackburn J, which defined the rule: 'A person who, for his own purposes, brings on his land and keeps there anything likely to do mischief if it escapes, must do so at his peril, and, if he does not do so, he is *prima facie* answerable for all damage which is the natural consequence of its escape.'

The justification for this rule, he explained, was that 'the person whose grass or corn is eaten down by the escaping cattle of his neighbour, or whose mine is flooded by the water from his neighbour's reservoir, or whose cellar is invaded by the filth of his neighbour's privy, or whose habitation is made unhealthy by the fumes and noisome vapours of his neighbour's alkali works, is damnified without any fault of his own . . .'

Despite the fact that the courts claimed a clear foundation for the rule in previous cases, these authorities did not go nearly as far as the decision in the case, and it is generally regarded as establishing a completely new principle at the time.

In order to succeed in a claim under **Rylands** *v* **Fletcher**, the claimant must therefore prove the following:

- The defendant must control the land from which the problem has come.
- The defendant must have brought or accumulated something in the course of some 'unnatural use' of the land.

- The thing brought or accumulated must be 'dangerous', meaning likely to do damage if it escapes from the land.
- There must be an escape of the dangerous thing.
- There must be damage as a result of the escape.

Legal Principle

A defendant who brings onto their land something which is likely to cause damage if it escapes is liable for the damage if it does escape.

The defendant must control the land

The tort will only apply where the land onto which the dangerous thing is brought is in the control of the defendant. In **Smith** *v* **Scott** (1973), a local authority let a house to a homeless family, on condition that they promised not to make any trouble. This promise was disregarded by the family once they moved in, and their behaviour was so intolerable that their next-door neighbour tried to sue the local authority on the basis of **Rylands** *v* **Fletcher**. However, it was held that the rule could not be applied to the landlord of tenants, as control of the land would lie with the tenants.

A defendant can also incur liability for bringing a dangerous thing onto the highway, if it then escapes onto someone's land. In **Rigby** *v* **Chief Constable of Northamptonshire** (1985), police attempting to capture a dangerous psychopath fired CS gas into the shop where he was, which was set on fire by the gas. It was decided that the rule did apply to the escape of things from the highway.

Bringing or accumulating for unnatural use

The dangerous thing must have been accumulated or brought onto the defendant's land in the course of some 'unnatural' use of the land; the rule does not apply to damage caused by anything which naturally occurs there (for such problems there will often be an action in nuisance or negligence). There has been much debate over what does amount to natural and non-natural use of land. It is clear that a defendant will not be liable for damage caused by trees or plants which grow naturally, nor for the escape of water which is naturally present on the land. In **Giles** *v* **Walker** (1890), the defendant ploughed up forest land, with the result that a large crop of thistles grew there. The seeds from these blew onto neighbouring land, causing the same problem on that land. The defendant was held not liable under **Rylands** *v* **Fletcher** because thistles grew naturally, and had not been introduced by him.

From the late nineteenth century, increasing industrialisation in Britain led the courts to hold, in a series of cases, that industrial activity was a natural use of land, so that problems arising from such activity could not be dealt with under **Rylands** *v* **Fletcher**.

In **Rickards** *v* **Lothian** (1913), the defendant leased the upper part of a building. A tap there was turned on by an unknown person and caused a flood, which damaged stock kept by the claimant on the floor below. The defendant was held not liable, since he was making an ordinary and proper use of the building. The Court of Appeal defined non-natural use as: 'some special use bringing with it increased danger to others. [It] must not merely be the ordinary use of the land or such a use as is proper for the general benefit of the community.'

In a similar vein was **British Celanese** *v* **A H Hunt** (1969), where the defendants owned a factory on an industrial estate in which they manufactured electrical components. Strips of their metal foil escaped from the factory and blew onto an overhead cable, causing a power failure which stopped production at the claimant's factory. The defendants were held not liable under **Rylands** *v* **Fletcher** because, given where their factory was sited, theirs could not be called a non-natural use of land. There were no special risks attached to the storage of foil and the use was beneficial to the community. On the other hand, the defendants were held liable in both negligence and nuisance.

Such cases seemed to suggest that **Rylands** would be of little use in the field of environmental protection. However, **Rickards** and **British Celanese** had to be reconsidered in the light of the following House of Lords case.

Key Case **Cambridge Water** *v* **Eastern Counties Leather** (1994)

Case Navigator

In **Cambridge Water** *v* **Eastern Counties Leather** (1994) the defendants had carried out a leather manufacturing business for many years. In the tanning process they had used a particular chemical solvent until 1976, when they changed to another method of tanning. In carrying out the old tanning process there were frequent spillages of the solvent onto the concrete floor, amounting to over a thousand tons of solvent over many years. This then seeped through the concrete floor and into the soil below. It polluted an area where the claimants, a water company, had their pumping station, extracting water for domestic consumption.

The pollution was only discovered in 1983 when changes in EC regulations forced the water company to make tests for such pollution. On discovering the problem the water company were forced to move their pumping station further upstream at a cost of over a million pounds. They sued the leather manufacturers for the expenses they had incurred. The claim failed because the damage suffered was held to be too remote, but the importance of the case lies in what Lord Goff had to say on the issue of unnatural use. He stated that the storage of chemicals on industrial premises was a 'classic case of non-natural use'. Just because the activity benefited the community in that it created employment did not render such use of the land natural.

Legal Principle

Industrial processes can be an unnatural use of land, even if they benefit the community as a whole.

Although the **Cambridge Water** decision seemed to breathe new life into a tort that many thought was practically dead, it failed to provide a clear definition of natural and non-natural use of land.

Key Case **Transco plc** *v* **Stockport Metropolitan Borough Council** (2004)

Case Navigator

The latest House of Lords view on the issue of non-natural uses of land was delivered in **Transco plc** *v* **Stockport Metropolitan Borough Council** (2004). Here the defendant owned a water pipe, which carried water from the mains to a large block of flats. The pipe fractured, and huge amounts of water ran along an embankment, which contained the claimant's gas pipeline. The embankment collapsed, leaving the gas pipeline unsupported. The claimant repaired the damage, and claimed the costs of the repairs under **Rylands** *v* **Fletcher**. Their claim failed, because the House of Lords held that a water pipe was not an unnatural use of land. This in itself was no surprise, but their Lordships went on to talk about how they would decide that a use of land was unnatural.

Lord Bingham stated that the phrase 'unnatural user' was not very helpful, and that a better question might be whether the defendant was an 'ordinary user'. **Rylands** *v* **Fletcher** should only offer a cause of action where the defendant's use of the land was 'extraordinary and unusual'. However, said Lord Bingham, this test should not be applied inflexibly: 'a use may be extraordinary and unusual at one time or in one place, but not so at another time or in another place'. The question to be asked was whether the defendant had done something out of the ordinary, considering the time and place in which he did so. Lord Bingham also stated that the question of whether the defendant's use of land was of benefit to the community was not relevant, which suggests that the approach used in **Rickards** and **British Celanese** is definitely no longer in favour.

Legal Principle

Rylands v Fletcher should only offer a cause of action where the defendant's use of land was out of the ordinary, considering the time and place.

Transco was applied in **LMS International** *v* **Styrene Packaging and Insulation** (2005). The case concerned a fire which broke out in the defendants' factory, and spread to the claimants' premises next door. The defendants made expanded polystyrene, a process which releases an inflammable gas. The fire was caused when this gas was ignited by a spark. The defendants argued that there was no non-natural use of land, given that the premises were on an industrial estate and they were carrying out an ordinary industrial process. The court disagreed, pointing out that the nature of the process involved a very real risk of fire being caused and spread. Although apparently limited only to cases involving fire, this decision suggests that in practical terms there is definitely still life in the tort of **Rylands** *v* **Fletcher**.

A dangerous thing

The thing which the defendant brings onto their land must be likely to do damage if it escapes, even though it might be quite safe if not allowed to escape. In **Transco** (see above), Lord Bingham explained that this test was quite a strict one, which would not be easily satisfied; essentially, it had to be shown that the defendant had brought or accumulated on the land something which he or she recognised, or ought to have recognised, would give rise to an exceptionally high risk of danger or 'mischief' if it escaped. If this requirement was fulfilled, it did not matter that the risk of an escape happening was low.

Examples of 'dangerous things' from decided cases include gas (**Batchellor** *v* **Tunbridge Wells Gas Co** (1901)); electricity (**National Telephone Co** *v* **Baker** (1893)); poisonous fumes (**West** *v* **Bristol Tramways Co** (1908)); a flag pole (**Shiffman** *v* **Order of St John** (1936)); tree branches (**Crowhurst** *v* **Amersham Burial Board** (1878)) and one of the chairs, complete with occupant, from a fairground 'chair-o-plane' ride (**Hale** *v* **Jennings** (1938)).

Escape

The tort only covers damage caused when a dangerous thing escapes from the defendant's land; damage caused to someone else while they are on the defendant's land is not applicable. In **Read** *v* **Lyons** (1946), the claimant was an inspector of munitions, visiting the defendants' munitions factory. A shell being manufactured there exploded, injuring her, and, because there was no suggestion that the defendants had been negligent, she claimed under **Rylands** *v* **Fletcher**. The defendants were held not liable, on the grounds that, although high-explosive shells clearly were 'dangerous things', the strict liability imposed by **Rylands** *v* **Fletcher** requires an escape of the thing that caused the injury. The court defined an escape as occurring when something escapes to outside a place where the defendant has occupation and control.

It was traditionally thought the term 'escape' meant that the release of the dangerous thing had to be accidental. In **Crown River Cruises Ltd** *v* **Kimbolton Fireworks Ltd** (1996), however, it was suggested that **Rylands** could be extended to cover intentional releases of dangerous things (in that case letting off fireworks as part of a display), although the defendants in the case were held not liable under **Rylands**.

Damage

The tort is not actionable *per se*, so the escape of the dangerous thing must be proved to have caused damage. Clearly, this will usually be damage to land or other property, but until **Transco** (see p. 316), it was unclear whether, if an escape did cause death or personal injury, **Rylands** would allow a claim. **Transco** now makes it clear that it will not. The House of Lords made it plain that **Rylands** *v* **Fletcher** was to be seen as a 'sub-species' of nuisance, and for this reason it could only protect rights to and enjoyment of land.

The claimant must prove causation under the normal rules (see Chapter 3).

Who can sue?

It has traditionally been thought that a claimant under **Rylands** must have some kind of property interest in the land affected by the escape of the dangerous thing, and, although **Transco** does not specifically refer to this question, the statement that **Rylands** is to be seen as an aspect of nuisance law seems to confirm that an interest in land is required here, as it is in nuisance itself.

The mental element

As explained at the beginning of this chapter, **Rylands** was originally a tort of strict liability, which meant that a defendant could be liable even if they did not know there was a risk of damage, and/or could not have prevented it. However, this never amounted to absolute liability, as there were defences available which effectively introduced an element of fault-based liability (see below). The strict liability element was also compromised by the requirement for non-natural use, which in practice allowed the courts to make policy decisions based on the desirability of particular activities at particular times. In **Read** *v* **Lyons**, for example, the case about a munitions factory (explained above), it was argued that running a munitions factory during wartime could be considered a natural use of land. Lord Porter said that 'All the circumstances of the time and place must be taken into consideration, so what might be regarded as dangerous or non-natural may vary according to those circumstances.'

Most importantly, the case of **Cambridge Water** (see above) not only gave new life to the tort in **Rylands**, but also brought in a new element of fault. It established that a defendant could only be liable for a type of damage which was reasonably foreseeable, which means that liability can no longer properly be seen as strict.

Defences

The general defences of *volenti*, contributory negligence, and statutory authority are applicable to **Rylands** *v* **Fletcher**, along with the related defences of common benefit and default of the claimant, and other specific defences discussed below.

Volenti and common benefit

Consent to the dangerous thing being on the claimant's land is a defence, and such consent can be implied or express. Consent will be implied where the presence of the thing offers some benefit to the claimant, as in the case of, for example, water tanks and pipes in a block of flats (some authorities treat this as a separate defence called common benefit).

Contributory negligence and default of the claimant

Where a claimant contributes to causing the escape of the dangerous thing, their damages can be reduced under the normal rules of contributory negligence. A further defence, known as default of the claimant, applies if the escape of the dangerous thing is completely the fault of the claimant, or, more commonly, if the escape only causes damage because of some abnormal sensitivity on the part of the claimant's property. This was the case in **Eastern and South Africa Telegraph Co** *v* **Cape Town Tramways Co** (1902), where the defendants were held not liable when a very minor escape of electricity caused by them affected the claimants' extremely sensitive power cables.

Statutory authority

Defendants may escape liability under **Rylands** *v* **Fletcher** if the terms of a relevant statute clearly authorise their actions. However, many Acts which permit the performance of dangerous activities do not specify whether the rule should apply, and the question then becomes one of interpretation of the particular statute. In **Green** *v* **Chelsea Waterworks Co** (1894), a water main laid by the defendant burst, flooding the claimant's premises. The Court of Appeal held that the company was not liable because they were not only permitted but obliged by statute to maintain a water supply, and occasional bursts were an inevitable result of such a duty. By contrast, in **Charing Cross Electricity Co** *v* **Hydraulic Co** (1914), which featured similar facts, the defendants were found not to have a defence of statutory authority because the relevant statute did not oblige them to provide a water supply but only gave them the power to do so.

Act of a stranger

A defendant will not be liable where the damage is done by a third party who is not acting under the defendant's instructions (note that that person need not literally be a stranger; the fact that the defendant knows them does not prevent the defence applying). This defence was applied in **Box** *v* **Jubb** (1879), where defendants were held not liable for damage done when their reservoir overflowed because the flooding was caused by a third person who had emptied his own reservoir into the stream which fed the defendants' reservoir.

Where a defendant avoids liability under **Rylands** because the harm was caused by the act of a stranger, there may nevertheless be liability for negligence if the act of the stranger was such that the defendant should have foreseen it and taken precautions against it.

Act of God

This defence is available when the escape is caused purely by natural forces, in circumstances which the defendant could not have been expected to foresee or guard against. In **Nichols** *v* **Marsland** (1876), the defendant dammed a natural stream in his land, in order to create three artificial lakes. The whole thing was well built, and precautions against flooding were quite adequate for all normal circumstances. However, an exceptionally heavy thunderstorm – described by witnesses as the heaviest in living memory – burst the banks of the lakes, and the resulting rush of water down the stream swept away four bridges on the claimant's land. The defendant was held not liable because the thunderstorm was an 'act of God' which he could not reasonably be expected to predict, and without it the lakes would have been secure.

On the other hand, in **Greenock Corporation** *v* **Caledonian Railway Co** (1917), which involved similar facts, the defence was unsuccessful, even though the rain was exceptionally heavy. The corporation had built a concrete paddling pool for children, and in the process had changed the flow of a stream. After unusually heavy rainfall, the stream overflowed, and water poured down a public street into the town, damaging the claimant's property. The House of Lords concluded that the rainfall was not an 'act of God', and therefore the corporation were liable. Clearly these two decisions are difficult to reconcile, and the later case suggests that the availability of the defence will be rarer than the earlier case would imply.

Relationship to other torts

Nuisance

The rule in **Rylands** *v* **Fletcher** has its origins in nuisance; in the case itself, the claimants relied almost exclusively on authorities from the law of nuisance, so it is not surprising that the two torts overlap to a certain extent. **Rylands** *v* **Fletcher**, however, has a more restricted application than nuisance because of the specific requirements of accumulation and of a substance likely to cause injury if it escapes, neither of which are necessary for liability in nuisance. In addition, the requirement of a non-natural use, though similar to the unreasonable user in nuisance, normally involves some degree of exceptional risk, which the unreasonable user does not. Nevertheless, in many factual situations claimants will succeed equally well under **Rylands** *v* **Fletcher** or in nuisance.

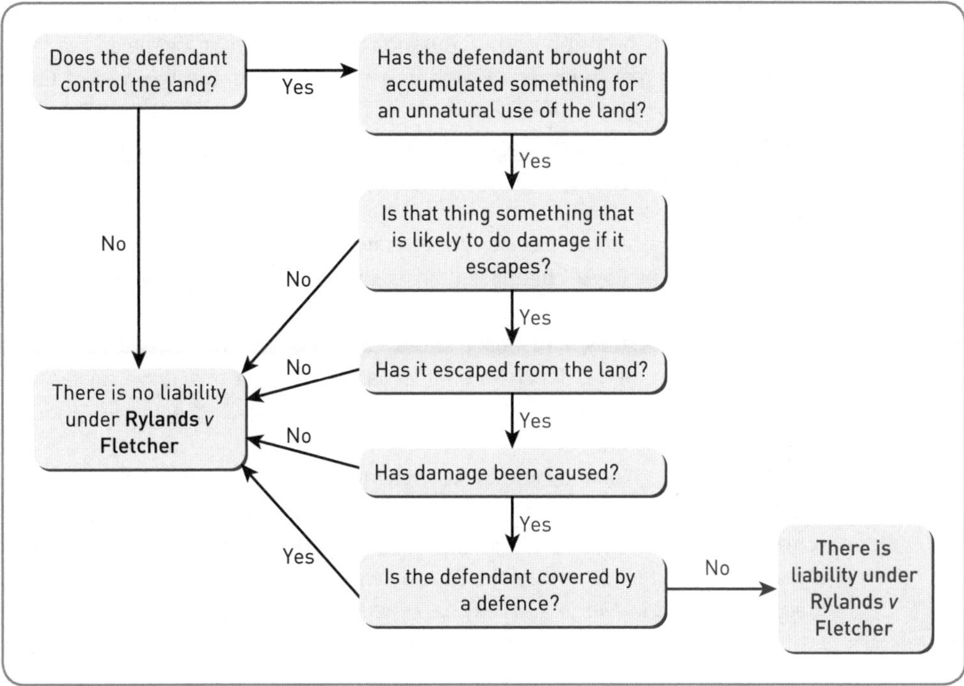

Figure 12.1 Is there a case under **Rylands** *v* **Fletcher**?

Negligence

In **Rylands** *v* **Fletcher**, the degree of care taken by the defendant to avoid the escape continues to be irrelevant, since liability is strict. However, where the defendant puts forward the defences of act of God, act of a stranger, common benefit or statutory authority, the courts must examine not only the reasonableness of the accumulation, but also the defendant's responsibility for its actual escape, and although the steps to their decision may be different from those where negligence is alleged, the result is likely to be the same, as suggested in **Mason** *v* **Levy Auto Parts of England Ltd** (1967).

Trespass

On occasion judges have regarded the rule in **Rylands** *v* **Fletcher** as a kind of trespass (discussed in the next chapter), but the main difference is that in most **Rylands** *v* **Fletcher** cases the damage done is not direct.

The role of Rylands *v* Fletcher

When **Rylands** *v* **Fletcher** was first decided, the tort could have been interpreted by future courts as a broad cause of action, imposing strict liability and available not just to injuries related to land but also to those concerning personal injury. However, the growing importance of mechanised industry led the courts to give the tort a highly restrictive interpretation, as seen in **Rickards**, and with negligence expanding to provide a cause of action for those who could prove someone else's fault, the strict liability approach of **Rylands** fell out of favour. By the end of the twentieth century it was thought that **Rylands** *v* **Fletcher** was all but dead, but the case of **Cambridge Water** in 1994 seemed to give it the kiss of life. It was widely predicted that, as a result, **Rylands** would be reborn as a defender against environmental pollution, but this does not appear to have happened (perhaps because this area is now the subject of so much government enforcement, leaving little gap for private actions).

As a result, it has been argued that the **Rylands** action should be abolished altogether. As far back as 1978, the Royal Commission on Civil Liability and Compensation for Personal Injury recommended that it should be replaced with a statutory scheme that would define activities considered particularly hazardous, and oblige those who engaged in them to pay compensation for any damage caused, under principles of strict liability. Neither this, nor a similar proposal by the later Royal Commission on Civil Liability for Dangerous Things and Activities, ever showed any serious prospect of being enacted.

The latest word on the importance of **Rylands** comes from the House of Lords in **Transco**. Their Lordships acknowledged that arguments had been made for absorbing the rule into the general rules of negligence, but they argued that, although it might be useful only in a very small number of cases, it still had a role to play and should be preserved. Lord Bingham stated that there was 'a category of case, however small it may be, in which it seems just to impose liability even in the absence of fault'. The categories Lord Bingham chose to illustrate his point were, however, somewhat confusing. He mentioned, for example, the 1966 Aberfan disaster, in which a slag heap collapsed onto a village school, as an example of a situation where compensation should be available even if fault could not be proved. Yet the tragedy of Aberfan was that it killed 144 people, 116 of them schoolchildren, rather than that it destroyed 20 houses and the school. Under Lord Bingham's 'sub-species of nuisance' formulation, **Rylands** would only have compensated the owners of the buildings for the damage to their property, which rather undermines its usefulness in this kind of case. However, the fact remains that allowing **Rylands** to continue breathing does at least provide some possibility of redress for damage caused by very hazardous activities where negligence cannot be proved.

Other protections against hazardous activities

Many of the activities which potentially could come under the rule in **Rylands** *v* **Fletcher** (and nuisance) are in fact regulated by statute, a recognition of the fact that an increasingly technological society brings risks as well as benefits. Some of these statutes impose strict liability for the escape of certain dangerous things, such as the Reservoirs Act 1975 regarding accumulated water, the Nuclear Installations Acts 1965 and 1969, which cover the escape of ionising radiation, and the Consumer Protection Act 1987, which imposes strict liability for injuries caused by defective products.

Answering questions

Give a critical explanation of the tort created in the case of **Rylands** *v* **Fletcher** (1868).

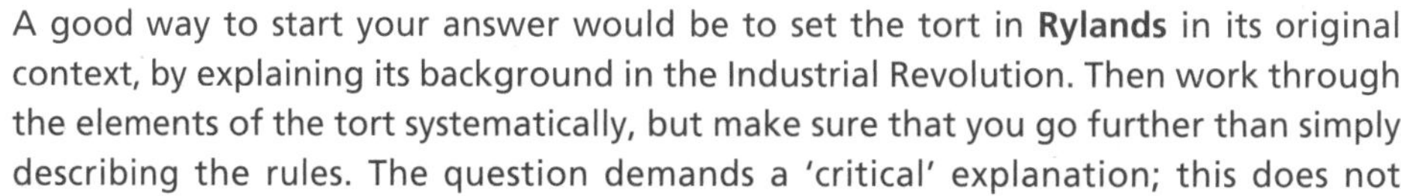

A good way to start your answer would be to set the tort in **Rylands** in its original context, by explaining its background in the Industrial Revolution. Then work through the elements of the tort systematically, but make sure that you go further than simply describing the rules. The question demands a 'critical' explanation; this does not necessarily mean you have to criticise the law, but you do need to examine the way it works, highlighting any problems or gaps, and bringing out its practical usefulness. Issues which you could discuss include whether the tort has been interpreted too strictly by the courts; whether it could or should play a greater role in protecting the environment; and to what extent it is, or should be, a tort of strict liability. You may want to refer back to some of the arguments for and against a requirement for fault, detailed in Chapter 1.

A good way to finish your essay would be to consider the tort's place in the wider law – does it fill a necessary gap or has it been superseded by other areas of law?

Summary of Chapter 12

The tort in **Rylands** *v* **Fletcher** dates from the Industrial Revolution, and was intended to provide redress for damage caused by increasing industrialisation.

Who can sue?

Claimants must prove:

- The defendant controls the land from which the problem has come.
- The defendant has brought or accumulated something in the course of some 'unnatural use' of the land.
- The thing brought or accumulated is 'dangerous'.
- The dangerous thing has escaped.
- Damage has been caused by the escape.

It appears that claimants must have an interest in the land affected by the escape.

The mental element

Traditionally **Rylands** was considered to impose strict liability, but:

- Defences effectively introduced an element of fault-based liability.
- The requirement for non-natural use allowed the courts to make policy decisions.
- The case of **Cambridge Water** (see above) established that a defendant could only be liable for reasonably foreseeable types of damage.

Defences

Available defences are:

- *Volenti*
- Contributory negligence
- Statutory authority
- Common benefit
- Default of the claimant
- Act of a stranger
- Act of God.

→

The role of **Rylands** *v* **Fletcher**

Rylands is rarely used and it has been argued that it should be abolished, but the House of Lords in **Transco** said it still has a role to play.

Reading list

Text resources

Amirthalingam, K (2004) 'Rylands lives' 63 *Cambridge Law Journal* 273
Bagshaw, R (2004) 'Rylands confined' 120 *Law Quarterly Review* 388
Fridman, G H L (1956) 'The rise and fall of Rylands *v* Fletcher' 34 *Canadian Bar Review* 810
Law Commission (1970) *Civil Liability for Dangerous Things and Activities.* Report No 32
Layard, F (1997) 'Balancing environmental considerations' 113 *Law Quarterly Review* 254
Murphy, J (2004) 'The merits of Rylands *v* Fletcher' 24 *Oxford Journal of Legal Studies* 643
Newark, F H (1961) 'Non-natural user and Rylands *v* Fletcher' 24 *Modern Law Review* 557
Nolan, D (2003) 'The distinctiveness of Rylands *v* Fletcher' 121 *Law Quarterly Review* 421
Simpson, A (1984) 'Legal liability for bursting reservoirs: the historical context of Rylands *v* Fletcher' 13 *Journal of Legal Studies* 209

Reading on the Internet

The House of Lords judgment in **Transco** *v* **Stockport** (2004) can be read at:
http://www.publications.parliament.uk/pa/ld200203/ldjudgmt/jd031119/trans-1.htm

Visit **www.mylawchamber.co.uk** to access tools to help you develop and test your knowledge of tort law, including interactive multiple choice questions, practice exam questions with guidance, weblinks, glossary flashcards, legal newsfeed and legal updates.

Use Case Navigator to read in full some of the key cases referenced in this chapter with commentary and questions:

Cambridge Water *v* **Eastern Counties Leather** (1994)
Transco plc *v* **Stockport Metropolitan Borough Council** (2004)

Chapter 13
Trespass to land

This chapter discusses:

- How the tort of trespass to land is committed
- Defences to trespass to land.

In the previous two chapters, we looked at two torts which are concerned with damage done to land. The tort covered in this chapter, trespass to land, is designed to protect a claimant's right to keep other people off their land, and it can be committed simply by someone entering land without permission, regardless of whether they do any damage there (as we saw earlier this is described as being 'actionable *per se*'). The idea behind the tort is that we all have a basic right to enjoy our own property without interference from anyone else, and to exclude people from the place where we live or work if we wish to.

Elements of the tort

The elements of the tort are:

- the claim must involve land;
- the land must be in the defendant's possession;
- the claimant must interfere with the land.

Land

Land includes not only the soil itself, but things under it, any building that is fixed to the surface, and such airspace above as is needed for the normal use and enjoyment of the land and the structures on it. This means that trespass may arise from tunnelling under land in possession of another, even though neither end of the tunnel is on that land, or from invading the air above it. In **Anchor Brewhouse Developments** *v* **Berkley House (Docklands) Developments** (1987), the arms of tower cranes situated on the defendants' land occasionally crossed the airspace above the claimants' land; the defendants were held liable for trespass, even though the cranes were at a height which meant that the normal use of the land was not affected.

The Civil Aviation Act 1982 provides that there is no trespass where civilian aircraft fly over property at a reasonable height; however, the Act imposes strict liability for damage caused by the taking off or landing of such aircraft, or by anything falling from them.

Possession

The defendant need not own the land, but must be in possession of it. In this context, possession means the right to exclude others from the land. Such possession must be immediate (meaning that it must exist at the time the trespass is committed). Therefore, for example, if someone trespasses on rented premises, it is the tenant who has the right to sue for trespass, and not the landlord.

Simply being on the land does not amount to possession for the purposes of trespass, and because possession must be exclusive, a lodger in someone's house or a guest in a hotel will not usually have possession in this context.

Interference

The interference must be direct and physical; indirect interference may give rise to an action for negligence or nuisance, but not for trespass. So if, for example, your next-door neighbour prunes their roses and throws the clippings into your garden, that may be trespass. However, if they simply fail to prune them, so that they overhang your garden, that may be nuisance, but is not trespass.

Interference can include entry onto land which is in the immediate and exclusive possession of another, remaining on such land when asked to leave or when permission to be there expires, abusing a right of entry to such land, and placing or throwing something onto such land.

Entering land

Even the slightest crossing of a boundary can be enough for liability here, such as putting your hand through a window.

Abuse of right of entry

A person who has permission to enter land, but does something which goes beyond what has been allowed, may be guilty of trespass. An example would be where students in a hall of residence have permission to go into their own rooms, and use the communal areas, but would commit trespass by going into another student's room without permission. Abuse of right of entry also applies where someone is allowed onto land for a certain purpose and then does something unrelated to that purpose – for example, if you allow someone into your home to paint the kitchen, and they then go and have a look round the bedrooms without your permission.

Remaining on land

A person who has lawfully entered land in the possession of another, and then remains there after the permission expires, or after being asked to leave, commits a trespass.

Placing things on land

It is a trespass to throw or place anything onto land occupied by another. It is not necessary that the boundaries are crossed, so long as there is some physical contact with the claimant's property, so trespass could arise from, for example, planting a vine so that it grows up the claimant's wall, piling rubbish against a fence, or leaning a bike against a shop window.

A common example of such trespass occurs when livestock stray onto land. In **League Against Cruel Sports** *v* **Scott** (1985) the defendant was the master of a hunt, and the claimants, an anti-bloodsports organisation, owned certain areas of Exmoor, which they had purchased for the purpose of creating sanctuaries for wild deer. On seven occasions, the hunt's hounds strayed onto the sanctuaries, and the court granted an injunction. It was held that persistent hunting near the prohibited land, when there was no effective way of preventing the hounds from straying onto it, could be evidence of an intention to trespass.

Trespass on highways

The owners of the soil on which a highway rests are treated as having possession of it for the purposes of trespass. There is no trespass where a person uses a highway to get from one place to another, or for anything which is incidental to that, such as stopping to look in a shop window, or consult a map.

It was traditionally thought that anyone who uses the highway for any other purpose becomes a trespasser. In **Hickman** *v* **Maisey** (1900) the claimant owned land on which racehorses were trained. A highway crossed this land, and while the horses were undergoing trials the defendant, who owned a racing newspaper, spent two hours walking up and down, watching the horses and taking notes on how well they were performing. It was held that this went beyond using the highway for its normal purpose, and he was liable for trespass.

Key Case **DPP *v* Jones (1999)**

However, the case of **DPP** *v* **Jones** (1999) has changed the law in this area. The case was actually a criminal one, in which a group of people were charged with the offence of trespassory assembly under the Public Order Act 1986, but it has relevance for tort law because the offence requires that the defendants have committed a trespass within the meaning of the tort. The defendants in the case had staged a demonstration at the side of the road adjoining the fence around Stonehenge. None of them was behaving in a destructive or violent way, and nobody else using the highway was obstructed by their presence. On the traditional view that it is trespass to do anything on the highway that amounts to more than getting from one place to another or the activities stemming from that process, the defendants would have been committing the tort of trespass. However, Lord Irvine, giving the leading judgment, held that this approach had become outdated. He presented a more modern test, concluding that:

> the public highway is a public place which the public may enjoy for any reasonable purpose, provided that the activity in question does not amount to a public or private nuisance and does not obstruct the highway by unreasonably impeding the primary right of the public to pass and repass; within these qualifications there is a public right of peaceful assembly on the highway.

The case makes it clear that there is a right to do more than simply pass along the highway, but quite what that right can comprise is unclear. Lord Irvine stated that in each case it will be for the trial court to decide whether the use of the highway is reasonable, and consistent with the right of other people to pass along it.

Legal Principle

Use of the public highway for any reasonable purpose, including peaceful assembly, is not trespass.

In **City of London** *v* **Samede** (2012), the Court of Appeal considered the issue of when an action will amount to lawful protest on the highway, and when it crosses the line and becomes trespass. The claimants were members of a group of protesters who had established a camp outside St Paul's Cathedral, on land owned by the defendants, including part of the highway in front of the church. The defendants brought a claim for trespass, to try to get the protesters to leave, but the protesters claimed they had a right to be there, because they were exercising the rights to freedom of expression and freedom of assembly under Arts. 10 and 11 of the European Convention on Human Rights. The court agreed that the Convention rights had to be weighed against the landowner's rights, but said that occupying the land for a long period of time and interfering with the rights of others using the highway, went beyond the rights protected by the Convention.

Continuing trespass

Trespass is said to be 'continuing' and can justify a series of legal actions for as long as it lasts. This arises mainly in cases of objects placed on the land, where the trespass continues until they are removed. In **Holmes** *v* **Wilson** (1839), the highway authorities had built a road which was supported by buttresses on the claimant's land. Building these buttresses was held to be a trespass, and they had to pay damages. However, they did not take the buttresses away, and so were found liable in a subsequent action for trespass.

Trespass by relation

A person who has a right to take immediate possession of land, and enters it in order to exercise that right, is regarded as having been in possession ever since the right of entry accrued. They may therefore sue for any trespass committed since the right of entry accrued. This principle allows a tenant to sue for any trespass committed between the time when the tenancy was agreed, and the time when they took possession of it; this is known as trespass by relation.

Trespass *ab initio*

Where a person's entry onto land is permitted by statute or common law, rather than merely by permission of the occupier, and the person does a wrongful act while there, that act makes the original entry a trespass, and not just the wrongful act. This is known as trespass *ab initio*. It was first defined in the old case of **The Six Carpenters** (1610). Here six carpenters went into an inn (which they had a lawful right to do), ordered bread and wine, and paid for it. Later, they ordered more wine, and this time refused to pay. The court held that a wrongful act committed at this stage could retrospectively render their original entry unlawful. However, the defendants were held not liable because they had not committed an act, only an omission, and this was not enough to create liability.

In **Cinnamond** *v* **British Airports Authority** (1980), the defendants sued a group of six taxi drivers who had been hanging about at the airport and touting for customers. The reason why the airport authority wanted to stop this was that the airport had an official taxi rank, where fares were regulated, and the defendants were catching passengers before they got to the rank, then charging them ridiculously high fares, and in some cases refusing to give them their luggage out of the boot unless they paid up. The drivers usually got access to the airport by dropping off a passenger there, and then hanging about to see if they could pick up departing passengers. Lord Denning said that it was lawful for them to enter the airport to drop off passengers, but that they had no legal right to loiter about in the hope of picking up passengers. This was therefore a wrongful act, so trespass *ab initio* applied, and they became trespassers from the time they entered the airport.

The main practical use of the trespass *ab initio* principle today is in the use of police search warrants. Where the police have a warrant to enter and search premises, but they do something there that is outside what is allowed by the warrant, the trespass *ab initio* rule could potentially make the initial entry unlawful. However, the courts have not been keen to use it in this way.

In **Elias** *v* **Pasmore** (1934), police officers wanted to arrest a man and had legally entered the claimant's land in order to do so. While on the land they seized a number of items, some lawfully and some unlawfully. It was held that they had committed trespass only with regard to the documents unlawfully removed; their wrongful act did not disturb the main purpose of entry, which was to make a lawful arrest.

In **Chic Fashions (West Wales) Ltd** *v* **Jones** (1968), another police search case, the Court of Appeal criticised the very existence of the doctrine, saying it ran counter to the principle that if an act was lawful when it was carried out, subsequent events cannot make it unlawful. In this case the police were searching the claimant's premises for stolen goods, and seized goods which they wrongly thought to be stolen. The seizure was held to be lawful because police entering premises with a warrant have authority to remove anything which they believe has been stolen.

The mental element

To be liable for trespass, the defendant must have intended to do the action that amounted to the trespass. In most cases of trespass, this is quite clear, because of the need for a direct action. If I throw rocks on your land, for example, or if I climb in through your window, clearly I intended to do those things.

However, it is important to note that the defendant only has to have intended to do the action they did; they do not have to have intended to commit a trespass, or to know that what they did would be a trespass. Nor do they need to have any intention to cause problems for the claimant, or have any kind of hostile purpose. Let's say, for example, that you have permission to enter a friend's garden shed to get a bike that they've offered to lend you. By mistake, you go into their next door neighbour's shed instead. That would be a trespass, because you intentionally walked into the shed, even though you did not intend to trespass because you thought it was somewhere you had permission to be. Similarly, if you were out walking in the countryside and wandered onto private land because you were lost, you would still be committing trespass because, by putting one foot in front of the other and walking on to the land, you acted intentionally. An example of this kind of situation was found in the old case of **Basely** *v* **Clarkson** (1681), where the defendant was cutting his grass, and without realising, went over the boundary onto his neighbour's land. This was held to be trespass, because he intended to cut the grass he was cutting, even though he did not intend to cross his neighbour's boundary.

By contrast, if someone pushes you onto land, or throws you there, you would not be committing trespass because you did not intend to enter.

Most trespasses are obviously intentional, and so the state of mind of the defendant is rarely an issue. However, the decision in **League Against Cruel Sports** *v* **Scott** (above) suggests that trespass to land can be committed negligently.

Where a person trespasses accidentally, either being unaware that the land is private, or mistakenly believing it is their own, liability is incurred nevertheless. However, it is well established that where a defendant unintentionally enters land adjoining the highway (perhaps where a car leaves the road as a result of an accident), the claimant must prove negligence (**River Wear Commissioners** *v* **Adamson** (1877)).

Defences

Licence

Where the person in possession of land gives someone permission, express or implied, to be on that land, there is no trespass, so long as the boundaries of that permission are not exceeded. This is called giving a person licence to be on the land.

Some licences are irrevocable and some statutes lay down restrictions on the revocation of licences such as residential licences, in order to protect the security of a person's home. However, a licence which is given without valuable consideration (that is, it is given rather than sold) can be revoked at any time. Where a licence is given by contract, it can also be revoked at any time, although this may result in liability for breach of contract. Once a licence is revoked, the person to whom it was granted must be allowed a reasonable time in which to leave and remove their goods; after that, they become a trespasser.

Justification by law

People sometimes avoid liability for trespass because the law provides some justification for their conduct. For example, much of the conduct of the police would amount to a trespass but for the provisions of the Police and Criminal Evidence Act 1984. Section 17 of this Act allows a police officer to enter and search premises in order to carry out an arrest.

Jus tertii

A defendant may have a defence to an action for trespass if it can be shown that the land rightfully belongs neither to the person in possession nor to the person claiming the land, but to a third person. This was established in **Doe d Carter** *v* **Barnard** (1849).

There is one exception to this rule. If a tenant takes a lease, and it turns out that the landlord had no right to grant the lease, the tenant cannot set up the defence of *jus tertii* against the landlord.

Necessity

Necessity has been allowed as a defence to trespass, for example in **Esso Petroleum Co** *v* **Southport Corporation** (1956), where a sea captain was forced to discharge oil, which then polluted the shoreline, in order to prevent his ship breaking up and endangering the crew after it ran aground. Similarly, in **Rigby** *v* **Chief Constable of Northamptonshire** (1985), the defendant successfully pleaded necessity after causing a fire by releasing CS gas into a shop in an attempt to eject a dangerous psychopath.

However, the courts have traditionally kept a tight rein on the use of necessity as a defence (in all torts, not just nuisance), and an example of this can be seen in **Monsanto plc** *v* **Tilly** (1999). The claimant, Monsanto, is a multinational firm which has spearheaded the development of genetically modified food. As part of this process, they were growing genetically modified crops on test sites throughout the UK. The defendant was a member of a group which considers genetically modified crops to be potentially harmful to the environment and to public safety, and they conducted a campaign in which they entered land where the trial crops were growing and uprooted part of them. When sued for trespass, the defendant claimed the defence of necessity, on the basis that their actions were essential to protect public health and the environment, but the Court of Appeal refused to accept this argument. They recognised that there might be occasions when pulling up a whole crop might be justified to protect others. However, in this case the defendant's group had only pulled up part of the crop as a symbolic gesture, and it was clear that the main purpose of the actions was to attract publicity for their campaign.

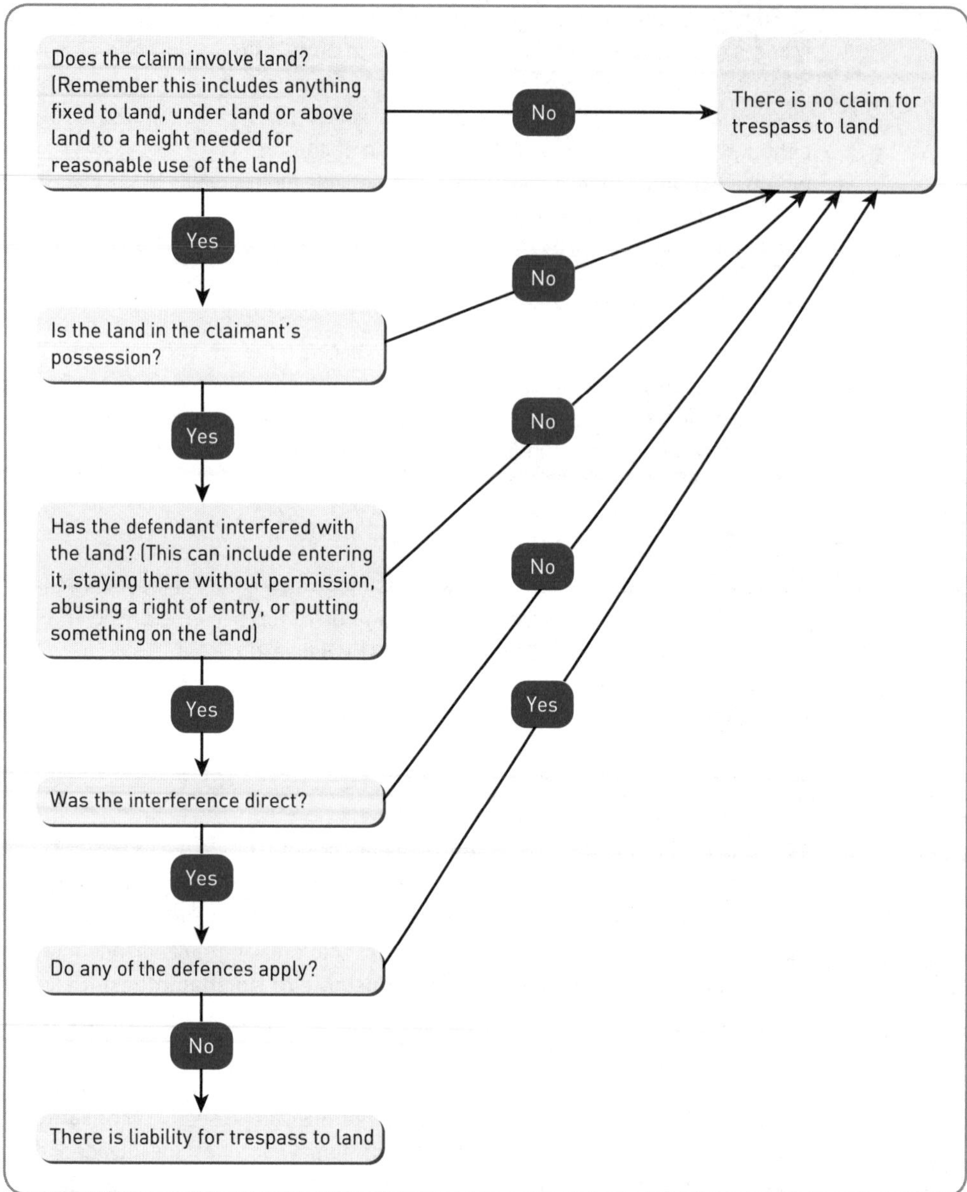
Does the claim involve land? (Remember this includes anything fixed to land, under land or above land to a height needed for reasonable use of the land)
No
There is no claim for trespass to land
Yes
No
Is the land in the claimant's possession?
Yes
No
Has the defendant interfered with the land? (This can include entering it, staying there without permission, abusing a right of entry, or putting something on the land)
No
Yes
Yes
Was the interference direct?
Yes
Do any of the defences apply?
No
There is liability for trespass to land

Figure 13.1 Is there a claim for trespass to land?

Remedies

As well as the usual remedies of damages and injunction, the tort of trespass to land allows some specific remedies.

Re-entry

Where a trespass involves excluding the rightful occupier from the land, he or she has the right to enter or re-enter the land. This is a form of self-help as the courts are not involved. But self-help is not encouraged by the courts and therefore there are considerable restrictions on when it can be resorted to. Only reasonable force can be used. In **Collins** *v* **Renison** (1754) the defendant found a trespasser up a ladder on his land. He said that he had reacted by gently shaking the ladder, which was a low one, and 'gently overturned it and gently threw the claimant from it upon the ground'. This amount of force was found to be unreasonable. Even where the force is reasonable and no tort has been committed, the person may still find that they have committed a statutory criminal offence.

Action for the recovery of land

This is sometimes called ejectment. It allows a person who has lost possession of their land to get possession back, provided they can establish an immediate right to possession. With the problems caused by squatters particularly in mind, a special summary procedure has been devised, which allows the claimant quickly to obtain an order for possession, and a writ for its enforcement, against anyone in occupation of their land who has entered or remained there without licence. This can be done even though the claimant cannot identify those in possession.

Table 13.1 Actions which can involve land

	Trespass to land	Rylands *v* Fletcher	Private nuisance	Negligence
Who can sue?	Only a claimant with an interest in the land	Only a claimant with an interest in the land	Only a claimant with an interest in the land	Anyone to whom a duty is owed
What kinds of action are covered?	Direct action	Indirect action (an escape of something dangerous)	Indirect action	Indirect action
Must the action be continuous?	No, continuous or one-off events covered	No, continuous or one-off events covered	One-off events not usually covered	No, continuous or one-off events covered
Must damage be caused?	No, actionable *per se*	Yes	Yes	Yes

Mesne profits

An action for mesne profits is a type of action for trespass. It allows the claimant to claim profits taken by the defendant during occupancy, damages for deterioration, and reasonable costs of regaining possession. An action for the recovery of land can be joined with a claim for mesne profits, and in this case it is unnecessary to have entered the land before suing. If the actions are brought separately, the claimant will have to enter the land before bringing the claim for mesne profits.

Distress damage feasant

Where an object placed or left unlawfully on the claimant's land causes damage, the claimant can keep it until the damage has been paid for. So if, for example, you hit a tennis ball through a neighbour's window, they are entitled to keep the ball until you pay to have the window replaced.

Trespass in the criminal law

In the past, despite signs on land saying 'Trespassers will be prosecuted', trespass was only a civil wrong and not a crime. However, the Criminal Justice and Public Order Act 1994 has created certain limited circumstances when trespass will now be a criminal offence as well as a tort. The Act was aimed at such people as animal activists opposed to hunting, and has been heavily criticised as increasing criminalisation and giving the police unnecessary powers.

Answering questions

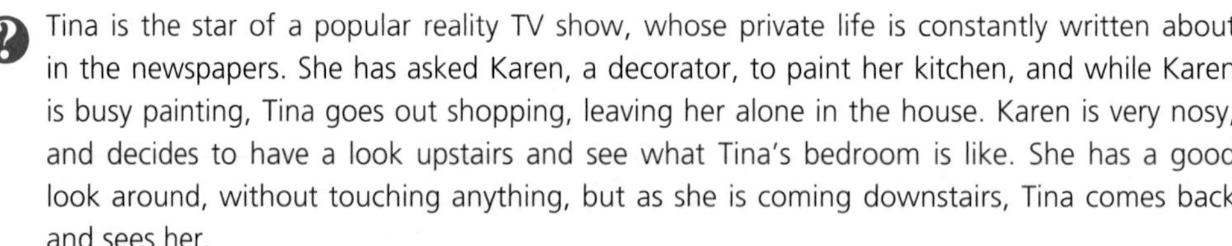

Tina is the star of a popular reality TV show, whose private life is constantly written about in the newspapers. She has asked Karen, a decorator, to paint her kitchen, and while Karen is busy painting, Tina goes out shopping, leaving her alone in the house. Karen is very nosy, and decides to have a look upstairs and see what Tina's bedroom is like. She has a good look around, without touching anything, but as she is coming downstairs, Tina comes back and sees her.

Tina is already annoyed, because when she arrived home, she found Gary, a press photographer, waiting outside her gate to try and take a picture of her. Tina dashed into her garden to avoid being photographed, so Gary leaned over her fence to try and get a picture. He lost his balance and fell over the fence into Tina's garden, crushing her favourite plants.

Tina decides to try and get some peace and quiet in her back garden, but when she gets out there, she finds that her neighbour, Steve, is burning some rubbish on a bonfire, and so much smoke is drifting across to Tina's garden that she is forced to go back indoors.

Advise Tina on any claims she may have in trespass to land or nuisance.

As usual with a problem question, you should work through each potential claim in turn, and here the possible claims are against Karen, Gary and Steve. Taking Karen first, she clearly has permission to be in the house, but does this permission cover her going upstairs and looking round the bedroom? If not, there is liability for trespass; remember that trespass is actionable *per se*, so it does not matter that Karen has not touched anything or done any damage.

Turning to Gary, we can reasonably assume that he does not have permission to be in Tina's garden, but the issue here is whether he had the necessary intention for trespass, given that he fell into the garden accidentally. However, remember that trespass can be committed just by putting a hand through a window, so in fact, just by leaning into the garden, he can be liable. However, he will not have to pay damages for destroying the plants, because that was the result of the fall, which was unintentional.

Finally, does Tina have a claim against Steve with regard to the smoke? Here, there is no direct interference with land, so there is no trespass. However, he may be liable in nuisance, so you should work through the elements of that tort to assess his possible liability.

Summary of Chapter 13

Trespass to land is unjustifiable interference with land in the immediate and exclusive possession of another.

- Land includes the soil, things under it, buildings fixed to the surface, and the airspace needed for normal use.
- The defendant must be in possession, but need not own the land.
- Interference must be direct and physical, including:
  - entering land;
  - abuse of right of entry;
  - remaining on land after permission expires;
  - placing things on land.
- Making reasonable use of the highway is not trespass.

Trespass is a continuing tort, and can give rise to a series of actions while it goes on.

Where entry is permitted by statute or common law, committing an unlawful act while there can make the original entry a trespass (trespass *ab initio*).

The mental element

Most trespasses are intentional, but accidental trespass can create liability.

Defences

Available defences are:

- Licence
- Justification by law
- *Jus tertii*
- Necessity.

Remedies

As well as damages/injunctions, specific remedies are:

- Re-entry
- Action for recovery of land
- Mesne profits
- Distress damage feasant.

Reading list

Text resources

Harlow, C (2005) *Understanding Tort Law*, 3rd edn, Chapter 5. Sweet & Maxwell
Weir, T (2008) *Casebook on Tort*, 11th edn, Chapters 8 and 9, Sweet & Maxwell
Williams, G (1936) 'A strange offspring of trespass *ab initio*' 52 *Law Quarterly Review* 106
Wiren, S (1925) 'The plea of *jus tertii* in ejectment' 41 *Law Quarterly Review* 139

Reading on the Internet

City of London *v* **Samede** (2012) can be read at:
http://www.judiciary.gov.uk/media/judgments/2012/cityoflondon-v-samede-appeal

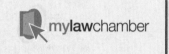

Chapter 14
Trespass to the person

This chapter discusses:

- How the tort of trespass to the person is committed
- Defences to trespass to the person
- Other protection from physical harm in tort.

Trespass to the person is a very old tort, which essentially protects what is called personal integrity, or in more modern terms, our personal space. The idea behind the tort is that we all have a right to be left alone by others, and not to have our freedom of movement restricted for unlawful reasons. For that reason, the tort is actionable *per se*, which, as you will remember, means that a defendant can be liable merely for committing the tort, even if no physical harm is done. That means that any form of unwanted touch, from a kiss to a haircut, can be a trespass to the person, as well as physical violence such as hitting or kicking.

Before the tort of negligence was created, trespass was the main way of getting compensation for physical injury. However, the growth of negligence and, more recently, the creation of statutory schemes to compensate victims of crimes against the person means that trespass is now much less often used for this purpose. In recent years, its main use has been in cases where someone has not been physically hurt, but has suffered some form of interference with their freedom of movement, or some unwanted contact; the most common examples are actions against the police by people who have been wrongly detained or mishandled during an arrest. However, as we will see later in this chapter, a change in the limitation period for trespass against the person has led to a new use of claims for trespass against the person, by adult victims of abuse that happened when they were children.

There are three types of trespass to the person: assault, battery and false imprisonment. In this section, we look at each of these in turn, followed by the defences available, which apply to all three. At the end of the chapter, we look at two related torts: the tort in **Wilkinson** *v* **Downton**, and the statutory tort of harassment.

Assault

In everyday language, to assault someone means to use physical violence against them, for example by hitting them. In tort law, however, the name given to this kind of behaviour is battery, which is discussed below. Assault in tort law is defined as an act which causes the claimant reasonably to apprehend that immediate physical violence will be used on him or her; in other words, you may commit assault if you do something that gives someone else reasonable cause to think you are about to use physical violence against them.

There are therefore two key elements to the tort:

- The defendant must act.
- The effect of the action must be a reasonable expectation of immediate physical violence.

Note that there is no requirement for the claimant to be caused any actual damage by the defendant. Assault, like all forms of trespass, is actionable *per se*.

The defendant's action

Obvious examples of actions that could amount to assault would be pointing a gun at someone, raising your fist to them, or picking up a rock as if to throw it at them. What about making threats in words, rather than actions? In the past, it was thought that there had to be some physical movement by the defendant, but it now appears that threatening words may be enough. The question has not been tested in a tort case, but the criminal offence of assault is very similar in definition to the tort, and in the criminal case of **R** *v* **Costanza** (1997) it was held that threats made by a stalker could be criminal assault, while in **R** *v* **Ireland** (1998), the House of Lords said that in the right circumstances even silence could be enough. The case concerned a defendant who had made silent malicious phone calls, and, as Lord Steyn pointed out, this could easily make a victim fear that the caller was about to appear at the door and commit violence against them. As the crime and the tort are so similar, most commentators believe that if the question were tested in a civil case the same rules would apply.

In some cases, a threatening act which would normally amount to an assault can be prevented from being one by the words which are spoken at the same time. In the old case of **Turberville** *v* **Savage** (1669), the claimant and the defendant had been arguing, and the defendant reached for his sword, and told the claimant: 'If it were not assize time, I would not take such language from you.' Assizes were travelling courts, so what the defendant was saying was that, with the judge in town, he would not take the risk of using his sword against the claimant. As this clearly meant that, despite the threatening gesture, the claimant was in no immediate danger, there was no assault. A more modern example might be raising your fist at someone while saying, 'I'd like to punch you, but you're not worth going to prison for.'

The effect of the action

The threatening act or words must be of a kind that could give the claimant a reasonable expectation that the defendant is going to use violence against them at that time. The claimant does not have to prove that he or she was actually afraid of violence, only that it was reasonable for them to expect that it was about to happen. In order for the belief to be reasonable, it must be (or appear to be) possible for the defendant to carry out the threat there and then. So, for example, it will usually be an assault to raise your fist at someone who is standing right in front of you, but not to do it from a train as it speeds past someone standing by the track, nor to do it from the window of a police van if you are in custody.

Of course, the latter two actions might well be taken to mean 'I'll get you later', but the case of **Thomas** *v* **National Union of Mineworkers** (1985) establishes that this would not be sufficient for assault. The case arose from the 1984 miners' strike, and the claimant was a miner who had refused to join his colleagues in the strike. He was among a group of such workers who were brought to the mine each day by special bus, so that they did not have to walk through the groups of striking miners who stood on the picket line outside. As the bus drove through, the strikers made violent gestures at those inside it, but the court held that those actions could not amount to assault. The pickets were held back by a police cordon, and the claimant was safe inside the bus; he had no reason to believe that immediate physical force could be used against him.

On the other hand, there may be an assault where the defendant's conduct gives the claimant good reason to expect immediate physical violence, but in fact the danger does not exist. For example, if you point a gun at someone and you know it is unloaded but they do not, you may still be liable for assault because it is reasonable for the claimant to expect immediate physical violence in that situation. This would be not be the case, however, if the claimant also knew the gun was unloaded.

Assault without battery

In practice, assault and battery often occur together, with the assault closely followed by the battery, but each is actionable in tort even if it occurs without the other. This means that if a situation is such that immediate physical violence clearly could be expected, there may be an assault, even though in fact the violence is prevented or for some other reason does not take place. This was the case in **Stephens** *v* **Myers** (1830), which arose from a parish meeting at which the Christian spirit was decidedly thin on the ground. The claimant was chairing the meeting when the defendant, who was sitting six or seven places away, started shouting. A majority of the members voted to have him sent out, at which point he came towards the claimant with a clenched fist. He was held back by the churchwarden, but was nevertheless liable for assault.

Battery

Battery is traditionally defined as the intentional and direct application of force to another person. There are therefore three elements to consider:

- Force
- Direct application
- Intent.

In addition, the courts have tended to add an extra element in an attempt to distinguish unacceptable physical contact from that which is merely part of everyday life. In some cases this has been described as 'hostility'; in others, it is addressed as an issue of consent, which is a defence to trespass to the person.

Like assault, battery is actionable *per se*, so the claimant does not have to show that they were caused any injury or damage. Unwanted contact or touching is enough.

Force

In this tort, any physical contact with a person's body or the clothes they are wearing can be sufficient to amount to force; there is no requirement for violence or physical harm. This means that in the right (or perhaps more accurately, wrong) circumstances, a kiss can be a battery, as can giving someone medical treatment that is designed to save their life. The essence of the tort is a belief that we all have a fundamental right to 'bodily integrity' or, to put it more simply, to be 'let alone' by others.

Direct application

Battery only applies to force that is direct. This is quite a difficult concept to explain and the courts have sometimes struggled with it, but an example that illustrates the basic idea is that hitting someone with a log or throwing a log at them would both be examples of direct force, whereas leaving a log on the floor for someone to trip over would be indirect. Similarly, holding someone so that they cannot move could be a battery, but standing in their way so they cannot get past would not.

Intent

Key Case **Letang *v* Cooper (1965)**

The defendant must intend to apply force; it was made clear in **Letang *v* Cooper** (1965) that doing so negligently was not a trespass. The claimant was sunbathing on a piece of grass outside a hotel, near to where cars were parked. The defendant was moving his car, and ran over the claimant's legs. He did not mean to do so, but the claimant argued that he did not take reasonable care to avoid her. The court held that in these circumstances the proper action was negligence, not trespass.

Legal Principle
Trespass to the person requires an intentional act.

The defendant need not intend to apply force to the claimant, as long as they intend to apply it to someone, and, as a result, it is applied to the claimant. This was the case in **Livingstone *v* Ministry of Defence** (1984), where the claimant successfully sued for battery after being hit by a bullet that was aimed at someone else.

Where a battery causes the claimant harm, the defendant must intend the application of force, but need not intend the harm, because the tort is actionable *per se*.

An extra element?

From the paragraphs above, you will realise that an enormous amount of perfectly ordinary everyday behaviour would appear to fit the definition of battery: jostling someone as you get on a train; touching someone's arm to get their attention; or putting an arm round someone to comfort them, for example. Most of us would agree that these forms of contact are usually acceptable, whereas punching someone or shooting at them is usually not. In between, however, there are areas where two parties may disagree on what is and is not acceptable: the uninvited kiss at the office party may seem like a friendly gesture to the person giving it, but an unwanted intrusion to the person receiving it, for example. Equally, most of us would want the right to prevent doctors from giving us medical treatment we did not want, even if they believed it was in our best interests.

For this reason, the courts have tried to pin down what it is that decides whether a particular application of direct force is a battery, or normal everyday contact. In early cases, it was suggested that jostling in a crowd and similar types of contact were not trespass because each of us gives implied consent to that kind of contact when we go about life in places where there are other people. However, in **Wilson *v* Pringle** (1987), the Court of Appeal said the extra element was 'hostility'. Both defendant and claimant were schoolboys, and the claim arose from an incident where the defendant jumped at the claimant to pull his schoolbag off his shoulder, which made the claimant fall and break his leg. The defendant argued that the incident was just the kind of playing about that is normal among boys (and therefore comparable to jostling on a train, for example), and the Court of Appeal held that whether it amounted to a battery depended on whether there was an element of hostility.

In normal language, we would take this to mean whether the defendant had some kind of aggressive or harmful intent, which might have been quite a useful definition, but the court went on to say that, by hostility, they did not actually mean ill-will. What they did mean was rather less clear. Most recently, in **Re F; F** *v* **West Berkshire Health Authority** (1990) Lord Goff dismissed both the 'implied consent' argument, and the requirement for hostility, which he said was too restrictive for a tort which was supposed to protect against any unlawful interference with bodily integrity. Lord Goff's view has since been backed up in other cases, notably **T** *v* **T** (1988), **R** *v* **Brown** (1994) and **R** *v* **Broadmoor Special Hospital** (1997), and most commentators now believe that hostility is not a required element. Where it exists, however, it is likely to be evidence of lack of consent, and so can be useful in that way.

In **Re F**, Lord Goff said that cases where direct physical contact was not to be considered trespass were best viewed as 'falling within a general exception embracing all physical contact which is generally acceptable in the ordinary conduct of everyday life'. This would seem to leave us back where we started, but remember that in a law exam you are not expected to know things that the courts themselves seem unable to get to grips with, as long as you can show that you know the uncertainty exists, and why it is important.

Table 14.1 Battery compared with negligence that causes personal injury

	Negligence	Battery
Type of action	Can be indirect, e.g. leaving a brick for someone to trip over	Must be direct, e.g. throwing a brick at someone, or hitting them
State of mind	Failing to take reasonable care to prevent foreseeable harm	Acting intentionally
Damage required	Must cause actual harm or damage	Actionable *per se*, so touching can be enough

False imprisonment

False imprisonment is defined as depriving the claimant of freedom of movement, without a lawful justification for doing so. The elements of the tort are:

- There must be an imprisonment.
- The imprisonment must be unlawful.

Imprisonment

The name of the tort is slightly misleading here, as 'imprisonment' means more than just locking someone in a room or building. It covers any restraint on freedom of movement, even for a short time, and can take place outdoors as well as in. In **Austin and another** *v* **Metropolitan Police Commissioner** (2005), the case arose from a demonstration which took place in London, where the police surrounded a section of the crowd in Oxford Circus, and prevented them from moving from the area for seven hours. Some members of the crowd sued, and it was accepted that this situation was a case of false imprisonment (though the police escaped liability as they were found to have the defence of necessity).

There must, however, be complete restraint; it is not sufficient to prevent someone using a particular route if they still have another open to them. In **Bird** *v* **Jones** (1845), a boat race was to be run on the Thames, and the defendants fenced off part of the footway on Hammersmith Bridge to provide a viewing point, charging for admission. The claimant was in the habit of walking along the footpath, and, insisting on his right to do so as usual, climbed into the enclosure without paying. The defendants refused to let him walk across the enclosure and out the other side, and said he could go out the way he came in, cross the road and walk past on the opposite side. Because this alternative route was available, they were not liable for false imprisonment. This would probably only apply, however, where it was reasonable to expect the claimant to use the alternative route, and not, for example, where the only other route was dangerous in some way.

The claimant need not actually make an attempt to leave; in **Grainger** *v* **Hill** (1838) it was held that there could be false imprisonment where the claimant was too ill to leave even if he had been allowed to. Nor, in fact, need the claimant even know that they are being prevented from leaving. In **Meering** *v* **Grahame-White Aviation Co Ltd** (1920), the claimant was an employee of the defendants, who suspected him of stealing paint. He was not told of their suspicions, but was asked to go with two police officers to the company's office. Without his knowledge, the officers stayed outside while he was questioned. The claimant sued for false imprisonment, and the defendants claimed that this could not apply because, as far as he knew, he was free to leave at any time, and he had merely chosen not to. The Court of Appeal disagreed. It said that as soon as the police were involved, the claimant was no longer free, and the fact that he did not know this was irrelevant. In fact, they said, the tort could be committed even when a claimant was asleep throughout, or was drunk or unconscious. This approach was confirmed by the House of Lords in **Murray** *v* **Ministry of Defence** (1988), though the court pointed out that where someone was unaware of being detained and suffered no harm as a result, only nominal damages (see p. 408) would usually be awarded.

By contrast, in **R** *v* **Bournewood** (1999), the claimant had a mental disorder which made him incapable of consent. The court held that there was no imprisonment when he was admitted to an unlocked ward, even though he was heavily sedated and the hospital gave evidence that if he had tried to leave they would have sought to use powers under the Mental Health Act to keep him there. In that situation the imprisonment had not actually happened; the fact that it could have happened if he tried to leave was not enough.

Conditional detention

It is not necessarily false imprisonment to impose a reasonable condition on someone before you allow them to leave. In **Robinson** *v* **Balmain Ferry Co** (1910), the claimant paid a penny to cross a river on one of the defendant's ferries. He entered the wharf, but realised he had just missed a ferry, and it was 20 minutes until the next one. He decided not to wait, but a notice on the wall stated that there was a one penny exit charge from the wharf. The defendants would not let him out until he paid this, but the court held that this was not false imprisonment. The charge was reasonable, and the claimant had entered a contract to leave the wharf by another route. One implication of this decision for modern life is that it would seem a bus passenger could not sue for false imprisonment if the driver refused to let them off before a scheduled stop.

However, a contrasting case is **Sunbolf** *v* **Alford** (1838), where an innkeeper was found liable for false imprisonment after he locked up a customer for not paying their bill. The distinction would appear to be that in **Robinson** the condition was considered reasonable because the claimant also had the choice of waiting for the next ferry if he did not want to pay the exit fee.

Cause of the imprisonment

The imprisonment must be caused by a deliberate act, and not just by carelessness. In **Sayers** *v* **Harlow Urban District Council** (1958), the claimant was trapped in a toilet cubicle by a defective lock, and injured herself trying to escape. She sued for false imprisonment, but the court found that there was no liability because there was no deliberate act which had caused her to be trapped (the council were, however, liable in negligence).

In **Iqbal** *v* **Prison Officers Association** (2009), the Court of Appeal suggested that liability for false imprisonment would only apply where the imprisonment was caused by the defendant's act, and not where it was caused by an omission to act. The case was brought by a prisoner against prison officers, who had gone on strike. Because of the strike, he was locked in his cell all day, rather than being allowed out into the common areas of the prison for three hours in the morning and two in the evening, which was the usual practice. He claimed that this amounted to false imprisonment. The Court of Appeal said that this claim offended against the general principle that there is no liability in tort for a failure to act, unless there is a specific duty to act. The prison officers had a duty to comply with their employment contracts, but this duty was owed to the prison service, not to prisoners. They had not done any act which had caused his false imprisonment, but had merely omitted to do their jobs. This in itself had not caused the claimant to be stuck in his cell; the cause of that was the prison governor's decision not to let prisoners out of their cells while there were insufficient staff due to the strike. However, Lord Justice Sullivan gave a dissenting judgment which said that the prison officers' behaviour could not reasonably be described as a 'mere omission' and that it was clear that their actions caused the governor's decision to keep the prisoners in their cells, and that the officers were aware that this would happen. There are clearly strong policy elements involved in a case like this, and it seems unlikely that it would form authority for a principle that omissions could never result in liability for false imprisonment.

Unlawfulness

The imprisonment must be unlawful, so a criminal who is lawfully convicted and kept in prison as decreed by a court has no case against the prison service for false imprisonment. However, if that same prisoner were to be trapped in his or her cell by another prisoner, they may have a claim against that person.

Where a person is carrying out a lawful arrest, no false imprisonment is committed, even if the person arrested has done nothing wrong. This applies whether the claimant is a police officer or an ordinary citizen. In order for an arrest to be lawful, the person making the arrest must follow the procedure set down by law, most of which is set out in the Police and Criminal Evidence Act 1984 and the Serious Organised Crime and Police Act 2005. These rules are beyond the scope of this book, but can be found in the book *English Legal System*, by the same authors.

The mental element

Both assault and battery require intention on the part of the defendant, but the case of **R** *v* **Governor of Brockhill Prison** (2000) makes it clear that false imprisonment is a tort of strict liability, which means that someone can be liable even though they could not have acted in any other way. The claimant had been convicted of a number of offences, and was sentenced to different lengths of time in prison for them. The sentences were to run concurrently (meaning at the same time, rather than one after the other), which meant that she should have spent no longer in prison than the longest sentence.

She had already spent time on remand for some of the offences, so the calculation of how long she should be in prison after the sentencing was a complex one. In working it out, the prison governor used rules set down in case law, but these were rules later declared to be wrong by the Divisional Court. That decision meant that the time the claimant was supposed to spend in prison was too long.

The claimant then sued for false imprisonment, arguing that she had been detained for longer than was lawful (and that therefore she was falsely imprisoned for all the days she was in prison after she should, by her calculations, have been released). The House of Lords accepted that the prison governor had been following rules which at the time were thought to represent the law, and that he had no choice but to do so. However, they held that even so he was liable because strict liability applied.

Brockhill was distinguished, however, in the apparently similar case of **Quinland** *v* **Governor of HM Prison Belmarsh** (2002). Here, the claimant had been convicted of a number of offences, and the total of the sentences imposed for them was two years and three months. However, the judge miscalculated, and said it was two years and six months. The mistake was soon spotted, but delays in the process of getting it officially corrected meant that by the time that was done the claimant had already served six weeks more than he should have done. He sued the governors of the prison, arguing that he had been falsely imprisoned for those six weeks, but the claim failed. The Court of Appeal said that the governors could not be liable because they had not made the miscalculation and they had no authority to disobey the order of the court.

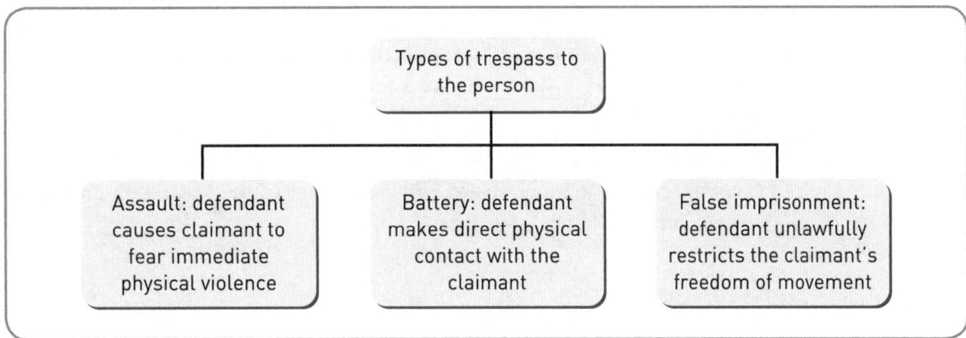

Figure 14.1 Trespass to the person

Defences

The defences which may apply in cases of trespass to the person are:

- *Volenti*, or consent
- Self-defence
- Contributory negligence
- Statutory authority
- Inevitable accident
- Ejection of a trespasser
- Parental authority.

Volenti (consent)

If the claimant agrees to what the defendant does, there is no liability for trespass. In some circumstances, consent may be given explicitly, as, for example, when a patient signs a form agreeing to have an operation. More often, however, it will be implied by behaviour: if you go into a hairdresser's and sit down in the chair, for example, you are signalling that you consent for the stylist to touch you in the process of doing your hair. Similarly, someone who takes part in sports or games is giving implied consent to the kind of physical contact that is within the rules of that sport, so if you enter a boxing match you cannot sue for battery just because your opponent hits you, even though you did not actually say that they could.

In **Herd** *v* **Weardale Steel Coke and Coal Co** (1915), a miner was part-way through a shift when he was asked to do some work he considered dangerous. He refused, and asked to be taken back to the surface, but was kept waiting for 20 minutes. He sued for false imprisonment, but the claim was refused on the grounds that he had given implied consent to stay underground for the length of the shift.

Consent only applies to the specific act for which permission is given. In **Nash** *v* **Sheen** (1953), the claimant asked her hairdresser for a perm, but the hairdresser applied a colourant, which caused a skin complaint. This was held to be a battery because the claimant had only consented to a perm. Note that the issue here is not the damage done: that was the reason why the claimant sued, but not the reason why she won. If the hairdresser had applied a perm as requested, and it had caused the skin complaint, the claimant would have had no case because she had consented to a perm. Equally, if the hairdresser had applied the colourant and not caused any problem, the claimant would still technically have had a claim because the hairdresser had applied direct force to which she had not consented, and there is no requirement for damage to be caused in trespass.

In sports, the general rule is that players are deemed to have consented to any activity that is within the accepted rules of the game, but not to any trespass (usually battery) that occurs as a result of behaviour outside the rules. So, to give an extreme example, a contestant in a boxing match cannot sue for a punch that is within the rules of the sport, but could sue if their opponent were to pull out a knife and stab them.

Self-defence

Under common law, a person is protected by this defence when they commit a trespass against the person as a result of using reasonable force which they honestly and reasonably believe is necessary to protect themselves or someone else, or property. What degree of force is 'reasonable' will depend on the situation, but the basic principle is that the amount and type of force must be balanced against the need for protection. So, for example, a degree of force which might be considered reasonable in protecting a person could be considered unreasonable if used merely to protect property. This principle was applied in **Lane** *v* **Holloway** (1968), which concerned a dispute between neighbours. The claimant had been drinking, and got into an argument with the defendant's wife, during which he called her a 'monkey-faced tart'. Hearing this, the defendant came out and said he wanted to see the claimant alone. Believing he was about to be hit, the claimant smacked the defendant on the shoulder. The defendant responded by punching him in the eye, causing a wound which needed 19 stitches. The claimant sued for battery. The court accepted that the defendant had reasonable grounds to believe he needed to defend himself, but said that his blow was out of proportion to the danger, so he was not covered by self-defence.

A similar defence exists in the criminal law, but there the defence will apply if the defendant honestly believes the force was necessary, even if there are no objective reasonable grounds for that belief. In **Ashley** *v* **Chief Constable of Sussex Police** (2008), the House of Lords confirmed that the defence in civil law is different, and the defendant must show reasonable grounds for their belief that force was necessary. The claimant was shot dead by a police officer during a drugs raid on his home in the early hours of the morning. After police entered the flat, they went into a bedroom, where Mr Ashley and his girlfriend had been asleep. The girlfriend had been woken by the noise of the police entering the front door, and had woken up Mr Ashley, and by the time the police came into the bedroom, he had got up and was standing by the bed. There was no light on in the room. The police argued that the officer who shot him was acting in self-defence, because he reasonably believed that he might be at risk from Mr Ashley, even though, as it turned out, Mr Ashley was not armed. This would have been enough to give him a defence under criminal law, but the House of Lords held that, in civil law, it was not enough simply to honestly believe there was a danger; there had to be reasonable grounds for such a belief. A related defence is contained in s. 329 of the Criminal Justice Act 2003, which provides that a person who is convicted of an imprisonable offence can only sue for trespass against the person relating to the same incident where the force used is 'grossly disproportionate' given the circumstances. This provision was introduced partly in response to claims that householders were afraid to tackle burglars in case they were sued afterwards.

Contributory negligence

The normal rules on contributory negligence apply in cases of trespass to the person (see Chapter 3).

Statutory authority

There are a number of statutes which authorise trespass to the person in particular circumstances. One of the most important is the Criminal Law Act 1967, which in s. 3(1) provides that no trespass to the person is committed when a reasonable amount of force is used to lawfully arrest a person, prevent a crime or assist in the lawful detention of a person unlawfully at large (such as an escaped prisoner). A sentence of imprisonment passed by a court provides a complete defence to an action for false imprisonment.

Statutes also authorise certain medical examinations and tests, such as the breathalyser test under the Road Traffic Act 1988, and blood tests under the Family Law Reform Act 1969. If taken without consent, any of these tests would normally amount to battery, but statutory authority provides a defence.

Inevitable accident

A defendant will not be liable in trespass to the person for an event over which they had no control, and could not have avoided by using even the greatest care and skill. In **Stanley** *v* **Powell** (1891), the defendant was part of a shooting party, and the claimant was employed to carry their cartridges. The defendant fired a shot in the usual way but, through no fault of his own, the bullet ricocheted off a tree and injured the claimant. It was held that the injury was an inevitable accident and the defendant was not liable.

Ejection of a trespasser

An occupier of land, or anyone with the authority of the occupier, may use reasonable force to prevent a trespasser from entering, or, after entry, to control their movements or eject them.

Before an ejection will be justified, the trespasser must have been requested to leave, and given a chance to do so peaceably.

Limitation periods

Both trespass to the person and negligence can result in personal injury, but, until recently, they were subject to completely different limitation periods. Negligence actions for personal injury were covered by s. 11 of the Limitation Act 1980, which provides for a three-year limitation period, but allows the courts to use their discretion to extend this period in suitable cases (see p. 135). Claims for personal injury caused by trespass to the person, on the other hand, were covered by s. 2 of the Limitation Act, which provided a non-extendable limitation period of six years. This difference was criticised by the Law Commission in 2001, on the grounds that it made no sense to have such different limitation periods for what could be the same kind of injury, depending on whether it was caused by an intentional act, or by negligence.

In more practical terms, the limitation period for trespass caused particular problems in cases of sexual assault, which often took place when the victim was young, and where it might take many more years than six for the victim to realise the damage that had been done, and summon the courage to sue the person who assaulted them. This was raised in the case of **Stubbings** *v* **Webb** (1993), brought by a woman who had been sexually abused 20 years earlier by her father and brother, but the House of Lords at that time insisted that the limitation period for assault could not be extended.

Key Case A *v* Hoare and others (2008)

However, the issue was raised again in **A** *v* **Hoare and others** (2008), in which six claimants all sought to sue for unrelated incidents of sexual assault. One of the claimants, whose case was widely reported in the press, was suing a rapist, Iorworth Hoare, who was serving a prison sentence for the rape when he won £7 million on the National Lottery. He had not been worth suing at the time of the rape because he had few financial assets, but the lottery win clearly changed that.

The House of Lords decided to exercise its power under the 1966 Practice Statement to depart from its own previous decision, and overruled **Stubbings**. The result is that cases of personal injury caused by trespass to the person are now subject to the same three-year limitation period as negligence claims, and this can be extended at the courts' discretion.

Legal Principle

Cases of personal injury caused by trespass to the person are now covered by s. 11 of the Limitation Act 1980, which provides for a three-year limitation period, which can be extended at the courts' discretion.

Topical issue

Trespass to the person and child abuse cases

The **Hoare** case was widely reported in the press because there had already been an outcry when the defendant, Iorworth Hoare, won £7 million on the National Lottery after buying a ticket when on day release from a prison sentence for attempted rape. However, very few newspapers reported the real legal significance of the case, which was much better represented by the other four cases heard alongside the claim against Hoare. These all involved claims of sexual abuse which had taken place when the (now adult) claimants were children, and they highlighted what had increasingly been seen as a problem with the limitation periods for trespass. As children, the victims had kept silent about what had happened to them, or had not been believed if they did try to expose their abusers. The abuse caused psychiatric problems which lasted into their adult life, but it was not until they got treatment for those problems that they were made aware of the connection between the problems and the abuse, and realised they might have a civil case against the abuser. Where the claimant was a child at the time of the tort, the Limitation Act provides that limitation periods do not begin to run until they are 18 but, even so, the victims – like many other adults who were abused as children – were outside the limitation period by the time they realised they might have a claim and/or summoned up courage to go to court.

In recent years, solicitors had begun to see increasing numbers of people in this situation. Many of the claims involved abuse which had taken place in care homes or schools, and in some cases, lawyers were able to frame the cases as breaches of duty by the authorities running the homes or schools, and sue in negligence. This meant they could ask the courts to use their discretion to extend the limitation period. But to prove such a case in negligence, they essentially had to show that the authority's entire system was at fault, which required a substantial amount of investigation into how the relevant authority had been working decades earlier. And at the same time, very similar cases, involving exactly the same sort of damage, but whose facts could not be squeezed into a negligence claim, were stuck outside the time limits for trespass.

A striking example of how illogical this situation was came in the case of **S** *v* **W** (1995), where a woman who had been abused by her father sued both him for the abuse, and her mother for failing to prevent it. The abuse had happened many years before, but because her claim against her mother was in negligence, the court used its discretion and the claim succeeded. Yet the claim against her father, who actually carried out the abuse, had to be in trespass, so it was ruled out of time.

This situation was widely considered to be unsatisfactory and unfair on claimants, and it is in these sorts of cases that the decision in **Hoare** has really made a difference. A solicitor for one of the child abuse claimants in **Hoare** estimated that around 6,000 cases had been awaiting the result of **Hoare** and could now go ahead, and that at least the same number of victims might now be encouraged to come forward.

Other protections from physical harm

There are two further torts concerned with causing intentional harm to the person, which are usually discussed alongside trespass to the person, even though they differ from it in important respects. The first is a common law tort, defined in the case of **Wilkinson** *v* **Downton**, and the second is the statutory tort of harassment created in the Protection from Harassment Act 1997, which we discuss later on in this chapter.

The tort in Wilkinson *v* Downton

In the case of **Wilkinson** *v* **Downton** (1897), the defendant, who clearly had a dubious sense of humour, had played what she saw as a practical joke on the claimant, by telling her that her husband had been seriously injured in an accident. The claimant believed her and suffered serious psychiatric illness as a result. The defendant could not be liable for trespass to the person, as there was no direct interference with the claimant's person. However, the court found that she was nevertheless liable in tort. The judge explained the basis for the ruling as:

> The defendant has . . . wilfully done an act calculated to cause physical harm to the plaintiff [claimant] . . . and has in fact thereby caused physical harm to her. That proposition, without more, appears to me to state a good cause of action, there being no justification for the alleged act.

Until recently, the ruling had only been followed in one other English case, **Janvier** *v* **Sweeney** (1919). The claimant was engaged to a German, and the defendants threatened that, unless she stole a particular letter from her employer and gave it to them, they would tell the authorities that her fiancé was a spy. Although that was not true, the political climate at the time, just after the end of the First World War, made this a frightening threat, and she suffered a nervous illness as a result. The Court of Appeal held that the defendants' behaviour fell within the tort explained in **Wilkinson** *v* **Downton**.

Since then, although the rule in **Wilkinson** had been mentioned in some modern cases, it was widely believed that it had effectively become obsolete, and that trespass, negligence and, more recently, the Protection from Harassment Act 1997 (see below) had replaced it. However, the tort resurfaced in the case of **C** *v* **D** (2006). Here the headmaster of a school had committed incidents of sexual abuse against a pupil which did not involve touching, and therefore could not be trespass. One of the incidents had caused the pupil psychiatric injury, and the school (which was vicariously liable for the headmaster's acts) was successfully sued for the tort in **Wilkinson** *v* **Downton**.

Elements of the tort

Because of the lack of decided cases, it is not easy to establish the boundaries of liability for the tort in **Wilkinson** *v* **Downton**. We do know from the definition in **Wilkinson** that there must be harm to the claimant, so the tort is not actionable *per se*, but the issues open to question concern the defendant's behaviour, the kind of harm caused to the claimant, and the mental state of the defendant.

The defendant's behaviour

As far as the first issue, the defendant's behaviour, is concerned, we know from the two decided cases that threats and false statements fall within the tort. However, in principle there seems to be no reason why other acts which are calculated to cause physical harm and do cause such harm should not be covered, such as perhaps shocking the claimant with a loud noise, or even intentionally infecting them with a contagious disease (but remember that a direct act which causes harm would be more likely to be sued as a trespass). Similarly, a true statement rather than a false one might be sufficient, so long as the person making it intended to harm the claimant by doing so.

Type of harm

In **Wong** *v* **Parkside Health NHS Trust** (2003), it was stated that the required damage for liability under **Wilkinson** *v* **Downton** was 'physical harm or recognised psychiatric illness' and not merely 'distress, inconvenience or discomfort'. The case concerned an employee who said she had been subjected to a sustained campaign of harassment by three fellow employees. This was followed in **Wainwright** *v* **Home Office** (2002). Here the claimants were a mother who had gone to visit her son, Patrick, in prison, taking with her another son, Alan, who had some learning difficulties. The prison officers subjected Mrs Wainwright and Alan to an embarrassing and upsetting strip-search, which was said to be necessary in order to make sure they were not smuggling in drugs. As a result of the incident, Mrs Wainwright's existing depression was made worse, and Alan suffered post-traumatic stress disorder. The court accepted that this was damage within the definition of **Wilkinson** *v* **Downton**, though the claimants lost for other reasons (see below).

Case Navigator

What about other types of harm? In an Australian case, **Smith** *v* **Beaudesert Shire Council** (1966), an attempt was made to extend the tort to cover economic loss, but the House of Lords firmly ruled this out in **Lonrho Ltd** *v* **Shell Petroleum** (1982).

The mental element

The term generally used for the mental element in **Wilkinson** is that the behaviour must be 'intentional', but what does this mean? Does the defendant have to intend harm, or merely intend the behaviour which in fact causes harm? If viewed as normal everyday language, the phrase 'calculated to cause physical harm' used in **Wilkinson** suggests the former explanation, but the facts of the case lean more towards the latter. The question has now been addressed in **Wainwright**, where the Court of Appeal approved a definition provided by Hale LJ in **Wong**. Beginning from the standpoint that the defendant's conduct must have caused physical harm or recognised psychiatric illness, she said that:

> The conduct complained of has to be such that that degree of harm is sufficiently likely to result that the defendant cannot be heard to say that he did not 'mean' it to do so. He is taken to have meant it to do so by the combination of the likelihood of such harm being suffered as a result of his behaviour and his deliberately engaging in that behaviour.

The issue was re-examined in **C** *v* **D**, where Field J stated that there were three states of mind which could lead to liability: first, where the defendant's acts were 'calculated' to cause psychiatric harm, and done with the knowledge that such harm was the likely result; secondly, where psychiatric injury was so likely to result from the defendant's acts that they could not reasonably claim that they did not mean to cause the harm; and, thirdly, where the defendant was reckless as to whether psychiatric harm was caused by their acts. In **C** *v* **D**, the judge found that psychiatric injury was not foreseeable as a likely consequence of what the defendant did, but that he was reckless as to whether he caused psychiatric injury, and was therefore liable.

The Protection from Harassment Act 1997

This Act was passed following public concern over the problem of 'stalkers', after a number of much-publicised cases in which individuals became obsessed with an ex-girlfriend or -boyfriend, a celebrity or even a mere acquaintance, and subjected them to constant and often long-term harassment. It imposes both criminal and civil sanctions for 'harassment'. Civil remedies allowed under the Act include injunctions and damages; damages can be claimed for mental distress and even pure economic loss resulting from the harassment.

What is harassment?

The Act does not specifically define harassment, but says that it can include alarming someone or causing them distress, by conduct which can include mere speech. Section 1 states that the offence consists of pursuing a 'course of conduct' which amounts to harassment, and which the defendant knows or 'ought to know' amounts to harassment. The phrase 'ought to know' is explained as applying where a reasonable person, who knows what the defendant knows, would think the behaviour amounted to harassment. In **Trimingham *v* Associated Newspapers** (2012), it was held that, in deciding whether a defendant 'ought to know' that their behaviour amounts to harassment, it was relevant to look at what the defendant knows about the claimant's personality, and how likely they are to be caused distress by the behaviour. The claimant in the case was the partner of an MP, whose affair with him was known to have broken up his marriage. She complained that a series of articles in the *Daily Mail* which constantly referred to her as bisexual, and made disparaging remarks about her appearance and her past sex life, amounted to harassment. In deciding that they did not, the court took into account the claimant's 'robust personality', the fact that she had not claimed to be distressed about the reports of her breaking up the marriage, and the fact that she herself had on occasion sold stories about the personal lives of other people.

Some light on what will be considered a course of conduct amounting to harassment has come in two cases decided since the Act was passed. In **Pratt *v* DPP** (2001), the course of conduct complained of was by a husband to his wife, and covered two occasions: on the first, he had a row with his wife which ended with him throwing a mug of water at her. Three months later, he lost his temper and chased his wife through the house, shouting, swearing and repeatedly questioning her. He was convicted by magistrates of harassment, and appealed, on the grounds that this did not amount to a 'course of conduct'. The Court of Appeal held that it did – but only just. They said it was 'close to the borderline' and recommended that prosecuting authorities should be hesitant about a charge of harassment under the Act where the number of incidents complained of was small (even though the Act itself says that two occasions is sufficient). In **Singh *v* Bhakar** (2006), the claimant moved into her in-laws' house, after an arranged marriage. Her mother-in-law treated her like a slave, making her do housework until her hands became infected. She also restricted her contact with her own family, made her cut her hair, which was against her religious beliefs, and forced her to wear an amulet from another religion. After four months, the claimant left, by which time she was suffering from depression. She successfully sued for harassment.

In **Thomas *v* News Group Newspapers Ltd** (2001), the case arose from an incident involving a Somali asylum seeker who had called at a police station to ask for directions to an asylum centre in Croydon. The claimant, a clerk at the police station, overheard one of the police sergeants on the desk joking about the asylum seeker afterwards; she claimed he had said 'She found her way here 8,000 miles from Somalia, surely she can find her way back?' (which was denied by the sergeant, who said that he had in fact said 'She found her way here 8,000 miles from Somalia, surely she can find her way to Croydon?'). Ms Thomas felt that the remark was racist and made a complaint about it. As a result, the sergeant was demoted. The *Sun* newspaper got hold of the story, and ran a series of articles criticising the decision to demote the officer after what – the paper said – was a harmless joke that was not even heard by the asylum seeker. They identified the clerk by name, and pointed out that she was black. The clerk began receiving racist hate mail, which left her too frightened to go to work. She brought an action against the newspaper under the Protection from Harassment Act.

The paper applied to have the action struck out, but the Court of Appeal held that the claimant had an arguable case, and that the publication of articles in the press could amount to harassment. They acknowledged that it was necessary to take into account the right to freedom of expression under the ECHR, but said that this had to be balanced against the right to freedom from harassment. The 1997 Act, they said, allowed for this balance by providing that a course of conduct that amounted to harassment could be lawful if the defendant could show that the conduct was reasonable.

The court said that a press article would only amount to harassment if there were exceptional circumstances that justified legal sanctions, and an example of such exceptional circumstances was where the articles were calculated to incite racial hatred. It was arguable that this was the case here, given that the paper had described the claimant as 'a black clerk', which seemed to suggest they thought it was because of her own race that she had complained about the remarks made.

In **Howlett** *v* **Holding** (2006), the claimant had been a local councillor and, as part of her duties, had heard an application for planning permission from the defendant, which she opposed. The defendant was so angry that he subjected Ms Howlett to a campaign of victimisation, following her to shops and restaurants, and even flying aircraft over her home, with banners alleging that she was a thief and unfit to hold public office. Ms Howlett twice sued successfully for defamation over the banners, but the campaign continued, and so she sued for harassment. Mr Holding said that he was exercising his right to freedom of expression under Art. 10 of the European Convention on Human Rights, but the judge rejected this argument and granted an injunction against him.

In **Conn** *v* **Sunderland** (2007), the case concerned two incidents which happened in the workplace. In the first, the claimant's foreman lost his temper, and threatened to smash a window with his fist, and to report the claimant and two other men to the personnel department. Evidence was given that the other men present were not bothered by this. In the second incident, the foreman threatened to give the claimant 'a good hiding' and said he did not care if he got the sack as a result. The claimant sued their employer, as being vicariously liable for the foreman's actions, but his claim failed. The court said that when considering whether conduct could give rise to damages for harassment it was necessary to ask whether the conduct was serious enough to amount to the criminal offence of harassment under s. 2 of the Protection from Harassment Act 1997. The boundary, the court said, was that between behaviour which was unattractive or even unreasonable, but not serious enough to justify criminal sanctions, and behaviour which went beyond that and was oppressive and unacceptable. In this case, the first incident was not serious enough to warrant criminal sanctions, which left only one incident, and that was not enough for a course of conduct.

Scope of the Act

Two recent decisions have widened the scope of the tort under the Protection from Harassment Act 1997, creating two new areas in which it can be used. **Majrowski** *v* **Guy's** (2006) established that an employer can be vicariously liable when their employees are subject to harassment from bosses or colleagues. In many cases, this will be an easier claim to bring than a case for psychiatric injury caused by stress at work, which is subject to quite strict limits.

In **SmithKline Beecham plc and others** *v* **Avery and others** (2009), the court found that it was lawful to grant an injunction to prevent harassment to a company, rather than an individual. The case was brought by a pharmaceutical company, whose employees were being harassed by animal rights campaigners seeking to stop the company from conducting experiments on animals. Such companies are now able to get an injunction to keep the campaigners away from their sites.

Statutory harassment and Wilkinson *v* Downton

Clearly the statutory tort of harassment under the 1997 Act has considerable potential overlap with the tort in **Wilkinson** *v* **Downton**, which, along with the fact that **Wilkinson** is so rarely used, has led to some suggestions that it will now quietly wither away; Lord Hoffmann is one who has suggested that the 1997 Act means that there is no longer any need for the common law to develop in this area. However, it can also be argued the tort in **Wilkinson** still has a role to play in dealing with intentional, indirect harm which might not be covered by the term 'harassment' – an example being the conduct in **Wilkinson** itself, which, being limited to one occasion, would not amount to a 'course of conduct' as required by the Act, as well as the sexual assault in **C** *v* **D** (see p. 348).

Answering questions

Tom and Gary are neighbours, who do not get on. One night, they both arrive home at the same time, and there is only one parking space in their street. Tom quickly nips in and takes the space. Gary rushes up to him, waving his fist, and shouts 'I'm not going to thump you this time, because I don't want to miss the start of *Eastenders*, but if you take my space again, I'll make you sorry!' Tom, who has just been to get a takeaway, throws a handful of chips at Gary, and rushes indoors. The chips hit Gary in the face, but he is not hurt.

The next morning, Gary is working in his shed, when Tom climbs over the garden wall, and locks him in. Gary is listening to the radio, and doesn't hear the key turn. He is so engrossed in what he is doing that he does not even realise he is locked in until his wife, Valerie, comes to call him in for lunch, and unlocks the door. There is a window in the shed, which would have been large enough for Gary to escape through if he had broken it.

Valerie is very cross, and decides to go next door and tell Tom what she thinks of him. As she leaves the house, she slips on a banana skin that Tom has deliberately left on their doorstep, and hurts her ankle.

Advise Gary, Tom and Valerie as to any claims they may have in trespass.

Taking Tom first, the first potential claim he has is against Gary for assault, as Gary threatened him with violence. However, you need to consider the effect Gary's word might have on his potential liability; the case of **Turberville** is one to look at here.

Gary may, however, be able to sue Tom for false imprisonment, for the time that he was locked in the shed. In assessing this claim, you need to look at the cases on claimants who did not know they were imprisoned and also, given that there is a window, on situations where there is an alternative way to get out.

Then consider Tom: does he have a claim against Gary for throwing the chips at him? Remember that trespass to the person is actionable *per se*, so it does not matter that he was not injured. You will also need to consider whether Gary could plead self-defence.

Finally, does Valerie have a claim against Tom for leaving the banana skin where it was clear someone might slip on it. We know he has acted intentionally, but it would appear that she has no claim in trespass, because the force used was not direct. She may have a claim in negligence.

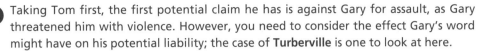

Summary of Chapter 14

There are three types of trespass to the person:

- Assault
- Battery
- False imprisonment.

Assault

Assault is defined as an act which causes the claimant reasonably to apprehend that immediate physical violence will be used on them.

- Words may be sufficient.
- It must be possible for the defendant to use immediate physical violence, but they need not actually use it.

Battery

Battery is the intentional and direct application of force to another person.

- Any direct physical contact can amount to force.
- The defendant must intend to apply force.
- The normal contact of everyday life is not a battery.

False imprisonment

False imprisonment is depriving the claimant of freedom of movement, without a lawful justification for doing so.

- Imprisonment covers any total restriction on freedom of movement, outside or in.
- There must be no reasonable means of escape.

- The claimant need not know their movement is restricted.
- Imposition of a reasonable condition for leaving is not imprisonment.
- The cause must be a deliberate act.
- The imprisonment must be unlawful.

The mental element

- Assault and battery require intention.
- False imprisonment is a tort of strict liability.

Defences

The defences which may apply are:

- *Volenti*, or consent
- Self-defence
- Contributory negligence
- Statutory authority
- Inevitable accident
- Ejection of a trespasser.

The role of trespass to the person

The tort has become less significant in practical terms, and now mainly arises in connection with actions for false imprisonment against the police.

Other protections from physical harm

*The tort in **Wilkinson** v **Downton***

This applies where the defendant 'willingly does an act calculated to cause physical harm' and harm is caused.

- Threats and false statements are sufficient for 'an act'.
- Only personal injury (including psychiatric) is covered.
- The mental element is intention, defined as:
  - where the defendant knew that injury was the likely result of their act;
  - where injury was so likely that the defendant could not reasonably claim they did not mean it to happen;
  - where the defendant was reckless as to whether psychiatric harm was caused.

The Protection from Harassment Act 1997

Creates a cause of action where the defendant pursues a course of conduct which amounts to harassment of the claimant.

The harassment must take place on at least two occasions.

Reading list

Text resources

Cane, P (2000) 'Mens rea in tort law' 4 *Oxford Journal of Legal Studies*, 533

Handford, P (1976) 'Tort liability for threatening or insulting words' 54 *Canadian Bar Review*' 563

Lunney, M (2002) 'Practical joking and its penalty: *Wilkinson* v *Downton* in context' 10 *Tort Law Review* 168

Marchant, S (2004) 'The right to treatment' 154 *New Law Journal* 1316

Prosser, W (1955) 'False imprisonment: consciousness of confinement' 55 *Columbia Law Review* 847

Trindade, F (1982) 'Intentional torts: some thoughts on assault and battery' 2 *Oxford Journal of Legal Studies* 211

Reading on the Internet

A *v* **Hoare** (2008) can be read at:
http://www.publications.parliament.uk/pa/ld200708/ldjudgmt/jd080130/hoare.pdf

The Protection from Harassment Act can be read at:
http://www.legislation.gov.uk/ukpga/1997/40/contents

Visit **www.mylawchamber.co.uk** to access tools to help you develop and test your knowledge of tort law, including interactive multiple choice questions, practice exam questions with guidance, weblinks, glossary flashcards, legal newsfeed and legal updates.

Use Case Navigator to read in full some of the key cases referenced in this chapter with commentary and questions:

Wainwright *v* **Home Office** (2002)

Chapter 15
Liability for animals

This chapter discusses:

- Liability under common law for damage done by animals
- Liability under the Animals Act 1971
- How the Act classifies different species
- Defences under the Act.

While most of the cases in this book concern damage done by people, it is equally possible for many forms of damage to be caused by animals: straying cattle might get into your garden, causing damage to your property, for example, while a dog could cause you personal injury. Since there is little point in suing a cocker spaniel, the law imposes liability for the damage caused by animals on their owners, or the person in control of them at the time the damage was done.

This liability is imposed in two different ways. The first is that damage caused by animals comes within the scope of several common law torts, and in these cases the normal rules associated with those torts apply, as we shall see below. The second is the Animals Act 1971, which provides specific statutory rules about damage caused by animals and is the main subject of this chapter.

Liability for animals at common law

In theory, almost any tort might be committed as a result of something done by an animal – the renowned tort academics Winfield and Jolowicz point out, for example, that a person could be liable in defamation for training a parrot to make defamatory remarks about someone in public. However, the torts most likely to be committed in connection with animals are negligence, nuisance, and trespass against the person.

Negligence

Aside from the specific forms of action provided in the Animals Act, negligence is the most likely form of tort claim for damage caused by animals. The normal rules of the tort apply, so, for example, the owner or controller of an animal will be liable for personal injury or property damage if it was reasonably foreseeable that the animal might cause that kind of damage. This was the case in **Draper** *v* **Hodder** (1972), where the claimant was a child who had been savaged by a pack of Jack Russell dogs from the premises next door. Although the dogs had never attacked anyone before, they did have a habit of running next door in a pack. The court held that as the owner was an experienced dog breeder, he should have known that Jack Russells as a breed had a tendency to attack moving persons or objects when they were travelling in a pack, and that as he did know that the dogs were in the habit of running next door, he should have fenced them in. It was therefore foreseeable that someone might be injured by the dogs.

Similarly, in **Pitcher** *v* **Martin** (1937), a dog owner was walking his dog on a long lead, and when the dog ran off, the claimant, who was walking nearby, got tangled in the lead and tripped, injuring herself. The dog owner was held to be negligent.

Nuisance

Animals can be a source of noise, smells and general disruption and, where this affects neighbouring land, there may be a cause of action in nuisance, subject to the normal rules of the tort. In **Leeman** *v* **Montagu** (1936), for example, the noise made by cockerels from about 2 a.m. every morning was held to be a nuisance, as was the smell of pigs in **Wheeler** *v* **J J Saunders** (1996).

Trespass to the person

As we saw in Chapter 14, trespass to the person includes both assault (meaning to put someone in fear of violence) and battery (which means to intentionally apply force to another person without their consent). Both of these can be committed using an animal: threatening someone with a snarling dog can lead to liability for assault just as threatening someone with a gun would, while inciting a dog to bite someone could constitute a battery. The normal rules and defences apply.

The Animals Act 1971

The Act divides animals into two different groups: dangerous species and non-dangerous species – although, as we shall see, these classifications do not necessarily correspond to what most of us would think of as dangerous or non-dangerous (camels, for example, are classified as dangerous and dogs as non-dangerous).

The two groups are subject to different rules under the Act: s. 2(1) governs dangerous animals, and s. 2(2) non-dangerous animals.

Dangerous animals

Section 6(2) of the Act defines dangerous species as:

(a) a species not commonly domesticated in the British Isles; and
(b) whose fully grown animals normally have such characteristics that they are likely, unless restrained, to cause severe damage or that any damage that they may cause is likely to be severe.

This category therefore covers animals which are not usually kept as pets or working animals in this country, so, as well as foreign animals such as lions and tigers, it includes wild animals that are native to this country, such as foxes and wildcats. The fact that an animal is commonly domesticated in other parts of the world is irrelevant: camels, for example, are widely domesticated in Arab countries, but under English law they still come under the category of dangerous animals.

Section 6(2)(b) also states that to be considered a dangerous animal, a species must either be likely to cause severe damage if not restrained (for example, a lion or tiger), or must be the kind of species that may be unlikely to cause damage, but, if they did, would probably cause serious damage. An example of this kind of species was given in **Behrens** *v* **Bertram Mills Circus** (1957), where the court held that although an elephant was not an aggressive or violent animal, and was therefore not likely to cause serious damage if unrestrained, its sheer size meant that if it did cause damage, the damage was likely to be serious.

The classification into dangerous or non-dangerous for the purposes of the Act applies to whole species, not individual animals. In **Behrens**, above, the owner of the elephant argued that his particular elephant was placid and 'no more dangerous than a cow', but the court held that an elephant was a dangerous species and therefore this particular elephant was covered by s. 2(1).

Liability for dangerous animals

Section 2(1) provides that:

> Where any damage is caused by an animal which belongs to a dangerous species, any person who is a keeper of the animal is liable for the damage, except as otherwise provided by this Act.

The reference to 'as otherwise provided' refers to the fact that the Act lays down three defences for keepers of wild animals (see below). However, if a defendant cannot claim one of these, liability is strict, which means that it does not matter whether the animal's keeper was at fault, or whether he or she did their best to prevent their damage; if they are the keeper of the animal that caused the damage, and they have no defence, they will be liable.

Section 6(3) specifies that a person will be considered to be the 'keeper' of a particular animal if:

(a) he owns the animal or has it in his possession; or
(b) he is the head of a household in which a member under the age of 16 owns the animal or has it in his possession.

Section 6(3)(b) covers cases where the animal is owned or kept by a child, and essentially makes their parent or guardian liable for the damage done.

Note that although the animal has to be one which makes it likely that the damage done will be severe, it is not necessary that the damage done is actually severe in order for liability to arise. It is therefore theoretically possible for someone to sue under the Act for merely trivial damage caused by an animal, though the fact that damages would tend to be low means this is unlikely in practice.

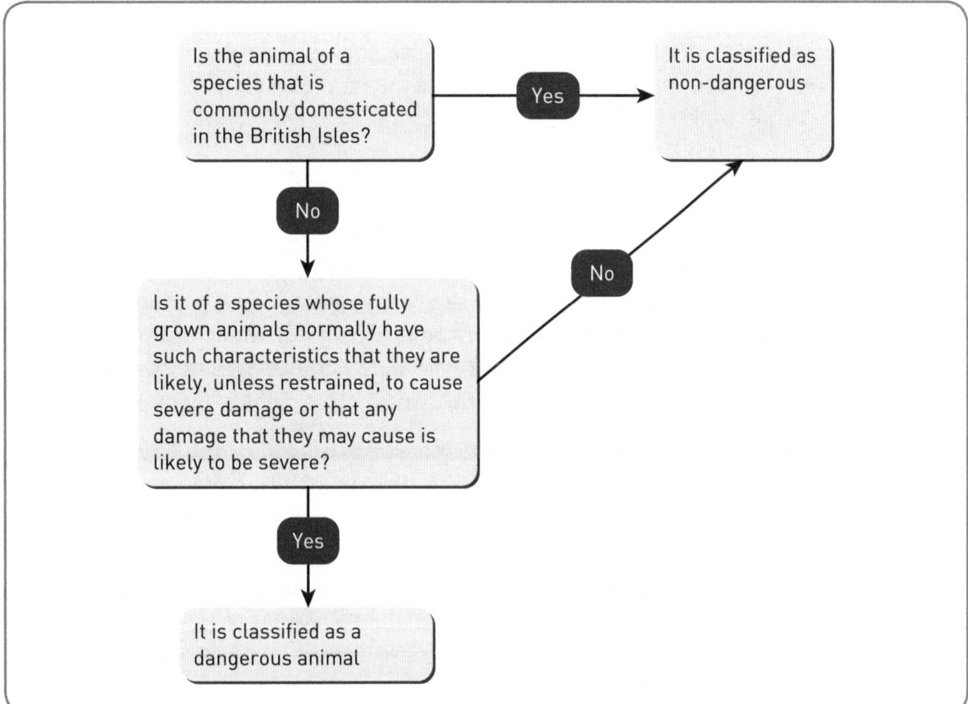

Figure 15.1 Dangerous and non-dangerous animals under the Animals Act 1971

Non-dangerous animals

All species which do not fall within the category of dangerous, as explained above, are classed as non-dangerous, and covered by the provisions of s. 2(2). Again, it is the species which is classified as dangerous, not the individual animal: damage or injury caused by a dog, for example, no matter how vicious, will always be judged under s. 2(2), because dogs are commonly domesticated in this country and therefore do not fit the legal definition of dangerous.

Liability for non-dangerous animals

Section 2(2) provides that the keeper of a non-dangerous animal will be liable for damage caused by it if each of the following three requirements is satisfied:

(a) the damage is of a kind which the animal, unless restrained, was likely to cause, or which, if caused by the animal, was likely to be severe; and
(b) the likelihood of the damage or of its being severe was due to characteristics of the animal which are not normally so found in animals of the same species or are not normally found except at particular times or in particular circumstances; and
(c) those characteristics were known to that keeper or were at any time known to a person who at that time had charge of the animal as the keeper's servant or, where that keeper is the head of a household, were known to another keeper of the animal who is a member of that household and under the age of 16.

Since all three of the requirements must be satisfied, it is sensible to work through them in turn when considering whether someone has incurred liability under the Act. As with s. 2(1), liability is strict – even if the animal's keeper did their best to prevent their damage, if they fall within the definition of liability, and have no defence, they will be liable. However, as we shall see, this part of the Act is worded in such a way as to attempt to restrict liability to situations where the owner/keeper could be expected to take more care.

Section 2(2)(a) requires that the damage caused has to be of a kind that that sort of animal was likely to cause, or, if the animal was not likely to cause that kind of damage, the damage that was caused was likely to be severe. In **Curtis** *v* **Betts** (1990), a bull mastiff attacked and injured the claimant when he went up to talk to it as it was being loaded into its owner's car to go off on a journey. Section 2(2)(a) was easily satisfied, as a bull mastiff is a big dog with a powerful bite. By contrast, in **Gloster** *v* **Chief Constable of Greater Manchester Police** (2000), a police dog attacked someone, but the court held that s. 2(2)(a) was not satisfied because, thanks to its training, it was not likely that this dog would cause damage if unrestrained.

Section 2(2)(b) provides two different branches of liability. The first ('characteristics of the animal which are not normally so found in animals of the same species') means that the animal concerned must have permanent or habitual characteristics which you would not usually expect in that sort of animal. In **Kite** *v* **Napp** (1982), a dog which habitually attacked people who were carrying handbags was held to fall within this category. The characteristic does not necessarily have to be a tendency to attack, however; it merely has to be a characteristic which is present in that particular animal and not normally in others of the same species, and which causes damage or injury. In **Wallace** *v* **Newton** (1982) the claimant was a groom, who was injured while looking after the defendant's horse. The horse was known to be nervous, and, while being loaded onto a trailer, it jumped forward and injured the claimant's arm. The court held that the horse did not need to have a tendency to attack people; s. 2(2)(b) was satisfied by the fact that the horse had a tendency to behave in a particular way when nervous, which was not found in most horses.

The second branch ('characteristics . . . which are not normally found except at particular times or in particular circumstances'), refers to the fact that it may be normal for a particular type of animal to behave in a dangerous way in certain situations, even if it is not normal for them to do so most of the time. An example would be that it is quite normal for a dog with puppies to attack anyone she thinks is threatening them, even though attacking people would not be normal behaviour for a dog at any other time.

The effect of s. 2(2)(b) was examined in **Curtis** *v* **Betts** (see above). The dog was not normally vicious, and had always been friendly with the young claimant, but was said to have attacked him because he approached it when it was being put into the owner's car. The dog saw this as its territory, and there was evidence that it was normal for such dogs to attack when defending their territory, though not at other times. The court held that the case came within s. 2(2)(b) because the behaviour was only normal in the particular circumstance of being in a situation where it felt compelled to defend its territory.

Key Case **Mirvahedy** *v* **Henley (2003)**

This approach was confirmed by the House of Lords in **Mirvahedy** *v* **Henley** (2003). The claimant in the case was seriously injured when his car collided with a horse owned by the defendants. The horse had been kept, with three others, in a field with an electric fence and a wooden fence. On the night in question, something (it was never discovered what) had frightened them, and they stampeded their way out of the field and ended up on the busy road where the accident happened. Evidence was given that although it was not generally normal for horses to behave in this way, it was normal for them to do so when they had been badly frightened. Therefore, the behaviour which caused the damage could be described as 'characteristics . . . which are not normally found except at particular times or in particular circumstances', falling within s. 2(2)(b). The defendants were therefore liable for the damage.

It was argued in **Mirvahedy** that s. 2(2)(b) should not apply, because it would be wrong to impose strict liability on an owner for behaviour which was quite normal; the Act, it was suggested, was only ever intended to impose strict liability where an animal had unusual characteristics that meant it was reasonable to expect that the owner would take care to restrain it. The House of Lords rejected this view, stating that s. 2(2)(b) also related to situations where an owner could be expected to take more care in ensuring that their animal did not cause damage or injury – if a dog owner knows that bitches with puppies are likely to bite, it is just as reasonable to expect them to take extra care when their dog has puppies, as it is to expect an owner of a dog known to be generally vicious to take extra care all the time.

Legal Principle

The keeper of an animal can be liable under the Animals Act for damage caused by characteristics of the animal only found in certain circumstances, even if those characteristics are normal for that species in those circumstances.

In **Welsh** *v* **Stokes** (2007), the Court of Appeal looked further at the issue of characteristics found in a species at certain times. The claimant in the case was a teenager who fell from a horse, after it reared up as she was riding along the road. The Court of Appeal held that any horse was capable of rearing up 'in certain situations if not handled properly' and that a characteristic like this, which was natural but might be unusual, could count as a characteristic which was 'normally found' in particular circumstances. They further held that the horse's owners would have known that horses in general could rear up in certain circumstances, and therefore they had the required knowledge to satisfy s. 2(2)(c), and were liable.

In **Clark** *v* **Bowlt** (2006), the Court of Appeal pointed out that there must be a link between the argument made under s. 2(2)(a), and that made under s. 2(2)(b). The case involved a horse, called Chance, which was being ridden along a public road. As the claimant drove slowly past in his car, the horse veered out from the verge; the rider could not control it, and it hit the claimant's car. At first instance, it was found that s. 2(2)(a) was satisfied because Chance weighed 600 lb, and so it was clear that if she caused damage, it was likely to be severe, while s. 2(2)(b) was satisfied because, in particular circumstances, horses had the characteristic of ignoring their rider and moving where they wanted to. The Court of Appeal rejected this view, stating that it was not possible to use one characteristic for the first test, and a different one for the second. If it was the weight of the horse that satisfied the test of whether damage was likely to be severe, then weight had to be the characteristic used for s. 2(2)(b) as well. As Chance was not abnormally heavy, and the weights of horses do not vary according to times or circumstances, the s. 2(2)(b) test was not satisfied. The claim therefore failed.

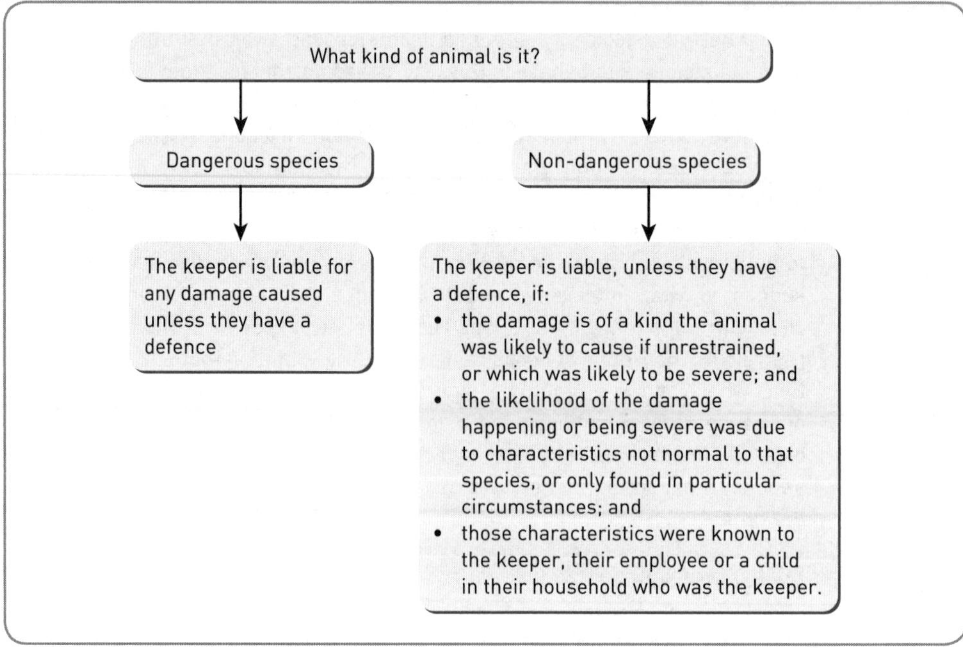

Figure 15.2 Liability under the Animals Act 1971

Section 2(2)(c) essentially means that the keeper of the animal will not be liable unless he or she was aware of the possibility that the animal might be dangerous, or unless an employee or a child for whom the keeper is responsible knew about this possibility of danger. Again, this is because the Act is only intended to impose strict liability in circumstances where it was reasonable to expect an owner to take extra care.

Defences

Section 5 of the Animals Act provides three defences, which can be used to escape liability for damage done by both dangerous and non-dangerous animals.

Section 5(1) states that a defendant will not be liable for damage done by an animal which was wholly the fault of the person who suffers it. In **Nelmes** *v* **Chief Constable of Avon and Somerset** (1993), the defence was held to apply where the claimant had kicked a dog which then bit him. Note that this section does not provide a defence where the claimant was only partly to blame for the damage (that is, it does not operate like the defence of contributory negligence, although it sounds similar).

Section 5(2) provides that the owner or keeper of an animal will not be liable for damage done by that animal if the person who suffers the damage voluntarily accepts the risk of it. In **Cummings** *v* **Grainger** (1977), the claimant was bitten by an Alsatian, which was used as a guard dog in the defendant's scrapyard. The claimant had gone to the yard late at night with her boyfriend, who knew the defendant and had a key. There was a sign saying 'Beware of the Dog', and the claimant admitted that she had seen it. The Court of Appeal held that she knew of the risk and decided to take it; therefore the defendant was covered by s. 5(2).

In a couple of recent cases, the courts appear to be using the consent defence as a way to mitigate the effects of the Act's strict liability. In **Turnbull** *v* **Warrener** (2012), the Court of Appeal found that if knowledge of how a species generally behaves is enough to make the keeper liable, the same level of knowledge can also be enough to mean that the claimant was accepting the risk of that behaviour. The defendant owned a horse called Gem, and made an arrangement with the claimant that allowed the claimant to ride Gem at weekends. This arrangement had been going on for four months when the accident that gave rise to the claim happened. Due to some problems with the horse's teeth, a vet had advised that Gem should be ridden with a bitless bridle, which meant a bridle without anything in the horse's mouth. Gem was not used to this kind of bit, and in that situation, horses will sometimes refuse to obey instructions. Knowing about the new bit, the claimant took Gem for a ride, and when they were cantering in an open field, he veered to the right, and she fell off and was injured. The court held that, as an experienced horsewoman, Ms Warrener would have known that this kind of thing could happen when a horse used a bitless bridle for the first time, and so it was established that she knew of a characteristic that was only present in certain circumstances, and could therefore potentially be liable. But, the court said, Ms Turnbull was equally experienced with horses, and had the same knowledge. Therefore, she could be said to have voluntarily accepted the risk, and Ms Warrener was not liable. A similar approach was taken in **Goldsmith** *v* **Patchcott** (2012), where the claimant was injured when the horse she was riding bucked, after being startled. The keeper was experienced with horses and knew that horses had the characteristic of bucking when they were startled, but so did the claimant, and so the defence applied.

Section 5(3) says that a defendant will not be liable for damage caused by an animal to a trespasser on the premises where the animal is kept, provided that either:

- the animal was not kept there for the protection of persons or property; or
- the animal was kept there for the protection of persons or property, but it was not unreasonable to keep it for that reason.

This effectively means that there is a defence where a trespasser is injured by an animal that is not a guard dog, or, where the animal is a guard dog, and it is reasonable for the defendant to keep one (the provision actually applies to all animals, not just dogs, but clearly it is most likely to be applied to dogs). This provision was accepted as offering an alternative defence in **Cummings** *v* **Grainger**, since the fact that the scrapyard was in an area that made it likely to be a target for thieves made it reasonable to keep a guard dog there.

Trespassing livestock

The Animals Act also covers liability for livestock which stray onto someone else's land. Livestock is defined by s. 11, and includes cattle, horses, donkeys, hinnies (a horse–donkey cross), mules, sheep, goats, poultry and farmed deer (but not wild deer).

Section 4 provides that where livestock belonging to one party stray onto land belonging to someone else, and cause damage to the land or property, the person owning the animals will be liable. There is no liability under this section for personal injury or damage to property belonging to anyone other than the landowner or occupier; where such damage is caused by straying livestock, a claimant would only be able to claim damages if they had a case under s. 2, or in a common law tort.

In addition, the owner of straying livestock will be liable for any costs incurred by the landowner or occupier in keeping the livestock before it is returned to its owner. Liability for both damage and expenses is strict; the owner of the livestock will be liable regardless of whether he or she knew that the livestock were liable to stray, and regardless of any precaution taken to prevent them doing so, unless he or she has a defence.

Defences

The defences under s. 5(1) and (2), described above, also apply to straying livestock, as does the defence of contributory negligence. However, it is important to note that it is not possible to use s. 5(1) to argue that damage is wholly the fault of the claimant because he or she did not fence off their own land (and therefore prevent other people's livestock from getting in). This is because there is traditionally no duty in law to fence off your land. This does not apply, however, where the claimant or someone else had a 'duty to fence' the claimant's land, for example under the contract for renting the land.

There is also an additional defence, in s. 5(5), which provides that the owner of straying livestock will not be liable where the livestock had strayed from a highway, and their presence there was a reasonable use of the highway.

Remedies

As well as the usual remedy of damages, s. 4 allows an extra remedy to landowners or occupiers when livestock stray onto their land. The landowner/occupier can keep the livestock until any damage is paid for, though they must notify the police and, if known, the livestock owner, within 48 hours. They must feed the livestock while they are kept, but the cost of this can be reclaimed from the owner. If the livestock owner offers to pay for the damage, the livestock must be given back, but if after 14 days no such offer has been made, or the owner has not been identified, the landowner/occupier may sell the livestock. He or she can then keep the cost of feeding the animals, any costs associated with the sale, and the cost of the damage done; anything extra must be returned to the owner.

Animals on the highway

Section 8 provides that where animals stray from unfenced land onto a highway, liability will be decided using the ordinary rules of negligence (before the Act was passed, animal owners were not liable for damage caused by their animals straying onto roads, a rule which originally existed when there were many more animals and far fewer vehicles). However, if the animals wander onto the highway from land that is unfenced, the act of leaving them on that land will not in itself incur liability, so long as the land is common land, or is situated in an area where fencing is not customary, or is a town or village green, and the owner had a right to place the animals there.

Special liability for dogs

Two sections of the Animals Act make special provision for the situation of dogs who are, or may be, about to worry livestock.

Section 3 provides that where a dog kills or injures livestock, the keeper of the dog will be liable for the damage, unless he or she is covered by a defence. The relevant defences are those defined in s. 5(1), covering fault of the claimant, s. 5(2) covering voluntary assumption of risk, and contributory negligence, plus a specific defence detailed in s. 5(4). This states that a dog owner will not be liable where his or her dog kills or injures livestock which have strayed onto land occupied by the dog owner, or where the dog's presence on the land was authorised by the occupier.

Section 9(3) provides that it is lawful for a person to kill a dog which is worrying, or is about to worry, livestock where there is no other reasonable means of preventing it from doing so. It is also lawful to kill a dog which has been worrying livestock, is still in the vicinity of the livestock, is not under the control of any person, and there are no practical means of discovering who owns it. In both cases, the person killing the dog must also show that he or she was entitled to act to protect the livestock (which will usually mean being the owner of the livestock or the land it was on, or being authorised by the land or livestock owner). He or she must also notify the police within 48 hours.

Remoteness of damage

A claimant must prove that the animal concerned actually caused the damage, both factually and legally. As you will remember, there are two possible tests of legal causation, or remoteness of damage: direct consequence and reasonable foreseeability (see Chapter 3). The Act does not specifically state which test should apply, but as liability is strict it is generally assumed it is the direct consequence test.

Topical issue

During 2008, newspapers reported that the decision in **Mirvahedy** had caused insurance costs to soar, which was putting many rural businesses at risk. Organisations representing those who work with animals and the public, such as riding schools and farms, claimed that the case extends liability beyond what Parliament must have intended, and the strict liability the case imposes was increasing the risk of being sued so much that insurance companies were no longer willing to cover businesses against that risk at a reasonable cost. The issue had been concerning the industry even before it hit the news; and, in 2007, the Conservative MP Stephen Crabb introduced a Private Member's Bill, which attempted to resolve the problem by amending the Act so that keepers of animals which do not belong to dangerous species would be liable only in situations where they know that the animal in question might be dangerous at the time the damage is caused, for example because it was protecting young, or was ill. Where the owner could not have known that the animal was likely to cause harm, they would not be liable under the Act, but could still be liable under the law of negligence if they had breached a duty of care. The Bill was supported by a number of organisations, but it failed to get through its second reading in March 2007.

Answering questions

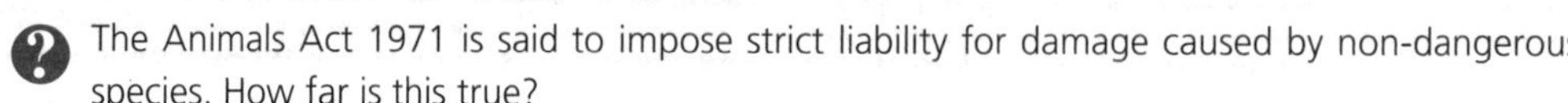

The Animals Act 1971 is said to impose strict liability for damage caused by non-dangerous species. How far is this true?

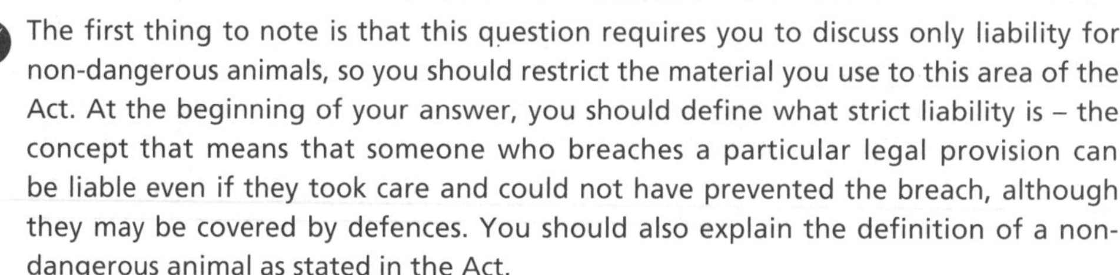

The first thing to note is that this question requires you to discuss only liability for non-dangerous animals, so you should restrict the material you use to this area of the Act. At the beginning of your answer, you should define what strict liability is – the concept that means that someone who breaches a particular legal provision can be liable even if they took care and could not have prevented the breach, although they may be covered by defences. You should also explain the definition of a non-dangerous animal as stated in the Act.

You should then explain how liability for non-dangerous animals can arise under the Act, referring to relevant cases. Discuss the fact that damage must be of a kind which was likely to happen if the animal was not restrained, or was likely to be severe (s. 2(2)(a)); that damage must be due to the peculiar characteristics of the animal (s. 2(2)(b)); and that the keeper or a member of their household must have knowledge of the characteristic (s. 2(2)(c)). You should give the definition of 'keeper'.

In explaining each requirement, you should assess how far it fits in with the concept of strict liability. The first requirement, about the type or severity of damage, for example, is clearly an aspect of strict liability, because liability does not rely on anything the keeper does or does not do; it is merely about the existence of a risk. If that risk exists, the requirements of s. 2(2)(a) are fulfilled. When discussing the second requirement, the animal's characteristic, you should talk about the argument made in **Mirvahedy** *v* **Henley**, that this section should not impose strict liability for normal animal behaviour, and the conclusion that the House of Lords came to in that case.

With regard to the third requirement, knowledge, you could argue that this in a sense reduces the possible harshness of strict liability because a defendant cannot be liable unless he knows of a risk, and, if he knows of a risk, he should take precautions to prevent it. In this sense, therefore, it could be argued that is not possible to be liable without a degree of fault.

You should also discuss the fact that there are defences which allow defendants to escape liability, and you should explain what these are.

Summary of Chapter 15

Liability for damage caused by animals can arise under common law, and also under the Animals Act 1971.

Liability under common law

The torts most likely to be committed in connection with animals are:

- Negligence
- Nuisance
- Trespass to the person.

The Animals Act 1971

The Act divides animals into two groups:

- Dangerous
- Non-dangerous.

In both cases, liability is strict.

Dangerous animals

Dangerous species are defined in s. 6(2) as species not commonly domesticated in Britain, which when fully grown:

- are likely to cause severe damage unless restrained; or
- if they do cause damage, it is likely to be severe.

The classification applies to whole species, not individual animals.

Section 2(1) provides that keepers of such animals are liable for any damage caused, unless they have a defence.

The keeper is:

- the owner; or
- the person in possession of the animal; or
- the head of the household where a child owns or has possession of the animal.

Non-dangerous animals

This covers all other species.

Section 2(2) provides that the keeper of a non-dangerous animal is liable for damage it does if:

- The damage is of a kind which the animal was likely to cause if unrestrained, or which was likely to be severe if the animal caused it.
- The likelihood of the damage happening or being severe was due to characteristics not normally found in that species, or only found at particular times and circumstances.
- Those characteristics were known to the keeper, the keeper's employee or a child in their household who was a keeper of the animal.

Defences

Section 5(1) and (2) of the Act provides that a keeper is not liable for damage:

- which is wholly the victim's fault;
- of which the victim voluntarily assumed the risk;
- which is caused by a trespass to the premises, provided that
  - the animal was not kept there for protection; or
  - if kept there for protection, it was reasonable to do so.

Trespassing livestock

The Act also imposes liability for livestock which stray onto another's land and cause damage to property or land. Liability is strict and covers the cost of keeping the livestock until they can be returned.

Defences

Applicable defences are:

- the defences under s. 5(1) and (2) of the Act (subject to there being no duty to fence off land);
- contributory negligence;
- under s. 5(5), that the livestock strayed from the highway when it was reasonable to be there.

Landowners can keep trespassing livestock until damage is paid for, and may sell them after 14 days if the owner cannot be found, or no offer of payment is made.

Animals on the highway

The Act provides that liability is covered by the ordinary rules of negligence.

Special liability for dogs

Under s. 3, keepers are liable when a dog kills or injures livestock, unless:

- they are covered by a s. 5(1) or (2) defence, or contributory negligence;
- the livestock have strayed onto land occupied by the dog owner;
- the dog's presence was authorised by the land occupier.

Under s. 9(3), it is lawful to kill a dog which is worrying or about to worry livestock, or has been doing so and the owner is not known.

Remoteness of damage

The claimant must prove the animals caused the damage. The test of remoteness is thought to be the direct consequence test.

Reading list

Text resources

Amirthalingam, A (2003) 'Animal liability – equine, canine and asinine' 119 *Law Quarterly Review* 565

Chevalier-Watts, J (2007) 'Civil liability for animals' 11 *Mountbatten Journal of Legal Studies* 56

Howarth, D (2003) 'The House of Lords and the Animals Act: closing the stable door' 62 *Cambridge Law Journal* 548

North, P (1972) *The Modern Law of Animals*. Butterworths

Samuels, A (1971) 'The Animals Act 1971' 34 *Modern Law Review* 550

Reading on the Internet

The House of Lords judgment in **Mirvahedy** *v* **Henley** (2003) can be read at:
http://www.parliament.the-stationery-office.co.uk/pa/ld200203/ldjudgmt/jd030320/mirva-1.htm

Visit **www.mylawchamber.co.uk** to access tools to help you develop and test your knowledge of tort law, including interactive multiple choice questions, practice exam questions with guidance, weblinks, glossary flashcards, legal newsfeed and legal updates.

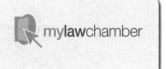

Chapter 16
Joint and several liability

This chapter discusses:

- The ways of assigning liability when a tort is committed by two or more parties
- Differences between independent, joint and several liability.

In some cases, a claimant suffers damage as a result of the activities of more than one person. Take, for example, a situation in which two motorists, both of them driving negligently, crash at a zebra crossing, injuring a pedestrian who is crossing the road. Who does the pedestrian sue, and how does the law make sure each party bears a fair share of both blame and the cost of damages? To deal with these and other cases involving more than one tortfeasor, the law has developed three different forms of liability, which are the subject of this chapter.

Types of liability

There are three basic forms of liability which allocate responsibility between two or more tortfeasors:

- Independent liability
- Several liability
- Joint liability.

Which form will apply depends on how the damage was done, and whether or not the tortfeasors were acting together.

Independent liability

This occurs where the victim suffers damage which is caused by two completely separate torts, as, for example, where a lorry is involved in two completely separate accidents, each causing damage to the car or injury to the driver. In such cases, each tortfeasor is liable for the damage they inflict, and has no connection with the other tortfeasor.

Several liability

Where two or more tortfeasors act independently, but the result of their acts is damage to the claimant for which they are both responsible, they are severally liable. The example in the introduction of two careless motorists crashing and injuring a pedestrian would be covered by several liability. The practical result is that each tortfeasor is separately liable for the whole of the damage, so the claimant may choose which to sue, but cannot get damages twice.

In most cases of several liability, the damage caused would be a result of the combination of the tortfeasors' actions, as in the car accident example. However, it is possible for the same damage to be caused in two separate incidents by different tortfeasors, as the case of **Vision Golf Ltd** *v* **Weightmans** (2005) shows. In that case, the claimants were tenants of a piece of land. There was a legal dispute over the land, which resulted in the landlord taking it back. In May 2000, the claimants instructed the defendants, a firm of solicitors, to deal with the problem, but they failed to make a court application which would have enabled the claimants to get their land back. In December the same year, the claimants later instructed another firm to make the application, but that firm advised that there was little chance of the application being successful at this stage. In fact, this advice was wrong, and the application probably would have succeeded then. When the application was eventually made in December 2001, it was dismissed on the grounds of delay. The result was therefore that the defendants' failure had resulted in the loss of the land, but this could have been put right if the second firm had not given the wrong advice. That wrong advice had then caused exactly the same damage. Did the second firm's breach of duty mean that the first firm was no longer liable?

The Chancery Division held that it did not. The 'but for' test of causation was satisfied, in that if the defendants had not breached their duty by failing to make the application, the claimants would have got the land back. The fact that the second firm had gone on to cause the damage might mean that the defendants could claim a contribution from them (see below), but it did not mean they could avoid liability for their breach of duty.

Joint liability

Where the same wrongful act is committed by two or more people, they are described as joint tortfeasors, and are jointly and severally liable. This means that the claimant can sue both (or all) of them, or recover the whole amount from just one, regardless of the extent to which each participated. Even where all are sued, judgment will be given for a single sum, and this may be enforced in full against any one of them. The claimant can only get damages once.

The two situations in which joint liability mainly arises are vicarious liability, where an employer and employee may be held jointly liable for the employee's negligence (which is covered in the next chapter), and where the tortfeasors had a common design. The latter covers cases where the defendants are acting together, with the same purpose in mind. In **Brooke** *v* **Bool** (1928) the claimant had leased a shop from the defendant. A lodger in the shop smelt gas, so the lodger and the defendant went to investigate whether there was a gas leak. The defendant told the lodger to light a match, which he did, and there was an explosion. They were held jointly liable for the damage caused by the lodger's negligence.

Three situations can cause problems in the areas of joint and several liability: where successive actions are brought by the claimant; where one of the tortfeasors is released from liability; and where the question of contribution arises.

Successive actions

Where more than one tortfeasor has caused loss or injury to the claimant, there may be circumstances where it is difficult or impossible to sue them all in the same action. In the past, under common law, a claimant could sue each in turn where there was several liability, but not where there was joint liability; in that case only one action could be brought in respect of the injury or loss in question. However, this distinction has been removed by statute. Under the Civil Liability (Contribution) Act 1978, s. 3, if a claimant has already successfully sued a joint tortfeasor, but has been unable to enforce the judgment, they can still sue any remaining joint tortfeasor, whether liability is joint or several.

Clearly, as far as the courts are concerned, it is preferable that a claimant should, if possible, sue all the tortfeasors who are liable for the same damage in one action. To encourage this, s. 4 of the 1978 Act provides that, if successive actions are brought, the claimant can only recover costs in the first action unless the court decides there were reasonable grounds for bringing the separate action(s).

Where a claimant settles out of court with one tortfeasor, this can have the effect of extinguishing any claims against other tortfeasors, so long as the settlement is intended by the parties to be a full and final settlement. This was the case in **Jameson** *v* **Central Electricity Generating Board**

(1999). The claimant, Mrs Jameson, was the wife of a man who had contracted a fatal lung disease at work. There were two potential tortfeasors liable for the injury: his own employer and the owners of the power station where his employer sent him to work. Mr Jameson reached an out-of-court settlement with his employer, worth £80,000, but he died before the money could be paid, and it was inherited by his widow. She then brought a claim under the Fatal Accidents Act 1976 against the power station owners, this claim being worth £142,000. The House of Lords held that this claim could not be successful unless it was clear that the earlier settlement had only ever been intended to settle part of Mr Jameson's claim. Given that the parties had said it was to be 'in full and final settlement', this could not be the case, and therefore settling the claim with the first tortfeasor meant there could be no further claim against the second one.

Release of a joint tortfeasor

If the potential claimant agrees that one of the joint tortfeasors will not be liable for a tort committed, all the others are released too, even though this may not have been the intention of the parties. The reasoning behind this rule is that, in cases of joint liability, only one tort has been committed, and there is only one cause of action. If this cause of action is terminated, everyone's liability must be terminated. By contrast, where liability is several, the release of one tortfeasor does not affect the liability of the others. The harshness of this rule for claimants in cases of joint liability has been reduced by the courts distinguishing between a mere agreement not to sue, in which the other tortfeasors remain liable, and a release by contract, which extinguishes the liability of the other tortfeasors.

Contribution

The Civil Liability (Contribution) Act 1978 provides that where there is joint or several liability and one tortfeasor is sued and pays damages, they may recover a contribution or indemnity from any other who is liable in respect of the same damage. This is a matter between the defendants and does not affect the claimant, who remains entitled to recover the whole loss from whichever defendant they choose.

Where an out-of-court settlement is reached, a contribution can still be sought, provided it was an honest settlement.

In each case, the court will decide the contribution to be claimed on the basis of what is just and equitable regarding each tortfeasor's proportion of responsibility for the damage, though the contribution recoverable will not exceed the amount that the claimant could have recovered from that particular defendant. The courts appear to take a similar approach to this issue as they do in relation to the reduction of an award of damages for contributory negligence. In **Fitzgerald** *v* **Lane** (1988), the claimant walked out onto a busy road, and was hit by a vehicle, which pushed him into the path of another vehicle. Both drivers were found to have been negligent. The House of Lords held that the claimant's behaviour had to be considered in the light of the totality of the two drivers' conduct. The claimant was considered to be 50 per cent to blame, and the court then had to decide how much contribution had to be made. It was held that both drivers were equally to blame, and should contribute equal shares of the remaining 50 per cent of the damage.

The Limitation Act 1980 provides that the contribution must usually be sought within two years of the original award or settlement.

Answering questions

The issues raised in this chapter are unlikely to form the main subject of an exam question, but they do sometimes arise as a small part of problem questions. Therefore whenever a problem talks about two people causing the same damage to a claimant, you should consider whether there are issues of joint and several liability.

Summary of Chapter 16

Types of liability

To deal with cases involving more than one tortfeasor, the law has developed three different forms of liability:

- Independent liability
- Several liability
- Joint liability.

Independent liability

- Arises where the victim is caused damage by two completely separate torts.
- Each tortfeasor is liable only for the damage they caused.

Several liability

- Arises where two or more tortfeasors act independently, but the combined effect of their acts is damage to the claimant.
- Each tortfeasor is liable for all of the damage, but the claimant cannot recover twice.

Joint liability

- Arises where the same wrongful act is committed by two or more people acting together, or where one person/organisation is vicariously liable for another.
- The claimant can sue all or any of them, but can only recover the full amount once.

Successive actions

Under the Civil Liability (Contribution) Act 1978, where there is joint or several liability, a claimant who sues one tortfeasor but cannot enforce the judgment can bring a later action against another of the tortfeasors.

Settling out of court with one tortfeasor also ends claims against the others.

Release of a joint tortfeasor

If a claimant releases one tortfeasor from liability, this releases the other(s) too.

Contribution

Where liability is joint or several and one or more tortfeasors are not sued, the Civil Liability (Contribution) Act 1978 allows those who are sued to recover a contribution from them.

The courts decide the contribution on the basis of what is just and reasonable, regarding each party's responsibility for the damage.

Reading list

Text resources

Weir, T (2001) 'The maddening effect of consecutive torts' 60 *Cambridge Law Journal* 231

Reading on the Internet

The House of Lords judgment in **Jameson** *v* **Central Electricity Generating Board** (1999) can be read at:

http://www.publications.parliament.uk/pa/ld199899/ldjudgmt/jd981216/james01.htm

Visit **www.mylawchamber.co.uk** to access tools to help you develop and test your knowledge of tort law, including interactive multiple choice questions, practice exam questions with guidance, weblinks, glossary flashcards, legal newsfeed and legal updates.

Chapter 17
Vicarious liability

This chapter discusses:

- How vicarious liability arises
- Who is considered an employee for the purposes of vicarious liability
- When vicarious liability will and will not apply
- Why vicarious liability exists.

There are some situations in which one person will be held legally liable for torts committed by someone else; this is known as vicarious liability. Vicarious liability arises where there is a relationship between the tortfeasor and the party who becomes vicariously liable which justifies giving the latter responsibility for the acts of the former. In the modern law, this is usually a relationship of employee and employer, and so vicarious liability cases usually involve events which happen at or in connection with work.

The principle is sometimes justified by the moral idea that if you have some degree of authority over another's actions, you should bear some responsibility for their mistakes, especially if you profit from their work. In reality, however, vicarious liability has become a practical tool to help compensate victims, since it allows liability to be placed with a party who is likely to be insured, in situations where the actual tortfeasor will probably not have the resources to meet a claim.

Vicarious liability is a form of joint liability, in that both the person who committed the tort, and their employer, can be sued (though in practice usually only the employer is sued, because they are most likely to have insurance). In addition to being sued as vicariously liable for a tort committed by an employee, the employer may also have their own original liability – for example, if an employee negligently injures a colleague, the employer may be vicariously liable for the employee's actions, but may also be personally liable for negligence, in failing to provide supervision that was adequate to prevent the risk of injury.

In order to decide whether vicarious liability applies in a particular situation, the courts address two questions: was the person who committed the tort an employee of the defendant, and was the tort committed in the course of that person's employment? Employers are only liable if the answer to both questions is yes.

Who is an employee?

At first glance this may seem a strange question: either you do work for a particular person or company, or you do not. Traditionally, a distinction was made between employees, whose actions could give rise to vicarious liability, and independent contractors, whose actions could not. In many cases the distinction was, and still is, obvious; in a factory, for example, a staff member who works full-time helping to produce the goods the company sells is likely to be an employee of the company that owns the factory, whereas someone called in from time to time to fix the plumbing is probably going to be an independent contractor, as far as the factory is concerned. However, modern working practices have blurred the edges in many areas. Companies increasingly prefer to give themselves maximum flexibility by hiring casual, temporary or freelance staff, and although these people may do the same work as others in the workplace, they are not always considered to be employees. Similarly, in industries such as the media and computing, many workers prefer to be self-employed, but may in fact end up doing most of their work for one or two companies, in the same workplace as company staff and often under the same sort of supervision; can they then be considered employees, at least for the time they are at the workplace?

Over the years, the courts have developed a number of different tests for deciding whether a particular individual is an employee or not. Many of these tests come not from tort cases, but from tax and employment law, as the question of whether someone is an employee affects the way they are taxed, and their rights at work. These same tests are, however, applied to cases where the question is whether vicarious liability should be applied.

Tests for employee status

In the past the usual way of deciding whether a person was an employee was to look at the degree of control exercised over that person's work by the supposed employer. Where the employer had control over the work, and was in a position to lay down how and when tasks should be done, the person doing the work would be an employee. If, on the other hand, the person was engaged to do a particular task, but allowed discretion as to how and when to do it, they would be an independent contractor.

However, as many types of work became increasingly skilled and specialised, the test became less useful. In industry, for example, many managers would have no idea how their computer technicians should do their work, and so are not in a position to give directions on the subject, yet it is obvious that in common-sense terms this does not make a salaried computer technician an independent contractor. The control test is still used, but clearly, in the light of these developments, it can no longer be conclusive. The courts now accept that no single test could cover the variety of work situations, and instead they look at all the circumstances of the particular case, including the level of control.

In **Ready Mixed Concrete (South East) Ltd** *v* **Minister of Pensions** (1968), the claimants were lorry drivers who did work for a concrete-manufacturing company, using their own lorries. The lorry owners were required to wear the company's uniform, and to paint their lorries with its colours and logo, so they certainly looked as though they were employed by the company, but their contract with the firm referred to them as 'owner-drivers', and stated that they were self-employed contractors, who would transport the company's concrete for a fixed rate per mile. In deciding whether they were employees or not, the court applied what came to be called the 'economic reality test', which looked at how the arrangement really operated from a business perspective. They found that the drivers were not employees but independent contractors, and the key reasons for this were that the drivers owned and maintained the lorries themselves, were free to hire other drivers to do the work if they needed to, and were not guaranteed any income – they took the risk of whether they made a profit or not. To be considered an employee the criteria to be satisfied are, first, that that person agrees to provide work and skill for the employer in return for payment. Secondly, that he or she agrees (expressly or by implication) to be subject to the employer's control. Thirdly, that the other terms of the contract are consistent with the existence of a contract of service. Terms which would be inconsistent with such a conclusion might to be that the person is required to pay for their own materials, or is allowed to employ staff to help do the job.

A test that has grown in popularity with the courts is whether a worker was in 'business on his own account'. This was used by the Court of Appeal in **Hall** *v* **Lorimer** (1992). The case was concerned with whether the defendant, a freelance television technician, was an employee for the purposes of tax law; as an employee he would have had to pay more tax than if he was self-employed. The Inland Revenue argued that he was an employee because he was subject to the control of the television companies in that they told him where, when and for how long to work. The Court of Appeal took a slightly different approach. They held that the crucial factor was that he was not in business on his own account. Workers will be viewed as in business on their own account if, for example, they provide their own equipment, take financial risks (such as doing work on credit), hire helpers, have managerial and investment responsibilities, charge varying amounts for different jobs, send out invoices for their work and have quite a few clients.

Nolan LJ said in **Hall** *v* **Lorimer** that just because people do highly-skilled work does not mean they are more likely to be self-employed, for a brain surgeon is usually an employee while a window cleaner is usually self-employed. Nor, in this day and age, does the fact that a person is on short-term contracts with different employers matter. He pointed out that the label that people give themselves is relevant but never decisive. He concluded that the 'business on their own account' test is not the exclusive test in deciding whether workers are employees:

> [T]he question whether the individual is in business on his own account, though often helpful, may be of little assistance in the case of one carrying on a profession or vocation. A self-employed author working from home or an actor or a singer may earn his living without any of the normal trappings of a business . . . The extent to which the individual is dependent on or independent of a particular paymaster for the financial exploitation of his talents may well be significant.

In many cases there will be a written contract detailing the relationship between the worker and the person using their services but, although the courts will usually look at this, it is not treated as decisive, and the courts may find that a person is an employee even in the face of an express contractual term describing them as self-employed. This was the case in **Ferguson** *v* **Dawson** (1976), where it was held by the Court of Appeal that a building labourer was an employee and therefore protected by certain safety legislation, on the basis of the type of work done and the degree of control exercised over it. This was despite a specific contractual term stating that he was self-employed, and it means that employers cannot evade certain responsibilities simply by choosing to describe their workers as self-employed.

In **JGE** *v* **Trustees of the Portsmouth Roman Catholic Diocesan Trust** (2012), the Court of Appeal looked at an unusual situation where, under the normal understanding of the law, the tortfeasor was neither an employee nor an independent contractor. The person concerned was a Catholic priest, and as a priest, he had no employment contract (priests are considered to work for God, rather than the Catholic Church), but given the work he did, which was only for the Church, was clearly not an independent contractor either. The Court of Appeal decided that the correct approach was to apply the tests usually used to decide whether someone was an employee, but to use the tests to decide whether the priest's relationship to the bishop (who the claimant sought to make vicariously liable) was sufficiently similar to an employer–employee relationship to make it fair and just to impose vicarious liability. They concluded that it was, and that vicarious liability could therefore apply.

Agency workers

In many industries, it is common for employers to use temporary staff through agencies, rather than hiring them directly. The advantage of this situation is that the agency does all the work of finding suitable staff, and the company can keep them for as long as they need them, and then simply end the arrangement without having either to sack them or to make them redundant, both of which can only legally be done under certain conditions. What happens, then, if an agency worker commits a tort? Can the company which is hiring their services from the agency be vicariously liable? In most cases, the answer is no, because it is usually very clear that the employee is actually employed by the agency: they recruit the worker and have the power to end their employment, and the payment arrangement is usually that the agency pays the worker and charges a fee to the company using the worker, rather than the company paying the worker directly.

However, the courts have found instances where a company using agency staff can be deemed to be their employer, and therefore vicariously liable for torts committed by them in the course of their employment. This was the case in **Hawley** *v* **Luminar Leisure** (2006). The case arose when a nightclub bouncer, Mr Warren, assaulted the claimant, Mr Hawley, causing him permanent brain damage. The assault was found to be within the course of his employment but there was a question as to who was his employer. Luminar were the owners of the nightclub, but they had not employed the bouncer themselves, but got staff from a security company, ASE Security Services. However, he worked at Luminar's premises on a day-to-day basis and had done so for two years. ASE had gone bust, so the claimant sued Luminar.

The Court of Appeal said that the question was 'who was entitled and therefore obliged to control Mr Warren's act so as to prevent it?' They found that it was Luminar. ASE's only role in the situation was to employ Mr Warren in the first place, send him to Luminar at their request, and pay his wages for as long as Luminar wanted to use his services. It was Mr Warren's line manager at the nightclub who had the power to control his behaviour. The court also highlighted two further factors which, in their view, made it right to impose vicariously liability on Luminar. The first was that Mr Warren would have been recognised by members of the public as working for Luminar, as he had been standing on their door, wearing their uniform, for two years. The second was that Luminar did not have to use an agency to supply door staff; they could have employed their own bouncers. The fact that they chose not to was clearly because they wanted to avoid certain aspects of employment law, which would have restricted the way they could manage the club. The court was not willing to allow this to prevent liability. Therefore, Luminar were vicariously liable for the assault.

Casual workers

Increasingly, companies now use workers on a casual basis, which means they are asked to work when the company needs them, but cannot demand to work and be paid when the company chooses not to use them. In **Carmichael** *v* **National Power** (1999), the House of Lords looked at whether someone working this way could be considered an employee. The claimants in the case worked as tour guides, showing visitors round a power station owned by the defendants. National Power would call them and ask them to work when they needed them, and usually the claimants did so. However, it was clear that if, on any occasion, the claimants were asked to work and chose not to, National Power did not take any disciplinary action against them; in other words, they could choose whether or not to work. The House of Lords held that they could not be employees, because there was no mutual obligation between them: the company was not obliged to give them work, and they were not obliged to take it if it was offered.

The loan of an employee

In some cases, one employer may 'lend' another the services of an employee. If an employee who is on loan commits a tort, who will incur vicarious liability for it?

The rules governing this situation were those laid down in **Mersey Docks and Harbour Board** *v* **Coggins & Griffiths (Liverpool) Ltd** (1947). The Harbour Board had hired out one of their crane drivers, with his crane, to Coggins, a company of stevedores. As a result of the crane driver's negligence, someone was injured, and it was necessary to decide who was the crane driver's employer (and therefore who was vicariously liable). According to the terms of the contract between the Harbour Board and Coggins, he was an employee of Coggins, but the Harbour Board paid his wages, and retained the power to sack him. The House of Lords held that this meant that the Harbour Board was his employer, and, in doing so, they laid down a number of principles to be used in deciding future cases:

- The permanent employer would usually be considered liable, unless they can show good reason why responsibility should be placed on the employer who has borrowed the worker.

- In deciding whether there is good reason to place responsibility on the borrowing employer, a key question is who had the immediate right to control the employee's method of working.
- Courts should identify the act which caused the negligence, and ask who had responsibility for preventing that act.
- Other important questions to consider were: who paid the worker, who had the right to dismiss him or her, and for how long was the employee borrowed?
- The terms of the contract between the two employers were not to be considered conclusive.

On the facts of the case, the court concluded that the Harbour Board had not shown good reason for liability to be placed on Coggins, and so the Board were held to be the crane driver's employer.

The principles laid down in **Mersey Docks** were traditionally used to enable the courts to choose between two possible employers, so that one or the other would end up taking full responsibility. However, in **Viasystems (Tyneside) Ltd** *v* **Thermal Transfer (Northern) Ltd** (2005), the Court of Appeal decided that in some cases it would be more appropriate to use those principles to share liability between two possible employers. The claimants in the case owned a factory, where they were having some construction work done. During the work, a fitter's mate, Mr Strang, damaged the sprinkler system, causing a flood which damaged the property. The claimants had hired a company, Thermal Transfer, to do the work; they had sub-contracted some jobs to a second company, Darwell, and a third company, CAT Metalwork, had supplied the fitter and his mate, Mr Strang, to Darwell. It was not in dispute that Viasystems had a claim against Thermal Transfers in contract, but they also sought to sue Darwell and CAT Metalwork in negligence, claiming they were vicariously liable for Mr Strang. The court therefore had to decide whether Mr Strang was employed by Darwell, or CAT Metalwork.

Mr Strang worked alongside, and under the instructions of, CAT Metalwork's fitter, but both of them were under the supervision of a foreman employed by Darwell. The Court of Appeal found that both of them had the right, and the responsibility, to control the way Mr Strang did his work, and so it was fair that both their companies were found to be vicariously liable for him. The Court held that both should contribute equally to the damages.

It now seems that joint vicarious liability will apply in many 'borrowed employee' cases, since there will often be shared responsibility for controlling the employee. Even if the permanent employer is not present at the time of the negligence, they will usually have instructed the employee about how to do the job, and perhaps given training, while the borrowing employer will usually give day-to-day instructions. However, it will not apply in every case. In his article 'Vicarious liability and joint employees' (see Reading list), Andrew Tettenborn suggests that, for example, a company which hires a JCB and driver from another company to do some work on their premises would be unlikely to share vicarious liability for the driver's negligence, because they are unlikely to be able to exercise a realistic amount of control over the driver. Conversely, if an employment agency supplies a secretary to a company, the employment agency is unlikely to share vicarious responsibility for his or her negligence because they would not usually have sufficient control over the day-to-day work.

In the course of employment

An employer will only be responsible for torts committed by their employees if those torts are committed in the course of the employment, rather than, as the courts have put it, when the employee is on a 'frolic of his own'. The traditional test for whether an act is committed in the course of employment was taken from the classic textbook on tort, *Salmond on Torts*, first published in 1907. Salmond stated that a wrongful act would be classified as done in the course of employment:

> if it is either (a) a wrongful act authorised by the master [the old-fashioned legal term for the employer] or (b) a wrongful and unauthorised mode of doing some act authorised by the master.

This means that the employer will be liable not only where they have permitted the employee to do the wrongful act, but also in some cases where they have not given such permission. This will be the case where the wrongful act is so closely connected with the task the employee has been asked to do that it could be considered merely part of doing that task, even if not in the way the employer had wanted or authorised. An example of this occurred in **Century Insurance** *v* **Northern Ireland Road Transport** (1942). The defendants' employee, a petrol tanker driver, was unloading petrol from his tanker to underground storage in the claimant's garage, when he struck a match to light a cigarette and then dropped the lighted match onto the ground. This caused an explosion, damaging the claimant's property. The defendants were found to be vicariously liable for his negligence, on the basis that what he was doing at the time was part of his job, even if he was doing it in a negligent way. It was agreed that the match was struck for his own purposes, not those of the employer, but nevertheless, in the circumstances in which it was done, it was still in the course of his employment.

In **Bayler** *v* **Manchester Railway Co** (1873), a railway porter employed by the defendants thought the claimant was on the wrong train and, meaning to be helpful, pulled him off it by force. The defendants were held vicariously liable because the porter was trying to do what he was authorised to do, in helping a passenger to get to his destination, even though he was doing it so badly as to have completely the opposite effect.

Express prohibition

An employer who expressly prohibits an act will not be liable if an employee commits that act. However, the employer may be liable if the prohibition can be regarded as applying to the way in which the job is done, rather than to the scope of the job itself. In **Limpus** *v* **London General Omnibus Co** (1862) a bus driver had been given written instructions not to race with or obstruct other buses. He disobeyed this order and, while racing another bus, he caused a collision with the claimant's bus, which damaged it. The court held that he was doing an act which he was authorised to do: driving a bus in such a way as to promote the defendants' business. This meant that he was within the course of his employment, even though the way he was doing the job was quite improper and had been prohibited. The defendants were vicariously liable.

A common situation arising in this area has been that of employees giving lifts to people. In **Twine** *v* **Bean's Express Ltd** (1946), the defendants' employee gave the claimant's husband a lift in a van and, as a result of the employee's negligence, he was killed. The driver had been told not to give lifts to anyone who was not within a group of authorised passengers, and there was a notice on the side of the vehicle stating who could be carried. The deceased was not among them. The defendants were held not to be vicariously liable because the driver was doing an unauthorised act and was therefore outside the course of his employment.

By contrast, in **Rose** *v* **Plenty** (1976) a milkman had been told by his employer not to permit passengers on his float, nor to let children help him deliver the milk. He disregarded these orders, and paid the claimant, who was 13, to help him. The claimant was injured while riding on the vehicle, as a result of the milkman's negligent driving. The defendants were held vicariously liable because the prohibition did not affect the job which the milkman had to do, only the way in which he should do it. He was doing his allocated job of delivering the milk, even though in a way that his employers disapproved of. Certainly there is a very fine division between this case and **Twine**. The majority of the Court of Appeal pointed to the fact that in **Twine** the lift was not given for a purpose which would benefit the employer, but in **Rose** the boy was helping with deliveries, and therefore furthering the employer's business. However, it is likely that the court was influenced by the fact that compensation for the child could only be secured by making the employer's insurance available to meet the claim.

Criminal acts

When we talk about vicarious liability for criminal acts committed by employees, we do not mean that the employer is prosecuted for the crime instead of the employee. The cases referred to in this section concern situations where an employee has done something which is both a crime and a tort. He or she will have been prosecuted for the crime by the state but, if their actions also fall within the definition of a particular tort, they can also be sued by the victim. Since few individuals have enough money to make them worth suing, the victim will try to impose vicarious liability and sue the employer in tort instead.

Having read so far in this chapter, if you were asked whether an employer was likely to be found vicariously liable for a criminal act done by an employee, you would probably feel quite confident in saying 'no'. On the basis of the Salmond definition alone, it is difficult to think of many situations in which committing a crime could be described as just a different way of doing your job, and certainly up until recently the courts would only find vicarious liability for acts amounting to crimes where there was clearly some actual fault of the employer. In **Lloyd** *v* **Grace, Smith & Co** (1912), for example, a solicitors' clerk defrauded a client out of property, and his employers were found vicariously liable, but largely because it was their lack of supervision over his work that allowed him to commit the fraud. By contrast, in **Warren** *v* **Henley's Ltd** (1948), the managers of a petrol station were held not to be vicariously liable for the actions of an employee who punched a customer on the nose during a row; the court held that this was an act of personal vengeance and not part of the course of his employment.

Key Case **Lister** *v* **Hesley Hall (2001)**

Case Navigator

Today, however, the area of vicarious liability for criminal acts is not quite so tidy, thanks largely to the case of **Lister** *v* **Hesley Hall** (2001). The claimants in the case were boys at a school for children with emotional difficulties, who had been sexually abused by the warden, an employee of the defendants. They claimed that the defendants were vicariously liable for the abuse. Clearly, the abuse could not be described as the warden merely doing his job in an unauthorised way, as stated in the Salmond test, but the House of Lords departed from this approach, saying that the basic Salmond test did not actually work very well in cases where the wrongdoing was intentional rather than careless. They referred instead to a phrase used by Salmond in explanation of the test, that 'a master . . . is liable for acts which he has not authorised, provided that they are so connected with acts which he has authorised, that they may rightly be regarded as modes – albeit improper modes – of doing them'. The key element here, according to the House of Lords, was the phrase 'so connected', and the

question to ask was whether the connection between what the employee had done, and what he was supposed to do as his job, was so close that it would be fair to impose vicarious liability.

To answer this, it was necessary to look at the task an employer had delegated to their employee. In this case, the school had the job of looking after the boys in its care, and it had delegated part of this task to the warden. The sexual abuse had been 'inextricably interwoven' with his performing this task, since it was carried out on the defendants' time, on their premises, and during the day-to-day routine of looking after the children. Merely having access to the place where the children were would not have been enough, but the close link between the warden's work and the abuse made it fair, in the House of Lords' opinion, to make his employers vicariously liable for the abuse.

Legal Principle

Vicarious liability may be imposed for illegal acts, where the act was so closely connected with the employee's job as to make it fair to impose vicarious liability.

Lister was followed, and further explained (although without shedding very much useful light) in **Dubai Aluminium Co Ltd** *v* **Salaam** (2002). The case itself is fairly straightforward in terms of vicarious liability: Dubai Aluminium had been defrauded of $50 million by two people referred to as Mr S and Mr T, with the help of a solicitor, Mr A. Mr A was a partner in a firm called Amhersts, and the Partnership Act 1890 provides that where a partner in a firm commits a wrongful act 'in the ordinary course of business of the firm', the firm effectively has vicarious liability for that act. Accordingly, Dubai sued Amhersts for compensation, and Amhersts settled the case for $10 million. They then sought to get back some of this from Mr S and Mr T, under the Civil Liability (Contribution) Act 1978 (see p. 372). Mr S and Mr T, however, claimed the Act did not apply because Amhersts were not vicariously liable for the fraud; one of their reasons was that the fraud had not been committed in the course of business. The House of Lords held that it had, and confirmed that the correct test was whether there was a 'close and direct connection' between the employee's duties and the criminal act: 'The wrongful conduct must be so closely connected with acts the . . . employee was authorised to do that . . . the wrongful conduct may fairly and properly be regarded as done while acting on the ordinary course of . . . the employee's employment.'

Unfortunately, all this phrase really tells us is that the test of closeness will be passed when it is fair for liability to be imposed. What exactly makes it fair or unfair to impose liability is not explained, and in fact Lord Nicholls admits this, commenting that determining what is 'fair and proper' inevitably involves a 'value judgment' based on all the circumstances and 'assistance' from previous court decisions. The Salmond test, their Lordships concluded, was just that – one test. It did not provide a conclusive answer in every circumstance, and it was possible that an employee's behaviour might satisfy the Salmond test, and yet 'the facts, taken as a whole', might still suggest that there was no vicarious liability. In addition, several of the factors which, in previous cases, had been taken to mean that there was no vicarious liability, were not to be viewed as decisive:

> It is no answer to a claim against the employer to say that the employee was guilty of intentional wrong-doing, or that his act was not merely cautious but criminal, or that he was acting exclusively for his own benefit, or that he was acting contrary to express instructions, or that his conduct was the very negation of his employer's duty . . . Vicarious liability is not necessarily defeated if the employee acted for his own benefit.

The approach was followed again in **Bernard** *v* **Attorney-General of Jamaica** (2004), where the Privy Council said that the correct approach is 'to concentrate on the closeness of the connection between the nature of the employment and the tort, and to ask whether, looking at the matter in the round, it is just and reasonable to hold the employers vicariously liable'. In this case a plain-clothes police officer approached a man using a public phone, said that he was a police officer, and told the man to let him use the phone instead. The man refused, and the officer pulled a gun and shot him. The police officer was not thought to be on duty at the time, but nevertheless the Privy Council held that his employers were liable for his actions. The shooting happened immediately after he had presented himself as a police officer, the gun was supplied by the police, and this made the shooting so closely connected with his employment that it was fair and reasonable to consider that it was done in the course of his duties. The court also said that employers should be liable for risks which are reasonably incidental to their business. In this case, the police had created the risk by supplying guns and allowing officers to take them home and carry them while off-duty.

In **Gravell** *v* **Carroll and another** (2008), the Court of Appeal held a rugby club vicariously liable for an assault by one of its semi-professional players, during a match. Following a scrum, the claimant had got involved in a row with the defendant, who was on the other team. The defendant threw a punch, which broke a bone in the claimant's face. The Court of Appeal held that the defendant's club was vicariously liable for the assault because there was a sufficiently close connection between the punch and what he was employed to do. He was employed to play rugby, and the altercation which developed between the two players, including the throwing of punches, was the kind of thing that regularly happened during a rugby match, and which both clubs could expect to occur.

In **Mattis** *v* **Pollock (trading as Flamingos Nightclub)** (2003) the Court of Appeal stated that vicarious liability for an act of violence was more likely to be found in cases where using violence was an expected part of the employee's job than where it was not. The case concerned a nightclub bouncer who stabbed a customer, leaving him paralysed. The act was the culmination of a series of incidents in which the bouncer had behaved in an intimidating way to a particular group of customers. On the night in question, his behaviour had led to a fight, in which the bouncer came off worse and had to flee the club. He later headed back towards the club, armed with a knife and apparently looking for revenge. The customers had left the club, but the bouncer met them in the street, and stabbed one of them.

The bouncer was found guilty of causing grievous bodily harm, and the victim sued the owner of the nightclub, Mr Pollock, as vicariously liable for the actions of the bouncer. Mr Pollock argued that the stabbing did not take place in the course of the bouncer's employment, not least because it was not in the club, although it did happen during the bouncer's working hours. However, the Court of Appeal held that it was not a separate incident, but part of the whole series of events springing from the bouncer's violent behaviour towards this group of customers. There was evidence that Mr Pollock had encouraged the bouncer to be intimidating and use violence; in fact other bouncers had warned Mr Pollock that the man's behaviour had gone beyond acceptable levels, but he had ignored the warnings. The Court of Appeal therefore held that Mr Pollock was vicariously liable.

In **MAGA** *v* **Trustees of the Birmingham Archdiocese of the Roman Catholic Church** (2010), the Court of Appeal examined a case that was in some ways similar to **Lister**, but with some important differences. The claimant alleged that, when he was a teenager, he had been sexually abused by a Catholic priest, Father Clonan, and sought to sue the church as being vicariously liable for the priest's actions. What made the claim significantly different from that in **Lister** was that the boy was not a Catholic, and the occasions on which he was abused were not directly to do with the church. He and Father Clonan had met when he was admiring the priest's sports car one day, and Father Clonan had invited him to a church disco that he ran, which was open to all local young people and not just Catholics. The claimant later began doing small jobs for Father Clonan, such as washing his car or cleaning the house where he lived, which was owned by the church. It was on these occasions that much of the abuse happened. The claimant did not attend the church and Father Clonan apparently did not attempt to persuade him to do so.

The church therefore argued that the abuse could not be said to be so closely connected with Father Clonan's work that it would be fair and just to hold them liable. They pointed out that although his position as a priest gave him the opportunity to abuse the claimant, it was made clear in **Lister** that there had to be a closer connection than mere opportunity.

The Court of Appeal took a different view. Lord Neuberger pointed out that whenever Father Clonan met the claimant, he was dressed in his priest's robes, and that symbolised the fact that he had a role involving trust, responsibility and moral authority. In addition, part of his job was to spread the Catholic faith, and an element of this involved getting to know and befriend non-Catholics, and to spend time alone with them, which was what he had done with the claimant. It did not matter that his reason for doing so was not to spread the faith but to commit abuse; the relationship with the claimant was still brought about under the guise of his duties as a priest. It was also relevant that Father Clonan had been given special responsibility by the church for working with young people, and that the event which drew the claimant in (the disco) was held on church premises and organised on behalf of the church. The abuse itself had also frequently happened on church premises, when the claimant was cleaning the priest's house. Taken together, these factors meant that the abuse passed the **Lister** test, and the church was vicariously liable.

The principle in **Lister** has now been extended in a landmark decision from the Supreme Court. In **Catholic Child Welfare Society and others** *v* **The Institute of the Brothers of the Christian Schools** (2012), the claim was brought by a group of 170 men who had been at a children's home, St William's School, in Yorkshire, during the years from 1958 to 1992. They alleged that they had been abused by members of the defendants' religious order, known as Christian Brothers, who worked there as teachers. The home was managed by the Catholic Child Welfare Society, but the religious order was responsible for placing the Christian Brother teachers there. The managers of the school had already been found vicariously liable for the abuse, but the question for the Supreme Court was whether the Institute should also share liability. The Institute argued they were not employers, because the brothers were bound by vows, not a contract, and did not personally earn wages. The Supreme Court disagreed. They said there was a two-stage test: was the relationship between the Institute and the abusers capable of producing vicarious liability, and what connected their relationship to the abuse? They said that the relationship was capable of creating vicarious liability, because it was just like that of an employer and employee: the brothers were sent to the school and their work directed by the Institute. There was a sufficiently close connection between that relationship and the abuse, because the Institute put the Brothers into a position where they had close physical proximity with vulnerable victims, and where they would be trusted because they were men of God.

'Frolics of their own'

An employer will not be responsible for acts done by employees which have nothing to do with their employment – judges often refer to this as employees going off on 'frolics of their own'. In many of these cases, the employee's job may give them the opportunity to commit the wrongful act – they may do so during work time, or using their employer's equipment, for example – but without a connection between the act and the job there will be no vicarious liability. In **Heasmans** *v* **Clarity Cleaning Co** (1987) the employee of a cleaning contractor was employed to clean telephones, and while doing so used the phones to make private long-distance calls from clients' premises. The defendants were held not vicariously liable; the Court of Appeal held that the unauthorised use of the telephone was not connected with cleaning it, and could not be regarded as the cleaning of it in an unauthorised manner.

Journeys and detours

One area that has caused problems for the courts is where a tort (usually negligence which causes an accident) happens on a journey that may or may not be taken in the course of employment. In **Hilton** *v* **Thomas Burton (Rhodes) Ltd** (1961), four workmen were out in their employer's van, which they were allowed to use for travelling to a demolition site out in the countryside. After half a day's work, they decided to stop and go to a café seven miles away for tea. On the return journey, there was an accident, caused by the van driver's negligence, and one of the passengers was killed. His widow sought to make the employer vicariously liable for the negligence, but the court held that there was no vicarious liability. Although the driver was using the van with the employer's permission, he was doing something he was not employed to do when the accident happened. However, in **Williams** *v* **Hemphill** (1966), a lorry driver who took a long detour was held to be acting within the course of his employment. It was his job to carry passengers to Glasgow and, while they were on board, he took a detour, during which part of the journey there was an accident. Were his employers liable for the accident? The House of Lords said they were, because it was his job to transport the passengers, and they were on the lorry at the time, so it could not be said that he was taking the detour merely for his own purposes. Lord Pearson said:

> Had the driver in the present case been driving a lorry which was empty or contained nothing of real importance, I think that so substantial a deviation might well have constituted a frolic of his own. The presence of passengers, however, whom the servant is charged . . . to drive to their ultimate destination makes it impossible . . . to say that the deviation is entirely for the servant's purposes. Their presence and transport is a dominant purpose of the authorised journey, and, although they are transported deviously, continues to play an essential part . . . [T]heir transport and safety does not cease at a certain stage of the journey to be the master's business, or part of his enterprise, merely because the servant has for his own purposes chosen some route which is contrary to his instructions.

In **Smith** *v* **Stages** (1989), the House of Lords took the opportunity to clarify the issue. The case involved a road accident involving two of the defendant's employees. They were usually based in the Midlands, but their employer had asked them to do a job at a power station in Wales. It was agreed that they would be able to claim travel expenses, and would be paid for the time it took to get to and from the job, as well as the time they spent working. Negligent driving by one of them caused an accident on the way home, and the other one was injured. Was the employer vicariously liable? The House of Lords said that, in most cases, travelling to and from work would not be considered within the course of employment, but in this case, because of the arrangements about being paid for the travelling time, the men were 'on duty' at the time of the accident, and what happened was within the course of their employment. Lord Lowry then went on to clarify the whole issue of vicarious liability arising from journeys:

- An employee travelling from home to their regular place of work is not acting within the course of their employment, even if the vehicle is provided by the employer, unless the contract of employment states that he or she must use transport provided by the employer. If the contract does say he or she must use transport provided by the employer to get from home to work and back, the employee will be in the course of employment during such journeys, unless the contract says otherwise.

- An employee will be acting in the course of employment when they are travelling between two workplaces. This would cover both an employee who usually works at one place but occasionally has to go to another, or employees such as meter readers or salespeople, whose job may take them to lots of different workplaces.
- If an employee is paid for time spent travelling, then the travelling will be within the course of their employment, even if the employee is able to choose when and how to travel. However, being able to claim travel expenses does not mean that a journey is within the course of employment.
- An employee travelling during the employer's time (meaning time the employer is paying them for) will be within the course of their employment if they are travelling from home to a workplace other than their regular one, or if they are travelling between different workplaces due to the nature of their job (such as a travelling salesperson), or if they are travelling to the scene of an emergency related to their work.
- If an employee is on a journey that is within the course of their employment, and they take a detour or interrupt the journey, they will no longer be within the course of their employment, unless the detour or interruption is 'merely incidental'.
- If an outward journey is within the course of employment, the return journey will be too.
- Any of the above principles can be displaced by express agreements between employer and employee.
- Where an employee is salaried, the issue of whether they were travelling on the employer's time may not be significant. The distinction here seems to be between jobs where the employee can claim overtime for extra hours worked, and those (usually in professional and managerial occupations), where the salary remains the same even if extra hours are worked, so it is harder to say whether the journey is on the employer's time.

Vicarious liability and statutory duties

Most cases of vicarious liability involve breach of a common law duty, such as the duty of care in negligence. In **Majrowski** *v* **Guy's and St Thomas' NHS Trust** (2005), it was held that an employer can also be liable for an employee's breach of a statutory duty, even if the statute appears to impose liability only on individuals. The claimant in the case, Ms Majrowski, worked for the NHS Trust. She claimed that her manager there had subjected her to a course of conduct which amounted to harassment under the Protection from Harassment Act 1997. As you will know (from reading Chapter 14), the Act provides a civil right to sue for harassment, and so Ms Majrowski sued her employers, claiming they were vicariously liable for the manager's behaviour.

The Court of Appeal agreed that it was possible for an employer to be vicariously liable in this situation, and the test to be applied was the same as that applied in **Lister** and subsequent cases, looking at the closeness of the connection between the breach of duty and the employment, whether the risk was incidental to the business, and whether it was fair and just to hold the employer responsible. The courts would also need to look closely at the words of the statute, to determine whether it was intended to exclude vicarious liability, and in this, the Court of Appeal held, they could be guided 'where appropriate' by questions of policy.

Violence between employees

As we have seen, the 'close connection' test established in **Lister** *v* **Hesley Hall** has meant that employers can be liable even for violence committed by one of their employees against someone else. In two recent cases, **Weddall** *v* **Barchester Healthcare** (2012) and **Wallbank** *v* **Wallbank Fox Designs** (2012), which were heard together, the Court of Appeal looked at the issue of vicarious liability where one employee uses violence against another. In the **Weddall** case, the claimant was employed by the defendants as deputy manager of one of their care homes. One night, one of the care assistants at the home called in sick. It was part of Mr Weddall's job to get cover if this happened, so he telephoned another employee, Mr Marsh, to ask him to come in and do an extra shift. Mr Marsh happened to be drunk at the time, and he got the impression that Mr Weddall was mocking him for this. When the conversation was over, Mr Marsh got on his bike, rode to the home and violently attacked Mr Weddall.

In the **Wallbank** case, Mr Wallbank was the managing director of a company which made metal bed frames. He was assaulted by a Mr Brown, who was an employee of the company. There was evidence that Mr Brown was not a very satisfactory employee, and often had to be reminded of how to do his job properly. On the day of the assault, he was operating a conveyor belt, which took spray-painted bed frames into an oven which set the paint. In order for the process to work efficiently and economically, the frames had to be fed through regularly and at a certain speed, and when Mr Wallbank noticed that this was not happening, he told Mr Brown off, and then said 'come on', indicating his intention to come and help with loading the frames. When he got to where Mr Brown was standing, Mr Brown threw him against a table, causing a fracture in his back.

Both Mr Marsh and Mr Brown were convicted of assault, and Mr Weddall and Mr Wallbank then sought to sue their employers, arguing that they were vicariously liable for the injuries which the other employees had caused them. In both cases, they argued that what had happened was a response to a lawful instruction or request, and that responding to such instructions or requests was a part of the employee's job. The Court of Appeal applied the 'close connection' test, as explained in **Lister** *v* **Hesley Hall**. In the **Wallbank** case, they held that the violence did have a sufficiently close connection with Mr Brown's job to justify vicarious liability. The factors which led them to this conclusion were that the incident happened during work time and at the workplace, and that the assault was an instant and spontaneous reaction to the employee being given an instruction, when being given such instructions was clearly part of his job. It was also important that the workplace was a small factory, where instant instructions and quick reactions to them were required; this, said Pill LJ, meant that: 'Frustrations which lead to a reaction involving some violence are predictable. The risk of an over-robust reaction to an instruction is a risk created by the employment.' Mr Wallbank therefore won his appeal.

In Mr Weddall's case, however, the Court of Appeal held that the connection between the assault and Mr Marsh's employment was not sufficiently close to justify vicarious liability. The factors which influenced this decision were that Mr Marsh was off-duty and at home when the request that triggered his violence was made, and that, rather than reacting spontaneously as Mr Brown did, he had had to get on his bike and cycle to the care home, and 20 minutes elapsed between the request being made and the assault happening. The assault was not, said Pill LJ, an instant response to the request, but an 'independent venture', which Mr Marsh had made for his own personal reasons. He therefore lost his appeal.

This contrasting pair of cases shows that there can be a very fine line between when the courts will and will not find a close connection. Remember that if you are given a problem question which raises this issue, you do not have to be able to say for certain whether a court would find a close connection or not; if it was that obvious, cases like the two above would not come to court. What you need to be able to do is identify when a problem requires the 'close connection' test, explain what it is, and point to factors which the courts would use to help them decide.

Employer's indemnity

Because vicarious liability makes employer and employee joint tortfeasors, each fully liable to the claimant, an employer who is sued on the basis of vicarious liability is entitled to sue the employee in turn, and recover some or all of the damages paid for the employee's tort. This is called an indemnity, and the employer's entitlement to sue may derive either from the provisions of the Civil Liability (Contribution) Act 1978, or in common law under the principle in **Lister** *v* **Romford Ice and Cold Storage** (1957). In that case, a lorry driver drove negligently in the course of his employment, and ran over his father, who was also employed by the company. The father recovered damages on the basis of the employer's vicarious liability for the driver's negligence; the damages were paid by the employer's insurers. The employer then exercised its right to sue the driver for an indemnity. The House of Lords held that the lorry driver's negligent driving was not only a tort against his father, but also a breach of an implied term in his employment contract, to the effect that he would exercise reasonable care in performing his contractual duties. It was decided that the employer was entitled to damages equivalent to the amount which it had had to pay to the father.

The House justified the decision on the basis that the employee who had committed the tort should not be able to avoid paying damages for the wrong. But the case was widely criticised as undermining the whole principle of vicarious liability, which is based on the assumption that employers are best placed to take out insurance, and therefore to meet the risk. Allowing insurers effectively to reclaim money from the employee means that the employers are paying premiums for a risk which may cost the insurance company nothing. In fact, since **Lister** *v* **Romford Ice** was decided, companies providing insurance to employers have informally agreed that they will not pursue their rights under the **Lister** principle unless there is evidence that employer and employee colluded together, or evidence of other misconduct with regard to the insurance cover.

Independent contractors

An employer is generally not liable for the acts of an independent contractor, as opposed to an employee. However, there are circumstances in which the acts of an independent contractor may give rise to the employer having primary liability because the employer was breaching their own duty to the claimant. The employer will then be liable as a joint tortfeasor with the independent contractor. The type of duty that the employer must have breached is described as a non-delegable duty. This means that while the work can be delegated to someone else, the liability for doing it properly cannot be delegated. For example, a water authority may have a non-delegable duty to repair a burst main. If it arranges for a private firm to carry out that repair, rather than its own employees, the firm will be its independent contractors. If that firm then carries out the repairs negligently so that several homes are seriously flooded, the firm can be liable for negligence, but the water authority will also be liable.

Whether a duty is delegable or not is always a question of law, but the answer is not always obvious. Strict liability torts tend to involve non-delegable duties, and in other cases the position may be clear from statutory provisions. For example, the Occupiers' Liability Act 1957 provides that an occupier may delegate the duty of care to make premises reasonably safe when a competent independent contractor is employed to deal with a potential risk, such as electrical maintenance. However, there are many situations where it is not clear whether a duty is delegable.

An employer can also be liable for the torts committed by an independent contractor where they have delegated a delegable duty but failed to take reasonable steps to find a competent person to do the work, or make sure it was done properly. In this situation the employer may incur primary liability in negligence for this failure.

Where there is potential liability for something done by an independent contractor, the employer will only be liable if the act was part of the work the contractor was engaged to do. Acts which are completely outside their role as an independent contractor (called collateral negligence) impose no liability on the employer. In **Padbury** *v* **Holliday and Greenwood Ltd** (1912), sub-contractors were employed by the defendants to do work on the windows of a house the defendants were building. While doing this, the sub-contractor placed on the window sill an iron tool, which subsequently fell off and injured the claimant in the street below. Placing the tool on the window sill was not part of the ordinary course of doing the work which the sub-contractor was employed to do, and so it was held that the claimant's injuries were caused by an act of collateral negligence, for which the builders were not liable. In order to make them liable, the negligence would have had to be central to the work the sub-contractors were doing for them, not merely casually connected to it.

Why is vicarious liability imposed?

Vicarious liability obviously conflicts with a basic principle of tort, that wrongdoers should be liable for their own actions. Why then do we have it? Various explanations have been put forward, including the following.

Employers have the necessary control

It can be argued that the employer is in control of the conduct of employees, and therefore should be responsible for their acts. While this may have been persuasive in the past, in modern industrial society, with its increasingly sophisticated division of labour, it is very difficult to believe. In many cases employees may have technical skills and knowledge not shared by their employers; to say, for example, that the manager of a hospital controls the work of a surgeon is simply not true. However, the modern application of this principle can be seen in the fact that employers set profit and/or performance targets, either formally or informally, and if these mean that there is insufficient time or staff to do a job properly, with the result that someone is, for example, injured by negligence, it is the employers who should be responsible.

Benefits to employers

Employers benefit from the work of their employees, and so ought to be liable for any damage the employee may cause in its performance. This is linked to the point about profit targets above; it would be very unfair if employees were sued for negligence when effectively they had been forced to be negligent by a cost-cutting employer, who would thereby profit from that negligence.

Financial resources

It is obvious that in the majority of cases, an employer will be in the best financial position to meet a claim, either because its resources are simply greater than those of an individual employee, or, more often, because it has relevant insurance cover. Many employers are large companies; placing liability on them effectively means that losses can be transferred to the consumer through higher prices, and so spread very thinly over a lot of people, rather than imposed on one.

Preventing negligent recruitment

It has been suggested that commission of a tort by an employee in the course of their employment implies that the employer was negligent in selecting that employee, and incurs liability on that basis. There is, however, no evidence that the courts approach the issue in this way, and in any case one negligent act does not necessarily mean that an employee is unfit for the work.

Promotion of care

There is some evidence to show that the imposition of liability on employers encourages them to take care to prevent work practices that could result in accidents; there could be a temptation for employers to 'turn a blind eye', especially if the practices have a benefit to themselves, if they knew liability would be restricted to the employee.

Answering questions

Micky works as a delivery driver for Supersavers Supermarket and has been told by his boss that he is not allowed to have passengers in his van. On the way back from delivering some books, he sees his granny, Daisy, struggling home with her shopping, and, as it is his lunch hour, he stops and offers her a lift home, two miles in the opposite direction from the office. Daisy knows that Micky is not supposed to take passengers, but her shopping is very heavy, so she agrees. Along the way, there is an accident, caused by Micky's negligence, and Daisy is badly injured.

Micky's wife, Minnie, works on the checkout at Supersavers. One day she accidentally gives the wrong change to a customer, Donald, who complains loudly, calling Minnie a thief. Minnie is furious, and punches Donald on the nose.

Can Daisy or Donald sue Supersavers to get compensation for their injuries?

Daisy will only be able to sue Supersavers if she can establish that they were vicariously liable for Micky's negligence. We know that he is an employee, so the first hurdle is cleared, but the key issue will be whether what he did was within the course of his employment. We are told that he has been expressly forbidden to carry passengers, so you need to discuss the cases of **Twine** *v* **Bean's Express** and **Rose** *v* **Plenty**. Clearly Supersavers will want to argue that **Twine** applies, while Daisy will seek to establish that **Rose** should be followed; you should point out any differences between them that make the court more likely to apply one than the other, such as the fact that, unlike in **Rose**, Micky giving Daisy a lift provided no benefit to his employer.

You should also consider the issue of whether Micky could be said to be 'on a frolic of his own', considering that he was in his lunch hour, and had gone in the opposite direction from the journey he was supposed to be on. The cases of **Hilton** *v* **Thomas Burton (Rhodes) Ltd** (1961) and **Storey** *v* **Ashton** (1869) are relevant here.

If Supersavers are liable, you need to consider whether they might be covered by a defence. Daisy knows that Micky is banned from taking passengers, so she could be said to be consenting to the risk, but you should point out that the provisions of the Road Traffic Act 1988, and subsequent cases such as **Pitts** *v* **Hunt** (1991), mean it is unlikely that the defence of *volenti* would be allowed to apply in this kind of case.

Regarding Donald, Minnie has clearly committed an illegal act, so you need to explain that **Lister** establishes that the court will ask whether her act was so closely associated with her job as to justify vicarious liability. The case of **Mattis** *v* **Pollock** is relevant here, as it points out that vicarious liability for a violent act is more likely to be found where physical violence was part of the job; clearly that is not the case here. Consider, too, the cases of **Warren** *v* **Henley's** and **N** *v* **Merseyside Police**, which would seem to have similarities with the situation involving Donald.

The principle of vicarious liability has been described as based on 'social convenience and rough justice'. Giving examples from case law, explain how far you think this is true, and whether it is satisfactory.

You should begin your essay with a clear and comprehensive definition of what vicarious liability is: the principle that allows an employer to incur legal liability for the acts of their employees. Then expand the definition by explaining how the law defines an employee, covering the tests which distinguish between an employee and an independent contractor. You should also explain that vicarious liability applies only where the employee is acting in the course of their employment, and discuss the cases that decided when this will and will not be the case, including the rules that apply when the act done by the employee has been forbidden by the employer, and when it is a criminal act.

The second half of your essay should be a critical discussion of the reasons behind the imposition of vicarious liability (discussed on p. 391), pointing out which of these can be said to be based on social convenience and/or 'rough justice' (it would be useful at this point to explain what you understand to be meant by rough justice – one definition might be that it means an approach which gives a roughly fair outcome considering all the circumstances, even though it could be argued to be unfair to individuals). You should relate the reasons given to the practical application of vicarious liability in the cases – for example, when discussing the idea that vicarious liability should apply because an employer has control of their employees, you might want to put forward one of the cases of express prohibition, where liability has been applied even though the employer has done their best to prevent the offending behaviour, as an example of 'rough justice' – the injured person gets compensation but the employer might well have reason to feel unjustly treated. You might also want to discuss the fact that modern working practices may be compromising the ability of vicarious liability to achieve even rough justice. The cases on criminal acts, particularly **Lister**, are also very relevant to this debate. You should also point out that, legally, the employer does have a right of indemnity from the employee, even though in practice it is rarely used. Your conclusion should sum up whether you agree that vicarious liability is based on 'social convenience and rough justice', and whether that is a satisfactory situation.

Summary of Chapter 17

Vicarious liability is a form of joint liability, which arises where there is a relationship between the tortfeasor and another that justifies making the other liable for the tortfeasor's acts.

In most cases, vicarious liability arises when a tort is committed in connection with the tortfeasor's work, with the employer vicariously liable for an employee's actions.

The courts use a two-stage test to judge whether vicarious liability should apply:

- Was the tortfeasor an employee of the defendant?
- Was the tort committed in the course of their employment?

Who is an employee?

The courts distinguish between employees and 'independent contractors', but modern working practices mean it is not always easy to tell which group a person falls into.

Tests used by the courts include:

- who had control over the work;
- the terms of the contract;
- whether the tortfeasor is 'in business on his own account'.

However, no single test is decisive.

Problematic situations include:

- Agency workers
- Loans of employees.

In the course of employment

Employers are liable only where the tort was committed during the course of employment.

- A wrongful act authorised by the employer, or an unauthorised way of doing an authorised act will be in the course of employment.
- The employer need not have permitted the act.
- Employers can be liable for prohibited acts, if the prohibition applies to the way the job is done rather than the job itself.
- Employers can be liable for criminal acts, if they are so closely connected to the job that it is fair to impose liability.
- Employers are not liable for acts done by employees which have nothing to do with their work, even if in work time.

Employer's indemnity

An employer sued for an employee's tort can sue the employee in turn, but this rarely happens in practice.

Independent contractors

Employers are not vicariously liable for the torts of independent contractors, but can be jointly liable with them if:

- the employer owes a non-delegable duty to the claimant; and
- the contractor's act puts them in breach of that duty.

Employers may also be liable where a duty is delegable, but they have not taken reasonable steps to ensure the contractor is competent.

Reasons why vicarious liability is imposed

- Control of employees
- Benefits to employers
- Resources
- Preventing negligent recruitment
- Promotion of care.

Reading list

Text resources

Atiyah, P (1967) *Vicarious Liability in the Law of Torts*. Butterworth

Barak, A (1966) 'Mixed and vicarious liability: a suggested distinction' 29 *Modern Law Review* 60

Brennan, C (2003) 'Third party liability for child abuse: unanswered questions' *Journal of Social Welfare and Family Law* 25

Brodie, D (2006) 'The enterprise and the borrowed worker' *Industrial Law Journal* 35

Cane, P (2000) 'Vicarious liability for sexual abuse' 116 *Law Quarterly Review* 21

Ferguson, E (2006) 'Blaming the boss' *Solicitors Journal* 53

Giliker, P (2006) 'The ongoing march of vicarious liability' 65 *Cambridge Law Journal* 489

Kidner, R (1995) 'Vicarious liability: for whom should the employer be liable?' 15 *Legal Studies* 47

Newark, F (1954) 'Twine *v* Bean's Express Ltd' 17 *Modern Law Review* 102

Stevens, R (2006) 'A servant of two masters' 122 *Law Quarterly Review* 201

Tettenborn, A (2005) 'Vicarious liability and borrowed employees' *New Law Journal* 1750

Weekes, R (2004) 'Vicarious liability for violent employees' 64 *Cambridge Law Journal* 549

Reading on the Internet

The Court of Appeal judgment in **Viasystems** *v* **Thermal Transfer** (2005) can be read at:
http://www.bailii.org/ew/cases/EWCA/Civ/2005/1151.html

The Court of Appeal judgment in **Mattis** *v* **Pollock** (2003) can be read at:
http://www.bailii.org/ew/cases/EWCA/Civ/2003/887.html

The House of Lords judgment in **Lister** *v* **Hesley Hall** (2001) can be read at:
http://www.publications.parliament.uk/pa/ld200001/ldjudgmt/jd010503/lister-1.htm

Visit **www.mylawchamber.co.uk** to access tools to help you develop and test your knowledge of tort law, including interactive multiple choice questions, practice exam questions with guidance, weblinks, glossary flashcards, legal newsfeed and legal updates.

Use Case Navigator to read in full some of the key cases referenced in this chapter with commentary and questions:
Lister *v* **Hesley Hall** (2001)

Chapter 18
Remedies in tort

This chapter discusses:

- The types of damages available in tort actions
- How damages are calculated
- Types of injunction and how they work
- When damages will be ordered instead of an injunction.

So far, we have looked at the rules on whether a defendant can be liable in tort. In this chapter, we look at the remedies that are available to the claimant once that liability is proved. The main remedies in tort are damages, which aim to compensate the claimant financially, and injunctions, which aim to stop or prevent the behaviour which comprises the tort. There are also a number of other remedies which are specific to particular torts; these have been discussed in the relevant chapters.

Damages

In the vast majority of cases where damages are claimed, they are what is known as compensatory (there are some types of non-compensatory damages, which are discussed on p. 408). The principle behind compensatory damages is that they should put the claimant in the position they would have been in if the tort had never been committed.

An award of compensatory damages may be composed of either general or special damages, or both. General damages are designed to compensate for the kinds of damage which the law presumes to be a result of the tort, such as pain and suffering from a personal injury, and loss of future earnings where the claimant's injuries mean they cannot return to a previous employment, or cannot work at all. Obviously, the amount of such damages cannot be calculated precisely, but the courts use the awards given for similar injuries in the past as a guideline. Special damages are those which do not arise naturally from the wrong complained of, and must be specifically listed in pleadings, and proved in court; they might include, for example, specific expenses incurred as a result of an accident.

Note that special damages are not the same as the special damage referred to in connection with slander or public nuisance.

Compensatory damages

The principle of restoring the claimant to the position they would have held if the tort had not been committed is called *restitutio in integrum*. There are essentially two different sorts of losses: pecuniary, which simply means financial, and non-pecuniary, which means losses other than those of money. Examples of pecuniary losses would be loss of earnings as a result of an injury, or a house being worth less than you paid for it because your surveyor negligently failed to spot defects in it. Non-pecuniary losses include pain and suffering after an injury, and what is called loss of amenity, which essentially means loss of the ability to enjoy life as you did before.

Calculating the loss

Pecuniary damages are clearly easier to calculate than non-pecuniary ones, since the claimant's loss can be measured in money. Even so, there are cases where the loss is purely financial, but the issue of what will amount to *restitutio in integrum* is not straightforward.

Key Case South Australia Asset Management Corporation *v* York Montague Ltd (1996)

In **South Australia Asset Management Corporation** *v* **York Montague Ltd** (1996), the House of Lords heard three appeals, each arising from similar facts: the defendants had each negligently valued a property, and the claimants lent money for the purchase of the property on the strength of those valuations. Soon afterwards, property prices dropped, and the borrowers in each case defaulted on the loan, leaving the lenders with a property worth less than the money they were owed on it. Each of the lenders gave evidence that they would not have granted the loans if they had known the true value of the property, and claimed that therefore their damages should include the loss that they had made through the general drop in property prices, since if they had not made the loan, they would not have made that loss either. For our purposes, the details of one of the cases is sufficient: here the lenders lent £1.75 million on a property that was valued at £2.5 million, but was actually worth £1.8 million. By the time the property market had dropped, it was worth only £950,000.

The Court of Appeal analysed the cases on the basis of whether the loans would have been granted if the true valuations had been known, and said that where the lenders would not have gone ahead with the loans had it not been for the negligent valuation, the lenders were entitled to recover the difference between the sum lent, and the sum recovered when the property was sold, together with a reasonable rate of interest, so that they would be compensated for the drop in market prices. Where a lender would still have gone ahead with the loan even if the correct valuation had been given, but lent a smaller sum, they would only be able to recover the difference between what they actually lost and what they would have lost had they lent a lesser amount; any fall in the market could not be compensated.

The House of Lords rejected this argument. Their Lordships said that in order to calculate damages for breach of a duty of care, it was first necessary to determine exactly what the duty consisted of; a defendant would only be liable for consequences arising from negligent performance of that duty. In this case, the defendants did not have a duty to advise the claimants whether or not to make the loan; their duty was to inform the claimants of the value of the property offered as security, and so their liability was limited to the consequences of that advice being wrong, and not to the entire consequences of the loan being made. The consequence of the advice being wrong was that the claimants had less security for the debt than they thought, and that loss should be compensated; in the case detailed above, the correct figure would be £700,000. This would give the claimants the amount of security they thought they had at the time the loan was made, but would not compensate for the drop in property prices, since this was not a consequence of the negligent valuation, but would have happened anyway. If the defendants had had a duty to advise the claimants whether or not to make the loan, they would have been liable for all losses arising from the fact that the loan was made, including the drop in property prices, but here their duty did not extend that far so their liability could not either.

Legal Principle

In order to calculate damages for a breach of duty, it is necessary to refer to what the duty consisted of. A defendant will only be liable for consequences arising from negligent performance of that duty.

Compensating property damage

Where the tort has caused damage to or loss of property, the defendant will be liable for the cost of putting the claimant back in the position they would have been in if the tort had not happened. If the property is destroyed, the defendant will have to pay the cost of replacing the property, at current prices, even if this is more than the item cost the claimant. If it is damaged, they will be required to pay the amount by which the damage has decreased the property's value; typically, this will be the cost of repairs. In either case, they will also be liable for any costs which arise from the loss or or damage to the property, providing these are not too remote. A common example is that where a car is damaged in an accident, the defendant may be liable for the costs of hiring a replacement while it is repaired.

Mitigation

A person who falls victim to a tort is expected to take reasonable steps to mitigate any loss; the defendant will not be liable for compensatory damages in respect of any losses that could have been prevented by such steps. However, since the situation is the fault of the defendant, not the claimant, the standard of reasonableness is not particularly high, and the claimant is certainly not required to make huge efforts to avoid a loss that is the defendant's fault.

In **Ronan** *v* **J Sainsbury plc** (2006), the claimant was injured while working for Sainsbury's, at the age of 19, and had to have a number of operations as a result of his injuries. He started a career in banking, and was doing well, but still needed further surgery. Eventually, his injury began to cause more problems, which surgery was unable to solve, and this caused depression, leading him to leave his job. He decided to have a change of career, and went to university. There was evidence that about a year later his health improved to the extent that he could have gone back to his old career. His case against Sainsbury's came to court after he had finished university, and as part of his compensatory damages the court included a sum to cover loss of earnings for the three years at university. Sainsbury's argued that this money should not have been included because the claimant should have mitigated his loss by giving up his studies and going back to his old job once his health allowed it. The court disagreed: the decision to change careers had been a direct result of the injuries caused by the accident, and once Mr Ronan had started his course it was unreasonable to expect him to leave it.

Compensation for personal injury

Damages for personal injury (which covers physical or psychiatric harm, disease and illness) raise problems not encountered with other types of loss. In the case of damage to property, for example, financial compensation is both easy to calculate and an adequate way of making good the loss, by allowing the claimant to buy a replacement or pay for repairs. It is not so easy to calculate the value of a lost limb, or permanent loss of general good health, and, even if it were, money can never really compensate for such losses. In addition, the court may be required to estimate the amount of future earnings which will be lost, and the future development of the injury; even though personal injury cases may take years to come to trial, the degree of recovery to be expected may still be unclear, and new symptoms may not appear until years later.

Damages for personal injury are divided into pecuniary and non-pecuniary losses. Pecuniary damages are those which can be calculated in financial terms, such as loss of earnings, and medical and other expenses, while non-pecuniary damages cover less easily calculable damages, such as pain, shock, suffering and loss of physical amenity.

Pecuniary damages

The courts have divided financial (or pecuniary) losses made by claimants in personal injury cases into the following 'heads of damage'.

Pre-trial expenses

The claimant is entitled to recover all expenses actually and reasonably incurred as a result of the accident up to the date of the trial. This includes, for example, loss of, or damage to, clothing and any medical expenses.

Expenses incurred by another

The most common example here is where a claimant has had to be looked after by a partner or relative, who has had to give up paid work as a result. Such carers cannot bring an action themselves directly against the defendant to seek compensation. But in **Donnelly** *v* **Joyce** (1972) the Court of Appeal recognised that the claimant could normally claim for this loss as part of his or her own claim. In that case the claimant was a child and his mother had to give up work to look after him when he was seriously injured by the defendant's negligence. The claimant succeeded in claiming for the financial loss that his mother had suffered as a result of caring for him.

The House of Lords decided in **Hunt** *v* **Severs** (1994) that any damages received under this head are awarded to the claimant to compensate the carer and not to the claimant themselves. When the claimant receives this award, he or she should hand the money over to the carer, and until he or she did so the money was held under an obligation to do so, known as being held on trust (for the facts of **Hunt** *v* **Severs**, see p. 407). This conclusion runs counter to the approach preferred by the Pearson Commission, which argued that damages should be the absolute property of the claimant. They pointed out that any duty to hand some of it over to someone else, such as a carer, would be extremely difficult to supervise. It might also constitute an incentive for members of a family not to help each other but to employ people from outside the family to care for their relations.

Pre-trial loss of earnings

The claimant can receive damages for the loss of the earnings or profits which would otherwise have been earned up to the date of the judgment. The amount awarded will be that which the claimant would have taken home after tax and National Insurance contributions have been deducted.

Future losses

Claims for future pecuniary loss usually comprise loss of future earnings, and, in cases of serious injury, the costs of care. They are regarded as general damages. Obviously they are difficult to calculate, since there is no real way of knowing what the future would have held for the claimant if the accident had not happened: they might have been promoted and earned a higher salary, for example, or, on the other hand, might have become unemployed.

Damages are usually awarded as a lump sum, but obviously the purpose of damages for loss of future earnings caused by personal injury is usually to give the claimant an income to replace the one they would have had if the injury had not happened. The courts therefore calculate a figure which, given as a lump sum, would be sufficient to buy an investment called an annuity that would give the claimant the right level of income for life, or however long the effects of the injury were expected to last (an annuity is an arrangement under which a lump sum is invested so as to produce an income).

The starting point for calculating future loss of earnings is the difference between income before the accident and afterwards, which is called the net annual loss. Obviously in some cases the claimant may be so badly injured that no income can be earned, but the principle also covers those who can work, but at lower paid employment than before. Predicting future earnings can be a matter of guesswork, especially in what are known as 'loss of a chance' cases, where the claimant alleges that there was a significant chance that their financial prospects would have improved in the future. An example is **Doyle** *v* **Wallace** (1998). In this case the claimant was badly injured in a road accident and was unable to work. She had been planning to train as a drama teacher if she could get the necessary qualifications, and if not she planned to get a clerical job. Her income would have been substantially higher as a teacher than as a clerk, but at the time of the accident it was too early to know whether she would have obtained the necessary qualifications. The trial judge found that she had a 50 per cent chance of qualifying as a drama teacher, and calculated the damages for loss of future earnings on the basis of an income that was half-way between that of a drama teacher and that of a clerical worker. The Court of Appeal upheld this approach.

Once the court has the net annual loss figure, it adjusts that sum to take into account factors which might have altered the claimant's original earnings, such as promotion prospects, and the figure that they reach as a result of doing so is called the multiplicand. The court then takes the number of years that the effects of the accident are likely to continue (which may be the rest of the claimant's life) and reduces this number by taking into account what are called the 'contingencies (or vicissitudes) of life' – basically, the fact that, even if the accident had not happened, the claimant might not have lived or worked until retirement age.

At this stage, the court has before it the annual amount that will compensate the claimant, and the number of years for which this amount should be payable. However, simply to multiply the first figure by the second would actually over-compensate the claimant. If we take, for example, an annual loss of £10,000, to be payable over 20 years, simple multiplication of these figures gives us £200,000. But a claimant does not actually need a lump sum of £200,000 to produce an annual income of £10,000 over 20 years, because the assumption is that the lump sum is invested and so makes more money during the 20 years, with the result that the claimant would end up over-compensated. To avoid this, the court assumes that the investment will earn a particular rate of return (called the discount rate), and reduces the lump sum to one which, on the basis of the assumed rate of return, will provide the right rate of compensation, nothing more and nothing less. The figure arrived at is called the multiplier, and the multiplicand multiplied by the multiplier gives the sum necessary to compensate the claimant for loss of future earnings.

Within these calculations, the rate of return on investments that the court assumes is very important – the higher the assumed rate of return, the smaller the lump sum, and if for some reason the claimant in practice is unable to achieve this rate of return on their investments, they will be under-compensated.

Until recently, the courts generally assumed a rate of interest of 4–5 per cent per year. This practice was criticised by, among others, the Law Commission in its 1995 report *Structured Settlements and Interim and Provisional Damages* (Law Com No 224). It said that the assumed rate of interest was an arbitrary figure; it was possible to achieve this rate of interest, but only with a relatively sophisticated understanding of investments which few claimants would possess, and so many claimants were likely to end up under-compensated. The Commission recommended that the courts should use as their guideline the return given to investors on a type of investment called an Index Linked Government Security (ILGS), which would give a more accurate picture of the kind of returns claimants could hope to get on their lump sums. The practical effect of this would be that multipliers would go up and so, as a result, would damages.

The Damages Act 1996 responded to this recommendation by providing that the Lord Chancellor can prescribe a rate of interest for the purposes of calculating multipliers, and in June 2001 the rate was set at 2.5 per cent. To appreciate how important the precise figure is, it might help to know that if we take for example a 20-year-old man who is awarded a multiplicand of £70,000, the difference between the damages paid with a discount rate of 2 per cent and the amount paid with one of 2.5 per cent would be £225,400.

The Damages Act provides, in s. 1(2), that a court may use a different discount rate 'if any party to the proceedings shows that it is more appropriate to the question'. An attempt to make use of this provision was made in **Warriner** *v* **Warriner** (2002). The claimant had suffered serious brain damage in a road accident and was claiming damages of over £2 million. His lawyers wanted to put forward expert evidence to show that a different discount rate should be used because the amount claimed was large and the claimant's life expectancy was long; it was claimed that the effect of a 2.5 per cent discount rate in this situation would be to under-compensate the claimant. The Court of Appeal refused to hear the evidence, stating that this was not the kind of circumstance intended to be covered by s. 1(2).

They held that the Lord Chancellor had given very careful consideration to setting the discount rate, and that the certainty offered by a set rate was extremely important. This being the case, the court said that a case could only activate the discretion allowed in s. 1(2) if there was material that supported changing the rate of return, and the Lord Chancellor had not considered that material when setting the rate. That was not the case here: the Lord Chancellor had considered the problems raised by large sums intended to cover long periods and allowed for them when setting the rate; the set rate assumed a relatively low level of investment performance, and, in practice, claimants could do better, with prudent investing, and so even out the problem of under-compensation.

In **Cooke** *v* **United Bristol Healthcare NHS Trust**; **Sheppard** *v* **Stibbe and another**; **Page** *v* **Lee** (2003), the Court of Appeal heard three similar cases in which the claimants had all been very severely injured and were likely to need care for the rest of their lives. They argued that, in their circumstances, using the conventional method of assessing damages with the discount rate would leave them substantially under-compensated because, although the discount rate took into account the effects of inflation, the costs of care were increasing at a much faster rate than that of inflation. Again, the Court of Appeal held that it was not possible to take evidence of this into account. Parliament had authorised the Lord Chancellor to set the rate, he had done so, taking inflation into account, and the courts had to respect that.

Topical issue

£4.3 million damages for a reckless tackle

The difficulty of assessing damages for future earnings can be seen on a larger than usual scale in the case of **Collett** *v* **Smith and Middlesbrough Football Company** (2008), which hit the news when it was heard by the Court of Appeal. It involved a young footballer, Ben Collett, whose career was ended by a reckless tackle and who won record damages of £4.3 million. Mr Collett, who was 18 at the time of the accident, had been playing in Manchester United's Youth Academy, and had been given a one-year professional contract. He was making his first appearance for Manchester United reserves, when he was tackled by a Middlesbrough player, Gary Smith, and his leg was broken in two places. The injury meant that he would not be able to play professional football again, and he successfully sued both Middlesbrough and Gary Smith.

In assessing the damages, the courts had to look at what Mr Collett could have been expected to earn had he not been injured, and this meant looking at what kind of career he could be expected to have as a professional footballer; clearly his income would be very different if he ended up spending his career in League Two, than if he went on to gain a regular place with a Premier League team. The Manchester United manager, Sir Alex Ferguson, was called to give evidence, and said that 'I thought the boy showed fantastic focus, a great attitude to work hard, and they are qualities to give any player an outstanding chance in the game.' This and other evidence about his previous performance led the courts to conclude that Mr Collett had been on course to spend most, perhaps all of his career in the Premier League, and could have expected to earn more than £16 million. However, experts in sports law questioned this conclusion, pointing out that of Mr Collett's ten teammates in the 2003 FA Youth Cup Final, fewer than half were playing for Premier League clubs by 2008. Sports lawyer Ian Blackshaw, quoted in *The Times*, said: 'Just because someone has come through the academy and has started to play, it doesn't necessarily follow that the next ten years will be brilliant, and that has to be reflected in the level of damages.'

Calculating lost years

As we have seen, the courts take into account how long a person could normally be expected to live, bearing in mind the 'vicissitudes of life', to calculate how long the claimant will need their income for. But what happens if, as a result of the tort, the claimant is expected to die earlier than they otherwise might have? In such a case it would clearly be unfair simply to reduce the amount of damages because the income would not be needed for so long, when this was the defendant's fault and therefore should not benefit them. In **Pickett** *v* **British Rail Engineering** (1978), it was decided that the correct approach was to use the claimant's predicted life expectancy if the accident had not happened, but reduce it by the amount that they would have spent on supporting themselves during that time. This means, for example, that if a claimant would have been expected to live a normal lifespan and retire at 65, but because of the accident is only likely to live to 30, they can still claim loss of earnings for the period between ages 30 and 65, but with an amount deducted to represent what it would have cost them to support themselves during those years.

Non-pecuniary losses

These are losses which are not financial, although the courts can only compensate for them in a financial way. They do this by reference to guidelines produced by the Judicial Studies Board, based on awards in previous cases. The Law Commission's 1995 Report No 225, *How Much is Enough?*, argued that compensation paid for these losses had fallen behind inflation and should be substantially increased. The Commission suggested that there was no real problem with the very smallest awards, those currently under £2,000, but that above that claimants were being under-compensated.

In **Heil** *v* **Rankin and another and Other Appeals** (2000), the House of Lords took the opportunity to look into this claim, and agreed with the Law Commission that there was a problem. However, they held that only those awards currently worth £10,000 or more needed adjustment, with the biggest problem being at the very top end of the scale, with the compensation for what the House of Lords called 'catastrophic injuries'. Where previously £150,000 had been regarded as the top level, this should be raised to £200,000; below that, there should be a tapering scale of increases down to awards of £10,000 or less, which would stay at current levels. The next Judicial Studies Board guidelines, published in 2000, followed the line taken in this case.

Non-pecuniary losses fall into the following heads of damage.

The primary injury

Damages for the actual injury are usually calculated with reference to a tariff, so that recognised values are placed on similar injuries. For example, minor or temporary eye injuries are 'worth' £1,000–£2,500, a broken leg £4,000–£7,000, lung disease £1,000–£65,000, and quadriplegia £160,000–£200,000. For most sorts of injuries there is a broad range within which damages can fall, allowing courts to take into account factors such as the seriousness of the injury, and how long the effects are likely to last.

Pain and suffering

Damages will be awarded for any pain and suffering which results from the injury itself, or from medical treatment of that injury. The claim may cover pain which the claimant can expect to suffer in the future, and mental suffering arising from the knowledge that life expectancy has been shortened or that the ability to enjoy life has been reduced by disability resulting from the injury.

Where the injury has caused a period of unconsciousness, that period will be excluded from any claim for pain and suffering, as it is assumed that an unconscious person is unaware of pain.

Loss of amenity

Loss of amenity describes the situation where an injury results in the claimant being unable to enjoy life to the same extent as before. It may include an inability to enjoy sport or any other pastime the claimant enjoyed before the injury, impairment of sight, hearing, touch, taste or smell, reduction in the chance of finding a marriage partner, and impairment of sexual activity or enjoyment. Calculation of these damages is based on a tariff laid down by the Court of Appeal, although the tariff figure can be adjusted to take into account the claimant's individual circumstances.

Damages for loss of amenity are not affected by whether the claimant is actually aware of the loss, so unconscious claimants may claim damages as if they had not been unconscious. This was the case in **West & Son** *v* **Shephard** (1964). The claimant was a married woman, who was 41 when she was injured. Serious head injuries left her at least partially unconscious, and paralysed in all four limbs. There was no hope of recovery, and her life expectancy was only five years. She was unable to speak, but there was evidence to suggest that she had some awareness of her circumstances. An award of £17,500 for loss of amenity was upheld by a majority in the House of Lords.

Alternative methods of payment

The standard method of paying damages is as a single lump sum, paid after the trial, but this can cause problems in certain cases. There are three alternative methods of payment, each aiming to deal with a different problem:

- Interim awards
- Structured settlements
- Provisional damages.

Interim awards are designed to deal with the problems caused by the fact that personal injury cases can take years to come to trial, which often leaves claimants without financial help when they most need it. In situations where the defendant has admitted liability, but there is still a dispute about the level of damages, the Supreme Court Act 1981 allows the courts to award interim damages before the case comes to trial. This provision can only be used where the defendant is insured, is a public body, or has the resources to make an interim payment.

Structured settlements are made not as a one-off sum, but in the form of a series of regular payments for the whole of the claimant's life. This form of damages is particularly useful in cases where the claimant has a serious injury which will mean they need lifelong care, but which does not shorten their lifespan. In these cases, providing a lump sum means there is a risk that at some point the money will run out, whereas payments from a structured settlements continue throughout their life. Even in less serious cases, lump sums almost always either over- or under-compensate the claimant because (as we saw on p. 401) they rely on an assumption of their lifespan, which is unlikely ever to be completely accurate.

Until April 2005, courts could only order structured settlements with the consent of both parties, and because defendants tended not to like the idea of such long-term liability such settlements were used only in around 100 cases a year. However, ss. 100 and 101 of the Courts Act 2003, which amend s. 2 of the Damages Act 1996 and came into force in April 2005, now give the courts a duty to consider whether a case is suitable for a structured settlement, and a power to order that damages should be paid this way, either wholly or partly. They can also order that damages for past losses are paid as a structured settlement, with the parties' consent. An example of a case considered for use of this power was **Walton** *v* **Calderdale Healthcare NHS Trust** (2005), where the claimant was 19 years old, would need lifelong care, and had a life expectancy of 70 years.

Provisional damages are designed to address the problem that, in some personal injury cases, the long-term effect of the injuries may not be known at the time of the trial. Where there is a possibility that the injured person will, as a result of the tort, develop a serious disease, or serious physical or mental deterioration in the future, the court can award initial damages based on the claimant's condition at the time of trial, but retain the power to award further damages if the possible future deterioration does in fact happen. The award can only be adjusted once.

Set-offs

As we have said, tort damages are generally calculated to put the claimant in the position they would have enjoyed if the tort had never been committed. They are not designed to put the claimant in a better position than if the tort had never been committed, and so the courts will generally take steps to make sure that any other money paid as a result of the injury will be deducted from the damages: this is known as a set-off. The following principles are followed.

Tax

Where a claimant is awarded damages for loss of earnings, the amount payable will be what the claimant would have earned after paying tax and National Insurance (**British Transport Commission** *v* **Gourley** (1956)).

Payments by an employer

Sick pay from an employer is taken into account in assessing damages, and damages are reduced accordingly. In **Hussain** *v* **New Taplow Paper Mills Ltd** (1988) the House of Lords stated that long-term sick pay from the employer according to the terms of the employment contract could be deducted, as such payments were the equivalent of receiving a salary.

Social security benefits

When the social security system was first set up, the Law Reform (Personal Injuries) Act 1948 provided that the value of certain social security benefits received by claimants should be deducted from the compensation payable to them, and, as time went on, the courts extended this approach, so that all benefits were covered by the rule. This prevented claimants being double-compensated, but it meant that the social security system (and therefore the taxpayer) was in effect subsidising defendants. From the late 1980s, new legislation was enacted, which deducted the value of social security benefits from the compensation received, but gave it to the state, rather than back to the defendant.

The situation is now covered by the Social Security (Recovery of Benefits) Act 1997. This provides that the value of social security benefits received by the claimant during the five years immediately following the accident or until the making of the compensation payment (whichever is the earlier) should be deducted from the compensation ordered by the court, and paid back to the state.

The Act treats compensation as having three elements – loss of earnings, cost of care, and loss of mobility – and the value of benefits received can only be set off against the corresponding element in the damages award. This means, for example, that if a claimant who has received £7,000 in income support and £3,000 in attendance allowance is awarded £10,000 for loss of earnings and £2,000 for cost of care, they will end up with £3,000, because the Scheme will not take the outstanding £1,000 in attendance allowance away from the sum awarded for loss of earnings. In addition, no part of the value of social security benefits can be deducted from damages awarded for pain and suffering. The previous legislation did not apply to awards of up to £2,500, but the 1997 Act brings such payments within the Scheme.

Exceptions

Apparent exceptions to the rule that damages should not make a claimant better off than they would have been if the tort had not been committed are made in the case of disability pensions paid by a claimant's employers, insurance pay-outs and payments made on a charitable basis. Sometimes known as the 'benevolence exception', this was established in **Parry** *v* **Cleaver** (1970), where Lord Read explained the decision on the grounds that set-offs of these kinds of payments would discourage charity and sensible investment in insurance, and might allow tortfeasors to benefit.

The rule has been criticised by the Law Commission in its 1997 consultation paper *Damages for Personal Injury: Collateral Benefits*. The Commission argued that it overcompensates victims, which is both contrary to the aims of tort law, and a waste of resources. It doubted that anyone would be put off buying insurance by the prospect of set-offs, since people buy insurance against income loss generally, not just loss as a result of a tort, so they would still want the cover.

Benefits provided by the tortfeasor

In **Hunt** *v* **Severs** (1994), the claimant was very seriously injured in a car accident caused by her fiancé, who she went on to marry. She sued him (which may seem odd, but bear in mind it would actually be his motor insurance company that stood to pay damages), and the issue arose of whether she could claim the cost of care that had been provided by him, and would continue to be given by him in the future. There is usually no problem with compensating the cost of care, even if that care is provided by a relative and so not actually paid for, but in this case the House of Lords held that such compensation could not be awarded because it would amount to double compensation, just as if the defendant had, for example, given the claimant a wheelchair and then been asked to pay compensation for the cost of it.

Fatal accidents

When a claimant dies as a result of a tort, the claim they would have had against the tortfeasor passes to their estate, meaning that it becomes part of what is inherited as a result of the death. Whoever inherits the estate can recover the losses that the claimant would have claimed for the period between the injury and the death, provided that it is not too brief – Law Reform (Miscellaneous Provisions) Act 1934, s. 1. So if, for example, someone is injured in an accident and dies six months later, the estate can claim damages for pecuniary and non-pecuniary losses, based on the usual principles, for that six-month period.

In addition, the Fatal Accidents Act 1976 establishes two further claims: a claim by dependants of the deceased for financial losses and a claim for the bereavement suffered. Claims can be brought by a spouse, dependent children and certain other close relatives who can prove they were financially dependent on the person who has died. Claims can also be brought by unmarried partners where the couple had lived together as husband and wife for at least two years, and the Civil Partnership Act 2004 amends the Fatal Accidents Act to include partners of the same sex. Dependants will only have a claim if the deceased would have had one, and any defence which could have been used against the claimant can be used against them.

Dependants can claim for financial losses to themselves caused by the death, including earnings spent on the dependants, savings made for their future use, non-essential items such as holidays, and the value of services rendered. So, for example, a man who loses his wife can claim the value of any domestic services she provided for the family. In **Martin and Browne** *v* **Grey** (1998), a 12-year-old girl was awarded a record amount of damages for loss of the services provided by her mother, who had been killed. The court held that in calculating the award it was necessary to look at the cost of providing the services a mother would normally provide, whether or not these services had actually been replaced; this might include, for example, the costs of employing a housekeeper, or the loss of earnings of the father if he gave up work.

The second claim allowed by the Fatal Accidents Act 1976 is for a fixed award of £10,000 damages for bereavement, which is designed to provide some compensation for the non-pecuniary losses associated with bereavement. It is only available to the husband or wife of the deceased, or, if the deceased was unmarried and a minor, to the parents. It does not give children a claim for the death of a parent.

Topical issue

Are bereavement damages high enough?

In 2007, researchers at the University of Warwick published an interesting study on bereavement damages, which suggested that the methods courts used to calculate such damages meant that the amounts ordered did not come close to compensating claimants for the loss suffered. As we have seen, the calculations tend to look mainly at the economic value of the dead person to the family, and the Warwick researchers found that this approach could not take into account the level of unhappiness caused by the death of a close relative. They proposed a new approach, which would examine the effect on mental well-being of particular life events, including bereavement.

The researchers used the British Household Panel Survey, which is a yearly survey of the same 5,000 households, chosen to represent a cross-section of British society. Among other things, it asks people about significant events that have happened over the past year, and also includes questions which are designed to measure mental well-being. The survey can therefore be used to measure the effect on mental well-being in those who mention that they have suffered a bereavement. In addition, it asks about changes to household income which, when cross-referenced to the mental well-being data, can measure the effect of particular amounts of money on mental well-being. By putting these two pieces of information together, the researchers came up with a set of sums which they said would be a true reflection of the emotional impact of bereavement, and the amount of money needed to compensate for that impact.

Non-compensatory damages

As we have seen, compensatory damages are carefully calculated to put the claimant in the position they would have enjoyed if the tort had never been committed. In some cases, however, damages may be awarded for different reasons, and these may be less, or much more, than is required to compensate the loss directly. There are four types of non-compensatory damages: contemptuous, nominal, aggravated and exemplary.

Contemptuous damages

Where a court recognises that the claimant's legal rights have technically been infringed, but disapproves of their conduct, and considers that the action should never have been brought, it may order contemptuous damages. These will amount to no more than the value of the least valuable coin of the realm (currently 1p). A claimant awarded contemptuous damages is also unlikely to recover costs. Contemptuous damages are not often awarded; their main use is in defamation actions.

Nominal damages

An award of nominal damages is normally made where there has technically been an infringement of a person's legal rights but no actual damage has been done. It comprises a small sum of money, normally £20, and its purpose is to acknowledge that the defendant has violated the claimant's rights, rather than to compensate for loss. In **Watkins** *v* **Secretaryof State for the Home Department** (2006), the House of Lords ruled that nominal damages should only be used in cases involving torts which are actionable *per se* (meaning that no actual damage need be done), such as trespass.

A claimant who secures nominal damages will not necessarily be awarded costs as well.

Aggravated damages

Where a defendant has behaved in such a way that the claimant has suffered more than would normally be expected in such a case, the court can show its disapproval by awarding damages which are higher than would normally be appropriate. These are called aggravated damages. An example of the kind of case where aggravated damages are considered appropriate is **Khodaparast** *v* **Shad** (1999). The claimant, an Iranian woman, had sued her ex-boyfriend for libel after he created photomontages that appeared to show her advertising pornographic telephone lines, and distributed the images throughout the local Iranian community. As a result, the claimant lost her teaching job at an Iranian school, and had little or no prospect of finding further work within the Iranian community; as her English was poor, this had been her main source of employment. In his pre-trial statements, and later in court, the defendant persisted in denying that he had created the montages, and insisted that they were real pictures of the claimant and quite likely to have come from pornographic magazines; in support of this allegation, he made a number of other untrue claims, including that she 'slept around', associated with prostitutes, and had had 'an improper relationship' with her solicitor. As a result of this behaviour, the trial judge awarded aggravated damages, and his decision was upheld by the Court of Appeal.

In **Rowlands** *v* **Chief Constable of Merseyside** (2006), the Court of Appeal examined the role of aggravated damages as compensation. The claimant, Mrs Rowlands, had complained to police about a persistently noisy party opposite her home, and got into a row with one of the police officers who had come to try to sort out the situation. She was arrested, handcuffed in front of her children, and taken to a police car, and, when she asked to have the handcuffs loosened because they were causing excruciating pain, the police officer deliberately tugged them, increasing the pain. After being detained for an hour and a half, she was charged with assaulting a constable in the course of his duty. At her trial, the magistrates did not accept that the police evidence was true, and Mrs Rowlands was acquitted. She sued Merseyside police for assault, false imprisonment and malicious prosecution, and the Court of Appeal decided that she should receive aggravated damages, even though the police had argued that this would amount to compensating her twice because her compensatory damages included an amount for psychological injury. The court acknowledged the danger of double compensation but said that, given the amount of humiliation and distress the arrest caused, and the willingness of the police to give false evidence against her, aggravated damages were appropriate.

Exemplary damages

Exemplary damages also involve paying the claimant more than would normally be appropriate, but they differ from aggravated damages in that their purpose is actually to offer a serious punishment to the defendant, and to deter others from behaving in the same way.

The punitive nature of exemplary damages means that they stray into an area which is generally thought to be more appropriate to criminal law, where of course there is a higher standard of proof.

Rookes *v* Barnard (1964)

As a result, their use is very carefully controlled, and in **Rookes** *v* **Barnard** (1964), the House of Lords laid down strict rules about when they could be ordered. The case must fall within one of the following categories:

- Statutory authorisation
- Conduct calculated to make a profit
- Oppressive conduct by government servants.

Legal Principle

Exemplary damages may only be ordered when they are authorised by statute, the defendant's action was calculated to make a profit, or in cases of oppressive conduct by government servants.

Statutory authorisation

There are a few cases in which exemplary damages are expressly allowed by statute.

Conduct calculated to make a profit

There are clearly some cases, usually involving defamation, where a defendant may calculate that it is worth committing a tort, even at the risk of being sued, because the profit to be made will exceed the cost of compensating the claimant if they do sue. For example, an unscrupulous newspaper may calculate that the revenue from increased sales may make it worthwhile to print a libellous story.

It is not necessary for the defendant to calculate precisely the potential profit and compensation, so long as they deliberately risk causing damage in order to make a profit. This was the case in **Cassell & Co Ltd** *v* **Broome** (1972). The claimant was a retired naval officer, and the defendants published a book about a wartime convoy with which the claimant was involved. The claimant successfully sued for libel and was awarded £25,000 exemplary damages. This was upheld by the House of Lords, taking into account the profit which the defendant would have made.

Oppressive conduct by government servants

Exemplary damages may also be awarded where there has been oppressive, arbitrary or unconstitutional action by government servants, which includes people exercising governmental functions, such as police officers. The purpose here is to mark the fact that government servants are also supposed to serve the community, and must use their powers accordingly.

An old example of such a case is **Huckle** *v* **Money** (1763). The claimant was detained under a search warrant. The detention was for six hours, and involved no ill-treatment; in fact food and drink were provided. Even so, the court upheld an award of £300 damages, stating that entering a person's home with a search warrant that did not have his name on it was a serious breach of civil liberties.

Much more recently, the Court of Appeal upheld the application of exemplary damages in **Muuse** *v* **Secretary of State for the Home Department** (2010). The case involved a man who

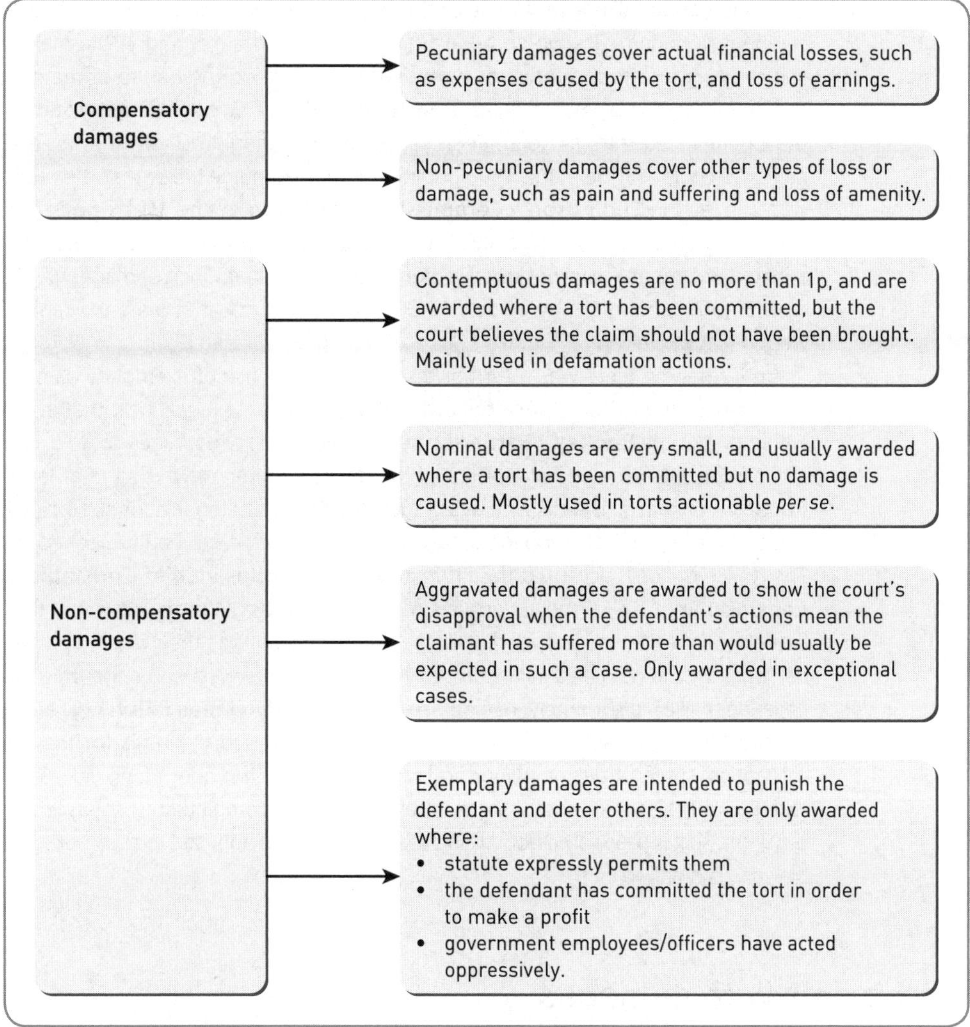

Figure 18.1 Types of damages

had been unlawfully detained while the Home Office considered whether to deport him to Somalia, which, it turned out, it had no right to do because although born in Somalia, he was a Dutch national. The court heard that during his detention, his treatment by Home Office officials had been 'high-handed, insulting, malicious and oppressive'. They ignored the obvious evidence that he was Dutch (such as his passport!), failed to answer letters from his solicitor, and even when they eventually accepted that there was no right to deport him to Somalia, kept him in detention for a further month. During all this time, Mr Muuse was terrified that he might be deported. The Court of Appeal agreed with the trial judge that exemplary damages were justified in order to show strong disapproval of the officials' behaviour. Modern cases have also involved local authorities which have practised sexual or racial discrimination in recruiting employees, such as **Bradford City Metropolitan Council** *v* **Arora** (1991), and exemplary damages were also awarded in **Rowlands** *v* **Chief Constable of Merseyside** (discussed at p. 409).

In addition to falling within one of these categories, it must be clear that the case is one where compensatory damages would be insufficient, and, if there is a jury, the members must be fully and carefully directed. Later cases have shed more light on the nature of the direction to be given to juries in particular types of case. In **John** *v* **Mirror Group Newspapers** (1995), the Court of Appeal stated that, in defamation cases, the jury should be told that an award of exemplary damages could only be made if the publisher had no genuine belief that the published information was true, and in **Thompson** *v* **Commissioner of Police of the Metropolis** (1997), the Court of Appeal stated that, in cases of unlawful conduct by the police, juries should be told that they can award damages at a level designed to punish the defendant. Such damages were unlikely to be less than £5,000, and might be up to £50,000 where officers of at least the rank of superintendent were directly involved.

Until recently, there was a further restriction on the use of exemplary damages, established in **AB** *v* **South West Water Services Ltd** (1993). In that case it was held that even where a case fell within one of the **Rookes** *v* **Barnard** categories, exemplary damages could only be awarded if the tort committed was one for which such damages had been awarded in at least one case before **Rookes** *v* **Barnard**. The decision was much criticised as being irrational, since whether exemplary damages were available would depend entirely on which cases had happened to come up before. The House of Lords accepted this criticism and, in **Kuddus** *v* **Chief Constable of Leicestershire Constabulary** (2001), they overruled **AB** *v* **South West Water**. However, this decision did not entirely clarify the issue. Their Lordships made it clear that they did not intend that exemplary damages should now be available for any tort, since there were some for which such damages had never been available (namely, negligence, nuisance and **Rylands** *v* **Fletcher**) and they did not want to make them available in these areas. They also criticised the basis for the **Rookes** *v* **Barnard** categories, stating that they were no longer in step with modern law; yet they were reluctant to take the radical step of abolishing exemplary damages completely. This has left nobody very much the wiser, so it is probably a good thing that in real life, as opposed to textbooks, exemplary damages play a very small role.

Problems with damages

Lump sums

As we have seen (on p. 404), the fact that damages are paid in a lump sum has disadvantages for the claimant, particularly where the effects of injury worsen after the award is made. The introduction of provisional damages has gone some way towards dealing with this problem, but still does not cover cases where at the time of trial there is no reason to believe that further deterioration will occur.

As well as the future prospects of the claimant's health, the lump sum system requires the court to predict what the claimant's employment prospects are likely to be; in reality this can never be known, so the compensation may well turn out to represent much more or less than the claimant should have had. Perhaps more importantly, it is impossible to predict the result of inflation on the award, so that, when inflation is high, the award's value can soon be eroded.

A further problem is that there is no way to ensure that the claimant uses the lump sum in such a way as to make sure it provides a lifelong income, where necessary. If the money is used unwisely, the claimant may end up having to live on state benefits, which partly defeats the object of making the tortfeasor compensate for the damage caused. The courts' new power to order structured settlements may go some way towards solving this problem, depending on whether they restrict its use to the most serious cases, or extend it more widely.

Degrees of fault

Because the aim of tort damages is to compensate the claimant, rather than punish the defendant, compensation does not take into account the degree of fault involved in the defendant's action. As a result, a defendant who makes a momentary slip may end up paying the same damages as one who shows gross carelessness. The system as it stands seems unable to provide justice for the claimant without injustice to some defendants.

West & Son *v* Shephard and loss of amenity

The case of **West & Son** *v* **Shephard** (1964), and the principle that a person who is unaware of their loss of amenity can still be compensated for it, has been strongly criticised. The main criticism is that the compensation cannot actually be used by the unconscious person, and in most cases will simply end up forming part of their estate when they die. This being the case, it seems inequitable that relatives in this situation may end up with considerably more than the relatives of someone killed immediately as the result of a tort. But if no such award was made the court would be treating the claimant as if they were dead.

The Law Commission has recommended that this aspect of the law should be kept, but the Pearson Commission suggested that awards for non-pecuniary loss should no longer be made to unconscious claimants. The Pearson Commission recommendation has not been implemented.

Damages for bereavement

The standard payment for bereavement (see p. 407) was raised from £7,500 to £10,000 in 2002, but the Association of Personal Injury Lawyers (APIL) has criticised this as inadequate and unfair. The Association had been pushing for a complete review of bereavement damages, arguing that such damages should be at least equal to those for the most serious injuries; at £10,000, bereavement compensation is a fraction of the £35,000 typically awarded for loss of one eye, for example, or the £200,000 for paralysis. The current situation means that it is cheaper for defendants to kill than to injure.

APIL has also criticised the fact that parents are denied damages for children over 18, which means that unless the child has another next of kin – such as a spouse – defendants do not have to pay anybody bereavement compensation.

Injunctions

Injunctions are the other main remedy the courts can order in tort cases, and are mainly used to deal with continuing or repeatable torts such as defamation and nuisance. In issuing an injunction, the court prohibits the defendant from committing, continuing or repeating a particular tort. Injunctions are an equitable remedy, which means they are not available as of right to a successful claimant, but are issued at the discretion of the court, where it is considered to be 'just and convenient' (Supreme Court Act 1981, s. 37). An injunction will not be granted where damages would be an adequate remedy.

Most injunctions prohibit the defendant from doing something: these are called, not surprisingly, prohibitory injunctions. Injunctions may also be mandatory, in which case they order the defendant to do something. These are subject to special guidelines, laid down in **Redland Bricks Ltd** *v* **Morris** (1970). The defendants had been digging on their own land, and this work had caused subsidence on the claimants' land, and made further subsidence likely if the digging continued. The claimants were awarded damages for the damage that had already been done, and a mandatory injunction ordering the defendants to restore support to their land. This restoration work was to cost more than the total value of the claimants' land, and the defendants appealed against the injunction.

The House of Lords allowed the appeal and laid down some general guidelines on the issue of mandatory injunctions, although they stressed that the decision on whether to grant such an order remained one for the court's discretion, bearing in mind the individual circumstances of a case. In general, they said, mandatory injunctions should be ordered only where damages would not be adequate to remedy the harm done to the claimant. Where the defendant has acted reasonably, though wrongly, the fact that carrying out a mandatory injunction would, as in the case of **Redlands**, be very costly may be a reason not to grant such an injunction; however, if the defendant has acted unreasonably, and particularly if the defendant has in some way tried to gain an advantage over the claimant or the court, the cost of carrying out the injunction should not be taken into account. Should a mandatory injunction be ordered, the court must ensure that the defendant knows precisely what is to be done, so that accurate instructions for carrying out the work can be given.

Interlocutory injunctions

In some cases a court may order an injunction (which may be either mandatory or prohibitory) before the case is actually heard. This is called an interlocutory or interim injunction, and is designed to prevent potential harm, or continued harm, during the period before the case comes to court (an injunction granted as a result of a decided trial is called a perpetual injunction).

The fact that an interlocutory injunction has been granted does not mean that the claimant has won; when the case is tried, the defendant may be found to have been in the right, and the injunction unjustified. For this reason, the courts do not give interlocutory injunctions easily, and in some cases the claimant may be required to give an undertaking in damages – a promise to pay damages for any loss incurred by the defendant while the injunction was in force, should the claimant lose the case. In **American Cyanamid Co** *v* **Ethicon Ltd** (1975), guidelines for the use of interlocutory injunctions were laid down. The claimant does not have to establish a *prima facie* case, but the court should be satisfied that there is a 'serious question' to be tried. If damages are an adequate remedy for the alleged wrong, no interlocutory injunction should be granted. On the other hand, if the adequacy of damages is questionable, the court should decide on the basis of the balance of convenience, weighing what the claimant stands to gain from an interlocutory injunction against what the defendant stands to lose.

One of the most obvious potential uses for interlocutory injunctions is that of libel cases, as clearly once a statement has been made public the damage can never truly be undone. However, in assessing whether to allow interlocutory injunctions, the courts are very aware of the need to protect free speech, and such injunctions are in practice uncommon in libel cases.

Damages in lieu of injunction

Key Case **Shelfer *v* City of London Electric Lighting Co (1895)**

The High Court has a discretion to order damages instead of an injunction. In **Shelfer *v* City of London Electric Lighting Co** (1895), it was stated that this discretion should generally be exercised where an injunction could have been issued, but would be oppressive to the defendant, and the harm done to the claimant is minor, and capable of being calculated in and compensated by money. Damages in such cases would generally be calculated using the normal principles discussed at the start of the chapter.

Legal Principle

A court should usually exercise its discretion to award damages instead of an injunction where an injunction would be oppressive to the defendant, and the harm done is minor and can be compensated for with damages.

An example of the way the courts apply **Shelfer** can be seen in **Daniells *v* Mendoca** (1999). The parties were neighbours, and Ms Daniells had had a bathroom extension built on her property. Some years later, she went away for three months, and when she came back, she discovered that Mr Mendoca had built an extension too, which was supported by the wall of hers and joined to her roof. The London Building (Amendments) Act 1939 requires that neighbours be informed of plans to build, but Ms Daniells had known nothing of the work that was taking place while she was away. Mr Mendoca admitted trespass, but the issue of remedies could not be agreed; Ms Daniells wanted an injunction, but Mr Mendoca argued that this was a case where **Shelfer** suggested that damages should be ordered instead. Applying the **Shelfer** principles, the court allowed the injunction: it was true that the extent of trespass was small, but this was offset by the fact that it was permanent, and other additions were planned; the injury could be compensated for by money, but this would not be a small amount, given the nuisance, the fire danger and the risk of structural damage; and the injunction could not be said to be oppressive to the defendant, given his own behaviour in building the extension in the first place, and failing to comply with the Act.

The issue of when an injunction will be considered 'oppressive' has been discussed in two recent cases. In **Jacklin *v* Chief Constable of West Yorkshire** (2007), West Yorkshire police had some construction work done, which involved placing a container on land over which the claimant had a right of way. Although it was still possible to walk across the land, the container meant that the claimant could not drive across it. The claimant complained against the proposed alterations but the police went ahead anyway. Three years after the container was first put there, the claimant sued in nuisance, and wanted an injunction to get the container removed. The police argued that an injunction would be oppressive, given the time the claimant had taken to sue, and the difficulty, three years on, of putting the site back to the way it was. The Court of Appeal disagreed. The trial judge had apparently taken note of the fact that the police had ignored the claimant's protests and gone ahead with the work without even checking what the problem was, and, as a result, considered that it was not unfair for them to be made to undo the damage. The Court of Appeal held that there was no reason to disturb that decision.

In **Regan** *v* **Paul Properties** (2006), the defendant was constructing a building near the claimant's maisonette. Part of the planned building would have reduced the light coming into the claimant's living room, and this would reduce the value of the house by around £5,000. The claimant wanted an injunction forcing changes to the plans, which would have reduced the value of the new building by around £175,000. Despite complaints from the claimant, and his assertion that he did not want damages but wanted to keep the light, the defendant continued with the original plans, and by the time the case came to court a large part of the building had been completed. The defendant claimed that an injunction would be oppressive because it would cost a substantial amount of money to change the building after so much work had been done. The Court of Appeal disagreed: the losses were only substantial because the defendants had pressed on with the project, and it was therefore not oppressive to order an injunction.

Answering questions

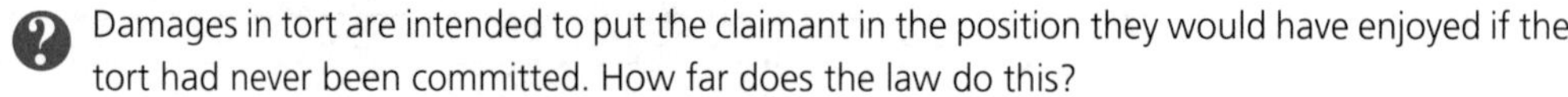

Damages in tort are intended to put the claimant in the position they would have enjoyed if the tort had never been committed. How far does the law do this?

A good way to start this essay would be to summarise briefly the principle of *restitutio in integrum*; if you have studied contract law, you could mention briefly how tort damages differ from the principle of damages in contract – one seeks to make good a loss, and the other to protect an expected gain.

You should then go on to discuss the rules on how tort damages are calculated and awarded. As you work through the rules, highlight the cases which reveal the problems associated with these calculations, including disputed loss cases such as **South Australia Asset Management** *v* **York Montague Ltd**, the 'loss of a chance' cases such as **Doyle** *v* **Wallace**, and the controversy over the discount rate, as highlighted in **Warriner** *v* **Warriner**. You should also cover the issues of possible over-compensation examined in **Parry** *v* **Cleaver**, with the criticisms made by the Law Commission; the problems with the principle in **West** *v* **Shephard**; and the problems associated with giving damages as lump sums.

In order to look further at the issue of how far *restitutio in integrum* is achieved, you could talk about the areas of tort law where damages simply cannot undo the harm done: the non-pecuniary damages associated with personal injury, and the damage to reputation done by defamation, for example. You should point out problems which arise from these – for the problem of juries awarding excessive damages for defamation may in part be caused by the fact that there is no way to put a price on damage to reputation.

Your conclusion should sum up how far you feel the law achieves the aim of *restitutio in integrum*, but you might also choose to say how far you feel this should be its aim in tort cases – you might mention, for example, the fact that in choosing this aim, the sum of damages cannot take into account degrees of fault.

Summary of Chapter 18

The main general remedies in tort are:

- Damages
- Injunctions.

Damages

Damages may be compensatory or non-compensatory.

Compensatory damages

Compensatory damages are designed to put the claimant in the position they would have been in if the tort was not committed. They comprise:

- general damages, which are presumed to result from the tort;
- special damages, which do not arise naturally from the tort.

Calculating compensatory damages

- Pecuniary damages compensate for financial losses.
- Non-pecuniary damages compensate for other losses, such as pain and suffering.
- Pecuniary damages are easier to calculate, but there may still be difficulties working out how much would put the claimant back in the pre-tort position.
  - The courts take steps to avoid over-compensation.
  - The claimant is expected to take reasonable steps to mitigate their loss.

Compensation for personal injury

Personal injury damages are pecuniary and non-pecuniary.

Pecuniary damages

- Pre-trial expenses
- Expenses incurred by another
- Pre-trial loss of earnings
- Future losses.

Non-pecuniary damages

- The primary injury
- Pain and suffering
- Loss of amenity.

Alternative ways of paying damages

Most damages are in the form of a one-off payment after trial, but this can cause problems for claimants. There are three alternatives:

- Interim awards are made before trial where liability is admitted, and only the amount of damages is in dispute.
- Structured settlements are a series of regular payments for the whole of the claimant's life, useful in cases where lifelong care is needed.
- Provisional damages can be awarded where the claimant's condition may worsen after trial.

Set-offs

Damages are designed to compensate for loss, not make the claimant richer, so other money paid as a result of the injury may be deducted from damages, including:

- Tax;
- Payments by an employer;
- Social security benefits.

Disability pensions, insurance pay-outs and charitable payments are not deducted.

Benefits provided by the tortfeasor cannot be compensated.

Fatal accidents

- If a victim of tort dies, their estate inherits their claim.
- The Fatal Accidents Act 1976 creates two further claims for dependants:
  - for the bereavement;
  - for financial losses.

Non-compensatory damages

There are four types:

- Contemptuous damages, used when the claimant's rights are infringed but the court feels the action should not have been brought.
- Nominal damages, used where a tort is committed but no damage is caused.
- Aggravated damages, used where the court wishes to show disapproval of the defendant's conduct.
- Exemplary damages, used in three categories of case:
  - where statute authorises them;
  - where the defendant has deliberately committed a tort in order to make a profit;
  - where there has been oppressive or unconstitutional action by government employees.

Problems with damages

Key issues are:

- Lump sums;
- Degrees of fault;
- Rules on loss of amenity;
- Damages for bereavement.

Injunctions

An injunction is an order from the court.

- Prohibitory injunctions order the defendant not to do something.
- Mandatory injunctions order the defendant to do something.

Injunctions are issued at the court's discretion, not as of right.

Interlocutory (or interim) injunctions are given before a case is tried. They should only be given in cases where there is a serious question to try, and damages are likely to be inadequate if the claimant wins.

The courts can order damages instead of an injunction.

Reading list

Text resources

Brennan, C (2006) 'An instrument of justice?' 17 *Child and Family Law Quarterly* 1

Cane, P (2006), *Atiyah's Accidents, Compensation and the Law*, 7th edn, Chapters 7 and 18. Cambridge University Press

Conaghan, J and Mansell, W (1998) *The Wrongs of Tort*, 2nd edn, Chapter 5. Pluto

Harlow, C (2005) *Understanding Tort Law*, 3rd edn, Chapter 4. Sweet & Maxwell

Kemp, D (1998) 'Damages for personal injuries: a sea change' 114 *Law Quarterly Review* 570

Law Commission (1997) *Aggravated, Exemplary and Restitutionary Damages*, Report No 247

Law Commission (1999) *Damages for Personal Injury: Non-Pecuniary Loss*, Report No 257

Law Commission (1999) *Claims for Wrongful Death*, Report No 263

Lewis, R (2001) 'Increasing the price of pain: damages, the Law Commission and Heil *v* Rankin' 64 *Modern Law Review* 100

Sands, A and Martin, N (2006) 'Period pieces' *Solicitors Journal* 457

Spencer, J (2005) 'Damages for lost chances: lost for good?' 64 *Cambridge Law Journal* 282

Reading on the Internet

The Law Commission's 1999 report *Damages for Personal Injury: Medical, Nursing and Other Expenses; Collateral Benefits* can be read at:

http://lawcommission.justice.gov.uk/docs/cp144DamagesPersonalInjuryMedicalNursingConsultation.pdf

The Law Commission's 1999 report *Damages for Personal Injury: Non-Pecuniary Loss* can be read at:

http://lawcommission.justice.gov.uk.docs/lc257DamagesPersonalInjuryNon-pecuniaryLoss.pdf

The Judicial Studies Board Guidelines for the Assessment of General Damages in Personal Injury Cases (2006), can be read at:

http://fds.oup.com/www.oup.co.uk/pdf/0-19-920757-7.pdf

Visit **www.mylawchamber.co.uk** to access tools to help you develop and test your knowledge of tort law, including interactive multiple choice questions, practice exam questions with guidance, weblinks, glossary flashcards, legal newsfeed and legal updates.

Appendix: Answering examination questions

At the end of each chapter in this book, you will find detailed guidelines for answering examination questions on the topics covered. Many of the questions are taken from actual A-Level past papers, but they are equally relevant for candidates of all law examinations, as these questions are typical of the type of questions that examiners ask in this field.

General guidelines

Citation of authorities

One of the most important requirements for answering questions on the law is that you must be able to back the points you make with authority, usually from either a case or a statute. It is not good enough to state that the law is such and such, without stating the case or statute which says that that is the law.

Some examiners are starting to suggest that the case name is not essential, as long as you can remember and understand the general principle that that case laid down. However, such examiners remain in the minority and the reality is that even they are likely to give higher marks where the candidate has cited authorities by name; quite simply, it helps give the impression that you know your material thoroughly, rather than half-remembering something you heard once in class.

This means that you must be prepared to learn fairly long lists of cases by heart, which can be a daunting prospect. What you need to memorise is the name of the case, a brief description of the facts, and the legal principle which the case established. Once you have revised a topic well, you should find that a surprisingly high number of cases on that topic begin to stick in your mind anyway, but there will probably be some that you have trouble recalling. A good way to memorise these is to try to create a picture in your mind which links the facts, the name and the legal principle – the more bizarre the image, the more likely you are to remember it.

Knowing the names of cases makes you look more knowledgeable, and also saves writing time in the exam, but if you do forget a name, referring briefly to the facts will identify it. It is not necessary to learn the dates of cases, although it is useful if you know whether it is a recent or an old case. Dates are usually required for statutes.

You need to know the facts of a case in order to judge whether it applies to the situation in a problem question. However, unless you are making a detailed comparison of the facts of a case and the facts of a problem question, in order to argue that the case should or could be distinguished, you should generally make only brief reference to facts, if at all – long descriptions of facts waste time and earn few marks.

When reading the 'Answering questions' sections at the end of each chapter in this book, bear in mind that, for reasons of space, we have not highlighted every case which you should cite. The skeleton arguments outlined in those sections must be backed up with authority from cases and statute law.

There is no right answer

In law exams, there is not usually a right or a wrong answer. What matters is that you show you know what type of issues you are being asked about. Essay questions are likely to ask you to 'discuss', 'criticise', or 'evaluate', and you simply need to produce a good range of factual and critical material in order to do this. The answer you produce might look completely different from your friend's but both answers could be worth 'A' grades.

Breadth and depth of content

Where a question seems to raise a number of different issues – as most do – you will achieve better marks by addressing all or most of these issues than by writing at great length on just one or two. By all means spend more time on issues which you know well, but at least be sure to mention other issues which you can see are relevant, even if you can only produce a paragraph or so about them.

The structure of the question

If a question is specifically divided into parts, for example (a), (b) and (c), then stick to those divisions and do not merge your answer into one long piece of writing.

Law examinations tend to contain a mixture of essay questions and what are known as 'problem questions'. Tackling each of these questions involves slightly different skills so we consider each in turn.

Essay questions

Answer the question asked

Over and over again, examiners complain that candidates do not answer the question they are asked – so if you can develop this skill, you will stand out from the crowd. You will get very few marks for simply writing all you know about a topic, with no attempt to address the issues raised in the question, but if you can adapt the material that you have learnt on the subject to take into account the particular emphasis given to it by the question, you will do well.

Even if you have memorised an essay which does raise the issues in the question (perhaps because those issues tend to be raised year after year), you must fit your material to the words of the question you are actually being asked. For example, suppose during your course you wrote an essay on the advantages and disadvantages of limiting compensation for nervous shock, and then, in the exam, you find yourself faced with the question 'Should compensation for nervous shock be subject to the same rules as for physical damage?' The material in your coursework essay is ideally suited for the exam question, but if (after briefly explaining what the rules on compensation for physical damage and for nervous shock are) you begin the main part of your answer with the words 'The advantages of limiting compensation for nervous shock include . . .', or something similar, this is a dead giveaway to the examiner that you are merely writing down an essay you have memorised. It takes very little effort to change the words to 'There are a number of good reasons why compensation for nervous shock should not be subject to the same rules as physical damage . . .', but it will create a much better impression, especially if you finish with a conclusion which, based on points you have made, states that special rules are a good or bad idea, the choice depending on the arguments you have made during your answer.

During your essay, you should keep referring to the words used in the question – if this seems to become repetitive, use synonyms for those words. This makes it clear to the examiner that you are keeping the question in mind as you work.

Plan your answer

Under pressure of time, it is tempting to start writing immediately, but five minutes spent planning each essay question is well worth spending – it may mean that you write less overall, but the quality of your answer will almost certainly be better. The plan need not be elaborate: just jot down everything you feel is relevant to the answer, including case names, and then organise the material into a logical order appropriate to the question asked. To put it in order, rather than wasting time copying it all out again, simply put a number next to each point according to which ones you intend to make first, second and so forth.

Provide analysis and fact

Very few essay questions require merely factual descriptions of what the law is; you will almost always be required to analyse the factual content in some way, usually highlighting any problems or gaps in the law, and suggesting possible reforms. If a question asks you to analyse whether individuals are adequately protected by the law on defamation, you should not write everything you know about defamation and finish with one sentence saying individuals are or are not adequately protected. Instead you should select your relevant material and your whole answer should be targeted at answering whether the protection is adequate, by, for example, pointing out any gaps or problems in it, and highlighting changes which have improved protection.

Where a question uses the word 'critically', as in 'critically describe' or 'critically evaluate', the examiners are merely drawing your attention to the fact that your approach should be analytical and not merely descriptive; you are not obliged to criticise every provision you describe. Having said that, even if you do not agree with particular criticisms which you have read, you should still discuss them and say why you do not think they are valid; there is very little mileage in an essay that simply describes the law and says it is perfectly satisfactory.

Structure

However good your material, you will only gain really good marks if you structure it well. Making a plan for each answer will help in this, and you should also try to learn your material in a logical order – this will make it easier to remember as well. The exact construction of your essay will obviously depend on the question, but you should aim to have an introduction, then the main discussion, and a conclusion. Where a question is divided into two or more parts, you should reflect that structure in your answer.

A word about conclusions: it is not good enough just to repeat the question, turning it into a statement, for the conclusion. So, for example, if the question is 'Are the rules on compensation for negligence causing economic loss satisfactory?', a conclusion which simply states that the rules are or are not satisfactory will gain you very little credit. A good conclusion will often summarise the arguments that you have developed during the course of your essay.

Problem questions

In problem questions, the exam paper will describe an imaginary situation, and then ask what the legal implications of the facts are – usually by asking you to advise one of the parties involved.

Read the question thoroughly

The first priority is to read the question thoroughly, at least a couple of times. Never start writing until you have done this, as you may well get halfway through and discover that what is said at the end makes half of what you have written irrelevant – or, at worst, that the question raises issues you have no knowledge of at all.

Answer the question asked

This means paying close attention to the words printed immediately after the situation is described. If a question asks you to advise one or other of the parties, make sure you advise the right one – the realisation as you discuss the exam with your friends afterwards that you have advised the wrong party and thus rendered most of your answer irrelevant is not an experience you will enjoy. Similarly, if a question asks about possible remedies, simply discussing whether a tort has been committed will not be enough – you need to say what the injured party can claim as a result.

Spot the issues

In answering a problem question in an examination you will often be short of time. One of the skills of doing well is spotting which issues are particularly relevant to the facts of the problem and spending most time on those, while skimming over more quickly those matters which are not really an issue on the facts, but which you clearly need to mention.

Apply the law to the facts

What a problem question requires you to do is to spot the issues raised by the situation, and to consider the law as it applies to those facts. It is not enough simply to describe the law without applying it to the facts. So in a question raising issues of negligence, for example, it is not enough to say what constitutes a duty of care and breach of it. You need to say whether, in the light of those rules, there was a duty of care and breach of it in the situation described in the problem.

Do not start your answer by copying out all the facts, or keep referring to them at great length. This is a complete waste of time, and will gain you no marks.

Unlike essay questions, problem questions are not usually seeking a critical analysis of the law. If you have time, it may be worth making the point that a particular area of the law you are discussing is problematic, and briefly stating why, but if you are addressing all the issues raised in the problem you are unlikely to have much time for this. What the examiner is looking for is essentially an understanding of the law and an ability to apply it to the particular facts given.

Use authority

As always, you must back up your points with authority from case or statute law.

Structure

The introduction and conclusion are much less important for problem questions than for essay questions. Your introduction can be limited to pointing out the issues raised by the question, or, where you are asked to 'advise' a person mentioned in the problem, what outcome that person will be looking for. You can also say in what order you intend to deal with the issues. It is not always necessary to write a conclusion, but you may want to summarise what you have said, highlighting whether, as a result, you think the party you have advised has a strong case or not.

There is no set order in which the main part of the answer must be discussed. Sometimes it will be appropriate to deal with the problem chronologically, in which case it will usually be a matter of looking at the question line by line, while in other cases it may be appropriate to group particular issues together. If the question is broken down into clear parts – (a), (b), (c) and so on – the answer can be broken down into the same parts.

Whichever order you choose, try to deal with one issue at a time. Jumping backwards and forwards gives the impression that you have not thought about your answer. If you work through your material in a structured way, you are also less likely to leave anything out.

Glossary

Act of God An event can only be an Act of God if it is caused entirely by natural forces, with no human intervention. There is no liability in tort for acts of God.

Actionable *per se* In the case of a tort which is actionable *per se*, the claimant only has to prove that the tort has been committed; they do not have to prove damage.

Assault In tort, assault is defined as an act which causes another person reasonably to apprehend immediate violence to their person.

Battery This is the direct and intentional application of force to another person without that person's consent.

Breach of contract This occurs when two parties make a contract, and one of them fails to do what they promised to do.

'But for' test In order to decide whether a defendant's breach of duty was, as a matter of fact, a cause of the damage suffered by the claimant, the question to be answered is whether the damage would not have occurred but for the breach of duty. This is known as the 'but for' test.

Compensatory damages The majority of damages awards in tort are compensatory, i.e. they are designed to compensate the claimant for damage done by the defendant. The basic principle behind them is that, so far as possible, the claimant should be put into the position they would have enjoyed if the tort had never been committed.

Contemptuous damages Where a court recognises that the claimant's legal rights have been infringed technically, but disapproves of their conduct and considers that the action should not have been brought, it may order contemptuous damages. These will amount to no more than the value of the least valuable coin of the realm (currently 1p).

Contract damages Unlike most tort damages, these generally try to put the claimant in the position they would have enjoyed if the contract had been performed as agreed.

Contribution The Civil Liability (Contribution) Act 1978 provides that where there is joint or several liability, and one tortfeasor is sued and pays damages, they may recover a contribution or indemnity from any other person who is liable in respect of the same damage. This is a matter between the defendants and does not affect the claimant, who remains entitled to recover the whole loss from whichever defendant they choose.

Contributory negligence A claimant who it has been shown has, by their own lack of care, contributed to the harm done to themselves, will be considered contributorily negligent. In such a case the damages can be reduced, at the discretion of the court, to take account of the contributory negligence involved.

Defamation This is the publication of a statement which tends to lower a person in the estimation of right-thinking members of society generally, or which tends to make them shun or avoid that person. There are two types of defamation: libel and slander.

Dependant For the purposes of a claim under the Fatal Accidents Act 1976 by the dependants of the deceased, the word 'dependant' can include not only the spouse and children of the deceased but also other relatives, provided that they can prove financial dependence on the deceased.

Distress damage feasant Where an object placed or left unlawfully on the claimant's land causes damage, they can keep it until the damage has been paid for.

Economic loss In tort the term is usually used to cover losses which are 'purely' economic, i.e. those where a claimant has suffered financial damage but has incurred no personal injury or damage to property.

'Eggshell skull' rule This states that defendants must take their victims as they find them, including any health problems which make the harm suffered more serious than it would otherwise be.

Ex turpi causa non oritur actio (Latin for 'No right of action arises from a base cause') This is a defence that may be used against a claimant whose claim arises from their own criminal actions.

Exemplary damages Also known as punitive damages, these are awarded, in addition to compensatory damages, when a court wishes to mark its extreme disapproval of the defendant's conduct and to deter both that defendant and others from similar conduct in the future.

False imprisonment This is the unlawful prevention of another from exercising their freedom of movement. In this context 'false' really means wrongful.

Fault principle Most torts require some element of fault, i.e. in addition to proving that the defendant has committed the relevant act or been guilty of an omission (and, where necessary, that damage has been caused as a result), it is necessary to prove a particular state of mind on the part of the defendant (for example, intention or negligence).

Intention This has various meanings depending on the context but essentially it involves deliberate and knowing behaviour.

Interim damages Under the Supreme Court Act 1981 the court can award interim damages before trial, where the defendant admits liability and is only contesting the amount of damages claimed.

Interlocutory injunction The court may award an interlocutory (or interim) injunction before the action is heard. It is designed to prevent potential harm, or continued harm, during the period before the case comes to court.

Joint tortfeasors Where the same wrongful act is committed by two or more people, they are described as joint tortfeasors and are jointly and severally liable. This means the claimant can sue both (or all) of them, or recover the whole amount from just one, regardless of the extent to which each participated. Even where all are sued, judgment will be given for a single sum and this may be enforced in full against any one of them. The claimant can only recover once.

Jus tertii (Latin for 'The right of a third party') A defendant may have a defence to an action for trespass if it can be shown that the land rightfully belongs neither to the person in possession of it nor to the person claiming it but to a third person.

Libel This is the publication of a defamatory statement about a person, made in some permanent form. This usually means in printed or written form, but it also covers films, pictures, broadcasts, statues and effigies.

Licence Where the person in possession of land gives someone permission, express or implied, to be on that land, there is no trespass, provided the boundaries of that permission are not exceeded. This is called giving a licence.

Limitation of actions The Limitation Act 1980 lays down time limits within which tort actions must be brought. The standard limitation periods are three years in a case which involves personal injury or death and six years in other tort actions.

Loss of amenity This term describes the situation where an injury results in the claimant being unable to enjoy life to the same extent as before. It may include an inability to enjoy sport or any other pastime they engaged in before the injury, impairment of sight, hearing, etc., reduction in the chance of finding a marriage partner or impairment of sexual activity.

Malice In tort, to act maliciously means acting with a bad motive. Normally malice – and motive in general – is irrelevant in tort law but there are a few torts (e.g. malicious prosecution) where it is an essential ingredient. It may also be relevant to the calculation of damages, making them higher than they would otherwise be if the same act was committed without malice.

Mesne profits An action for mesne profits is a type of action for trespass. It allows the claimant to claim profits taken by the defendant during occupancy, damages for deterioration and reasonable costs of regaining possession.

Mitigation of loss A person who falls victim to a tort is expected to take reasonable steps to mitigate any loss; the defendant will not be liable for compensatory damages in respect of any loss which could have been prevented by such steps.

Necessity This defence applies where a defendant intentionally causes damage in order to prevent greater damage. It may turn out that the defendant need not have taken action at all, but so long as the action taken was reasonable in the circumstances the defence will still apply.

Negligence (1) As a state of mind, this generally means carelessness – doing something without intending to cause damage, for example, but not taking care to ensure that it does not. (2) It is also a tort, which concerns the breach of a legal duty of care, with the result that damage is caused to the claimant.

Neighbour principle In **Donoghue** *v* **Stevenson** the House of Lords attempted to lay down a general criteria as to when a duty of care in negligence would exist. Lord Atkin stated that the principle was: 'You must take reasonable care to avoid acts or omissions which you can reasonably foresee would be likely to injure your neighbour.' He said that by 'neighbour' he meant 'persons who are so closely and directly affected by my act that I ought to have them in contemplation as being so affected when I am directing my mind to the acts or omissions which are called in question'.

Nervous shock Lawyers often use the term 'nervous shock' to describe psychiatric damage caused by a person suffering a sudden or unexpected shock. Such illnesses include anxiety neurosis, clinical depression and post-traumatic stress disorder. In this book we usually use the term 'psychiatric injury'.

Nominal damages An award of nominal damages is normally made where there has technically been an infringement of a person's legal rights but no actual damage has been done. Such damages are for a small sum (normally £20) and tend to arise in relation to torts which are actionable *per se* (such as trespass and libel).

Non-pecuniary damages These cover damages which are not always easily calculable, such as pain, shock, suffering and loss of physical amenity.

Novus actus interveniens (Latin for 'A new act intervening') If the chain of causation between a defendant's act and the damage done is broken by the intervening act of a third person, the defendant will not be liable for the damage unless it could be foreseen that it would necessarily follow from their original act.

Occupier For the purposes of the Occupiers' Liability Acts 1957 and 1984 an occupier is the person who controls the premises. They do not have to be the physical occupier nor the owner; the critical issue is whether they exercise a sufficient degree of control to allow or prevent other people entering.

Pecuniary damages This kind of damages can be calculated in financial terms, such as loss of earnings, and medical and other expenses.

Personal injury This term covers physical or psychiatric harm, disease or illness.

Prescription A defendant may be held to have acquired the right to commit a private nuisance by prescription. This applies where it can be shown that the nuisance has been actionable for at least 20 years and that the claimant was aware of that during the relevant period.

Provisional damages The Supreme Court Act 1981 gives the courts power to award provisional damages. Where there is a possibility that the injured person will, as a result of the tort, develop a serious disease, or serious physical or mental deterioration in the future, the court can award initial damages based on the claimant's condition but retain power to award further damages if the possible future deterioration does in fact happen. The award can be adjusted only once.

Punitive damages *See* **Exemplary damages**.

Recklessness For the purposes of the tort of deceit, recklessness means that the defendant must have been consciously indifferent as to whether a statement which they have made was true or not. Mere negligence, in the sense of failing to make sure it was true, is not enough.

Remoteness of damage This is a legal test which decides whether a tortfeasor should be liable for the results of their actions.

Res ipsa loquitur (Latin for 'The facts speak for themselves') Where, in negligence cases, it is clear that the harm caused was such that it could not possibly have arisen unless the defendant was negligent, the court may be prepared to infer that the defendant was negligent without hearing detailed evidence of what was or was not done.

Restitutio in integrum This is the principle of restoring the claimant to the position which they would have held if the tort had not been committed.

Rylands v Fletcher, rule in The rule is that an occupier of land who brings onto it anything likely to do damage if it escapes, and keeps it there, will be liable for damage caused by such an escape.

Several liability Where two or more tortfeasors act independently, but the result of their acts is damage to the claimant for which they are both responsible, they are severally liable. The practical result is that each tortfeasor is separately liable for the whole of the damage, so the claimant may choose which to sue, but cannot recover twice.

Slander Defamatory statement about another made in a transitory form, i.e. orally or by gestures, not in writing or in print.

Special damage (1) In an action for slander, the claimant must normally prove that the slander has caused some actual damage (known as 'special damage') over and above the loss of reputation, usually a financial loss. (2) In a tort action for public nuisance, special damage means damage beyond that suffered by other members of the affected group.

Special damages These are losses which do not arise naturally from the wrong complained of and must be specifically listed in pleadings and proved in court. They generally cover the claimant's financial loss up until the date of trial, and any expenses incurred up to that point.

Strict liability A tort of strict liability is committed simply by the performance of the relevant act or omission; there is no requirement for the tortfeasor to have been at fault.

Tort In general terms a tort occurs where there is a breach of a general duty fixed by civil law.

Tortfeasor The wrongdoer, i.e. the person who committed the tort.

Trespass *ab initio* Where a person's entry onto land is permitted by statute or common law, rather than merely by permission of the occupier, and the person entering does a wrongful act while there, that act makes the original entry a trespass. This is known as trespass *ab initio*.

Trespasser A trespasser is someone who goes onto private land without any kind of permission to do so.

Vicarious liability There are some cases where one person will be held liable for torts committed by someone else; such liability is said to be vicarious. It only arises where there is a particular relationship between the two, usually (in fact, almost exclusively) that of employer and employee. An employer is vicariously liable for the torts committed by his employees if they are acting in the course of their employment.

Visitor For the purpose of the Occupiers' Liability Act 1957 a visitor is someone who has express or implied permission from the occupier to enter premises. Where permission to enter is given and then withdrawn while the entrant is still on the property, they are allowed a reasonable time in which to leave; once that expires, they become a trespasser.

Volenti non fit injuria (Latin for 'No injury can be done to a willing person') This defence applies where the claimant has consented to what was done by the defendant, on the grounds that they have voluntarily assumed the risk of injury. An obvious example is a boxer, who, by the fact of entering into a match with an opponent, voluntarily consents to be hit.

Index

Page numbers in **bold** refer to entries appearing in the glossary

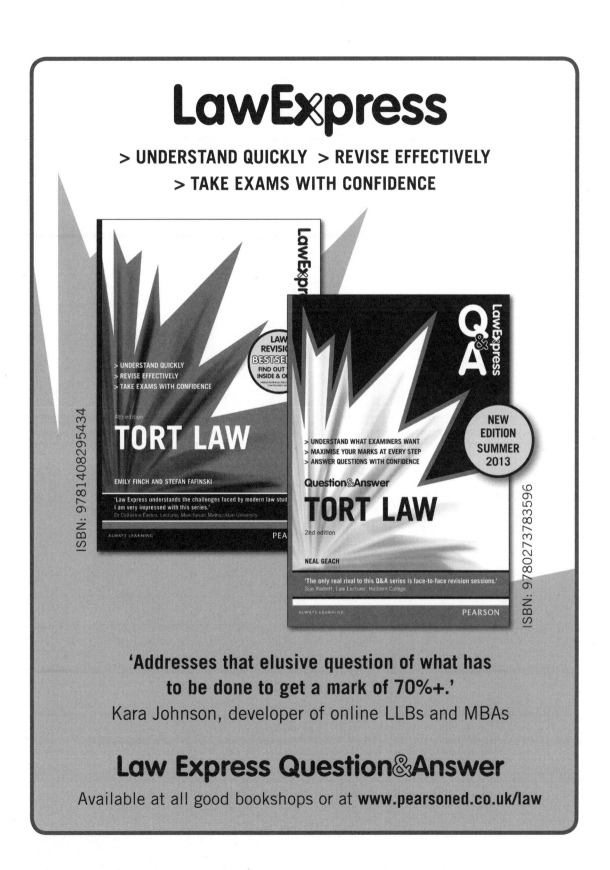